Nonverbal Communication in Everyday Life

Fourth Edition

Nonverbal Communication in Everyday Life

Fourth Edition

Martin S. Remland
West Chester University of Pennsylvania

Los Angeles | London | New Delhi
Singapore | Washington DC | Melbourne

FOR INFORMATION:

SAGE Publications, Inc.
2455 Teller Road
Thousand Oaks, California 91320
E-mail: order@sagepub.com

SAGE Publications Ltd.
1 Oliver's Yard
55 City Road
London EC1Y 1SP
United Kingdom

SAGE Publications India Pvt. Ltd.
B 1/I 1 Mohan Cooperative Industrial Area
Mathura Road, New Delhi 110 044
India

SAGE Publications Asia-Pacific Pte. Ltd.
3 Church Street
#10-04 Samsung Hub
Singapore 049483

Acquisitions Editor: Matthew Byrnie
Editorial Assistant: Janae Masnovi
Production Editor: Olivia Weber-Stenis
Copy Editor: Erin Livingston
Typesetter: C&M Digitals (P) Ltd.
Proofreader: Carole Quandt
Indexer: Marilyn Augst
Cover Designer: Candice Harman
Marketing Manager: Ashlee Blunk

Printed in the United States of America

Library of Congress Cataloging-in-Publication Data

Names: Remland, Martin S., author.

Title: Nonverbal communication in everyday life / Martin S. Remland.

Description: Fourth Edition. | Thousand Oaks, California : SAGE, [2016] | Includes index.

Identifiers: LCCN 2015051098 | ISBN 9781483370255 (pbk. : alk. paper)

Subjects: LCSH: Nonverbal communication. | Body language.

Classification: LCC P99.5 .R45 2017 | DDC 302.2/22—dc23
LC record available at http://lccn.loc.gov/2015051098

This book is printed on acid-free paper.

16 17 18 19 20 10 9 8 7 6 5 4 3 2 1

BRIEF CONTENTS

DETAILED CONTENTS

Chapter 8 • Nonverbal Communication in Intimate Encounters 285

Chapter 9 • Nonverbal Communication in Deceptive Encounters 331

PREFACE

I first became interested in the subject of nonverbal communication as a graduate student in 1973, a time when the scientific study of physical appearance, eye contact, personal space, touch, facial expression, voice, and gesture was still in its infancy. Today, countless researchers from most academic disciplines are doing research on these topics, making it a tremendous challenge to stay abreast of the latest discoveries and applications.

This new, fourth edition of *Nonverbal Communication in Everyday Life* endeavors to present the latest developments in the field. Written for a wide audience, it presents the research in a way that is interesting and highly readable without sacrificing the need to be comprehensive and critical.

Instructors can use this book as the primary text in any undergraduate course that introduces students to the subject of nonverbal communication, regardless of whether that course is taught at the freshmen/sophomore level, or at the junior/senior level. In addition, graduate-course instructors should find the book very useful as a supplementary text, providing a basic foundation, a conceptual framework, and an extensive up-to-date review of the literature, particularly for students with little or no background in the subject.

By far, the biggest challenge in writing new editions of this book is the need to make difficult choices about what to include, what to add, and what to delete from previous editions. As in the past, I have tried to make these choices guided by my belief in the need to include the seminal works most often cited in other introductory textbooks, along with my own judgment of what is most interesting, relevant, and useful to readers. I also believe that it is vital to provide balanced coverage of the foundations, codes, functions, and applications of nonverbal communication.

CONCEPTUAL APPROACH AND ORGANIZATION

Part I of the text, *Foundations*, consists of two chapters that give readers the general background needed to appreciate the significance of nonverbal communication in everyday life. It also introduces many of the key concepts and principles needed to understand the material presented in subsequent chapters.

The first chapter addresses the key issues involved in defining nonverbal communication and differentiating it from verbal communication; it also introduces and discusses the four basic functions of nonverbal communication as well as the connection between each nonverbal communication code (i.e., physical appearance, eye contact, touch, personal space, facial expression, voice, and gesture) and its primary function. The second chapter introduces the concept of nonverbal communication skills and discusses the various types of sending and receiving skills. It also reviews the research on the development of these skills from infancy into adulthood and includes important studies of how individuals differ in the development of nonverbal communication skills and the impact of education and training.

While other textbooks tend to organize the subject according to either (1) the *codes* (channels) of nonverbal communication (e.g., physical appearance, gestures, personal space, voice, etc.) or (2) the *functions* of nonverbal communication (e.g., signaling identity, expressing emotion, building relationships, etc.), Part II of this text tries to integrate codes and functions by showing how each of four nonverbal signaling systems serve a different primary function. Chapter 3 focuses on physical appearance primarily as a way of signaling identity; Chapter 4 highlights the use of personal space, eye contact, and touch (i.e., contact codes) as a means of building relationships; Chapter 5 stresses the emotion function of facial expression; and Chapter 6 focuses on how voice and gesture replace speech and work in tandem to facilitate speech (i.e., the delivery function).

Part III, *Applications*, offers an in-depth treatment of how nonverbal communication is relevant in our everyday lives. This part of the text contains five chapters focusing on non-intimate encounters (Chapter 7), intimate encounters (Chapter 8), deceptive encounters (Chapter 9), workplace encounters (Chapter 10), and mediated encounters (Chapter 11). Taken together, these chapters consider how nonverbal communication influences our ability to accomplish a number of important interaction goals:

- Building conversational rapport
- Getting help
- Attracting a romantic partner
- Maintaining an intimate relationship
- Managing relational conflict
- Providing emotional support
- Catching liars
- Projecting strength and confidence
- Achieving workplace goals

- Staying connected through social media
- Resisting media influence
- Absorbing the popular culture

SPECIAL FEATURES

To assist the reader in understanding and retaining the information presented in this text, I've tried as much as possible to use plain English instead of academic jargon. In addition, each chapter contains an abundance of definitions, explanations, concrete examples, and vivid illustrations. As in previous editions, clarity continues to be my highest priority. To further assist the reader, each chapter also contains an outlined preview of main topics, a list of key terms that are boldfaced in the chapter, and a summary of main ideas at the end of each chapter. A new feature in this edition is a list of specific learning objectives that follow the chapter outlines.

Every chapter also contains a variety of boxed inserts to promote learning and to prompt in-class discussion. Instructors can also use these boxed inserts for graded or extra-credit assignments. The *Try This* boxes ask students to participate in an out-of-class activity relevant to a topic covered in the chapter; the *Can You Relate to This?* boxes encourage students to reflect on the personal experiences of other students. New to this edition are the *Find Out More* boxes found in each chapter. These boxes provide a brief, easy-to-read synopsis of a recently published study and then prompt students to answer a series of questions about the study. Students can answer these questions and learn more about the study by visiting the publisher's student website, where they will find full-text copies of each study. The *Find Out More* boxes also encourage students to review the brief essay on "Approaches to the Study of Nonverbal Communication," found in the textbook's Appendix.

An instructor's resource manual is also available. The manual provides sample course syllabi, guidelines for assigning and evaluating a research project, and useful Internet websites. Also, for each chapter, it includes a detailed topic outline, test questions, in-class activities, recommended readings, instructional videos, and relevant feature films.

CHANGES IN THE FOURTH EDITION

This fourth edition of *Nonverbal Communication in Everyday Life* continues to reflect the changing landscape of the field. Readers of previous editions will find new discoveries and applications in every chapter. In a few chapters, readers will notice slight modifications in the chapter outline where certain topics receive more or less in-depth treatment. This edition also adds some new key terms and deletes some others and adds a new series of boxes on recent scholarship that replaces the boxed readings found in previous editions. In keeping with the goal of introducing students to the best and latest research on nonverbal communication in a way that does not create information overload, this edition leaves out some of the material contained in previous editions. The most notable changes in this edition are listed below:

- The Chapter 1 section on downplaying the difference between nonverbal and verbal communication has been deleted.
- Chapter 2 has been deleted. Key information about the functions of nonverbal communication has been added to Chapter 1.
- The chapter on non-intimate encounters (formerly Chapter 8, now Chapter 7) has been shortened to include only the sections on building rapport and getting help. The section on deception has been expanded into a full chapter (Chapter 9).
- Chapter 11 has been revised, updated, and expanded to include the latest research and developments on the social uses of interactive media (e.g., texting, Facebook, etc.).
- A new section addressing scientific and humanistic approaches to the study of nonverbal communication, as well as the many different methods used by nonverbal communication researchers, has been added as an Appendix.

ACKNOWLEDGMENTS

I'd like to begin by thanking the outstanding editorial staff at SAGE: Matt Byrnie, for giving me the opportunity to work on a new edition of the book and for his many helpful suggestions; Janae Masnovi and Anna Villarruel, for their editorial assistance during the initial stages of development; and Olivia Weber-Stenis, for guiding me through the production process. I'd also like to thank Erin Livingston, for her highly professional copy editing of the manuscript.

I am indebted to the reviewers of this edition for their useful feedback and thoughtful suggestions.

I also want to express my gratitude to the students in my nonverbal communication classes at WCU for testing many of the ideas and activities that have gone into this book and for giving me plenty of feedback on the first three editions.

Finally, my work on this new edition literally would not have been possible without the love, support, patience, and comfort I have received from my wife, Tricia, and my son, Alex. This book is dedicated to them.

SAGE Publications gratefully acknowledges the contributions of the following reviewers:

Todd Lee Goen, Christopher Newport University

Tricia S. Jones, Temple University

David T. Kottenstette, Metropolitan State University of Denver

Dennis Patrick, Eastern Michigan University

Karl Payton, LeTourneau University

Elena Steiner, Regis University

Barbara J. Tarter, Marshall University

Jane B. Teel, Auburn University

ABOUT THE AUTHOR

Martin S. Remland is a professor of communication studies at West Chester University of Pennsylvania. He has been teaching undergraduate and graduate courses in nonverbal communication for nearly four decades and continues to teach at least three sections of the undergraduate nonverbal communication course at WCU every year.

In addition to this fourth edition of *Nonverbal Communication in Everyday Life*, he is a contributing author of the *SAGE Handbook of Nonverbal Communication* (2006), coauthor of *Intercultural Communication: A Peacebuilding Perspective* (Waveland, 2015), coauthor of *Interpersonal Communication through the Life Span* (Pearson, 2007), and coauthor of *Argumentation and Debate: A Public Speaking Approach* (Kendall Hunt, 2015). His research on nonverbal communication has appeared in several book chapters and numerous academic journals, including *The Journal of Nonverbal Behavior*, *The Journal of Social Psychology*, *International Journal of Conflict Management*, *Communication Quarterly*, *Sex Roles*, *Perceptual and Motor Skills*, *Journal of Business Communication*, *Southern Communication Quarterly*, and *Argumentation and Advocacy*, among others.

PART I

FOUNDATIONS

istockphoto.com/Yuri_Arcurs

Chapter Outline

1

THE NATURE AND FUNCTIONS OF NONVERBAL COMMUNICATION

People sometimes make judgments about us that are not accurate. Jennifer, a student in one of my classes, described one such experience:

> During the winter semester in my freshman year, I took a history class that I really enjoyed. One day in class, I noticed that the instructor kept looking at me in a negative way. After class, a friend of mine, Angela, complained about how boring she thought his lecture was. I told her I liked it and that I was surprised at her reaction. Her response was, "Well, you sure didn't look interested." When I questioned her, she told me that I looked bored and even annoyed. I told her I wasn't feeling well and didn't get much sleep the night before. Then it occurred to me that the instructor must have gotten the same impression my friend did. I guess my posture and facial expressions gave them the wrong idea.

Jennifer's experience illustrates several important points about the subject of this book, **nonverbal communication**, or *communication without words*. First, it shows how a facial expression, a glance, or a posture can shape our opinions of others. In fact, these nonverbal cues usually have a greater impact on our judgments of a person's attitudes, intentions, and emotions than spoken words do. Second, it demonstrates

Learning Objectives

After reading this chapter, you will be able to do the following:

1. Understand the role and importance of intentionality in attempting to define communication.
2. Identify and define the basic elements of a communication code.
3. Compare and contrast the intrinsic, iconic, and arbitrary codes of nonverbal communication.
4. Explain the four basic properties of verbal communication—communicating with words.
5. Explain the four basic properties of nonverbal communication—communicating without words.
6. Identify and discuss the four functions of nonverbal communication—signaling identity, building relationships, expressing emotion, and delivering symbolic information—and how each contributes to the survival of a species.
7. Indicate how humans use nonverbal signals for each of the functions.

how easily we can misinterpret these actions. Compared to verbal messages, the meaning of most nonverbal messages is more ambiguous and more dependent upon the overall context in which they occur. Jennifer's friend Angela assumed that Jennifer's facial expressions and posture expressed the same negative feelings she had about the class; and Jennifer only assumed that the instructor's look meant that he interpreted Jennifer's behavior the same way Angela did. Third, it shows how unaware we are of how others are interpreting our actions. Finally, it raises a fundamental question about when nonverbal communication between individuals takes place: *Do we send nonverbal messages whether we intend to or not*? In this case, did Jennifer send a message to her instructor and her friend or did they merely think that she did? Did the instructor send a message to Jennifer when he glanced at her or did Jennifer only imagine it?

You may think there is a single answer to the question raised above, that experts on the subject have long agreed on when nonverbal communication occurs. But there are different points of view regarding the importance of intentionality, as well as other relevant factors such as mutual understanding and the presence or absence of feedback (Andersen, 1991; Motley, 1990). Despite these differing viewpoints, however, a growing consensus seems to be emerging that favors less rather than more restrictive definitions of nonverbal communication (Manusov & Patterson, 2006). In the sections that follow, we'll discuss when communication occurs, explore the distinction between nonverbal and verbal communication, identify the primary functions of nonverbal communication, and conclude the chapter by briefly introducing the four basic nonverbal signaling systems discussed in detail in Part II (Chapters 3–6).

▸ We often send nonverbal messages, whether we intend to or not. While texting sends a verbal message to the recipient of the text, does it send any nonverbal messages during a class or on a date?

istockphoto.com/adamkaz

istockphoto.com/JenniferPhotographyImaging

EXERCISE 1.1

TRY IT

Has Communication Taken Place?

Instructions:

For each of the scenarios described below, note whether you believe communication has occurred. Circle *yes* if you think it has, *no* if you think it hasn't, and *it depends* if you think important information is missing. Be prepared to present your position in class.

Scenario 1:

As he walks toward the store, Frank sees a good friend of his, Ben, in the parking lot. Frank waves at Ben, but because Ben is looking away, he doesn't see Frank waving. Is Frank communicating to Ben?

Yes *No* *It depends*

Scenario 2:

While standing in line in front of a movie theater, Darla overhears a conversation between a man and a woman standing behind her. They are yelling at each other in loud, angry voices. Darla can't believe how rude they are to be acting this way in public. Is the couple communicating to Darla?

Yes *No* *It depends*

Scenario 3:

Peter and Alyssa are having lunch together during their break from work. Peter listens attentively as Alyssa tells him about her previous job. At one point during the conversation, Alyssa reaches across the table and touches Peter on his hand. Although she meant nothing by it, Peter sees her touch as a sure sign of romantic interest in him. Has Alyssa communicated this message to Peter?

Yes *No* *It depends*

WHEN DOES COMMUNICATION OCCUR?

When people use words, there is little doubt that they intend to send a message. But can we be sure someone is sending a message just because he or she chooses to dress or act in a certain way? Also, much of what we take to be nonverbal communication—facial expressions, eye contact, hand gestures, and so forth—happens automatically and outside our conscious awareness. There is some disagreement about when communication occurs in situations not involving the use of a formal language.

The position we develop here focuses on the use of a **communication code**. That is, *communication takes place whenever two or more individuals, using a socially shared or biologically shared signaling system, send and receive a message*. A communication code (signaling system) includes certain kinds of **signs**, which individuals use to exchange information. Generally speaking, a sign is anything that stands for or indicates something else. When one or more signs carry information that gets through to a receiver, communication occurs. Nonverbal communication scholars usually use the term ***signal*** when referring to such signs. Of course, this distinction also implies that not all signs are signals. For example, eye blinking is an involuntary sign of stress (i.e., a result of stress), but if eye blinking doesn't generally convey information that gets through to people (i.e., decoded by receivers) and has no clear social function, it is not a signal. In contrast, blushing, as an involuntary sign of embarrassment that occurs in the presence of other people, is a signal because the message usually gets through and it serves a social-emotional function. Nonverbal signals convey information in different ways. Paul Ekman and Wallace Friesen (1969b), pioneers in the study of nonverbal communication, have identified three primary types of communication codes, which we discuss below.

Intrinsic Communication Codes

Natural signs, or **symptoms** (Cronkhite, 1986), represent cause-and-effect relationships between the sign and what the sign indicates: Gray hair is a sign of aging, crying is a sign of distress, yawning is sign of boredom, and so on. Much of our nonverbal communication consists of symptoms. Many of our facial expressions are symptoms of emotional or motivational states and often occur automatically as part of a *spontaneous* communication system (Buck & VanLear, 2002). Also, there is compelling evidence that these expressions of anger, sadness, fear, and so forth are part of an inherited signaling system that evolved as an essential means of communication (Fridlund, 1994). On the other hand, sneezing may be a symptom of an allergy, but that does not mean sneezing evolved in large measure as a form of communication (i.e., that sneezing is less likely without an audience).

An **intrinsic communication code** is a biologically shared, innate signaling system in which a particular species uses symptoms for its communication with other members of the species. Much of the animal kingdom sends and receives messages in this way. Using a wide array of postures, movements, calls, scents, touches, and appearance displays, animals communicate important information about themselves and their environment. According to Michael Argyle (1988),

> Animals conduct their entire social life by means of nonverbal communication: they make friends, find mates, rear children,

cooperate in groups, establish leadership hierarchies, and get rid of enemies entirely by the use of nonverbal signals. This elaborate signaling system has mainly been built up in the course of evolution, as a result of its value for the survival of the species. (p. 27)

Humans and other primates take advantage of this intrinsic communication code to signal multiple identities; expedite relationships; exchange messages of emotion; and deliver symbolic messages through physical appearance, facial expressions, vocalizations, spatial behavior, gestures, and postures.

Iconic Communication Codes

Many of our nonverbal signals only resemble or appear to be symptoms. Picture this scene: You discover that some of the people you work with are planning a surprise party for you. Obviously, you don't want them to know that you know. When you arrive at work and they shout, "Surprise!" you pretend to look surprised. Your jaw drops; your eyes bug out; you're speechless. Your facial expression mimics the look of surprise but is not symptomatic of genuine surprise. These posed facial expressions exemplify a *pseudo-spontaneous* form of communication (Buck & VanLear, 2002). More broadly, communication scholar Jo Liska (1993) referred to these signs as **semblances**. Semblances include a wide variety of nonverbal signals: putting on a happy face, pretending to be afraid, wearing makeup to look younger, miming the act of drinking from a glass, drawing a picture of something in the air, getting a tattoo of a snake on your shoulder, and so on.

▸ An iconic signal looks like the real thing but isn't. Pretending to be afraid, wearing makeup to look younger, drawing a picture of something in the air, or getting a tattoo of a snake are all iconic signals.

istockphoto.com/webphotographeer

Humans and many animal species use an **iconic communication code** for various communication functions. An iconic code represents a signal system, either learned or inherited, in which semblances are used to communicate with others. Often, we use these signals for the sole purpose of deception; we try to mislead others into believing we may do something we do not plan to do (fight or cooperate) or feel an emotion that is not felt (happy, sad, etc.). Of course, humans are not the only animals capable of such dishonesty. Observations of monkeys and apes, for instance, have shown that they occasionally pretend not to be interested in some preferred object while a dominant member of the group is watching, but later sneak back to get it (Argyle, 1988). Similarly, researchers have observed young male elephant seals acting like females so they can enter a harem and copulate with the female of a harem master (Wiley, 1983).

But the iconic code can also facilitate accurate communication. Gestures that resemble their **referents** are much easier to decode than are abstract gestures (it's easy to understand pantomime if you are familiar with the actions portrayed). Also, many nonverbal signals, known as **intention movements**, are easy to decipher because they represent a small segment of some anticipated action (Argyle, 1988). Opening your mouth and taking in a breath to signal your desire to speak or looking toward an exit as a signal that you want to leave are examples of intention movements. Among animal species, a bird will spread its wings as a signal that it is preparing for flight; a dog will bare its teeth when communicating its readiness to bite; a gorilla will pound the ground as a display of aggression.

PERSONAL EXPERIENCE 1.1

CAN YOU RELATE TO THIS?

Intention Movements Send a Clear Message

Practically every time I go to my girlfriend's house after work, I use an example of an intention movement without thinking much about it. When I enter the house, I try not to show that I am anxious to leave. However, once some time has passed, I begin playing with my car keys, which signals to my girlfriend, "I am ready to leave and go to my house." She almost always gets the message.

Brian

Arbitrary Communication Codes

An **arbitrary communication code** is a socially constructed, learned signaling system that uses **symbols** to convey messages. Unlike symptoms and semblances, the relationship between a symbol and what the symbol represents is a matter of agreement among members of a social community. The words we use in a written or spoken language are symbols, with agreed-upon meanings called **referents**. But gestures can also be symbols because many have agreed-upon referents (the thumbs-up gesture, the head nod, the handshake, etc.). A language can even consist entirely of gestures, as it does for those who learn to use sign language as a means of communicating. In addition, much of what we wear on our bodies is symbolic of social class, occupation, age, nationality, and so forth.

Compared to the use of intrinsic and iconic codes, there is much less evidence that nonhuman animals use arbitrary codes for communication. Of course, research has been accumulating that many animals learn to send and receive messages in ways that are remarkably similar to human symbolic communication (Rogers & Kaplan, 2000). But, despite a capacity for the use of symbols, there is no convincing proof that the ability to invent and learn a complex language built entirely on the use of symbols exists in nonhuman species. Yet animals are capable of communicating in ways that contain many of the essential properties of language. For instance, primates can learn the rudiments of sign language (i.e., simple one- and two-word expressions). Much has been written over the years, for example, about the extraordinary accomplishments of Washoe the chimpanzee and Koko the gorilla. Both learned to sign in remarkable ways.

▸ An arbitrary code is a learned, socially constructed form of communication that can differ from one culture to another. Greeting rituals, which have shared meaning among the members of a cultural group, are an example of such a code.

istockphoto.com/btrenkel

For example, Koko the gorilla demonstrated an astonishing ability to use signs that revealed imagination and emotion: naming her pet kitten, warning an aide that she would be attacked by an alligator if Koko's lunch wasn't made faster, acting embarrassed when caught encouraging her dolls to kiss and tickle, advising a woman to drink orange juice for an upset stomach, and signing to herself when alone (Masson & McCarthy, 1995).

Because the connection between a symbol and its referent is arbitrary, the meaning we attach to symbols is rarely fixed. To illustrate, consider the diversity of gestures we use to replace speech to say things such as "Good job," "Come here," "He's crazy," "Be quiet," "Shame on you," "I don't know," and the like. Many of us would not recognize the meaning of gestures used in other countries. For example, in parts of the Middle East, people signal agreement by pressing the forefingers together, side by side. In Italy and South America, you can call someone a miser by pressing a clenched fist against your chest (Morris, 1994). Likewise, persons outside the United States might not understand some of the gestures we use every day. Occasionally, we find that an ordinary gesture taken for granted here would be offensive elsewhere, such as the gesture for okay (making a circle with thumb and forefinger), which is an obscenity in many countries around the world (Morris, 1994). Misunderstandings also arise because the same gesture can mean different things from one country to another. For example, the cheek screw gesture (screwing the forefinger into your cheek) means "superb" or "beautiful" in Italy, "He is effeminate" in southern Spain, and "You're crazy" in Germany (Morris, 1994).

One of the earliest discussions of the communication code perspective limited communication to "(a) a socially shared signal system, that is a code, (b) an encoder who makes something public via that code, and (c) a decoder who responds systematically to that code" (Weiner, Devoe, Rubinow, & Geller, 1972, p. 186). Notice that the starting point in this definition is the presence of a signal system or code used by encoders and decoders of messages. Although this definition has its limitations—a socially shared signal system excludes the use of intrinsic codes—it highlights the fact that not all behavior is communication. For instance, unlike those who claim that we are always sending messages (i.e., the idea that "we cannot not communicate"), this is a narrower view of what constitutes communication. Communication scholar Judee Burgoon (1980) argues that this perspective, with its focus on the code rather than the encoders and decoders, rules out idiosyncratic mannerisms, behaviors that do not occur with any regularity, actions or attributes that are merely informative (i.e., serve as a basis for inferences by an observer but are clearly not communication), and activities that do not regularly evoke the same interpretations across members of the social unit engaging in them (p. 180).

In addition, instead of trying to figure out whether each individual in an interaction is sending a message with intent, this perspective sidesteps the issue by looking only at the larger and more central question of whether a code is being used. This allows for the possibility that a person may communicate without intent, even when using an arbitrary communication code. In one episode of the television series *Seinfeld*, Jerry accidentally squirts some grapefruit into George's left eye. This causes George to shut his left eye throughout the day in a way that looks as though he is winking at people. But he is not aware of doing it and this complicates George's ability to be understood. One person thinks he is kidding when he is trying to be serious, another thinks he is flirting, and another thinks he is trying to hide something. Each person interprets his wink in a different context. Is George communicating nonverbally by winking? According to our definition, he is. Although the wink was unintentional, winking is a symbolic gesture typically done on purpose to send a message.

This approach to nonverbal communication also addresses the issue of responsibility by implying that ignorance is no excuse. In other words, even if you do something with absolutely no intention of communicating, you may still be held accountable. Consider how it may be possible to use symbolic gestures, which we usually perform deliberately to send a message, without any such awareness. For example, although we think it's ill-mannered to pick your nose in public, we do not regard it as a communicative act; yet it is an insulting gesture in some Arab countries. Similarly, placing your hands on your hips (known as the *arms akimbo* gesture) is a relatively unconscious action, but in Malaysia and the Philippines, it is often a deliberate expression of anger. Perhaps the best example of how we can get into trouble performing a symbolic action without the intention of communicating is the foot-show gesture. While sitting, a person shows the sole of the shoe by crossing his or her legs in the ankle-on-knee position. In parts of the Middle East and the Orient, showing another person the lowliest and dirtiest part of the body is extremely insulting and often leads to serious altercations (Morris, 1994). No doubt, important consequences result from accepting the idea that when we unwittingly use the signal system of another culture, we are responsible for the messages we send and may be held accountable. This clearly underscores the importance of learning about the communication codes used by other people.

PERSONAL EXPERIENCE 1.2

CAN YOU RELATE TO THIS?

The Meaning of a Behavior Depends on One's Culture

When I was a kid, my dad used to be involved with a lot of foreign business clients for his company. Many of them were Chinese. One night, he had to take about ten Chinese clients out to dinner and he brought along my younger sister and me. My sister and I were trying to be well behaved, being in the presence of so many adults. After we all finished eating, many of the Chinese clients began to belch. My sister and I, being nine and six years old, found this absolutely hysterical, since we were taught that belching was not appropriate at the dinner table. My dad shot us a stare that said, "Stop laughing." We tried out best to stop but found it hard to resist. On the way home, we asked my dad, "Didn't they know it was impolite to belch at the table?" My dad explained to us that in their culture belching after a meal was considered a compliment to the chef. I've always remembered that night for some reason. It was probably my first experience realizing how arbitrary rules are. After that, my sister and I belched often during dinner, laughing and saying, "Well, they're allowed to do it in China."

Chris

WHEN IS COMMUNICATION NONVERBAL?

Now that we have addressed the fundamental question of when interpersonal communication takes place, we need to discuss further the question of when, and even whether, communication is not verbal. In the beginning of this chapter, we defined nonverbal communication simply as communication without words. This is the most common definition and the one generally regarded as reasonable. However, it is much

EXERCISE 1.2

TRY IT

A Rush to Judgment

INSTRUCTIONS: Sometimes we may be too quick to judge others based on the way they look or act. All too often, this rush to judgment has serious consequences. Each of the situations below represents a common misunderstanding based on a misreading of nonverbal signals. Try to think of one that has happened to you. Be prepared to share these experiences with others in your class.

Situations

1. You form an impression of someone's personality based on the way they look or dress, but your impression turns out to be wrong.
2. You decide someone doesn't like you because of the way they behave in your presence. It turns out that you were mistaken.
3. Others misread you because of something about your appearance or demeanor.

easier to say that nonverbal communication is communication without words than it is to apply the definition to the various signals usually regarded as nonverbal. In short, are all nonverbal signal systems truly communication codes that do not contain words? To answer this question, we must first examine whether the essential properties of verbal communication actually distinguish it from nonverbal communication.

Communicating with Words

As used here, **words** are *the units of meaning upon which a language is built*. Although a word is a symbol, can we say that all symbols are words? The answer to this question probably depends on one's definition of the term *language*. In the broadest sense of the term, there is almost no difference between a language and any signal system, as long as communication takes place. Based on this view, any nonverbal symbol—gestures with agreed-upon meanings, the clothes we wear, and so forth—can be considered a *word*. Usually, however, an attempt is made to discuss those properties of verbal language that seem most likely to differentiate it from nonverbal forms of communication. Yet, as Burgoon, Buller, and Woodall (1996) discovered in their analysis of these properties, nearly all of them are true, in varying degrees, of either iconic or arbitrary codes. On the other hand, if we limit our discussion of nonverbal communication to intrinsic codes (innate, symptomatic, spontaneous, and nonpropositional), the similarities end. Let's briefly consider some of these basic properties.

WORDS ARE DISCRETE, MEANINGFUL UNITS As noted above, a word is a single unit in a language. Dictionaries allow us to learn the meaning and use of words. To some extent, this is also true of nonverbal communication. As we have already seen, many single gestures have explicit meanings. Certain kinds of vocalizations—yawning, saying *uh huh*, throat clearing, laughter, and so on—are easy to understand, as are most facial expressions. We know what it means to kiss, shake hands, or pat someone on the back. We can identify the occupation, nationality, social status, or personal values of many people based solely on their attire. And the many stereotypes we hold about people based on their physical attributes (weight, facial features, hair color, etc.) confirm the symbolic nature of these particular signals. Despite the fact that we do not have dictionaries, we can still learn the meaning of nonverbal signals with very little difficulty.

LANGUAGE MUST ADHERE TO GRAMMATICAL RULES To use a language, we must learn its grammar (rules of syntax, punctuation, composition, etc.). Not following the rules of grammar will often render what we say or write to others meaningless or at least difficult to comprehend. Likewise, much of our nonverbal communication depends on our adherence to various sets of rules. Unlike language, however, these rules have much less to do with the structure and sequencing of signals than they do with the appropriateness of the signals in a given context. Since we do not learn these rules in the same way we learn grammar, they often go unnoticed until they are broken. Imagine the following scenarios:

- Nine-year-old Brent wants to show his interest in Tricia, a classmate, so he walks over to her and pushes her several times. He is surprised when she becomes upset and runs away.
- Charles is introduced to a new coworker at the company picnic. They shake hands with each other, but Charles doesn't smile or make any eye contact.
- Laura gives an oral report in her history class but speaks so quickly and softly that many of her listeners cannot understand her.
- Steve is ejected from a basketball game after gesturing obscenely toward a referee with whom he vehemently disagreed.
- Malik is so disappointed that he didn't win first place in the poetry contest that he becomes visibly angry when the winner is announced.

In each of the above scenarios, someone is violating a rule governing the use of nonverbal signals. Brent doesn't know how to express his interest in Tricia—his inappropriate use of touch serves only to send the wrong message. As an adult, Charles should know the importance of smiling and eye contact when greeting someone. Laura's speaking style breaks a fundamental rule about how to use your voice in a public presentation. Steve's temper may have kept him from following a rule that prohibits participants from using obscene gestures in athletic competitions. Finally, Malik disregards a well-known rule about displaying emotion in public: Don't be a sore loser.

Perhaps the difference between verbal language and nonverbal signals has less to do with the need to follow rules than it does with the consequences of breaking the rules. According to Duke, Nowicki, and Martin (1996) in their book, *Teaching Your Child the Language of Social Success*, most of us will think of a person using poor grammar as unintelligent, whereas we regard an individual unskilled in the use of nonverbal communication as odd or just socially awkward. As a result, they believe our educational system has plainly overlooked the need to teach young children the rules (or grammar) of nonverbal communication.

> The very informality of the process, compared to the structured lessons of grammar, often makes the learning of nonverbal skills a hit-or-miss affair in which some children have much training and others relatively little. Great gaps in knowledge can result in broad differences in social success, ranging from the child who moves through life with relative grace and ease to the youngster who is rejected by peers "for no apparent reason." (p. 4)

LANGUAGE CAN REFER TO THINGS REMOVED IN SPACE AND TIME Proponents of the view that nonverbal communication is not a language are quick to note that only words can take us to distant places and transport us to other times. Nonverbal messages, on the other hand, bind us to the here and now. Certainly this is true of most nonverbal signals, particularly symptoms of our emotions and inclinations (the intrinsic code). Yet there are exceptions. We can tell stories through the language of gesture, most notably with sign language (arbitrary code) or pantomime (iconic code). However, because the essential properties of sign language resemble spoken or written language, we usually regard it as a type of verbal rather than nonverbal communication. To a lesser degree, the symbolism of clothing and other elements of body adornment—cosmetics, jewelry, tattoos, and so forth—can also evoke reflections of the past or images of faraway lands.

LANGUAGE CONTAINS PROPOSITIONS THAT CAN BE PROVEN TRUE OR FALSE
Language users can utter various kinds of statements that may or may not be true. Propositions of fact are statements that assert the existence of something in the past, present, or future (for example, "Jefferson City is the state capital of Missouri"). Propositions of meaning express the nature of something (for example, "America is

a democratic nation"). Value statements assert the relative worth of something (for example, "Deceptive advertising practices are unethical"), and policy propositions argue that something should be done (for example, "Capital punishment should be prohibited").

It is difficult to see how nonverbal signals can express any of the ideas stated above. This is not to say that gestures and other signals are entirely nonpropositional. Phony facial expressions (semblances) allow us to lie about our feelings as we pretend to be happy, angry, sad, and so forth. We can use intention movements to bluff someone into believing that we will do something we do not plan to do, as a quarterback does when faking a pass. In addition, many gestures can convey messages that may be false ("Good job," "I have a headache," "I don't know," "He's crazy," etc.). But clearly, the range of propositions, as well as the capacity for combining them into complex arguments (for example, "Capital punishment should be abolished because it doesn't deter crime"), differentiate language from nonverbal signal systems.

Communication with words (language) differs from nonverbal signal systems in important ways. Perhaps many of the differences are far less substantive than we might have thought. The more we include iconic and arbitrary codes into our discussions of nonverbal communication, the more we begin to accept the idea of a nonverbal language. Some studies show, for instance, that the gestures used by deaf children who have never learned any kind of sign language still contain many of the properties of verbal communication (Clay, Pople, Hood, & Kita, 2014; Goldin-Meadow, 2003). On the other hand, when we focus on the nonverbal signal systems humans share with many other species, we invite a sharp contrast between communication with words and communication without words.

Communicating without Words

Compared to communication with words, is there anything unique about nonverbal communication? The most obvious answer is that much of what is unique stems from the properties of our biologically shared signal system.

MANY NONVERBAL SIGNALS ARE UNIVERSAL Some of our signaling systems evolved because of their survival value for our species. Our physical features identify us (gender, geography, maturity), protect us (babyish features evoke a caretaking response, intimidating features deter potential aggressors), and facilitate courtship and mating (availability, attractiveness). Facial expressions motivate us to act (doing something that makes us happy) and allow us to influence others. Our ability to decode facial expressions determines the behaviors we choose in response to others (avoiding an angry person, helping a depressed person, etc.). Our use of personal space, touch, and eye contact indicates whether we are connecting with others or rejecting them. Therefore, it is not surprising that all humans and many other species as well use these basic signaling systems. It's simply a matter of survival. In contrast, the arbitrary nature of verbal communication codes means that they will vary from culture to culture. At present, there is no universal language.

SOME NONVERBAL SIGNALS ARE SENT AND RECEIVED SPONTANEOUSLY Although we do not always choose our words carefully, we still have a choice. Nonverbal symptoms such as blushing, dropping our jaw, and trembling occur involuntarily. It would not make much sense to say that we choose to do these things for communication purposes. Nevertheless, each seems to constitute a nonverbal signal: We blush when embarrassed, drop our jaw when surprised, and tremble when afraid. As is the case with all symptoms, the message sent cannot be false because of the necessary cause-and-effect relationship between these signs and their referents. This statement is not meant to imply, however, that we cannot mimic a symptom with a semblance (for example, pretending to cry), but only that many symptoms are tough to fake, and most are tough to fake convincingly (e.g., genuine facial expressions). For this reason, we frequently try to read these actions to determine how someone feels or whether someone is telling us the truth.

On the receiving end of these signals, we often react spontaneously as well. And these reactions occur even before we interpret the signal. For example, researchers have discovered various physiological as well as behavioral responses to acts of staring, touching, and spatial invasion (Argyle & Dean, 1965; Ellsworth, Carlsmith, & Henson, 1972; Patterson, 1977). Apparently, some degree of arousal or discomfort precedes any meaning we attach to the signal, such as "She must like me," "He's being rude," or "That person's acting strangely." In contrast, words generally elicit a cognitive, less automatic response whereby we interpret the meaning of what we hear or see.

The spontaneous rather than deliberate and controlled nature of nonverbal communication contributes to the idea that nonverbal behavior is more stable and thus a more reliable indicator of our personality than is verbal communication. In fact, one recent study found that across different situations, verbal communication tended to vary significantly more than nonverbal communication did (Weisbuch, Slepian, Clarke, Ambady, & Veenstra-VanderWeele, 2010).

NONVERBAL SIGNALS CAN RESEMBLE WHAT THEY REPRESENT Words do not look like the things they represent. The word *chair* does not resemble an actual chair; the word *Cindy* looks nothing like a person named Cindy. While this property of iconicity is missing from language, it characterizes much of our nonverbal communication and fosters mutual understanding, even between individuals who speak a different language. If you visit a foreign country, for example, you can ask for a drink of water, find out the time of day, or get directions to the nearby gym without speaking a word because of the ease with which you can mime those particular activities (try doing Exercise 1.3).

EXERCISE 1.3

TRY IT

Miming Your Own Business

INSTRUCTIONS: This exercise can be done in small groups or in front of the whole class. Imagine being in a place where no one can speak English. Since you can't speak their language either, how will you communicate if you must? Try finding out how well you can communicate the following messages without uttering a single word.

Messages:

1. My friend is very sick; where is the nearest hospital?
2. Do you work here?
3. My car just broke down and I need help getting it repaired.
4. I'm looking for an electronics store so I can buy a notebook computer.
5. Is there a zoo here in the city?
6. I think someone just stole my train ticket.
7. Where is the nearest restroom?
8. I'm very thirsty. Where can I get a drink of water?
9. I need directions to the hotel I'm staying in.
10. Is there a pay phone near here?

NONVERBAL SIGNALS CAN OCCUR SIMULTANEOUSLY When we use language, we must speak, write, or sign one word at a time. This is not true of nonverbal communication. While we are speaking to another person, we are also communicating through body movement, posture, facial expression, appearance, touch, eye contact, and tone of voice.

▸ Without the use of words, professional mimes use body movement and facial expressions to get their messages across.

istockphoto.com/VladartDesign

Because many of these signals are capable of producing the same basic message—saying "I like you," for instance—the likelihood that the message will get through may be increased significantly if the signals are consistent. On the other hand, inconsistency among signals, which may reflect mixed feelings, can lead to confusion or miscommunication. Sometimes, our communication strategies are based on this ability to send mixed messages. In the dating game, for instance, it is not unusual for men and women to equivocate deliberately and thus appear cool and coy. The man might convey interest through tone of voice, facial expression, and touch but simultaneously communicate disinterest through lack of eye contact, increased distance, and physical relaxation. The woman might express her interest in him with smiles, giggles, and flirtatious speech, but at the same time signal her detachment by avoiding touch, keeping her distance, turning away, and breaking eye contact (see Chapter 8). These mixed signals serve to keep the other person guessing. Revealing your intentions, in no uncertain terms, puts an end to the game—the game itself may be a source of pleasure—and risks rejection or exploitation by the other person. On the positive side, it may speed up the process of getting together.

In everyday situations, we often use verbal and nonverbal channels simultaneously to convey sarcasm. Consider the following case:

> Maria suggests to her roommate, Wendy, that they clean up the house before going out to the movies. Wendy frowns and then moans sarcastically, "Sure, why not?" Oblivious to Wendy's disapproval and sarcasm, Maria begins cleaning but gets confused and upset when Wendy is slow to join in. "You just agreed it was a good idea. What's the problem?" shouts Maria.
>
> Clearly, Maria and Wendy are not adequately attuned to each other's feelings and intentions. The true message in this case is a product of mixed signals, contradictory verbal and nonverbal messages: Verbally, Wendy said she agreed with Maria's suggestion to clean the house but nonverbally, she disagreed.

WHAT ARE THE FUNCTIONS OF NONVERBAL COMMUNICATION?

As used here, the functions of nonverbal communication are the communication-related activities that are necessary for the survival of a species. Nonverbal signal systems evolved to perform these basic functions. It's easy to see why we must be able to recognize each other or at least be able to tell the difference between males and females and between humans and other animals (the identification function). It's also easy to see how we benefit as a species from forging relationships with others in ways that are mutually advantageous (relationship function), send and receive messages about our feelings and intentions (emotion function), and deliver verbal messages about ourselves and the outside world (delivery function).

PERSONAL EXPERIENCE 1.3

CAN YOU RELATE TO THIS?

Nonverbal Signals Often Resemble Their Referents

A couple of weeks ago, I was in a large music store doing some Christmas shopping. I was in there for a while and eventually had to use the restroom. The door to the restroom had a sign saying "KEY AT FRONT DESK." I went to the front desk and the gentleman was on the phone with another customer. I waited patiently for a minute or so but finally waved my arm to get his attention and then made a gesture that resembled turning a key. Immediately, he handed me the key to the restroom. Using this gesture enabled me to communicate with him without interrupting his phone conversation.

Bryan

As we'll see in this chapter, each function appears to be universal. In other words, all animals have developed unique signaling systems that enable members of a species to identify themselves, relate to others, express their internal states, and deliver vital information about their environment. Thus, it should come as no surprise that humans have acquired the same capacity as well. We'll examine each of these functions in the sections that follow. In subsequent chapters, we review the research on human nonverbal communication as it relates to each of the functions (Part II).

The Identification Function

A simple fact of life is that all creatures have a distinct identity. Either as an individual, a male or a female, a member of a group, or a representative of a particular species, an animal must be able to signal its identity to others. Even among the lowest of animals, a case of mistaken identity could have disastrous consequences (failing to recognize a natural predator, trying to mate with an individual of a different species, not being permitted to join other members of the group, etc.). Because identity signals enhance the survival of any species, they have become an integral part of the communication systems used by all animals. They include various sounds, calls, songs, scents, and physical features. As is the case with other animals, humans must also signal identity. Through appearance and behavior, we signal our age, race, gender, ethnic origin, social class, occupation, values, and more. Various nonverbal signatures also identify us as unique individuals (facial features, body shape, voice, etc.). Like other species, we inherit much of this nonverbal repertoire because of its survival value. Unlike other animals, however, humans have been able to fashion many of the ways identity is expressed to others. In this section, we'll take a brief inventory of the myriad ways we communicate who we are without words.

Even before birth, we can read many of the signs that will later identify us (for example, biological sex and physical fitness). In time, genetic and cultural forces will combine to create multiple identities, some more important than others in shaping the way we are judged and ultimately treated. Certainly gender is a case in point. Just as soon as we say, "It's a boy" or "It's a girl," we are already beginning the lifelong process of gender discrimination, a process that will do much to determine the kind of person the infant becomes. What are these innate gender signals? Zoologist Desmond Morris (1977) attributes many of the observable, anatomical differences between males and females to the ancient division of labor that once existed between the sexes: males as hunters, females as breeders and food gatherers.

From this evolutionary perspective, many of the differences we take for granted between male and female physiques are the product of specialized sex roles that are little more than relics of the distant past. Compared to the female, the male is designed as a "running, jumping, and throwing machine" (Morris, 1977, p. 231). For example, male bodies are taller and heavier than female bodies, with bigger bones and more muscle, larger feet, broader shoulders, longer arms, bigger hands with thicker fingers, a larger skull, and stronger jaws.

These biological gender signals illustrate the inherent connection between our physical features and the pressures of natural selection that mold them. Another example of natural identity signals is the appearance of cuteness in people. What is it about someone that makes him or her look cute rather than handsome or beautiful? Ethologist Konrad Lorenz (1950) was the first to recognize formally the important role played by baby-faced signals in parent–infant bonding. He observed that certain age-specific physical characteristics of infants across different species elicit nurturing responses; that is, the appearance of the infant stimulates the urge to protect and care for the infant—to love it. Among humans, these physical features include relatively large heads; prominent and protruding foreheads; pudgy cheeks; large, low-set eyes; small, button noses; and more. As the individual matures, he or she loses many of these features. To the extent that some are retained into adulthood, the individual may continue looking cute to others.

To be sure, nature exercises a great deal of control over our identity signals. But one of the distinguishing attributes of all humans is the capacity and the desire to alter appearances. What are some of the many arbitrary ways we communicate our different selves to others? Of course, the most obvious way is through clothing and cosmetics. Sometimes the body is modified or adorned to augment natural differences. Examples of these enhancements include pads that make the shoulders look larger, blush to enhance a woman's natural color, tight-fitting attire that accentuates a woman's hourglass figure or holds in a man's belly, shoes that add inches to a person's height, wigs, false eyelashes, and so forth.

RESEARCH 1.1

FIND OUT MORE

How Do Tattoos Signal Our Identity?

In this study, the authors conducted in-depth interviews with undergraduate tattooed women aged 18–35 in order to find out why they decided to get tattoos and how their tattoos were related to their sense of self. For example, one of the women who was interviewed by the researchers said,

> It reminds me where I come from. It defines who I am. You don't wear traditional clothes anymore, so it is to show who you are, and it is always on your body in contrast to jewelry, which is not part of you. Tattoos become a secret thing to yourself. It is a good comfort to be there for yourself. (Ronda, age 20)

Another woman said,

> I think I just wanted something to represent me, to make me an individual because, I don't know, my dad did call me a conformist. But, I just feel like it's just something that I've always kind of wanted to do, to express myself and to have something meaningful on me. (Katie, age 18)

To find out more about this study and answer the following questions, see the full text of this study (cited below).

1. How did the researchers find the women to participate in the study?
2. What do you think was the most important finding in this study?
3. What were the main limitations of the study?
4. What type of nonverbal communication research is this? (See Appendix.)

Source: Mee Mun, J., Janigo, C. A., & Johnson, K. P. (2012). Tattoo and the self. *Clothing and Textiles Research Journal*, 30, 134–148.

There are also creative uses of clothing and cosmetics that represent—among other things—our culture, occupation, social class, age, and values. Perhaps nothing epitomizes the identification function of attire more than uniforms do. Think of all the people, for example, who must wear a uniform on the job: doctors, athletes, police officers, postal workers, restaurant employees, nuns, nurses, and so on. Resistance to the wearing of uniforms illustrates dramatically the tension that exists in this country between the need for affiliation and solidarity on the one hand and the need for autonomy and individuality on the other. Efforts to require uniforms in public schools illustrate this kind of tension clearly. As historian Elizabeth Ewing (1975) observes:

> Uniformity is not natural to humankind, but everywhere, people are in uniform. Few of those living in the western world today have not worn it at some time, yet to many it seems an aberration from that uniqueness of the individual which is his highest quality. (p. 11)

Perhaps somewhere between order and chaos lies the best rationale for the wearing of uniforms and the best explanation for their presence throughout history and across cultures.

A less obvious but no less important way we acquire identity signals is through **stereotyping**—making generalizations about a class of people based on certain attributes they have in common. Because we learn from personal experiences or secondhand accounts to see a connection between overt cues (the way a person looks or behaves) and internal traits (the kind of person they are), these stereotypes are quick to form. Examples abound: "People who wear eyeglasses are intelligent," "Fat people are lazy," "People who don't make eye contact are not trustworthy," "People who don't smile are unfriendly," "People with tattoos are rebels," and so on. One of the most pernicious of these stereotypes is known as the *halo effect*. In general, the halo effect is an inclination to form positive judgments about others simply because they possess some other positive, although unrelated, attribute. A great deal of research confirms the existence of this halo effect for physical attractiveness; that is, good-looking people are often perceived more favorably—as smarter, friendlier, happier, and so on—than are their less attractive counterparts. Of course, given the absence of any evidence that these judgments are true, this kind of everyday discrimination against unattractive individuals is both misguided and unfortunate (Part II presents evidence of this discrimination).

We tend to think much less about behavior than we do about appearance when it comes to identification. Yet our actions can also signal our identity to others. Some of these nonverbal signals may be inborn, behavioral symptoms of who we are, such as the higher-pitched voices of women compared to men and the gaze avoidance of people who are shy. Some actions are theatrical in the sense that they merely mimic behaviors based on natural differences: acting like a child, acting like an old man, acting like a disabled person, and so on. Still other behaviors are conventional, arbitrary actions based on socially derived standards of conduct—how a person is "supposed" to act. Certainly, many of the behavioral differences between men and women are based more on sex roles than they are on biology. For instance, because women are expected to be more nurturing than men, they tend to smile more, make more eye contact while listening, and use comforting forms of touch more often than men do. Another conventional difference in nonverbal signals that serves to identify various cultures and subcultures is accented speech. We can often tell where someone was raised just by listening to the way they speak their language (see Chapter 6 for a review of this research).

The Relationship Function

Among all social animals, individuals must form relationships with others to survive and reproduce. The dynamics of this process always involve negotiating and settling two fundamental issues: intimacy and control. Intimacy involves questions of attachment and closeness; it includes courtship as well as companionship. Control is a matter of influence and deference; it becomes paramount under conditions of scarcity when individuals must compete for valued resources.

Like other animals, we communicate nonverbally to make friends and fall in love, to intimidate some adversaries and appease others. So fundamental are these nonverbal signals that it is impossible to engage in any face-to-face interaction without communicating some degree of interest or disinterest and some degree of dominance or submissiveness.

Many of the physical features we're born with attract the opposite sex. Since the most basic part of courtship is getting the interest of a potential mate, it's not surprising that both men and women are biologically equipped to do so. Women are attracted to tall men with broad shoulders, slim waists, and narrow hips. Men are attracted to women with youthful and shapely figures. Both sexes prefer facial features that signal youth, health, and sexual maturity. There is also evidence of a mutual preference for facial symmetry and familiarity or "averageness" in the appearance of most facial features. Many of our physical characteristics (height, body build, etc.) also convey to others some degree of strength or weakness (see Chapter 3 for a review of this research).

In addition to physical appearance, many nonverbal behaviors evolved to expedite our relationships with others. Among those behaviors that signal approach–avoidance are various actions involving the use of touch, personal space, and gazing (see Chapter 4 for a review of the research on these signals). Picture a scene in which Vanessa is talking to Greg: She's standing close to him, she's directly facing him, she touches him often, and she makes nearly continuous eye contact with him. Does she like him? Perhaps. The signals are certainly positive. But she might have some reason for pretending to like him (e.g., he's her employer), or she might have learned that this is the way a polite person is supposed to behave. Now let's change Vanessa's behavior. Picture this scene: She's standing far from him, she's not facing him, she never touches him, and she makes very little eye contact with him. Clearly, Vanessa's nonverbal signals in this scene tell a much different story about her attitude toward or her relationship with Greg than they did in the first scene. In addition to touch, personal space, and gazing behavior, signs of conversational involvement also indicate positive or negative attitudes. Had Vanessa talked very little or had she appeared detached when she did speak (few gestures, little vocal intonation, few facial expressions), she would be signaling an even more negative attitude toward Greg than she was above.

Like nonhuman animals, we also use nonverbal behaviors during courtship to gain the attention, interest, and ultimately the affection of another individual. Some of the ways that men do this aren't much different from the tactics employed by many other species, such as body enlargement, swaggering, and preening. But women actually bear the heavier burden when it comes to initiating the courtship sequence, which they do through both their appearance and their behavior. Anthropologist Monica Moore's (1985) observations of women in different contexts suggests that numerous behaviors—hair flipping, head tossing, caressing, parading, and more—may serve to entice a potential mate (see Chapter 8 for a discussion of the research on courtship signals).

Thus far, we've addressed the intimacy consequences of nonverbal communication. What about the issue of relational control? Here also nonverbal signals are crucial in resolving questions of dominance and submissiveness. Like many animals, we stare, growl, and enlarge our bodies when attempting to intimidate our adversaries. Other threat displays include actions that invade the space or territory of another, such as getting too close, shouting, or touching as well as angry facial expressions. In contrast, many of our appeasement displays are just the opposite: avoiding the gaze of another, speaking softly, shrinking our bodies, backing away, smiling, and so forth. For example, in a recent study of Olympic judo competitors, Hwang and Matsumoto (2014) found that the winners produced more of certain behaviors—arms above shoulders, arms away from body, chest out, making fists, head tilted back/up, shouting, and facial aggression—compared to the losers.

The Emotion Function

In the broadest sense of the term, emotion is a fundamental stimulus-response process that motivates an organism to engage in behavior that is essential for the survival of the species. The study of emotion includes (1) the kinds of stimuli that tend to evoke different emotional responses, (2) the kinds of emotions that can be evoked, (3) behaviors or activities essential for the survival of a species, (4) the overt expression of emotions, and (5) the covert experience of an emotion.

The prevailing theory of emotional expression draws heavily on the seminal work of Charles Darwin. As a simple matter of survival, this process is, to some extent, automatic in nearly all animal species (Buck, 1984; Izard, 1977; Plutchik, 1980). To illustrate, Helen opens the refrigerator door and grabs a carton of milk. She pours the milk into a bowl of cereal, sits down at the table, and begins eating. To her horror, the milk has gone sour and she spits it out immediately: not much thinking, just stimulus (sour milk) and response (spitting out the milk). Her reaction also probably included a look of disgust on her face and maybe a gagging sound (overt signals), along with any of the thoughts, feelings, and sensations she had about the incident (covert experience). In this case, her act of spitting out the milk represents one of the basic ways we adapt to our environment: rejection of something undesirable.

The idea that animals express emotions is not new. In his classic text, *The Expression of the Emotions in Man and Animals*, published in 1872, Charles Darwin documented countless instances of animals—from lizards to lemurs, birds to baboons—using their voices, faces, and bodies to convey their emotions. More controversial than whether they express emotion is the degree to which their covert experience of emotion is similar to our own. Although fascinating, this question has been explored elsewhere (see Masson & McCarthy, 1995) and will not be addressed here. In this section, we'll focus on how animals signal their emotional state to others (overt expression). Some emotions seem to be more basic for survival than are others. As a result, more elaborate and detectable signal systems have developed for those emotions, as seems to be the case in particular for anger and fear and to a somewhat lesser degree for joy and grief. Among higher animals, there is also evidence of signaling systems for emotions such as astonishment, guilt, shame, pride, and embarrassment. Like humans, many primates use various facial expressions to communicate emotion. But a lack of facial muscles prevents most other animals from doing the same. See Chapter 5 for a review of the research on facial expressions.

▸ The emotion function of nonverbal communication allows us to express our feelings and makes it possible for us to recognize and respond to the feelings of others.

istockphoto.com/Juanmonino

Along with many other species, humans also use nonverbal signals to express emotion. Unlike most other species, however, we count on a complex set of facial expressions to get the message across. While our voices, gestures, and postures play a role, they are not as fully involved in the process as are facial expressions. Like the signals we use to identify ourselves and to establish relationships, we inherit some and learn others.

RESEARCH 1.2

FIND OUT MORE

Are Facial Expressions of Emotion Universal?

While there is little doubt that signaling emotions is a primary function of all animals, what do we know about the use of facial expressions of emotion among all animals? Do nonhuman animals also use facial expressions to express anger, fear, sadness, joy, surprise, and disgust?

In their review of the scholarly research available on this subject, the authors of this article focus primarily on nonhuman primates while acknowledging some examples of facial expressions of emotion among non-mammalian species. Among nonhuman primates there is little debate, for example, of whether chimpanzees use facial expressions in ways similar to humans. There is much less certainty and research among other groups. Even among chimpanzees, there is some disagreement about whether facial expressions signal emotions or whether they signal an animal's social intentions. In this article, the authors also address some of the most important difficulties involved in researching facial expressions among nonhuman primates. What are some of these limitations?

To find an answer to this question above, see the full text (cited below).

Source: Waller, B. M., & Micheletta, J. (2013). Facial expression in nonhuman animals. *Emotion Review*, 5, 54–59.

Some signals of emotion are more involuntary than others. As evidence of shame or embarrassment, for example, blushing is a natural and spontaneous reaction. The evidence has been mounting for decades that some of our facial expressions are innate signals of emotions or social motives and can occur spontaneously (see Chapter 5). Researchers Mark Knapp and Judith Hall (2002) reviewed several studies on the facial expressions of children deprived of hearing and sight, infants, nonhuman primates, and persons from both literate and preliterate cultures. Given the remarkable similarities observed in the expressions of these groups, they concluded, "A genetic component passed on to members of the human species seems probable for this behavior" (p. 72).

As we've seen above, primates are not alone when it comes to expressing emotion. Nearly all animals have a need to signal anger, distress, and fear. The obvious survival value of emotion signals is twofold: first, they may instigate behaviors necessary for survival (Izard, 1977); second, they communicate one's intentions to others (Fridlund, 1994; Halliday, 1983). Exactly how many emotions we have inherited is not known, although the general consensus is that the number of primary emotions—those that are signaled the same way by all humans—is probably in the range of six to ten. Researchers Paul Ekman and Wallace Friesen (1975) have identified anger, happiness, sadness, surprise, fear, disgust, and contempt as the primary emotions. Other emotions considered candidates for the primary emotions are shame, guilt, and interest (Izard, 1977; Tompkins, 1962).

Our social lives would be far less complex (though not necessarily more successful) if we always expressed our true feelings. Imagine not being able to control your emotions. You feel bitter, so no matter where you are or who you're with, you look and sound bitter. Of course, we learn two facts of life at a very young age: We have a lot of control over our nonverbal expressions and there are rules to be followed—two lessons that contribute to our social and emotional intelligence (Duke, Nowicki, & Martin, 1996; Goleman, 1994, 2006). In fact, many of our expressions are not symptoms of our emotions at all (intrinsic code) but merely semblances of them (iconic code). We can mimic a look of surprise when we are not at all surprised. We can pretend to be sad when we're not.

Often, the decisions we make about how to behave are based on rules that we learn. These display rules can prompt us to misrepresent our true feelings. Ekman and Friesen (1969b) identified several ways this can happen (see Chapter 5). Taboos against showing anger in public, for example, are very common. Someone who feels enraged might show only mild disapproval or might even cover up the anger with a social smile. This seems to be especially true among Asian populations, where people routinely use masking smiles to conceal feelings of anger or depression.

The Delivery Function

Thus far, we have focused our discussion on how nearly all living creatures use nonverbal signals for self-expression, that is, to communicate information about one's identity or one's intentions (motivational state). But most species also use nonverbal signals to exchange information about the outside world and, in some cases, the manner in which this is done raises provocative questions about whether nonhumans use symbolic forms of communication. The delivery of symbolic messages is one of the primary functions of nonverbal communication. In this section, we will consider how animals and humans use nonverbal channels of communication to exchange these messages.

Do animals other than humans deliver symbolic messages? Do they have the capacity to use an arbitrary communication code with the properties of a human language?

To be sure, the intricate signaling systems many species use to send alarm calls and to exchange information about sources of food come closer to a language than any of the other more symptomatic forms of expression (Argyle, 1988).

Many of these signals involve what communication scholar Jo Liska (1993) calls "proper symbols"—signals that are readily decoded and learned through a process of simple conditioning. Much like human words, these symbols refer to things. Chickens use "tck, tck, tck" calls to announce the presence of food (Milius, 1999). Chimpanzees use pointing gestures. And by checking back and forth between the object they are pointing at and the individual who is supposed to be paying attention, they demonstrate that their pointing is an intentional act of communication. These actions imply an awareness of what another individual needs to know and a desire to see whether that individual is getting the message (de Waal, 2001). Studies also indicate that chimpanzees use gestures that have different meanings in different contexts. For instance, a chimp in a fight might extend its hand toward another chimp in a plea for help but use the same gesture to request food when it sees another chimp eating (Than, 2007).

Some animals use signals in other ways that mimic the properties of language. Researchers have discovered, for instance, that the grunts, moans, and belches of humpback whales appear to have a complex syntax similar to that found in the sentences of a human language ("Whale Chat," 1999). But despite these similarities, there seems to be at least one critical difference: There is presently no compelling evidence that nonhuman animals can escape the "here-and-now," that they can use symbols for the purpose of referring to things removed in time and space, one of the primary features of verbal communication (Corballis, 2001).

Even with the advent of modern technology, humans still spend a lot of time every day in face-to-face interactions. As we've seen thus far, nonverbal communication plays a primary role in signaling our identity, structuring our relationships, and expressing our emotions in these encounters. But we also depend greatly on the nonverbal mode of communication, through speech and gesture, to get our verbal messages across. Some of these abilities are inborn. Others we learn over the years.

When we write a letter or send an e-mail, we don't depend on our voice or body to get the message across. When we talk to someone over the phone, we use our voice but not our body. When we speak to others face to face, we use both our voice and body to carry the verbal content of our message. And each plays an important role.

All of us are born with the capacity to speak. To begin with, this involves a complex process of vocalization: Exhaled air travels through our windpipe, throat, and voice box (where our vocal cords are located). Air passes through a small regulated opening between our vocal cords called the *glottis*. When muscular tension tightens our vocal cords, they vibrate as the air goes through. The vibration of our vocal cords produces a sound similar to the vibrations of a violin string. This activity determines the *pitch* of our voice, or how high or low it sounds. Our vocal cords produce a sound that resonates (amplified and modified) in our chest, throat, mouth, and nasal cavities. This gives our voice its distinctive sound. The final step involves articulation—using our lips, tongue, teeth, palate, and jaw to utter words clearly (enunciation) and correctly (pronunciation).

When we speak, we also move our bodies in ways that alter the meaning and impact of our words. Much of this movement is so closely tied to speech production that it's hard to imagine talking without moving. In fact, most theories of speech-related gestures (see Chapter 6) view speech and movement as two parts of the same symbolic process, implying that our natural inclination to speak includes a similar predisposition to gesture (Freedman, 1972; McNeil, 1995). Invariably, when I ask students in my nonverbal communication classes to participate in a small-group exercise in which they must express their opinions without speech-related gestures, very few of them are unaffected.

While speaking and gesturing may come naturally, effective speaking clearly does not. Some people are better at it than others. To be sure, some individuals are born with more pleasant or more authoritative voices but, for the most part, we learn the rules of effective delivery: Make eye contact, don't speak too fast, gesture, don't pace back and forth, and so on. Becoming an effective speaker means not only learning the rules but practicing them: increasing our eye contact if our natural amount is inadequate, slowing down if our natural speech rate is too fast, or using gestures if our natural style doesn't incorporate them. (Of course, the real quandary surfaces when such advice is accompanied by the admonishment that, above all else, it's important to be yourself.)

The meanings of most gestures are also learned. Symbolic or emblematic gestures have verbal translations and function effectively as word substitutes. As we saw earlier in this chapter, their meanings can vary tremendously from one culture to another; a gesture that we take for granted in the United States may in fact mean nothing in many other countries.

THE BASIC NONVERBAL SIGNALING SYSTEMS

The basic nonverbal signaling systems are the communication codes that were used by our prehistoric ancestors and are still being used today. As long as we engage in face-to-face interaction, these nonverbal signals will continue to be an essential part of our everyday lives.

The Human Body: Signaling Multiple Identities

Long before we utter a single word or make a single move, our bodies are communicating. In Chapter 3, we will take a close look at the human body as a signaling system designed to express our many selves. These multiple identities include our gender, race, ethnicity, age, occupation, social class, personality, and more. There are three ways our bodies send these messages. The first is through body endowment—the physical features we inherit at birth. These relatively stable attributes include body shape, skin color, height, hair, facial features, and so on. The second is through body modification. Although we are all destined to look a certain way, we can alter our appearance through diet, exercise, cosmetic surgery, tattooing, body piercing, and the like. Body modification involves changes in our appearance that are relatively enduring as opposed to the momentary, short-lived changes we make through the process of body adornment, which includes clothing, cosmetics, and accessories. Through body endowment, body modification, and body adornment, we let those around us know who we are, who we think we are, who we would like to be, or (as is often the case) who we want them to think we are.

Space, Eye Contact, and Touch: An Approach–Avoidance Signaling System

Chapter 4 examines the three interrelated signals we use to engage others or to disengage, to signal our interest in others or our lack of interest, to let others know we like or dislike them, and to intimidate others or to be intimidated by them. In short, although we use space, gaze, and touch for other reasons as well, they are used fundamentally to define our relationships with others and to communicate our attitudes toward them. Albert Mehrabian (1972) referred to these signals as *immediacy behaviors*, which increase the mutual sensory stimulation between individuals in a face-to-face interaction. They include leaning toward, directly facing, moving close to, maintaining eye contact with, and touching another person. Each time we interact with someone face to face, these signals reflect positive and negative attitudes, degrees of intimacy, and feelings of inferiority and superiority.

The dynamics involved in our face-to-face encounters demand that we address approach–avoidance signals as part of a larger communication system. As Burgoon, Buller, and Woodall (1996) correctly observe, "It is not sensible to talk about what meanings are being expressed by touch or distance alone without taking into account what is happening with other immediacy components such as eye contact" (p. 53).

Facial Expression and the Communication of Emotion

The human face is our most expressive organ. As Desmond Morris (1977, p. 27) points out, "The human face has the most complex and highly developed set of facial muscles in the entire animal world," so our ability to manipulate these muscles makes it possible for us to show others a nearly infinite number of distinct faces. Chapter 5 focuses on facial expressions of emotion. It appears that our capacity to encode and decode these facial expressions, which convey emotions such as anger, fear, joy, sorrow, surprise, and disgust, is inborn and universal. There are striking similarities between human expressions and those of many other primates.

Understanding facial expressions, however, requires much more than knowing the emotional content of a particular face. While many of our expressions are spontaneous and thus symptomatic of our emotional state, perhaps many more are posed or deliberately shown to others for some purpose. This difference reflects our need to learn the many display rules that literally shape the face we choose to show in social situations. We learn at a young age what kind of behavior is appropriate or inappropriate, and this includes facial expressions. Although these rules are unwritten, they are well understood. Perhaps the best example of this is smiling. Think of how many times you deliberately smile in a single day. Most of us will smile nearly every time we think it is the polite or courteous thing to do (for example, when greeting someone). Many people smile just to be friendly. Clearly, a smile may reflect our desire to do what we think is appropriate more often than it will express how we actually feel.

Voice and Gesture: Speaking and Replacing Speech

When we speak to others face to face, we use language to exchange our thoughts and ideas. In so doing, we supplement our speech with a complex repertoire of gestures, postures, and vocalizations designed to enhance or replace the spoken word. Chapter 6 introduces this basic connection between speech and body movement. For instance, we use some gestures and postures instead of words. These emblematic gestures have well-known meanings. We don't have to speak when we use gestures to say "yes" or "no," "come here," "goodbye," "okay," "stop," and so forth. Other gestures are such an integral part of our speech that many of us could not speak effectively without them. Gestures that naturally accompany speech, called *illustrators*, include the wide array of body movements that visualize, emphasize, and synchronize what we say to others.

Sometimes referred to as *vocal paralanguage*, the nonverbal elements of speech include everything except spoken words: the unique sound of our voice (our vocal signature), pitch, volume, rate of speech, pronunciation, and more. Taken together, these signals serve multiple functions. Most importantly, however, they constitute the channel we use for delivering spoken language. Vocal cues can take the place of words, and they can emphasize, punctuate, and add rhythm to what we say. If we expect to be understood by others, we must learn the rules of effective delivery just as we must learn the rules of grammar.

SUMMARY

When two or more people exchange messages that are expressed in words, there isn't any doubt that communication is taking place. But are we communicating every time someone interprets what we do or the way we look? In this chapter, we tried to answer this question and thus shed some light on the nature of *nonverbal communication*, defined generally as communication without words. Taking a communication code perspective, we settled on a definition of communication that replaces earlier concerns over intentionality and responsibility with a focus on the use of a signaling system. We introduced three different codes, each consisting of a different kind of signal. Intrinsic codes are the natural signal systems that consist of symptoms; iconic codes contain signals called *semblances*; and arbitrary codes make use of symbol systems.

We also explored the question of when communication is nonverbal. Usually, this means that words aren't used. Since we tend to think of words as the basic units of language, it follows that nonverbal communication is not a language. We examined the many features of *language*, or communication with words, and discovered that although there are fundamental differences between language and nonverbal communication (for example, language is syntactical and propositional), there are some important similarities as well (both are governed by rules; gestures can substitute for words). We also considered the main features of *nonverbal signal systems*, communication without words. Unlike nonverbal codes, languages are neither universal nor spontaneously sent and received. Words don't resemble their referents and are never uttered simultaneously (more than one word is not spoken at a time).

The functions of nonverbal communication are the communication-related activities necessary for the survival of a species. These include the identification function, which signals an individual's gender, fitness, culture, group affiliation, age, religion, and so forth; the relationship function, which negotiates levels of control and intimacy in a relationship; the emotion function, which allows persons to express and recognize the emotional state and intentions of others; and the delivery function, which carries verbal or symbolic messages.

In Part II, we'll explore in more detail the four basic nonverbal signaling systems that were introduced in this chapter:

- signaling multiple identities such as gender, ethnicity, occupation, personality, and so on, through body endowment, modification, and adornment;
- communicating interpersonal attitudes with the immediacy behaviors of touching, gazing, and distancing;
- expressing our emotions and more with a variety of spontaneous and posed facial expressions; and
- delivering spoken messages with gesture and voice.

KEY TERMS

Arbitrary communication code 8
Communication code 6
Iconic communication code 7
Intention movements 8
Intrinsic communication code 6
Nonverbal communication 3
Referents 8
Semblances 7
Sign 6
Signal 6
Stereotyping 22
Symbols 8
Symptoms 6
Words 12

istockphoto.com/gpointstudio

Chapter Outline

2

THE DEVELOPMENT OF NONVERBAL COMMUNICATION: ACQUIRING EVERYDAY SKILLS

Nine-year-old Brian Stevenson wasn't expecting a pair of pajamas as a birthday gift from his favorite aunt and uncle. He tries to hide his disappointment, but it's obvious to everyone how upset he really is.

After a dreadful day at work and a two-hour commute home through rush-hour traffic, Tisha feels awful. "How was your day?" her husband, Jake, inquires as she walks through the front door. "Okay, I guess," she replies, her slumped posture, deadpan voice, and vacant look suggesting otherwise. "If you didn't feel well, why didn't you just say so?" Jake shouts an hour later, after dinner, when Tisha asks him why he didn't care about what was upsetting her.

Mindy's friends like to pick on her because she's fun to tease—she always takes things seriously. The other day, one of her friends, Kara, asked Mindy jokingly—but with nearly a straight face—if she was putting on a few pounds. Apparently not realizing that Kara was kidding, Mindy became visibly upset.

Perhaps you've witnessed incidents similar to these, in which individuals just don't seem to have the social skills it takes to make the best of a difficult situation. In the first scenario, Brian struggles to put on a good face but can't quite pull it off. In the second case, Jake seems unable to read his wife's feelings. Finally, Mindy's inability to pick up on her friend's jokes continues to be a source of amusement for them and a source of embarrassment to her. What Brian, Jake, and Mindy share is a need for greater skill in the practice of nonverbal communication.

Learning Objectives

After reading this chapter, you will be able to do the following:

1. Differentiate simple encoding and decoding nonverbal communication skills from complex encoding and decoding nonverbal communication skills.
2. Trace the major milestones in the development of both simple and complex nonverbal communication skills from infancy to adolescence.
3. Consider how the general competence in one nonverbal communication skill relates to general competence in other nonverbal skills.
4. Critically examine the notion that women possess greater abilities in nonverbal communication than men do.
5. Review the research on the effects of age and personality on nonverbal communication skills.
6. Review the research on whether interpersonal success and failure depends on nonverbal communication skills.
7. Consider whether one's early family environment has an impact on nonverbal communication skills later in life.
8. Evaluate the impact that training and education programs have on the potential to enhance a person's nonverbal communication skills.

This chapter introduces the key elements that constitute the everyday practice of sending and receiving nonverbal signals. It considers the development of these abilities, the kinds of people who become skilled, and whether formal education or training makes a difference.

NONVERBAL COMMUNICATION SKILLS

Ordinarily, when we think of people who are good with words, we imagine them as good speakers or good writers. As receivers of verbal messages, they may also have skills in listening and reading. But what does it mean to be good with nonverbal signals? As with any communication ability, it means being competent in sending messages but also in receiving them, being able to send and receive the many nonverbal signals we use every day to present ourselves, relate to others, express emotion, and deliver verbal or symbolic information. In the sections that follow, we'll distinguish between simple and complex skills. This distinction is not meant to imply that simple skills are easy to acquire, only that they focus on single rather than multiple channels of communication, develop earlier in life, and require less critical thinking than do the more complex skills (see Table 2.1).

Sending Skills

As we have seen in previous chapters, we send some nonverbal signals spontaneously; we send others on purpose. The difference is a matter of what we can control and thus do strategically. For example, when a four-month-old infant cries for food, the cry is a spontaneous signal, produced automatically as a symptom of hunger. A year later, however, the same baby may be crying on purpose—part of a planned strategy of getting what he or she wants. Despite the fundamental difference between spontaneous and strategic action, both kinds of signals contribute to our overall competence as message senders. In discussing these abilities, we'll begin first with the simple capacity to encode messages accurately. Signal accuracy implies that the message sent is essentially the same as the message received. Next, we'll consider the more complex skills of adapting to the situation and coordinating multiple signals.

Table 2.1 Nonverbal Communication Skills

	Simple Skills	Complex Skills
Sending Messages	Spontaneous signaling Deliberate signaling	Adapting to the situation Coordinating signals
Receiving Messages	Attunement Deciphering signals	Contextualizing signals Integrating signals

SIMPLE ENCODING SKILLS These are single-channel skills that involve the accurate transmission of messages. A facial expression is easy to read, a gesture sends the intended message, and so forth. There are two such skills. The first is the capacity to send messages spontaneously. We send many signals automatically as part of our intrinsic communication system. When these signals are not inhibited, modified, or simulated in some way, they express our true identity and feelings. Gray hair indicates our relative age, voice quality usually signals our gender, gaze avoidance frequently expresses our attitude or personality, facial expressions represent our emotional state, and so on.

EXERCISE 2.1

TRY IT

Self-Assessment: How Expressive Are You?

INSTRUCTIONS: The following items should be rated on a six-point scale ranging from 0 (not at all descriptive of me) to 5 (very descriptive of me). If you score near or more than 30 points, you tend to see yourself as an expressive person—someone who shows how he or she feels. Please respond to the following statements as accurately and honestly as possible with the following:

0 = not at all descriptive of me
1 = rarely descriptive of me
2 = occasionally descriptive of me
3 = regularly descriptive of me
4 = frequently descriptive of me
5 = very descriptive of me

1. I can't help but let other people know when I'm glad to see them.
2. People can tell I have a problem from my expression.
3. I tend to touch friends during conversation.
4. I laugh a lot.
5. People have told me that I am an expressive person.
6. I show that I like someone by hugging or touching that person.
7. I get excited easily.
8. People can tell from my facial expression how I am feeling.
9. When I am alone, I can make myself laugh by remembering something from the past.
10. Watching television or reading a book can make me laugh out loud.

Source: Klein, C. L., & Cacioppo, J. T. (1993). *The Facial Expressiveness Scale and the Autonomic Reactivity Scale* (Unpublished manuscript). Ohio State University, Columbus, Ohio.

But much of our nonverbal communication is not automatic. A second simple skill is sending messages deliberately. We choose the clothes we wear and much of our behavior. While we may not be very conscious of the ordinary things we do out of habit, these choices collectively determine how good we are at getting others to interpret our actions the way we want them to. To the extent that we are successful communicating who we are and how we feel—either real or imagined—we have mastered the **simple encoding skills** of sending nonverbal messages.

COMPLEX ENCODING SKILLS People describe Bill as a genuine guy—blunt but always aboveboard. When he talks about himself, without fail, he says, "What you see is what you get." Most agree that there isn't anything mysterious about him. Bill is a prototype of the candid or open style of communicating, someone who invariably sends signals that are honest and easy to read. In the extreme, these people are unable (or unwilling) to cover up who they are or how they feel; they become transparent to others. Of course, this ability can be both a blessing and a curse. On the positive side, we appreciate them for their frank and straightforward demeanor. And they need not worry about being misunderstood. But when it comes to doing what is

EXERCISE 2.2

TRY IT

The *Dos* and *Don*'ts of Nonverbal Communication

INSTRUCTIONS: Much of our nonverbal communication is governed by the rules we follow. Some rules are so obvious, nearly everyone knows them; other rules are less apparent. Knowledge of these rules can separate those who are competent communicators from those who are not. For each of the situations listed below, can you list three rules of nonverbal communication that could determine whether someone in that situation is successful or not? Where do these rules come from? Must these rules always be followed? Be prepared to discuss these questions in class.

1. Interviewing for a job
2. Going out on a first date
3. Conducting a meeting
4. Giving a speech
5. Interacting with a stranger
6. Talking to your boss

socially appropriate or even most effective in a particular context, their misguided belief in "always being me" can put them at a real disadvantage. In a rule-governed society, this kind of rigidity is often looked upon as a sign of immaturity rather than as an indicator of social skill. While there is a time and a place for spontaneity, adapting to the demands of the situation is one of the most important yet difficult nonverbal communication skills we can learn.

▸ An important nonverbal communication skill is having the knowledge and the ability to adapt to the demands of different situations. In what ways would you expect a person to dress and behave differently in a job interview, for instance, than in other social situations?

istockphoto.com/andresr

Most of us practice adaptation skills every day. We don't dress the same way for a job interview as we do for an evening out with our friends. We don't speak the same way while delivering an oral report as we do while speaking to someone sitting next to us on an airplane or in a crowded theater. We don't act the same way with our boss at work as we do with our siblings at home. The list could go on, but it's plain to see that, whether we are mindful of it or not, adaptation is a necessary part of daily living. Still, some people are better at it than others. They have superior knowledge of what to do, how to do it, and when to do it. In other words, they know the rules of nonverbal communication. And they possess superior performance skills by following these rules when necessary.

Another **complex encoding skill** is coordinating nonverbal and verbal signals. Only rarely do we rely on a single nonverbal signal when sending a message. Usually, our messages contain multiple signals, verbal and nonverbal. For instance, if we want to tell someone we don't feel well, we may do this with words, facial expressions, vocal intonations, sounds, postures, and so forth. How well we get our message across depends on the combined impact of the signals we choose to send. Psychologists Paul Ekman and Wallace Friesen (1969b), in discussing the interdependence that exists between nonverbal and verbal messages, identified six important ways that nonverbal communication directly affects our verbal discourse.

First, we can use nonverbal signals to emphasize our words. All good speakers know how to do this with forceful gestures, changes in vocal volume or speech rate, deliberate pauses, and so forth. These actions allow a speaker to highlight the words, phrases, or statements that may be critical to his or her message.

Second, our nonverbal behavior can repeat what we say. We can say yes to someone while nodding our head; we can order three drinks in a restaurant while holding up three fingers; if someone asks us where the telephone is, we can point to it while saying, "Over there." If our aim is to make sure the message gets through, certainly

PERSONAL EXPERIENCE 2.1

CAN YOU RELATE TO THIS?

Adapting to the Situation with Vocal Volume

I walked into the reference room of the library the other day to begin studying for my finals. The room was silent and signs were posted: "In the interest of those studying for exams, please maintain silence." However, I did not see the signs right away and began talking to some friends of mine who were walking in as I was. I could feel everyone staring at me. I quickly stopped talking and quieted my friends. Then I found an empty table and we sat down to study.

Matt

two signals are better than one. The repetitive nature of nonverbal signals allows us to build emphasis into our messages in a less clumsy way than by saying something twice.

Third, nonverbal signals can substitute for words. Often, there isn't much need to put things in words. A simple gesture can suffice (e.g., shaking your head to say *no*, using the thumbs-up sign to say "Nice job," etc.). But we also use nonverbal signals to express things that we can't afford to say in words. Coaches and players on a football team, for example, use a secret code of nonverbal signals in place of words so they can exchange messages that won't be understood by opposing players and coaches. Moreover, speech is not well suited for communicating at a distance, particularly in a crowd. And sometimes we use a well-timed gesture when we can't find the words (see Personal Experience 2.2).

PERSONAL EXPERIENCE 2.2

CAN YOU RELATE TO THIS?

Gestures Can Help When Words Fail Us

My brothers-in-law came to visit my family from Sweden this past summer. While we were having dinner my brother's sister-in-law started making a hand motion, like she was pulling on a rope. She said, "Can you pull the . . . um . . . um . . ." She did not know the word for blinds. We did not understand what she was asking until she squinted, showing that the sun was shining in her eyes and that she wanted us to pull down the blinds.

Jilanna

Fourth, we can use nonverbal signals to regulate speech. Called **turn-taking signals**, these gestures and vocalizations make it possible for us to alternate the conversational roles of speaking and listening, without the need for crude verbal declarations (e.g., "It's my turn to talk"). Someone who fails to send these nonverbal signals may experience difficulty warding off unwanted interruptions, getting a turn to speak, terminating a conversation, and so on.

Fifth, nonverbal messages sometimes contradict what we say. A friend tells us she had a great time at the beach, but we're not sure because her voice is flat and her face lacks emotion. A new boss emphasizes his open-door policy but we're unconvinced because he ignores us when we visit. In commonplace situations such as these, inconsistencies between verbal and nonverbal signals breed skepticism—we don't believe what they say, we believe what they do. Nonverbal signals are more difficult for a speaker to control than words are, so we tend to trust them more. In fact, research on how adult listeners interpret these kinds of contradictory messages shows that they place more weight on the nonverbal message than they do on the verbal message (Mehrabian & Ferris, 1967; Mehrabian & Weiner, 1967). Of course, we often send contradictory messages on purpose. One way is through the use of **sarcasm**, putting a negative nonverbal spin on a positively worded message: Lenny tells Jackie that he thought the service at the diner was truly exceptional, but he rolls his eyes when he says it. Similarly, we can use nonverbal signals to say things facetiously, to put people on. An example of this is telling someone you had a lousy time with a grin on your face (to signal that you really had a good time).

Finally, we can use nonverbal signals to complement the verbal content of our message. For the most part, the language of feelings is nonverbal. If we tell someone that we're very upset, they won't get the full message from words alone. Unless they can see it in our faces, hear it in our voices, and so on, they may not appreciate how upset we really are (the intensity of our feelings). In fact, they might not even get the right message. Being upset could mean we feel angry, depressed, disappointed, or just a bit on edge. Nonverbal signals can help to clarify the words we use and reveal the true nature of our feelings.

Receiving Skills

These skills enable us to read people: to identify them, to infer their attitudes and emotions, to decipher intended meanings, to consider the context in which a message is sent, and to unravel mixed messages. Clearly, some receiving skills are not as complex as others are—they require less critical thinking and develop earlier in life. We'll begin by identifying these **simple decoding skills**. Then, in the following section, we'll examine the skills that are more complex.

SIMPLE DECODING SKILLS Chris is very affected by the feelings of those around her; she not only seems to have a sixth sense when it comes to knowing how others feel, but she claims often to feel the way they do. If she's with someone who is angry, she can feel herself getting angry. If she's with someone who is giddy, she becomes giddy herself. Being with someone who is depressed can put her in a mood that will ruin the rest of her day. This kind of receptivity to others represents a simple decoding skill—being attuned to the emotions and attitudes of others. With this capacity, we are better able to connect and empathize with people. As a result, we may be more likely to help them, console them, or pay attention to them. In this way, **attunement** may be fundamental to the process of building supportive relationships—from the establishment of rapport to the development of strong emotional ties—that can last a lifetime. The questionnaire in Exercise 2.3 may give you some idea of how attuned you are to the feelings of other people (see Chapter 5 for more information).

Another simple decoding skill is deciphering the meaning of a nonverbal signal—the ability to interpret the meaning of a gesture, a vocalization, a facial expression, a touch, and so forth. When there is widespread agreement on the meaning of a particular signal, this ability requires little critical thinking. Yet the task of deciphering a nonverbal signal is complicated by attempts to deceive, challenging us to discriminate between the natural and the theatrical in a person's presentation. Is there something about the person's appearance or demeanor that doesn't seem genuine? In some cases, it may be obvious—a phony laugh, an insincere gaze, an awkward gesture, and so on. In other cases, it may be nearly impossible to tell. Still, some people have a more discerning eye (or ear) than others do; they can pick up the subtle differences that distinguish a performance from the real thing.

COMPLEX DECODING SKILLS Unlike the simple skills noted above, these skills require some degree of critical thinking. In addition, the development of these skills occurs much later in childhood. Trying to figure people out is a common everyday pastime. At some point in our dealings with others, we may find ourselves wondering about their true feelings or motives: "Is she really depressed?" "Does he really like me?" Or we may be forced to make sense of a confusing or ambiguous message: "Was he putting me down or was he just kidding?" "Is she getting defensive or am I reading too much into her reaction?" Of course, since we aren't mind readers, how can we expect to answer such questions? Well, in a strict sense, we can't. We have no direct access to another person's inner thoughts and feelings. Nonetheless, we can make inferences based on what we see or hear. And the quality of these inferences is directly related to how well we can comprehend the information we receive from various channels.

EXERCISE 2.3

TRY IT

Self-Assessment: Do You Catch the Feelings of Others?

This questionnaire measures your susceptibility to emotional contagion—the tendency to "catch" the feelings of other people. There are no right or wrong answers, so try to be completely honest in your answers. Read each question and indicate the answer that best applies to you. Please answer each question carefully. A score near or greater than 20 points means that you see yourself as susceptible to emotional contagion.

Use the following key:

4 = always true for me

3 = often true for me

2 = rarely true for me

1 = never true for me

1. I often find that I can remain cool in spite of the excitement around me. 4 3 2 1
2. I tend to lose control when I am bringing bad news to people. 4 3 2 1
3. I have trouble remaining calm when those around me worry. 4 3 2 1
4. I cannot continue to feel okay if people around me are depressed. 4 3 2 1
5. I get upset just because a friend is acting upset. 4 3 2 1
6. I become nervous if others around me are nervous. 4 3 2 1
7. The people around me have a great influence on my moods. 4 3 2 1

Source: Adapted from Stiff, J. B., Dillard, J. P., Somera, L., Kim, H., & Sleight, C. (1988). Empathy, communication, and prosocial behavior. *Communication Monographs*, 55, 198–213. Used by permission of the National Communication Association.

One **complex decoding skill** is contextualizing nonverbal signals: When interpreting a signal, taking into account the overall context in which the signal occurs. With few exceptions, various elements of the context make a difference: who the people are, where they are from, what their relationship to you is, what they are talking about, where they are, and so forth. For instance, imagine two women, Danielle and Roberta, having a conversation. Roberta is talking about an automobile accident she witnessed the other day. The accident shook her up. Danielle says nothing, but she reaches out and touches Roberta on the arm. In this context, how would you interpret the touch? It seems to be a comforting gesture, a show of concern by Danielle. But what if we alter key elements of the context? Would you interpret the touch differently? Consider the following:

- Danielle and Roberta are having a heated argument. (Danielle says nothing, but she reaches out and touches Roberta on the arm.)
- Danielle is listening to Murray go on and on about the history of professional wrestling. (Danielle says nothing, but she reaches out and touches Murray on the arm.)
- Danielle is Roberta's boss. She wants Roberta to stop being late for. Roberta threatens to go to Danielle's supervisor. (Danielle says nothing, but she reaches out and touches Roberta on the arm.)
- Danielle and John are having dinner at a romantic restaurant. John compliments Danielle on her appearance. (Danielle says nothing, but she reaches out and touches John on the arm.)

Sometimes contextual factors can render a nonverbal signal nearly meaningless—there is little need for interpretation. The signal may become so embedded in the context that only the absence of the signal seems to mean anything. To illustrate, when we enter the showroom of an automobile dealer, a smiling salesperson will greet us. In this context, what does the smile mean? Some possibilities are the salesperson is happy to see us, the salesperson is a friendly individual, the salesperson wants to make a good impression, the salesperson thought about something amusing. Of course, if we think of the smile as merely part of the overall context, it may mean only that the salesperson is acting as a salesperson—salespeople are supposed to smile when they greet prospective customers. In such cases, the absence of a smile—violating the norm—may be more telling than the smile itself (e.g., the salesperson is not doing a good job, the salesperson doesn't feel well, the salesperson doesn't regard us as a prospective customer, etc.).

A second complex skill is integrating multisignal messages. Competence in this skill means being able to sort through an array of nonverbal and verbal signals. Some of the signals may be unclear; some may have several different meanings; some may be contradictory. And the fact that many of the signals are sent simultaneously makes the task of interpretation that much more difficult.

Thus far, we've seen how the practice of nonverbal communication involves a number of simple and complex skills in both sending and receiving messages. Table 2.1 summarizes these skills. The next section in this chapter considers the development of these skills—the simple ones that emerge in the first year of life and the more complex ones that develop gradually during childhood.

PERSONAL EXPERIENCE 2.3

CAN YOU RELATE TO THIS?

We Integrate Signals to Figure Out the Real Message

One day, a few of my friends and I went to the mall and we forgot to ask our friend Nicole if she wanted to go. When we were all together that night, Nicole asked us why we didn't ask her to go to the mall. She said we should have remembered that she needed to go to the mall because she was constantly telling us about all of the things she needed to return. I told Nicole that I was sorry I forgot to ask her to go and I asked her if she was mad. She said that she wasn't, but her angry tone of voice made me think otherwise. The rest of the night, Nicole was not as talkative as usual and seemed a little standoffish. Even though she would smile and say she wasn't upset whenever I asked if she was, I didn't really believe her.

Marlena

THE DEVELOPMENT OF NONVERBAL COMMUNICATION SKILLS

All of us are born with a built-in capacity to communicate nonverbally. In fact, numerous studies suggest that infants demonstrate all of the simple encoding and decoding skills by the time they celebrate their first birthday. They express their feelings spontaneously, send messages deliberately, become attuned to the feelings of others, and discriminate among various nonverbal stimuli (e.g., faces, voices, gestures, etc.). Of course, it takes time to make the transition into the world of symbolic communication. And with time, children learn the more complex skills involved in sending and receiving nonverbal signals. Before we discuss these complex abilities, we need to examine what we know about the development of nonverbal communication during the first year of life as well as the simple skills that come soon after.

The Development of Simple Encoding and Decoding Skills

Most parents know that communication takes place between them and their infant. But they might be surprised to find out how much. In fact, so much happens during the first year that we can easily monitor these communication milestones by the month. We'll begin by considering the development of simple encoding skills and then discuss the corresponding development of an infant's decoding abilities (see Table 2.2 for a brief summary of these findings).

Table 2.2 Development of Simple Encoding and Decoding Skills

Age	Vocal Expressions	Facial Expressions	Gaze, Touch, Personal Space	Gestures
0–3 months	Produces reflexive sounds (distress cries, noises) Responds to parents Recognizes voices	Shows interest in faces Imitates some expressions, smiles often Differentiates positive and negative expressions	Grasping and gazing instincts Positive responses to touch and eye contact	Emergence of protogestures (hand and arm movement synchronized with vocalization)
3–6 months	Produces reactive sounds (e.g., cooing, giggling, simple babbling) Mimics some vocal expressions	Mimics most and shows some of the primary emotions, such as happiness, surprise, and disgust	Gaze avoidance with strangers Turns head to display interest in others	
6–9 months	Activity sounds (grunting, advanced babbling) Awareness of turn taking	Comprehends positive and negative emotions Begins showing fear, anger, and sadness	Crawling to approach and avoid others	
9–12 months	Communicative sounds (shouting, word-like utterances) Crying takes on speech-like features Purposeful crying	Shows most of the primary emotions	Tracking gaze of others (perspective taking) Sense of personal space and privacy	Uses and responds to pointing (deictic) gestures and some iconic gestures
12–18 months	Acquires speech (single-word utterances)		Purposeful gazing, touch, and proximity as signs of interest or disinterest in others	
18–24 months		Shows all of the primary emotions	Beginning awareness of link between immediacy behavior and like/dislike toward others	Uses and responds to some emblematic gestures

Age	Vocal Expressions	Facial Expressions	Gaze, Touch, Personal Space	Gestures
2–3 years		Begins controlling expressions Labels positive and negative emotions	Deliberate use of distance, touch, and gaze to signal like and dislike	Gestures synchronized with speech production
3–4 years		Labels some primary expressions		Uses and decodes/ interprets abstract emblematic gestures
4–6 years	Labels some expressions of emotion	Labels most primary expressions	Inferences of like/ dislike based on distance, gaze, touch	

SIMPLE ENCODING SKILLS From the start, newborns tell us a lot about who they are (i.e., identification signals). Various physical features communicate their gender, ethnicity, physical condition, individuality, and age. Not until much later, however, do children develop the sense of self needed for them to begin playing a role in fashioning their own identity, which they ultimately do through appearance and demeanor. Of course, long before then, we make sure to outfit them in the attire appropriate for their age, gender, culture, and social standing.

A baby's first cries are especially important signals, indicating pain, discomfort, or hunger. As an infant's primary form of communication, crying enables her to get the help she needs and, when she gets a little older, the help she wants. Some experts believe, and many parents confirm, that we can tell from the unique sound, tempo, pitch, and duration of a cry whether the baby is hungry, uncomfortable, bored, angry, frustrated, or afraid (Argyle, 1988; Wolff, 1969). Others, citing a lack of solid research, remain unconvinced (Baron, 1992). Speech pathologist Thomas Murry (cited in Roberts, 1987) claims that, at around three to four months of age, crying helps in the development of speech by providing infants with an awareness of their lips, tongue, palate, jaw, and voice. The pitch variations that occur while crying enable babies to practice the intonation patterns they will use later when speaking (Lieberman, 1967). As they get older, they cry for shorter periods, with each cry approaching more closely the sound of words. Crying becomes most speech like, in terms of rate and rhythm, by the time the infant is about nine months old, a time when he or she also begins to cry out of anger or frustration. In addition, infants learn that crying is a good way to get attention, something they begin doing well before their first birthday.

To many parents, crying might seem like the only sound an infant makes during the first months of life. But quite a lot of vocalizing other than crying does take place. Based on their observations of infant vocalizations during the first 18 months of life, speech scientists Rachel Stark, Lynne Bernstein, and Marilyn Demorest (1993) argue that vocal communication follows an orderly developmental sequence: (1) reflexive sound making, which includes distress cries and noises such as sneezing, burping, wheezing, and so forth, predominates from birth until two months; (2) from two to five months, the infant engages in reactive sound making, vocalizations produced during face-to-face interactions with an adult or while gazing at various objects (e.g., cooing, simple **babbling**, giggling, imitating sounds); (3) this is followed by a period of activity sound making, the noncommunicative sounds that occur between five and nine months while the baby is actively exploring his or her environment (e.g., grunting, advanced babbling); (4) communicative sound making reflects the vocalizations that occur late in the first year and well into the second—at this point, there's little doubt that she has something she wants you to hear (e.g., shouting) and the babbling begins to sound more and more like real speech. Intricate word-like utterances, such as *ah-dee-dah-boo-maa*, begin to replace simpler sounds (e.g., *dadada* or *gagaga*). Now she is on the verge of talking.

The development of an approach–avoidance signaling system—behaviors such as eye contact, touch, and proximity—also begins early. Infants only a few days old gaze longer at the faces of their parents or caregivers than they do at strangers, and eye contact is evident at three to four weeks after birth (Wolff, 1963). Newborns use touch immediately, holding and grasping their mother or caregiver. These early instincts to use eye contact and touch strengthen the emotional ties that already exist between infant and parent.

At around six months, infants will avert their gaze from that of a stranger (LaFrance & Mayo, 1978). And between 11 to 14 months, they start tracking the gaze of other people to see where they are looking, thus demonstrating an early capacity to take another person's point of view (Scaife & Bruner, 1975). During the first three months, a baby begins to show signs of interest in other people by turning his or her head in their direction. In their laboratory study of infants three, 6.5, 10, and 13.5 months old, developmental psychologists Mary Rothbart, Hasan Ziaie, and Cherie O'Boyle (1992) found that 10- and 13.5-month-old infants were much more likely to use gaze and body lean while interacting with their mothers than were the younger three- and 6.5-month-old babies—a sign of early developmental changes in the use of approach–avoidance signals. By the end of the first year, most infants have begun to develop a limited sense of personal space and privacy (Caplan, 1973).

After the first year, children learn quickly that relating to others involves purposeful acts of gazing, distancing, and touching (Mueller & Rich, 1976). They begin to make choices about who to make eye contact with, who to get close to, and who to touch. The connection between these behaviors and attitudes toward other people becomes firmly established and readily observed. In one field study of nursery school children, researchers observed that four-year-olds unfamiliar with those in a group maintained greater distances with the group members than did other four-year-olds who were already acquainted with those in the group (McGrew & McGrew, 1975). And a study of three- to five-year-olds found that friendly pairs tended to stay closer together than did unfriendly pairs (King, 1966).

Infants also express emotions nonverbally. While babies have the facial muscles they need to express all the primary emotions at birth (Oster & Ekman, 1978), these early expressions are little more than reflex responses (e.g., a startled expression). Many of them may resemble mature adult expressions of emotion, but it takes time before such expressions truly emerge (Camras, Sullivan, & Michel, 1993). Gradually, they appear and eventually come under voluntary control; the baby starts to use them strategically. The earliest examples of this are crying and smiling. By inhibiting these expressions when they are alone and by exaggerating them when people are present, babies come to grips with the process of exerting influence over others, learning how to get their way (Argyle, 1988).

RESEARCH 2.1

FIND OUT MORE

When Do Children Begin Reading Facial Expressions?

The prevailing theory about children's ability to read facial expressions of emotion is that eventually, they acquire some understanding of how the face signals specific primary emotions such as fear, anger, happiness and so on. In this review of the research that has been done, the authors take a somewhat different position about how and when children develop this skill. How does the author's position differ from the prevailing theory?

To answer the question above and to find out more, see the full text of this article (cited below).

Source: Widen, S. C. (2013). Children's interpretation of facial expressions: The long path from valence-based to specific discrete categories. *Emotion Review*, 5, 72–77.

Other than reflexive actions, many facial expressions are the result of imitation. This ability to mimic the facial behavior of others—mouth opening, tongue protrusion, head bobbing, and so on—is innate and prepares the infant for the facial expressions that develop later (Bjorklund, 1987; Caplan, 1973). By the time they are two months old, many infants begin imitating some of these expressions (Meltzoff & Moore, 1977).

No facial expression is more welcome to parents than is a baby's smile. A reflex at first—indiscriminate smiling doesn't stop until the infant is nearly six months old (Spitz & Wolf, 1946)—it develops quickly into an expression of joy, an invitation to play, a gesture of affiliation. Recent studies show that infant smiling may be more informative than was previously thought. Developmental psychologist Alan Fogel and his colleagues have reported the presence of three different types of smiles observed during mother–infant interactions. The frequency of the smile depended on the type of activity taking place between infant and mother: A simple smile (lip corner retraction only) indicated the least positive emotions, an enjoyment smile (simple smile with cheek raising) indicated greater positive emotions, and a big smile (simple plus cheek raising and jaw dropping) indicated the most positive emotions (Fogel, Nelson-Goens, & Hsu, 2000; Messinger, Fogel, & Dickson, 2001).

By the time a baby is nearing his or her first birthday, he or she has expressed most, if not all, of the primary emotions (Argyle, 1988; Izard, 1978). Some researchers claim that even newborns can produce facial expressions of interest, joy, fear, disgust, and sadness (Field, 1982). Stronger evidence indicates that while infants younger than four months show happiness, interest, and surprise, they are not yet able to make facial expressions for fear, disgust, anger, or sadness (Camras et al., 1993; Oster, Hegley, & Nagel, 1992), which are more likely to appear in varying degrees after the sixth month (Argyle, 1988; Izard, 1978). Before most children enter nursery school, they have learned to control their facial expressions (e.g., pretending to be sad or angry). Some research suggests that this ability to put on a facial expression develops in the third year and improves steadily thereafter (Profyt & Whissell, 1991). From that point, children also begin learning from parents and peers the importance of following the *dos* and *don'ts* (i.e., display rules) of emotional expression (Malatestra, 1985).

▸ Mutual involvement, reciprocity, and mimicry characterize much of the face-to-face communication that takes place between the infant and parent.

istockphoto.com/sdominick

Preverbal infants can also communicate with simple gestures. Between 10 and 14 months, the time during which their social interactions involve objects, infants begin using **triadic gestures**—attempts to direct another person to some outside entity, not to the self (Tomasello & Camaioni, 1997). These early appearing gestures, which coincide with the infant's ability to follow another person's gaze (joint attention occurs when they look at the same thing) demonstrate an awareness that others are willing to pay attention to objects or events of interest to the infant and that they can be enticed to do so. The simplest kind of triadic gestures are **deictic gestures**—direct, physical references to something, usually through pointing. Among the most common are

> (1) pointing, in which infants use an extended arm-hand-finger to direct the adult's attention to an outside entity; (2) showing, in which they hold up an object manually in the adult's line of sight in order to share attention to it; (3) offering, in which they hold out an object to an adult, intending that she take it; and (4) ritualized requests, in which they request an object by extending the arm with hand open, palm up. (Tomasello & Camaioni, 1997, p. 13)

While infants often use simple pointing gestures when they want something, recent research shows that they also point for less selfish ends, such as indicating the location of something another person is trying to find (Liszkowski, Carpenter, & Tomasello, 2007).

Deictic gestures mark the infant's transition to the use of single words and soon thereafter to the use of two-word utterances, paving the way for language development (Iverson & Goldin-Meadow, 2001). After the first year, children learn through imitation to use other kinds of gestures for communication. **Iconic gestures**, which resemble something (e.g., waving arms like a bird, making a face like a fish, etc.) and simple **emblematic gestures** (e.g., symbolic gestures such as waving goodbye) are common.

▸ Babies use a variety of simple gestures, such as pointing and reaching, to communicate their interests and desires.

istockphoto.com/Linda Kloosterhof

Without any encouragement to use them, the repertoire of emblematic gestures among children remains quite limited, particularly during the first few years. But recent studies suggest that infants may be able to learn this type of communication much sooner than expected and that such learning may have beneficial results beyond improved infant–parent communication (Acredolo & Goodwyn, 1996). In one experiment, for instance, researchers found that 11-month-old infants who were taught and encouraged to use simple gestures, as symbols for objects and requests, outperformed a control group of 11-month-old infants on most measures of language acquisition when they were tested at 15, 19, 24, and 36 months (Goodwyn, Acredolo, & Brown, 2000).

The use of gestures that accompany speech begins at a very early stage of language development. In one study, Italian and Japanese two- and three-year-olds were shown pictures of objects, animals, and people performing various actions and then asked questions such as *What is this?* and *What is he or she doing?* The researchers found a strong tendency among the children to gesture along with their speech, and there were little cultural differences in both the frequency and types of gestures used by the children to depict the objects and actions in the pictures. Moreover, in both groups of children there was a tendency for them to use the gesture before they spoke and to complete the gesture after they spoke, supporting the idea that gestures in some way facilitate speech production (see Chapter 6) (Pettenati, Sekene, Congestri, & Volterra, 2012).

SIMPLE DECODING SKILLS Infants demonstrate a remarkable capacity for responding to nonverbal signals. As we have seen, an infant during the first year can express emotions. At first, some of this expressiveness takes the form of mimicry in response to adult behavior. But the mutual involvement and responsiveness of both infant and adult combine to create patterns of interaction based on synchrony and reciprocity. This kind of interpersonal attunement is characteristic of adult–infant communication during much of the first year. Mutual smiling is a good example. As child development expert Penelope Leach (1995) points out,

> His early smiles are an insurance policy against neglect and for pleasant social attention. The more he smiles and gurgles and waves his fists at people, the more they will smile and talk to him. The more attention people pay him, the more he will respond. He will tie them ever closer with his throat-catching grins and his heart-rendingly quiverly lower lip. His responses create a self-sustaining circle, his smiles leading to your smiles and yours to more from him. (p. 112)

Research confirms the existence of this cyclical kind of interaction. Much of it results from a phenomenon known as **emotional contagion** (see Chapter 5), in which the baby and the parent catch the emotions of the other. In fact, soon after birth, an infant will cry in response to a tape recording of a crying baby. And after only a few months, they respond in kind to the facial expressions, movements, vocalizations, and gaze of their caregivers (Dolgin & Azmita, 1985; Field, 1982; Sagi & Hoffman, 1976; Tronick, Als, & Brazelton, 1980).

Although infants may lack the ability to interpret the meaning of most nonverbal signals, they display a capacity for both reception (receiving and responding to a signal) and differentiation (recognizing the differences among signals). They smile at faces, pay attention to voices, and respond favorably when picked up and cuddled (e.g., they may stop crying). More surprisingly, their responses seem to vary according to whose voice or face it happens to be. Only a few days old, they can recognize their mother's voice (Van Lacker, 1981), and they respond more favorably after one to three months to the faces of their parents than they do to the faces of strangers (LaFrance & Mayo, 1978). Research also shows that infants prefer higher-pitched voices to lower-pitched ones (Argyle, 1988), that they pay more attention to faces with a direct gaze than to faces with an averted gaze (Bower, 2002), and that they gaze longer at attractive faces than they do at unattractive faces.

Numerous studies also suggest that infants only a few months old can differentiate expressions of emotion (Ekman, 1982; Haviland & Lelwica, 1987) and appear to comprehend the positive versus negative meaning of these expressions by about seven months (Phillips, Wagner, Fells, & Lynch, 1990). Developmental psychologist Tiffany Field (in Trotter, 1987) believes that even newborns demonstrate these basic differentiation skills. Based on the amount of time three-day-old babies gazed at various facial expressions—they spend more time looking at novel expressions than at those they already know—her research suggests that newborns may learn to recognize differences among facial expressions of emotion, such as happiness, surprise, and sadness. In one experiment, researchers observed the reactions of four-month-old infants to adult facial expressions of emotion in the context of a peekaboo game. The infants' gazing patterns in combination with their expressions of surprise provided evidence that they were responding in a meaningful way to adult facial expressions of anger, sadness, fear, and happiness (Montague & Walker-Andrews, 2001). In fact, recent studies confirm that the brains of four-month-old infants process angry facial expressions, particularly when direct eye gaze accompanies the facial expression (Striano, Kopp, Grossman, & Reid, 2006). But while infants only a few months old may be able to differentiate facial expressions of emotion, the same cannot be said of their ability to comprehend vocal expressions of emotion. In one study, researchers found that five-month-old infants could not discriminate between vocal expressions of happiness and sadness without the accompanying facial expression of the same emotion (D'Entremont & Muir, 1999). Of course, there seems to be little doubt that the ability to differentiate positive versus negative facial expressions of emotion is firmly in place by the end of the first year. In one particularly compelling study, researchers found that one-year-olds placed on a "visual cliff" were more likely to cross over to their mother on the "other side" when she had a happy facial expression than when she exhibited a fearful one (Sorce, Emde, & Klinnert, 1981).

For the most part, deciphering nonverbal signals is an ability that gradually improves with age. The ability to correctly label emotional expressions may not surface until a child is at least three to five years old (Bretherton, Fritz, Zahn-Waxler, & Ridgeway, 1986; Gross & Ballif, 1991; Stifter & Fox, 1986). Research indicates that this ability continues to improve until late adolescence (Buck, 1981; Herba, Landau, Russell, Ecker, & Phillips, 2006; Morency & Krauss, 1982). In one early study, children ranging in age from five to 12 years old were able to identify the emotions conveyed in a speaker's voice, but the older children were more successful than were the younger children (Dimitrovsky, 1964). Philippot and Feldman (1990) found that the ability to recognize facial expressions of happiness, sadness, and fear increased from three to five years old; happiness was recognized by all five-year-olds, but sadness was recognized by only slightly more than half of the five-year-olds. In another study, Harrigan (1984) found a steady improvement with age in the ability to label six primary emotions: accuracy was 48% for the three-year-olds, 62% for the six-year-olds, 73% for the nine-year-olds, and 82% for the 12-year-olds. And, in a more recent study, researchers found a clear improvement in recognizing facial expressions of sadness when comparing seven-year-olds and 10-year-olds, with error rates of 17% and 8% respectively (De Sonneville et al., 2002).

Cross-cultural investigations also confirm the importance of age in learning to decode facial expressions. In a study of American and Japanese children, researchers found that six- and seven-year-olds were better able to identify facial expressions of emotion than were four- and five-year-old children (Matsumoto & Kishimoto, 1983). In a study of Chinese and Australian children four, six, and eight years old, the overall ability to decode facial expressions improved with age, with the children having the least difficulty identifying happy faces, followed (in order of difficulty) by sadness, anger, surprise, fear, and disgust (Markham & Wang, 1996).

At some point, children also learn to spot the difference between a sincere facial expression of emotion and a false one, a skill that gradually improves with age. In one laboratory experiment, Robert Feldman and his colleagues (1978) arranged for third graders to watch videotapes of other third graders who were instructed to praise the work of students they were tutoring. In some cases, the work being praised was very good (genuine praise); in other cases, it was very poor (insincere praise). Seeing only the facial expressions of the tutors, the third graders rated the expressions of genuine praise as "happier" than those of insincere praise. But other studies raise doubts about whether young children really notice a difference between a genuine expression and a phony one. In a follow-up experiment, Feldman and White (1980) studied five- to 13-year-old children. The children served as both encoders and decoders. As encoders, their facial expressions were videotaped while they pretended to like a good- and bad-tasting drink and while they pretended to dislike both drinks. As decoders, they watched videotapes of the facial expressions and identified the ones they thought were truthful and the ones that weren't. The children were correct only 51% of the time and, surprisingly, the older children did not perform significantly better than did the younger children. In a recent experiment testing the ability of eight-year-olds to discriminate between genuine and fake smiles of enjoyment, researchers found that the children were much less able to recognize genuine smiles than adults were (Del Giudice & Colle, 2007).

It doesn't take long for children to begin interpreting many other nonverbal signals. An understanding of distance and eye contact as signs of liking or interest becomes well established in the preschool years. In one study, four- to six-year-old children were shown pictures of a man and a woman close or far apart from each other and with or without eye contact. The four-year-olds were able to use distance cues to decide which pairs liked each other best. But when six-year-old girls made inferences about who liked each other, they were better able to use both distance and eye contact as indicators of attraction than were the younger children (Post & Hetherington, 1974). In another study, five-year-olds were better able than four-year-olds to accurately infer how much a person liked an object based on how long that person looked at the object (Einav & Hood, 2006). More recent research confirms that older children are more skilled than younger children. In a series of experiments comparing four-, five-, and six-year-olds, researchers found that only the five- and six-year-olds were able to infer friendship based on different patterns of eye contact among animated cartoon children; but only the six-year-olds were able to offer an explanation of which cartoon children were the best friends based on differences in eye contact among the cartoon children (Nurmsoo, Einav, & Hood, 2012).

Infants comprehend the meaning of pointing gestures. In one study, 14-month-olds were able to locate a hidden toy when an adult either pointed or gazed at the container holding the toy (Behne, Carpenter, & Tomasello, 2005). By the time they are three years old, children can also decode simple gestures (e.g., waving goodbye). And this ability increases considerably between ages three and five (Kumin & Lazar, 1974; Michael & Willis, 1969). In their research, for instance, Boyatzis and Satyaprasad (1994) found that four-year-olds could decode common gestures for *yes*, *no*, *come here*, *quiet*, *goodbye*, and so forth.

Children also learn at a very young age to form stereotypes based on physical appearance. For example, kindergarten children hold very negative stereotypes of people who are fat or skinny (Lerner & Korn, 1972), stereotypes that may start developing in children three to five years old (Cramer & Steinwert, 1998). And preschool children see tall men and women as stronger and more dominant than their shorter counterparts (Montepare, 1995). Furthermore, research on perceptions of color shows unequivocally that gender stereotypes develop early. Child development researchers Martha Picariello, Danna Grennberg, and David Pillemer (1990) asked preschoolers to identify the sex of six toy pigs, which were identical except for their color. They found a strong association between color and gender. Specifically, 91% of the children said the brown-colored pig was male, 85% said the blue pig was male, and 70% believed the maroon-colored pig was male. In contrast, 94% of the children said the light pink pig was female, 79% said the pink pig was female, and 79% called the lavender pig female. When asked to select their favorite animal, 70% of the children picked a pig whose color matched the stereotype for their gender.

The Development of Complex Encoding and Decoding Skills

▸ Young children learn many of the rules of nonverbal communication during the grade-school years.

istockphoto.com/Susan Chiang

It takes time for children to learn complex nonverbal communication skills. And, certainly, the lack of formal education and training slows the progress that might otherwise take place. Still, research shows that children as young as two years old are beginning to develop some of these abilities: the encoding skills of adapting to the situation and coordinating nonverbal and verbal signals, the decoding skills of contextualizing nonverbal signals and interpreting multisignal messages. Even more surprising are the findings of recent studies suggesting that the building blocks of some complex skills may emerge during the first year. One study found that four-month-olds engage in precisely timed vocal interactions with adults: They take turns in a way that is similar to the give-and-take that occurs between listeners and speakers in conversations (Bower, 2001). Other studies show that by age three months, well before they begin to babble, infants communicate by coordinating vocalizations with facial expressions, such as emitting a growling noise in conjunction with an angry facial expression. And by the time they start to babble, at around six months, they begin to use rhythmic hand and arm movements, the first stage in coordinating gestures with speech (Bower, 2000).

COMPLEX ENCODING SKILLS At some point, children learn the importance of adapting to the demands of the situation—following rules about what is appropriate or inappropriate in a particular situation. When do children learn these rules? Some rules are learned early. In one study, 18-month-olds who were observed while their mothers interacted with other adults altered their behavior to fit the situation they were in: They approached their mother when she wasn't talking, stayed away when she was talking, and came the closest when she was playing cards; they also vocalized the least when the adults were talking and the most when the adults were not talking (Fein, 1975).

Psychologists Marianne LaFrance and Clara Mayo (1978) claim that children learn to control their emotional expressions after age two. But it takes much longer to really learn this complex skill. As one group of researchers put it,

> Although necessary on a daily basis for smooth social interaction in adulthood, control of affective expression appears to be acquired only gradually during development, probably because of the cognitive sophistication necessary for that control. For example, showing what you don't feel and not showing what you do feel require children to be aware of the emotions they are actually feeling as well as those they ought to be showing they are feeling. The "ought" indicates a third property of the ability, an understanding of the display rules embedded in the social situation. (Halberstadt, Grotjohn, Johnson, Furth, & Greig, 1992, p. 215)

Research suggests that some learning occurs among preschool children. For example, between ages four and six, boys become less expressive than girls do (Buck, 1977)—a sign that reflects the early development of traditional gender stereotypes of stoic males and emotional females.

But some rules take longer to learn and are more difficult to follow. Observations of nursery school children engaged in various competitions, for example, show plenty of sore losers (Blurton-Jones, 1967). For the most part, children abide by emotional display rules during the elementary school years (Barrett, 1993; Gnepp & Hess, 1986), despite evidence that they are aware of these rules at younger ages (Misailidi, 2006). For instance, they appropriately inhibit the display of negative emotions. In one study, when six- to 10-year-olds were deliberately given an undesirable gift (a baby toy) for helping a researcher, the six- to eight-year-olds were more likely to show displeasure than the older children were (Saarni, 1979). In a related study, one team of researchers found that first graders were unable to convince others that the unpleasant slides they were looking at were pleasant, but fifth graders could (Morency & Krauss, 1982). Another group of researchers discovered that 11-year-olds could pretend that they liked a bad-tasting drink more skillfully than six-year-olds could (Feldman, Jenkins, & Popola, 1979). But not all studies suggest early grade-school performance deficiencies. Halberstadt and colleagues (1992) found that when asked to describe various activities (e.g., swimming, going to the dentist, doing homework, playing video games, etc.)

in ways that did not express their real feelings (e.g., "I like going to the dentist," "It's no fun playing videogames"), second and fourth graders were equally effective in managing their emotional expressions.

Young children also use approach–avoidance signals by the rules. Perhaps the best example of this is the use of touch. The overall frequency of touch declines steadily from kindergarten through the sixth grade (Willis & Reeves, 1976). Beginning in preschool and well into adolescence, same-sex touching is more common than is opposite-sex touching (Berman & Smith, 1984). These patterns reflect societal norms regarding the use of touch; they suggest that rules are being learned, such as "Touching other people can be rude" and "Boys and girls shouldn't touch each other."

Children also learn rules about other approach–avoidance behaviors. One example is, "It's not polite to stare." Another is that you shouldn't get too close to someone else. These rules reflect a code of conduct that stresses the need to respect the privacy and personal space of other people. Studies show that children get the message. In fact, on average, the distance maintained while interacting with others steadily increases from preschool into adulthood (Aiello & Aiello, 1974; Burgess, 1983). For instance, Lomranz and colleagues (1975) observed preschoolers in small work groups. They found that while three-year-olds sat close enough to touch each other, five- and seven-year-olds sat farther apart. In general, most researchers believe we begin adapting to the situation—who we are with, where we are, and so forth—when we are five or six years old and that by the time we are 10 years old, we've learned most of the basic lessons (Aiello & Jones, 1971; Berman & Smith, 1984; Hutt & Vaizey, 1967; Wolfe & Laufer, 1974). And adults expect these lessons to be learned. In one study, for example, researchers arranged for a child to deliberately invade the personal space of adults who were standing in line. They found that when the child was a five-year-old, adults were tolerant; but when the child was a 10-year-old, the adults were visibly upset (Fry & Willis, 1971).

Sending messages effectively not only means adapting to the situation. It also means being able to coordinate nonverbal and verbal signals. Of course, this takes experience. According to LaFrance and Mayo (1978),

> During the first year, children use one nonverbal channel at a time. This suggests that the integration of the nonverbal system may emerge as part of a developmental process. As children mature, they develop the skills needed to combine and coordinate the different nonverbal channels in more differentiated and hierarchically integrated ways. (p. 143)

The development of this skill coincides with a child's awareness that (a) the same basic message can be communicated through several different nonverbal channels

RESEARCH 2.2

FIND OUT MORE

How Do Children and Adolescents Learn the Rules of Physical Appearance?

The authors of this study wanted to learn more about the process of appearance management that develops in early childhood and continues through adolescence. Included under the idea of appearance management were activities related to decisions about the clothes to wear as well as whether to get tattoos and piercings. Undergraduate students were asked to write about their experiences during a specific period in their lives during childhood and adolescence and also asked to find photographs that showed how they usually looked during that period. Using this method of research, the authors found out about the kinds of rules they followed, where these rules came from (e.g., mothers, peers), and the conflicts that were experienced. For instance, when emphasizing peer pressure, one research participant said,

> Looking back to 8th grade, I was definitely a follower and a conformist. All I wanted was to fit in and be cool. . . . [M]y friends were significant because they saw me every day and I cared the most about what they thought. They believed that if you wore something out of the ordinary that did not fit the group, you were not cool and everybody talked behind your back. (ID 14)

To find out more about this study and to answer the following questions, see the full text of the article (cited below).

1. What type of research are the authors doing? (See Appendix.)
2. Specifically, what did the authors do to collect their data?
3. In your opinion, did any of their results surprise you?
4. What are the major limitations of the authors' study?

Source: Johnson, K. P., Kang, M., & Kim, J. E. (2014). Reflections on appearance socialization during childhood and adolescence. *Clothing and Textiles Research Journal*, 32, 79–92.

(e.g., saying "I'm angry" with facial expression, tone of voice, and gaze avoidance) and (b) it's possible to communicate contradictory nonverbal messages (e.g., the face looks angry, but the voice doesn't sound angry). But the task of coordination isn't limited to nonverbal signals. Eventually, children learn to combine nonverbal and verbal messages (e.g., to emphasize, repeat, complement, etc.). Before long, they come to accept the well-known adage, "It's not just what you say that counts, but how you say it."

Learning to coordinate nonverbal and verbal signals is important for a child's development. The sooner children learn this skill, the sooner they can participate fully in the business of social influence and impression management—whether that means trying to persuade someone with a consistent performance (e.g., getting away with a lie) or trying to puzzle someone with an inconsistent one (e.g., kidding, teasing). Of course, this ability doesn't show up completely until a child learns to use symbolic forms of communication. For example, the most basic kind of nonverbal–verbal coordination is using a gesture instead of a word. And children begin using symbolic gestures with the onset of language. These signaling systems are related in early development because both rely on a common underlying symbolic code (Bates, Thal, Fenson, Whitesell, & Oakes, 1989).

During this early transition period, most gestures are concrete expressions of a child's physical state (e.g., "I'm tired) as well as simple requests (e.g., "Give me that toy"). After age four, however, their gestures start to become more abstract (Boyatzis & Watson, 1993). Apparently, some gestures take much longer to learn than others do. Communication researcher Allen Dittman (1972) observed young children conversing with each other. He discovered that listener responses—gestures such as head nods that are used to show you are paying attention to a speaker—were almost never used among elementary school children but were very common among eighth graders.

When do children learn to coordinate nonverbal and verbal signals in more complex ways? For example, when do they learn to make sarcastic comments? When do they learn to say things in jest? And when do they acquire the ability to tell, convincingly, an untrue story? Unfortunately, given the lack of research on these questions, we can't say for certain. Some research seems to suggest that first graders can't tell convincing lies, third graders have trouble, but by the fourth and fifth grade, children can fool others successfully (DePaulo & Jordan, 1982). An exception may be in the telling of simple "white lies." In one study, three- to seven-year-old children were told to take a photograph of an experimenter. Before taking the picture, the experimenter asked, "Do I look okay for the photo?" For one group of children, the experimenter's nose had a visible mark; for the other group, it did not. Most of the children who saw the mark on the experimenter's nose told white lies, saying that the experimenter looked okay. Undergraduates who saw videotapes of the children were unable to discriminate between the liars and the truth tellers, thus supporting the idea that even very young children can get away with a lie in certain situations (Talwar & Lee, 2002). For the most part, however, the sophistication needed to use these strategies doesn't develop until late adolescence (Burgoon, Buller, & Woodall, 1996; Feldman, Tomasian, & Coats, 1999).

COMPLEX DECODING SKILLS Mastering these skills means going beyond instantaneous reactions to nonverbal stimuli, such as catching someone's emotions or compensating when someone invades your space. It also requires more than the simple interpretations of a single behavior (e.g., labeling a facial expression, translating a gesture, identifying a foreign accent, etc.). Rather, it means being able to read between the lines when someone says something you don't really believe, to take into account the overall context in which a behavior occurs, or to recognize and unravel mixed messages. In sum, these skills help us get the real message when that message may not be readily apparent.

At some point, we learn that people routinely don't mean what they say and don't say what they mean. We learn that pretense—lying, posing, bluffing, kidding, and so on—is part of our everyday lives. Psychologists Bella DePaulo and Audrey Jordan (1982) discuss two kinds of fabrications we are exposed to at an early age: **nonliteral messages** and **deceptive messages**. A nonliteral message is not meant to be taken seriously; a speaker uses nonverbal signals (e.g., winking, vocal intonation, facial gestures, etc.) to let us in on the lie. Sarcastic statements, kidding remarks, fanciful stories, and so on, are examples of nonliteral messages. With a deceptive message, however, the aim is most definitely to be taken seriously—to get away with the lie. From a developmental standpoint, this distinction is important because the ability to decode a nonliteral message is more directly a sign of maturity than is the ability to detect deception.

When exposed to contradictory verbal and nonverbal messages, we learn that actions speak louder than words. Numerous studies suggest that very young children tend to take things literally; that is, if a speaker's words contradict her facial or vocal expressions, a three- or four-year-old child will believe the speaker's words (Burgoon et al., 1996). But the results of one study suggest that even children in this young age group are more likely to believe a speaker's facial and vocal expressions over the speaker's words when the speaker *exaggerates* the nonverbal message with obvious facial and vocal expressions, making the contradiction between actions and words easier for the children to notice (Eskritt & Lee, 2003). Of course, this ability improves with age. When they have access to both verbal and nonverbal cues, older children (i.e., at least 11 years old) can detect certain kinds of deception, such as lying about what you like or dislike, better than younger children can, and during late adolescence, older teens (17- and 18-year-olds) demonstrate greater skill than do younger teens (DePaulo, Rosenthal, Green, & Rosenkrantz, 1982).

Often, the real meaning of a message depends on the overall context in which the message is sent. The role of contextual cues becomes more apparent to children as they mature. Increasingly, they witness a mismatch between public displays of emotion, which conform to certain rules about how we're supposed to behave, and private feelings, which reflect our true emotional reactions. Some studies indicate that older children are, in fact, more likely than younger children to minimize the importance of facial expressions when those expressions conflict with contextual cues (Gnepp & Hess, 1986; Hoffner & Badzinski, 1989) as would be the case when someone smiles upon receiving an unwanted gift. The same conclusion also applies to vocal expressions. In one experiment, researchers Nuran Hortacsu and Birsen Ekinci (1992) asked Turkish children from kindergarten, second grade, and fifth grade to figure out how someone's mother was feeling when her tone of voice contradicted her situation. For example, in one scenario, the child breaks a vase while playing with a ball in the living room. His mother sees him break the vase and asks in a happy tone of voice, "What are you doing?" Only four of the 26 fifth graders reported any contradiction. The children simply relied on one of the two sources of information: voice or context. As the researchers expected, the older children relied more on the context for their judgments than did the preschoolers.

PERSONAL EXPERIENCE 2.4

CAN YOU RELATE TO THIS?

Interpreting and Using Gestures Comes with Age

When I was a little girl—about seven years old—I saw this man stick up his middle finger at my neighbor. I had no idea what it meant, but I was fascinated that this man could hold down all of his other fingers and release only his middle finger. After practicing for a little while, I was finally able to do it. I was going around in the neighborhood showing everyone my new skill when my mother saw me and started screaming at me. I had no idea what she was talking about—she just kept saying that was a bad thing to do. I never understood until I got a little older.

Casi

The ability to integrate multisignal messages also improves with age. Confronted with the task of trying to make sense of a message containing inconsistent signals, young children use much less sophisticated ways of resolving the inconsistencies than do older children, adolescents, and adults. According to developmental psychologists Cynthia Lightfoot and Merry Bullock (1990), these less sophisticated ways generally discount rather than account for discrepant signals—signals that contradict the accepted message. They studied the ability of preschoolers, grade-school children, and adults to construct meaning from messages in which verbal and facial expressions were inconsistent. For example, one film clip showed a girl receiving a disappointing gift from her aunt. As the girl takes the gift, her face looks unhappy while she says in a neutral tone, "I like it." The results of the study showed that only 4% of the preschoolers were able to reconcile the inconsistency in a way that allowed for the possibility of a single situation producing mixed signals (i.e., the girl didn't like the gift but she was trying to be polite, or she didn't like it at first but then changed her mind). In contrast, more than 50% of the second and fourth graders and well over 75% of the sixth graders and adults were able to do so. The typical reaction among preschoolers was to discount one of the contradictory signals (e.g., she said she liked the gift and she frowned for some other reason). These findings, as well as those of the studies above, demonstrate that complex decoding skills develop gradually as children learn from repeated experiences to accept the reality of both nonliteral and deceptive communication strategies—that people often don't mean what they say or say what they mean.

PERSONAL EXPERIENCE 2.5

CAN YOU RELATE TO THIS?

Young Children Are Less Able to Interpret Nonliteral Messages

One of the little boys I babysit is almost four years old. Sometimes I joke around with his older brothers, who are both seven, when a TV commercial advertises a doll or princess toy. I say in a kidding way, "How about I get you one of those for your next birthday?" They always pick up on my teasing, but the younger one gets really mad and yells at me that he's not a girl and princess toys are dumb.

Gabby

INDIVIDUAL DIFFERENCES IN NONVERBAL COMMUNICATION SKILLS

Not everyone develops the same level of skill in sending and receiving nonverbal messages. For nearly four decades, researchers have been trying to find out what kinds of people have more skill in the practice of nonverbal communication than others have. Below, we examine the results of these investigations. Before proceeding, however, we should bear in mind that most of the standardized assessment methods researchers have used to measure nonverbal skills measure simple encoding and decoding skills, such as expressing and identifying emotions; none measure the complex encoding skills of adapting to the situation and coordinating nonverbal and verbal signals. Additionally, researchers using standardized assessment methods typically focus on the emotion function of nonverbal communication. Consequently, we know little about skill differences in the use of nonverbal signals for the identification, relationship, and delivery functions. How do we know how skilled we are? Over the years, researchers have devised numerous ways of measuring differences in sending and receiving abilities. Many of these methods, although useful in a particular investigation, never became widely used. Since the lack of any single standardized assessment procedure makes it difficult to accumulate knowledge about differences in skills, researchers have been developing standardized instruments. The following are some of the most widely used multichannel assessment methods (i.e., face, voice, body).

The Profile of Nonverbal Sensitivity (PONS): Researchers at Harvard University, Johns Hopkins University, and the University of California introduced, in 1979, the first major systematic effort to measure nonverbal decoding skill. This test consists of videotaped clips of a 24-year-old female actor's face and/or body (with no sound) and audiotaped segments (with no audible words) of a male voice and a female voice portraying different situations (e.g., threatening someone, ordering food in a restaurant, asking forgiveness, etc.). It assesses the simple ability to decipher facial, bodily, and vocal signals. Scoring is based on how well a receiver can correctly identify each situation being portrayed by the actor (Rosenthal, Hall, DiMatteo, Rogers, & Archer, 1979). A modified version, the nonverbal discrepancy test, combines different nonverbal channels to produce inconsistent presentations (e.g., a submissive voice paired with a dominant facial expression). Test takers receive scores indicating how well they are able to recognize contradictory messages.

The Interpersonal Perception Task (IPT): Researchers Mark Costanzo and Dane Archer (1989) developed this unique method of assessing decoding skill. The IPT shows 30 videotaped clips of unscripted interactions representing five types of situations: status, kinship, deception, intimacy, and competition. In one scene, for example, a man and two women are conversing. The test asks respondents which woman is engaged to the man (intimacy). In another scene, one person tells two different stories. Respondents note which story is true (deception). In another scene, two individuals talk about the chess match they just played. Respondents identify the person they believe won the match (competition). The total number of correct answers on the IPT is a measure of one's decoding abilities.

The Diagnostic Analysis of Nonverbal Accuracy (DANVA): In 1989, Emory University psychologists Stephen Nowicki and Marshall Duke introduced this method of assessing the "social processing difficulties" of children six to 10 years old. Designed as a screening instrument to identify children who may lack the social skills needed for successful interactions with others, it measures both receptive and expressive nonverbal skills (Nowicki & Duke, 1994). The reception component shows slides of facial expressions, postures, and gestures and plays audiotapes of children saying the same sentence but altering their vocal tone to convey different emotions. As decoders, children try to identify the emotions of anger, sadness, happiness, and fear from each of the nonverbal channels. For the assessment of expressive skills, children try to communicate each of the four emotions with facial expressions, gestures, and vocal intonations. They imagine being in a particular situation (e.g., inviting someone to play) and then use a facial expression, gesture, or tone of voice to convey the feelings they would have in that situation.

General Competence

The question of general competence in sending and receiving nonverbal messages asks whether skill in one area is related to skill in another area. In other words, are good senders also good receivers? Or if you possess one particular skill, such as decoding facial expressions, are you likely to possess other skills as well, such as decoding vocal expressions, interpreting gestures, detecting deception, and so on? Communication scholar Mark Knapp and social psychologist Judith Hall (2002) report mixed findings on the question of whether nonverbal communication skills are related. It appears that some are, to a modest degree, such as the overall ability to encode and decode emotions. Yet some studies reveal negative relationships between the ability to encode and decode particular emotions such as anger, suggesting perhaps a problem of overconfidence—if we can express the emotion, we can easily read it—or merely a lack of curiosity (i.e., we may be more interested in emotions we don't show than we are in those we do show). It appears that the research on sending emotions is more consistent.

Two researchers attempted to tackle this decades-old question of whether there is any consistent relationship between expressing emotions and interpreting the emotions of others. By analyzing the results of 40 studies of more than 2,000 participants, they concluded that there is a positive correlation, but only for emotions that are expressed on purpose (intentionally) and not for those that are expressed naturally (spontaneously). This finding has considerable importance, as the authors point out: "Our results suggest that theorists are justified in linking emotional display and perception performance together within a single model of emotional intelligence or social skill if they specify that the former refers to individuals' purposeful attempts to express themselves" (Elfenbein & Eisenkraft, 2010, p. 314). So people who are themselves good at deliberately expressing emotions also tend to be good at recognizing the deliberately expressed emotions of others.

EXERCISE 2.4

TRY IT

Self-Assessment: Testing Your Knowledge of Nonverbal Communication

Included below are sample true/false questions taken from the Test of Nonverbal Cue Knowledge (TONCK) developed by Janelle Rosip and Judith Hall (2004). Scores on the complete test are predictive of accuracy in decoding nonverbal cues.

Indicate whether you believe each statement is true (T) or false (F).

1. _____ Widening of the eyelids while speaking signifies emphasis on what was said.
2. _____ Human beings can recognize the identity of a speaker with a high degree of accuracy.
3. _____ You maintain greater interaction distances with unknown adults than with familiar adults.
4. _____ The size of the pupil in a person's eye can influence interpersonal attraction to that person.
5. _____ Rapid head nods are a signal to the speaker to finish quickly.
6. _____ People are more likely to touch themselves while telling the truth than while lying.
7. _____ Blinking is not an indicator of physiological arousal.
8. _____ Men are more likely than women to pay attention to nonverbal cues that they can see compared to nonverbal cues in the voice.
9. _____ Your seating position in a classroom is not related to your participation level.
10. _____ Observers can tell pretty well whether someone's facial expression reflects real or faked enjoyment.
11. _____ Social anxiety is related to higher levels of gazing at another person during conversation.
12. _____ Under stress, the pitch of the human voice gets lower.
13. _____ Anger in the voice is revealed by a decrease in speech rate.
14. _____ To tell if someone is truly feeling amusement or enjoyment, you need to look at his or her eyes.
15. _____ A speaker's age can be estimated fairly accurately from his or her voice.
16. _____ Men are better at judging facial cues than women are.

EXERCISE 2.4

17. _____ Lowered brows are not a common sign of an angry feeling.

18. _____ Interpersonal attraction is not a predictor of how close people stand to each other.

19. _____ In a conversation, a more dominant person is likely to show relatively more gazing while speaking than while listening, compared to a less dominant person.

20. _____ The eyebrow flash (raising and lowering of the eyebrows) is found in greeting rituals and signals a desire to interact.

21. _____ Shy people gaze more.

22. _____ Sadness is not easily identified from a person's voice.

23. _____ You gaze more at strangers when you are physically close to them.

24. _____ People approach both high- and low-status others more closely than they approach equal-status others.

25. _____ When judging emotions from facial expressions, observers often confuse surprise and fear.

Answers: 1. T, 2. T, 3. T, 4. T, 5. T, 6. F, 7. F, 8. F, 9. F, 10. T, 11. F, 12. F, 13. F, 14. T, 15. T, 16. F, 17. F, 18. F, 19. T, 20. T, 21. F, 22. F, 23. F, 24. F, 25. T

Source: Adapted from Rosip, J., & Hall, J. (2004). Test of Nonverbal Cue Knowledge (TONCK). *Journal of Nonverbal Behavior, 28*(4), 267–276. Copyright 2004. Reprinted with permission from Springer Science and Business Media.

The Female Advantage

When it comes to the general practice of nonverbal communication, women outperform men in both encoding and decoding tasks. A sizeable body of research has demonstrated this female advantage for the spontaneous expression of emotion and for the ability to decipher various nonverbal signals (Buck, Savin, Miller, & Caul, 1972; Costanzo & Archer, 1989; Fujita, Harper, & Wiens, 1980; Gallagher & Shuntich, 1981; Hall, 1984, 2006; Harper, Wiens, Fujita, & Kallgren, 1981; McClure, 2000; Rosenthal et al., 1979; Rotter & Rotter, 1988; Swenson & Casmir, 1998; Wagner, Buck, & Winterbotham, 1993). Other studies suggest that after participating in a conversation, women can recall the nonverbal cues in the conversation with more accuracy than men can and that they possess greater general knowledge about nonverbal communication (Hall, 2006). Taken together, these findings lend support to the widely held belief that women are more skilled nonverbal communicators than men are, that they are more sensitive to the emotional nuances of an interpersonal encounter. We usually attribute this difference to the process of socialization. For instance, boys generally learn to

▸ Studies show that when it comes to the general practice of nonverbal communication, women tend to demonstrate greater skill than men, particularly in recognizing and responding to emotional cues.

istockphoto.com/Wavebreakmedia

conceal their emotions while girls are expected to reveal theirs (Buck, 1975, 1977; Zuckerman & Przewuzman, 1979). We expect girls to be more attentive and supportive than we expect boys to be. But before concluding that women are always better nonverbal communicators than men, we ought to consider some important exceptions.

First, the available research doesn't allow us to form any generalizations about differences between males and females in the complex skills such as adapting to the situation, coordinating verbal and nonverbal signals, and so on. Second, the female advantage in decoding is significant mostly for deliberately sent messages, implying that women are more accommodating receivers than men are (Buck, 1984; Rosenthal & DePaulo, 1979); that is, women are especially adept at reading signals that senders want them to read (e.g., posed expressions) but no better than men at reading some signals that aren't meant to be read (e.g., phony expressions). Third, the decoding advantage for women may depend partly on the purpose of the decoding task. For instance, in one recent study, women outperformed men on the IPT when they believed it assessed judgment skills needed by social workers, but men outperformed women when they believed it assessed judgment skills of use to military interrogators (Horgan & Smith, 2006). Third, there are exceptions to the general rule that women are more expressive. For example, girls learn to mask negative emotions in public—to be nice to others. In fact, studies show that when receiving an unwanted gift, girls hide their disappointment more than boys do (Davis, 1996; Saarni, 1984). Finally, there are exceptions to the overall finding that women are superior to men at decoding posed expressions. For instance, some research indicates that this may not be true for decoding negative emotions such as anger (Rotter & Rotter, 1988), and it may not be the case when comparing males and females who are also extroverted and socially competent (Zuckerman, Larrance, Hall, DeFrank, & Rosenthal, 1979).

Age Makes a Difference

With some exceptions, we must learn to communicate nonverbally, so it isn't surprising that most of our skills improve with age. This is especially true of the complex skills such as following display rules, telling lies, and interpreting signals in context (Feldman et al., 1979; Gnepp & Hess, 1986; Josephs, 1994; Lightfoot & Bullock, 1990). A child's understanding of the need to control emotions, for example, steadily improves until around age 10 and remains relatively stable thereafter. Similarly, the ability to deceive others, which requires skills in coordinating multiple signals and controlling emotions, is much less developed at age six than it is at age 10. But even simple skills are affected by age, such as the ability to decipher (label) emotions, which seems to follow a curvilinear pattern: It begins to emerge at age three, improves until adulthood, levels off, and deteriorates somewhat in old age (Lieberman, Rigor, & Campain, 1988; Nowicki & Duke, 1994; Nowicki, Glanville, & Demertzis, 1998; Rosenthal et al., 1979; Soppe, 1988; Sullivan, Ruffman, & Hutton, 2007; Thompson, Aidinehad, & Ponte, 2001).

In particular, there is a great deal of research, using typical standardized measurements, documenting a relative decline in older adults' ability to recognize facial expressions of emotion compared to younger adults (Ruffman, 2011). Of course, we should also keep in mind that the poorer performance of older adults on such tests may be due in part to the method of assessment used by researchers (e.g., looking at static pictures), since there is less evidence that these differences exist in the context of real-world interactions, which may be more helpful to older adults than it is to younger adults (Isaacowitz & Stanley, 2011). In addition, there is some evidence that older adults perform better than younger adults at recognizing specific emotions, such as happiness and disgust, as compared to emotions of anger, fear, and sadness (Ruffman, 2011).

Additional support indicating that older adults have more difficulty recognizing expressions of emotion than younger adults comes from studies on the vocal expression of emotion. In one study, for example, older adults were less able than younger adults were to match vocal expressions of fear, sadness, happiness, anger, and fear with the corresponding facial expression of those emotions. They were also less able to use the correct emotion label for identifying the emotions of sadness and anger (Ryan, Murphy, & Ruffman, 2010). So it would seem that the poorer performance of older adults in recognizing emotions from nonverbal cues is not limited to facial expressions alone.

A Personality Profile

The personal qualities of individuals with skills differ markedly from those without. With respect to encoding skills, research indicates that expressive people tend to experience emotion more on the outside than they do on the inside, whereas non-expressive people may simply not show on the surface what they are feeling inside. These types of individuals are known as *externalizers* and *internalizers*, respectively (Buck et al., 1972). Expressive people are also likely to have more outgoing and extroverted personalities than are less expressive persons (Buck et al., 1972; Buck, Miller, & Caul, 1974; Riggio & Friedman, 1982). The ability to communicate emotions deliberately is related to a personality trait known as *self-monitoring*, an awareness of and the tendency to control one's own behavior (Snyder, 1974). Good actors are high self-monitors (Riggio & Friedman, 1982). Finally, some research suggests that deception skill is related to dominance. Studying nursery school children as well as university undergraduates, researchers Carolyn Keating and Karen Heltman (1994) discovered that those who were best able to get away with a lie also tended to be more dominant in free-play periods (preschoolers) or in task-oriented groups (male undergraduates). Confirming what many no doubt already believe, the authors conclude, "If leaders chose to mislead us, their deceptions would be very difficult to detect" (p. 320).

Studies on decoding skills also reveal personality differences. As is the case with skilled encoders, skilled decoders tend to be higher in self-monitoring than persons with less skill are (Costanzo & Archer, 1989; Rosenthal & DePaulo, 1979). There is also some evidence that a high need to belong correlates positively with accuracy judging vocal and facial expressions of emotion (Picket, Gardner, & Knowles, 2004). Research also shows that social anxiety is related to some decoding abilities. In one study, researchers found that socially anxious children had more difficulty identifying vocal expressions of emotion than non-anxious children had (McClure & Nowicki, 2001). Another study found that when judging facial expressions of emotion, socially anxious children were more likely to see emotions in neutral facial expressions than were the non-anxious children (Melfsen & Florin, 2002). Research also supports a link between introversion–extroversion and decoding skill, but the nature of that link may be more complex than was previously thought. In several recent experiments, psychologists Matthew Lieberman and Robert Rosenthal (2001) found support for their hypothesis that when it comes to decoding nonverbal cues, the only difference between introverts and extroverts is that extroverts are better at multitasking: They can decode nonverbal cues and do something else at the same time. Lieberman and Rosenthal argue that the arousal resulting from multitasking is more likely to be debilitating for introverts than it is for extroverts. (In their experiments, they repeatedly found no differences between introverts and extroverts when decoding the vocal cues of another person was the only task the participants were asked to do.) But when the experimenters instructed them to focus on another, more important task, such as having a good conversation with another person, introverts were less accurate in judging the vocal cues of that person than were the extroverts. Finally, studies of children show that skilled decoders tend to have greater self-esteem, do better academically, and are less likely to be emotionally disturbed than their less skilled peers (Nowicki & Duke, 1994). With respect to children with emotional problems, for example, one recent study found that children with psychopathic tendencies were less able to identify fear and sadness in facial expressions than were the children in a comparison group (Stevens, Charman, & Blair, 2001).

Interpersonal Successes and Failures

Based on the available evidence, there is little doubt that persons with skills in sending and receiving nonverbal messages experience greater interpersonal successes than do those without such skills. People who can accurately communicate their feelings are so gifted in this regard that the term *charismatic* is an apt label, according to social psychologist Ronald Riggio (1992). Indeed, research shows that such people, when compared to less expressive persons, make a better first impression, are liked more, are seen as more physically attractive, and become more popular (Boyatzis & Satyaprasad, 1994; Friedman, Prince, Riggio, & DiMatteo, 1980; Larrance & Zuckerman, 1981; Friedman, Riggio, & Casella, 1988; Sabatelli & Rubin, 1986). Being able to tell a convincing lie is a complex encoding skill that requires the liar to coordinate the spoken verbal message with a variety of nonverbal behaviors in a way that makes the verbal message seem truthful. After classifying a group of 11- to 16-year-old boys and girls on a measure of social competence, one study found that the best liars—the ones who could convince listeners that they either liked an unpleasant-tasting drink or disliked a pleasant-tasting drink—also tended to be the most popular in the group (Feldman et al., 1999).

Decoding skill is also related to interpersonal success. Almost all the standardized assessments support this claim. Studies indicate that skilled decoders, when compared with their less-skilled counterparts, are not as lonely, are more satisfied with their marriages, report more successes in their social relationships, are perceived as more physically attractive, and, as children, are more popular with their peers (Carton & Kessler, 1999; Hodgins & Zuckerman, 1990; Koerner & Fitzpatrick, 2002; Noller, 1981; Nowicki & Duke, 1992b; Philippot & Feldman, 1990; Rosenthal et al., 1979; Sabatelli & Rubin, 1986; Spence, 1987; Zakahi & Goss, 1995).

From Different Environments

Several investigations by Amy Halberstadt and others suggest that family socialization plays a prominent role in determining one's expressive skills. First through imitation and later through more advanced modes of learning, children tend to pick up the behavior of their parents. In her review of the research, Halberstadt (1991) found considerable support for the simple hypothesis that "when the family environment is high in expressiveness, younger family members also develop similarly high expressiveness, and when the family environment is low in expressiveness, younger family members develop similarly low expressiveness" (p. 110). But more surprising is the finding that adults with expressive parents tend to be poorer decoders of emotional expressions than are adults with less expressive parents (Halberstadt, 1991; Halberstadt, Dennis, & Hess, 2011). How can this be? According to the researchers, it would seem that those from less expressive homes have to work harder over the years to decipher the emotional expressions of family members than those from more expressive homes, and they gain increased skills as a result of this greater effort.

Another feature of the home environment that influences nonverbal skills is the presence of an abusive parent–child relationship. A longitudinal study of British

▸ Family socialization as well as gender plays a prominent role in determining one's ability to send and receive nonverbal messages.

istockphoto.com/Attila Barabas

children found that children who were physically abused in the first four years of life had more difficulty four years later interpreting high-intensity expressions of emotion that did children who were not abused in their first four years (Bowen & Nowicki, 2007). Similarly, developmental psychologist Linda Camras and her associates (1983) found in their investigations that physically abused children had greater difficulty recognizing facial expressions of emotion than did non-abused children. Camras (1985) explains how this deficiency could develop:

> The facial behavior of abusing parents may deviate from the behavior of nonabusing parents in several important ways. First, abusing parents may be facially inexpressive; they may tend to use fewer facial expressions than other persons when placed in an emotional situation. In addition (or alternatively), abusing parents may be inappropriate or inconsistent in their use of facial expressions; for example, they may smile when scolding their children, rather than frown. A third possibility is that abusing parents are not atypical in their use of facial expressions, but that they are atypical with regard to their frequency of parent–child interactions. Thus, their children do not get adequate experience with facial expressions because they engage in fewer social exchanges with their parents overall. (p. 146)

There is also some evidence that children exposed to interparental violence may suffer a loss of nonverbal communication skills. One study found that undergraduates from such homes were less able to recognize facial expressions of happiness and more likely to use inappropriate facial expressions of emotion than were undergraduates with no exposure to domestic violence (Hodgins & Belch, 2000).

EDUCATION AND TRAINING

In their book, *Helping the Child Who Doesn't Fit In*, Stephen Nowicki and Marshall Duke (1992a) say that skill deficits in the practice of nonverbal communication represent a special type of learning disability called ***dyssemia*** (difficulty with nonverbal signals). For example, a child with "receptive facial dyssemia may misread a sad face as an angry one, and as a result may respond to downcast eyes with a frown or glare" (Duke,

Nowicki, & Martin, 1996, p. 12). They estimate that about one in ten children suffer from this condition and experience interpersonal problems severe enough to cause social rejection. If education and training make a difference, their research suggests that we ought to begin teaching children nonverbal communication skills at a young age. Children requiring early diagnosis, and intervention in the form of education and training, also include those afflicted with a mild but often socially debilitating form of autism known as **Asperger's syndrome**. This neurological disorder was added to the American Psychiatric Association's Diagnostic and Statistical Manual of Mental Disorders, 4th edition in 1994 but, at present, is classified on the high-functioning scale of autism spectrum disorders (ASD). This particular disorder generally interferes with the development of all the nonverbal communication skills, including the simple ones we take for granted. Persons with Asperger's exhibit at least two of the following symptoms: (1) impairment in the use of multiple nonverbal behaviors such as eye-to-eye gaze, facial expression, body postures, and gestures to regulate social interaction; (2) failure to develop peer relationships appropriate to developmental level; (3) lack of spontaneous seeking to share enjoyment, interests, or achievements with others, such as not showing or pointing at objects of interest; (4) lack of social or emotional reciprocity (Barnhill, Cook, Tebbenkamp, & Myles, 2002; Kutscher, 2002).

Studies generally confirm that ASD or Asperger's syndrome interferes with the ability to recognize facial expressions of emotion. This tends to be the case in studies of children, adolescents, (Demopoulos, Hopkins, & Davis, 2013) and adults, particularly for the recognition of complex emotional states such as guilt, boredom, and interest (Sawyer, Williamson, & Young, 2012, 2014). Asperger's may also interfere with the ability to recognize the feelings of others from other nonverbal cues, such as posture and body position. In one study, researchers found that persons with Asperger's were less able to recognize postures of boredom and took significantly longer to label postures of boredom and interest compared to a control group of individuals without Asperger's (Doody & Bull, 2011).

Studies also show that individuals with depression are less receptive to positive facial expressions (Joorman & Gotlib, 2006), and persons with social anxiety disorder and ADHD may be less sensitive to facial expressions of anger, disgust, or sadness (Demopoulos et al., 2013; Montagne et al., 2006; Pelc, Kornreich, Foisy, & Dan, 2006). Yet despite the social setbacks experienced by individuals who suffer from various conditions that limit their nonverbal communication abilities, help is available. Research shows that, with plenty of coaching and feedback, children and adults can improve their nonverbal communication skills (Barnhill et al., 2002; Camargo et al., 2014; Nowicki & Duke, 2002).

The idea that nonverbal communication is a skill represents a shift in thinking away from an interest in abstract traits, such as empathy, intuition, friendliness, and charisma, to a focus on the observable behaviors that make up such traits, such as facial expressions, gestures, eye contact, and so on (Friedman, 1979). From a learning standpoint, this makes sense. We can teach people to improve the way they communicate (i.e., behaviors) more readily than we can teach them to change their personality (i.e., traits). There appears to be growing sentiment that the practice of nonverbal communication in everyday life is vital for social and professional success (Argyle, 1988; Duke et al., 1996; Goleman, 1994, 2006; Nowicki & Duke, 2002; Pentland, 2008; Riggio, 1992). Despite this belief, as well as the popularity of courses and workshops in the subject, more research is needed to find out whether efforts to educate and train people make a significant difference. Some argue that the practice of nonverbal communication is far enough outside our awareness and so ingrained that any efforts to enhance basic skills are destined to fail (e.g., can you teach someone to be more expressive?). The argument is certainly not without some merit. Many of us would find it difficult to change the habits of a lifetime. But change is possible, as we will see, and even likely under certain conditions. In this section, we'll consider the impact of education and training.

Research indicates that oral performance courses help students develop communication skills. First, studies have found that students believe their skills can improve. For instance, they report greater competence communicating with others after completing a basic communications course, which includes lessons on nonverbal communication in various contexts (e.g., interviewing, listening, public speaking, etc.), than they report during the first week of classes (Ford & Wolvin, 1993; Rubin, Rubin, & Jordan, 1997). Second, coursework improves student performance. Using a standardized assessment instrument that she developed to measure student performance (Rubin, 1985), communication researcher Rebecca Rubin and her colleagues investigated the impact of a one-semester basic speech course on ninth- and tenth-grade students (Rubin, Welch, & Buerkel, 1995). Ratings of extemporaneous speeches delivered before and after instruction revealed that student performances improved in several key areas, including vocal skills related to a speaker's tone of voice (e.g., pitch variation, volume).

Nonverbal communication training programs often target specific populations—managers, physicians, job applicants, counselors, married couples, shy or lonely people, children, and so forth—to help them cope with the daily demands of their personal or professional lives. More often than not, these programs make a difference. For example, studies show that with proper instruction—providing practice and feedback—trainees become more articulate and dynamic speakers (Seibold, Kudsi, & Rude, 1993), better able to detect deception (deTurck & Miller, 1990; Fiedler & Walka, 1993), more sensitive counselors (Grace, Kivlighan, & Kunce, 1995), more adept in selling (Peterson, 2005), better at decoding facial expressions of emotion (Beck & Feldman, 1989; Elfenbein, 2006), and more skilled at reading social signals in various contexts (Costanzo, 1992; Nixon & Bull, 2005). In his review of the literature on nonverbal skills and the impact of training, Ronald Riggio (1992) concludes:

> One encouraging aspect of nonverbal skill training programs is their dramatic effectiveness. For example, in our own experimental attempts to "train" people in nonverbal communication skills, we often see substantial gains in relatively short periods of time (e.g., Friedman, Nelson, & Harris, 1984; Riggio, 1987). We are convinced that this is due to the fact that nonverbal skills are so critically important for all forms of social interaction that even slight improvements in one's nonverbal interaction skills are immediately reinforced by others in one's social network. Close friends and family members respond favorably to increased attempts to communicate and to the clearer and more effective nonverbal sending of messages. This leads to further improvement. (p. 23)

SUMMARY

The practice of nonverbal communication is an important part of our everyday lives. Some skills are relatively simple and develop early in life. These include the encoding skills of expressing messages spontaneously as well as deliberately and the decoding skills of being attuned to others—picking up their feelings—and being able to decipher nonverbal signals. Other skills are more complex—they involve multiple channels of communication, develop much later in life, and require some degree of critical thinking. As message senders, we need an understanding of how to adapt to various situations and how to coordinate nonverbal and verbal signals so that our messages are understood. As receivers, we use skills that help us to get a person's real message; that is, we learn to take into account the context in which a signal occurs and to integrate the various signals into a meaningful message.

The development of nonverbal communication skills has attracted a great deal of scientific study. Most of these investigations show that the simple skills emerge in some way during the first year of life. Infants express emotions; they deliberately communicate through vocalization, gaze patterns, gestures, and so on; they become attuned to the feelings of those around them; they recognize familiar faces; and they acknowledge cues of emotion. They also learn to decipher simple gestures, facial expressions, and approach–avoidance signals. Later in their development, children acquire the complex skills. They learn the importance of adapting to the situation—for instance, that it is sometimes necessary to show an emotion one doesn't feel or to suppress an emotion that one does. With the onset of speech, they begin to acquire skills in coordinating their messages and figuring out what someone is saying to them when the signals are insincere, inconsistent, or context dependent.

Studies indicate that certain kinds of people become more skilled than others do. Various assessment methods suggest that women tend to be more proficient than men; age makes a difference; certain personality types—such as extroverts, people who can self-monitor, and dominant persons—are more skilled than others; skill in nonverbal communication contributes to academic success, higher self-esteem, and more satisfying relationships; and those with skill come from different home environments than those with less skill. People can learn to become more effective in the practice of nonverbal communication. Research has demonstrated that education and training, under the right circumstances, can make a difference.

KEY TERMS

Asperger's syndrome 73
Attunement 42
Babbling 48
Complex decoding skills 43
Complex encoding skills 39
Deceptive message 61
Deictic gestures 51
Dyssemia 72
Emblematic gestures 51
Emotional contagion 52
Iconic gestures 51
Nonliteral message 61
Sarcasm 41
Simple decoding skills 41
Simple encoding skills 38
Triadic gestures 51
Turn-taking signals 41

PART II

CODES AND FUNCTIONS

istockphoto.com/wernerimages

Chapter Outline

3

THE HUMAN BODY: SIGNALING MULTIPLE IDENTITIES

At one time, it was against the law in many places to make yourself look better than you were supposed to look. Naturally, any society firmly committed to the belief that one's outer appearance is meant to reflect one's station in life—a belief that says, "You wear what you are"—would have a difficult time accepting the modern-day notion that "You are what you wear." Not surprisingly, laws were passed to keep people in their place, thus protecting the social order of the day. These **sumptuary laws** restricted a person's dress to clothes that represented that person's class, rank, or status and, by doing so, protected the identities of the privileged few—the aristocracy of the day—from the liberties and excesses of the wealthy bourgeoisie. This has been the case throughout much of human history. During the reign of Charles IX in France, only high-ranking women were allowed to wear dresses of silk and to carry fur muffs. In England, Edward III prohibited the use of pearls outside the royal family. Henry VIII decreed that no one below the rank of countess could wear a train, and Queen Elizabeth insisted on unpopular laws regulating the length of a man's hair and beard according to rank (Horn, 1975). Closer to home, in early New England, a woman was not permitted to wear a silk scarf unless her husband was worth at least $1,000 (Morris, 1977). But according to fashion historian James Laver (1969), sumptuary laws, whenever and wherever they are tried, inevitably give way to the rising tide of animosity they foster. People, it seems, are just never satisfied with the way they're supposed to look.

Learning Objectives

After reading this chapter, you will be able to do the following:

1. Understand how the human body represents intrinsic, iconic, and arbitrary communication codes.
2. Discuss the primary function of the human body as a signaling system; for example, how it signals multiple identities related to physical beauty, age and fitness, individuality, race, ethnicity, character, and personality.
3. Recognize a secondary function of the human body as a signaling system, contributing to the two basic dimensions of all relationships: intimacy and control.
4. Understand how the human body contributes to the delivery function of nonverbal communication, sending a variety of verbal or symbolic messages.
5. Consider how the human body, to a limited degree, can express some emotions through clothing and physiological changes, such as blushing.

Our appearance certainly expresses much more than our social standing. As we will see shortly, it is a form of communication that serves many different functions, although identification is the primary one. In this chapter, we'll begin by introducing the human body as a signaling system. Then we'll examine how physical appearance expresses multiple identities and, to a much lesser degree, also facilitates relationships, conveys emotions, and delivers verbal or symbolic messages.

COMMUNICATION CODES

Our bodies send messages in various ways. **Body endowment** includes the natural and enduring physical features that identify us, such as the color of our skin, hair, and eyes; the shape of our body and face; the size of our nose, ears, and feet; and so on. **Body modification** refers to the many semipermanent ways we alter our physical appearance. In addition to the widespread practices of dieting, exercising, and shaving, body modification includes tattooing, piercing, and scarification (e.g., branding). Until recently, these latter practices, while common in many parts of the world and restricted in this country to small subcultures, were largely shunned in mainstream American society. As is often the case, what was once taboo is now fashionable among large segments of the population. We see tattoos everywhere. People are piercing noses, bellybuttons, eyebrows, and tongues as well as ears. And individuals proudly display on shoulders, arms, or thighs the burned-on insignia of their respective groups. **Body adornment** is another way of altering our physical appearance. All of us experience the everyday routine of getting dressed and fixing ourselves up. These short-lived changes in our appearance—clothing, cosmetics, jewelry—reflect our daily need to balance the sometimes-conflicting demands for modesty, self-expression, conformity, and comfort. In the following section, we'll examine physical appearance as a form of communication consisting of intrinsic, iconic, and arbitrary codes.

Intrinsic Codes

Intrinsic codes are the natural signaling systems we inherit rather than learn. Our capacity to send and receive these signals evolved as a matter of survival. Some physical features communicate our identity to others, signaling our gender, race, or individuality, for example. Visible differences in body shape, hair distribution, facial features, and so forth allow us to recognize someone we know or to categorize someone as a woman rather than a man, an adolescent rather than a senior citizen, an Asian American rather than a Native American, and so on. Some facial features, such as those associated with baby faces—large eyes, small nose, bulbous forehead, chubby cheeks, and the like—elicit nurturing responses from parents and caregivers. Observations that these features are shared among the young in many different species supports the claim that these particular signals probably constitute an intrinsic communication code (see Chapter 1). Other physical features of the face and body make people look attractive to us (e.g., high cheekbones, facial symmetry, youthful skin, etc.), which promotes courtship and mating. And still others contribute to judgments of maturity (e.g., facial hair, wrinkling skin, gray hair, balding, etc.) or perceptions of power (e.g., strong jaw, height, broad shoulders, muscularity, etc.), fostering relationships based on differences in status.

Investigating a field of study sometimes referred to as *human social anatomy* (Guthrie, 1976), scientists from various disciplines (e.g., biology, zoology, anthropology) claim that many of our physical features are social organs because they evolved largely to transmit messages about how we compare to others (i.e., sexuality, beauty, power, and seniority). Questions about why we look the way we do lead to answers based on studies of fossil records and/or animal behavior. Eyebrows are a case in point. Ethologist R. Dale Guthrie (1976) speculates that these hairy patches evolved to do more than keep the rain out of our eyes or highlight our facial expressions. Some explanation, he contends, is needed for age and gender differences (e.g., brow hair grows during puberty and males have hairier brows than females do). According to Guthrie's argument,

> Disproportionate brow hair development among older males seems to provide a false contour to the underlying bony brow. This brow ridge was an important sexually distinctive character of our early ancestors. It seems to have a role in the threat display, among primates, of permanently accentuating the lowered brow. Even to us the exaggerated, protruding bony brows of an old male gorilla connote awesome intimidation. Hence fiction writers portray it as a dangerous beast, even though it is a rather shy vegetarian. The thick row of hair across the brow ridge in older human males gives the underlying structure a more permanently lowered appearance. (pp. 60–61)

Although not universally practiced, the widespread routine of cosmetically plucking, thinning, or arching their eyebrows is one way the women of many cultures try to make themselves appear less aggressive as well as less masculine than the opposite sex.

Another example of a social organ is the female breast. That women's breasts transmit a sexual signal is hardly news. More surprising is the apparent origin of this female-to-male form of human communication. One theory is based on the concept of automimicry: that over the course of evolution, it can become adaptive (i.e., advantageous) for one part of the body to resemble another part of the body. Desmond Morris (1967, 1977) has shown how this phenomenon occurred in the sexual signaling of some nonhuman primates (e.g., the gelada baboon) as well as in humans. As human copulation became a face-to-face encounter, it became advantageous, according to this theory, for sexual signaling to shift in some way from the rear to the front of the female's body. Since the rump display is the primary sexual signal in most primates, the rounded shape of the human female breast evolved to mimic the general shape of the buttocks. Curiously, the fact that female faces are more childlike in appearance than are male faces (Zebrowitz, 1997) has also led to speculation over whether some process of automimicry has taken place—adult female faces mimicking baby-faced features—one that would reinforce the age-old gender roles of man-as-protector and woman-as-protected (Guthrie, 1976; Morris, 1977).

Returning to the more general question of intrinsic communication codes, evidence is mounting that many signals once thought to be learned may in fact be part of an inborn signaling system. Consider the case of good looks. Recent research challenges the relativistic notion that beauty is solely in the eye of the beholder. First, studies of two- to three-month-old infants show that they prefer attractive over unattractive faces (Langlois, Ritter, Roggman, & Vaughn, 1991), a preference that cannot be explained adequately by socialization. Second, research is beginning to show that people from many different cultures tend to agree on the faces they regard as attractive, a finding that appears to back the claim that certain features may be universally appealing (Cunningham, Roberts, Barbee, Druen, & Wu, 1995; Langlois & Roggman, 1990).

Iconic Codes

When it comes to the way we look, humans have a special talent for picking up where nature left off. Padding creates the illusion that our shoulders are broader than they really are. Belts, buttons, and bands help to create fit figures. Wigs and hair weaves mimic the real thing. Shoe lifts and high heels give us that needed boost. Artificially arched eyebrows can change our fixed expression from off-putting to inviting. Blush adds a touch of color to the face. These enhancements (i.e., semblances) alter our appearance superficially and often with the desired result: projecting an image of a person who is stronger, shapelier, taller, younger, or even more receptive and vibrant than the real person. The drive to look younger is singularly responsible for the creation of a multibillion-dollar industry that provides us with cosmetics, wrinkle creams, hair replacements, hair dyes, push-up bras, facial peels, teeth whiteners, and the like.

Even a cursory study of women's fashion finds instances of iconic signaling. Perhaps none is more telling than the preoccupation with creating an hourglass figure. In their book, *Mirror, Mirror: The Importance of Looks in Everyday Life*, authors Elaine Hatfield and Susan Sprecher (1986) remind us that during most of the nineteenth century (i.e., the Victorian era), beautiful women were expected to wear heavy corseting.

> Extremely fashionable women had their lower five ribs removed to insure that they had a properly tiny wasp waist. The whalebone

corset compressed the waist into a circumference of a few inches. Breasts and buttocks gained in prominence. A bustle completed the illusion. (p. 231)

▸ Cosmetics, designed to make us look younger and healthier, typify the use of iconic communication codes.

istockphoto.com/PeopleImages

In many ways, the corset and bustle, mimicking (albeit, exaggerating) the natural contours of the female human body, represent the quintessential case of how clothing functions as a form of iconic communication. But the not-long-ago, everyday wearing of these garments also illustrates the changing standards of dress and the symbolism invariably attached to those changes. What was once regarded as beautiful and necessary may be seen by subsequent generations as peculiar, perverse, or, as in the case of tightly laced corsets, downright oppressive (i.e., an arbitrary code).

Each morning, millions of men remove the hair growing on their faces. Why do they do it? Since beardedness is a natural male condition—left uncut, the average beard will grow about 20 inches—shaving is a form of body modification that makes the adult male face resemble somewhat the hairless face of a prepubescent boy. Whatever the reasons given for shaving—cleanliness or conformity, for instance—the undeniable effect of mimicking a more juvenile face is to make the man's face younger, less intimidating, more revealing, and more feminine (Guthrie, 1976). This softened image has its advantages in societies striving to balance the conflicting values of cooperation on the one hand (i.e., not everyone is a rival) and competition on the other (i.e., a powerful presence is sometimes important).

Another example of iconic signaling accomplished through body modification is the practice of skin coloring. All of us are familiar with the way women use blush to redden their cheeks, mimicking the appearance of natural youth and vitality, and with the way women powder their faces to avoid the look of a person who labored in the sun, but less well known is the cosmetic practice of skin bleaching—using various pharmaceutical products to whiten the skin—which has become quite popular in many parts of Africa, particularly among the young people seeking a brighter, higher-status complexion (Didillon, Bounsana, & Vandewiele, 1988). In addition to skin coloring, all of us are familiar with tattooing as a form of iconic signaling.

Arbitrary Codes

Most of our bodily communication is rooted in the symbolism of physical appearance; that is, some aspect of our appearance—a hairstyle for instance—means something to us, but the meaning is not fixed in time or place. Even though there is widespread agreement about the attractiveness of some physical features (such as youthful-looking skin), the beauty of many other aspects of our appearance, as we will see shortly, remains in the eye of the beholder (e.g., style of dress, body shape, etc.). Aside from individual self-expression, variations in appearance generally reflect societal norms. Not surprisingly, these norms change over time and differ from place to place. In her book, *The Second Skin*, Marilyn Horn (1975) identified four ways a society perpetuates its ideas about how one ought to look: **folkways**, **customs**, **mores**, and **laws**.

PERSONAL EXPERIENCE 3.1

CAN YOU RELATE TO THIS?

Rules Dictate What Is an Acceptable Appearance

When my brother was in fifth grade, the style was to grow a "tail," a piece of hair that formed at the base of the neck and extended as long as the wearer desired. In the school at the time, no rules were established on hairstyles, especially those of males. When the time to receive report cards rolled around, my brother and his friend didn't receive theirs because of their hairstyle. The report cards were held without even confronting the boys or their parents. The parents didn't see the big deal where the hair was concerned. The boys and their parents argued with administrators over the matter but were unsuccessful. The parents made the boys cut their "tails" in order to receive their report cards.

Melissa

Folkways represent the conventional way of doing things—the ordinary routines we take for granted, such as wearing a belt with a pair of pants, a necktie with a jacket, or a pair of dress shoes to a nice restaurant. To a large extent, the way we dress is determined by our unquestioned obedience to these simple rules. But when a folkway is disregarded, only the puzzlement, amusement, or mild disapproval of others is likely to result (e.g., reacting to someone who forgets to comb his hair or whose socks don't match). Customs differ from folkways in two fundamental respects: They are more deeply anchored in tradition and they are safeguarded more actively and consistently.

Because the clothing customs of any social community are invariably linked to basic questions of gender, status, beauty, and the like, they represent a strong stabilizing influence, making changes in fashion piecemeal at best. The cut of a man's trousers may change every few years, but he still wears them; the length of a woman's skirt may rise and fall, but she continues to wear them.

When expectations about how one should look become strong enough to carry moral connotations of right and wrong, they take the form of *mores*. Adherence to mores comes from the pressure to avoid the taboos of a society as well as the desire to be one of its model citizens. You won't get arrested for wearing a bathing suit to a funeral, attending a party in blackface, or showing up at an awards ceremony in smelly sweats, but you'll no doubt be on the receiving end of much more than mild disapproval for exhibiting such crude and offensive behavior. On the other hand, you may get arrested for violating the laws that are enforced to discourage those physical appearances likely to threaten the public's welfare and safety. Most of us know it is against the law to impersonate a police officer, and laws against public nudity are commonplace. Although the sumptuary laws described in the chapter opening are almost unheard of today, other laws may seem equally bizarre when judged by persons unfamiliar with the values and practices of a people who lived long ago or who live in a foreign culture. Even in our own country, we witness endless debates over the pros and cons of enforcing bans on fashions such as long hair, facial hair, shoe styles, and the like. Mark Knapp and Judith Hall (2002) report numerous cases involving bans against wearing beards, mustaches, long hair, ponytails, and so on. In a 1996 Texas case, for example,

> A state appeals court ruled [that] school officials were out of bounds when they sent a ponytailed eight-year-old to the equivalent of solitary confinement. The school district's claims that its hair rule was needed to prevent gangs, teach gender identity, and maintain discipline were sheer nonsense. (p. 227)

Clashes between schools and parents over how students should look are not limited to hairstyles. In 1997, parents sued a Kentucky elementary school for repeatedly suspending their 13-year-old girl because she wore black lipstick to school (Breed, 1997). Uniforms and dress codes often reflect more severe restraints on what we can and cannot wear. In these cases, the penalties are designed to make potential violators think twice.

Folkways, customs, mores, and laws represent a kind of grammar that needs to be learned by the members of a culture who wish to be fluent in the "language of the body." But like any learned language, the code is an arbitrary one that can change with the passage of time and with each visit to another locale. To illustrate, consider how definitions of attractiveness vary over time. Today, being thin is a symbol of an attractive body. This hasn't always been the case. In fact, the desire for a thin physique is essentially a twentieth-century phenomenon, contradicting the much older standard of attractiveness that equated a big body with a good life (Cogan, Bhalla, Sefa-Dedeh, & Rothblum, 1996). Rubenesque women—fat by today's standards—were the ideal in the seventeenth century. Even today, in many different cultures, obesity represents physical beauty as a sign of affluence or as a symbol of the good life. Recent research documents a shift in the popular media to a leaner model of feminine beauty. In a study of Playboy centerfolds and Miss America Pageant contestants, for example, Garner and colleagues (1980) found a significant trend over a 20-year period toward a thinner female body. They also found that the shift coincided with a substantial increase in the number of diet-related articles found in several popular women's magazines. Another example of changing definitions of beauty is skin color. Before the twentieth century, tanned skin indicated outdoor labor and therefore a lower class. But the popularity of leisure time associated with outdoor sports created a new standard of tanned good looks, one that represented a healthy, wealthy standard of living.

Fashion cycles also demonstrate the arbitrary and capricious meanings of physical appearance symbols. Historian James Laver (1945) proposed the idea that judgments of fashion follow a recurring pattern: Ten years before a particular outfit is in style, it is seen as indecent; five years later, it's considered merely shameless; a year before it becomes popular, it's regarded as a bit daring; then it's smart, while in fashion; a year after being in style, it's dowdy; ten years later, it's hideous; thirty years later, it's just amusing; a century later, and it's romantic; and after 150 years, it's beautiful. Although not illustrative of Laver's theory, men's hats are a good example of changes in fashion and in definitions of what constitutes the well-dressed man. Prior to World War II, a man wouldn't think of being seen in public without a hat. Few men wore hats in the 1960s, but now they are popular again in the form of baseball caps. Researcher Nigel Barber (2001) claims that men's facial hair comes and goes according to a fashion cycle tied to the availability of single women. Using annual data on British beard and mustache fashions from 1842 to 1971, it was discovered that beards and mustaches are more common when the marriage market favors women (difficult times) and less common when the market favors men (good times). According to Barber, in difficult times, men may be trying to entice women by using facial hair as a sign of their masculinity. In good times, men may be shaving their faces, conveying an impression of trustworthiness, in order to reassure women who might fear sexual exploitation and desertion (Barber, 2001).

In addition, what is seen as beautiful in one culture may look hideous to people in another culture. In much of Western Africa, for instance, calling someone "fat" is a compliment (Cassidy, 1991). The many exotic rituals we often see in documentaries or in the pages of *National Geographic*, such as neck stretching, lip enlargements, earlobe plugs, teeth filing, and so on, represent the beautifying practices common in many parts of the world. Of course, liposuction, hair implants, facelifts, laser surgery, and the like, while not the least bit extraordinary to many Westerners, may seem abhorrent to people from other parts of the world.

COMMUNICATION FUNCTIONS

Our bodies serve various communication functions. In this section, we'll examine the role of physical appearance in signaling our identity, the primary function. We'll also consider the more limited role of physical appearance in establishing relationships with others, expressing emotions, and delivering verbal messages.

▸ Changing our physical appearance can change the way others see us as well as the way we see ourselves.

istockphoto.com/Maartje van Caspel

Identification: The Primary Function

More than any other nonverbal communication code, our physical appearance tells others who we are or who, at first sight, we appear to be. This includes

PERSONAL EXPERIENCE 3.2

CAN YOU RELATE TO THIS?

A Change in Appearance Can Be a Change in Identity

When I first entered high school, I wore glasses and braces. Yes, I was a cool kid but I did not look the part. Quickly, I convinced my parents to allow me to get contacts and things changed. I am sure, nonverbally, I conveyed new messages because inside I felt better about myself. But people treated me differently. I was no longer a good guy with glasses, but someone to pay attention to. When I entered college, I never wore my glasses and always donned a baseball hat. The first time I didn't wear a hat and put my glasses on, people did not recognize me. I felt like Dr. Jekyll and Mr. Hyde. Jokingly, people said, "Oh, you have hair," and "You look smarter with glasses." What a simple change to produce such surprising results. I felt as if I had two identities: a cool college student (hat and no glasses) and a studious college student (glasses, no hat).

Justin

▸ What are the consequences of casual-attire dress codes in the workplace? How is the culture at a casual-dress workplace affected by the attire?

istockphoto.com/Geber86

physical beauty, individuality, gender, age, fitness, culture, race, occupation, social class, character and personality, values, and beliefs. Despite what some may regard as society's obsession with physical appearance and the obvious fact that we are much more than that which meets the eye, it is difficult to separate, particularly in the minds of others, who we are from how we look.

PHYSICAL BEAUTY In almost all societies, the prevailing standards of physical beauty determine whether or not an individual is regarded as attractive. And the benefits bestowed on those who fit the mold can be more than enough to justify the often grueling ordeal of modifying and adorning one's body. What are the physical features that identify a person as beautiful? Recent studies lend support to the claim that some elements of physical beauty are probably universal. Several cross-cultural studies of facial attractiveness, for instance, show that people all over the world tend to agree on the faces they see as beautiful, although there is more agreement when people judge faces representing their own race than when they judge faces from other races (Etcoff, 1999). What is it about faces that might account for such agreement? Research suggests several possibilities, including **sexual dimorphism**, **straightness**, **proportionality**, **symmetry**, and **averageness** (Etcoff, 1999; Fink & Penton-Voak, 2002; Rhodes, 2006; Zebrowitz, 1997).

In a society desperate to turn back the clock on the physical effects of aging, it's not hard to believe that youth and beauty go hand in hand. As applied to facial appearance, however, it's not just youthfulness (a face with youthful features such as smooth skin, large eyes, and small nose) that accounts for an attractive face, but hormones. Sexual dimorphism states that an attractive face contains some optimum blend of masculine and feminine characteristics of the face; it does not suggest that younger is necessarily better. If faces looked more attractive simply because they were younger looking, men and women with baby faces would look better than everyone else. While this is truer of women's faces than it is of men's—a nonthreatening appearance is more important in women than in men—it overlooks the importance of adult feminine and masculine facial features, which add a measure of sexual competence to the appearance of the face. In fact, research shows that women across racial and cultural lines—Hispanic, Asian, black, and white—appear attractive with distinctly feminine features, including the mature features of prominent cheekbones

RESEARCH 3.1

FIND OUT MORE

How Much Does Our Dress Influence Our Sense of Self?

In this study, the authors examined how three different styles of business dress (casual, business casual, and formal business) affected how employees viewed themselves. Based on prior theory and research, they hypothesized that (1) employees will feel more competent, authoritative, trustworthy, and productive when wearing formal attire but (2) more creative and friendlier in casual or business casual attire.

After analyzing their data, the authors found some support for their first hypothesis: Employees reported feeling more competent and authoritative when wearing either formal business attire or business casual attire than when wearing casual attire; employees also felt more trustworthy when wearing business casual than when wearing casual attire. Regarding their second hypothesis, the researchers found that employees felt the least friendly and creative when wearing formal business attire.

To find out more about this study and answer the following questions, you can visit the full text (cited below).

1. What research or theory supported their hypothesis?
2. How did they get a sample of employees for their study?
3. How did their hypotheses differ from their findings?
4. What kind of research study is this? (See Appendix.)

Source: Karl, K. A., Hall, M. N., & Peluchette, J. V. (2013). City employee perceptions of the impact of dress and appearance: You are what you wear. *Public Personnel Management*, 42, 452–470.

and narrow-looking faces combined with immature features of large, wide-set eyes and a small nose (Cunningham et al., 1995). Studies also show that female faces are more attractive with fuller lips, weaker jaws, and smaller chins than the population average—features that suggest high amounts of female hormones such as estrogen and low amounts of male hormones (Johnston & Franklin, 1993). In short, an attractive female face, which contains a mix of immature and mature features, is a face that is both youthful and extremely feminine, appealing to males because it advertises innocence and fertility.

The research showing a strong female preference for masculine male faces is much less consistent than the research showing a strong male preference for feminine features in female faces. Some studies show that an extremely masculine face can make the male face appear too dominant and unapproachable to females and that a blend of feminine and masculine features is more attractive (Keating & Doyle, 2002). But other studies show that masculine features are seen as more attractive to certain groups of females, such as those from less developed societies (DeBruine, Jones, Crawford, Welling, & Little, 2010), those at the fertile peak of their menstrual cycle (Wang, Hahn, Fisher, DeBruine, & Jones, 2014), those seeking short-term rather than long-term relationships, and those with certain sociosexual attitudes toward heterosexual relationships (Boothroyd & Brewer, 2014).

The idea of *straightness* comes from the model that guides the work of cosmetic and orthodontic surgeons, which views a straight profile as an attractive ideal. Accordingly, the jaw should be vertically aligned with the forehead. Researchers have found not only that straight-profiled faces are perceived as more attractive than out-of-alignment faces (Carello, Grosofsky, Shaw, Pittenger, & Mark, 1989; Dongieux & Sassouni, 1980; Lucker & Graber, 1980) but that beautiful people—contest winners, professional models, and actors—generally possess this physical attribute (Peck & Peck, 1970). Of course, the appeal of a straight profile does little to explain why some faces, when viewed frontally, as they are in most studies of attractiveness, are better looking than other faces.

Another perspective on attractive faces, *proportionality*, maintains that the key to good-looking faces is the ratio of the size of one segment of the face to another. One proposal, based on the golden proportions ideal of the ancient Greeks, is that three vertical segments of the face should be approximately equal in height: one segment extends from the hairline to the brow ridge, another from the brow ridge to just under the nose, the third from under the nose to the tip of the chin. In addition, the distance between the top of the face to the tip of the nose is "golden" if it is approximately two-thirds of the total length of the face. Although the idea of equal proportions seems to have some aesthetic appeal, little systematic research has been done to test its validity. One supportive study found that adolescent girls were rated as less attractive when the lower half of their faces was lengthened in proportion to the upper half (Dongieux & Sassouni, 1980).

Much more evidence is available to support the idea of *symmetry*: that the size, form, and arrangement of facial features are relatively symmetrical in attractive faces. Most of us are familiar with the aesthetic value of symmetry in art and architecture, but people also seem to like symmetry in the human face. In a landmark study, ethologist Karl Grammer and biologist Randy Thornhill (1994) discovered that both males and females preferred faces with greater symmetry, which they rated as more attractive, healthier, sexier, and more dominant than less symmetrical faces. Other researchers have since reached similar conclusions (Fink, Neave, Manning, & Grammer, 2006; Rhodes, Proffitt, Grady, & Sumich, 1998; Shackelford & Larsen, 1997). Interestingly, the attractiveness of facial symmetry may be limited to the perception of natural-looking faces. In a recent experiment, researchers found that computerized images of perfectly symmetrical left-sided and right-sided faces were rated as *less* attractive than were the natural faces (Zaidel & Deblieck, 2007).

If symmetrical faces are attractive, why is this so? The most popular but still contested theory is that human mate selection favors healthy over unhealthy individuals—we are naturally attracted to healthy-looking people—and since symmetrical faces imply healthier genes than do asymmetrical faces, we prefer them over the latter (Grammer & Thornhill, 1994). Some studies have supported this "good genes" hypothesis, finding that we perceive symmetrical faces to be healthier than faces with less symmetry (Rhodes et al., 2001; Zebrowitz & Rhodes, 2004), particularly when judging opposite-sex faces (Jones et al., 2001). There is also some evidence that persons with symmetrical faces may, in fact, be healthier. In one study, participants with more facial symmetry reported experiencing fewer physiological, emotional, and psychological problems than persons with less symmetrical faces (Shackelford & Larsen, 1997). The link between health and physical attractiveness, including facial symmetry, has attracted a great deal of interest among social scientists in recent years. The conclusion emerging from this body of research is that the link between health (actual and perceived) and attractiveness depends on a number of factors, some of which we address in the next section on age and fitness.

The research on averageness maintains that faces with average features are attractive. Some research indicates that composite faces—artificially created by averaging numerous computer images of individual faces—tend to be rated as better looking than any one of the individual faces. And the more faces that go into the composite, the more attractive it looks (Langlois & Roggman, 1990). One possible explanation is that average-looking faces are more familiar to us and we tend to prefer the familiar. Another is the fact that average faces also tend to be more youthful, symmetrical, and free of blemishes, all of which are seen as attractive qualities (Zebrowitz, 1997). Another explanation argues that faces containing a composite of average features constitute prototypes of a population of faces and are more visually pleasing to look at. According to this theory, faces are attractive not because they signal health, fitness, or reproductive potential (the evolutionary view) but because our brain processes these face more easily and with fewer disruptive stimuli than it does when looking at faces containing atypical or fewer average features. Unlike the evolutionary view, this theory contends that average faces contain the features both necessary and sufficient to appear attractive, and some recent research seems to support these claims (Trujillo, Jankowitsch, & Langlois, 2014). But studies also show that composite faces slightly exaggerating those features considered to be attractive for women, such as large eyes, high cheekbones, and a narrower lower jaw, are even more attractive than composites of more ordinary looking faces, suggesting that averageness is not the whole story. The favorable impact of average facial features seems more the case for female faces than it is for male faces (Grammer & Thornhill, 1994). This may be due to the fact that some male features are more attractive when large than when only average (e.g., a strong jaw).

At one time or another, or somewhere in the world, many aspects of our physical appearance are seen as beautiful. As noted above, judgments vary tremendously. Thus, any attempt to compile a comprehensive list of "beautiful features" would be pointless (Hatfield & Sprecher, 1986). In many cases, studies confirm our suspicions about what we regard as good looking. For example, research shows that bald men are seen as less attractive than are men with hair (Cash, 1990; Muscarella & Cunningham, 1996). Medium to longer hairstyles for women are often seen as more attractive than shorter hairstyles (Mesko & Bereczkei, 2004). Women's faces are rated as less attractive with eyeglasses than they are without them (Edwards, 1987; Hamid, 1972; Terry & Krofer, 1976) and while some studies suggest that makeup enhances the attractiveness of a woman's face (Cash, Dawson, Davis, Bown, & Galumbeck, 1989; Graham & Jouhar, 1981), the findings of other studies do not agree (Huguet, Groizet, & Richetin, 2004).

In general, there also seems to be some consensus on what makes for an attractive body. Survey research shows that overall body build is especially important to both sexes when judging male or female attractiveness (Pedersen, Markee, & Salusso, 1994). Men are attracted to curvaceous women as specified by a woman's waist-to-hip ratio (Singh, 1993). A woman's waist-to-hip ratio (WHR) in the range of .67 to .80—the waist is about .70 to .80 as large as the hips—takes shape after puberty under the influence of estrogen and signals health and fertility. Indeed, studies confirm that women with WHRs under .80 are almost twice as likely to become pregnant as are women with ratios above .80 (Etcoff, 1999). All over the world, men seem to take notice. Psychologist Devendra Singh's (1993) research in 18 different cultures revealed a strong preference for a WHR of .70. Some cross-cultural studies provide additional support for the attractiveness of a low WHR (Furnham & Baguma, 2002; Marlowe, Apicella, & Reed, 2005). But other cross-cultural studies raise questions about the universality of the findings and suggest taking into account measures of body weight, such as the body mass index (BMI), which affects judgments of attractiveness differently across cultures (Fisher & Voracek, 2006; Swami, Caprario, Tovee, & Furnham, 2006).

Women are attracted to men with V-shaped physiques and especially dislike pear-shaped bodies (Lavrakas, 1975). Research shows that a man's waist-to-chest ratio (WCR) is important in this regard. In one recent study, Greek and British women preferred images of men with lower ratios, and the WCR was a much stronger predictor of the men's attractiveness than other measures of physical attractiveness, such as the WHR and the BMI (Swami et al., 2007).

Despite the health risks of overexposure to the sun, tanned skin is often viewed as good looking. In one study, college students rated a person more attractive if he or she was described as having a dark suntan than when no such description was given (Miller, Ashton, McHoskey, & Gimbel, 1990). In another experiment, researchers showed to secondary school students slides of four models professionally made up—they applied liquid body makeup to the models—to have either a dark tan, medium tan, light tan, or no tan. Perhaps reflecting a greater awareness of the dangers of a dark tan, medium-tan models were rated as healthier and more attractive than any of the others (Broadstock, Borland, & Gason, 1992). Health risks aside, tattooing also garners support among many people as a beautifying ritual. In his ethnographic study of "tattoo enthusiasts" in Canada, Michael Atkinson (2004) offered the following commentary from one such enthusiast, named Jim:

> An ugly body I can forgive as long as you're trying to look better. Not everyone is beautiful, but if you don't try to enhance yourself, you're lazy. You work at being attractive, it doesn't come naturally. . . . My tattoos get so many compliments, and part of it comes from people's realization of how much effort I put into them. And since they're art and not just Post-It notes tacked onto my body, I know people admire the way I look. I mean, don't we all treat gorgeous, carefully sculpted bodies better than hideous ones? (p. 130)

AGE AND FITNESS As we grow older, changes in our physical appearance are a constant reminder to us and a bold announcement to others that we belong to a certain age group. In fact, most observers are very accurate in guessing someone's age, misjudging by only a few years (Henss, 1991). Aside from the highly visible changes in height, body size, physique, skin, and hair, the face contains many key signals. From birth to maturity, some of these changes include a smaller, more backward-sloping forehead; smaller (in proportion to the face), higher-placed eyes; a larger, more protruding chin and nose; and an enlarged jaw (Zebrowitz, 1997). Interestingly, evidence that the various signs of aging constitute an intrinsic signaling system comes from studies of infants as young as four months old, whose reactions indicate that they can discriminate between the approach of an unfamiliar child and the approach of an unfamiliar adult. Reactions to the child tend to be more positive—even when the size difference between the child and the adult is not a distinguishing factor (Lasky, Klein, & Martinez, 1974).

Clothing, too, is an indicator of age. Of course, since we have far greater control over the clothes we wear than we have over the physical signs of age, it is a much less reliable indicator. Nevertheless, as Marilyn Horn (1975) points out, "[E]very society maintains some differentiation in clothing norms for each stage in the life cycle. Most often these are broadly defined in terms of dress that is considered appropriate for children, adults, or the aged" (p. 205). Although the sanctions against age-inappropriate attire amount to little more than disapproving glances and snide remarks, most people tend to dress their age. In the past, age distinctions were often more carefully drawn. During the Victorian era, for example, the length of a boy's trousers was a sign of his age. Boys younger than six or seven were restricted to short pants; prepubescent boys wore knickers; and a boy couldn't wear long pants until he was considered a young man (Horn, 1975). In her book, *Dress Codes*, sociologist Ruth Rubinstein (1995) describes how teenagers in the workforce near the end of the 20th century began using their incomes for self-expression through clothing. Affluent times made this type of self-expression among the young more possible than ever before, giving rise to trendy styles of dress, characterized as youthful, fleeting, and distinctly different from mainstream fashion. Some examples of these youthful looks include hip-hop and rap styles, gothic attire, body piercings, mock hippie clothing, and rave styles.

Physical appearance also signals a person's health and level of fitness. In addition to the physical symptoms of disease and the visible signs of a disability, an individual's general well-being often registers on the face and body. A person who is in good shape advertises the youth and vigor associated with a healthy lifestyle. Most of us probably believe we can tell by sight alone if someone is in good health. In fact, some research suggests that we can. In one study, college students were asked if they could accurately rate, on a scale from poor to excellent, the health of 18-year-old men and women shown in black-and-white portrait photographs. The ratings turned out to be in general agreement with the medical records of the individuals in the photographs (Kalick, Zebrowitz, Langlois, & Johnson, 1997).

As we noted earlier, there may be a link between physical attractiveness and the signaling of health and fitness. A great deal of research shows, for instance, that a woman's WHR and BMI are somewhat reliable signals, not only indicating health and fitness but shaping observers' judgments of health and fitness as well (Weeden & Sabini, 2005). Facial attractiveness may also signal health and fitness, though this claim remains controversial (Grammer, Fink, Moller, & Manning, 2005; Weeden & Sabini, 2005). In their effort to examine the link between facial attractiveness and fitness (i.e., health and intelligence), Zebrowitz and Rhodes (2004) found support for a "bad genes" hypothesis rather than a "good genes" hypothesis. That is, health and intelligence correlated positively with facial attractiveness ratings, facial averageness, and facial symmetry, but only for the faces that were average and below average in these attributes. Thus, attractiveness is not predictive of good genes. Instead, less attractiveness is predictive of bad genes. On the other hand, *perceptions* of health and intelligence did not differ in this way. Judges rated attractive faces as healthier and as more intelligent than less attractive faces. Women often use cosmetics to boost perceptions of facial beauty, and some research suggests that we judge the same faces with makeup as healthier and more confident than without the makeup (Nash, Feldman, Hussey, Leveque, & Pineau, 2006).

INDIVIDUALITY One feature of the human body that signals our individuality is body odor. A brief review of the "dirty T-shirt" experiments that were done in the 1980s reported an ability to recognize the odor of another person. In these experiments, participants smelled the cotton T-shirts of individuals who wore the shirts from one to seven days. Seventy-five percent of the participants could pick out their own shirts; parents could identify the shirts of their children with accuracy rates reaching 90% and higher; and 50% of spouses could identify the T-shirts of their mates (Knapp & Hall, 2002). For many of us, what we look like is very much part of who we are as an individual. No two people look exactly alike, and there are no limits to the things we can do, through modification and adornment, to bring out our uniqueness. What we choose to do says a lot about how we would like to be seen by others. Self-expression and physical appearance are, in a word, inseparable.

Our ability to recognize people we've met before is probably the best evidence that physical appearance signals individuality. While there may be something special about the way a person dresses or the shape of a person's physique, most of us are drawn to faces. Indeed, no other aspect of our appearance identifies us more completely. Research indicates that we are very good at remembering faces. In one study, people had no difficulty identifying faces taken from their own high school yearbooks rather than other yearbooks—fifty years after they had graduated (Bahrick, Bahrick, & Wittlinger, 1975). But this capacity is greatly diminished in cases of cross-race identifications. In fact, several studies have demonstrated that whites, blacks, and Orientals recognize faces of their own race more accurately than the faces of other races (Bothwell, Brigham, & Malpass, 1989; Brigham & Malpass, 1985; Ng & Lindsay, 1994; Shapiro & Penrod, 1986). Although this phenomenon has not yet been fully explained, Leslie Zebrowitz (1997) offers one possibility:

> Perhaps extracting identity information from faces is like language acquisition: Just as experience with a particular language very early in life is necessary to become truly fluent, so may early experience with a particular set of faces be essential to facial recognition. (p. 25)

Despite pressures to conform and dress like others, we usually express our individuality in some way through the clothes we choose to wear. Many people have also taken up the more daring and sometimes risky practices of tattooing, piercing, and scarification. In some cultures, tattooing has a long history of expressing one's identity. In New

▸ Many people get tattoos to signify their affiliation with a group, their belief in an idea, or their individual sense of self.

istockphoto.com/mapodile

Zealand's Maori tribes, for example, each family wore a facial tattoo known as a *moko* that individual family members were able to personalize. As Bell (1999) points out, "Their moko was like a signature, which they actually used when signing documents; that is, instead of signing their names they drew their moko, which was a true representation of self" (p. 53). In their search for more lasting and creative forms of personal and group identification, increasing numbers of young people are challenging the customs of the older generation. As one psychiatric assessment points out, however, the desire for self-expression may sometimes mask more deep-seated needs.

> Tattoos and piercings can offer a concrete and readily available solution for many of the identity crises and conflicts normative to adolescent development. In using such decorations, and by marking out their bodily territories, adolescents can support their efforts at autonomy, privacy, and insulation. Seeking individuation, tattooed adolescents can become unambiguously demarcated from others and singled out as unique. The intense and often disturbing reactions that are mobilized in viewers can help to effectively keep them at bay, becoming tantamount to the proverbial "Keep Out" sign hanging from a teenager's door (Martin, 1997, p. 2)

Of course, while some adolescents may be distancing themselves from others with tattoos (or piercings), there is no evidence to date of a significant problem in this regard. One study estimates that 10% of the population in modern Western societies has some form of body modification (Wohlrab, Stahl, Rammsayer, & Kappeler, 2007). Tattooing in particular is becoming a common medium of expressing one's individuality. As one "tattoo enthusiast" interviewed in Atkinson's (2004) study said:

> There's something about a tattoo that screams individuality. First, not everyone does it, so it's still tricky. . . . Plus, you completely style the way it looks. No one else, probably ever, will look like you afterward. With every person I know running out to buy the spring line at the Gap, . . . I see my tattoos as statements about who I really am. When my friends say, "Wow, your tattoo looks fantastic," the key word is your. They don't say "That tattoo you have is amazing." . . . Most people I know wouldn't ever copy someone else's

> tattoo. The whole point of redesigning your body is to make it your own, so why destroy it by stealing someone else's? (p. 130, Carl)

In one study comparing individuals with tattoos and individuals without tattoos, researchers in Australia found that the tattooed group scored higher on a questionnaire measuring "need for uniqueness" than did the non-tattooed group. Additionally, among those without tattoos, the scores predicted the likelihood of getting a tattoo (Tiggeman & Golder, 2006). Similar results from more recent studies showing a correlation between having a tattoo and need for uniqueness were obtained with sample of respondents from Austria, Germany, and England (Swami, 2012a, 2012b).

GENDER AND SEXUAL ORIENTATION Some of Hollywood's top actors have taken up the challenge of portraying the opposite sex: Julie Andrews in *Victor, Victoria*; Dustin Hoffman in *Tootsie*; Robin Williams in *Mrs. Doubtfire*; and Tyler Perry in *Madea's Family Reunion* all gave it their best shot. Despite the excellent makeup, wardrobe, and acting, many natural signs of gender were still apparent. One exception was actor Jaye Davidson's stunning portrayal in *The Crying Game*. Anatomically, men's physical features are generally larger than women's. Compared to women, men have bigger bones, muscles, shoulders, arms, hands, chests, heads, jaws, noses, and so on. Other natural signals include male–female differences in hair distribution and overall body shape.

In many cases, the desire to accentuate these natural gender differences directly influences the clothes we wear (i.e., iconic signals). In some Oriental cultures, painful foot-binding techniques made women's feet appear much smaller than they actually were; exotic male headdresses are used in some cultures and large hats have been used in others to increase a man's height; women used to wear uncomfortable corsets and bustles to emphasize their feminine shape; the use of shoulder pads and epaulettes widen the look of a man's shoulders.

But many gender differences in our appearance have no relation at all to any natural differences (i.e., arbitrary signals): Women wear skirts, men wear pants; women have long hair, men have short hair; women carry handbags, men use pockets; women apply makeup, men don't. Indeed, exceptions to the rule can be found in each of these cases, depending upon where you look—or when. We also tend to believe that women are more interested in their appearance than men are, yet this is hardly a biological fact. Throughout the animal kingdom, the male of the species usually inherits a more flamboyant appearance. And prior to the eighteenth century, men's attire was just as decorative as (if not more so than) women's attire (Horn, 1975). Even today, there is evidence that things are changing. According to one survey, three in four men report using facial moisturizers, seven in ten have their clothes tailored and get manicures or pedicures, and two-thirds have had their teeth capped or whitened ("Men Acting Badly," 1997). One especially revealing trend is the growth in cosmetic surgeries for men. The American Society of Plastic Surgeons reported that 200,000 men had cosmetic surgery in 1999. Compared to 1997, this included an 87% increase for liposuctions, a 47% increase for breast reductions, and a 30% increase for face-lifts (Muhammad, 2001). Another recent trend, tattooing, has been closing the gap between body modification practices appropriate for men and appropriate for women. Historically, men and not women got tattoos. But now, more women than men are getting tattoos, even though there may be some lingering prejudice against visible tattoos on women compared to men (Hawkes, Senn, & Thorn, 2004).

Sometimes the differences between men's and women's clothing that we take for granted and don't think about turn out to have origins linked to traditional sex roles. For instance, why are the buttons on female garments on the left side, whereas the buttons on male garments are on the right side? Morris (1977) explains:

> This behavior has been going on for centuries and is usually referred to simply as traditional. The true explanation, however, appears to be that males prefer left-over-right because it means they can tuck their right hands into the fold of the garment. This began in a pocketless epoch and was supposedly a way of keeping the dominant weapon-hand warm and ready for action, and has persisted ever since. Females, by contrast, preferred the wrapping over of the longer right side of their garment because they tended to carry their babies more often on the left breast than the right, and it meant that they could wrap the long fold over the infant as it slept or sucked. Again the pattern is thought to have persisted long after the original reason for it became obsolete. (p. 236)

Male–female distinctions in dress are commonplace everywhere in the world. Occasionally, we find attempts to downplay these distinctions. In post-revolutionary Russia, for example, to display their allegiance to the state and their solidarity as a people committed to the goals of a classless society, women adopted the same uniform attire of men. This experiment in sexless garb was relatively short-lived, however, as both men and women eventually returned to more masculine and feminine styles of dress (Horn, 1975).

Recent research also examines the potential of physical features to signal one's sexual orientation and the ability of persons to make accurate judgments based on nonverbal cues, sometimes referred to as "gaydar." One source of nonverbal cues is the physical features of a person's face. Some studies show that people can make accurate judgments of sexual orientation by looking at an individual's face (Rule & Ambady, 2008) Stereotypes exist regarding the facial features of persons presumed to be gay—feminine features in men and masculine features in women. People have a tendency to apply these stereotypes when making judgments about whether an individual is gay or straight (Freeman, Johnson, Ambady, & Rule, 2010). Of courses, the reliance on these stereotypes, like the reliance on any simple stereotype, can lead to false judgments. On the other hand, one study found that the use of this stereotypical information led to accurate judgments about a person's sexual orientation (Lyons, Lynch, Brewer, & Bruno, 2014). Some research also shows that the use of these simple stereotypes is affected by many factors, such as a person's political orientation. The results of a recent study found, for example, that when shown faces of males with feminine features and females with masculine features (stereotypical information about gays), conservatives exhibited more of an inclination than liberals to rely on these stereotypes, labeling the masculine female faces and the feminine male faces as being gay rather than straight (Stern, West, Jost, & Rule, 2013).

RACE AND ETHNICITY Our racial and ethnic identity is closely tied to our physical appearance (e.g., skin color, facial features, style of dress). Although racial classifications are widely regarded as scientifically invalid, the judgments we make about a person's race are part of everyday life. Physical features we generally attribute to differences in race are the natural byproducts of geography. As Nancy Etcoff (1999) points out in her book, *Survival of the Prettiest*,

> [The features that signify our identity and ancestry evolved partly as adaptations to climactic conditions, just as body shapes and skin tones did. Noses carry air into the lungs. They evolved into long narrow shapes in climates where the air was cold or dry and needed to be warmed and moistened before reaching the lungs. People of northern European or Middle Eastern ancestry often inherit long noses with narrow nostrils (perfect for restricting air flow). In humid environments, the short wide noses common to many African and Asian people are more efficient. (p. 134)

Regarding ethnicity, the work of some physical anthropologists suggests that there may be global differences in the preponderance of two facial types (Zebrowitz, 1997). The DC face (dolichocephalic), which predominates in northern Europe, northern Africa, India, and the Middle East,

> is a relatively angular face, narrow, long, and protrusive, with close-set eyes; a relatively thin, longish, and protrusive nose with a high bridge; and a relatively receding chin. The forehead in this face tends to slope backward and to jut out over the eyes, which consequently appear deep set. (p. 20)

▸ Physical appearance is an important marker of one's racial and ethnic identity. Rachel Dolezal received a great deal of media attention when it was learned that she had changed her natural appearance as a white person to coincide with her newfound identity as a black activist for the African American community.

Arakathman/Wikimedia

The BC face (brachycephalic), which is found more generally in middle Europe and the Far East, "is short, broad, and flat with wide-set eyes, a short puglike nose, and a prominent chin. The forehead in this face tends to be upright, the eyes are bulging, and the cheekbones are squared and prominent" (p. 20).

In addition to physical characteristics, clothing can communicate racial and ethnic identity. Although Western dress has spread in popularity throughout much of the industrialized world, we still see traditional costumes being worn faithfully by members of many religious and ethnic groups (e.g., the Japanese kimono, the Indian sari, the Scottish kilt, the African dashiki, etc.). And most of us have seen the clothing associated with any number of well-known subcultures that are spread across the United States (e.g., the Amish, Hasidic Jews, Rastafarians). People all over the world alter their appearance to celebrate important life events. Ceremonies and rituals typically prescribe certain forms of body adornment. A particular costume thus becomes a symbol of the occasion (e.g., wedding, graduation).

OCCUPATION AND SOCIAL CLASS Sometimes it is possible to identify a person's line of work solely from their attire. Uniforms are worn by people in many occupations: police officers, waitresses, postal workers, airline pilots, nurses, priests, and firefighters, to name a few. Often, the uniform becomes so much a part of the job that the wearer may become less effective without it. In one recent study of the white coat worn by physicians, patients reported that white-coat wearing improved virtually all aspects of doctor–patient interaction and that when doctors wore white coats, patients rated them as more hygienic, professional, authoritative, and scientific (Gooden, Smith, Tattersall, & Stockier, 2001). Obviously, it is much more difficult to identify a person's occupation when it doesn't require any particular outfit. Yet stereotypes still prevail. Whether from personal experience or movie portrayals, most of us have an image in our mind of what someone is supposed to look like if he or she is a lawyer, professor, artist, or engineer. In reality, however, these stereotypes usually aren't true. For years, students in my nonverbal communication classes have tried, with very little success (about a 30% accuracy rate), to match photographs of individuals with the individual's occupation and personality. As they discuss the reasons for their guesses, typical comments that surface include "She doesn't look like a cab driver," "He can't be a nurse," or "I never had a teacher who looked like that."

Social class refers to one's station in life as determined by factors such as education, income, and occupation. Research suggests that various physical appearance cues are related to these indices of social class. During the preindustrial era, obesity was a status symbol—a sign of the good life. Today, in developing countries there is still a positive association between a woman's weight and her socioeconomic status (Sobal & Stunkard, 1989). But in relatively affluent societies, which value thinness, an inverse relationship exists: As weight goes up, socioeconomic status goes down (Lapidus, Bengtsson, Haellstroem, & Bjoerntorp, 1989; Sobal & Stunkard, 1989). One study in the black community, for example, discovered an inverse relationship between the BMI—a widely used standardized measure of obesity—and socioeconomic status, but only among women (Croft, Strogatz, James, & Keenan, 1992). A study in England, Scotland, and Wales found that girls in the heaviest 10% of their age group at age 16 earned 7.4% less than their nonobese peers by the time they reached age 23. Girls in the heaviest 1% earned 11.4% less at age 23 (Coleman, 1994).

Abundant evidence shows that social class is tied to race and ethnicity. It is widely known that a disproportionate number of those in the low socioeconomic strata of society are black, Hispanic, and Native American. And even within these traditionally disadvantaged groups, physical features can become markers of social class. In their analysis of the data obtained from a nationwide survey of Mexican Americans, one group of investigators discovered that respondents with a European physical appearance were higher in socio-economic status than were those without European features (Arce, Murguia, & Frisbie, 1987). Other studies suggest that lighter skin may be related to greater privilege. One study found that skin tone variations among Mexican Americans living in San Antonio, Texas, reflected social class distinctions (Relethford, Stern, Gaskill, & Hazuda, 1983). And some evidence suggests an association between complexion and socioeconomic status in the black community as well (Keith & Herring, 1991).

Other aspects of our natural appearance are also related to social class. To some extent, beauty pays off when it comes to occupation and income. Analysis of data obtained from several national surveys conducted at the University of Michigan's Survey Research Center (Quinn, 1978) revealed that the incomes of good-looking men and women were substantially higher than those who were rated as plain or homely. After taking into account differences in jobs, education, work experience, race, and other factors related to income, one economist found that female hospital and school district workers who rated themselves as attractive earned about 8% more than did the female

PERSONAL EXPERIENCE 3.3

CAN YOU RELATE TO THIS?

Skin Color Can Influence Judgments of Social Class

If you are a light-skinned black person, you are looked upon as "uppity" or thinking that you're too good. This is something I have come across a lot. For my first year of college, I attended the first historically black college, Lincoln University. It was my first time being around that many African Americans (the high school I attended was mostly Caucasian). I am naturally shy, so I would walk around not speaking to anyone. In many cases, I would walk around looking at the ground or just with no expression on my face whatsoever. I was viewed as the "uppity" light-skinned girl who thought she was too good for everyone else.

Ami

workers who did not rate themselves as attractive (Morin, 2002). Additionally, the jobs of attractive persons were considered more prestigious than those of their less attractive counterparts. Research on height also reveals a pattern of discrimination: Tall men are more likely than shorter men to occupy positions of status and to earn higher starting salaries (Deck, 1968; Quinn, 1978).

Clothing choices reflect disparities in wealth as well as in occupational demands. As cues to status, differences in dress emerge at an early age. In one study, observations of Midwestern elementary school children revealed that high status was symbolized by clothing items that were aesthetically rather than functionally oriented, multipurpose, and gender-specific; low-status clothing was merely functional and utilitarian. In poor communities, clothing is often used to elevate one's social standing in the eyes of others. As one group of researchers explained, "African American youth are disproportionately poor, and face social class devaluation and discrimination in society. They may want to communicate wealth and status to compensate for their actual situation" (LaPoint, Holloman, & Alleyne, 1992, p. 22).

In many cultures, attire is an unequivocal symbol of where one stands in the hierarchy. Among the Kalabari in Nigeria, for example, men's style of dress corresponds closely to their position in society, indicating whether one is a young worker, "gentleman of substance," corporate chief, or ruler of state (Michelman & Erekosima, 1992).

Whether physical appearance is a reliable indicator of social class or not, most of us see a connection. Studies demonstrate that we form opinions about other people's income, occupation, and education based on the way they look. In a clothes-conscious society, it's not too difficult to notice the value of what someone is wearing. But we also form opinions as a result of subtler signals. For instance, we tend to view attractive people as coming from a better background than those who are less attractive (Kalick, 1988). Even a person with an attractive individual may be seen differently. Research suggests, for instance, that we judge men who are seen with attractive women as more successful and intelligent (Bar-Tal & Saxe, 1976). Height also influences us to the extent that we think a tall man has a more prestigious job than a shorter man does. In one well-known experiment, the same person is introduced to three different groups of students. Each time he's introduced, his position is described differently: a graduate student, a new instructor, or a professor. The researcher discovered that student estimates of the man's height increased along with his apparent rank at the university (Wilson, 1968).

CHARACTER AND PERSONALITY The practice of physiognomy, which proffered the view that our facial features reveal our true character, is no longer taken seriously. Yet not long ago, face reading was widely practiced and revered. Ironically, Charles Darwin, who pioneered the modern study of facial expression, nearly failed to gain passage on the HMS Beagle—the ship that set sail on the voyage that led to Darwin's theories of natural selection—because the captain thought the shape of Darwin's nose suggested a lack of energy and determination (Zebrowitz, 1997). A more fitting testimonial to the pseudoscience of face reading would be hard to find. What research does tell us about the relationship between character and physical appearance is that we are stereotyped in particular ways because of our physical appearance and that sometimes, through self-fulfilling prophecies, we may become the kind of person others expect us to be.

People certainly make snap judgments about our character and personality because of the way we look. Our physical appearance is a salient (i.e., conspicuous) source of information to those who see us, especially if they lack information from other sources. And the nearly endless associations that we all form between a person's inner qualities and outward appearances make these first impressions an inevitable part of daily life. Many of these knee-jerk reactions probably result from inborn tendencies, such as perceiving a baby-faced adult as a nice person, while others result more from cultural conditioning, such as regarding a tattooed person as rebellious.

Numerous studies show that a host of inferences stem from facial features alone. People with attractive faces appear to benefit from what social scientists call a **halo effect**, the tendency to judge good-looking people more positively than those who are less attractive. Social psychologist Leslie Zebrowitz (1997) summarized this body of research. She reports that attractive people are seen as more socially skilled and sexually warm than are less attractive persons. They are also rated as more sociable, persuasive, honest, poised, warm, strong, kind, outgoing, and, to a lesser degree,

EXERCISE 3.1

TRY IT

People Watching

OBJECTIVE: All of us are guilty of making snap judgments about people we see or meet based solely on their physical appearance. The purpose of this exercise is twofold: first, to encourage you to focus on your own personal biases about the relationship between looks and personality; second, to share with others in the class the way these biases shape our first impressions of other people.

INSTRUCTIONS: By yourself or with another person, go to a nearby shopping mall for some people watching. Using a tape recorder or notes, select three different people for observation. For each person you observe, note the following: (1) the kind of person you think they are (i.e., personality), (2) what it is about their appearance that contributes to your first impression—be as specific as you can (e.g., their hairstyle, shoes, body weight, article of clothing, jewelry, etc.). Be prepared to discuss each of these observations in class.

intelligent. But some judgments depend more on the type of attractiveness cues found on a person's face than other judgments. For instance, the inclination to label someone as warm, kind, sociable, and honest is much greater when a woman's face is attractive in a cute way than in a mature, sexy way. On the negative side, Zebrowitz (1997) reports some research that good-looking women may also be seen as more egotistical, vain, snobbish, and materialistic than their less attractive counterparts. Overall, the halo effect seems to benefit both men and women, develop early in life, and affect people regardless of their age.

Studies also show that the effect is present across cultural and racial groups, although the specific traits attributed to attractive people may vary according to the values of the particular group (i.e., what they regard as positive qualities). For example, Koreans are likely to see good-looking Koreans as having integrity and being concerned for others. This reflects their high regard for these personal qualities—a characteristic of most collectivistic cultures. These qualities are much less likely to be part of the attractiveness halo found in individualistic cultures such as the United States. Recent studies of undergraduates in Taiwan—a collectivistic culture—confirm this tendency to stereotype attractive faces in a culturally desirable way (Chen & Shaffer, 1997; Shaffer, Crepaz, & Sun, 2000).

Although the halo effect confirms a "beauty bias" in favor of attractive faces, one recent study of children and adults suggests that the preference for attractive faces is actually weaker than is the dislike of unattractive faces. In other words, the disadvantage of being unattractive probably outweighs the advantage of being attractive (Griffin & Langlois, 2006). In addition, while attractive faces influence judgments of character, one study found that judgments of character also influence perceptions of attractiveness. Participants in the experiment who believed a person was honest judged that person as having a more attractive face than did participants who believed the person was dishonest (Paunonen, 2006).

Much of the research on the halo effect focuses on its ramifications—discriminatory practices found in almost all walks of life. We review this research in Part III of the text. The consequences of this type of discrimination are particularly troublesome because of the automatic and difficult-to-monitor nature of the response. For instance, research in the field of social neuroscience shows that the perception and appraisal of facial attractiveness occurs at speeds that defy thoughtful reflection. Participants respond favorably to attractive faces even when they have little or no conscious awareness of having seen the faces (Olson & Marshuetz, 2005).

▸ The baby-faced overgeneralization effect says that regardless of physical beauty, we tend to perceive adults with babyish features—small nose, large eyes, round faces, protruding forehead, small chin, pouting lips, and so forth—as having more childlike qualities than adults with mature facial features. In this regard, how do the facial features of actress Reese Witherspoon compare to those of actress Cate Blanchett?

istockphoto.com/EdStock

PERSONAL EXPERIENCE 3.4

CAN YOU RELATE TO THIS?

Baby-Faced People Are Innocent Looking

My close friend, Joe, who I've been close with since the third grade, fits the definition of a baby face perfectly. He has a round baby face with chubby cheeks, long dark eyelashes, big round blue eyes, a button nose, and a big forehead. Because of his, he always seems to get out of trouble. Joe and I played soccer together when we were younger and I remember whenever he and the other troublemaker, Tom, were acting out that it was always Tom and never Joe who got into trouble. All of the parents of my friends in high school thought he was "such a nice, sweet boy," and they never complained when we hung out at his house. Yet, in reality, we hung out there because he held the wildest parties!

Denise

Some other aspects of the face that trigger character judgments are the appearance of baby-faced features, racial features, hair, eyeglasses, and cosmetics. Our natural reactions to baby-faced features seem to carry over to our perceptions of adults who also possess some of these features. This **baby face overgeneralization effect** is well supported. We tend to perceive persons with babyish features—small nose, large eyes, protruding forehead, light hair, and so on—as having many childlike qualities. As a result, we see them as cute, innocent, nice, naïve, and weak (Zebrowitz, 1997). But there is no evidence that baby-faced people possess these traits or live up to the expectations of others (Zebrowitz, Collins, & Dutta, 1998). To the contrary, there is evidence that they may be trying to shatter the stereotypes imposed on them. And this may be the case regardless of whether the stereotype is socially desirable or not. In one study, Leslie Zebrowitz and her colleagues found that baby-faced adolescent boys demonstrated higher academic achievement than their mature-faced peers, disconfirming the stereotype that baby-faced people are intellectually weak. In another study, they discovered that baby-faced boys from low socioeconomic backgrounds were more likely than their mature-faced peers to be delinquent, despite the opposing stereotype that baby-faced people are innocent, warm, submissive, and physically weak (Zebrowitz, Andreoletti et al., 1998). Another kind of overgeneralization effect, based on facial features, may be found in the snap judgments people make about individuals with Afrocentric-looking faces. In a series of experiments, one team of researchers wanted to find out if the negative stereotyping of black males in general also occurs in response to any individuals with Afrocentric facial features (i.e., coarse hair, dark skin, full lips, and a wide nose). In one experiment, the researchers asked participants in the study to match photographs of black men with written descriptions of black men. One of the descriptions contained information typical of the negative stereotype: The person grew up in the inner city, was attending college on a basketball scholarship, had failed several classes, had been involved in fights on the basketball court, and was waiting to talk to his coach about a drug charge. The photographs matched up with this description tended to be of men with stronger Afrocentric facial features. In a follow-up experiment, the researchers found that photographs of European American faces were matched up in a similar way: The faces with stronger Afrocentric features were more likely to be seen as the ones fitting the negative stereotype (Blair, Judd, Sadler, & Jenkins, 2002).

EXERCISE 3.2

TRY IT

The Implicit Association Test (IAT)

OBJECTIVE: To assess your implicit bias in judging people based on their physical appearance

INSTRUCTIONS: The IAT measures your nonconscious tendency to favor some people over others based on their physical attributes, such as race, skin color, age, and body weight. The test presents pictures of people along with positive and negative concepts and asks you to make split-second decisions about which pictures and concepts belong together. How quickly you make these decisions is a measure of your *bias* or inclination to hold a positive attitude or negative attitude toward people with those physical attributes. You can go online and take a demonstration test at implicit.harvard.edu

Some studies suggest that men with a beard are perceived in more masculine terms than are men without one: aggressive, independent, extroverted, self-confident, mature, dominant, and courageous (Addison, 1989; Freedman, 1969; Kenny & Fletcher, 1973; Pancer & Meindl, 1978; Wogalter & Hosie, 1991). Women with long hair may be seen as younger looking and, as a consequence, less mature and forceful (Terry & Krantz, 1993). And one (perhaps outdated) study found that short-haired men were viewed as more intelligent, moral, masculine, mature, wise, and attractive than long-haired men (Peterson & Curran, 1976). Even hair color can make a difference. One study reports that people actually do expect blondes to have more fun and redheads to act like clowns (Clayson & Maughan, 1986). Eyeglasses are related to judgments of increased intelligence but decreased social forcefulness (Terry & Krantz, 1993). And women use cosmetics to appear more youthful and attractive. As noted above, it generally seems to have the desired effect. Studies also suggest that we perceive women in a more gender-stereotypical manner when they wear makeup than when they do not (e.g., talkative and sociable) and that they may be seen as more popular, poised, and self-confident (Graham & Jouhar, 1981; Workman & Johnson, 1991).

To be sure, we read a lot into people's faces. But what about a person's body and style of dress? One area of research that has attracted some interest focuses on **somatotypes**, different kinds of human physiques that may be related to an individual's temperament or personality (Sheldon, 1940; Sheldon, Dupertuis, & McDermott, 1954). Some studies reveal persistent stereotypes of people based on the general shape of their bodies. An endomorphic physique (which is soft, round, and fat) tends to be seen as lazy, weak, sympathetic, agreeable, dependent, and good-natured; an ectomorphic physique (which is tall, thin, and fragile) is regarded as tense, nervous, suspicious, ambitious, quiet, and pessimistic; and a mesomorphic physique (which is muscular and athletic) is considered to be masculine, strong, good looking, adventurous, and self-reliant (Wells & Siegel, 1961). Occasionally, these stereotypes turn out to be true, not because of some inborn connection between personality and physique but as a result of a self-fulfilling prophecy; that is, a person may become quiet, adventurous, or lazy if he or she gradually conforms to the expectations of others. More often than not, we will unfairly misjudge someone if we assume they have a certain personality trait simply because they happen to be thin, chubby, or athletic.

Not surprisingly, there is a definite relationship between our personalities and the way we dress. Clothing not only expresses some measure of our personality, but it also exerts a rather strong influence on how others judge us. One widely cited study, conducted by communication researchers Lawrence Rosenfeld and Timothy Plax (1977), determined that certain attitudes we hold about clothing may be related to our personality. In part, they found that women who were very clothes conscious—they believe clothes are important and spend a lot of time thinking about their clothes—tended to be inhibited, deferential to authority, anxious, kind, sympathetic, and loyal, whereas women who were not the least bit clothes conscious had forceful and independent personalities. Another attitude toward clothing, called *exhibitionism*, measured individuals' approval of skin-revealing attire. Exhibitionistic women were radical, detached from interpersonal relationships, and had a high opinion of themselves. Exhibitionistic men had aggressive, outgoing, unsympathetic, and impulsive tendencies. Many people hold a very practical view of clothing—it should be functional and comfortable. Practical men were inhibited, rebellious, and had little motivation to make friends. Practical women were confident, enthusiastic, outgoing, and had feelings of superiority. Men who scored low on this practicality dimension were success oriented, mature, forceful, and analytical; women who scored low were self-centered, independent, and detached.

Have you ever instantly labeled someone as egotistical, sloppy, conscientious, rebellious, or conservative simply because of what that person was wearing? Most of us hold stereotypes of people based on little more than their clothing preferences. In one study, 15- and 16-year-old girls were asked to make judgments about the kinds of people who would wear various outfits pictured in magazines. The girls showed considerable agreement in matching an outfit with a person they described as either snobbish, fun loving, rebellious, or shy (Gibbins, 1969). One clear-cut example of stereotyping involves the snap judgments people make of women who wear "sexy" clothes. In an experiment that showed college students a slide of the same female model wearing either provocative or conservative clothing, the students rated the model as more likely to be unfaithful, to use sex for personal gain, to have had sex at a younger age, and to be more promiscuous when she was dressed provocatively than when she was dressed conservatively (Cahoon & Edmonds, 1987). Similarly, college students in another study were more likely to blame the victim of marital rape when she was described as having worn "seductive" attire (Whately, 2005).

Another well-known example of stereotyping is the inclination to label people with multiple tattoos and body piercings as rebellious risk-takers, people outside the mainstream (Bell, 1999). In fact, there is some evidence of a disproportionately higher number of "impulsive sensation-seekers" in this group of individuals compared to the general population (Roberti, Storch, & Bravata, 2004; Swami, 2012a, 2012b; Wohlrab et al., 2007). Numerous studies also show that college students and other young adults and particularly adolescents with tattoos and body piercings are more likely than their peers without these body modifications to engage in some kind of risk-taking behavior, such as greater use of alcohol and illegal drugs, more unprotected sex, more run-ins with the law, and more disordered eating (Burger & Finkel, 2002; Carroll, Riffenburgh, Roberts, & Myhre, 2002; Drews, Allison, & Probst, 2000; Forbes, 2001; Frederick & Bradley, 2000; King & Vidourek, 2013; Koch, Roberts, Armstrong, & Owen, 2009; Nowoseleski, Sipinski, Kuczerawy, Kozlowska, & Skrzpulec, 2012; Suris, Jeannin, Chossis, & Michaud, 2007).

Despite the results of these studies, however, the more widespread these body modification practices become, the more imprudent it becomes to stereotype individuals on first sight.

RESEARCH 3.2

FIND OUT MORE

What Factors Are Associated with Tattoos and Piercings?

The purpose of this study was to identify the lifestyle factors most predictive of body modification practices (tattoos and piercings) among young people. The researchers contacted all of the high school students in one of the school districts in Colorado, asking for their participation in the study. Of those contacted, more than 1,500 students between Grades 9–12 agreed to participate (a response rate of 76%). Most of the participants reported that they had neither a tattoo nor a piercing (62%), but among those participants who said they did, the researchers findings included the following: Older students were more likely to have tattoos and piercings than younger students; there were no differences between boys and girls in having tattoos, but girls (42%) were much more likely than boys (16%) to have piercings (not counting earrings); pierced girls were less likely to be school oriented than girls that didn't report having piercings; and pierced girls were the most likely group to report use of substances such as marijuana, alcohol, tobacco, and other substances such as cocaine.

To find out more about this study and to answer the following questions, see the full text (cited below).

1. What three theories are briefly cited to explain their predictions and results?
2. How diverse is their sample of participants in terms of race, ethnicity, and so forth?
3. What are the limitations of the study?
4. What method of nonverbal communication research is this study? (See Appendix.)

Source: Dukes, R., & Stein, J. (2011). Ink and holes: Predictive associations of body modifications among adolescence. *Youth and Society*, 43, 1547–1569.

Most people have an image of the kind of person they want others to think they are. And whether that image happens to be hip, rebellious, conservative, young, religious, affluent, or healthy, we can use our physical appearance to project the desired image. At the same time, we also recognize the need to alter our appearance according to the situation. We may want to dress one way for a job interview, another way at a party, and another way relaxing at home or shopping at the mall. Today, we have the capacity to change the way we look in more ways than ever before. On the positive side, this affords us tremendous flexibility in conveying the image we choose. On the negative side is the danger of becoming overly concerned—even obsessed—with projecting the "right" image, no matter the cost. And there are many costs involved in altering our appearance: continued dissatisfaction, financial losses, health risks, and wasted time, to name a few. To be sure, there may be a fine line between being concerned about our appearance and being overly concerned. While most people would probably like to experience the so-called halo effect that often results from being attractive, studies indicate that, in the long run, things tend to even out: Attractive people are no happier than their less attractive counterparts (Hatfield & Sprecher, 1986).

Establishing Relationships

Through body endowment, modification, and adornment, we signal a great deal about our multiple identities: attractiveness, individuality, gender, age, fitness, social class, occupation, race, ethnicity, character, and personality. Identification is the primary function of the human body's signaling system. But our bodies can also—although to a limited degree—contribute to the other essential functions of nonverbal communication, to which we now turn.

An important secondary communication function of our bodies is facilitating interpersonal relationships. This is a secondary rather than a primary function because it merely stems from and is not independent of the identification function. We may choose to initiate a relationship with someone, for example, because of the kind of person we think they are—attractive, intelligent, warm, generous, outgoing, and so forth—which may be based partly on what they look like. On the other hand, we may choose to avoid someone because something about that person's appearance puts us off. These snap judgments represent the first step we take in our quest for intimacy (see Chapter 8). The appearance of a person also contributes to perceptions of dominance and submissiveness, which in turn can determine who takes control in a relationship (see Chapter 10 on status reminders).

Physical appearance plays an important role in the formation of friendships and in the initiation of the courtship process. What is it about someone that moves us to pursue a relationship with him or her? There are many popular opinions on the subject. One says that we are drawn to people who are good looking: There is a beauty bias in our decision making. Another one says that opposites attract: We form relationships with people who are very different from us. A third opinion says that we are attracted to people who are similar to us: Birds of a feather flock together. A fourth says that each of us is attracted to a particular type of person whom we may or may not be able to describe, a sort of "I'll know them when I see them" approach. As we'll see in Chapter 8, most of the available research supports a similarity effect—that we are drawn to people who are similar to us in various ways, including physical appearance (Berscheid & Walster, 1978). Not surprisingly, when we look around at people congregating in couples or groups, they appear quite similar in terms of attractiveness, age, clothing, race, ethnicity, and even stature. For heterosexual couples, however, one intriguing exception may be in the smell of their genes. Studies by Swiss researcher Claus Wedekind suggest that women are sexually attracted to the scent of men—the scent is picked up by smelling unwashed T-shirts—who have immune system genes most dissimilar from their own (this smells the least like them). The odors of men with similar immune system genes reminded them of fathers or brothers; they didn't find these men sexually attractive. The explanation is that women are naturally averse to inbreeding and unconsciously attracted to men whose differing immune systems contribute to the vitality of their offspring (Etcoff, 1999). A related, though different, line of inquiry focuses on the sexual scent of a woman, underarm secretions thought to be human **pheromones** (olfactory signals, common throughout the animal kingdom, that influence sexual behavior). Some researchers have discovered that women whose perfume is laced with a synthetic pheromone report more formal dates, intimate encounters, and sexual activity than women whose perfume is laced with a placebo (Cutler & Genovese, 2002; McCoy & Pitino, 2002).

Our physical appearance can go a long way toward the creation of dominance and submissiveness in relationships. Deference to authority is often a reaction to status displays—nonverbal signals that communicate one's apparent superiority over another. Many of these displays are related to a person's appearance—height, physique, facial features, clothing, and so on—and can intimidate or simply influence other people, whether they are consciously aware of it or not. (See Chapters 7 and 10 for a review of this research.) In one classic experiment, for example, researchers found that pedestrians were more willing to follow a jaywalking stranger when the stranger was well dressed than when poorly dressed (Lefkowitz, Blake, & Mouton, 1955). In another study, a researcher observed greater deference toward well-dressed than toward casually dressed persons. Passersby were more likely to walk around rather than through two individuals talking to each other in a hallway if the two individuals were well dressed (Fortenberry, Maclean, Morris, & O'Connell, 1978).

Delivering Verbal or Symbolic Messages

For the most part, we deliver verbal messages through speech and gesture (see Chapter 6). But, increasingly, people are finding other ways of getting their messages across. We use T-shirts to display a prestige brand, advertise a product or service, convey humor, express a political belief, and much more. One study found that men may be more inclined to wear them than women are (Behling, 1988), and another suggests that individuals with shy personalities are less likely to wear them than are persons with more outgoing personalities. In addition to T-shirts, more people are turning to tattoos, brandings, hats, and the like to deliver verbal or symbolic messages (Spicer, 1981).

Communicating Emotion

Since we communicate emotion primarily through dynamic (i.e., behavioral) rather than static (i.e., appearance) signals, we'll examine this function of nonverbal communication in subsequent chapters, particularly in Chapter 5. Yet it is possible in a limited way to convey emotion through appearance, such as wearing black to signal grief. Moreover, some involuntary changes in our appearance accompany certain emotions. We blush when embarrassed, perspire when afraid, and redden when angry.

PERSONAL EXPERIENCE 3.5

CAN YOU RELATE TO THIS?

Clothing Can Deliver Messages That Offend Others

This guy I know wears some pretty weird clothes, but he has this one shirt that I feel is indecent. It's a devil shirt that's supposed to be like a hockey jersey, with a big 666 where the number should be. The team logo says Devil Worshippers and the name on the back of the jersey is Lucifer. I think the shirt speaks for itself. I refuse to be around him when he wears it (he's a nice guy, actually) because the one time I was with him, I felt ashamed. We were at the mall on a little spending spree and everyone looked at him with disgust. Old people would stare and mutter, along with everybody else. He was just causing a major ruckus the entire time. I think he enjoyed the attention he got.

Wendy

SUMMARY

The human body is an important signaling system, communicating our multiple identities in three ways. First, body endowment includes the natural and enduring physical features we inherit: body shape, facial features, hair color, and so forth. Second, body modification consists of the semipermanent alterations we make, changing our appearance with surgery, diets, and exercise or decorating our bodies with tattoos, piercings, and scarification. The third way, body adornment, includes the everyday changes we make with clothing, cosmetics, jewelry, and the like.

Bodily communication codes can be intrinsic, iconic, or arbitrary. Many of the identity messages we exchange, such as those pertaining to beauty, sexuality, gender, age, race, and individuality, depend on the efficiency of inborn signaling systems: facial proportions, hair distribution, skin color, and so forth. The exchange of other messages benefits from the clarity of iconic signals that mimic natural features: shoulder pads, wigs, makeup, tailored suits, surgical enhancements, and more. But most of the messages we exchange consist of the endless array of stereotypical meanings that we attribute to a person's looks. These messages represent the symbolism of physical appearance, a communication code that reflects the folkways, customs, mores, and even laws of a society. Standards of physical beauty, for example, often reflect little more than contemporary tastes and cultural preferences.

As a signaling system, the primary function of the human body is communicating our multiple identities. Among many other aspects of our appearance, facial features, body shape, and dress combine to send basic messages about how attractive we are, our individuality, gender, age, level of fitness, race, ethnicity, occupation, social class, character, and personality. Bodily signals can also send messages that influence the course of our relationships with others. How a person looks can determine whether or not we view that person as a potential friend or as a romantic partner. A person's appearance also elicits judgments that can lead to deferential behavior on the one hand or disrespectful behavior on the other. Finally, although it is possible for our appearance to express basic emotions such as grief and joy and to deliver verbal messages, we communicate feelings primarily through dynamic facial and vocal expressions and we rely mainly on voice and gesture to deliver verbal messages.

KEY TERMS

Averageness 88
Baby face overgeneralization effect 106
Body adornment 80
Body endowment 80
Body modification 80
Customs 84
Folkways 84
Halo effect 103
Laws 84
Mores 84
Pheromones 112
Proportionality 88
Sexual dimorphism 88
Straightness 88
Symmetry 88
Somatotypes 108
Sumptuary laws 79

istockphoto.com/BraunS

Chapter Outline

4

PERSONAL SPACE, EYE CONTACT, AND TOUCH: AN APPROACH–AVOIDANCE SIGNALING SYSTEM

It happened innocently enough at an HIV-AIDS news conference in New Delhi, India. Movie actor Richard Gere, in a moment of unbridled enthusiasm, embraced and kissed one of Bollywood's most popular actresses, Shilpa Shetty. A photograph of the kiss made the front page of newspapers across the country amid protests condemning the act as disgraceful and obscene. Outraged protesters beat burning effigies of Gere and set fire to photographs of Shetty. India is one of many countries in the world where large numbers of people frown on public displays of affection. In 2007, Pakistan's tourism minister said she feared for her life after clerics at a radical mosque issued an edict accusing her of committing a great sin by hugging her French parachute instructor at a fundraising event.

Incidents such as these should remind us of an important principle: The meaning and significance of nonverbal communication—in this case, a kiss or a hug—can vary dramatically from culture to culture. What may be routine and expected in one culture can be taboo and shocking in another. In this chapter, we'll examine the approach–avoidance signals associated with our use of personal space, eye contact, and touch. We use approach–avoidance signals in two basic ways: (1) to express our interest or disinterest in others and (2) to communicate our respect or disrespect for others. Sometimes only a fine line separates the two. For instance, we can let others know we are interested in them by getting close to them, looking at them, or touching them (i.e., approach signals). Yet in certain contexts, the same behaviors

Learning Objectives

After reading this chapter, you will be able to do the following:

1. Understand how personal space, eye contact, and touch operate as intrinsic, iconic, and arbitrary communication codes.
2. Consider the primary function of personal space, eye contact, and touch as an approach–avoidance signaling system that establishes intimacy and control in relationships with others.
3. Recognize an important secondary function of personal space, eye contact, and touch as a form of communication that signals one's identity such as culture, gender, and personality.
4. Understand how the use of personal space, eye contact, and touch can function as part of a delivery system that communicates verbal messages.
5. Consider how the use of personal space, eye contact, and touch are capable of expressing emotions.

can be disrespectful. It depends on whether the behavior violates a particular rule (e.g., getting too close, **staring**, inappropriate touching). In the next section, we'll introduce the communication codes that we use to convey these messages. In the following section, we'll consider the communication functions of these codes.

COMMUNICATION CODES

As a communication system, approach–avoidance signals are complex and interrelated. Unlike the relatively static cues of the body that we discussed in Chapter 3, these behaviors are extremely dynamic. Our spatial and gaze behaviors in particular—and touch, to a lesser degree—frequently shift from moment to moment, depending on who we're with, what we're talking about, where we are, how we feel, and so on. Understanding these signals is thus a complex matter, requiring some awareness of the many factors accounting for the sudden shifts that occur. In addition, the signals are interrelated. Generally, what affects one may well affect the others in a similar way.

As originally conceived by social psychologist Albert Mehrabian, the term **immediacy** refers to the degree of mutual sensory stimulation between people, which is influenced directly by the combinations of proximity, gazing, and touching that take place. For example, a shy person tends to stand farther away from, use less **eye contact** with, and touch others less often than does a person who is not shy. Thus, shyness produces a collection of behaviors characterized as low in immediacy. In contrast, numerous studies have demonstrated that individuals from certain cultures prefer closer distances, more eye contact, and more touch than do individuals from other cultures—a composite of high immediacy signals. Gender, too, seems to have this kind of impact, affecting our use of space, gaze, and touch in similar ways.

In addition, each of these behaviors represents a way of making contact with the outside world. As noted anthropologist Ashley Montagu (1986) observes, "Seeing is a form of touching at a distance, but touching provides the verification and confirmation of reality. That is the reason why eye contact is the perfect example of touching at a distance" (p. 124). In this section, we'll address the nature of this approach–avoidance signaling system, first by introducing fundamental concepts and then by showing how we use intrinsic, iconic, and arbitrary communication codes.

One way we signal approach–avoidance is through the use of space. The general subject of spatial behavior is often called **proxemics**, a term coined by the pioneer anthropologist Edward T. Hall (1959, 1966). In our everyday encounters, we use the space around us in various ways. These include changes in **interpersonal distance**, **body orientation**, **positioning**, and **territorial behavior** (Argyle, 1988).

Changes in *interpersonal distance* are adjustments in the physical distances maintained between people. The concept of *body orientation* refers to the angle at which individuals face one another. A direct orientation places two people across from each other, with the front of their torsos facing directly. Standing side by side is an indirect body orientation. *Positioning* is where one is located with respect to others in a given area. At a social gathering, for example, a person may be more centrally located than others are. In a classroom, some people like sitting up front while others prefer the back of the room.

The final concept is *territorial behavior*. This refers to the myriad ways we signal ownership and defense of an area. Some behaviors simply delineate the territory. Sitting at a table and spreading out your possessions is one way of doing this. Sometimes the simple act of taking up space, such as sprawling out in a chair, walking around while conversing with someone, or using expansive gestures sends the same message. Other behaviors are intended to prevent intrusions during the "owner's" absence. The use of **territorial markers** is one way of doing this. A marker announces ownership of an area. Leaving your books on a table or putting your coat on a chair lets others know that the area is taken. Still other behaviors are meant to ward off intrusions (i.e., threat displays) or to invite them (i.e., submissive displays) while they are taking place. Usually thought of as the invisible and portable bubble of space we carry around with us, we may be more territorial about our **personal space** than we are about any other single area. The apparent size of these body buffer zones may vary considerably from person to person. Getting too close to someone means that you have penetrated this personal zone, an act of spatial invasion.

PERSONAL EXPERIENCE 4.1

CAN YOU RELATE TO THIS?

Territorial Markers Prevent Unwanted Intrusions

I used to take a trolley and bus to and from high school every day. I didn't want anyone to sit in the seats next to me in the morning because I was so tired and bitter about going to school. So I would place my jacket on one side of me and my backpack on the other side. If I could, I would sit at a window seat so I'd only have to worry about blocking one side. Doing this worked most of the time, unless the bus or trolley was crowded, in which case, people would ask me to move my belongings so they could sit down.

Gloria

Eye contact is another way we signal approach or avoidance. The subject of eye contact includes the study of **nonreciprocal gaze**, mutual gaze (eye contact), **gaze aversion**, staring, and **pupil dilation**.

Nonreciprocal gaze is a one-sided expression of interest. Someone catches our attention for some reason (e.g., her hair is an unusual shade of green) and we look. But she doesn't look at us; the gaze is not returned. Nonreciprocal gaze can sometimes be frustrating. Have you ever tried unsuccessfully to catch the attention of your server in a restaurant by repeatedly trying to make eye contact? When two people look at each other, they are engaged in eye contact or mutual gaze. If the eyes really are the "windows to the soul," then making eye contact with another person must be the single most important act of interpersonal communication. Another frequently used term is *gaze aversion*. In general, this occurs when one person deliberately looks away from another person. Everyday situations often prompt instances of gaze aversion. A stranger catches you looking at him. Looking away assures the stranger that you respect his right to privacy; it's the polite thing to do. In contrast, if you don't look away when the stranger catches you looking, you would be staring at him, an act of spatial invasion or threat display, which often triggers a fight-or-flight response in the target—he might leave the area or he might confront you to find out why you are staring at him. The topic of gazing behavior sometimes includes other forms of eye behavior, such as *pupil dilation*. Laboratory experiments demonstrating that the pupils in our eyes enlarge when we gaze at something we consider very pleasant and that even our attraction to a person can be influenced by the size of that person's pupils attest to the remarkable subtlety that exists in approach–avoidance signaling systems (Hess, 1975).

PERSONAL EXPERIENCE 4.2

CAN YOU RELATE TO THIS?

Staring Can Produce a Fight-or-Flight Reaction

On Sunday, my friend Brian and I were riding in his car. We were behind a nicely restored Volkswagen Bug (which I hate) and Brian was admiring it. Then the guy driving the Bug started staring at us. I didn't care, but Brian was getting really pissed off. He got to the point where he was going to get out of the car at the next stop and "find out what the guy's problem is." I had to convince him that that was stupid, and then the guy ended up turning anyway. He was willing to put himself in physical danger just because someone was looking at him!

Greg

Touch is arguably the most profound of the approach–avoidance signals. Perhaps no other single action says as much about where a relationship is heading than does the simple act of reaching out to someone or pulling away from them. Early attempts to develop a vocabulary for the language of touch—sometimes called **haptics**—tended to focus on common types of touch such as patting, squeezing, stroking, brushing, pinching, shaking, and the like (Argyle, 1975; Nguyen, Heslin, & Nguyen, 1975) or on the intimacy of a touch, ranging from professional touching to sexual touching (Heslin & Alper, 1983).

As with eye contact, we can distinguish between touching that is nonreciprocal and touching that is mutual. **Nonreciprocal touch** is initiated by one person but not returned by the person who is touched. This concept is important because of what one-sided touching can tell us about a relationship (e.g., like or dislike, differences in status). It is also important because many social touches are not meant to be returned. The touch may complement what someone says (e.g., "Thanks"), it may take the place of words (e.g., "Don't worry, it'll be okay"), or it may be initiated to gain compliance with a request (e.g., "Excuse me, could you help me carry this?"). But **mutual touch** is also revealing. One special category of mutual touches that focuses on the symbolism of physical contact is known as **tie signs** (Morris, 1977). A tie sign is a public display of togetherness between two persons. Ranging from casual to very intimate, these social touches include handshakes, arm links, embraces, handholds, kisses, and more. They advertise to onlookers that some sort of bond exists between the touchers. Another important characteristic of most tie signs is that the touch usually lasts longer than other kinds of social touching.

Of all the attempts to classify touch signals, communication researchers Stanley Jones and Elaine Yarbrough (1985) have come the closest to giving us a comprehensive vocabulary for understanding the meanings of touch. Listed below are the five most meaningful categories:

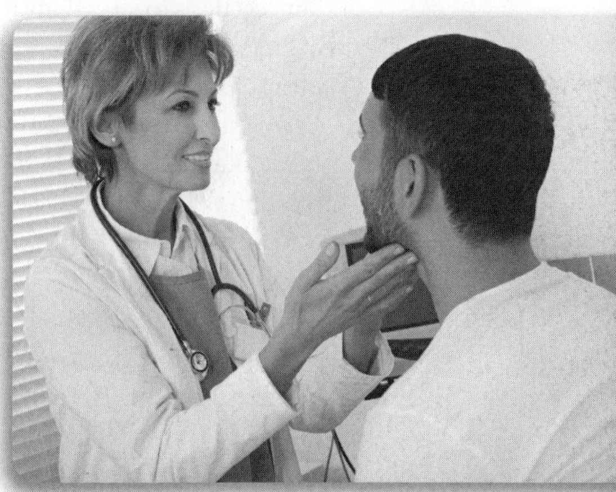

▸ A physician examines her patient. Our relationship with another person determines both the meaning and the appropriateness of interpersonal touching.

istockphoto.com/Lajos Repasi

1. ***Positive affect touches***—these touches signal some degree of liking toward another person and include expressions of appreciation, support, affection, sexual interest, and so forth.
2. ***Playful touches***—playful touches signal a nonserious, joking, or teasing attitude toward another person either in the form of mock aggression or quasi-affection and include tickling, punching, grabbing, pinching, shoving, and so on.

3. ***Control touches***—these touches are intended to influence another person in some way, such as getting someone's attention or compliance.
4. ***Ritualistic touches***—these touches are an integral part of certain rituals, such as greetings and departures.
5. ***Task-oriented touches***—these touches occur while trying to accomplish a particular task (e.g., inspecting someone's clothing, handing someone a telephone, helping someone out of a car, etc.).

Intrinsic Codes

Much of our approach–avoidance signaling seems to be innate, emanating from the natural tension that exists between the need for affiliation and comfort on the one hand (approach) and the need for privacy and space on the other (avoidance). In Chapter 2, research demonstrated how eye contact, distance, and touch—as well as smiling and baby-faced features—reinforce the bonding process that occurs naturally between infant and parent. Thus, the development and maintenance of intimacy is closely tied to this basic form of communication. In addition, the need to claim and defend one's territory, which appears to be universal as well, requires a signaling system that minimizes the likelihood of unnecessary or mutually destructive conflict. Fundamental issues of control are resolved, at least temporarily, when one individual willingly submits to the wishes of another.

Claims regarding the innate character of approach–avoidance signaling receive support from studies on human territorial behavior, which document similarities in our reactions to spatial invasions. The underlying premise is that we experience some degree of stress, a protective response, under such circumstances. The invasion sets off a sort of built-in alarm system known as the **general adaptation syndrome** (Selye, 1956). In their summary of the research on this phenomenon, communication scholars Judee Burgoon, David Buller, and W. Gill Woodall (1996) identify a number of typical reactions: (1) physiological responses, such as increased heart rate, blood pressure, skin conductance, and electroencephalogram (EEG) activity; (2) behavioral symptoms of anxiety, such as gaze aversion, nervous gestures, self-touching, body blocking, indirect body orientation, and body lean; (3) taking flight, often as a sign of desperation, in situations where an intrusion continues unabated; (4) task performance decline from a decreased ability to think clearly or to concentrate; and (5) the surfacing of an array of negative feelings, such as feeling crowded, hostile, angry, irritable, unsocial, and so on.

Paradoxically, our need for space is rivaled by no less a need for physical contact. Although not taken seriously for most of this century, the need for touch is now firmly established. In his remarkable book, *Touching: The Human Significance of the Skin*, Ashley Montagu (1986) traces the scientific work that has transformed our thinking about the biological significance of touch. Decades of scientific study confirm the devastating consequences of touch deprivation and the existence of a "skin hunger" for touch. Studies of nonhuman primates show that touch-deprived chimpanzees suffer an array of physiological, psychological, and emotional problems. Compared to their comforted counterparts, they experience brain damage, immune system deterioration, depression, aggressiveness, and poor social functioning. Studies of human infants provide compelling evidence of the benefits of gentle touching, which include the immediate effects of weight gain and diminished stress and the long-term effects of emotional well-being and improved social relations.

RESEARCH 4.1

FIND OUT MORE

Is Hugging Good for Your Health?

In a recent study at Carnegie Mellon University, researchers interviewed 404 healthy adults over 14 consecutive evenings to find out how much social support they thought they received from others, which included how many hugs they received. Then the participants were exposed to a common cold virus and were monitored in quarantine to assess infection and signs of illness. The researchers discovered that both perceived social support and hugs reduced the risk of illness.

To find out more about this study and answer the following questions, see the full text (cited below).

1. Do the authors address the ethical implications of what they did in their study?
2. What theory or theories do the authors discuss to justify doing this study in the first place?
3. What kind of research is this study? (See Appendix.)
4. What are the strengths and limitations of this study?

Source: Cohen, S., Janicki-Deverts, D., Turner, R. B., & Doyle, W. J. (2015). Does hugging provide stress-buffering social support? A study of susceptibility to upper respiratory infection and illness. *Psychological Science, 26,* 135–147.

As we learned in the previous chapter, some aspects of our physical appearance automatically convey information about our identity (e.g., gender, attractiveness, and age). These signals comprise an innate signaling system because sending and receiving these messages is highly adaptive for humans. New research suggests that gaze behavior also contributes to this process of identification. That is, we are better equipped to identify people who look at us than we are people who don't look at us. As one social scientist has observed,

> [I]t makes . . . sense that we should be hypersensitive to when another organism is watching us, since this is about the best early warning system that another organism may be about to attack us, or may be interested in us for some other reason. (Baron-Cohen, 1995, p. 98)

Studies confirm this natural hypersensitivity to mutual gaze. In one set of experiments, for instance, participants made much quicker judgments about the gender and the masculine or feminine stereotypes associated with the gender of faces in photographs, when the faces displayed a direct gaze than when they displayed an averted gaze (looking to the right) or closed eyes (Macrae, Hood, Milne, Rowe, & Mason, 2002). Another team of researchers discovered that direct eye contact with an attractive stranger was more likely to stimulate a response in the pleasure receptors of the brain (the ventral striatum) when the attractive stranger was making eye contact rather than looking away (Kampe, Frith, Dolan, & Firth, 2001); and researchers recently found that participants in an experiment were more likely to blush (increased blood flow to the forehead area) while making eye contact with a person asking potentially embarrassing and threatening questions than while not making eye contact with the person (Drummond & Bailey, 2013).

Iconic Codes

Approach–avoidance signaling systems are often iconic; that is, the signal mimics the real thing. This is done in four ways. First, the behavior may be deceptive: The actor's behavior is carefully orchestrated to appear spontaneous and truthful, but the objective is to get away with the performance. A person may feign attention to someone who is speaking, pretend to care for someone by moving close and touching, or act unfazed by not backing down when someone approaches in an intimidating fashion. Since the particular behavior is a counterfeit version of the real thing, an astute observer may be able to spot the deception: an awkward movement, forced eye contact, revealing facial expression, and so forth. Second, an action may be a put on. Unlike deception, there is nothing disingenuous about a put on—no attempt to hide the truth. Examples of this include the playful aggression that only looks somewhat like a real fight, an exaggerated stare that resembles real anger, a condescending pat on the head that mimics a parent–child encounter, and so forth. Third, iconic gestures can take the place of the actions they resemble. The goodbye kiss of a baby is one example. Finally, intention movements represent abridged versions of some anticipated action. Some people use movements, called "touch invitations" (Jones, 1994), to signal their desire to touch or be touched. One example would be holding out your arms in anticipation of embracing. Many departure signals are intention movements, expressing in a subtle way our desire to leave (e.g., looking at the door, turning away, glancing at other people, etc.). While someone is talking to us, we could simply say, "Gotta go," or we could just walk away. Believing it is more polite not to interrupt, however, we use nonverbal signals to express our intentions without causing much embarrassment (when the signals work, that is).

Arbitrary Codes

In many ways, our use and interpretation of spatial behavior, gaze, and touch depends on where we are, who we are with, what we are doing, and when we are doing it. This is because we learn to follow rules. We learn what is and is not appropriate or meaningful in a particular context. But not everyone learns the same set of rules, and sometimes the rules change. Consider the case of touch. Despite what may be a universal need to be touched, a touch can often send the wrong message. Laws against sexual harassment and more frequent reporting of child-abuse cases, for example, have combined in recent years to change dramatically the climate in which social touching occurs. In the modern workplace, touches that in the past may have been ignored are now often seen as crude and ill-mannered. Examples of this new intolerance are common and widespread. In El Paso County, Colorado, an undersheriff was fired for violating departmental policy on sexual harassment by hugging several lower-level employees ("Undersheriff Fired for Hugging," 1999). In New Zealand, issuing a statement that his intentions were irrelevant, the government found a naval instructor guilty of sexual harassment and fired him for hugging a former student, touching her hair, calling her "darling," and telling her she was beautiful ("Navy Issues Warning on the Dangers of Hugging," 2002). In Singapore, school principals, counselors, and social workers have been warned to avoid physical contact with children unless it is absolutely necessary. They have been told that it's okay to shake hands or pat a child on the back, but hugs are not allowed ("No Hugging or Kissing—They're Counsellors," 2002). Another example of changing norms concerns sexual touching, which at one time was taboo outside marriage. Perhaps the most dramatic illustration of our shifting sensibilities regarding the use of touch involves the way parents touch their children. Not long ago, parents were cautioned against the use of touch with their children; such indulgences, pediatricians warned, would spoil the child and create a condition of excessive dependency. Today, we generally shun such advice. But consider the words of then-professor of psychology at Johns Hopkins University, John Watson, who wrote in his 1928 textbook, *Psychological Care of Infant and Child*:

> There is a sensible way of treating children. . . . Never hug and kiss them, never let them sit in your lap. If you must, kiss them once on the forehead when they say good night. Shake hands with them in the morning. Give them a pat on the head if they have made an

▸ The uses, interpretations, and appropriateness of hugging, kissing, and other forms of touch vary considerably from culture to culture. Is some form of touching an important part of your family's day-to-day interactions?

istockphoto.com/meshaphoto

extraordinary good job of a difficult task. Try it out. In a week's time, you will find how easy it is to be perfectly objective with your child and at the same time kindly. You will be utterly ashamed of the mawkish, sentimental way you have been handling it. (quoted in Montagu, 1986, p. 151)

In addition, many of the cultural norms that govern approach–avoidance signals operate outside our level of awareness—that is, until someone's behavior surprises us. Anthropologist Edward Hall's (1959, 1966) research on cultural differences in the use of space raised our consciousness about the existence of these norms. Among his findings was the observation that some cultures rely on tactile (touch) and olfactory (smell) modes of communication more than other cultures do. Members of these **contact cultures** (e.g., Arab, Latin American, and Southern European nations) use more touch and less personal space than do members of so-called **noncontact cultures**, who prefer the visual mode of communication (e.g., North American, Asian, and Northern European nations). These differences underscore the arbitrary nature of an approach–avoidance signaling system that relies as much on nurture as it does on nature. We review this research below in the section on culture.

PERSONAL EXPERIENCE 4.3

CAN YOU RELATE TO THIS?

Contact Cultures Differ from Noncontact Cultures

My mom's side of the family is Italian. They live in California, so we rarely see them. When we do, there is so much physical contact. They are constantly hugging, kissing, touching, and using their hands when they speak. My dad's family is English and Irish. They live in Pennsylvania, and I see them much more. At family functions, nobody hugs or kisses each other. It is almost awkward if one attempts to have physical contact.

Karrie

COMMUNICATION FUNCTIONS

All of us use personal space, gaze, and touch in our everyday interactions because these signals help us carry out our most important communication goals. We begin the next section by considering the vital role played by approach–avoidance signals in charting the course of our relationships with others. Then we examine the secondary functions. We look at the ways we differ, the identification function. Extensive research shows that gender, culture, and personality greatly influence the use of approach–avoidance signals. Finally, we'll address the role of personal space, gaze, and touch in communicating emotions and in delivering verbal messages.

Establishing Relationships: The Primary Function

Establishing relationships is the primary function of approach–avoidance signals. While all of our nonverbal signals influence our relationships with others, none does so as fundamentally as the way we use space, gaze, and touch. We manage our personal space, direct our gaze, and touch other people in ways that signal varying degrees of interest, involvement, and attraction. The signals combine to convey messages that encourage or discourage the growth of intimacy in our relationships with others. But these behaviors also send messages designed to prevent or instigate conflict or merely to remind us of differences in status. Depending on the situation, for example, the same actions that signal dislike or disinterest—such as gaze aversion, backing away, or reluctance to touch—can also be interpreted as a message of submissiveness, appeasement, or deference to authority.

INTIMACY Can you tell if someone likes you? Since most of us don't routinely express in words our attitudes toward others, we must rely on nonverbal communication. For the past five decades accumulating research shows how we use nonverbal signals to express positive or negative attitudes and how these signals both reflect and regulate the degree of intimacy that exists in a relationship (see Chapter 8).

During the early stages of a relationship, politeness norms exert pressure on us to behave in a friendly but reserved manner—even when we hold strong positive or negative feelings. On the surface, this means being attentive, involved, and responsive. Most important, it means not being rude. We may use modest amounts of eye contact, proximity, and body orientation to get the message across. But momentary deviations from these politeness signals may reveal more genuine attitudes just below the surface. And deviations from the norm that occur only during interactions with certain people help us figure out where an individual really stands.

▸ We use varying degrees of eye contact, touch, and interpersonal distance to connect with others and to build intimacy in our relationships with them.

istockphoto.com/Christopher Badzioch

In the 1960s, social scientists became interested in studying the extent to which we communicate our interpersonal attitudes nonverbally. Social psychologist Albert Mehrabian was one of the first to conduct laboratory experiments of people sending and interpreting nonverbal messages. Often in role-playing situations, a person would be instructed to act friendly or unfriendly toward another individual. The person's nonverbal signals would be carefully observed and quantified. One overall conclusion that emerged from these early experiments was that certain specific nonverbal signals—immediacy behaviors—consistently communicate a positive attitude. These immediacy behaviors include eye contact, physical proximity, touching, a forward lean rather than a reclining position, and a direct body orientation (Mehrabian, 1972). In-depth reviews of numerous studies confirm the basic proposition that we tend to approach what we like and avoid what we dislike (Andersen, 1999; Argyle, 1988; Burgoon et al., 1996).

While it's easy to see how our attitudes shape the behaviors we use, research on self-perception theory suggests that our simple use of these behaviors may help shape our attitudes as well. In one experiment, for example, subjects were told to listen to a speaker for five minutes. For half the subjects, their chair was placed 12 feet away from the speaker; the other half sat in a chair four feet from the speaker. All subjects were instructed to adopt a single set of listening behaviors: those 12 feet away were told they might lean back, fold their arms across their chest, and not look at the speaker (the low-immediacy condition); for those four feet away, the experimenter suggested leaning forward, maintaining eye contact, and facing the speaker (high-immediacy condition). The researchers found that the subjects assigned to the high-immediacy condition liked the speaker more than did the subjects who were assigned to the low-immediacy condition, thus supporting the idea that the way we act can influence the way we feel (Slane & Leak, 1978).

Research also shows that we readily make inferences about a person's attitudes based solely on these approach–avoidance signals. Depending on the context in which they occur (what's appropriate in one context may not be in another), gazing, touching, and proximity all lead to judgments associated with positive attitudes (Burgoon, 1991; Burgoon, Buller, Hale, & deTurck, 1984; Mehrabian, 1968, 1969; Patterson, 1977;

Wellens & Goldberg, 1978). Not surprisingly, we may believe someone likes us if that person faces us directly, stands or sits close to us, makes eye contact with us, and touches us. Sometimes a single nonverbal signal is enough to alter our judgment one way or the other. And these judgments can influence dramatically the path we choose to follow in a particular relationship (see Chapter 8).

Early attempts to classify approach–avoidance signals recognized the importance of relational context: They took into account the way different levels of intimacy affect the signals we use. Edward Hall's (1959, 1966) ideas on the **zones of interpersonal distance** is one example. These zones, which represent the distances people maintain between each other in social situations, correspond to distinct changes in the kinds of face-to-face interpersonal activities people engage in, the changes in closeness that occur in their relationships, and the way they feel toward each other at a given point in time. Working with linguistics researcher George Trager, Hall became interested in the voice modulations that seemed to coincide with different distances within whispering and shouting ranges. His investigations of middle-class Americans helped him to settle on four distinct zones—each with a near and a far range—that seem to characterize our use of space (although he cautions repeatedly against generalizing to other cultures and subcultures):

- ***Intimate distance*** (contact to 18 inches): This distance is reserved for those with whom we are very intimate. At close ranges, we use this zone for some kind of physical involvement with another that relies very little on the use of speech (e.g., comforting, love making, wrestling, protecting, etc.). Our visual image of another person at this distance is distorted; facial features look overlarge. Persons from contact cultures may enter this area, which would constitute an invasion of space for many Americans. When crowded together, we often use tactics designed to minimize anxiety levels, such as not moving, looking away, tensing up, or regarding another individual as a nonperson. We use and expect a soft speaking voice, even at the far range of this zone.
- ***Personal distance*** (18 inches to four feet): We use the expression "keeping someone at arm's length" to represent this distance, which minimizes the likelihood of physical contact. In a sense, for many Americans, this zone represents interactions that are warm and involving but not hot and arousing. Unlike the intimate zone, our visual perception of others—particularly at the far range of this zone—is relatively free of distortion, our voice level is moderate, and our ability to pick up another person's scent is greatly diminished.
- ***Social distance*** (four to 12 feet): At the closer ranges, Americans speak in a normal tone of voice, which is probably louder than that of the English upper class or the Japanese and softer than that of the Arab or Spaniard (Hall, 1966). We use this

distance for relatively impersonal, businesslike transactions. Eye contact plays a vital role in keeping the lines of communication open, and we spend more time looking at each other at far than at close ranges.

- ***Public distance*** (12 to 25 feet and beyond): Because this distance is outside our social sphere, we are less likely to become involved in conversations with others who inhabit this zone. If we do, we tend to engage in the more formal style of speaking—loud voice, large gestures, sharp enunciation, and slow cadence—associated with public presentations.

RESEARCH 4.2

FIND OUT MORE

Does Interpersonal Distance Reflect Our Need for Privacy?

Machines in public places offer a convenient way of purchasing tickets, making deposits, withdrawing cash from personal accounts, and so forth. Because these machines vary in the amount and kind of information requested from users, the authors of this study predicted that there would be a correlation between a machine's need for personal information (e.g., PIN numbers) and the distance between the user of a machine and the next person waiting, which is what was observed by the researchers at numerous public places. In addition, interviews revealed that a user's desired interpersonal distance tended to be greater than the actual distance between users observed by the researchers.

To find out more about this study and to answer the following questions, see the full text (cited below).

1. What kind of study is this? (See Appendix.)
2. Where was this study conducted and who were the participants in the study?
3. How did the researchers measure interpersonal distance?
4. What were some of the main limitations of the study?

Source: Li, S., & Li, L. (2007). How far is enough? A measure of information privacy in terms of interpersonal distance. *Environment and Behavior*, 39, 317–331.

In addition to our use of space, we use contact codes in ways that signal varying degrees of intimacy. Social psychologist Richard Heslin (1974) devised a taxonomy of touches based on the context in which touching takes place. The categories range from distant and impersonal to intimate and highly personal:

- ***Functional/professional:*** This kind of touching takes place in the context of a professional relationship, in which physical contact of some sort is part of the task. Examples include a doctor touching a patient, a ski instructor touching a student, a hair stylist touching a customer, and so forth.
- ***Social/polite:*** The common, ritualistic touches prescribed by cultural norms suggesting how, when, where, and whom one should touch. The various forms of touch that occur during greetings and departures are good examples.
- ***Friendship/warmth:*** We often touch others to express warm feelings and positive regard. These are the touches that are most likely to be misinterpreted as more intimate than intended and that occur more regularly in some cultures than in others. In addition, the incidence of these touches is affected by differences in gender, personality, and age (see identification section in this chapter).
- ***Love/intimacy:*** The most personalized kind of physical contact, these touches convey strong feelings of affection or represent close emotional ties. Certain types of touch are not appropriate and will arouse considerable discomfort if initiated by nonintimates. Various hand-to-head and hand-to-body touches fall in this category.
- ***Sexual arousal:*** This kind of touching, which usually targets the erogenous zones, is used primarily for sexual stimulation, even though the parties involved may perceive love/intimacy connotations.

Because our use of space, eye contact, and touch automatically conveys some degree of liking and intimacy, there is always the risk, in any encounter, that the signals may not be appropriate. Just as we wouldn't expect two lovers to shake hands when greeting, we would be surprised to see two strangers holding hands minutes after meeting. In less extreme cases, we expect other people to behave only in ways that don't make us feel uncomfortable. Yet when they do not, rarely do we put our feelings into words. And many of our visible reactions often go unnoticed (e.g., changes in eye blinking, body lean, positioning, body orientation, etc.). How people respond to these unexpected moves is a question that has intrigued and bewildered social scientists for more than three decades.

Systematic study of this phenomenon began in 1965 with the **equilibrium theory**—also called *affiliative conflict theory*—proposed by social psychologists Michael Argyle and Janet Dean. According to their theory, in our face-to-face interactions with others, we strive for a comfortable balance in approach–avoidance behaviors—an equilibrium point—which for us involves comfortable levels of eye contact, distance, smiling, and topic intimacy. If someone's behavior is too intimate and makes us feel uncomfortable, such as standing too close, we will *compensate* by decreasing the level of intimacy in some way (e.g., backing up, reducing eye contact, changing the topic, etc.). This compensatory reaction is an attempt to restore equilibrium, to return the interaction to a comfortable level of intimacy.

In their first experiment, Argyle and Dean (1965) found support for their model when comparing the reactions of subjects placed in chairs at different distances from a continuously gazing conversational partner. Those closest (two feet) exhibited more avoidance behaviors—backward lean and reduced eye contact—than those placed at greater distances of six feet and 10 feet. Experiments in support of equilibrium theory usually find that individuals, in response to the close approach of another, compensate with gaze aversion, indirect body orientation, and increased distance (Patterson, 1983). Less research shows that a compensatory pattern may occur in response to decreases in intimacy, such as one person increasing eye contact or moving closer if the other person moves farther away (Cappella, 1983).

EXERCISE 4.1

Too Close for Comfort

Try It

What happens when you get too close to someone? Many studies reveal that our reactions are somewhat predictable. Most of the time, the victim of a spatial invasion will become uncomfortable and try to compensate in some way by backing up, turning to the side, reducing eye contact, or changing the topic of conversation (if it was personal). But, of course, this doesn't always happen, for one reason or another. Try this experiment on your own to see what happens:

1. Select a target, someone you know well enough not to offend.
2. Start a casual conversation with this person while the two of you are both standing.
3. Gradually inch closer to this person, head on. Try to get as close as you can—within 16 inches or so.
4. Note as many reactions as you can. Specifically, do you see any of the following?

____ Backing up, leaning away
____ Turning to the side
____ Looking away
____ Changing the topic
____ Defensive arm crossing
____ Rapid eye blinking
____ Fidgeting, swaying
____ Self-touching

For discussion, be prepared to report what you observed. If none of the above occurred, why do you suppose this person did not try to compensate in this particular situation?

The basic principle of **compensation** is well supported and easy to observe firsthand. Just watch how people behave in a crowded elevator (e.g., body orientation, eye contact, etc.) or notice what happens when you move closer and closer to someone talking to you. But compensation doesn't always occur. And in some situations, it is very unlikely. Often, there is no appreciable reaction. On many occasions, **reciprocity** takes place. Reciprocity—responding in kind to another's behavior—is common when we're interacting with people we like. For example, imagine being on a third date with someone you want to get to know better. How would you respond if that person suddenly moved closer?

Social psychologist Miles Patterson (1976) developed an **arousal-labeling model** to account for reactions other than compensation. Briefly, his model suggests how we may become aroused by another person's immediacy behavior: If the arousal is perceived positively (e.g., liking, love, relief), we will reciprocate; if our arousal is labeled negatively (e.g., dislike, embarrassment, anxiety), we will compensate. Despite its commonsense appeal, the model doesn't explain our behavior adequately in many situations. For example, in a superior–subordinate encounter, we might reciprocate the immediacy behaviors of the boss to make a good impression or to avoid making a bad one, even if the boss's behavior made us feel uncomfortable (i.e., negative arousal).

Communication scholar Judee Burgoon (1978) proposed a model designed to consider more fully our relationship with the person whose behavior violates our expectations. Her **expectancy violations model** suggests that our reaction to someone's unexpected move, such as standing too close or too far, will arouse us and direct our attention to that person's reward value (e.g., status, attractiveness, etc.). We will respond favorably to a rewarding violator (i.e., reciprocate) and unfavorably to a violator with little reward value (compensate). Thus, we might reciprocate the behavior of the boss solely because of his or her reward value to us. But this model also has trouble predicting reactions in certain situations. For instance, how would you react if someone you liked a lot—a person with high reward value—suddenly became very distant? The model predicts that you would reciprocate, which means you would also become more distant. Yet a compensatory response, such as moving closer, isn't hard to imagine (Burgoon et al., 1996). Unlike other models, however, since the expectancy violations model focuses on whether a reaction is favorable and not merely on whether a reaction is compensatory or reciprocal, it has implications for successful communication (e.g., building credibility, gaining compliance) that surpass other approach–avoidance theories (see Chapter 7).

Another theoretical development took place when communication researchers Joseph Cappella and John Greene (1982) proposed an alternative explanation, one designed to explain reactions that occur too quickly to be explained adequately by earlier models. The **discrepancy arousal model** argues that our reactions depend more on how aroused we become when a person's actions violate our expectations than on how we label the arousal or on what we think about the individual who aroused us. Moderate arousal produces a positive effect and results in reciprocity; high arousal leads to a negative effect and compensation. Building on this link between how aroused one becomes and the nature of one's reaction, communication theorist Peter Andersen (1989) proposed a **cognitive valence theory** of nonverbal immediacy behavior (see Chapter 8). Like the Cappella and Greene model, it predicts that compensation is likely under conditions of high arousal. But it also specifies an array of factors called *cognitive schemata* that determine whether reciprocity or compensation occurs under conditions of moderate arousal (low arousal produces no change in behavior). If any of these factors (e.g., culture, predisposition, situation, etc.) is unfavorable (i.e., negatively valenced), compensation is expected. In a recent study pitting cognitive valence theory against both the expectancy violations and discrepancy arousal models, Andersen and colleagues (1998) found that while each of the models could account somewhat for the way people reacted to nonverbal immediacy behaviors, none of the models could predict the many mixed signals that occurred (both reciprocal and compensatory reactions).

These early models provided a much needed set of explanations for the occurrence of noncompensatory behaviors, which was lacking in the equilibrium model. But their confinement to the study of nonverbal behaviors that signal positive–negative feelings (intimacy) left unexplained the many contexts in which we use approach–avoidance behaviors to signal dominance and submission (control). For instance, imagine Jana and Greg in a heated argument. Jana stares at Greg; Greg gets in Jana's face. According to the arousal-labeling model, compensation should occur. In response to her stare, Greg should have looked away, backed up, or behaved in like fashion. The other models are also ill-equipped to make satisfactory predictions. The problem is that, in a competitive context such as an interpersonal conflict, staring is an act of intimidation or defiance rather than one of intimacy. And any avoidance behavior on Greg's part could be interpreted as acquiescence—a sign of weakness rather than a rejection of intimacy.

The fact that individuals use approach–avoidance behaviors to attain goals other than intimacy led, in part, to Patterson's (1983) **sequential-functional model** of nonverbal exchange, an ambitious elaboration of how our reactions to the nonverbal involvement behaviors of another person may be affected by an array of factors, such as our motivations (functions) for using a particular behavior, our relationship with the other person, our personality and behavioral tendencies, and more. Like Patterson's earlier model (1976), it includes a process of arousal assessment as a predictor of how one will respond. But it also allows for the possibility that some degree of cognition may precede and even cause the arousal that one experiences (e.g., "She's trying to embarrass me"). In addition, the model attempts to explain nonverbal behaviors (i.e., involvement behaviors) not limited to the simple approach–avoidance signals we have been discussing in this chapter. More recent theoretical advancements include

Patterson's (1995) parallel-processing model and Burgoon, Stern, and Dillman's (1995) **interaction adaptation theory**.

As we have seen so far, we use space, eye contact, and touch to communicate positive and negative attitudes toward others. These signals can reflect and regulate (albeit superficially) the intimacy in a relationship. In one interesting application of this idea, researchers found that nonverbal intimacy regulation even occurs when people interact with others via avatars in online environments. As in face-to-face encounters, people typically respond to decreased distances by compensating with reduced gaze (Yee et al., 2007). But we should keep in mind what communication scholar Mark Knapp (1983) has pointed out: These stereotypical immediacy behaviors—close distances, eye contact, touch, body lean, and so forth—are more evident during the early stages of intimacy than they are during later stages (see Chapter 8). When people become comfortable with each other, they may become more selective in their use of nonverbal immediacy signals, using them during a personal crisis, after a fight, on special occasions, at particular social gatherings, and the like. They may also adopt other more idiosyncratic ways of showing their affection—a unique gesture or a special touch, for instance—and they may feel less obliged overall to display their affections in public (e.g., tie signs).

CONTROL Whether it's in a brief encounter or in a long-term relationship, we frequently use approach–avoidance signals, not for the sake of building or discouraging intimacy, but for the purpose of showing who's in charge. In this section, we'll examine the three ways this is done: **territorial invasions**, **threat displays**, and **status reminders**.

The well-known sociologist Erving Goffman (1971) described the penetrating gaze as an act of territorial invasion. Our use of space and touch can also represent such acts, particularly when uninvited and unwelcome (e.g., sexual harassment). Territorial behavior is an ordinary part of our everyday lives. On the freeway, someone cuts us off. At the movies, someone takes our seat. Waiting in line, someone breathes down our neck. In extreme cases, such actions can provoke a fight-or-flight response (e.g., road rage). For example, many years ago in Wildwood, New Jersey, a man was beaten to death in a fight that erupted outside a bar after three young men became angry at the man because, they say, he was staring at their girlfriends (Campbell, & Urgo, 1997). In a far less serious incident recently reported in the news, a United Airlines flight from Newark to Denver was forced to land in Chicago when an in-flight altercation occurred over a device, called a "knee defender," which prevents the seat in front of you from reclining (Hunter & Ahlers, 2014).

In less dramatic instances, victims of territorial invasion may become annoyed, uncomfortable, and eager to leave. These reactions were the subject of study in a classic early experiment on territoriality in a college library (Russo, 1967). Over a two-year period, researcher Nancy Russo observed the behaviors of women who had been sitting alone until she sat down at their table. Sometimes she took the seat next to them, moving to within 12 inches; sometimes she took the one directly across from them; and sometimes she took the seat diagonal to them. Compared to control subjects (women sitting alone at tables she didn't occupy), the women exhibited all sorts of defensive gestures, shifts in posture, and efforts to move away. Among the women she inched closer to, most of them (70%) left the table at some point.

Under such circumstances, the real question may not be whether they leave, but how long it takes. In one study, researchers visited a large suburban shopping mall on several weekends and measured the departure times of individuals sitting on benches after experimenters sat next to them (Young & Guile, 1987). The average individual took flight about 5 minutes after the intrusion, compared to an average departure time of nearly 10 minutes for individuals who were only observed (control subjects).

Other studies of territorial invasion document various avoidance and withdrawal reactions, supporting the idea that some kind of compensation is a likely response to the unwelcomed invasion of a stranger (Patterson, Mullens, & Romano, 1971). Even staring at someone can elicit similar reactions. Observing drivers stopped at traffic lights and pedestrians at crosswalks, one team of researchers discovered that those who were stared at left more quickly than did those who were not stared at (Ellsworth, Carlsmith, & Henson, 1972). One interesting exception to these flight reactions may be in situations where a victim is able to retaliate by not leaving (e.g., taking one's time on a public telephone while someone is waiting impatiently to use it). One team of researchers discovered that drivers took longer to exit their parking spaces when another driver was waiting for their space than when no one was waiting (Ruback & Juieng, 1997).

▸ Sitting too close to someone, especially someone we don't know, is likely to make that person feel very uncomfortable. What are some of the factors that determine when a violation of one's personal space occurs?

istockphoto.com/szelmek

While approach–avoidance behaviors generally signal like and dislike, they take on relational control connotations in threatening contexts, such as those characterized by competition and criticism. Maintaining eye contact while trying to win an argument, posturing expansively while trying to impress a rival, or attempting physical contact while ridiculing someone are not actions meant to gain affection. People often use these threat displays to intimidate an adversary or to reinforce an unflattering appraisal.

RESEARCH 4.3

FIND OUT MORE

Is Eye Contact between a Speaker and Listener Always Good?

Few people would question the importance of eye contact in face-to-face interactions. In most public speaking courses, for example, instructors routinely tell their students about the need to make eye contact with your audience and how it makes a speaker more effective with his or her audience. But is this always the case? Is eye contact always beneficial? In fact, the authors of this study discovered that sometimes eye contact has the opposite effect, making a speaker less rather than more effective with his or her audience.

To find out more about this study and to answer the following questions, see the full text (cited below).

1. According to the authors of this study, what is the most important difference between the way they studied eye contact and the way previous researchers studied eye contact?
2. What is their reasoning as to why eye contact sometimes backfires on a speaker?
3. What type of study is this? (See Appendix.)
4. What are the limitations of this study?

Source: Chen, S, F., Munson, J. A., Shöne, M., & Heinrichs, M. (2013). In the eye of the beholder: Eye contact increase resistance to persuasion. *Psychological Science, 24*, 2254–2261.

A third way approach–avoidance signals communicate control rather than intimacy is when they underscore differences in status between people. More than the overt acts of territorial invasion or the threat displays associated with certain contexts, status reminders are the ritualized forms of behavior that come to symbolize status in a particular culture (i.e., we expect a person to act according to his or her rank). For this reason, we sometimes notice irregularities in the expression of status. In many Asian and Latin American countries, for example, when a parent scolds a child, the child shows respect by looking down and avoiding eye contact. In the United States, a scolding parent declares, "Look at me when I'm talking to you."

Researchers have discovered that many status differences exist in the uses of space, gaze, and touch, and several reviews of this research have been available for quite some time (Andersen & Bowman, 1990; Argyle, 1988; Burgoon et al., 1995; Edinger & Patterson, 1983). From these studies, we can reasonably conclude that high-status individuals in this culture are afforded key privileges not ordinarily granted to low-status persons. When invoked, these privileges constitute important status reminders that not only reflect the pecking order but reinforce it as well (see Chapter 10). These actions seem to fall generally into three main categories.

The first kind of status reminder is exercising the privilege to occupy an area. Studies show that persons of higher status usually take up more space than do low-status individuals. Aside from larger offices, these status reminders include expansive postures, larger body buffer zones, much greater mobility during an interaction, holding positions of authority (sitting at the head of a table, at the front of a room, or in the biggest chair), and being at the center of attention.

The second kind of status reminder is exercising the privilege to intrude. Whether through close distances, touch, or gazing, a person of higher status generally retains the prerogative to initiate some form of contact. But what distinguishes these actions from the other territorial invasions is the fact that the victim is much less likely to signal discomfort and resentment (you don't want to alienate the boss). In fact, from the perspective of the higher-status person, these actions might not seem like intrusions at all, but entitlements. Social psychologist Nancy Henley (1977), and sociologist Erving Goffman (1967) before her, observed how the initiation of touch seemed related to status: The person of higher status did most of the touching.

Studies show that, when observing photographs and videos of people interacting, we tend to perceive the person who touches as more dominant than the person who receives the touch (Forden, 1981; Major & Heslin, 1982; Summerhayes & Suchner, 1978). But these judgments do not necessarily generalize to situations in which the judge is also the person being touched (Storrs & Kleinke, 1990). One investigator recently took up the question of whether social touchers are in fact more likely to be high-status individuals (Hall, 1996). Observations of participants at various professional meetings revealed that high-status individuals didn't touch more but used different kinds of touches—casual spot touches to the arm or shoulder—than did their low-status associates (e.g., handshakes, and other formal touches). Despite not finding any difference in the frequency of touch, this study still appears to support the status reminder thesis, given the more obligatory kinds of touches initiated by low-status persons.

The third type of status reminder is exercising the privilege to disengage. In their interactions with low-status persons, individuals of high-status often demonstrate little vigilance. Given their more powerful position, they enjoy greater freedom to express any detachment they might feel. Specifically, they signal a lack of interest in obtaining feedback from low-status persons and a disregard for politeness norms by using more indirect body orientations, increased distances, and less looking-while-listening behavior. Not paying attention to another person represents a kind of fearlessness ordinarily associated with status and power (Mehrabian, 1972).

PERSONAL EXPERIENCE 4.4

CAN YOU RELATE TO THIS?

Not Paying Attention Can Be a Status Reminder

I once had difficulty in a class and decided to go and talk to the professor. He always said in class that we should go see him during his office hours. However, when I went to see him, it didn't seem as though he had any interest in me. He never looked up from his desk, he took a phone call, and he was constantly looking at his watch. I don't think he realized all the messages he was sending. But that was the last time I went to speak with him.

Beth

Identification: A Significant Secondary Function

Unlike the bodily signals we discussed in the previous chapter, approach–avoidance signals alone do not enable us to identify a person. While there is a rather sizeable body of research supporting the claim that certain people use these signals differently than others do, this research tells us only about group tendencies. For example, some studies may give us an idea of how the average man compares to the average woman in their reactions to touch. Other studies may suggest that introverts are more likely than extroverts to avoid eye contact with strangers. What are we to make of these studies? Aside from demonstrating that our behavior is somewhat predictable, this body of research cautions us to temper our judgments about whether someone likes or dislikes us, respects or demeans us. The person might be acting only as a typical male, a typical Latin American, or a typical shy person.

GENDER DIFFERENCES Risking overstatement as well as oversimplification, one basic conclusion we can draw from the research comparing men and women is that, overall, women exhibit more immediacy behaviors than men do. Many studies indicate that women generally prefer closer distances, more direct body orientations, more eye contact, and more touch. Studies also suggest that, compared to men, women are somewhat more likely to be the target rather than the instigator of territorial invasions, threat displays, and status reminders. There is also some evidence that males and females differ in their interpretations of various approach–avoidance signals.

▸ As a general rule, research supports the claim that men tend to be more distant in their interactions with other men than women are in their interactions with other women.

istockphoto.com/Xavier Arnau

Gender differences in the use of immediacy behaviors are almost always accepted at face value. They seem to reflect what we learn early in life about sex roles: Females are supposed to be supportive, nurturing, warm, and people oriented; males are supposed to be assertive, competitive, cold, and task oriented (LaFrance & Mayo, 1979). Watching men and women in everyday situations, it may strike us that men seem more aloof in their body language than women do. Some observational studies support this conclusion. For instance, in her popular book, *You Just Don't Understand: Women and Men in Conversation*, linguistics researcher Deborah Tannen (1990) reports the results of a study in which she observed pairs of children and adults who were videotaped entering a room, sitting down, and starting a conversation. As she notes,

> [d]ifferences in physical alignment, or body language, leap out at anyone who looks at segments of the videotapes one after another. At every age, the girls and women sit closer to each other and look at each other directly. At every age, the boys and men sit at angles to each other—in one case, almost parallel—and never look directly into each others' faces. (p. 245)

Although Tannen's discovery only corroborated the findings of much earlier studies of interpersonal distance (for reviews of this research, see Hall, 1984; Hayduk, 1983) and body orientation (Jones, 1971; Jones & Aiello, 1973; Mehrabian & Friar, 1969), other investigations raise as many questions as they answer. Leslie Hayduk (1983), in an extensive summary of the research on interpersonal distance, identified a total of 27 studies that found gender differences, 54 studies that were inconclusive, and 29 studies that failed to detect differences. But in another review of the research, limited to studies that used unobtrusive measures of interpersonal distance, such as observations in public settings, Judith Hall (1984) found strong support for the general claim that males use greater distances than female do. Regarding gender differences in body orientation, Hall's review found that women faced each other more directly than men did. These differences may also depend on the context in which an interaction occurs. In a series of naturalistic observations in several European countries, for instance, Remland, Jones, and Brinkman (1991, 1995) found no gender differences in body orientations among adults interacting at train stations. As a potent signal of conversational involvement, men and women may align their bodies in similar ways when conversation is not the primary activity and when the environment is filled with distractions that compete for our attention. Yet there are still other naturalistic observations that find gender differences under such circumstances. For instance, a recent observational study of more than a thousand adolescent and young adult small groups in an urban environment walking from one place to another found that male dyads and triads tended to walk abreast less often and at a faster rate of speed compared to female dyads and triads (suggesting less intimacy), a finding that disappeared in larger groups of people (Costa, 2010).

Similar conclusions apply to the research on touching and gazing. Surveys suggest that women share a more positive attitude toward same-sex touch than men do (Andersen & Leibowitz, 1978; Willis & Rawdon, 1994). And studies comparing males and females in their use of touch usually show more frequent touching between females than between males (Hall, 1984; Hall & Veccia, 1990; Roese, Olson, Borenstein, Martin, & Shores, 1992), although these gender differences don't always show up when researchers observe people in other countries (Remland et al., 1995). As for the amount of touch that occurs in opposite-sex encounters, it depends primarily on the couple's relationship (Guerrero & Andersen, 1991; McDaniel & Andersen, 1998). Researchers have also observed gender differences in gazing behavior. One fairly consistent finding is the presence of more other-directed gaze between females than between males (Dindia, Fitzpatrick, & Attridge, 1989; Exline, 1963; Hall, 1984; Mulac, Studley, Weimann, & Bradac, 1987). There is some evidence that this difference appears very early in development. Researchers in one study found that, although there were no differences at earlier ages, female infants only 13 to 18 weeks old engaged in more mutual gaze with unfamiliar adults than did male infants of the same age (Leeb & Rejskind, 2004).

Despite these differences in how often males and females use touch or eye contact, it may be more fruitful to consider what these behaviors mean. Jones (1994) points out that women are more apt than men to exchange affectionate touches such as hugs and kisses (Derlega, Lewis, Harrison, Winstead, & Costanzo, 1989) and to use touch when offering social support (e.g., consoling, complimenting, etc.). In contrast, men are more likely to exchange playful touches (e.g., mock aggression, teasing, etc.). Studies also suggest that men and women interpret touch differently. Overall, women tend to find it more pleasant than men do (Hall, 1984), but their reactions depend on how well they know the toucher. For men, touch often carries sexual overtones and, as a result, their reactions seem to depend on whether the toucher is male or female (Heslin & Alper, 1983; Heslin, Nguyen, & Nguyen, 1983). In fact, researchers mainly attribute the fact that men, compared to women, avoid same-sex intimate forms of touch and possess a more negative attitude about such touching (Derlega et al., 1989). After observing same-sex couples and recording how often they touched, one team of researchers found that those who touched least scored the highest on a questionnaire measuring negative attitudes toward homosexuals (Roese et al., 1992). Recent research also supports the claim that homophobia in men produces negative judgments of certain kinds of touching between men (Floyd, 2000).

PERSONAL EXPERIENCE 4.5

CAN YOU RELATE TO THIS?

Men and Women Differ in Their Use of Eye Contact

I always experience this with my boyfriend. I will be telling him a story and he'll be looking around the room. Sometimes I'll get really frustrated because I think he's not listening to me and I'll stop telling my story. I live with eight girls so I am so used to getting the full attention of the person I am talking to. Whenever my roommates and I are talking, we look each other in the eyes to show our interest and that we are listening.

Cari

We also use approach–avoidance signals to control others as well as to encourage intimacy with them. Some research implies that in opposite-sex interactions, men are more likely than women to engage in acts of territorial invasion, use threat displays, and invoke status reminders. In the workplace, unwelcome touches and other intrusions of a sexual nature constitute sexual harassment, and more men than women are implicated in such actions. In everyday opposite-sex encounters, research indicates that women are more likely than men to be the victim of spatial invasion (Hall, 1984; Henley, 1977). In one study, researchers found that people were more inclined to walk between rather than around two women conversing in a hallway than they were to do the same with male pairs or opposite-sex pairs (Lomax, 1994). Another study compared the efficacy of male and female territorial markers and found that males were more likely to disregard women's territorial markers than the other way around (Shaffer & Sadowski, 1975). Women may also be less willing to defend their territory following an invasion. A study conducted in a college library found that more women than men got up and left after a stranger sat at their table (Polit & LaFrance, 1977). Another study found that, when men and women approached each other directly on a sidewalk, in 12 of 19 encounters, women—not men—were the ones who moved to avoid a collision. In only three encounters did the man move out of the woman's way (Silveira, 1972).

It may be more than coincidental, as some scholars have argued, that male–female interaction patterns resemble those typically found in superior–subordinate exchanges (Henley, 1977). The contention is that nonverbal signals often reflect traditional sex roles; the patterns serve to remind us that men have been in charge for a long time. These status reminders carry the implication that power comes with privileges, and research demonstrates that men tend to exercise these privileges. Reviews of the literature show that in opposite-sex interactions, men take up more space, position themselves in superior ways, are more likely to intrude, and are less attentive than women are (Argyle, 1988; Burgoon et al., 1996; Hall, 1984; Henley, 1977; LaFrance & Mayo, 1979).

Men often assume positions of authority. In one study, researchers observed couples walking from place to place and noticed that women tended to walk behind the men (Grady, Miransky, & Mulvey, 1976). In addition, observations of the way men and women touch in public (i.e., tie signs) often reveal that men get the upper hand (e.g., guiding and directing). In fact, researchers have confirmed the idea that men literally get the upper hand when men and women hold hands in public. Observations of more than 15,000 couples showed that men had the "dominant" hand position, even when taking into account male–female differences in height (in couples with a taller woman, more men than women still had the upper hand). Moreover, the finding seems to hold up across cultures. Men had the upper hand in Asian, black, Hispanic, and Japanese couples as well as European American couples (Chapell & Beltran, 1999). Studies also show that men take up more space, sprawling out when seated or moving around when standing (Hai, Khairullah, & Coulmas, 1982; Mehrabian, 1972).

Some researchers claim that men touch women more than women touch men and that touch-initiation in these cases constitutes a status reminder (Henley, 1973, 1977, 1995). But many observations of touching in opposite-sex interactions have failed to corroborate this. Researchers find that women initiate touch more than men do (Jones, 1994; Stier & Hall, 1984; Willis & Dodds, 1998). One extenuating circumstance may be the age of the couple. One study of couples in public places found that men initiated more touch than women did in younger couples, whereas women touched more in older couples (Hall & Veccia, 1990). Another related factor is the kind of touch one uses. Research shows that males initiate more hand touches, whereas women tend to initiate more non-hand touches, such as hugs and kisses (DiBiase & Gunnoe, 2004). One possible explanation is that touch in these situations may be a status reminder—signaling possessiveness—in less secure relationships. In addition, if touch does count occasionally as a status reminder, it probably makes more sense to investigate how touch is used instead of how often. A touch that attempts to control (i.e., directing someone), for example, seems more indicative of status than is a touch that is meant only to show concern or affection. Another explanation offered by some researchers is that differences in the use of touch between men and women reflect an evolutionary model of reproductive strategies: Men use touch for sex and women use touch to maintain resources and parental involvement. This theory may explain why researchers sometimes find that men who are dating or newly married are much more likely to initiate touch than men who have been married longer than a year. But for women, there are no reported differences in the use of touch between courting and married couples (Willis & Briggs, 1992; Willis & Dodds, 1998).

EXERCISE 4.2

TRY IT

Observing Men and Women

As we have seen, many studies report differences between men and women in their use of space, gaze, and touch. The purpose of this exercise is to find out whether your own observations confirm any of these differences. Select one of the following questions. Find a good location for your observations (e.g., a classroom, the student center, an airport, a shopping mall, etc.) and record what you see. Be prepared to share your findings in class.

1. Do men use more space than women do? Observe men and women sitting in chairs and note whether the men are more sprawled out than the women. Or observe men and women in opposite-sex interactions and note whether the men move around more than the women do.
2. Who initiates more touch, men or women? Observe several opposite-sex couples as they are conversing. Try to record who touches first and who touches most often.
3. Are women more attentive than men are? Observe male pairs, female pairs, and opposite-sex pairs and note their typical body orientations and how often they look at their partner.

CULTURAL DIFFERENCES As we saw earlier, approach–avoidance codes can be arbitrary, varying greatly from one time and place to another. Sometimes visitors from other countries are astonished at the differences they encounter. Several studies support Edward Hall's basic thesis that certain cultures use more distant styles of communication than others.

In an early laboratory study, researchers observed that Arabs sat closer together than Americans did and that Arabs and Middle Easterners touched more than Americans, Britons, and Australians (Watson & Graves, 1966). Another early study found that Latin American individuals adopted closer distances in their conversations than did Americans (Hall & Whyte, 1966). Similarly, in a more recent laboratory study, Mediterranean and Latino participants used less distances in their interactions than did participants representing Asian and Anglo-Saxon cultures (Beaulieu, 2004). In two field studies, communication researcher Robert Shuter (1976, 1977) photographed couples in Italy, Germany, the United States, Costa Rica, Panama, and Colombia. Among his findings were the observations that Italians and Germans stood closer to each other than Americans did, Italian men touched more than German or American men did, and Costa Ricans used closer distances and more touch than Panamanians or Colombians did. In a study of cultural differences in Europe, my colleagues and I (Remland et al., 1991, 1995, 1999) found that southern Europeans were more inclined to use touch than northern Europeans. Brief observations of nearly 1,000 couples at numerous train stations in 15 countries revealed differences in the percentages of couples in which one person touched the other. For example, among countries with at least 50 observed couples, the highest incidence of touch occurred for those in Greece (32%), Spain (30%), Italy (24%), and Hungary (23%). The lowest was found in the Netherlands (4%), Austria (9%), England (11%), Belgium (12%), and Germany (16%).

Of course, while culture certainly has some impact on our use of approach–avoidance signals, other factors, such as context, relationship, and personality, may be more important in determining whether we touch, gaze at, or move toward someone. This would explain why many studies looking for cultural differences fail to find them or find only limited evidence of them (Forston & Larson, 1968; Jones, 1971; Keating & Keating, 1980; Mazur, 1977; McDaniel & Andersen, 1998; Noesjirwan, 1978; Remland et al., 1991, 1995; Sussman & Rosenfeld, 1982).

Sometimes cultural differences are most visible to us when we see individuals participating in rituals, such as greetings and departures, or in everyday situations governed by rules different from our own. We shake hands when we greet someone. And handshaking for this purpose is common throughout much of the world. But not everyone does it (e.g., the Japanese bow). Other forms of touch—hugging and kissing, for instance—are more common in some cultures, particularly among friends and acquaintances (e.g., South America, Italy, France, Russia). In many Latin American countries, hand kissing is still a widely performed greeting. Customs in other parts of the world differ as well. For example, in India, a common greeting—the *wai*—involves placing the palms together in prayer-like fashion and bowing. It is still customary in Arab countries to touch your forehead and chest, the *salaam*, when meeting someone. In other cultures—the Maoris in New Zealand, Lapps in Finland, Bedouin in North Africa, Eskimos, Polynesians, and Malays—many people rub their noses together or against the other person's face when greeting (Morris, 1994). Some researchers report cultural differences in public displays of affection. Field (1999) observed peer interactions among adolescents in Paris, France and Miami, Florida. She found that American adolescents spent less time leaning against, stroking, kissing, and hugging their peers than did the French adolescents. Compared to the French, the Americans also displayed more self-touching and more aggressive physical behavior. In another study, a team of researchers observed male–female couples walking on a college campus. They found no differences in hand-holding when comparing Latino couples with Asian couples, but arm embracing was much more prevalent among the Latinos than it was among the Asians (Regan, Jerry, Marysia, & Johnson, 1999). In another study, researchers observed the most male-female affectionate touching (hugging, kissing) in Italian dance clubs and the least in American dance clubs (DiBiase & Gunnoe, 2004). There may also be learned cultural differences in the use of gaze as a conversational signal. Observing individuals responding to interview questions, researchers found that Japanese respondents used the least amount of eye contact and tended to look down while thinking of answers, whereas Canadian and Trinidadian respondents tended to look up while thinking (McCarthy, Lee, Itakura, & Muir, 2006).

The meaning of touch often depends on one's culture. In some Middle and Near-Eastern countries, shaking hands is an act of bargaining rather than a form of greeting. In much of the Middle East, holding hands is a sign of friendship and is a common practice among male friends (unlike in the West, where such an act between men implies homosexuality). In fact, same-sex touching in public is more acceptable in many Asian and Middle Eastern countries than is opposite-sex touching (Jones, 1994). Some forms of touch have meanings that are unique to a particular culture. In Saudi Arabia, for example, an individual will sometimes kiss the nose of another person after an argument to say, "I am sorry" (Morris, 1994). It would be a mistake to underestimate the importance of cultural differences in the meaning of touch. Consider the tragic case of Sam and Kathy Krasniqi, Albanian Muslim immigrants living in the United States since 1971, who lost their children over allegations of sexual abuse. It all began in 1989, when Sam Krasniqi took his five-year-old daughter to a karate tournament in their hometown of Dallas, where his son was competing. Witnesses alleged that Krasniqi was touching his daughter, who was sitting on his lap at the time, in a sexual way. Based on these allegations, the Krasniqis ultimately lost custody of their two children. Did he touch his daughter in a sexual way, as the witnesses alleged? The answer, which came during Sam Krasniqi's criminal trial in 1994, was no. It was all just a cultural misunderstanding over the use of touch. Unfortunately, however, the Krasniqis were never able to regain custody of their children (Zimmerman, 1998).

Subcultural differences in the United States also exist. Studies by social psychologist Frank Willis and his colleagues (reported in Jones, 1994) suggest that blacks use touch more than whites do. Other studies indicate that the gaze patterns of blacks may also differ from whites. Early lessons that looking people in the eyes is disrespectful may prompt blacks to develop a tendency to use less eye contact with others than whites do (Ickes, 1984; Vrij & Winkel, 1992). And some early studies found that whites look more while listening than while speaking, whereas blacks may look more while speaking than while listening (LaFrance & Mayo, 1976). If this is true, one possible ramification is that whites might think blacks are not paying attention to them while blacks might think whites are staring.

Different norms and rules governing the use and acceptability of approach–avoidance behaviors can affect how we judge the people we meet. Behavior that may be viewed positively in one culture may be viewed negatively in another culture. For example, in one recent study, a team of researchers found that individuals in Japan, an East Asian culture, were more likely to judge a person making direct eye contact with them as angrier, less pleasant, and less approachable than were persons from Finland, a Western culture (Akechi et al., 2013).

PERSONAL EXPERIENCE 4.6

CAN YOU RELATE TO THIS?

Rituals Involving Touch Are a Product of Culture

In 1995, I traveled with an international organization. We stayed with host families all over the world. I recall saying goodbye to a particular family in Germany. They fed me breakfast that morning and handed me a bag lunch. I packed my bags and was ready to go. In this particular family, there was an older woman, a grandmother, who lived with them. When I went to lean in and give her a hug, she put her face next to mine and kissed my cheek, then went to kiss the other. It was awkward because I wanted to hug her and she wanted to kiss me.

Wendy

PERSONALITY DIFFERENCES Aside from gender and culture, personality plays a part in shaping the way we use approach–avoidance signals. In addition, we often attribute personality traits to people based on their willingness to touch, get close, or make eye contact. One line of research shows that we may be able to characterize individuals who exhibit a contact style of interaction (i.e., proximity, gaze, and touch) as more impulsive, expressive, self-disclosing, sociable, extroverted, assertive, and democratic than individuals with a noncontact style (Argyle, 1988; Burgoon et al., 1996; Fromme et al., 1989). Studies also indicate that persons who connect with others through touch, distance, and gaze are more likely to have higher self-esteem (Andersen, Andersen, & Lustig, 1987; Jourard, 1966; Silverman, Pressman, & Bartell, 1973) than are persons who avoid such contacts. Paralleling male–female differences, some research suggests that masculine individuals use greater distances when interacting with each other than feminine individuals do (Uzzell & Horne, 2006). Approach–avoidance signals also reveal differences in social anxiety. For instance, experimental studies of gaze behavior show that persons high in social anxiety tend to exhibit a vigilant avoidant pattern of gaze, characterized by looking more often at people's emotionally expressive faces (vigilant) but also looking away from those faces more quickly than persons with lower anxiety (Garner, Mogg, &

Bradley, 2006). This is especially the case when highly anxious persons are exposed to threatening faces. Research shows that highly anxious individuals look away from angry faces more quickly than persons who are not highly anxious (Terburg, Aarts, & van Honk, 2012). Even in virtual reality environments, highly anxious individuals avoid eye contact. In one recent study, researchers found that highly anxious young women were more likely to avoid the direct gaze of approaching male avatars on a computer screen than were young women low in social anxiety (Wieser, Pauli, Grosseible, Molzow, & Mulberger, 2010).

Another trait-like quality that directly affects approach–avoidance signals is self-construal, which reflects our sense of self in relation to others. An interdependent self-construal represents a general desire to be with others, whereas an independent self-construal represents a desire to be apart or separate from others. In a series of experiments, researchers confirmed that participants with an independent self-construal tended to select seats in a waiting room that were slightly farther away from another occupied seat than did participants with an interdependent self-construal. In addition, the researchers manipulated the self-construal of participants by priming them to feel independent or interdependent prior to selecting seats in the waiting room. Exposing participants to subliminal messages on a computer screen that primed them to feel independent (their own name flashed on the screen) caused them to take more distant seats than those taken by participants exposed to neutral subliminal messages (the word *apple* flashed on the screen). And in a subsequent experiment, the researchers found that participants asked to write four sentences noting differences between them and their close friends and family members (independent self-construal) chose more distant seats than did participants asked to write four sentences noting similarities between them and their close friends and family members (Holland, Roeder, van Baaren, Brandt, & Hannover, 2004).

Much like the physical attractiveness halo effect, numerous studies support the idea that we ascribe positive traits to people who use eye contact, close distances, and touch. For instance, in his review of numerous laboratory studies, social psychologist Chris Kleinke (1986) concluded that we judge people who use eye contact frequently much more favorably than we do people who don't. In part, we tend to rate the former as more friendly, assertive, credible, competent, and socially skillful. In one early experiment, the same actor varied his eye contact in two films. Keeping other factors constant, he established eye contact 15% of the time in one version and 80% of the time in the other. Judges rated him as more cold, pessimistic, defensive, immature, evasive, and submissive in the 15% film (Kleck & Nuessle, 1968). Research shows that even a fleeting glance, establishing or breaking eye contact, can affect our judgments. When female faces on a computer screen shifted their gaze, making direct eye contact with the participants viewing the faces, the participants rated those faces as more attractive and likeable than they rated the faces when the faces shifted their gaze away from the participants (Mason, Tatkow, & Macrae, 2005). Even the faces of computer agents are perceived as more attractive with a direct gaze than with an averted gaze (Palanica & Itier, 2012). Some research on eye contact also reveals a difference in perceptions of women compared to men. For instance, one study found that people were more antagonistic toward gaze-avoidant women than they were toward gaze-avoidant men. Photographs of women who avoided gaze were seen as disagreeable, unconscientious, unattractive, and less intelligent (Larsen & Shackelford, 1996). One possible explanation for this gender bias may be that because we expect more eye contact from women than we do from men, gaze avoidance in women seems more deviant, and therefore less desirable, when compared to the same behavior in men. Shifts in a person's gaze can also affect our personality judgments of that person.

Research on touch indicates a similar effect. In one study, for example, persons who initiated touch were regarded as more dominant, assertive, and expressive than were those who received touch (Major & Heslin, 1982). Perhaps the most common form of touch is the handshake. One recent study confirms the importance of handshaking as an expression of personality and as a behavior that influences first impressions. Examining the importance of a firm handshake, which depends on the strength, duration, vigor, and completeness of the grip (along with the use of eye contact), researchers found that women who used a firm handshake had different personalities than women who didn't. The firm handshakers were more extroverted, expressive, liberal, intellectual, and open to new experiences. They also made a better first impression. As the authors conclude,

> Our results provide one instance in which women who exhibit a behavior (a firm handshake) that is more common for men and that is related to confidence and assertiveness are evaluated more positively than are women who exhibit a more typical feminine handshake. (Chaplin, Phillips, Brown, Clanton, & Stein, 2000, p. 115)

Other Secondary Functions

The primary function of approach–avoidance signals is resolving fundamental issues of intimacy and control in relationships. Our use of space, gaze, and touch also reflects differences in gender, culture, and personality, and thus contributes (albeit in a limited way) to the identification function of nonverbal communication. In this concluding section, we'll consider the restricted role of approach–avoidance signals in the delivery of verbal messages and in the communication of emotions.

DELIVERING VERBAL OR SYMBOLIC MESSAGES Sometimes we use space, gaze, or touch to deliver verbal messages. They either enhance or take the place of spoken words. Some gestures substitute for words. Referred to as *emblems*, we use these symbolic gestures to convey specific messages. Because they are recognizable as such, there is much less uncertainty about whether one intends to send a message than there is about most other approach–avoidance signals. Some of these gestures include various acts of gazing or avoiding gaze. For example, an upward gaze often sends the message, "I'm thinking." Making eye contact while raising your eyebrows is a greeting gesture, a way of saying hello without speaking. Sometimes the context can turn a simple act of eye contact into a symbolic gesture, as it does in a restaurant when we make eye contact with our server or in the classroom when we avoid eye contact with the instructor. Many of our social touches also convey clear symbolic messages. As a widely understood greeting or departure gesture, handshaking is one obvious example. In some cases, the context helps clarify the meaning, as it does when we comfort a friend who is depressed or express our gratitude to someone who helps us out. In cases such as these, touch conveys unambiguous messages of support and appreciation (Jones & Yarbrough, 1985).

We also use space, gaze, and touch when we speak. These actions often punctuate, repeat, or regulate what we say. A speaker may lean forward to emphasize an important idea or highlight a transition point by physically moving from one position to another. Many speakers often try to connect with their audience by reaching out to them with outstretched arms (Morris, 1977). Try to imagine talking to someone without making any eye contact whatsoever. Gaze, body lean, and touch often regulate the turn taking that takes place in conversations. We make eye contact to let someone know we are finished speaking, we touch someone to ward off an interruption, we lean forward to signal our interest in speaking, and so on. In their research on touch, Jones and Yarbrough (1985) noticed that people often use touch to reinforce what they say. In such cases, it is difficult to separate the meaning of the touch from the words that are spoken. For example, many touches accompanied controlling statements such as, "Listen to this" or "We'd better get going." Others occurred when people were trying to be helpful, making statements such as "Don't worry, it'll be okay."

COMMUNICATING EMOTION In general, we do not express our emotions directly and spontaneously through approach–avoidance signals. Facial and vocal expressions, more than any other nonverbal channels of communication, tell others whether we are depressed, overjoyed, angry, and so forth (see Chapters 5 and 6). Although our eyes (i.e., brows, eyelids) play a vital role in signaling emotions, gaze alone does not. This should not imply that our use of space, gaze, and touch is unaffected by our emotions or that others cannot correctly infer emotions from approach–avoidance cues. In general, positive emotions motivate approach behaviors and negative

PERSONAL EXPERIENCE 4.7

CAN YOU RELATE TO THIS?

Speakers Can Use Touch to Control a Conversation

I was having a conversation with two of my friends. At one point, both of them were talking at the same time. Because I was the only one not talking, it felt as though I needed to decide who to pay attention to. One of my friends reached out and grabbed my arm, not forcefully, but just enough to "grab" my attention. Although this happened in a matter of seconds, I realized that her touching me was her way of staying in control of the conversation. And it worked. My other friend stopped talking and let her finish what she was saying.

Alexandra

emotions motivate avoidance behaviors. If we are happy, we may be more inclined to touch or make eye contact. And we tend to avoid eye contact and keep our distance when we feel embarrassed, guilty, fearful, sad, or disgusted. Of course, some emotions may lead to approach or avoidance reactions. What happens when you are angry at someone? Do you withdraw or do you confront? Also, there is some evidence that intentional acts of touch alone can signal specific emotions. In one series of studies, participants in Spain and in the United States were able to guess with much better than chance accuracy whether an instance of touch expressed anger, fear, disgust, love, gratitude, or sympathy (Hertenstein, Keltner, App, Bulleit, & Jaskolka, 2006).

SUMMARY

Approach–avoidance signals, which consist mainly of the ways we use interpersonal space, eye contact, and touch, express our interest or disinterest in others (intimacy) as well as our respect or disrespect for them (control). As a communication system, these signals are complex and interrelated. Typically, a change in one of these immediacy behaviors (reduced eye contact, for instance) coincides with a similar change in another (e.g., increased interpersonal distance, indirect body orientation, and/or decreased touch). For this reason, we discussed these behaviors as part of the same basic signaling system rather than as three distinct and separate forms of communication.

The study of spatial behavior, sometimes called *proxemics*, includes the messages we send and receive as a result of various actions related to interpersonal distance, body orientation, positioning, and territoriality. In particular, territorial behavior—the way we signal ownership and defense of an area—includes our use of territorial markers and the body buffer zone (our personal space) we carry with us. Gazing behavior includes acts of nonreciprocal gaze, mutual gaze, gaze aversion, staring, and the like. Similarly, the study of interpersonal touch includes acts of nonreciprocal as well as mutual touch, tie signs, and a host of other touches that signal positive feelings, attempts to control, playfulness, and so forth.

Reflecting basic needs for affiliation as well as privacy, much of our approach–avoidance signaling is intrinsic. For example, territorial intrusions seem to set off a kind of alarm system that leads to a range of physiological responses and defensive behaviors. The negative consequences of touch deprivation and the benefits of being touched suggest a biological need for physical contact, a "skin hunger," for all sorts of touches. Iconic signaling is also possible through the use of deception, put-ons, iconic gestures, and intention movements. The use of arbitrary communication codes is evident in the changes that have taken place in how we use and interpret touch and in the preferences for space that vary from culture to culture.

The primary function of approach–avoidance signals is establishing relationships. Studies show consistently that immediacy behaviors—eye contact, close proximity, direct body orientation, and touch—communicate positive attitudes toward others, supporting the basic principle that we tend to approach what we like and avoid what we dislike. But immediacy behaviors, such as touch, vary greatly with the intimacy of our relationships and with other features of the overall context. Researchers have proposed several theories to explain and predict reactions to immediacy behaviors. Each model attempts to specify the conditions most likely to produce compensation (e.g., a negative response to a positive behavior) or reciprocity (i.e., responding in kind).

Approach–avoidance signals also communicate dominance and submission. One way is through territorial invasions—the uninvited and unwelcome intrusions that evoke a range of fight-or-flight responses. Another way is through threat displays, the use of immediacy behaviors in a threatening context (e.g., competing, criticizing). A third way is through the use of status reminders, the various actions that symbolize one individual's power over another.

The most important secondary function of approach–avoidance signals is identification. Research shows that the use of immediacy behaviors varies significantly according to one's gender, culture, and personality. To a limited degree, we also use immediacy behaviors to deliver verbal messages and to express positive and negative emotions indirectly.

KEY TERMS

Arousal-labeling model 133
Body orientation 118
Cognitive valence theory 134
Compensation 133
Contact cultures 126
Discrepancy arousal model 133
Equilibrium theory 131
Expectancy violations model 133
Eye contact 118
Gaze aversion 120
General adaptation syndrome 122
Haptics 121
Immediacy 118

Chapter Outline

5

FACIAL EXPRESSION: COMMUNICATING EMOTION

Try doing the following with your face: Pull your eyebrows down and together, raise your upper eyelid and tighten your lower eyelid, narrow your lips and press them together. Hold your face like this for five seconds. How do you feel?

This brief exercise recreates part of an experiment that was conducted in 1983 by scientists who were interested in exploring the connection between our facial expressions, personal feelings, and physiological reactions. Asked to activate facial muscles that produce an angry expression—as you just did, if you followed the instructions above—subjects in the experiment reported feelings that were consistent with the faces they unwittingly created. More important, their autonomic nervous system (e.g., heart rate, skin temperature) showed a physiological pattern consistent with the emotion of anger. And the same results occurred for other facial expressions as well (Ekman, Levenson, & Friesen, 1983). Recent studies suggest that voluntary muscle movements that create prototypical facial expressions of fear, joy, sadness, disgust, and anger produce physiological changes, including brain wave activity, indicative of the emotion shown on the face (Ekman & Keltner, 1997). One possible implication? The way we look influences the way we feel.

Perhaps taking some of the mystery out of our emotional lives, these studies invite us to consider the links that may exist between how we experience emotion on the inside and how we show it on the outside. In this chapter, we'll introduce the facial expression signaling system. We'll begin by examining the communication codes we use with facial

Learning Objectives

After reading this chapter, you will be able to do the following:

1. Understand how facial expressions operate as intrinsic, iconic, and arbitrary communication codes.
2. Discuss the primary function of facial expressions, which involves the encoding and decoding of basic emotions such as anger, fear, happiness, surprise, disgust, and contempt.
3. Consider important differences in the use and interpretation of facial expressions based on one's culture, gender, personality, and behavior.
4. Discuss how facial expressions can function as a delivery system for the communication of verbal messages.
5. Consider the role of facial expressions in building interpersonal relationships.

expressions. Then we'll discuss emotion signaling as the primary communication function. But facial expressions also play an important although secondary role in the delivery of verbal messages, the expression of identity, and the formation of relationships, so we address these functions as well.

COMMUNICATION CODES

According to some estimates, with the complex set of muscles we have in our faces, we can produce more than 1,000 different expressions (Ekman, Friesen, & Ellsworth, 1972). We make these faces for various reasons. One reason is to express our emotions. These **affect displays** include specific facial expressions for basic emotions such as anger, joy, and fear. Sometimes referred to as **facial paralanguage**, we also use our faces in much the same way that we use other gestures (i.e., the delivery function): to replace, accompany, or supplement the spoken word (Fridlund, 1994).

According to one well-known classification system (Ekman & Friesen, 1969b), there are three main types of facial paralanguage, called **conversational signals**: emblems, illustrators, and regulators (Ekman, 1979). Facial emblems are symbolic gestures with clear, agreed-upon meanings. While speaking, we use facial illustrators, energizing and punctuating our words with eyebrow movements, head bobs, and the like. Facial regulators help us start or end conversations, and they allow us to negotiate the turn taking that occurs. A simple eyebrow raise sends an invitation to speak. An open mouth signals an intention to talk. Facial adaptors, which are not usually regarded as conversational signals, help satisfy our need for physical or psychological comfort. Yet any of these actions, such as lip biting, nose wrinkling, or lip licking, can become communicative (i.e., emblematic) in certain contexts if they are done on purpose and if their meaning is reasonably clear to most onlookers.

Intrinsic Codes

Many facial expressions are part of our biological inheritance, contributing to our survival as a species. Like most animals, we benefit from a signaling system that lets us declare our emotions and allows us to read the emotions of others. Showing anger, which announces hostile intentions, works well as a warning signal. Expressing sadness is a kind of SOS signal, soliciting help from others. Exhibiting fear works as an alarm signal. Displaying joy invites the company of others, a "let's play" signal. The expression of other emotions also helps us in our everyday encounters. Additionally, facial expressions of emotion are an integral part of a system that prepares us for action in response to life's daily predicaments. Our emotions motivate us to overcome obstacles, flee from danger, seek assistance, fall in love, and so forth.

Ample evidence exists that emotional signaling in general, and facial expressions in particular, are innate systems. Some of this evidence comes from observations of other species in which such communication is common. Some comes from research on human infants showing the early development of skills in sending and responding to facial expressions (see Chapter 2). And some comes from studies of individuals born without the ability to see or hear who nonetheless show many of the same facial expressions shown by everyone else (Eibl-Eibesfeldt, 1973, 1975). In this section, we'll focus on the commonalities researchers have discovered in the facial expressions of nonhuman primates and then we'll highlight cross-cultural evidence that particular facial expressions of emotion are probably universal.

FACIAL EXPRESSIONS IN NONHUMAN PRIMATES The signaling systems used by all primate species include facial expressions. While the lower primates (i.e., lemurs) have the facial muscles for only a few different expressions, rhesus monkeys (i.e., macaques) exhibit as many as 13, and some apes, such as chimpanzees, show up to 20 different facial expressions (Argyle, 1988). Among the most common, and the ones from which some human expressions may have originated, are the **cry face**, the **glare**, the **grimace**, the **play face**, and the **pout**.

The cry face expresses frustration or sadness and, particularly in chimpanzees, resembles the human expression of similar emotions. The glare is an easily recognizable look of anger, consisting of a tight-lipped, hard stare. Experts regard many other expressions as **bonding displays**, signaling affiliation, submission, and playfulness (Preuschoft & van Hooff, 1997). The grimace expression (in nonhuman primates, usually referred to as the *silent bared-teeth display*) originated as a show of fear but eventually took on meaning as an appeasement or submissive gesture. Dominant individuals also use this expression to reassure insecure subordinates. In some species, it occurs routinely in social contexts such as grooming, greeting, and huddling. The grimace (grin) in most monkeys and apes bears a striking resemblance to the human smile. The play face, as the name implies, occurs almost exclusively in playful contexts (e.g., rough and tumble play). This relaxed open-mouth display seems to be a spontaneous expression of joy and amusement and often resembles the face of laughter in humans. Another bonding display, the pout, is mainly an infant signal that expresses a need for motherly comfort.

Because of the similarities in both their appearance and function, scholars have long believed that the human smile evolved from the primate grimace (van Hooff, 1972). But not everyone agrees. Some contend that smiling is more likely an evolutionary product of the play face (Argyle, 1988). In fact, both schools of thought may be correct. Recent research disputes the notion that smiling is a single human expression but suggests instead that there are many different types of smiles (Ekman, 1986). In all

Figure 5.1 The Seven Basic Emotions and Their Universal Expressions

Source: Ekman, P., & Keltner, D. (1997). *Nonverbal Communication in Social Interaction*. New York, NY: Taylor & Francis Group, LLC Books. Reproduced with permission of Taylor & Francis Group, LLC Books in the format textbook via Copyright Clearance Center.

likelihood, the genuine smile of happiness—referred to as an *enjoyment smile*—evolved from the play face, whereas many other types of social smiles are traceable to the simple grimace expression.

FACIAL EXPRESSIONS IN HUMANS Charles Darwin was the first scientist to gather evidence in support of the claim that human facial expressions are inborn and universal. But the observations reported in his book, *The Expression of the Emotions in Man and Animals*, were not adequately tested until a century after its publication in 1872. In the interim, the prevailing view asserted that facial expressions, like most other gestures, were a product of culture rather than biology (Birdwhistell, 1970; Klineberg, 1940; LaBarre, 1947). This view, which garnered support from observations that people neither use nor interpret facial expressions the same way in all cultures, was not seriously challenged until researchers began to understand how cultural **display rules** that prompt us to inhibit or falsify a facial expression can trick us into believing that the same basic facial expressions mean different things to different people.

Cross-cultural investigations by psychologists Paul Ekman, Wallace Friesen, Carrol Izard, and others suggested that people all over the world use and interpret facial expressions in very similar ways (Figure 5.1) and that cultural differences in expressing basic emotions such as anger, disgust, and fear are due to different beliefs (i.e., rules) about whether or not it is appropriate to show an emotion in a particular situation and not on real differences in the facial appearance of the emotion (Ekman, 1972; Ekman & Friesen, 1969b, 1971; Ekman, Sorenson, & Friesen, 1969; Izard, 1971). In their classic experiment confirming the existence of cultural display rules, Ekman and Friesen showed stress-inducing films to a sample of Japanese and America college students. Some of the time, the students watched the film alone and some of the time, they watched the film in the presence of a person from their own culture. Ekman and Frieson discovered no differences in the facial expressions of the Japanese and American students when they watched the film alone. However, when another person was present, the Japanese students, following a cultural display rule to avoid showing negative emotions, were more likely to cover up their unpleasant facial expressions than the American students were (Ekman & Friesen, 1975).

Iconic Codes

As we have seen in previous chapters, iconic codes consist of signals (semblances) that look like their referents. We often use our faces in this way to deliberately mimic an emotional expression or to imitate part of some larger activity. One way we mimic emotional expressions is through deception. In these instances, we try to convince those around us that the expression on our face is genuine when it isn't. We begin doing this by the time we are three years of age, for instance, pretending to be sad or distressed to get what we want (see Chapter 2). Before long, we start showing other unfelt emotions: pretending to be happy when we get a gift we don't like, acting interested in what someone says when we aren't, and so forth. These phony faces may resemble genuine expressions of emotion but there are noticeable differences, as we'll see later in this chapter. Another way we consciously mimic emotional expressions is with a put-on. Unlike deceptive faces, put-ons are not meant to mislead; their exaggerated appearance lets everyone in on the drama. People often use these faces when telling stories, describing personal experiences, or identifying with speakers.

But posed or phony facial expressions of emotion are not the only way that facial expressions become iconic signals. Facial gestures are sometimes iconic too. A deliberate yawn, which mimics drowsiness, tells us that a person is bored. Puffing up our cheeks, which exaggerates the act of overeating, lets others know that we're stuffed. And by puckering our lips and imitating a kiss, we can tell loved ones that we care about them.

Arbitrary Codes

Many of our facial expressions convey other kinds of symbolic messages in two ways. First, as is the case with many other gestures, a facial expression can mean what we want it to mean. Rolling our eyes is one example. Neither an intrinsic nor an iconic signal, the meaning of this gesture is a matter of convention. Looking up to the heavens, we let others know how exasperated we feel. Sometimes a simple facial expression of this kind can transmit a message that would be difficult to send in any other way. For instance,

> [t]he wink is a deliberate, one-eyed blink that signals a shared secret between the winker and the winked-at. The collusion is based on the idea that the closed eye—aimed at the companion—is keeping their secret, while the open eye—aimed at the rest of the world—is excluding everyone else from the momentary intimacy. Performed between private friends it signals a moment of shared, private understanding. Performed towards a stranger it requests a shared intimacy that has yet to happen. In other words, between strangers, it becomes a flirtation signal. (Morris, 1994, p. 50)

A second way that facial expressions become symbolic forms of communication is when they adhere to the arbitrary display rules found in most societies. Learned when we are very young, these rules exert a tremendous influence over our use and interpretation of facial signals. Many of these rules are so deeply ingrained that we rarely stop to consider the possibility that everyone may not share the same rules. Smiling is a case in point. In his landmark study of bodily communication, anthropologist Ray Birdwhistell (1970) observed how the rules taken for granted about the appropriateness of a smile can lead to interesting geographical differences in the frequency and interpretation of smiling.

COMMUNICATION FUNCTIONS

The face may be the most significant channel of nonverbal communication. When we interact with another person, we direct much of our attention toward that person's face. This facial bias is hardly surprising, given the important role the face plays in almost all the functions of nonverbal signaling. Indeed, many of the misunderstandings that occur in everyday life are the result of misreading another person's face. In this section, we'll examine, in order of importance, how facial expressions convey our emotions, deliver verbal messages, communicate our identity, and affect our relationships.

Communicating Emotion: The Primary Function

Our facial expressions reveal much about how we feel. We can see anger, fear, or joy in a person's face more assuredly than we can hear those emotions in a person's voice or read them in a person's words. According to the position taken here, which represents the prevailing view, communicating emotions is the primary function of facial expressions.

Before we continue to elaborate this position, however, we should point out that some of the issues underlying the idea that our facial expressions reveal particular emotions have been sparking debate among social scientists for many years (Parkinson, 2005); a debate that shows no signs of slowing down (Fernandez-Dols, 2013). Some scholars, such as James A. Russell, reject the contention that our faces express a limited number of discrete emotions—known as the *categorical view*—and prefer a *dimensional view*, which asserts that facial expressions only reveal various states corresponding to how pleasant/unpleasant, aroused/unaroused, or strong/weak we happen to feel at a given point in time (Nelson & Russell, 2013; Russell, 1980, 1983, 1994; Russell & Bullock, 1986). Psychologist Alan Fridlund (1994) also takes exception to the prevailing view. As he sees it, facial expressions do not reveal our emotions at all but only signal our intentions to others and are therefore strictly social in nature. We briefly address this perspective (the *behavioral ecology* view) in the section below on the interpersonal domain.

Even the strongest advocates of the categorical view do not claim that all our emotions show on our faces. According to Ekman (1994), we may feel as many as 17 basic emotions: amusement, anger, awe, contempt, contentment, disgust, embarrassment, excitement, fear, guilt, interest, pride, relief, sadness, satisfaction, sensory pleasure, and shame. These emotions, which evolved because of their value in urging us to deal with the challenges of everyday life (Izard, 1977), share certain features, such as a quick onset, brief duration, distinctive physiology, involuntary occurrence, and presence in other primates (Ekman, 1994). Yet our facial expressions communicate only some of these emotions. In the next section, we'll take a look at the way our faces show emotion (encoding) and how well we are able to recognize these signals (decoding). Then we'll consider the significance of facial expressions as an intrapersonal as well as an interpersonal phenomenon.

SIMPLE ENCODING AND DECODING In their classic book, *Unmasking the Face*, Paul Ekman and Wallace Friesen (1975) developed a facial atlas that shows how six basic emotions appear on the human face: surprise, fear, disgust, anger, happiness, and sadness. The appearance of each emotion involves specific muscle movements in three regions of the face. The upper region includes the forehead and eyebrows; the middle

Table 5.1 Facial Expressions for Six Basic Emotions			
Emotion	**Upper Region**	**Middle Region**	**Lower Region**
Surprise	Brows raised, creating wrinkled forehead	Wide-opened eyes: upper lids raised and lower lids drawn down	Jaw drops, parting lips and teeth
Fear	Brows raised and drawn together, producing wrinkles in center of forehead	Upper eyelids raised, lower eyelids raised and tensed	Mouth opened, lips tensed and drawn back
Disgust	Brows lowered	Nose wrinkled, cheeks raised	Upper lip raised
Anger	Brows lowered and drawn together	Eyelids tensed, bulging eyes	Nostrils may be dilated, lips may be pressed together or open and tense
Happiness	Does not show	Cheeks raised, lower eyelids raised, wrinkles appear around eye corners and under eyes	Lip corners drawn back, wrinkles appear around mouth
Sadness	Inner corner of brows drawn up	Upper eyelid inner corner raised	Lip corners drawn down

Source: Adapted from Ekman, P., & Friesen, W. V. (1975). *Unmasking the face*. Englewood Cliffs, NJ: Prentice Hall.

region consists of the eyes and bridge of the nose; and the lower region includes the nose, cheeks, mouth, and chin. Table 5.1 briefly reviews the muscle movements involved in each of the three regions for the six basic emotions. (Figure 5.1 shows the general appearance of these expressions.)

Much less consensus exists for the facial expressions of other basic emotions. Some emotional displays include particular head and gaze actions in addition to facial expressions. Many researchers have long believed that there is a universal display for the emotion of contempt. Darwin (1872) described a look of disdain or sneering marked by a retracted upper lip corner and upturned head. Contemporary scientists have documented similar contempt expressions that include a backward head tilt with downcast gaze (Izard, 1971) and/or a slightly raised lip corner (Ekman & Friesen, 1986; Matsumoto, 1992). Research also suggests that appeasement displays may consist of distinct signals for certain self-conscious emotions such as embarrassment. Several experiments by psychologist Dacher Keltner (1995) showed that a downward gaze, controlled smile, head turn, gaze shift, and face touch combine to communicate embarrassment. There is also some evidence that interest may be encoded by head turning, direct gaze, eyelid widening, and lip parting (Reeve, 1993).

No doubt all of us have been in situations when our emotions got the best of us. Whether we were overcome with grief, anger, or joy, we couldn't disguise the look on our faces. Yet in many everyday situations, we can put on a happy face when we're sad, conceal our anger when we're furious, or dampen our delight when we're overjoyed. In short, facial expressions can be spontaneous (uninhibited) or posed (deliberate). A spontaneous expression reflects the way we really feel; the look on our face will correspond to the natural expression for that particular emotion. On the other hand, a posed expression only mimics the real thing. Often, there are telltale signs that a facial expression is spontaneous or that it is posed. Some facial muscles are relatively easy to control, whereas others are extremely difficult to control. A posed expression usually doesn't include the difficult-to-control muscle movements that are part of the natural expression. The best example of this is smiling.

▸ Not all smiles express genuine emotions of joy, amusement, and pleasure. How does a posed, deliberate smile differ from an authentic, spontaneous smile?

istockphoto.com/PeskyMonkey

Probably the most ubiquitous of all facial expressions, the posed smile often differs markedly from the genuine (i.e., felt) smile. Paul Ekman (1982) has shown that a real expression of positive emotions such as joy, amusement, pleasure, and so forth includes the action of two muscles, the zygomatic major and orbicularis occuli. Zygomatic major is responsible for pulling up our lip corners, putting a smile on our lower

PERSONAL EXPERIENCE 5.1

CAN YOU RELATE TO THIS?

A Misread Face Can Lead to a Misunderstanding

I was at work the other day and I was absolutely exhausted. I was caught in a daze (looking off into nowhere) by one of my coworkers who is also a good friend. He didn't realize that I wasn't looking at him, though my eyes were set in his direction. He thought that I was giving him a dirty look, which would imply that I was angry with him. At the time, I had no idea that anything was going on. For the rest of the night, he was acting "weird" to me. He was ignoring me and being really short with me. Finally, he came up to me at the end of the night to ask why I was so aggravated with him. By that time, I was aggravated because of the way he had been acting toward me. Well, in the end I found out that he thought that I was angry at him because of the dirty look I supposedly gave him. It was this great big deal over absolutely nothing at all.

Marissa

face. Oribularis occuli gives us smiling eyes by raising our cheeks and tightening our eyelids. These actions often produce the so-called crow's-feet around the outer corners of our eyes. Sometimes called *Duchenne smiles* (named after the French physician that Darwin credited for the discovery) or *enjoyment smiles*, these expressions differ from the less sincere variety that are usually limited to a smiling mouth, that is sometimes more asymmetrical—a stronger smile on one side of the face, fragmented, and more poorly timed than the former (Frank & Ekman, 1993). One study comparing lip movement in posed and spontaneous smiles found that onset and offset speed, amplitude of movement, and offset duration were greater in the posed smiles (Schmidt, Ambadar, Cohn, & Reed, 2006). While it may be difficult, however, to pose an enjoyment smile, studies show that some people are able to do so; that is, they can deliberately activate the muscles around the eyes as well as those pulling up the corners of the mouth (Gunnery, Hall, & Ruben, 2013; Krumhuber, Likowski, & Weyers, 2014).

Other emotions are also tough to fake. Take the infamous case of Susan Smith, the South Carolina woman who drowned her own two children in 1994 but claimed they were kidnapped by an unknown black man. As she continued to appear before the media, supposedly despondent over the alleged kidnapping of her young boys, it became increasingly difficult for her to perform in front of the camera. Eventually, as many observed, her face (and voice) seemed to show little real emotion. According to Ekman (1986), who would later describe Smith's facial expressions on an NBC Dateline program as showing no emotion, fewer than 10% of the people he tested have been able to pull the corners of their lips (depressor muscles) downward voluntarily without also moving their chin (mentalis muscle), an action necessary for an expression of grief.

PERSONAL EXPERIENCE 5.2

CAN YOU RELATE TO THIS?

Spontaneous Expressions Show Our True Feelings

One night, my friend Jeff and I went out to eat sushi. I was hesitant to try it, but he convinced me that I would like it. Because I didn't know exactly what to order, he ordered for me. When it arrived, I took my first bite and realized why I never had an urge to try it. It was horrible. However, I did not want to be completely rude and spit it out or tell Jeff I hated it, so I tried to pretend that it wasn't that bad. He obviously saw my facial expression while I was eating it (even though I tried to hide it) and just said, "Chrissy, you don't have to eat it. Just order something else."

Chrissy

Sometimes we try to conceal our real feelings, but muscle contractions that are difficult to control can give us away. One example is the expression of fear, which involves subtle movement of the eyebrow and eyelid muscles. We might try to look confident when we get ready to speak in front of a large audience, but our raised eyebrows and eyelids might tell a much different story. Furthermore, some facial expressions, known as **micro-expressions**, are especially difficult to control. While most expressions last one to four seconds, micro-expressions occur much more rapidly—they come and go in a fraction of a second (Ekman & Friesen, 1975). Because these expressions are so hard to inhibit, they provide a reliable source of information about how someone really feels. Yet most go unnoticed (see Chapter 9).

Thus far, we've seen how our faces express particular emotions. With a single expression, we can show how angry, happy, disgusted, sad, contemptuous, surprised, afraid, interested, or embarrassed we are. But this is only part of the picture. Imagine the following scenarios:

- Isaac has been laid off. At his office, while packing up his belongings, he exchanges stories with a couple of coworkers about some of the good times they've had.
- Karen is sitting on her favorite recliner at home reading a book. Suddenly, she feels something crawling down her back.

In the first scene, Isaac is depressed about leaving his job, but he can't help feeling amused as he recalls the fun he's had with his coworkers. At any given point in time, he may feel both sad and happy. In the second scene, Karen is jolted by the frightening sensation of feeling an insect crawling down her back. Most likely, she felt both surprise and fear. These examples illustrate what Ekman and Friesen (1975) referred to as **blends**, facial expressions that exhibit more than a single emotion at the same time. Thus, while smiling weakly, Isaac's eyes might reveal a bit of sadness. And Karen's mouth might drop in surprise while her eyes express fear.

As you can probably imagine, many blends are possible given the fact that we often feel more than one emotion at a time. Usually the appearance of a blend involves two different emotions displayed on two different parts of the face. Look carefully at the three pictures of the man shown in Figure 5.2. The two on the left represent the pure emotions of anger (a) and disgust (b). When the eyes of anger are combined with the mouth of disgust, the result is an anger/disgust blend (c) of emotions.

Now, after looking at the pictures in Figure 5.2, take a look at the three pictures of the woman shown in Figure 5.3. How well do you think you can pick out the two blended emotions that appear on each of her faces? (Answers in caption.)

Figure 5.2 Facial expression blend (c) of anger (a) and disgust (b). (Three photos of white male posing two emotions and one blended emotion.)

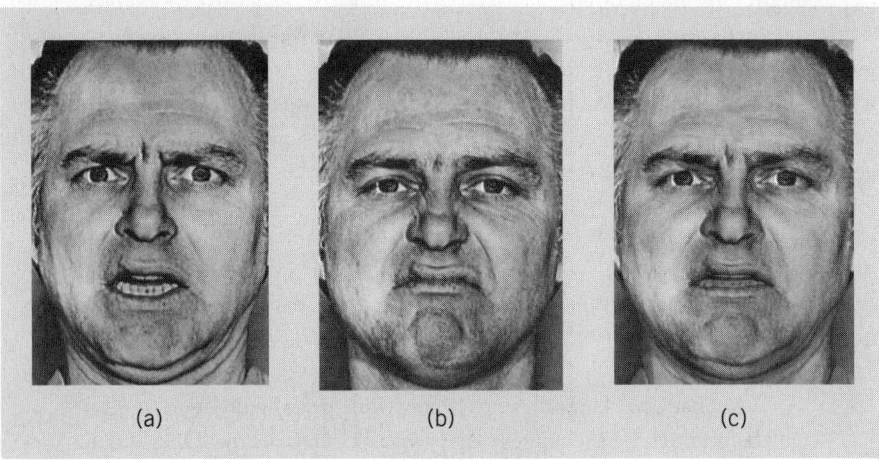

Source: Ekman, P., & Friesen, W. V. (1975). *Unmasking the Face* (p. 109). Englewood Cliffs, NJ: Prentice Hall.

Figure 5.3 Three examples of facial expression blends. (Three photos of white female posing three blended emotions.) Answers to question on previous page: Photo on left is happy and surprised; photo in center is afraid and disgusted; photo on right is angry and sad.

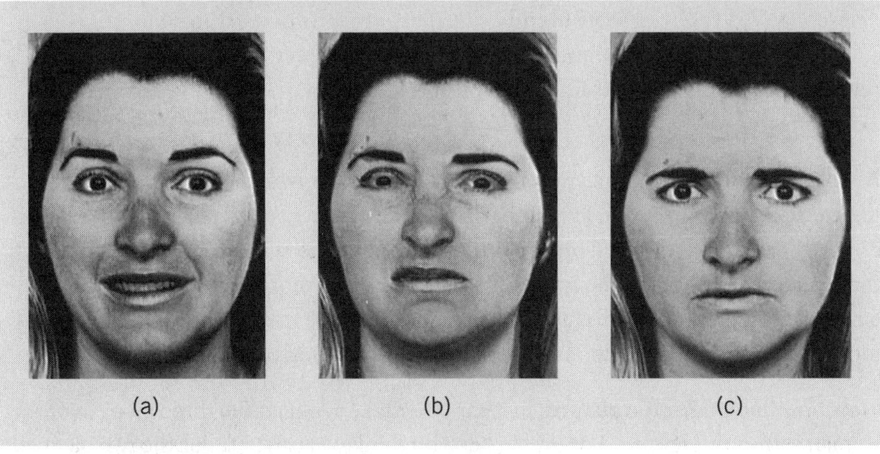

Source: Ekman, P., & Friesen, W. V. (1975). *Unmasking the Face*. Englewood Cliffs, NJ: Prentice Hall.

TRY IT

EXERCISE 5.1

Making Faces

OBJECTIVE: Although many of us would like to express our feelings spontaneously, it's probably more realistic to expect being in situations where we must show an emotion on demand. The purpose of this simple exercise is for you to see what you look like when deliberately showing an emotion on your face.

INSTRUCTIONS: Looking into a mirror, try to imagine the following:

1. Seeing a good friend you haven't seen in a long time (joy).
2. Taking a sip of milk that has gone sour (disgust).
3. Being shoved by someone standing in line behind you (anger).
4. Hearing about the accidental drowning of an infant (sadness).
5. Walking into a room and someone jumps up from behind a sofa (surprise).
6. Enduring job advice from someone you don't respect (contempt).
7. Camping in the wilderness and being confronted by a grizzly bear (fear).

Discussion Questions:

1. Did you experience any difficulty making these faces? Why?
2. How did your expressions compare to those presented in Figure 5.1 and in Table 5.1?
3. Were some emotions easier to convey than others were?

A considerable body of theory and research supports the fundamental claim presented in this chapter that facial expression prototypes exist for certain emotions (Buck, 1984; Darwin, 1872; Eibl-Eibesfeldt, 1975; Ekman, 1972, 1973, 1992; Ekman & Friesen, 1971; Ekman, Friesen, & Ancoli, 1980; Ekman, Sorenson, & Friesen, 1969; Izard, 1977; Tompkins, 1962). From a communication standpoint, the obvious implication is that when Person A feels a particular emotion, such as anger or joy, it shows on her face in a particular way (encoding), and when Person B sees Person A's face, he can correctly interpret how she feels (decoding). As simple and as straightforward as this principle sounds, however, it hasn't always been easy to confirm scientifically in either encoding studies or in decoding studies.

Encoding studies focus on the facial expressions that appear when persons experience particular emotions. They address the following question: Do the facial expressions correspond to those expected for that emotion (i.e., facial prototypes identified in Table 5.1)? When studying posed expressions, a researcher examines the facial expressions that appear as individuals try to look angry, sad, happy, and so on. When studying spontaneous expressions, a researcher tries to either elicit a genuine emotion from someone in a laboratory or capture natural expressions of emotion in real-life situations. Evidence of correspondence between an emotion and an expected facial display comes from various methods of assessment: facial EMG (electromyography), which measures specific muscle contractions; sophisticated coding systems that record visible muscle movements; and observer judgments of emotions shown on the face. While the first two methods can provide direct evidence of a correspondence, observer judgments offer only indirect proof that a particular facial expression prototype (e.g., an enjoyment smile) is or is not being used to convey a particular emotion.

Studies of posed facial expressions that rely on observer judgments show that observers tend to see the particular emotion that the actor is trying to portray (Ekman, 1972, 1973; Galati, Scherer, & Ricci-Bitti, 1997; Gosselin, Kirouac, & Dore, 1995; Motley & Camden, 1988; Tucker & Riggio, 1988; Zuckerman, Hall, DeFrank, & Rosenthal, 1976). Although they do so with less accuracy, observers are also capable of identifying spontaneously expressed emotions, such as those that occur in response to viewing emotionally charged slides (Buck, 1984; Tucker & Riggio, 1988; Wagner, 1990; Zuckerman et al., 1976). But observers may find it more difficult to interpret the kinds of spontaneous expressions of emotion that emerge in social contexts such as conversations (Motley, 1993; Motley & Camden, 1988).

Of course, whether they are accurate or not, observer judgments alone do not prove that people who encode particular emotions do so with the facial prototypes discussed earlier. One approach that researchers have used for this purpose is coding specific facial actions (i.e., noting visible muscle movements). Using an intricate measurement method developed by Ekman and Friesen (1976, 1978) called the *facial action coding system* (FACS), some studies have shown a correspondence between enjoyment smiles—contraction of zygomatic major and orbicularis occuli—and the presence of positive emotions (Ekman & O'Sullivan, 1991a). In one study, for instance, researchers found that individuals who were videotaped watching pleasant films exhibited more enjoyment smiles than other kinds of smiles. In addition, the more they reported being happy, the more likely they were to exhibit enjoyment smiles (Ekman, Friesen, & Ancoli, 1980). Researchers report similar findings in studies of individuals who imagine being in happy situations (Galati et al., 1997) and in studies using facial EMG measurements of muscle contractions (Hess, Banse, & Kappas, 1995).

Yet when it comes to facial expressions of emotions other than enjoyment (e.g., disgust, contempt, fear, etc.), the research often fails to confirm a complete and consistent correspondence between a particular emotion and its facial prototype, leading to questions about whether such a correspondence actually exists (Fernandez-Dols,

Sanchez, Carrera, & Ruiz-Belda, 1997; Galati et al., 1997; Reisenzein, Studtmann, & Horstmann, 2013) or to cautions about the need to consider factors other than emotion (e.g., social context) that directly affect our facial expressions (McIntosh, 1996). Additionally, when researchers fail to find a correspondence between an emotion and an expected facial expression, they remain vulnerable to questions about whether the participants in the study actually felt the emotion in the first place (Ekman & O'Sullivan, 1991a). Still, the controversy over correspondence continues. In a series of experiments, one team of researchers found only a partial correspondence between the emotion of surprise and the prototypical facial expression of surprise (Reisenzein, Bordgen, Holtbernd, & Matz, 2006). The typical expression consisted of eyebrow raises, and only a very small percentage included the full facial expression of surprise (raised brow, widened eyes, dropped jaw).

Shifting the focus away from how we show emotions to how we read them, decoding studies examine the link between a facial prototype and the inferences we make about it. For example, if we see the prototype of disgust (e.g., wrinkled nose, etc.), do we instantly see the person as expressing disgust? In these investigations, researchers usually show respondents pictures of faces conveying an emotion in the expected way (see Table 5.1) and ask them to match the expression with one of the terms provided by the researcher (e.g., disgust, anger, fear, etc.). Using this fixed-choice approach (Rosenberg & Ekman, 1995), studies generally find that respondents select the correct term for each facial expression, although some facial expressions, such as the one for happiness, appear to be more recognizable than are those for other emotions, such as disgust or anger (Ekman & Friesen, 1986; Kirouac & Dore, 1985). The ability to recognize a facial expression of emotion also seems to depend on how frequently we see that facial expression in everyday life (Calvo, Gutierrez-Garcia, Fernandez-Martin, & Nummenmaa, 2014). But the fixed-choice method alone isn't sufficient to substantiate the claim that everyone decodes facial prototypes the same way. By restricting the emotion labels a respondent can use, researchers lose the opportunity to find out whether the respondent's own (i.e., freely chosen) labels match those provided by the researchers. Thus, the fixed-choice approach runs the risk of greatly exaggerating the degree to which people actually recognize facial expression prototypes (Russell, Suzuki, & Ishida, 1993).

In response to this indictment, researchers use alternative methods. To illustrate, we'll highlight the decoding research that has been done on one particular facial expression, that of contempt. In 1986, Paul Ekman and Wallace Friesen announced the discovery of a new pancultural facial expression of emotion. When they asked people from ten countries around the world—Greece, Germany, Turkey, West Sumatra, Italy, Japan, Estonia, Scotland, the United States, and Hong Kong—to label each facial expression depicted in a series of photographs by selecting one of seven possible labels, they found high rates of agreement with the correct label for each expression (Table 5.2).

RESEARCH 5.1

FIND OUT MORE

What Do Facial Expressions Really Say about Our Emotions?

The authors of this article take the position that our recognition of a facial expression of emotion may depend to a considerable degree on the words available to us to label the facial expression. That is, language shapes our understanding of facial expressions, a premise referred to as the *construction hypothesis*.

To find out more about this essay and answer the following questions, see the full text (cited below).

1. What do the authors mean by the "common sense" view of facial expressions?
2. What do the language acquisition studies of children tell us about the importance of words in recognizing facial expressions?
3. What are the implications of the authors' position for lab studies of facial expressions?

Source: Lindquist, K. A., & Gendron, M. (2013). What's in a word? Language constructs emotion perception. *Emotion Review*, 5, 66–71.

Table 5.2 Percentage of Respondents from Ten Countries Correctly Labeling Facial Expressions

Facial Expression	Percentage Correct
Happiness	90.1
Surprise	89.5
Sadness	85.8
Fear	80.4
Contempt	75.0
Disgust	73.8
Anger	73.8

Source: Ekman, P., & Friesen, W. V. (1986). A new pancultural facial expression of emotion. *Motivation and Emotion*, 12, 164.

Of particular interest was the fact that 75% of their respondents selected the term *contempt* as a label for the photographs of a man raising the corner of his lip. As the authors concluded, "The results suggest that the unilateral contempt expression can be considered a pure signal that conveys a highly differentiated message recognized by most people in every culture we studied" (p. 166). Two years later, these results were replicated in an Indonesian sample (Ekman & Heider, 1988) and soon after in Japan, Poland, and Hungary and among Vietnamese immigrants in the United States (Matsumoto, 1992). But the following question persisted: Would as many people label that particular facial expression in the same way, or even in a similar way, if they were free to choose their own label?

James A. Russell decided to seek an answer to his own question (Russell et al., 1993). With two of his colleagues, he asked observers in Canada, Greece, and Japan to label the emotion shown in the same photographs that had been used in the Matsumoto (1992) study. But unlike the original studies, observers here were free to choose their own labels. As expected, this free-response method produced results that were much more difficult to interpret, and observers chose fewer correct labels—when "correct" meant using the same or nearly the same words provided by researchers in the earlier studies—than observers had chosen in the fixed-choice studies. For example, only 37% of Greeks, 58% of Canadians, and 62% of Japanese gave the correct label for the sad facial expression. Yet the rate of agreement jumped dramatically when the researchers used a less strict criterion for determining which labels would be counted as correct. When terms such as disappointment, grief, and regret were accepted, 75% of Greeks, 70% of Canadians, and 80% of Japanese got the right answers. But the facial expression of contempt did not fare well. Regardless of the criterion used, no more than 2% of the respondents answered with a correct label (responses included "indifferent," "skeptical," "bored," "frustrated," etc.).

That observers in the Russell et al. (1993) study, as well as in other free-response studies (Rosenberg & Ekman, 1995), fail to identify the raised lip corner photograph as an expression of contempt probably means that the proposed prototype is much more ambiguous than the fixed-choice investigations led us to believe. Yet, some research suggests that observers may have more trouble thinking of the right words to label the emotion than they have understanding the emotion itself. Erika Rosenberg and Paul Ekman (1995) demonstrated that when given the opportunity to match a facial expression with a situation in which such an expression might occur, observers make the right choices. For instance, 93.5% of their American sample paired the contempt expression with a situation in which "the person hears an acquaintance bragging about accomplishing something for which the acquaintance was not responsible" (p. 136). While the results of this study certainly bolster Ekman and Friesen's (1986) initial claim, questions remain and research continues (Wagner, 2000). In one study, for instance, Matsumoto (2005) found that American and Japanese participants asked to identify emotions in a range of facial expressions accurately judged expressions of contempt, although the American participants were more likely than the Japanese participants to see anger and disgust in the contempt expressions.

Decoding studies on the facial expression of contempt and other emotions demonstrate the importance of using different methods of research as a safeguard against premature conclusions. In addition, decoding studies have improved our understanding of the many factors that directly influence the meaning of a facial expression. One such factor is the *intensity* of the expression. Research indicates that with the exception of smiling faces, which we recognize easily, our ability to identify an emotion from someone's facial expression may depend partly on how intensely the pattern appears on that person's face (Hess, Blairy, & Kleck, 1997). This finding explains why studies routinely show that people have much less difficulty recognizing posed expressions (i.e., high intensity) than they have recognizing spontaneous expressions (i.e., low to moderate intensity). Another factor that alters our recognition and interpretation of a facial expression is the *context* in which it appears (Hassin, Aviezer, & Benin, 2013; Parkinson, 2013). Some experiments show that we may place more weight on the situation a person is in than on the facial expression we see on his or her face. For example, researchers in one study found that most individuals believed that a man shown with a fearful facial expression was in fact angry when they were told he just saw some kids stealing the hubcaps from his new car (Carroll & Russell, 1996). Interpretations of facial expressions also depend on emotions conveyed through other nonverbal channels. Researchers showed photographs of people with the people's faces conveying anger or fear while their bodies conveyed a matched (fearful face and fearful body) or mismatched (fearful face and angry body) emotion. Participants were more likely to see the person in the mismatched photographs as feeling the emotion conveyed through the body than through the face (Meeren, van Heijnsbergen, & Gelder, 2005).

Despite the complexities of accurately recognizing emotional expressions and the difficulties social scientists have encountered, the weight of evidence still seems to favor the long-standing view that certain facial expression prototypes are encoded and decoded essentially the same way by everyone (Frank & Stennett, 2001; Haidt & Keltner, 1999; Matsumoto & Hwang, 2014). But before we leave our discussion of the emotion function of facial expression, we need to consider several fundamental processes—intrapersonal and interpersonal—that explain further the unique way our facial expressions of emotion shape the way we communicate with others.

THE INTRAPERSONAL DOMAIN Although our central concern in this chapter is with facial expression as a form of interpersonal communication, this section briefly addresses the private, intrapersonal domain and the light it sheds on the role of facial expressions in social situations. As discussed here, the intrapersonal domain takes the perspective of either encoding or decoding, but not both, as does the interpersonal domain. For example, if we focus only on the encoder or expresser of emotions, we might include a discussion of (1) adaptive behavior—emotions motivate us to act in ways that have survival value (e.g., joy promotes bonding, anger helps us overcome obstacles, etc.), (2) antecedents—the various events that produce emotional reactions (e.g., what causes one person to feel sad may not cause another person to feel the same way), and (3) consequences—how we personally understand, experience, and cope with our emotions.

▸ Scientific studies show that changing our facial expression changes the way we feel.

istockphoto.com/Minerva Studio

To illustrate a focus on the encoder or expresser of emotion, you may recall that in the opening of this chapter, we introduced the idea that our facial expressions can affect the way we feel. This idea is not new. Known in the scientific literature as the **facial feedback hypothesis**, it was considered at length during the latter part of the nineteenth century in the emotion theories of both Charles Darwin (1872) and William James (1890). Put simply, it says that an individual's facial expression of an emotion can directly and immediately influence the individual's experience of that emotion. Despite the apparent simplicity of the idea and the fact that scholars have been speculating about it for well over a century, solid scientific backing has only begun to surface.

The impetus to begin testing the idea came from an early experiment conducted by psychologist John Lanzetta and his colleagues. They discovered that individuals who received electric shocks but who pretended not to feel any pain actually experienced less pain and showed fewer physiological reactions than another group of individuals who pretended to feel unbearable pain (Lanzetta, Cartright-Smith, & Kleck, 1976). Studies have shown a similar effect when examining how changes in facial expressions of basic emotions alter the experience of those emotions. The most convincing studies are those that devise ingenious ways of getting volunteers to form facial expression prototypes unknowingly, so that they are blind to the researcher's hypothesis and thus unable to tell the researcher simply what they think the researcher wants to hear.

In one such study, investigators found that individuals who were instructed to hold a pen between their teeth, which contracts the muscles, producing a smiling mouth, thought that the cartoons they read were funnier than did individuals who were instructed to hold a pen between their lips or in their hand (Strack, Martin, & Stepper, 1988). Other researchers have directed individuals to produce facial expressions by pronouncing certain vowels. In one study, individuals who read a story with a lot of *u* sounds, which create frowning or scowling expressions, reported being in a worse mood than were individuals who read a story with no *u* sounds (Zajonc, Murphy, & Inglehart, 1989). In another study, researchers learned that physiological changes associated with positive or negative emotions take place while just repeating certain vowel sounds. Voicing the *u* sound increased forehead temperature, which is associated with negative feelings, whereas voicing the *e* sound, which produces a smiling mouth, had the opposite effect. The participants in the study also enjoyed repeating the *e* sound more than they enjoyed repeating the *u* sound (McIntosh, 1996). More often than not, studies tend to support the main thesis underlying the facial feedback hypothesis (McHugo & Smith, 1996; McIntosh, 1996). The look on your face may indeed influence the emotions you feel.

The intrapersonal domain is not limited to a focus on the person who expresses emotions; it can also consider the decoder or interpreter of facial expressions apart from the encoder or expresser of emotions. One example of this perspective deals with how we sometimes read emotions into faces that aren't expressing or encoding any emotion. A person's face might be neutral; none of the muscles in the face are activated in a manner that represents an emotional expression. Yet we may see an emotion in the person's face because the face objectively resembles an emotion. This **emotion overgeneralization hypothesis** has been supported in numerous studies and certainly resonates with any of us who recalls seeing someone who looked sad, happy, or angry even though he or she denied feeling that way. In one study, for instance, researchers found a gender difference in emotion overgeneralization. Men's neutral faces were more likely than women's faces to objectively resemble anger, whereas women's neutral faces were more likely to objectively resemble surprise; and consistent with their hypothesis, participants in the study who viewed male neutral faces were more likely to infer that the men were angry than the women were and that the women were more surprised than the men were (Zebrowitz, Kikuchi, & Fellous, 2010).

THE INTERPERSONAL DOMAIN Thus far, we've looked at facial expressions of emotion while paying little attention to the social sphere in which these expressions occur. In this section, we'll highlight three ways that others become involved in the process of emotional communication, making it an interpersonal phenomenon: (1) catching the emotions of others, (2) following display rules, and (3) signaling intentions.

When you're with a friend who's depressed, do you find yourself getting the blues? When you see someone laughing, do you feel yourself starting to grin? These questions address a subject that came up briefly in Chapter 2: emotional contagion. **Emotional contagion** generally refers to a phenomenon in which emotions spread from person to person. While experts may not agree completely on how this happens, they tend to see the process as relatively automatic and unconscious. One theory, known as *primitive emotional contagion*, maintains that we catch others' emotions by means of a two-step process: (1) emotional mimicry and synchrony and (2) facial, vocal, and postural feedback (Hatfield, Cacioppo, & Rapson, 1994). Although the process involves much more than facial expression, our focus in this chapter will limit the discussion to those studies dealing only with **facial mimicry** (Step 1) and facial feedback (Step 2). Ample scientific evidence appears to have removed most doubt about whether the phenomenon takes place. Less clear, however, is our knowledge of how many emotions are involved, since most studies only show contagion for happiness and sadness (Hess, 2001; Wild, Erb, & Bartels, 2001).

▸ Emotional contagion represents one way that our facial expressions involve us in the process of interpersonal influence. Shared emotions create strong bonds between individuals and among the members of social groups.

istockphoto.com/pappamaart

Studies show that facial mimicry occurs quickly and automatically. Facial mimicry means mirroring the facial expression of another person. Sometimes it occurs in a way that's easy to see: cheering with others at a football game, sobbing with others at a funeral, yawning with others at a late-night meeting, and so on. Compelling evidence in support of facial mimicry has been accumulating for quite some time (Lishner, Cooter, & Zald, 2008). Developmental research shows that infants, even at birth, often mimic the facial expressions they see (Field, Woodson, Greenberg, & Cohen, 1982). Observations of many animal species support the notion that emotional mimicry may be a highly adaptive form of behavior (studies cited in Hatfield et al., 1994). But perhaps the most convincing evidence for the occurrence of facial mimicry comes from EMG studies that monitor facial muscle movements. In these studies, researchers can detect slight changes in facial expressions that might otherwise go unnoticed. In one of the first studies, psychologist Ulf Dimberg (1982) demonstrated that mere exposure to a facial expression is sufficient to produce muscle movements in observers that mirror the expression they see: Looking at an angry face activates the corrugator muscle (i.e., frowning); looking at a happy face contracts the zygomatic major (i.e., smiling mouth). Dimberg and his colleagues have replicated these findings in numerous studies (Dimberg & Ohman, 1996). And in a more recent study with a Japanese sample, researchers observed facial mimicry in response to happy, sad, angry, and disgusted expressions (Tamura & Kameda, 2006). Interestingly, new research shows that mimicry is more likely to occur in response to authentic rather than inauthentic facial expressions. For example, an enjoyment smile that activates the eye muscles as well as the mouth muscles is more likely to produce mimicry than a non-enjoyment smile that does not activate the muscles around the eyes (Krumhuber et al., 2014). It may also be the case, as one recent study demonstrated, that without some degree of facial mimicry, we may be less likely to notice the difference between a genuine enjoyment smile and a false non-enjoyment smile (Maringer, Krumhuber, Fischer, & Niedenthl, 2011).

What remains less clear than the occurrence of facial mimicry is the extent to which these rapid facial reactions are simply motor reflexes followed by an emotional response or whether they are the result of instantaneously shared emotions. For instance, researchers have shown that feeling fear while viewing an angry face is more likely to produce a fearful facial expression than a facial expression of anger (Moody, McIntosh, Mann, & Weisser, 2007). In addition, the occurrence of facial mimicry may depend to some extent on a person's mood. In a recent study, researchers found that participants were less likely to mimic a facial expression when they were in a sad mood (after watching a sad movie) than when they were in a happy mood (after watching a happy movie). To explain these results, the researchers theorized that being in a sad mood compared to being in a happy mood leads a person to pay more attention to one's self rather than to the actions of others, which might lessen the occurrence of mimicry (Likowski et al., 2011).

The process of emotional contagion also involves facial feedback. John Lanzetta and his coworkers have shown repeatedly how contagion occurs through facial mimicry and feedback. In one study, they examined participants' reactions to a televised comedy routine (Bush, Barr, McHugo, & Lanzetta, 1989). To study the occurrence of facial mimicry, they permitted half the participants to see reaction shots of laughing studio audience members; the other half did not see these shots. To study facial feedback, they instructed half the participants to inhibit their facial expressions (they were told that doing so would interfere with the electrodes attached to their faces), while the other half were told to be spontaneous, to relax and enjoy the show. EMG activity in the faces of participants who were allowed to be spontaneous revealed greater zygomatic major and orbicularis oculi activity (i.e., of the enjoyment smile muscles) among those who saw audience laughter than among those who didn't see audience laughter—clear evidence of facial mimicry. Those who saw the reaction shots thought the routines were funnier than did those who didn't see the audience—support for the occurrence of facial feedback. But stronger support came when comparing the spontaneous and inhibited participants: Spontaneous participants, who were allowed to smile, thought that the routines were funnier than did the inhibited participants.

Emotional contagion represents one way that our facial expressions involve us in the process of interpersonal influence. Another way is when we design a facial expression for the sake of others. We may choose to spare another person's feelings, for example, by not showing the hurt we feel when he or she lets us down. Or we may choose to put on a happy face even when we're feeling bitter or depressed. These choices reflect our ability to manage our facial expressions—to follow rules about what we regard as an acceptable public performance in a particular situation. These display rules put pressure on us to pose. We generally succumb to this pressure in four ways (Ekman & Friesen, 1969b). One way is by neutralizing an affect. This occurs when a felt emotion registers on the face as a blank or neutral expression, as in the case of a prize fighter who doesn't want to look afraid. Another way is by overintensifying an affect, or showing more of an emotion than what is actually felt. Imagine an attorney, for instance, who wants to intimidate a hostile witness and shows more anger on her face than she really feels. A third way is by deintensifying an affect. Sometimes we underplay or show less of an emotion than what is actually felt. An example of this is the college graduate who, overjoyed about landing a great job, is restrained in showing his feelings around his less fortunate friends. Masking an affect is a fourth way that display rules can shape our expressions. This occurs when we substitute one expression of emotion (mask) for another (felt). Smiling usually serves this purpose. For example, a good-natured husband is angry at his wife for making fun of him in public, but he smiles with everyone else. Everyday pressures to be polite, friendly, or to lighten up result in false smiles, the most common type of masking behavior.

EXERCISE 5.2

TRY IT

Lying Faces

OBJECTIVE: To identify and discuss the display rules people use every day.

INSTRUCTIONS: For each of the personal experiences below, indicate the kind of display rule that the person is following:

1. Neutralizing
2. Overintensifying
3. Deintensifying
4. Masking

Two summers ago, my best friend and I were both applying for a camp counselor position. The pay was great and it sounded like such a great time. Since there were many spots open for camp counselors, we both assumed we'd get the job. We had interviews and were very excited and eager to do it. She found out that she didn't get picked for the job and she was very disappointed. Well, I did get the job and I was thrilled, but when I told her, I pretended like it wasn't that big a deal because I didn't want to make her feel bad. (Christine)

One time when I was in my friend's car, he asked me how I liked the new CD he was playing. Even though I couldn't stand it, I told him it was pretty cool. I didn't want him

(Continued)

EXERCISE 5.2

(Continued)

to know how I really felt. I had to keep my face from giving anything away so I kept an interested look on my face to pretend that I really liked it. (Dan)

I'm involved in a sorority on campus. We had elections for the executive board for the next school year. I was running for vice president of committees, and the other candidate was one of my roommates, who has been in the sorority less than me and knows less than I do about it. Well, she won the election. I had to sit there all composed and act like I wasn't mad or upset, but I was fuming. (Jennifer)

Discussion Questions

1. Should each of the above persons have been honest in showing their feelings instead? Why?
2. Can you think of a personal experience that illustrates each of the four display rules?

EXERCISE 5.3

TRY IT

What Rules Do You Follow?

INSTRUCTIONS: Indicate the type of emotional display rule you generally follow when with family members, close friends, people you work with, and strangers. Please choose among the following list for each situation noted in the table below:

1. Express the feeling as is, without inhibition
2. Express the feeling, but with less intensity than your true feelings
3. Express the feeling, but with more intensity than your true feelings
4. Try to remain neutral; express nothing
5. Express the feeling, but together with a smile to qualify your feelings
6. Smile only, with no trace of anything else, in order to mask/hide your feelings

Emotion	Family	Close Friends	Colleagues	Strangers
Sadness				
Anger				

EXERCISE 5.3

Emotion	Family	Close Friends	Colleagues	Strangers
Happiness				
Disgust				
Contempt				
Fear				
Surprise				

Source: Adapted from Matsumoto, D., Yoo, S., Hirayama, S., & Petrova, G. (2005). Development and validation of a measure of display rule knowledge. *Emotion*, 5, 23–40.

Display rules explain why many of the facial expressions we exhibit in the presence of others may not reflect our true feelings. Although we might follow these rules without much thinking, our facial expressions are still more posed than they are spontaneous. But even spontaneous expressions of emotion often seem to require an audience. Some scholars believe the reason for these audience effects is that facial expressions evolved to signal our intentions to others. When understood as social signals, it's easy to see why facial expressions of emotion often don't show up without an audience. Known as the **behavioral ecology theory**, this view of facial expressions has attracted considerable attention in recent years (Fridlund, 1994).

PERSONAL EXPERIENCE 5.3

CAN YOU RELATE TO THIS?

A Facial Expression Can Mask Our True Feelings

My boyfriend recently came back from Ireland. Before he left, I joked about a present I wanted. I said, "Bring me back a leprechaun." I really didn't want or expect a leprechaun, so when he returned and handed me my present, I was excited to find out what it was. I opened the gift and unwrapped a ceramic leprechaun. It was the most ridiculous gift I had ever received. I was so disappointed, but I had to pretend that I loved it. With a surprised and happy look, I said, "Oh my god, you got me a leprechaun. It's so cute."

Amy

Studies confirm the presence of **audience effects**. In one provocative laboratory study, psychologist Janet Bavelas and her colleagues discovered that even spontaneous acts of facial mimicry, such as wincing in pain when seeing another person wincing in pain, was a more likely occurrence when eye contact could be made with the person than when no eye contact was possible (Bavelas, Black, Lemery, & Mullett, 1986). In everyday contexts, we also tend to show our enjoyment more when others can see us than when they can't. In a well-known series of field studies, two social psychologists, Robert Kraut and Robert Johnson (1979), found audience effects among bowlers, hockey fans, and pedestrians in Ithaca, New York. Bowlers were more likely to smile after making a strike or a spare when facing their friends than when facing the pins; hockey fans smiled more after their team made a good play when they were turned toward their friends than when they were not; and pedestrians smiled more in nice weather than in bad weather, but they still smiled more in the company of others—regardless of the weather. Some research leaves less doubt about whether these audience-induced smiles are really spontaneous (i.e., true enjoyment smiles) rather than false smiles. Using the FACS procedure for assessing facial expressions, one team of researchers observed that Olympic gold medalists at the 1992 Barcelona Games showed more genuine happiness during the awards ceremony when they were interacting with others than when they were not (Fernandez-Dols & Ruiz-Belda, 1995). A recent study on laughter also confirms the presence of audience effects. Participants who viewed a funny video clip were more likely to laugh in the presence of friends or strangers than they were when alone, regardless of how funny they thought the clip was. Thus, the presence of others had a much stronger effect on their facial expressions than did their emotional reaction to the stimulus (Devereux & Ginsberg, 2001).

But most of the research on audience effects focuses on positive emotions. One recent study on facial expressions of sadness failed to support the behavioral ecology view. In this study, participants who watched a sad film in the presence of others were less likely to show sadness than were the participants who watched the film alone (Jakobs, Manstead, & Fischer, 2001). In addition, a field study of Olympic medal winners of the judo competition at the 2004 Athens Olympics Games, in contrast to the Barcelona study noted above, did not reveal more genuine expressions of emotion in social contexts (Matsumoto & Willingham, 2006). In line with the notion of display rules, the researchers found that the gold medalists were equally happy at the end of the match and on the podium receiving their medals (enjoyment smiles), whereas the silver medalists showed no joy at the completion of their matches and showed much less genuine happiness on the podium receiving their medals but still showed no signs of being a sore loser (posed and masking smiles, happy/sad facial blends, and neutral expressions).

Table 5.3 Facial Expressions of Emotion as Social Signals

Emotion	Intention
Enjoyment smile	"Let's play."
False (social) smile	"Okay with me."
Sadness	"Help me."
Anger	"Back off or I'll attack."
Fear	"If you continue, I'll back off."
Contempt	"I can't even bother with you."

Source: Adapted from Fridlund, A. J. (1994). *Human facial expression: An evolutionary view*. New York, NY: Academic Press.

Supporters of the behavioral ecology view of facial expressions stress the social signaling function of facial expressions in lieu of the emotion function. The extreme view is that facial expressions do not convey emotions at all but only the intentions arising out of a social situation (Chovil, 1991; Fernandez-Dols & Ruiz-Belda, 1995; Fridlund, 1994, 1997). Advocates of this view see no connection between our true emotions and our facial expressions. Accordingly, they reject the idea that some facial expressions of emotion are genuine whereas others are phony (i.e., posed according to display rules). Instead, they suggest that facial expressions differ only according to the intention they communicate (see Table 5.3). A common reaction to the extreme behavioral ecology view is that facial expressions are influenced by both emotion and audience effects rather than one or the other (Buck, 1991; Hess et al., 1995) and that audience effects often depend on the role of the audience (a participant who shares our emotions will affect us differently than an observer will) and the particular emotion being expressed (Jakobs, Fischer, & Manstead, 1997).

We've devoted nearly all of this chapter to the emotion function of facial expression because of the prevailing and well-supported view that this is the primary function of facial expressions. In all likelihood, we encode and decode certain basic emotions in a way that is universally shared. Research on facial feedback, emotional contagion, display rules, and audience effects shows how facial expression of emotion is an important intrapersonal as well as interpersonal phenomenon.

The benefits of participating in a face-to-face interaction would be lost if we couldn't see each other's facial expressions. Because we use our faces not only to convey

RESEARCH 5.2

FIND OUT MORE

How Do Our Facial Expressions Affect Other People?

In this article, the author proposes a model that can be used to predict how people will respond to our emotional expressions. To support the model, the author discusses research that has been done on the effects of emotional expressions on the thinking patterns and behavior of people in everyday life. Included in this review of the literature are studies dealing with personal relationships, parent–child interactions, conflict, negotiation, and leadership.

To find out more about this research review and to answer the following questions, see the full text (cited below).

1. Identify any one of the basic processes involved in the Emotions as Social Information (EASI) model and explain how it works.
2. In his concluding remarks, the author poses a number of questions that arise from his model, which suggest future directions in research relevant to sports, parenting, and politics. What are these questions?

Source: Van Kleef, G. A. (2009). How emotions regulate social life: The Emotions as Social Information (EASI) model. *Current Directions in Psychological Science*, 18, 184–188.

emotions but to serve all the functions associated with nonverbal communication, we would miss out on a great deal. In the sections that follow, we'll examine how facial expressions can signal identity, deliver verbal or symbolic messages, and help establish relationships with others.

Identification

Another function of facial expression is identification. This is not to say that our facial expressions reveal who we are, only that differences in environment and heredity can explain why all of us are not the same when it comes to showing emotion, reacting to facial expressions, or following display rules. Despite the similarities in how people encode and decode facial expressions of emotion, researchers continue to discover important differences as well. In this section, we present the results of research on the impact of culture, gender, and personality and behavior.

CULTURE Cultural differences are particularly important because we may not be aware of them to the same extent that we are familiar with gender or personality differences. As we noted above in our discussion of facial emblems, there are cultural differences in the meaning of certain facial gestures. To some degree, there is also evidence of an ethnic bias in the recognition of facial expressions; that is, we may experience less difficulty labeling the expressions of those from our own ethnic group than we experience labeling the expressions of those from other ethnic groups. Comparisons among African, Asian, and white facial expressions provide some evidence of this bias (Derntl et al., 2012; Ducci et al., 1982; Izard, 1971; Kilbride & Yarczower, 1983; Weathers, Frank, & Spell, 2002). In a review and summary of these cross-cultural studies, one team of investigators confirmed an "in-group" advantage for recognizing facial expressions of emotion. But they emphasized that the advantage was smaller for cultural groups with greater exposure to one another, such as living in the same nation, having close physical proximity, and having access to telephone communication. Interestingly, they also observed a recognition bias related to differences in status: Members of lower status cultural groups were more accurate at decoding the facial expressions of individuals from higher-status cultural groups than the reverse. Lower-status persons generally need to pay more attention to the faces of higher-status persons, since the latter tend to have greater access to sources of power (i.e., rewards and punishments) than do the former (Elfenbein & Ambady, 2002). Some researchers have also suggested that there is less evidence of an in-group advantage for spontaneous compared to posed expressions of emotion (Matsumoto, Olide, & Willingham, 2009).

One proposed explanation for a cultural bias in recognizing facial expressions of emotion is the **dialect theory** of facial expressions (Elfenbein, Beaupré, Lévesque, & Hess, 2007). This theory, while accepting the principle that communicating emotion is universal, rests on two basic propositions: (1) As with other languages, different cultures can express themselves in different dialects and (2) the presence of dialects has the potential to make recognition of emotion less accurate across cultural boundaries. In a study comparing the posed facial expressions of participants from Quebec and from the West African nation of Gabon, researchers observed significant cultural variations in the participants' facial expressions of contempt, shame, and serenity and also in their facial expressions of anger, sadness, surprise, and happiness. The researchers also found support for an in-group bias. Participants were better able to recognize their own facial expression dialect than that of the other cultural group (Elfenbein et al., 2007). Like learning a new language, proponents of dialect theory believe that the in-group advantage is minimized or even eliminated with increased exposure to other cultural groups as well as greater assimilation into another culture (Elfenbein, 2013).

Cultural and racial stereotypes can also bias our perceptions of facial expressions, particularly in response to the faces of group members we regard as threatening in some way. In one experiment, white undergraduate students were primed by the researchers to feel fear by viewing a scary scene from the movie, *Silence of the Lambs*, and then asked to rate the intensity of emotions expressed on different faces. The researchers hypothesized that arousing fear in the participants would cause them to see more danger in the faces of some people than in others, based on cultural and racial stereotyping. As expected, the students perceived greater anger in black male faces and in Arab faces than in the faces of other "less threatening" groups (Maner et al., 2005).

RESEARCH 5.3

FIND OUT MORE

How Does Culture Influence Our Judgments of Facial Expressions?

This research was designed to study how culture can affect our interpretation of facial expressions. One finding from past research on facial expressions is that persons from East Asian cultures are more inclined than persons from Western cultures to incorporate elements of the *context* in their judgments of facial expressions. One important element of the context is the specific situation that makes a person feel angry, sad, disgusted, and so forth. When interpreting a facial expression, which is more important: the facial expression you see or the emotional context that may produce a particular facial expression? The authors hypothesize that one's culture may influence which factor is more important.

To find out more about this study and to answer the following questions, see the full text (cited below).

1. What do the authors mean by the term *context differentiation?*
2. In their study, how were vignettes and facial expressions used to test their hypotheses?
3. What was the main difference between U.S., Korean, and Japanese participants?
4. What type of research is this? (See Appendix.)
5. What were the main limitations of this study?

Source: Matsumoto, D., Hwang, H. S., & Yamada, H. (2012). Cultural differences in the relative contributions of face and context to the judgment of emotions, *Journal of Cross-Cultural Psychology*, 43, 198–218.

Another line of inquiry focuses on how certain sociopsychological dimensions of culture—shared values and beliefs—shape the way we use and interpret emotional displays. Early research on cultural display rules, for example, uncovered the reason why Japanese were more likely than Americans to conceal negative emotions with masking smiles: Japanese were following a rule that encouraged them to promote positive relations with others (Ekman, 1972). Recent studies continue to confirm differences in display rules. For example, a study of 2,000 photographs of individuals from 10 different countries posted on an Internet website indicated that individuals from Western countries were more likely to smile in their photograph than were individuals from Eastern European countries. This cultural difference seems to support the idea that Eastern Europeans regard a posed smile as insincere whereas Western Europeans are more likely to regard a posed smile as polite and friendly (Szarota, 2010).

In addition to these cultural display rules, research also indicates the existence of **decoding rules**, "culturally prescribed rules learned early in life that manage the perception and interpretation of others emotional expressions" (Matsumoto, Kasri, & Kooken, 1999, p. 202). For example, studies show that Japanese consistently rate facial expressions of emotion as less intense than Americans do. Researchers speculate that because Japanese learn to inhibit and mask emotional displays in everyday life, they may also tend to see less emotion in the faces of others (Ekman et al., 1987; Matsumoto, 1989, 1990; Matsumoto & Ekman, 1989). In a follow-up investigation, Matsumoto and his colleagues were interested in possible differences between intensity ratings among Japanese and Americans of both facial expressions (other's outward display of emotion) and felt emotions (other's inward experience of emotion). In line with earlier studies, they found that Japanese rated facial expressions of emotion as less intense than Americans did. But they also discovered that Americans tended to rate a person's facial expression of emotion as being more intense than that person's felt emotion. The researchers suggest that Americans may be following a decoding rule that accounts for their tendency to express more emotion in many situations than they actually feel, a tendency rarely found in Japanese culture (Matsumoto et al., 1999).

Taking as his starting point the basic idea that our facial expressions conform to cultural display rules, psychologist David Matsumoto (1990, 1991) used two well-known dimensions of cultural variability, individualism/collectivism and **power distance** (Hofstede, 1980, 1983), to develop a provocative and far-reaching theory of how culture influences facial expressions of emotion. **Individualistic cultures** promote the needs and interests of the individual, encouraging members to become unique and self-important. In contrast, **collectivistic cultures** promote group harmony and favor group over individual needs. A person's identity in collectivistic cultures is much more rooted in group affiliations than is the identity of a person in an individualistic society. According to Matsumoto's theory, because individualistic cultures encourage self-expression, its members are relatively free to display a range of emotions, positive or negative, toward others. In addition, the politeness rules most people follow prompt individuals to be friendly, smiling at others, regardless of who they are. But in collectivistic cultures, people learn to put the needs of the group ahead of their own needs. This pressures them to suppress negative emotions (e.g., anger, disgust, sadness) toward in-group members because the display of such emotions will upset the harmony of the group. Yet there is little pressure to conceal negative emotions or to show positive emotions toward out-group persons. The lack of group affiliation with such persons lessens the pressure to promote positive relations.

The second component in Matsumoto's theory focuses on the power distance orientation of a culture—the degree to which it promotes the maintenance of status differences among members. High power distance cultures endorse displays of emotion that reinforce hierarchical relations (i.e., status reminders), such as showing anger toward a low-status person or appeasing a high-status person (e.g., smiling). Low power distance cultures embrace egalitarian values and teach the importance of treating people as equals. Thus, there is less pressure in these cultures for members to adjust displays of emotion according to the status of another person. Although it isn't always the case, high power distance cultures tend to be collectivistic, whereas low power distance cultures tend to be individualistic. For instance, high power distance/collectivistic cultures include most Arab, Latin American, African, Asian, and southern European nations. Low power distance/individualistic cultures include South Africa, North America, Australia, and northern Europe (Hofstede, 1980, 1983).

Research confirms some of these cultural differences. In one study comparing Americans (individualistic/low power distance) and Japanese (collectivistic/high power distance), Matsumoto (1990) found that Americans were more likely than the Japanese to approve of showing disgust and sadness in the company of close friends and family members (in-group contexts). Americans were also more likely to endorse smiling in public (out-group context) and less likely to consider expressions of anger as appropriate with casual acquaintances (out-group context) or with low-status individuals. In another study comparing Americans with Costa Ricans (collectivistic), researchers found that Costa Ricans felt less comfortable expressing anger toward family members than did Americans (Stephan, Stephan, & DeVargas, 1996).

Studies also show an interesting difference between East Asian and Western cultures in recognizing and interpreting facial expressions of emotion. Persons in East Asian cultures tend to prefer holistic approaches when interpreting a message compared to persons in Western cultures. In other words, East Asian cultures, according to this view, are more likely to consider the overall context in their interpretation of a facial expression than Western cultures are. In two experiments, researchers found that when interpreting emotions, Japanese observers were more likely to gaze at surrounding individuals and to incorporate information from the facial expressions of surrounding individuals than Westerners were (Masuda et al., 2008).

GENDER We can't fully understand facial expressions without considering the impact of gender. As we discovered in Chapter 2, studies generally indicate that, compared to males, females are more expressive and somewhat better at recognizing facial expressions of emotion. For instance, a large-scale study of more than 7,000 participants confirmed that women were better able than men to correctly identify facial expressions of emotion, with men demonstrating a particular tendency to not see an emotion on the face when an emotion is shown compared to women (Sasson, Pinkham, Hughett, Gur, & Gur, 2010). Males and females also don't follow the same display rules. Societal expectations and stereotypes about how men and women are supposed to behave probably explain many gender differences. Studies show, for instance, that we expect women to express so-called feminine (i.e., submissive and nonthreatening) emotions, such as happiness, shame, fear, embarrassment, and sadness, more often than men do. In contrast, we expect more displays of "masculine" (i.e., dominant and threatening) emotions from men: anger, contempt, disgust, and pride (Algoe, Buswell, & DeLamater, 2000; Plant, Hyde, Keltner, & Devine, 2000). Several studies confirm these expectations. In one study, women who saw frightening pictures showed more fear on their faces than did men who saw the same pictures. But, as the researchers also discovered, the men and women did not differ on other measures of fear. Women may have shown more, but they didn't feel more fear than the men did (Thunberg & Dimberg, 2000). The ability to convey an emotion may also confirm gender expectations. Researchers in one study asked men and women to discuss with a same-sex experimenter three emotional experiences they have had. While the women did a better job conveying happiness, the men did a better job conveying anger (Coats & Feldman, 1996). Gender stereotypes may directly influence how we interpret the facial expressions of men and women. In one interesting experiment, researchers showed participants male and female pictures of anger and sadness facial blends—one image showed anger in the upper face and sadness in the lower face; another showed sadness in the upper face and anger in the lower face. Consistent with gender stereotypes, participants tended to see more anger in the male faces and more sadness in the female faces (Plant et al., 2000). A follow-up study using images of the same facial expression blends but digitally altering the gender of the image, produced the same results (Plant, Kling, & Smith, 2004). In a related study, researchers found that participants saw more anger and contempt and less fear in the posed facial expressions of men than they did in the same facial expressions of women (Algoe et al., 2000). Finally, there is some evidence that women are more likely than men are to catch the emotions of others, that they are more susceptible to emotional contagion (Doherty, Orimoto, Singelis, Hatfield, & Hebb, 1995). But in one recent experiment, gender differences were only slight (Wild et al., 2001).

Much of the research on gender and facial expression shows that females in various social situations and in posed photographs usually smile more than males do (Brennan-Parks, Goddard, Wilson, & Kinnear, 1991; Dovidio, Brown, Heltman, Ellyson, & Keating, 1988; Halberstadt, Hayes, & Pike, 1988; Hall, Horgan, & Carter, 2002; Hall, LeBeau, Reinoso, & Thayer, 2001; Henley, 1977; Mills, 1984;

▸ Gender differences in displays of emotion may reflect societal norms about the "feminine" behavior we expect from women and the "masculine" behavior we expect from men.

istockphoto.com/killerb10

LaFrance & Hecht, 1999), a finding not limited to male–female comparisons in the United States but in many other countries as well (Gueguen, 2010; Szarota, 2010). Some scholars contend that women have been smiling more than men have for a long time. Researchers Mark Desantis and Nathan Sierra (2000) examined photographs of adult females and males taken for various occasions in the United States throughout the twentieth century. They found that, in nearly every type of photographic category, women smiled more than men did, and when both sexes smiled, the female smile tended to be a fuller smile. These findings are consistent with the idea that there is more social pressure on females to smile than there is on males. They also raise the possibility that women are more likely than men to smile strategically, whereas men are more likely than women to limit their smiles to the expression of positive emotions (LaFrance & Mayo, 1979). Of particular interest is how we regard men and women who resist the pressure to conform. For example, in one study, researchers discovered that photographs of unsmiling women were judged more harshly (e.g., less happy, carefree, and relaxed) than were photographs of unsmiling men (Deutsch, LeBaron, & Fryer, 1987). Some scholars contend that the pressure placed on women to smile represents a subtle form of gender discrimination (Henley, 1977).

PERSONALITY AND BEHAVIOR Facial expressions as well as reactions to and interpretations of facial expressions reveal information about people other than their gender and culture. For instance, we have learned that certain types of people, known as *self-monitors*, seem to be especially good at posing and reading facial expressions. We also learned that individuals with outgoing, extroverted personalities tend to be more emotionally expressive than individuals who are withdrawn and introverted. In a study of American and German adults, researchers found that extroverts reported more of a tendency to laugh than did introverts (Ruch & Deckers, 1993). Observations of German preschool children at play showed that children whose parents described them as shy exhibited fewer facial expressions of interest and more negative facial expressions than did children who were not rated as shy by their parents (Unzner & Schneider, 1990).

One study found that extroverts' brains respond more emotionally to a smiling face than do the brains of introverts. There were no differences in brain responses to facial expressions of fear (Canli, Silvers, Gotlib, & Gabrieli, 2002). In addition, research on emotional contagion offers a personality profile of someone most likely to catch the emotions of others: reactive, emotional, sensitive to others, empathic, high in self-esteem, low in self-assertiveness, and low in alienation (Doherty, 1997).

A person's sense of self in relation to others (referred to as *self-construal*) may also influence the expression and recognition of facial expressions. Much like the research on culture reported earlier in this chapter (i.e., individualism and collectivism), persons with an independent sense of self (i.e., they feel less connected to other people) are less troubled with the expression of negative emotions by others compared to persons with an interdependent sense of self (i.e., feel more connected to other people) and, as a result, have been found by researchers to have less difficulty recognizing the facial expression of negative emotions (Kafestios & Hess, 2013).

Socially anxious individuals differ from those who report much less social anxiety. Some research indicates that higher levels of social anxiety in children and adults cause them to avoid faces that show negative emotions, such as anger and fear, compared to faces with neutral expressions (Stirling, Eley, & Clark, 2006). Yet despite this aversion to negative expressions, one study found that highly anxious individuals have a heightened sensitivity to fearful faces in particular, which they recognize more accurately than do persons low in social anxiety (Surcinelli, Codispoti, Montebarocci, Rossi, & Baldaro, 2006). In general, most people, including those with high social anxiety, recognize happy expressions with greater accuracy than other facial expressions; but one study found that social anxiety still hinders the ability to recognize positive emotions. Researchers found that highly anxious individuals took longer to recognize happy facial expressions than their less-anxious counterparts did (Silvia, Allan, Beauchamp, Maschauer, & Workman, 2006).

Individuals with hostile and aggressive tendencies differ in their use and recognition of facial expressions. In one study, researchers discovered that undergraduate students who scored high on a measure of hostility were much less likely to use non-enjoyment smiles in a structured interview than were undergraduates who scored low on hostility. Presumably, hostile individuals are less inclined to smile for various communicative purposes, such as being polite or as a listening response, than are their less-hostile peers. The researchers speculate that this lack of smiling may contribute to uncomfortable interpersonal relations and may deprive hostile individuals of social support from others (Prkachin & Silverman, 2002). Another study found that aggressive individuals are more likely than their less aggressive counterparts to see anger in the faces of people who are not expressing anger (Hall, 2006). One implication is that aggressive persons may feel justified acting aggressively in situations where they perceive a threat from others, even though no such threat may exist. Some researchers speculate that exposure to media violence may produce a similar effect, heightening viewers' sensitivity to displays of anger. In one study, participants viewed photos of expressionless faces morphing to either an angry or a happy face. Participants high in violent media consumption identified anger more quickly and happiness more slowly than did participants low in violent media consumption (Kirsh, Mounts, & Olczak, 2006).

Some studies suggest a possible link between individual levels of the male hormone testosterone and facial expressions. Research shows that, as an indicator of dominance, high levels of testosterone result in less social smiling (i.e., appeasement signaling) than do lower levels of testosterone (Cashdan, 1995; Dabbs, Hargrove, & Heusel, 1996). When they do smile, as in a posed photograph, one study found that men with low levels of testosterone exhibited bigger smiles than did those with high testosterone levels (Dabbs, 1997). More recent research raises the highly provocative question of whether testosterone levels interfere with facial mimicry and, as a consequence, the ability to empathize with others. In a double-blind placebo experiment, female participants who received a single dose of testosterone for two days were less likely to mimic happy and angry faces than a control group of female participants (Hermans, Putman, & van Honk, 2006).

Persons with social disorders may lack some ability to empathize with others due to brain malfunctions we are just beginning to understand. Research on *mirror neurons*—specialized cells in the premotor cortex of the brain's frontal lobe that activate imitative responses, such as facial mimicry—raises the possibility that persons with autistic spectrum disorders (e.g., Asperger's syndrome) and other social skills deficits may not have a fully functioning system of mirror neurons. For example, participants in one study viewed pictures of happy and sad facial expressions while EMG recorded the muscle activity over their cheek and brow area. Although all of the participants were able to voluntarily mimic the facial expressions they saw, only the autistic participants showed no signs of automatic mimicry (McIntosh, Reichmann-Decker, Winkielman, & Wilbarger, 2006). Developmental psychologist Mirella Dapretto and her colleagues discovered in their research that autistic children showed abnormally depressed activity in their premotor cortex while imitating and observing facial expressions, and the more severe the autism, the more depressed the activity was (reported in Nash, 2007). Other researchers have discovered similar deficiencies in children with disruptive behavior disorder. In one study, such children scored lower on a measure of empathy and also exhibited subnormal levels of facial mimicry in response to angry facial expressions compared to other children (de Wied, van Boxtel, Zaalberg, Goudena, & Matthys, 2006).

Psychological depression in some people may affect their ability to recognize emotions of happiness and sadness in the faces of others. In one study, participants viewed faces that expressed increasing degrees of emotional intensity. The images changed slowly from a neutral expression to a full-intensity happy, sad, or angry face. The researchers found that participants diagnosed with major depression were much quicker in identifying facial expressions of sadness but much slower identifying happiness compared to a control group of participants without depression (Joorman & Gotlib, 2006).

Some research shows that differences in facial expressions, as well as differences in recognizing facial expressions, may reveal altruistic tendencies and the likelihood of engaging in prosocial behavior. In one series of experiments, researchers videotaped individuals who scored high on a measure of altruism with those who scored low as the individuals participated in a role-playing exercise designed to reveal levels of cooperation and selfishness. As expected, altruists were more helpful and less selfish than the non-altruists were. When examining facial expressions, the researchers found that the altruists smiled in a more genuine (spontaneous) way than the non-altruists did (Brown, Palameta & Moore, 2003). In another series of studies, researchers discovered that participants who recognized facial expressions of fear more accurately also behaved in a more prosocial way, such as pledging more time and money to help a student in desperate need. Interestingly, the ability to recognize fearful expressions was a stronger predictor of altruism and prosocial behavior than was the participants' scores on a measure of empathy (Marsh, Ambady, & Kozak, 2007).

PERSONAL EXPERIENCE 5.4

CAN YOU RELATE TO THIS?

We Tend to Judge People Who Smile More Favorably

Recently, one of the other two people who parks next to me in my apartment parking lot wrote a nasty note and left it on my car, saying that I don't know how to park my car. I have seen both guys. One always smiles and waves when he sees me, while the other one barely nods and makes little eye contact. I assumed the one who always smiles did not write the note, because he seems so nice and friendly. I later found out that the one with the polite smile was the one who wrote the nasty note to me.

Emilie

We often form stereotypes of people based on their facial expressions. Much of this research focuses on perceptions of smiling faces. Some research suggests that we see smiling faces as more feminine than non-smiling faces (Kawamura & Kageyama, 2006). Other studies show that we judge a person as more sociable, sincere, intelligent, attractive, cooperative, and nicer when they smile than when they don't smile, raising the possibility of a halo effect for smiling faces (Godoy et al., 2005; Johnston, Miles, & Macrae, 2010; Lau, 1982; Otta, Abrosio, & Hoshino, 1996; Reis et al., 1990), an effect that becomes even greater when the smile is more authentic (Krumhuber, Manstead, & Kappas, 2007; Quadflieg, Vermeulen, & Rossion, 2013) and when the smiling face makes eye contact with the person judging the face (Jones, DeBruine, Little, Conway, & Feinberg, 2006). Some researchers also find support for what they call a *smiling familiarity bias*, or the tendency to see smiling faces as more familiar than faces with neutral or negative expressions (Lander & Metcalfe, 2007). But other researchers have begun to question whether the favorable judgments attached to smiling faces depend on culture, especially for the more variable judgments about competence and intelligence than the more consistent judgments related to warmth and friendliness (Krys, Hansen, Xing, Szarota, & Yang, 2014).

Research by LeeAnn Harker and Dacher Keltner (2001) offers some of the most far-reaching evidence to date that a big smile may carry a big reward (at least for women). In 1958 and again in 1960, most of the senior class of students at a private women's college in California participated in a study on personality and plans for the future. The researchers who were doing the study contacted these women to do follow-up assessments when the women were 27, 43, and 53. Harker and Keltner obtained the college yearbook photographs of these women and coded the intensity/fullness of the smiles in each of the faces. They found that smiling predicted personality as well as a range of positive outcomes later in life. Specifically, women with full smiles, compared with their less-smiling counterparts, were more likely to have an affiliative personality (e.g., warm, cheerful, pleasant, sociable, affectionate), be married by age 27, be satisfied with their marriage at age 53, and report a higher sense of well-being each time they were contacted. Cross-cultural research as well confirms the value of smiling. In one of the more intriguing investigations, a team of management and anthropology scholars found a benefit for smiling and laughter among men and women in a foraging and farming society in the Bolivian Amazon. Using the body mass index (BMI) as a proxy for income, they discovered that individuals who smiled, smiled and laughed, and laughed openly during interviews had 2.4%, 3.1%, and 5.4% higher BMI than interview participants who neither smiled nor laughed. Participants who smiled more also had more social capital and better self-perceived health (Godoy et al., 2005).

Some studies point to a connection between alcoholism and the ability to interpret facial expressions of emotion. These findings show that alcoholics have a tendency to overestimate the intensity of emotions appearing on the face and that they may be more likely than nonalcoholics to see anger and contempt in the faces of others (Kornreich et al., 2001; Philippot et al., 1999). If, in fact, this turns out to be one of the consequences of alcohol consumption, it may help to explain some of the interpersonal problems that often result when people have too much to drink.

Delivering Verbal or Symbolic Messages

Earlier in this chapter, we introduced the concept of *facial paralanguage*, which consists of the myriad of facial gestures we use to replace, accompany, or supplement speech. These conversational signals play an important part in our everyday face-to-face interactions. The most widely used classification system divides these gestures into three main types: emblems, illustrators, and regulators (Ekman, 1979; Ekman & Friesen, 1969b).

As we noted earlier, emblems take the place of words. Although most of these gestures are hand signals, we sometimes use our faces in the same basic way. Some of these expressions are well known to most people, such as sticking out your tongue or winking. The most recognizable facial gesture is the smile, a universal symbol of friendship. Less well known in non-Western nations is the facial shrug, the equivalent of saying, "I don't know" or "I don't care": raising our eyebrows and pulling down the corners of our mouth. Desmond Morris (1994) reports examples of facial emblems that are restricted to certain countries or geographical regions and are probably unknown to most outsiders. In Saudi Arabia, we can call someone a liar by rapidly moving our tongue in and out of our mouth; in Greece, we can say "no" by raising and lowering our eyebrows once. If we speak out of turn in southern China and Tibet and want to apologize, we can protrude the tip of our tongue and then immediately withdraw it.

Most of our facial paralanguage consists of illustrators and regulators, neither of which occurs outside the context of verbal discourse. Most often, facial illustrators such as eyebrow or head movements emphasize a spoken message. In one study, researchers determined that speakers often widen their eyelids while stressing certain words or phrases. Vocal intonation can serve the same purpose. Referred to as **eye flashes**, these momentary actions seemed to occur when a speaker was emphasizing an adjective or adverb in an utterance, such as "It was a *great* place to visit" (Walker & Trimboli, 1983). Facial regulators help us coordinate the turn taking that takes place in most face-to-face exchanges. As a speaker, we can invite a response with an eyebrow raise; as a listener, we can request the floor with an open mouth or raised brow. In fact, a recent study showed that the eyebrow movement of a listener was most likely to occur immediately before the listener spoke, thus signaling the listener's turn-taking intention (Guaitella, Santi, Lagrue, & Cave, 2009). But we also use facial regulators to affirm or reject what we hear (smiling in agreement or frowning in disapproval).

In his discussion of smiling, Paul Ekman (1986) identified four types of smiles that cannot be separated from the verbal context in which they occur and depend on whether the smiler is speaking or listening. A *qualifier* smile takes the edge off an unpleasant or critical message, making it difficult for the target of the message to avoid smiling in return. A *compliance* smile is a reaction to unpleasant news, acknowledging that the news will be accepted without protest. A *coordination* smile is a polite, cooperative smile that affirms another person by showing agreement, understanding, approval, and the like. A *listener response* smile is a specific kind of coordination smile that, much like head nods or vocalizations such as *mmhmm* or *yeah*, encourages a speaker to continue.

Research on smiling shows how it can alter our interpretation of a verbal message and our judgment of the speaker. In one experiment, participants saw computer-generated videos of female characters making angry, disgusted, happy, or neutral statements. In general, when a verbal statement was combined with a smile, the verbal statement was interpreted more positively. The speaker was seen as happier with a happy or neutral statement, and as trying to be funny (perhaps sarcastic) when smiling with a disgusted statement. But although an angry statement was perceived as more positive with a smile than without a smile, the speaker was also seen as less sincere, likely using a masking smile to conceal the anger expressed in the verbal statement (Krumhuber & Manstead, 2009).

PERSONAL EXPERIENCE 5.5

CAN YOU RELATE TO THIS?

Facial Expressions Can Take the Place of Words

My roommate was worried about taking an extremely challenging exam. She spent hours studying for it. I wished her luck before she went to take the exam. When she returned about an hour later, she looked at me and I raised my eyebrows as if to say, "Well, how did it go?" She rolled her eyes and shook her head, giving me the idea that she hadn't done very well. She didn't have to say a word.

Bridget

Compared to facial expressions of emotion, researchers haven't paid much attention to the subject of facial paralanguage. Psychologist Nicole Chovil is a rare exception. Her doctoral dissertation focused on the uses of facial paralanguage in dyadic interactions (Chovil, 1989). She arranged for same- and opposite-sex couples to each discuss topics meant to elicit facial reactions. One topic was to tell about a close call that they had either experienced or heard about. Another was to describe a conflict that had taken place with another person. She videotaped each of the five-minute conversations and coded facial expressions based on their appearance, when they occurred, the type of information they conveyed, the gist of the conversation at the time, and whether the person was speaking or listening. Because they occur so often, she decided not to include smiles in her analysis. This still left her with nearly 1,200 facial expressions, which she placed into five basic categories: syntactic displays, speaker illustrators, speaker comments, listener comments, and facial adaptors.

Syntactic displays are connected with our vocal intonation or with the syntax of our speech and consist mainly of eyebrow and eyelid movements. We use these movements while emphasizing words or phrases (e.g., "He's *really* bad,"), while asking questions (i.e., with raised intonation), or while signaling that we have more to say. We use speaker illustrators to depict or represent what we are saying. A grimace might accompany a statement about how much something bothers us. When recounting an experience, we might mimic the facial reaction we had at that time. Speaker comments offer information not contained in our utterances. These include personal reactions to what we're saying (e.g., a neutral statement might be accompanied by a smiling face), signs that we're thinking about what we're saying, invitations to respond to what we've said, and so on. Listener comments include an array of facial expressions that show we are paying attention, getting confused, empathizing, disagreeing, and so forth. Finally, facial adaptors include all sorts of mannerisms (lip biting, etc.) that have little connection to the process of speaking and listening.

Establishing Relationships

As we do with other nonverbal signals, we often use and respond to facial expressions in ways that influence the degree of intimacy and control we have in our relationships with others. When we think of facial expressions primarily as displays of emotion or as forms of paralanguage, we may too easily overlook their significance as approach–avoidance signals. Yet there is a fine line between what counts as an expression of emotion and what we perceive as a relational message. Demonstrating how the same facial expressions convey simultaneously both sorts of information (emotion and relationship messages), individuals in one series of experiments perceived angry and disgusted faces as high in dominance but low in affiliation, enjoyment smiles as high in dominance and high in affiliation, and fearful and sad expressions as low in dominance (Knutson, 1996).

In our everyday encounters with smiling and frowning people, we experience firsthand the impact of approach–avoidance signals. Probably all of us see a smile as a friendly sign. In fact, when a stranger smiles at us, many of us respond in kind, as though saying hello to someone who says hello to us. As a simple courtesy, people act out this norm of reciprocity every day. Watching people's reactions in various public places (e.g., shopping centers, grocery stores, sidewalks, etc.), one team of researchers

PERSONAL EXPERIENCE 5.6

CAN YOU RELATE TO THIS?

Facial Expressions Can Help You Relate to Others in a Positive Way

A simple expression such as a wink of the eye can go a long way to getting people together, especially if it is repeated back and forth between people. I had such an encounter while I was completing my high school graduation project at a nursing home four years ago. All of the patients and I were in the lounge playing bingo, and because this one lady was visibly senile and probably couldn't speak well, I think she kept making funny faces and winking at me, as I was the "odd man out" in the room because of my age. So after a few minutes of discomfort, I began to smile at her and even made some funny faces and winked. I think it made her feel more comfortable as it did the same for me.

John

observed that 53% of the people who were smiled at reciprocated the smile. Furthermore, a smile may invite communication from others, but a frown appears to discourage it. In the same study, 23% of the observed people smiled at a stranger who showed a neutral facial expression, but only 14% smiled at a stranger who frowned (Hinsz & Tomhave, 1991).

Whether we are aware of it or not, we respond to the facial expressions of others as relational signals that influence our approach-avoidance behavior toward them. In one study, researchers found that participants allowed individuals with happy expressions to get closer to them than individuals with sad and fearful expressions; and the participants kept individuals with angry expressions the furthest away (Miller, Chabriac, & Molet, 2013). Laboratory experiments show how approach-avoidance reactions to facial expressions operate below the surface in our communication with others. For example, researchers in one study asked participants to categorize facial expressions of fear and anger as they viewed each facial expression on a computer screen, by either pulling or pushing a joystick as quickly as they could in response to each image. One group of participants had to pull the joystick for fear and push the joystick for anger, while another group had to do the reverse, pulling the joystick for anger and pushing it for fear. Previous research has shown that pulling represents an approach response and pushing an avoidance response, and in this experiment, participants pushed the joystick more quickly than they pulled it in response to angry expressions, but pulled it more quickly than they pushed it in response to fear expressions. These results seem to show that an angry face, as a threatening stimulus, produces avoidance whereas a fearful face, seen as needy or appeasing, elicits an approach response (Marsh, Ambady, & Kleck, 2005). But as is often the case, the context in which a facial expression appears is important. So it is not surprising that researchers in another series of laboratory experiments found that participants were more likely to use approach behavior in response to an angry face in a socially challenging situation, suggesting that in an argument or conflict, for example, individuals are often more likely to respond by confronting (approaching) the angry person than by avoiding a confrontation (Wilkowski & Meier, 2010).

So facial expressions of emotion serve as potent approach–avoidance signals. But these expressions may not be the only ones that have evolved, in part, to manage our relationships with others. Certain facial gestures may in fact be universal signals of approach–avoidance, inviting people to interact or keeping them away. Eibl-Eibesfeldt's (1972) pioneering field studies of numerous cultures around the world revealed that people use what he called an **eyebrow flash**, a fraction-of-a-second raising of the eyebrows, as a greeting gesture. He also observed various flirting behaviors, facial movements that seem to register the inner conflict one feels in courtship encounters between approach on the one hand and avoidance on the other. Usually interpreted as signs of embarrassment, these coy behaviors include blends of approach (e.g., smiling, glancing) and avoidance (e.g., shutting eyes, covering face, wrinkling nose) (see Chapter 8).

We probably aren't aware of many approach–avoidance signals. Some are so subtle that they escape the notice of both the person who sent the signal as well as the person who received it. Perhaps the best example of such a signal is **tongue showing**. Many researchers believe that this slight protrusion of the tongue is both a sign of concentration by the tongue shower as well as a primate facial display performed when the displayer wants to discourage interaction with others (Dolgin & Sabini, 1982; Givens, 1978b; Jones, Kearins, & Watson, 1987; Smith, Chase, & Leiblich, 1974). Some research bears this out. In one clever experiment, test takers needed to approach the person who administered the test and request a test booklet from him because the one they had was missing a page. The test takers were more reluctant to get his attention—he was listening to headphones with his eyes shut—if his tongue was showing than if it wasn't (Dolgin & Sabini, 1982). In a similar experiment, another team of researchers replicated these findings and found that prospective customers were less willing to approach a salesperson who was reading a book if the salesperson was showing his or her tongue than if the salesperson was not (Jones et al., 1987).

SUMMARY

We use facial expressions to communicate basic emotions, but many facial expressions also facilitate and replace speech. Known as *facial paralanguage*, these conversational signals play an important role in our face-to-face interactions. Many facial expressions are part of our biological inheritance, contributing to our survival as a species. Expressions of basic emotions, such as anger, fear, and joy, represent an intrinsic communication code that signals our intentions to others and motivates us to cope with the challenges of everyday life. In part, evidence that facial expressions of emotion are universal comes from studies of similar expressions in nonhuman primates and from studies of human facial expression encoding and decoding in diverse cultures. In addition to intrinsic codes, iconic codes include the many facial expressions we use while pretending to show emotion and the ones we use as symbolic gestures (e.g., blowing someone a kiss). Arbitrary codes include emblematic facial gestures—those that do not resemble their referents—such as winking; they also include display rules that regulate public expressions of emotion.

Communicating emotion is the primary function of facial expressions. Ample evidence exists that humans everywhere have the capacity to encode and decode certain prototypical expressions of emotion: surprise, fear, disgust, anger, happiness, and sadness. Much less evidence suggests the possibility of universal signaling for other expressions of emotion, such as contempt, interest, and embarrassment. Research also indicates that spontaneous expressions, which reflect our true emotions, differ in appearance from posed or put-on expressions. A single facial expression called a *blend* can express more than one emotion. Despite strong evidence regarding the universality of certain facial expressions of emotion, important methodological questions in recent years have stirred some controversies over the existence of the six primary facial prototypes.

Some research suggests that our facial expressions influence our emotions, a phenomenon known as the *facial feedback hypothesis*. Other studies show how emotions seem to be contagious, spreading from person to person through a two-step process of facial mimicry and facial feedback. Display rules illustrate the social nature of facial expressions, helping us understand why some expressions mask, downplay, exaggerate, or neutralize our true feelings. Research also shows the existence of *audience effects* (the tendency to show some emotions only in the presence of others), a fact that provides some support for the view that facial expressions of emotion are primarily social signals.

Facial expressions also serve important secondary functions. Various conversational signals—facial gestures such as smiles and eyebrow movements—play an important role in delivering verbal messages. Research also documents differences in the sending and receiving of facial expressions based on culture, gender, and personality. Finally, some facial expressions function as displays of dominance or submissiveness, while many more seem to operate as approach–avoidance signals, encouraging or discouraging interaction with others.

KEY TERMS

Affect displays 156
Audience effects 180
Behavioral ecology theory 179
Blends 165
Bonding displays 157
Collectivistic cultures 185
Conversational signals 156
Cry face 157
Decoding rules 185
Dialect theory 183
Display rules 158
Emotion overgeneralization hypothesis 174
Emotional contagion 174
Eye flashes 193
Eyebrow flash 197
Facial feedback hypothesis 173
Facial mimicry 175
Facial paralanguage 156
Glare 157
Grimace 157
Individualistic cultures 185
Micro-expressions 165
Play face 157
Pout 157
Power distance 185
Tongue showing 197

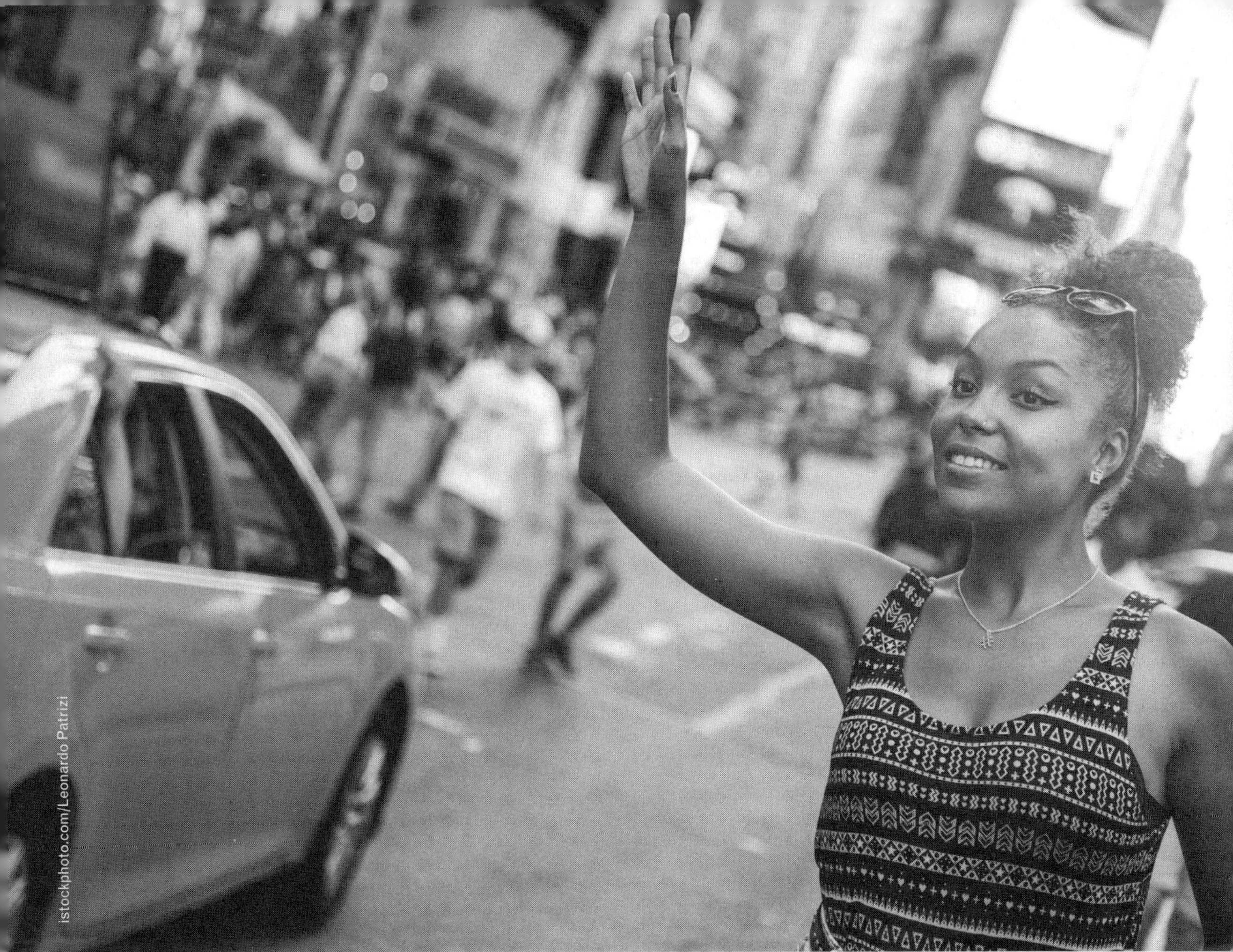

istockphoto.com/Leonardo Patrizi

Chapter Outline

6

VOICE AND GESTURE: SPEAKING AND REPLACING SPEECH

> I turned to face the jury, to show them my disgust. My eyes caught those of Juror 247, reportedly a former Black Panther. Earlier in the trial, Judge Lance Ito had asked Cochran to get tickets to the UCLA-Miami football game for Juror 247, and Simpson's lawyer had gladly obliged. That's what this trial was about. Juror 247 and I stared at each other while the courtroom erupted, all at once, in a collective gasp, a rejoicing shout, and the tortured hiss of Fred Goldman: "Murderer!" Finally, Juror 247 looked away from me, at the floor. As he left the courtroom, he raised his fist in a black power salute, and I was saddened that one of the symbols of my idealistic youth was being used to celebrate a killer's release. As the jury filed out of the box, my head swung around the courtroom until I settled on O. J. Simpson. (Darden, 1996, p. 4)

In describing perhaps the most memorable moment in the trial that captured the attention of the world, then-prosecutor Christopher Darden relives a scene that reminds us of how a single gesture can speak volumes. We often use gestures to replace speech. It's hard to imagine getting through a single day without nodding our head to say "yes," shrugging

Learning Objectives

After reading this chapter, you will be able to do the following:

1. Understand how voice and gesture operate as intrinsic, iconic, and arbitrary communication codes.
2. Examine the way that voice and gesture replace speech and operate in tandem to facilitate speech.
3. Identify key differences in the use and interpretation of voice and gesture according to individuality, age, personality, gender, race, culture, and social class.
4. Consider how voice and gesture are capable of expressing emotions and emotional messages.
5. Explain the role of voice and gesture in establishing and building interpersonal relationships.

our shoulders to say "I don't know," or pointing to say "over there." Although these are hardly the kinds of gestures that speak volumes, they are nonetheless part of the routine conversations we have in everyday life. But the fact that gestures often replace speech shouldn't allow us to overlook the underlying premise of this chapter: Much of our nonverbal communication is fundamentally a part of speech, facilitating, carrying, and elaborating the spoken word. This chapter examines the many ways we use voice and gesture to deliver verbal messages. Of course, like all nonverbal signaling systems, we use our voice and we gesture in ways that also serve secondary communication functions. In this chapter, we'll show how these vocal and gesture signals communicate multiple identities, convey emotions, and affect our relationships with others. We begin by introducing the communication codes that allow us to transform voice and gesture into meaningful messages.

COMMUNICATION CODES

One of the earliest and most widely cited taxonomies of **vocal paralanguage**, which refers to the nonverbal elements of speech, differentiates **voice qualities** from **vocalizations** (Trager, 1958). Voice qualities include all the features of speech not directly related to the verbal message. To elaborate, we'll take the advice of speech scientist Jeffrey Pittam (1994), who recommends drawing a distinction between *speech related features* such as speech errors and fluency and *vocal features* such as pitch and loudness. Speech-related voice qualities are essentially those pertaining to the articulation or utterance of speech that occur when we use our jaw, lips, tongue, teeth, and palate to form words. These **articulatory signals** include speech behaviors such as pronunciation, speech rate, tempo, hesitations, and so forth. Vocal features consist of the **acoustic signals** that result from the sound production process that takes place prior to speech articulation. These processes (e.g., exhalation, phonation, etc.) create the loudness, pitch, and distinctive sound (e.g., nasal, raspy, breathy, etc.) of our voice.

In addition to voice qualities, vocal paralanguage also includes various *vocalizations*, the sounds that replace or qualify the spoken word. There are three types of vocalizations. The first type, vocal characterizers, are the sounds we make while engaged in behavior unrelated to speech, such as laughing, crying, coughing, moaning, belching, yawning, and so on. Vocal qualifiers are the second type, consisting of changes in pitch, volume, and so forth that directly affect the content of what we say. One way we do this is by turning up the volume of our voice to emphasize a certain word or phrase in an utterance. Another way is by raising the pitch of our voice at the end of an utterance so the listener understands that we're asking a question and not making a statement. The third type of vocalization, vocal segregates, includes speech fillers such as *um* and *ah*, as well as the various sounds we use to replace words (vocal emblems), such as *shh*, ("be quiet"), *uh huh* ("yes"), and *yuk* ("that's disgusting").

We use vocal paralanguage to replace and facilitate speech. But we also use gestures in much the same way. The most comprehensive attempt to classify gestures was that of anthropologist David Efron (1941), who observed the gestures of Jewish and Italian immigrants living in New York City just prior to American involvement in World War II. Efron's interest in the study of gesture was, in fact, partly motivated by his desire to challenge the Nazi claim that one's gesturing style is an inherited part of one's racial identity, a claim Efron ultimately refuted by showing how such styles change as people assimilate into a new culture. Efron's classification system continues to lay the groundwork for more recent taxonomies (Bavelas, 1994; Ekman & Friesen, 1969b; Johnson, Ekman, & Friesen, 1975; McNeil, 1995; Rime & Schiaratura, 1991).

We use various gestures to deliver verbal messages, replacing and facilitating speech (McNeil, 1995; Rime & Schiaratura, 1991). In addition to **emblematic gestures**, which take the place of spoken words, we often use other kinds of gestures that do not require speech, such as **deictic gestures** for pointing at or referring to things, and **pantomimic gestures** for acting things out. But we also gesture while speaking. These **co-speech gestures** or *gesticulations* come in many forms (including deictic gestures). When we try to visualize in some way the content of our speech, we use illustrators or graphic gestures. Many speakers use their hands to visualize concrete referents with **iconic gestures** (sometimes called *representational gestures*). We might use our hands to show how the furniture inside a room is arranged, how an automobile accident happened, or how to plant a vegetable garden. Of course, we also use our hands to visualize abstract referents, to help the listener "see" the idea we're trying to get across. Sometimes these **metaphoric gestures** (also called *ideographic gestures*) present an abstract concept as though it were concrete. An example would be a speaker cupping each hand to represent two competing proposals for dealing with the problem of school violence while weighing the pros and cons of each. Finally, we use illustrators not only to visualize speech but to emphasize, punctuate, and synchronize our speech. With **batonic gestures**, a speaker can highlight an important point, introduce a new idea, or simply beat out the natural rhythm of his or her speech. We use all these gestures like we use our voices—primarily to replace or facilitate speech but also to communicate who we are, how we feel, and where we stand in relation to others.

Gestures that take the place of speech are often the preferred mode of communication when speech is either not possible, inefficient, or inappropriate (e.g., coaches using hand signals to their players, using gestures instead of speech in a noisy environment, etc.). But why do we need gestures while we speak? Although much less is known about the benefits of these co-speech gestures, studies are beginning to shed light on how speakers and listeners alike benefit greatly from the use of these gestures.

PERSONAL EXPERIENCE 6.1

CAN YOU RELATE TO THIS?

Deictic (Pointing) Gestures Can Improve Communication

I work as a personal fitness trainer and kickboxing instructor. The kickboxing class is taught aerobically (to the beat of music) and in sync with me, the instructor. I cannot stop the class to correct people if they are punching incorrectly, so I use pointing directions to get their attention and indicate proper body positioning. During my last class one of the participants was supposed to be doing a jab that ends at nose level. I kept saying, "Jab to nose level," but it was not working. Finally, because there are mirrors and they can see me, I first said "nose level," then pointed to my nose and threw a jab to my nose level. After that, I noticed that everyone jabbed to the correct level. I learned that just saying something doesn't always get attention. Sometimes it is more effective to use gestures, such as pointing, to direct attention as a means of getting people to notice and act accordingly.

Tammy

Intrinsic Codes

We are born with the capacity to speak. Our uniquely human vocal apparatus allows us to communicate in a way that cannot be duplicated by other animals. Speech is a human activity. When our prehistoric ancestors stood upright, they freed their hands from the job of locomotion, making it possible and expedient to use hand gestures as a means of communication (Morris, 1977). Of course, while we may have an innate ability to develop speech and to use gestures, we must learn the symbol systems that make it possible to speak and gesture meaningfully. But delivering verbal messages isn't the only way we use voice and gesture. Intrinsic codes have evolved to serve these crucial secondary functions. For example, our voices promote infant–parent bonding; express basic emotions such as anger and grief; signal our individuality, gender, and age; and communicate dominance or submissiveness. In each of these cases, automatic encoding and decoding suggest the use of an intrinsic signaling system.

Many human vocalizations have great survival value as social signals. As a result, they become part of the communication systems we inherit at birth. The best example is crying, which signals a need for help but may also tell us something about the health of the baby. Although programmed to react immediately, we nonetheless don't interpret all cries in the same way. The way we respond depends on the influence of both nature

EXERCISE 6.1

TRY THIS

Talking Hands

OBJECTIVE: To see how we use gestures while we speak

INSTRUCTIONS: Watch someone speak for about ten minutes. A professor giving a lecture, a stand-up comedian (or late-night talk show host) giving a monologue, and a politician giving a speech are good examples. As you watch, record five specific instances when the speaker uses a particular gesture. Describe each gesture as fully as you can. What was said while the gesture was made? What did the gesture look like? Using the gesture categories identified in this chapter (batonic, iconographic, etc.), classify each of these five gestures.

Discussion Questions:

1. Did the speaker's gestures help his or her presentation in any tangible way?
2. Were you able to classify each of the gestures easily?
3. Did the speaker use various gestures or did he or she stick to a certain type?

and nurture (Roberts, 1987). Another example is **parentese**, the kind of baby talk adults instinctively use when interacting with infants and young children. It consists of soft, high-pitched tones accompanied by various forms of simplified speech (e.g., elongated vowel sounds, duplicated syllables, etc.) that foster infant–parent bonding and promote the early development of communication skills in children. Our ability to process voice qualities also appears to be inborn. Like many other animals, we automatically discriminate between threatening (e.g., growling) and inviting sounds (e.g., cooing). For example, in one interesting study of eight different groups of people representing four different languages and cultures from around the world, scientists discovered that individuals were able to accurately predict a man's upper body strength and potential for aggression by listening only to the man's tone of voice (Sell et al., 2010). We also have the ability to recognize individuals from their distinctive vocal cues. Research shows that three-day-old infants can pick out their own mother's voice from a set of maternal voices (Van Lancker, 1987), leaving little doubt about the important role the voice plays in signaling our identity.

While a convincing case could be made regarding the natural communication codes involved in certain facial movements (e.g., eyebrow flash, nose wrinkling) and territorial behaviors (e.g., arm crossing, body orientation) that overlap with the general subject of gestures, any claim that most gestures represent an intrinsic communication code is more difficult to support. Certainly, the inclination to gesture, to point at objects, or to move to the beat of our own speech is as natural as is the inclination to speak. All humans use gestures. In fact, studies show the emergence of **protogestures**, the rudiments of our elaborate system of hand gestures, within the first few weeks of life (Trevarthen, 1977). According to researcher David McNeil (1995, p. 300), protogestures are "motions of the hands and arms, such as raising the hand above head level, that appear in the company of speech articulatory movements of the tongue and lips, although there may be no sound." As McNeil concludes,

> The linkage of the manual and vocal at so early an age suggests a biological connection of the two systems. . . . The infant is endowed with the raw materials with which such communication is effected—including the impulse to make communicative movements of the hands and arms along with speech. (p. 300)

Researchers Iverson and Goldin-Meadow (2001) believe that gesticulating is an inherent part of thinking and speaking and not simply a visual aid we learn to use by watching and modeling others. Their observations of congenitally blind children and adolescents show that blind speakers gesture as often and as fully as sighted speakers do—something they couldn't have picked up from watching others. Moreover, blind speakers even gesture as much when speaking to blind listeners, a finding that casts considerable doubt on the idea that we gesture solely for the benefit of our listeners.

Iconic Codes

Ionic expressions include those that mimic the real thing. As we've done in previous chapters, we can distinguish here between deceptive signals and put-ons. Some vocal expressions represent deliberate attempts to deceive a listener into believing that the behavior is real when it isn't. Whether someone pretends to sound angry or sad, to laugh or cry, the common denominator is that the person's vocalizations or voice qualities only resemble the real thing. With a put-on, there is no attempt to fool the listener, such as impersonating the voice of a famous celebrity.

Many of the gestures we use every day while speaking are what we earlier referred to as iconic gestures that mimic concrete referents: using a pushing motion while describing how a fight got started, your thumb and forefinger to illustrate how close you were to the edge of a cliff, your hands to demonstrate how you tried unsuccessfully to assemble a new toy for your neighbor's child, and so on.

In addition to these iconic gestures, which we use almost automatically while speaking, many emblematic gestures get their meanings across because of their iconic nature. It's not hard to come up with examples. Think of the gestures you would use to say each of the following: "I have a headache," "Come here," "He's very strong," "It's freezing in here," "She can't handle the pressure (she'll choke)." In each of these cases, the gesture closely resembles its referent. But many everyday gestures are iconic in more symbolic ways. Nearly all versions of the "screw you" gesture incorporate into the hand or arm movement some sort of phallic symbol (e.g., the middle finger). Even the popular thumbs up/thumbs down (good/not good) gesture carries the symbolism associated with the gladiatorial contests of ancient Rome, with the thumb symbolizing the sword of the gladiator. Because the meaning of these gestures is associated with a widely recognizable action, they can reach more people, quicker, and sometimes in more dramatic fashion than the arbitrary gestures that vary from one group of people to another. One example of this is the "hands up, don't shoot" gesture recently used by many people as a rallying cry to symbolize their outrage over police shootings of unarmed black men (McCallmont, 2014).

▸ We need to learn the meaning of many gestures, but iconic gestures that replace speech are not difficult to decipher. For instance, because the raised-arms gesture of the referee in a football game resembles the goalposts on the field of play, we can be fairly certain that the gesture signifies that a team has just scored a touchdown, extra point, or field goal.

istockphoto.com/stevecoleimages

Some gestures are **intention movements**—they mimic part of some anticipated action. In his autobiography, comedian Jay Leno describes how his father used such a gesture to get his message across:

> Whenever my dad got mad at me or my brother, he would never actually hit us. But he did have one of the great belt movements. He'd say, "Do I have to go for the belt?" Then he'd wiggle his waistband around a little—kind of a fatherly Morse code for impending doom. (Lyon, 2008, p. 133)

Arbitrary Codes

Much of our vocal and gestural communication comes from signaling systems that are neither natural nor artificial. Many signals come from the arbitrary conventions that determine what a behavior means and whether it's appropriate to use. Arbitrarily coded vocal cues include regional accents (e.g., a Boston accent, a southern accent, etc.) as well as the learned stereotypes associated with those accents. The use and interpretation of vocal emblems (e.g., whistling at someone; using the *shh* sound to say, "Be quiet"; etc.), the social etiquette rules we follow regarding the appropriateness of many vocal characterizers (such as laughing, crying, yawning, and belching), and the rules that pressure us to keep our voices down in certain places (such as libraries, theaters, museums, churches, and so on) demonstrate the prevalence of arbitrary vocal codes. Sometimes the appearance of an arbitrary speech code among certain members of a society can foster the kind of group identification that many individuals find appealing. During the early 1990s, for example, teenage girls began using a style of speech called *uptalk*, which involved a rising intonation at the end of an utterance and could make anything you said sound as if you're asking a question.

People also use gestures in arbitrary ways. In professional sports, for example, coaches must use hand signals that can't be decoded by opposing teams. The need for secrecy rules out the use of iconic signals, which would be easy to decipher. As we'll see later, there is also tremendous diversity in the meaning of emblematic gestures from one culture to another. An unsuspecting visitor to a foreign country who takes the meaning of a gesture for granted runs the risk of offending his or her host by inadvertently using a gesture that sends the wrong message. Some cases of cross-cultural miscommunication are so outrageous they become the next day's headlines:

- When Soviet Prime Minister Leonid Brezhnev visited the United States during the Nixon administration, he and Nixon used emblems in their public appearances to communicate the "spirit of détente." Nixon liked to use the American hand wave, a greeting emblem. Brezhnev would clasp his hands together and, with arms extended, raise his clasped hands up in front of his face—a Soviet emblem for friendship. In America, this gesture often means, "I am the winner" (Ekman, 1976).
- When President George Bush visited Australia in 1993, he drove by crowds of citizens showing what he thought was the *V for victory* sign from the backseat of his limousine. Apparently not knowing the difference, he gestured to onlookers with the back of his palm instead of the front. The next day, his picture appeared in newspapers alongside the headline, "President Insults Australians." In Australia, as in England, the *reverse V* sign is their equivalent of the American "screw you" gesture (Axtell, 1998).

COMMUNICATION FUNCTIONS

Voice and gesture serve more multiple functions than any other nonverbal signaling system, delivering verbal messages, communicating our identity, expressing our emotions, and influencing the course of our relationships with others. As we'll see in the section that follows, however, when voice and gesture work together as an interrelated system, they function primarily to facilitate and replace speech.

Delivering Verbal Messages: The Primary Function

▸ Voice and gesture play a crucial role in the delivery of verbal messages, working in tandem to produce, mark, visualize, synchronize, and replace the spoken word.
istockphoto.com/EdStock

Picture this scene: A student at the university, Aaron, is giving an oral report in one of his communication classes. In his presentation, he uses his voice and he gestures in ways that show how nonverbal communication facilitates and replaces speech. The effectiveness of his delivery is due in no small part to his compelling voice, which fills the room and commands the attention of his audience. He emphasizes key points with fluid hand and arm movements, vocal intonations, and well-timed pauses. He rarely hesitates, suggesting both knowledge of his subject and confidence in what he is saying. During the question-and-answer session following his speech, Aaron listens attentively to individuals, responding with the kinds of reassuring vocalizations that characterize active listeners. At one point, when an audience member makes an especially astute comment, he silently responds with a confirming *thumbs-up* gesture. In short, Aaron's voice and gestures worked together during his performance to produce, mark, visualize, synchronize, and replace speech.

PRODUCING SPEECH The physical production of speech is a truly remarkable human process that involves five distinct phases:

1. *Inhalation*—the air we breathe in through our nose or mouth travels down our pharynx (throat), larynx (the "voice box," where our vocal cords are located), trachea (a tube in our neck known as the *windpipe*), and bronchial tubes (located in our chest cavity) and enters our lungs.
2. *Exhalation*—by relaxing our diaphragm (the large, dome-shaped muscle that separates our chest cavity from our abdominal cavity) and contracting the muscles of our chest and abdomen, we force air up from our lungs, which accounts for the loudness of our voice.
3. *Phonation*—exhaled air enters our larynx, passing through a small regulated opening between our vocal cords called the *glottis*. Tightening our vocal cords with muscular tension vibrates the air going through, producing sound and determining the pitch of our voice.

4. *Resonation*—the sound produced by our vibrating vocal cords is amplified and modified as it passes through the cavities of our throat, mouth, and nose. This process determines the distinctive quality of our voice.
5. *Articulation*—our tongue, lips, teeth, palate, and jaw shape the sounds we make, enabling us to enunciate words clearly and to pronounce them correctly.

Of course, speech production involves much more than this. A speaker needs to come up with a message that he or she wants to communicate and then must put that message into words. Research indicates that this process of verbal encoding may get a boost from both voice and gesture. Have you ever wondered, for example, why speakers say *um* (or *ah*, *er*, etc.) between words? These vocal segregates, referred to as **filled pauses**, are the meaningless (i.e., non-semantic) vocalizations that signify a break in the fluency of our speech. Most people seem to believe that filled pauses are a sign of nervousness or a lack of skill on the part of a speaker. But the reality is more complex than that. Some researchers contend that speakers use all kinds of pauses, including *um*, as a break while they decide what to say (Goldman-Eisler, 1968). In an interesting application of this theory, psychologist Stanley Schachter and his colleagues (1991) reasoned that speakers who must access a relatively large vocabulary while delivering their speech will probably need to do more searching, and hence need more breaks, than will speakers who do not have to access as many words to get their points across. After determining that lecturers in the humanities routinely use a greater variety of words than lecturers in the sciences use, the researchers discovered support for their hypothesis: The speech of the former group contained more filled pauses than did the speech of the latter group.

Some studies show that the complexity of a message increases the number of pauses a speaker uses to communicate the message (Greene & Ravizza, 1995). Thus, it is tempting to conclude that whatever makes the production of speech difficult (e.g., searching for words) would increase a speaker's need for pauses and in turn increase his or her use of filled pauses. But studies show that speakers do not necessarily use more *um*s and *ah*s just because the speaking task is difficult (Christenfeld & Creager, 1996). More important, it seems, is the extent to which they pay attention to what they are saying. One team of researchers tested this self-consciousness theory of filled pauses and found that speakers who paid attention to their own voices used more filled pauses than did speakers who were less conscious of their own voices (Christenfeld & Creager, 1996). In the same study, the researchers also found a correlation between alcohol and *um*s. When asked a thought-provoking question, bar patrons who drank more used fewer filled pauses when answering the question than did bar patrons who drank less. Being intoxicated may have made it more difficult for them to think of the words, but they just didn't care (i.e., they were less self-conscious). Apparently, getting speakers to pay less attention to the content of their speech may reduce their use of filled pauses. In one study, for example, instructing speakers to synchronize their spoken words with the beats of a metronome, thus shifting their attention away from what they were saying to how they were saying it, dramatically reduced their use of filled pauses (Christenfeld, 1996).

Gestures also play a role in speech production. The next time you talk to someone, try speaking without any gestures. It's not easy. For several years, I've had students in my classes participate in this exercise, allowing them to engage in group discussions but not allowing them to gesture in any way. The outcome is always the same: They talk less than they normally do, their talk is less animated than usual (i.e., more monotone), and they report being either uncomfortable or disinterested. The fact that people talking on the telephone still gesture, even though their audience can't see them, demonstrates a need to gesture that goes well beyond the need for visual aids. In fact, controlled experiments show clearly how much we need to gesture while we speak. When one team of investigators restricted the head, arm, hand, and leg movements of individuals engaged in 50-minute conversations, they discovered increased activity in those parts of the body, such as the fingers and eyebrows, that were not restrained—an effect that occurred only when the individuals were speaking. Restricted movement even affected the content of the participant's speech, which was much less vivid while they were restrained than while they were free to move (Rime, Schiaratura, Hupet, & Ghysselinckx, 1984). In another experiment, researchers found that speakers paused

PERSONAL EXPERIENCE 6.2

CAN YOU RELATE TO THIS?

We Use Gestures Even When Talking on the Phone

In high school, my friend Tony worked at the local pizza shop. One day after school, I stopped by to visit him. He was behind the counter on the phone with a customer. Apparently, the customer must have asked some question regarding the size of the pie. "It's about . . ." Tony began, placing the telephone receiver on his shoulder and extending both hands, thus making a large round shape, "13 inches around." He completed the sentence only after looking at his pie gesture. When he hung up the phone, I jumped on the opportunity to tease him. "You know that person on the phone couldn't see you right?" "Shut up!" he laughed. "I'm Italian. I talk with my hands."

Adriane

▸ Gesturing is a natural part of thinking and speaking and is more than something we do just for the benefit of our listeners.

istockphoto.com/gruizza

more when they kept their arms folded than when they could gesture freely (Graham & Heywood, 1975). Other studies show that preventing speakers from gesturing while they are describing objects reduces the fluency of their speech (Morsella & Krauss, 2004; Rauscher, Krauss, & Chen, 1996). As one team of researchers put it, "[T]he gestural motor activity of a speaking person is inextricably linked to his or her verbal encoding activities" (Rime & Schiaratura, 1991, p. 241).

The results of experiments such as these raise the possibility that gesturing, by helping us find the right words, may actually help us speak (Chawla & Krauss, 1994; Krauss, Morrel-Samuels, & Colasante, 1991). If gestures do help us in this way, we should expect a speaker to use more gestures when he or she is having trouble thinking of the right words than when the words are coming with less difficulty. There is some evidence for this. In one study, for example, speakers who gave the same talk three times, one after the other, used fewer gestures each time and also used fewer gestures while discussing simple ideas than they did while discussing complex ideas (Cohen, 1977). Some research also indicates that speakers who are searching for a word that is on the tip of their tongue may be more likely to come up with the word when they are free to gesture than when they are not (Frick-Horbury & Guttentag, 1998). But research on this tip-of-the-tongue phenomenon also casts doubt on whether gestures increase the overall rate of *success* in coming up with the right words. For instance, one study found that, although gestures did help speakers when they experienced a tip-of-the-tongue situation, gestures did not help speakers avoid these situations. In fact, to the contrary, the speakers who could not gesture were more successful in coming up with the right words in the first place than were the speakers who were free to gesture (Beattie & Coughlin, 1999). Thus, there remains the possibility that only on some occasions will gestures help speakers come up with the right words (Goldin-Meadow, 2003).

There is less doubt about whether gestures facilitate speech production than there is about how and the extent to which they do it. One hypothesis is that gestures play a limited role in helping speakers access and utter words with spatial content (the lexical retrieval hypothesis). Recent research confirms a close connection between iconic gestures and the use of concrete words: The more concrete words we utter, the more iconic gestures we use (Pine, Gurney, & Fletcher, 2010). Another hypothesis is that gestures may be instrumental in helping speakers conceptualize spoken messages that convey spatial information (the information packaging hypothesis). This hypothesis implies that speakers need more gestures for explanations than they do for descriptions because gestures help speakers "package" spatial information into units appropriate for verbalization. In a recent experiment, researchers tested these two hypotheses by examining the speech and gestures of kindergarten children (Alibali, Kita, & Young, 2000). The children had two speaking tasks. In one, the children had to describe how two items looked different (two glasses of sand and two masses of playdough). In another, the children first had to indicate whether two quantities (i.e., two glasses of sand or two balls of playdough) were the same amount (e.g., "Do these two glasses have the same amount of sand or different amounts of sand?"). One quantity was then changed (sand poured into another glass; playdough shaped into another form). After the change, the children had to say whether the two quantities were the same or different and then explain their judgment (e.g., "How can you tell?"). Thus, the first task required only description of spatial content, whereas the second required explanation and consequently more conceptual planning than the first task did. In line with the information packaging hypothesis, children used more representational (iconic) gestures—there were no differences in the use of pointing (deictic) gestures—for the explanation task than they did for the description task. In addition, the children's gestures were less redundant during the explanation task (i.e., providing information not contained in the children's words).

Another interesting hypothesis is that gesturing helps a speaker's memory. Research shows, for instance, that speakers gesture more when describing something from memory than they do when describing something they can see (Wesp, Hesse, Keutmann, & Wheaton, 2001); and the more difficult it is to remember what they are describing, the more speakers will gesture (Morsella & Krauss, 2004). This seems to suggest that gestures create spatial images that facilitate a speaker's short-term memory. More evidence of this comes from a study of six- and seven-year-old children who answered interview questions assessing their recall of a "visiting the pirate" event they attended two weeks earlier. Children who received instructions to gesture while answering questions gestured more, used fewer redundant gestures, and recalled more information about the event than did the children who didn't receive the same instructions (Stevanoni & Salmon, 2005). Another, more recent study of preschool children showed that when retelling an unfamiliar story, the use of both iconic and pointing gestures improved the children's ability to remember the details of the story (Cameron & Xu, 2011).

Whatever the explanation happens to be, most studies show that speakers tend to use more gestures as the speaking task becomes more demanding and that gestures lighten the load, making the task a little easier. As Susan Goldin-Meadow (2003) says, "[I]t's clear that gesturing can help free up cognitive resources that can be used elsewhere. At the very least, we ought to stop telling people not to move their hands when they talk" (p. 166).

MARKING SPEECH Voice and gesture also provide the markers that give our speech the kind of shape and substance we take for granted. One way is by letting us emphasize or clarify what we are saying. We can give a statement added weight by raising our voice or by waving our hand. Indeed, the simultaneous occurrence of vocal stress and gesture is what marks emphatic speech. In a study of conversations between pairs of strangers, researchers found that most points of vocal emphasis were accompanied at precisely the same time by various gestures of the head, hands, or other parts of the body (Bull & Connelly, 1985).

Sometimes vocal intonation alone can even determine the underlying meaning of a spoken message. Mark Knapp and Judith Hall (2002) offer the following example:

- *He's* giving this money to Herbie. (He is the one giving the money).
- He's *giving* this money to Herbie. (He is not lending the money.)
- He's giving *this* money to Herbie. (The money is not from another source.)
- He's giving this *money* to Herbie. (This is not a check or something else of value.)
- He's giving this money to *Herbie*. (He's not giving it to someone else.)

One episode of the TV show *Seinfeld* provides an excellent illustration of how the meaning of a message can depend on this kind of vocal emphasis. George, Elaine, and Kramer are invited to a Thanksgiving eve party, but Jerry doesn't receive an invitation. He asks Elaine to find out if he is invited by asking the host in an indirect way. Following up on Jerry's request, she asks the host if Jerry should bring anything to the party. The host replies, "Why should Jerry bring anything?" When Elaine tells Jerry what the reply to the question was, Jerry is bewildered. He still doesn't know whether he was invited or not because he doesn't know how the reply was said: Two meanings are possible, depending on which of two different words in the reply was emphasized. If the host said, "Why should Jerry *bring* anything?" that would imply that Jerry was invited but that he didn't need to bring anything. However, if the host said, "Why should *Jerry* bring anything?" that would imply that Jerry was not invited.

Another way vocal intonation can change the meaning of a spoken message is sarcasm. When we say something sarcastically, it implies that we mean the opposite of what we're saying in words. Take the statement, "You wouldn't believe what a *great* time I had at work yesterday." Our vocal intonation in uttering the word *great* should be enough to let listeners know that we actually mean the opposite of what we're saying (i.e., not great). A final example is how we use vocal intonation to differentiate statements from questions, using a lower pitch at the end of a declarative and a rising pitch at the end of an interrogative.

Aside from emphasizing and clarifying speech, we also use vocal cues and gestures to mark the structure of our discourse. We organize the printed word into sentences, paragraphs, and so on, but we chunk our speech into basic units called **phonemic clauses**, defined as

> a string of words, averaging five in length, in which there is one and only one primary stress and which is terminated by a juncture, a barely perceptible slowing of speech, often with slight intonation changes at the very end. (Dittman & Llewellyn, 1967, p. 99)

For instance, when uttering the statement, "The man who called me yesterday / just telephoned again," we'll mark the break in the statement where the slash appears with a pause and with audible changes in vocal pitch, rhythm, and loudness. These changes in vocal intonation are sufficient to chunk the statement into two distinct phonemic clauses (Boomer, 1978, pp. 246–247). Gestures tend to occur just prior to a phonemic clause and, as noted earlier, may help launch the verbal encoding of these utterances (Dittman, 1972). Research showing that listener responses such as *uh huh* tend to occur at the end of phonemic clauses supports the idea that these are the basic decoding units of speech—the way we process what we hear—for us as listeners (Dittman & Llewellyn, 1967).

The gestures that mark speech are so much a part of our spoken discourse that on some occasions, we may use gestures to highlight the intended meaning of a word or phrase even when the person we're talking to isn't around to see the gestures. A student in one of my classes, Ryan, described an excellent example of this:

> I remember being on a bus in New York and stuck in traffic. I looked out the window down at this woman alone in her car, and I see she's talking on her cell phone. After watching her continue to talk for about twenty seconds or so, I see her suddenly put the cell phone between her ear and shoulder, release the steering wheel, and use both hands to give the "in quotes" gesture. I was amazed to see that even on the phone, people use gestures like they are talking to someone right in front of them.

VISUALIZING SPEECH (AND THOUGHT) Body movements add a visual dimension to our discourse, making it possible to "see" the words and ideas we're trying to communicate. As we noted earlier, iconic gestures picture in a limited way the concrete referents of a speaker (e.g., objects, actions); metaphoric gestures are abstract representations of a speaker's thoughts (e.g., making a fist while saying, "We must be strong"). According to one theory of spontaneous speech and gesture, our use of gestures depends on how easy it is for us to speak (Freedman, 1972; Freedman & Hoffman, 1967). To elaborate briefly, suppose Mitchell has a mental image of what he wants to communicate through speech. If he can translate that image easily into words, his speech will be fluent, with less need to use gestures. The more difficult it is for Mitchell to express himself in words, the more likely it is that he'll supplement his speech with gestures.

Illustrative movements can range from simple gestures to elaborate pantomimes (i.e., acting). They occur often in everyday life without much awareness on our part and with little or no planning. The iconic gestures we use to depict action in an unfolding story—a downward motion to show something dropping, a horizontal hand gesture to show someone running, and so on—probably seem as automatic as do the words themselves. On the other hand, we may use iconic gestures more thoughtfully when the speaking task demands it. And there is evidence that gestures enhance communication. In one of the earliest experiments on the effects of iconic gestures, researchers gave participants one minute to describe each of several shapes to another person, who in turn tried to draw each shape as accurately as possible. When the participants used hand gestures, they were much more successful in their communications than when they could not (Graham & Argyle, 1975). More recent studies also confirm the impact of iconic gestures on listeners. In one study, listeners who viewed video clips of social conversations that included speech-only segments recalled less about the speech than did the listeners who viewed co-speech segments (Church, Garber, & Rogalski, 2007). Support for the impact of iconic gestures also comes from a recent experiment demonstrating that because listeners gain a more complete picture of a story told by a speaker who uses iconic gestures compared to a speaker who does not, the listeners don't need to use as many iconic gestures themselves when they retell the same story to others, indicating a better mental image of the story (Cutica & Bucciarelli, 2011). The positive effect of iconic gestures on listener retention even extends to the use of animated agents in multimedia presentations. Researchers have found that viewers recall more information in an animated agent's presentation when the agent uses gestures that duplicated some of its speech content than when it doesn't (Buisine & Martin, 2007). More recently, research shows that listeners retain more information in human-robot interactions when the robot uses iconic gestures than when the robot does not (van Dijk, Torta, & Cuijpers, 2013).

Gestures also provide insights into a speaker's thoughts—insights that are sometimes not contained in the speaker's words (McNeil, 1995). This nonredundant feature of co-speech gestures increases the efficiency of the communication process. Some studies provide support for this idea (Beattie & Shovelton, 1999a, 1999b). In one study, a group of participants (narrators) were videotaped describing the stories contained in several different cartoons. Another group of participants (respondents) answered questions about the stories after being exposed to audio-only clips of the narration, visual-only clips, or clips from the full video. When respondents could see the gestures in addition to hearing the speech, they received significantly more information than they did when they could only see or hear the narration. Iconic gestures provided information about the size and relative position of objects. Typically, the speech would convey the action involved in the story (e.g., eating food), while the gestures would convey how the action was accomplished (e.g., bringing the food to the mouth with the right hand). Research also shows that increased communication and learning is most likely when speakers use gestures that add rather than merely duplicate information contained in the verbal part of their message; that is, when there is a mismatch between gesture and speech (Goldin-Meadow, 2003). For instance, researchers in one study of third- and fourth-grade children found that adding gestures to a lesson in mathematics encouraged the children to produce gestures of their own, and the children that gestured learned more than the children who did not (Cook & Goldin-Meadow, 2006).

As we noted earlier, gestures benefit the speaker as well as the listener, which explains why speakers use a range of gestures while talking on the telephone. Still, the presence of an audience increases a speaker's use of gestures, and even though speakers often have little awareness of their own gestures, research shows that they adapt their gestures according to the needs of their audience. For instance, a speaker's gestures are less redundant with a speaker's words in face-to-face conversations than in telephone or tape-recorded conversations. One team of researchers found that when a speaker and listener were face-to-face, fewer than 20% of the gestures conveyed only information contained in words (redundant). But without face-to-face contact, over 60% of a speaker's gestures were redundant (reported in Bavelas & Chovil, 2006,). Other studies show that a speaker uses no gestures or less informative gestures (e.g., smaller, less precise or complex) when talking to well-informed rather than uninformed listeners (Gerwing & Bavelas, 2004; Holler & Stevens, 2007). And another study found that speakers who told a story to inattentive listeners used fewer gestures than they did while telling the same story to listeners who paid more attention (Jacobs & Garnham, 2007). In sum, speakers use gestures with their audience in mind.

SYNCHRONIZING SPEECH Operating at a level outside our conscious awareness is the rhythmic coordination of speech and gesture. There is a cadence to our speech (manifested in stressed syllables and pauses) that is as real as the beat of a marching band. You can tap your finger to it. When a person speaks, much of that person's body movement is synchronized to the beat of his or her own speech (this is not true of individuals with neurological disorders). The gesture movement (called the *stroke*) coincides with the equivalent linguistic segment of speech and usually precedes the spoken segment. In a recent experiment, for example, researchers found that they could change the timing of a speaker's gestures by changing the vocal stress the speaker placed on a syllable (Rusciewicz, Shaiman, Iverson, & Szuminski, 2013). In addition, research suggests that the gap in time between the word and the gesture is larger for unfamiliar words than for familiar words (Morrel-Samuels & Krauss, 1992).

Psychologist William Condon began studying the phenomenon of speech synchrony in the early 1960s. His initial insights came from fine-grained analyses of 16-mm films depicting ordinary interactions; one consisted of a frame-by-frame breakdown of a 4.5-second film clip of a family dinner. Looking for the smallest visible signs of coordination between speech sounds and body movements (e.g., syllables, head nods, eye blinks, etc.), Condon ultimately found evidence, not only of **self-synchrony**, movement to the beat of one's own speech, but also of **interactional synchrony**, listeners moving to the beat of the speakers (Condon & Ogston, 1966). We'll discuss the subject of interactional synchrony later in this chapter.

Patterns of speech-movement synchrony tend to be hierarchical; that is, the size of a speech unit coincides with the size of a body movement. Most movements occur in single-second pulses. But within these pulses, smaller units of speech seem to match comparable body movement units. For example, a speaker might sweep her right arm away from her body as she asks, "So where are we going?" But when we break it down, we might find a wrist extension that coincides with the word *we* and even smaller movements, such as finger curls, coinciding with the syllable sounds in the word *going* (Douglis, 1987). Some researchers believe that these hierarchical patterns exist well beyond the level of syllables, words, and phrases. One of the pioneers on the subject of nonverbal communication, psychiatrist Albert Scheflen, showed how increasingly larger body movements accompany comparable changes in the content of a speaker's discourse (Scheflen, 1964, 1973). A slight postural shift, for example, might coincide with the introduction of a new point, while a more dramatic change in posture and positioning might correspond with the introduction of an entirely new issue or topic.

Synchronized movements may help listeners by making speech easier to comprehend. One study tested this hypothesis by focusing on the effects of rhythmic head movements that normally accompany speech. Japanese participants who viewed realistic talking-head animations uttering a series of barely audible sentences were better able to recognize the words contained in these sentences when natural head motion was present in the animation than when it was either eliminated or distorted (Munhall, Jones, Callan, Kuratate, & Vatikiotis-Bateson, 2004).

REPLACING SPEECH Speech is not always the best way to communicate in face-to-face situations. There are many good reasons why we may choose to gesture instead:

1. When separated by distances that would force us to shout, a gesture is a less intrusive way of sending a message;
2. in a noisy environment, it might be easier for us to see a gesture than it would be to hear a word or a phrase;
3. when speech is not permitted, we may be able to gesture instead;
4. arbitrarily coded gestures provide a convenient way for us to be secretive in our interactions with others;
5. we can use iconic gestures easily to communicate with individuals who do not speak our language; and
6. compared to speech, gesturing is often faster, less ambiguous, and more dramatic.

We use emblematic gestures to replace speech. Of course, not all movements that occur in the absence of speech qualify as emblems. For us to classify any gesture as an

EXERCISE 6.2

TRY THIS

Creating Gestures

OBJECTIVE: To consider the arbitrary nature of emblematic gestures

INSTRUCTIONS: Create your own unique gesture for each of the messages listed below. Be prepared to perform each gesture and to explain how it communicates the intended message.

1. I think he/she is very unattractive.
2. Later (not now).
3. I think I'm going to be sick.
4. You're an idiot.
5. You look great!
6. No way!
7. Where's the restroom?
8. I like you.

▸ Sign language demonstrates the use of gestures as a substitute for spoken language.

istockphoto.com/humonia

emblem, we must be able to answer *yes* to each of the following questions:

1. Is it an act that has a direct verbal translation, usually consisting of a word or two or a phrase?
2. Is the meaning of the gesture known by most or all members of a group, class, subculture, or culture?
3. Do individuals use the gesture deliberately and with the conscious intent to send a particular message?
4. Do persons who see the gesture believe it was performed deliberately to send a message?
5. Do the persons who use the gesture usually take responsibility for sending the message?
6. Can we decode the gesture, even out of context? (Johnson et al., 1975)

PERSONAL EXPERIENCE 6.3

CAN YOU RELATE TO THIS?

We Need Gestures When Speech Is Not Possible

This past summer, I went scuba diving in Cancun, Mexico. It was very spontaneous, and I hadn't realized that I would need to learn so much before actually doing it. We were taught a whole code to use for underwater communication. For example, a thumbs up meant that you wanted to swim up, and thumbs down meant the opposite. There were other, more complicated signals, which were interesting to learn. Some stood for the type of fish we were looking at, others dealt with checking out our scuba gear. Without this code, we would not have been able to communicate with each other underwater, which can lead to very dangerous, even fatal results. At one point, I wasn't breathing correctly and needed to get this across to the instructor. Thankfully, since I had learned how, I was able to swim to the top and get adjusted.

Nicole

Discovering the existence of emblematic gestures—compiling a kind of gesture dictionary—is no easy matter. In the first systematic study of American emblems, Harold Johnson, Paul Ekman, and Wallace Friesen (1975) developed a three-step procedure that is now widely regarded as the standard methodology: Step 1 involves emblem encoding—finding out if individuals use gestures to express certain verbal messages (e.g., "Go away," "I've got a headache," etc.); Step 2 is a visual analysis of the gestures—checking for similarities in the gestures different individuals use to express the same message; Step 3 is emblem decoding—verifying that observers' translations of a gesture are essentially the same. Using this basic three-step method, Johnson and colleagues identified more than 60 verified emblems, a few of which are listed in Table 6.1. Some reviews of the research on emblems conclude that people around the world use emblematic gestures to send only certain kinds of messages. In his review, Adam Kendon (1981) determined that more than 80% of these gestures (1) express a desire to control another person, (2) convey one's mental or physical condition, or (3) make an evaluative comment about another person.

▸ Saluting is a well-known emblematic gesture used in the military to convey respect to a person of higher rank and status.

istockphoto.com/Mie Ahmt

Most studies on the use of emblematic gestures reveal interesting and important cultural differences. We'll discuss these findings later in this chapter. For now, we conclude this section by presenting a short list of common American emblematic gestures. Using a list of message types similar to that of Johnson, Ekman, and Friesen's (1975) and the gesture names found in Morris's (1994) guide to gestures, Table 6.1 identifies a number of common American emblems that were verified in the study by Johnson, Ekman, and Friesen (1975) study.

Before leaving our discussion of gestures that replace speech, one final point deserves mention. While it is true that emblems are gestures we perform deliberately, a slip of the hand may be as possible, as a slip of the tongue. Paul Ekman recalls,

> In my first study of body movement in 1955, I observed such an emblematic slip. I had arranged for the director of the graduate program to subject one of my fellow students to a stress interview. He attacked and criticized her abilities, ethics, motives, etc. While she had volunteered for some abuse, it seemed clear that he succeeded in upsetting her. Importantly, the power relationship was such that the student could not fight back and had to contain

Table 6.1 Some Common American Emblematic Gestures

Message Type	Gesture	Meaning
Greetings/farewells	Hand wave	Hello or goodbye
	Handshake	Hello or goodbye
Insults	Showing the middle finger	Screw you.
	Temple circle	He/she is crazy.
	Forefingers rub	Shame on you.
Commands	Hand/finger beckon	Come here.
	Palms lower	Calm down.
	Ear cup	Speak up.
	Forefinger touches lips	Be quiet.
	Forefinger point	I'm warning you.
Replies	Head nod	Yes
	Head shake	No
	Thumbs up/thumbs down	Okay/not okay
	The ring	Okay
	Shoulder/hand shrug	I don't know.
Self-expressions	Belly pat	I'm full.
	Forehead slap	How could I be so dumb?
	Forehead wipe	That was close.
	Hand fan	It's hot. (I'm hot.)

> her anger and resentment. My film record showed that she held the "finger" emblem on one hand for a few minutes during the interview. Both the student and the professor were unaware of this emblem until I showed it to them on film (Ekman, 1976, p. 25).

Thus far, we've discussed voice and gesture as each contributes to the delivery of verbal messages: producing, marking, visualizing, synchronizing, and replacing the words we speak. But voice and gesture contribute much more: signaling our identity, expressing emotion, and charting the course of our relationships with others.

Identification

Second only to physical appearance, our voice communicates a great deal about who we are, both as an individual and as a member of a speech community. It not only expresses our uniqueness, it offers significant clues about our age, personality, gender, ethnicity, and more. Although gestures do not communicate our personal and group identity in the same way, they nonetheless reflect some of these differences.

INDIVIDUALITY Imagine hearing the telephone ring. You pick up the receiver and say "Hello." On the other end, you hear a familiar voice. Do you know who it is? Odds are that you do. Each of us has a unique voice. Although not nearly as accurate as fingerprints and easy to disguise, voiceprints (called *spectrograms*) can show us what our voice "looks" like and how it differs from other voices. Studies show consistently that we are remarkably accurate—more than 90% accurate—at the task of matching the names and voices of people we know (Pittam, 1994). Of course, how well we perform depends on several factors, such as how familiar we are with the speaker, how much the speaker says, how much time has passed since we last heard the speaker's voice, and whether the speaker is trying to fool us.

RESEARCH 6.1

FIND OUT MORE

How Does a Speaker's Age Affect What We Think of the Speaker?

In this study, the researchers were interested in finding out how the first impressions of young adult listeners were affected by the voices of young, middle-aged, and older adult speakers. Participants listened to speakers ranging in age from 22 to 79 delivering a neutral-content passage; then the participants completed a questionnaire asking them to judge the speakers on a variety of character traits.

To find out more about this study and to answer the following questions, see the full text (cited below).

1. What type of research is this? (See Appendix.)
2. How did the researchers get people to participate in this study? Is this a representative sample of young adult listeners?
3. What did the researchers discover about first impressions of older and younger speakers?
4. Did the results of this study support the stereotypes we have about older persons?

Source: Montepare, J. H., Kempler, D., & McLaughlin-Volpe, J. M. (2014). The voice of wisdom: New insights on social impressions of aging voices. *Journal of Language and Social Psychology*, 33, 241–255.

AGE Can you guess a speaker's age from vocal cues alone? Research suggests that we can, getting to within five years of a speaker's actual age (Hollien, 1987). There are some predictable biases in our guesswork, however, that reflect the age of both speaker and listener: We overestimate the age of speakers younger than us, accurately estimate the age of speakers the same age as us, and underestimate the age of speakers older than us (Hollien & Tolhurst, 1978; Shipp & Hollien, 1969).

Undoubtedly, our voice carries some information about our relative age. Differences in pitch, vocal quality, and speech rate provide much of this information. Research indicates that advancing age brings a slower rate of speech, more dysfluencies, a reduced pitch range, and greater moment-to-moment pitch variability (i.e., a trembling voice). The evidence is less consistent regarding the average pitch and loudness of our voice (Hummert, Mazloff, & Henry, 1999). Although average pitch decreases steadily from infancy to puberty, some research suggests a gender difference across the life span: Among males, it continues to decrease through middle age, but after age 80, it begins to increase; for females, there is less change with age (Mysak, 1959). But other studies have failed to confirm this (Benjamin, 1986; Chevrie-Muller, Perbos, & Guilet, 1983). In one recent study, researchers compared the voices of individuals reciting the beginning of the Declaration of Independence. The speakers represented three age groups, characterized as young-old (age 60–69), middle-old (age 70–79), and old-old (age 80–89). For the female speakers, higher pitch and greater variation in pitch were related to increased age; for the male speakers, volume and variations in volume increased with age (Hummert et al., 1999). There are other features of older voices that listeners use to infer a speaker's age. For instance, age-related changes in the muscular settings of the larynx act on the vocal cords, producing a voice that sounds somewhat like a stick being run along a railing—what researchers call a creaky voice (Catford, 1964). These changes also contribute to the breathy quality we sometimes hear in the voices of older adults (Hollien, 1987).

PERSONAL TRAITS AND BEHAVIOR Our voice communicates some aspects of our personality, but there is a sizeable gap between what our voice truly reveals about our personality (which is very limited) and what listeners think it reveals (which is quite a bit). In fact, studies generally show that listeners are not very accurate judges (Brown & Bradshaw, 1985). Perhaps the most convincing personality profile to emerge from studies of vocal cues is that of the extrovert (Argyle, 1988). Based on the available evidence, we would expect the speech of such a person to be moderately loud, fluent, slightly high-pitched (for males), dynamic (i.e., reflecting emotion), and relatively time-consuming (Scherer, 1978; Siegman, 1987). Less research shows that there are vocal signs of Type A personalities. These competitive, impatient, hard-driving, and aggressive individuals tend to speak loudly, fast, explosively, and dynamically (Friedman, Brown, & Rosenman, 1969; Jacobs & Schucker, 1981).

Most of the research on voice and personality looks at **vocal stereotypes**, the persistent judgments we make about a person's character based entirely on that person's voice. For example, research shows that listeners stereotype loud speakers as being more dominant than softer-sounding speakers (Tusing & Dillard, 2000). Speech researcher David Addington (1968) conducted one of the first scientific experiments to confirm the existence of vocal stereotypes. He arranged for trained speakers, two males and two females, to simulate seven different voice qualities (e.g., nasal, breathy, tense, etc.), to use three different speech rates (normal, fast, or slow), and to vary their vocal pitch (normal, more than normal, or less than normal). Listeners judged the speakers on a long list of personality traits. For both male and female speakers, nasal, tense, and flat voices produced the most unfavorable personality ratings. The most favorable stereotypes emerged for a resonant voice (e.g., energetic, lively, etc.), a fast rate of speech (animated and extroverted), and more than normal variation in pitch (dynamic). Addington also discovered some gender differences that might reflect different expectations we have—or had at the time, more than three decades ago—for acceptable male and female voices: (1) breathy sounding females were rated as feminine and pretty but shallow, while breathy males were rated as younger and artistic; (2) thin female but not male voices were rated as immature; and (3) throaty female voices received all sorts of negative evaluations (e.g., unintelligent, lazy, neurotic, boorish, ugly, unemotional, sickly, etc.) but throaty male voices were rated as mature, sophisticated, older, realistic, and well adjusted. In a much more recent study, researchers considered how nasal-sounding voices affected sex-stereotyped perceptions of male and female speakers (Bloom, Zajac, & Titus, 1999). They created audiotapes containing the voices of three men and three women, each saying the same sentence at low, medium, and high levels of nasality. Listeners rated the nasal voices as more undesirable than the less nasal voices. Specifically, nasal voices were associated with (1) fewer positive male stereotypes (assertive, intelligent, competent, and persuasive); (2) fewer positive female stereotypes (sensitive, understanding, and warm); (3) more negative male stereotypes (arrogant, demanding, boastful, and hostile); and (4) more negative female stereotypes (immature, weak, passive, and whiny).

The latest research on first impressions of a speaker, based solely on the sound of the speaker's voice, shows, remarkably, that we form these impressions in less than a second and after hearing only a single word. In this study, University of Glasgow Scotland psychologist Phil McAleer and his colleagues Alexander Todorov and Pascal Belin, recorded 64 speakers reading the same paragraph. Using only the spoken word "Hello" taken from the paragraph, the researchers obtained the first impressions of 320 participants. Listeners were surprisingly consistent in their personality ratings of the speakers. For example, low-pitched male voices were perceived as more dominant but less friendly and trustworthy than higher-pitched male voices were; a rising vocal intonation at the end of the word made females sound less trustworthy to listeners than female voices that dropped at the end of the word (McAleer, Todorov, & Belin, 2014).

One implication of this research is that we prefer certain kinds of voices to that of others. Pursuing this line of inquiry, psychologist Miron Zuckerman and his colleagues developed the idea of a **vocal attractiveness stereotype**, the inclination to assign positive attributes to speakers with attractive voices. They found that attractive-sounding speakers—those with resonant, articulate, moderately low-pitched, less monotone, and less nasal voices—tend to get high marks on all sorts of positive traits, such as being likeable, successful, dominant, secure, open, extroverted, and conscientious (Zuckerman & Driver, 1989; Zuckerman, Hodgins, & Miyake, 1990; Zuckerman & Miyake, 1993). However, the advantages of having an attractive voice, in this regard, only hold up if the speaker is not physically unattractive or if the listener has no knowledge of the speaker's physical appearance. In fact, research shows a negativity effect: We give more weight in our judgments to the unattractive source of information than to the attractive source of information, so that in the case of the vocal attractiveness stereotype, the speaker's physical appearance would influence our impressions more than the speaker's voice so that the speaker would be disproportionately penalized for not also being physically attractive (Zuckerman & Sinicropi, 2011).

In a related study on the vocal attractiveness stereotype, psychologist Diane Berry (1990) found that the sex of the speaker also determined some of the evaluations the speaker received: Attractive-sounding male but not female speakers received high ratings on masculine attributes such as strength, assertiveness, and dominance; in contrast, attractive-sounding female but not male speakers received high ratings on kindness and honesty (both got high marks on warmth). As is the case with good looks, we "see" an attractive-sounding man as masculine and an attractive-sounding woman as feminine (among other positive traits).

In addition to vocal attractiveness, researchers believe that two other vocal cues influence our perceptions of a speaker's personality. The first is vocal maturity. Studies show that we evaluate speakers with childlike voices (e.g., high-pitched) as weaker, warmer, and more approachable than speakers with more mature, adult-sounding voices (Berry, 1990; Montepare & Zebrowitz-McArthur, 1987). The second is turn-taking behavior. While most of us know about the negative stereotype of the "big mouth" who monopolizes a conversation, we may be less aware of the positive evaluations given to speakers who take more than their fair share of turns (Cappella, 1985). In one early experiment, for instance, researchers found that listeners rated both male and female speakers as warmer, friendlier, more intelligent, and more outgoing when they spoke 80% of the time in a conversation with an opposite-sex individual than when they spoke only 20% of the time. But the results were not all favorable for the big talkers: Males who spoke 80% of the time were also judged as inconsiderate, impolite, and inattentive. As the researchers surmised, we may be a bit tougher on a man who dominates a conversation with a woman than we are on a woman who dominates a conversation with a man (Kleinke, Lenga, & Beach, 1974). Our perceptions of turn taking may also depend on the speaking context. Opinions of big talkers in everyday conversations may differ from opinions of big talkers in business meetings. Numerous studies show, for instance, that we tend to judge participants who talk a lot in task-oriented groups as having more leadership attributes and being more dominant than speakers who don't talk as much (Mast, 2002).

Gestures and bodily movements can also signal certain personality traits. For example, studies of people with communication reticence—people who avoid communication as much as possible—give us a profile of someone who looks uncomfortable, uninvolved, and unemotional. Their profiles include uncoordinated or random movements, self-touching (i.e., **adaptors**), tense postures, and inhibited gestures (Burgoon, Buller, & Woodall, 1996). Our gestures and bodily movements may also influence the way others judge us. For example, we may appear more assertive if we use emphatic and graphic gestures than if we do not, especially if others perceive our use of such gestures as firm and composed (Leathers, 1997). Although these studies suggest a connection between personal traits and bodily movements in general, there has been almost no empirical research on the link between any specific hand or arm gesture and judgments of other people. But the exceptions are quite interesting and will likely encourage more research in the future. For example, in one experiment, participants who described the personal traits of a woman posed in a photograph in a sitting position with her hand over her heart used the term *honesty* in their descriptions of the woman (49% of the participants) significantly more than did the participants who described the same person posed in a sitting position with her hands resting on her stomach (18% of the participants). In a second follow-up experiment, the researchers told another group of participants they were going to listen to a woman job applicant in her interview for the job. Half of the participants were given a picture of the woman using the hand-over-her-heart gesture; the other half were given a picture of the same woman with her hands behind her back. The participants who saw the woman with her hand over her heart rated her as more credible than did the participants given the picture of the woman with her hands behind her back (Parzuchowski & Wojciski, 2014).

Our use of a gesture can also influence our judgments of other people. For instance, in one experiment, researchers told their participants that they were doing a study on the effects of hand movements on reading comprehension, which was their cover story for concealing the real purpose of the experiment: the effects of hand gestures on first impressions of other people. Some of the participants were asked to extend their middle finger while reading the text (hostility gesture), some of the participants were asked to raise their thumb (approval gesture), and some of the participants were asked to extend their index finger (control group). While following these instructions, all the participants read the same ambiguous description of a person and were then asked some questions about this person. The researchers found that the participants' impressions of the person described in the text were affected by the particular gesture they were making, even though they were unaware of making any meaningful gesture. Participants making the middle finger gesture were more likely to describe the person in the text in a negative way while those making the thumbs-up gesture were more likely to describe the person in the text in a positive manner (Chandler & Schwarz, 2009). In a similar experiment, following up on their hand-over-the-heart gesture experiment discussed above, the researchers found that participants asked to place their right hand on the left side of their chest (creating a hand-over-heart gesture) provided a more honest assessment about the physical appearance of another person (and cheated less on various tasks) than they did while placing their right hand on their hip or when placing their right hand on their left shoulder (Parzuchowski & Wojciski, 2014).

GENDER In most cases, we can tell whether a speaker is a male or a female because the voice emits reliable signals. In one experiment, researchers discovered that listening to a speaker recite vowels provided enough clues for listeners to identify the sex of the speaker 96% of the time. Even when the speakers whispered, listeners were accurate 76% of the time (Lass, Hughes, Bowyer, Waters, & Broune, 1976). In fact, the voice may carry some gender signals that are so automatic or so subtle a speaker cannot monitor them adequately, which would explain why speakers who try to sound like the opposite sex usually don't succeed (Lass, Trapp, Baldwin, Scherbick, & Wright, 1982). Among these signals are the higher-pitched, softer, and breathier voices of females compared to those of males (Pittam, 1994), signals that probably owe as much to culture (i.e., pressures exerted on females to sound nonthreatening, nurturing, etc.) as they do to nature (i.e., males have thicker, longer vocal cords than females do, which produce a deeper-pitched voice).

Most other gender differences in both vocal and gestural communication probably reflect the learned sex-role demands of the situation. For instance, research shows that women adhere more strictly than men do to the pronunciation standards of their group, which may indicate a stronger desire on their part to emulate the speech styles of the upper classes (Bonvillain, 1993). The intonation patterns of female speech also differ from those of males: They are less monotonous and incorporate more rising pitch contours (Bonvillain, 1993; LaFrance & Mayo, 1978). The more monotone delivery of men is yet another sign that women are more expressive communicators than men are (see Chapter 2). Although sometimes frowned on because it makes a speaker sound insecure, the use of a rising pitch contour at the end of an utterance that makes a statement sound like a question (known as *uptalk*), has nonetheless become a feminine-appropriate way of inviting communication from others (Fishman, 1983; McConnell-Ginet, 1983).

Stereotypical differences in the vocal cues of women compared to those of men contribute to what we regard as feminine and masculine styles of speech that vary within as well as between genders. That is, some women have more feminine or masculine styles compared to other women; and men also differ along the same lines. Typically, feminine voices are higher and more varied in pitch and less resonant than male voices. Research suggests that we stereotype people accordingly. In one experiment, participants tried to match a speaker's recorded voice with what they believed was the speaker's self-description. The researchers created descriptions that varied according to gender stereotype (feminine role vs. masculine role). An example of a feminine description was "As an elementary school teacher, I like to create an environment where students learn to cooperate and build self-confidence." An example of a masculine description was "As an engineer, I thrive on solving challenging problems." The results of the study confirmed the presence of gender stereotyping. Participants tended to match masculine descriptions with masculine-sounding voices and feminine descriptions with feminine-sounding voices for both male and female speakers (Ko, Judd, & Blair, 2006).

Female gestures also differ from those of males. The more expansive and relaxed postures and gestures of men relative to women (Argyle, 1988) can take many forms: when seated, the ankle-on-knee position, the sprawled-out arms and legs position, and the hands-behind-the-neck position; and when standing, the hands-on-hips (arms akimbo) position. These gestures, which are more likely a product of sex-role demands than of biological necessity (Eakins & Eakins, 1978; Henley, 1977), have become so much a part of our everyday behavior that we pay little attention to the signals until we encounter the unexpected: masculine behavior from a female or feminine behavior from a male. In addition, many flirting gestures are tied to traditional sex roles and are designed to attract the attention of a potential mate. Numerous observations of the heterosexual courtship ritual show that men and women use all sorts of stylized gestures (e.g., preening, head tossing, etc.) to signal their romantic intentions (see Chapter 8).

RACE, ETHNICITY, AND CULTURE Some studies show that listeners can guess with better-than-chance accuracy the racial identity of black and white speakers from vowel sounds alone (e.g., 83% accuracy in one study), thus supporting the idea that the vocal signal probably includes more than racial differences in dialect, pronunciation, speech rhythm, and so forth (Lass, Tecca, Mancuso, & Black, 1979; Roberts, 1966; Walton & Orlikoff, 1994). In one study, for example, researchers found that one-second samples of the /a/ vowel sounds of black speakers contained more "spectral noise" than did those of white speakers—a difference that could make black voices sound deeper, rougher, and harsher than white voices (Walton & Orlikoff, 1994).

More conspicuous vocal cues, such as those related to learned differences in speech articulation (e.g., pronunciation, fluency), help listeners identify a speaker's ethnic

▸ Differences in the meaning of vocal cues and gestures often reflect differences in culture and ethnic background.

istockphoto.com/visualspace

background. Persistent mass media stereotypes of **speech accents**—the sounds of speech that characterize a particular group—no doubt influence our ability to both encode and decode regional American accents as well as foreign accents. While we may feel confident in our ability to identify some gross regional (e.g., southern) and foreign accents (e.g., Hispanic, Asian), there is little empirical evidence to show that we are in fact accurate at even these simple tasks, let alone the more difficult ones of matching accents with specific places of origin (Burgoon et al., 1996).

To be sure, accents and dialects sometimes enable us to identify a speaker's roots. But there are other vocal behaviors that, while insufficient to announce one's birthplace, still reflect the everyday customs of a culture and therefore may differ from place to place. For example, vocal volume varies with culture. Some researchers claim that Arabs prefer loud speech because they regard it as stronger and more sincere than a softer tone of voice (Hall & Whyte, 1966; Watson & Graves, 1966). In contrast, Britons generally prefer a quieter, less intrusive volume than persons from many other cultures, including both Arabs and Americans (Hall, 1966). There is also some evidence that Latin Americans may sound loud when their speech is compared to that of Asians and Europeans (Watson, 1970).

PERSONAL EXPERIENCE 6.4

CAN YOU RELATE TO THIS?

Talking Too Loud May Depend on One's Culture

I participated in a study abroad program this past summer. When we were in Norway, we had the opportunity to interact with Norwegian college students. It was very apparent to us that our group of Americans talked much louder than the Norwegian did. I observed that the Norwegians spoke in a soft tone and I learned that in their culture, raising one's voice or talking very loud is considered rude. Later in the summer, we had the opportunity to interact with students from Morocco, where loud speech is considered stronger and more sincere than soft speech. Compared to the Arab students, our group of Americans was actually quiet!

Maureen

Another example of a cultural difference is the deliberate use of silence. Americans generally have little tolerance for silence. Especially when interacting with nonintimates, many Americans behave as though a major goal of speech is the prevention of silence (Ishii & Bruneau, 1988). Yet this is hardly the case among Native Americans, such as the Western Apache, for whom silence is the norm in many unscripted social situations: encounters with strangers, first dates, times of mourning, greeting people who have been away for a long time, reactions to angry outbursts, and so on (Basso, 1972). As linguistics researcher Nancy Bonvillain (1993) explains,

> These circumstances have a common theme: that an individual is interacting with someone who is unpredictable either because she or he is unknown, not known well, has been absent for some time, or is in a distressed psychic state. When interacting with such people, one must take care to observe them silently in order to pick up clues, and anticipate their likely behavior. (p. 49)

Culture can also influence our use of gestures. Aside from anecdotal evidence that the members of some cultures appear to gesture more than do the members of other cultures (e.g., southern Europeans compared to northern Europeans), studies point to differences in the kinds of gestures that are used. In his pioneering study of East European Yiddish-speaking immigrants and those from southern Italy, Efron (1941) discovered differences in their use of graphic gestures. While both groups made extensive use of hand and arm movements as they spoke, Italians favored sweeping iconic gestures, whereas Jewish speakers preferred smaller, metaphoric kinds. But the meanings of emblematic gestures, more than any other type, vary from one culture to another. As we've already seen, these differences can sometimes cause serious misunderstandings and subsequent embarrassment. We can trace most cross-cultural miscommunication of this kind to three sources: (1) **multi-message gesture**s, (2) **multi-gesture message**s, and (3) **unique gestures**. With few exceptions, most of the research on cultural differences in the use and interpretation of emblematic gestures has been anecdotal (Axtell, 1998; Morris, 1977, 1994). One of the rare exceptions is a recent study by Matsumoto and Hwang (2012) that surveyed six world regions (the United States, East Asia, South Asia, Latin America, Africa, and the Middle East) to compile a catalogue of cross-cultural emblems. In their survey, a gesture was only included on their list if 70% of the encoders (persons making the gesture) and decoders (persons seeing the gesture) agreed on the gesture's intended meaning.

A multi-message gesture has more than one agreed-upon meaning. Typically, its meaning in one culture differs from its meaning in another. The best example is the *forefinger-thumb circle* gesture, which means "okay" in America, but "zero" or "worthless" in France, "asshole" in parts of Latin America and the Middle East, and "money" in Japan. Even the well-known *thumbs-up* gesture has some meanings that could create problems for its users: In Japan, it can mean the number five, and in Germany, it can signify the number one. Other examples include the *hand purse* gesture in which the fingers are bunched together and the hand is jerked up and down several times with a wrist action, which is a request for clarity in Italy but means "good" in Greece and Turkey; a similar version means "be careful" in many Arab cultures. An erect little finger is a gesture that, in Japan, refers to a man's female companion. In parts of Europe and South America, it can mean that someone is very thin; in many places, particularly the Mediterranean region, it is an insulting reference to a man's small penis. In France and other European countries, when the little finger is held close to one's ear, it means, "I know your secret" ("A little bird told me"). A simple throat-grasping gesture can mean several different things: "I'll strangle you" (Arab cultures), "I could kill myself" (New Guinea), "I've had enough" (Italy), "He/she has been caught" (South America), "I performed badly" (North America), "I can't breathe" (North America).

Sometimes different gestures communicate the same basic message. Discovering a multi-gesture message is a clear reminder of the great cultural diversity that is so characteristic of emblematic gestures. Examples abound. Some people use beckoning hand gestures with the palm of the hand facing up while other people hold the palm facing down. The palm-up version is typical in North America, most of northern and central Europe, and much of the Middle East, but the palm-down version is preferred throughout most of southern Europe and Asia. People don't use the same insulting gestures everywhere. In a fit of rage, an American might give someone the finger (*raised middle finger* gesture), but to send the same message, an angry Italian would use a *forearm thrust* while an angry Briton would use a *palm-back V-sign*. And the widespread practice of ogling the object of one's sexual desires has produced various gestures commenting on the good looks of the person (usually a female) being ogled. An Italian man might use a *cheek screw* gesture as if he is creating a dimpled cheek with his forefinger; a Greek man strokes his cheek because in ancient times an egg-shaped face was considered especially beautiful; a Brazilian man mimes the act of looking through a telescope; many South American men place a forefinger against their lower eyelid and pull down slightly, signifying "That's an eyeful"; and in many countries, a man uses both hands to outline a female body.

Unique gestures are exclusive to a single location. In most cases, the deliberate action needed to perform an emblematic gesture rules out the possibility of inadvertent signaling. But our ignorance of unique gestures can be particularly troublesome in cases where an unintended gesture gets confused with an intended one, when a non-communicative action in one culture turns out to be a communicative action in another. Many self-touching movements fall into this category (i.e., adaptors). How do you cross your legs when you're seated? An innocent act of ankle-to-knee leg

PERSONAL EXPERIENCE 6.5

CAN YOU RELATE TO THIS?

Cultural Differences in Gestures Can Be Confusing

Last semester, I studied abroad in a program called Semester at Sea. One of the countries we traveled to was India. I did a "home stay" with an Indian family in Chennai (Madras) for two days. I was with two other girls from the United States. We often were confused when talking to our host family because they use the "head wobble" as a gesture that means they are listening and understanding what you are saying. At first, I thought they were saying "no." But when you really pay attention, you can see that their heads are not moving in a shaking movement; they are wobbling their heads. We were very confused by this. We actually had to ask our host mother the meaning of the gesture.

Robin

crossing, typical of most American males, could be mistaken for an insult (*sole show* gesture) in Saudi Arabia, Egypt, Singapore, or Thailand. Do you ever touch your ear lobe? Depending on how you touch it, you could be saying, "I don't like him" (Russia), "He is effeminate" (Italy), "Don't argue with me" (Saudi Arabia), "I don't believe you" (Scotland), or "Good luck" (Turkey). According to Matsumoto and Hwang (2012), an apology gesture, where the thumbs and forefingers of both hands grasp the earlobes, was found only in parts of South Asia.

Cultural differences in emblematic gestures reflect the arbitrary nature of these nonverbal signals. Like learning the words and phrases of a foreign language, learning gestures takes time and effort. Our knowledge of these gestures, like our knowledge of any other aspect of a foreign culture, is a sign of our familiarity with that culture. In one series of studies, researchers wanted to determine whether the ability to distinguish between genuine and phony gestures in a foreign culture indicates how well one is adapting to that culture. They administered a videotaped test of American emblematic gestures, including both real and fake gestures, to a large group of nonnative American students. Higher scores on the test predicted length of stay in the United States. In addition, persons who scored higher on the test rated themselves higher and received higher scores from others on a measure of intercultural communication competence (Molinsky, Krabbenhoft, Ambady, & Choi, 2005).

SOCIAL CLASS When it comes to the task of identifying a speaker's social class—one's relative station in life based on income, education, and occupation—we seem to do well (Brown & Lambert, 1976). Studies show that many vocal characteristics of speech

PERSONAL EXPERIENCE 6.6

CAN YOU RELATE TO THIS?

People Discriminate against Some Accents

I moved to the Poconos from Long Island, New York when I was in seventh grade. I had lived in New York all my life, so I had a very strong accent. I can remember going to school on the first day. If the teacher asked me a question, I would answer and the entire class would crack up. People imitated me all the time, even told me that I sounded stupid. I took the jokes well, but I could not believe how many stigmas are attached to a New York accent. People also assume that people with New York accents are mean and intimidating. A lot of people didn't like me at first because they thought I was mean.

Katie

convey messages of social class, meaning that either these vocal cues represent actual class distinctions or listeners perceive these vocal cues as indicators of social class. Among the conclusions we can draw from this body of research are the following:

- The speech of lower-class individuals is vocally more polite and less confident than that of the middle and upper classes. Lower-class speech includes more unfilled (silent) pauses, hesitations, and rising intonations (Baroni & D'Urso, 1984; Robbins, Devoe, & Weiner, 1978; Siegman & Pope, 1965).
- Lower-class speakers demonstrate less proficiency in the articulation of speech, uttering consonants less clearly, speaking less fluently, and pronouncing words less correctly than do their middle- to upper-class counterparts (Argyle, 1988).
- Listeners generally downgrade speakers with nonstandard accents (i.e., "incorrect" pronunciation) or speakers with foreign accents (Pittam, 1994).
- In the United States, as in many other countries, listeners stereotype some regional accents as less prestigious than the standard accent (i.e., the "received pronunciation"). These include southern Appalachian, New England, Brooklyn, west Texan, Mexican American, and black English accents (Bradford, Ferror, & Bradford, 1974; Giles, 1973; Ryan, 1979; Thakerar & Giles, 1981).
- American listeners judge some foreign accents (e.g., upper-class British accent) as more prestigious than the standard American accent (Stewart, Ryan, & Giles, 1985).

RESEARCH 6.2

FIND OUT MORE

Do We Discriminate Against People with Foreign Accents?

To some extent, we make judgments about people based on their speech accent or manner of pronunciation. A great deal of research shows that these judgments tend to be more negative for persons with a non-standard accent. In fact, studies confirm that second-language speakers are often victims of discrimination in all walks of life. But how aware are we of the judgments that we make? In this study, the researchers hypothesized a difference between the judgments that we are highly conscious of making (explicit attitudes) and the judgments that we may not be aware of making (implicit attitudes). In an experiment where participants heard only the audio portion of a scripted medical malpractice trial, researchers instructed participants to imagine that they are members of the jury and told to be unbiased in their judgments. One actor portraying the physician and an expert witness for one side or the other delivered his lines with a Korean accent while another actor delivered the same lines with a standard U.S. American accent.

The researchers found that participants had a more positive *explicit* attitude toward the Korean-accented speakers but a more negative *implicit* attitude toward the Korean-accented speakers, supporting the idea that attitudes toward accented speech may depend to a large extent on how aware we are of our biases and how controllable those biases are.

To find out more about this study and to answer the following questions, see the full text (cited below).

1. How did the researchers differentiate between explicit attitudes and implicit attitudes?
2. Who were the participants in this study? Could this have affected the results of the study?
3. Why were explicit attitudes of participants different than their implicit attitudes?
4. Might the results of the study been different if speakers used a different foreign accent?

Source: Pantos, A. J., & Perkins, A. W. (2012). Measuring implicit and explicit attitudes toward foreign accented speech. *Journal of Language and Social Psychology*, *32*, 3–20.

Few studies of social class and speech accent have taught us more than those of linguistics researcher William Labov. His 1966 book, *The Social Stratification of English in New York City*, provided the first evidence that even a single phonological variation in the speech of New Yorkers, the pronunciation of /r/ following a vowel (referred to as *postvocalic /r/*), could differentiate speakers according to their social class. Knowing in advance that the answer to his question would be "the fourth floor," Labov asked 263 employees at three department stores differing in prestige—Saks Fifth Avenue, Macy's, and S. Klein—where he could find women's shoes. What he found provided clear evidence that the pronunciation of /r/ is an indicator of social class: At S. Klein's, the low-prestige store, 21% of the employees pronounced an /r/ in "fourth floor," compared to 79% who did not; at the high-prestige Saks Fifth Avenue store, in sharp contrast, 62% of the employees pronounced an /r/ and 38% did not; and at Macy's, the middle-class store, the numbers were evenly split: 51% pronounced /r/ and 49% didn't.

Labov (1972) gathered even more compelling data in a follow-up study. He taped residents of New York's Lower East Side while they talked with family members, answered interview questions, read stories, and so forth. Based on occupation, education, and income, he classified each participant as lower class, working class, lower middle class, or upper middle class. As in the first study, he found a clear pattern: /r/ pronunciations increased with social class, regardless of the speaking situation. But he also discovered a strong tendency for the members of all classes to use more /r/ pronunciations in situations that focused greater attention on how words were being pronounced; the fewest /r/s occurred during casual conversations with family members, more occurred during interviews, more while reading out loud, still more while reciting word lists, and the most when reading pairs of similar words (e.g., dock/dark, sauce/source, etc.). The obvious implication is that in situations that make us self-conscious about how we sound, an awareness of proper pronunciation can be enough to make us change the way we speak.

Of course, Americans are not alone in their use of pronunciation as a status symbol. British researcher Peter Trudgill (1974) confirmed a connection between pronunciation and social stratification in his classic study of speech patterns in Norwich, England. He found that lower-class speakers were much more likely than upper-class speakers to use each of three stigmatized pronunciations: (1) replacing the /ng/ sound with /n/, as in *goin* instead of *going*; (2) dropping the /h/ sound, as in *ammer* instead of *hammer*; and (3) replacing /t/ sounds with a glottal stop, as in *bu'er* instead of *butter*.

Communicating Emotion

In the previous chapter, we learned how facial expressions communicate our emotions. Although we do so in a much more limited way, we also express feelings of anger, joy, grief, and the like through voice and gesture.

THE VOICE OF EMOTION Can you tell whether someone is sad or happy from that person's voice? At a rate of about four to five times better than what you would expect from guessing, listeners can identify the emotion in a speaker's voice (Pittam & Scherer, 1993). Of the five emotions researchers study most often, listeners are usually most accurate in detecting anger and sadness, followed by joy and fear. Disgust is almost always the toughest to identify from vocal cues alone (Pell, Monetta, Paulman, & Kotz, 2009; Pittam & Scherer, 1993). There is also some evidence in support of an in-group advantage for recognizing emotions; that is, it seems to be slightly easier to accurately identify an emotion from the vocal cues of speakers from one's own culture than it is from the vocal cues of speakers from a different cultural group, even when the listener is not aware of the speaker's culture (Laukka et al., 2008; Sauter, 2013).

Of course, trying to discover whether listeners can identify an emotion without being influenced by a speaker's words is no easy task. Among the techniques researchers use to remove the verbal portion of a message are the use of meaningless utterances (e.g., asking speakers to recite part of the alphabet or to count from one to ten), standardized speech (e.g., reciting some emotionally neutral statement in an angry voice, happy voice, etc.), and electronic filtering of the higher frequencies needed for word recognition (i.e., you can hear the voice but not the words).

EXERCISE 6.3

TRY IT

Voicing Your Feelings

OBJECTIVE: To see whether you can convey certain feelings through vocal paralanguage

INSTRUCTIONS: Say the following: "I have to go now, but I'll be back in about 15 minutes." Say this sentence eight times, each time trying to say it in a way that expresses each of the feelings listed below. See if someone you know can figure out which feeling you are trying to convey.

1. Anger
2. Depression
3. Fatigue
4. Elation
5. Nervousness
6. Disgust
7. Uncertainty
8. Fear

Discussion Questions:

1. Were you successful in conveying each feeling?
2. Were some more difficult than others?
3. How did you change your vocal behavior each time?

Psychologist Klaus Scherer has been investigating the voice of emotion for nearly four decades. He and his colleagues believe that listeners can determine a speaker's emotional state from vocal cues alone because when a speaker becomes angry, sad, panic-stricken, bored, and so forth, audible changes occur in the speaker's respiration, phonation, and articulation that are symptomatic of his or her emotional state (Scherer, 1986, 1989). When fear combines with stress to produce anxiety, for example, a speaker's vocal cords tighten, producing a higher-pitched voice. Anxiety also causes the speaker to experience verbal encoding difficulties that disrupt the flow of speech, such as silent pausing, stuttering, repeating a word, and so forth (but not *ums* and *ahs*). Scherer and his colleagues also believe that the vocal signals of an emotion depend on the intensity of the emotion: Hot anger doesn't sound like cold anger, elation doesn't sound like contentment, and so on. For example, the voice of cold anger is not as loud, is not as high pitched, is more monotone, and includes more downward pitch contours than does the voice of rage (Kappas, Hess, & Scherer, 1991; Pittam, 1994).

To investigate this theory, Scherer and his colleague, psychologist Rainer Banse, recruited 12 professional actors to recite a meaningless statement 14 times, each time portraying a different emotion (Banse & Scherer, 1996). With the single exception of disgust, they found that listeners were able to identify each of the emotions with better-than-chance accuracy. The easiest emotions to identify were hot anger, boredom, interest, contempt, and sadness. Aside from disgust, shame was the most difficult emotion to identify. They also confirmed that a speaker's pitch, loudness, and speech rate varied with the emotion and with the intensity of the emotion portrayed. For instance, panic-stricken speech was much higher pitched, louder, and faster than was anxious speech.

A study of speakers in Sweden identified vocal patterns that listeners reported as speakers tried to convey happiness, fear, anger, sadness, and disgust. These patterns included various combinations of three rated factors: activation, valence, and potency. *Activation* refers to the speaker's level of arousal, *valence* refers to the speaker's positive or negative affect, and *potency* refers to the speaker's level of power or control. Listener ratings of the speakers indicated that happiness was high in activation and potency and positive in valence; fear was moderate in activation, low in potency, and negative in valence; sadness was low in activation and potency and negative in valence. Anger and disgust produced a similar pattern: high in activation and potency and negative in valence. The researchers also identified vocal cues associated with each rated dimension. For example, high activation included high pitch, large pitch variability, few pauses, and precise articulation. High potency included low pitch, high volume, slow speech, and precise articulation. Positive valence included low pitch, large pitch variability, low volume, and fast speech (Laukka, Juslin, & Breslin, 2005).

To date, the research on vocal expressions of emotion indicates an ability to pick up a range of negative emotions, such as anger, sadness, and fear. In one study, listeners were able to hear anxiety in a speaker's voice based on the speaker's higher-pitched voice and increased use of silent pauses (Laukka et al., 2008). Research also shows an ability to recognize the positive emotion of happiness. But our ability to hear distinct emotions in a speaker's voice may be fine-tuned enough for us to distinguish among different positive emotions. A study of speakers in two different languages found that listeners were able to recognize emotional expressions of achievement/ triumph, amusement, contentment, sensual pleasure, and relief (Sauter & Scott, 2007).

GESTURES OF EMOTION Sometimes we can tell from the way a person walks or from the person's overall posture whether he or she feels sad, angry, or overjoyed (Crane & Gross, 2013; de Meijer, 1989; Montepare, Goldstein, & Clausen, 1987). Using trained actors, one team of researchers found that the actors could successfully convey particular emotions without the use of facial or vocal expressions, but through body movement alone (Montepare & Koff, 1999). Angry movements involved variations in velocity and force, accompanied by abrupt changes in tempo and direction (i.e., jerky, stiff, hard, fast, and action filled). For sadness, actors relied on a relative lack of movement; but when moving, the movements were rated as slow, smooth, and contracted. Happy movements were seen as action-filled, expanded, loose, fast, relatively soft, and somewhat jerky. Of the three emotions, anger was the easiest for viewers to identify. A person's anger, sadness, or happiness may not automatically trigger a particular hand or arm movement that, in turn, becomes a reliable (and universal) signal for that emotion. Yet there is accumulating evidence that our brain responds to the bodily expression of emotion much like it responds to facial expressions of emotion. Some studies show, for instance, that fearful bodies produce a similar reaction in the same part of the brain, the amygdala, that automatically responds to facial expressions of fear (de Gelder, 2006). In addition, we can make valid inferences based on gestures alone about how emotionally aroused an individual is and about how much anxiety she or he is experiencing. In this section, we'll identify several emblems of emotion, and then we'll discuss the difficult-to-control gestures that may reveal some of our inner feelings.

People around the world use emblematic gestures to communicate particular emotions. Some of these gestures are quite common, such as slapping your cheek for surprise, covering your face for embarrassment, wiping your dry eyes for grief, punching your fist for anger, or pointing your thumb at someone for whom you feel contempt. Other gestures may be unique to a country or region. For example, many Europeans and North Americans show pride by hooking their thumbs into their armpits and spreading out their fingers (symbolically puffing up the chest); people in Belgium, France, and Portugal express fear by opening and closing the bunched fingertips of one hand (symbolizing the opening and closing of the sphincter muscles); and Saudi Arabians can communicate contempt by slapping the back of the palm of one hand (Morris, 1994).

But some gestures may be symptomatic rather than merely symbolic of our inner feelings. Occurring automatically and often escaping our awareness, these private gestures may show how we really feel and not just how we want others to think we feel. Adaptors refer to the various self- or object-touching actions we use to satisfy our physical or psychological needs. Although these actions take many forms and occur under different circumstances, they are all related in some way to the management of stress. In fact, ethologists have observed similar behaviors, called **displacement activities**, in many animal species. Displacement activities are patterns of behavior (mostly body care activities) that seem to be irrelevant to the situation in which they appear (Tinbergen, 1952). Among nonhuman primates, these actions—scratching, self-grooming, body shaking, yawning, and the like—occur in various stressful situations involving some degree of uncertainty, inner conflict, or frustration. Ethologists observing monkeys usually notice a sudden increase in these behaviors when the monkeys encounter a higher-status individual, engage in a territorial squabble, or wrestle with a difficult decision (Maestripier, Schino, Aureli, & Troisi, 1992). In humans, displacement activities consist of the nervous fill-in actions we perform to relieve tension: finger tapping, head scratching, nail biting, leg shaking, clothes fiddling, paper shuffling, and so on (Morris, 1977). Not surprisingly, social scientists have known for a long time that an increase in anxiety can produce an increase in displacement activity (Freedman & Hoffman, 1967; Ruggieri, Celli, & Crescenzi, 1982; Wolff, 1945).

Closely related to displacement activities are self-intimacies, the soothing self-touch actions that unconsciously give us the comfort we'd like to receive from others. Head holding, face touching, arm folding, and leg crossing are all examples. As Morris (1977) explains,

> When we perform a self-intimacy, we use part of our body as if it belonged to a comforting companion. During our infancy, our parents cuddle and hug us, and rock us gently back and forth if we are frightened or hurt. They pat us, stroke us, and caress us, and make us feel safe and secure, loved and wanted. When we are adults, we often feel insecure and in need of gentle loving, but the parental arms are no longer there to protect us. Our own arms are there, however, and so we use them as substitutes. (p. 102)

Establishing Relationships

As we've seen, voice and gesture work together to deliver verbal messages. But they also work independently to express who we are and how we feel. Voice and gesture also help shape and are shaped by the intimacy we share with others as well as the control we have in our dealings with them. In the following sections, we'll examine how this happens.

INTIMACY Vocal and gestural signals can invite or reject communication from others. Some of these signals make implicit requests for a person to speak (e.g., raised pitch) or for a person to continue speaking (e.g., vocalizations such as *uh huh* and gestures such as head nodding). These are important conversational signals that we'll examine in the next chapter. Some signals exhibit varying degrees of involvement in an interaction and, as a result, send a positive message of interest. These signals include increases in vocal volume, speech rate, intonation (i.e., expressiveness), speech duration, interruptions, and speech-related gestures (Cappella, 1983; Coker & Burgoon, 1987; Patterson, 1983).

Other signals convey some measure of warmth and openness toward another person (e.g., soft vocal tones, relaxed laughter, open body positions). While an open body position, for instance, generally conveys a receptive attitude, closed body positions tend to signal the opposite. Many closed body positions occur in response to interpersonal encounters that produce momentary feelings of discomfort, such as meeting new people, losing an argument, being embarrassed, and so forth. Certain types of positions, which Morris (1977) calls **barrier signals**, construct a kind of temporary barrier between us and others. As Morris explains,

> People feel safer behind some kind of physical barrier. If a social situation is in any way threatening, then there is an immediate urge to set up such a barricade. For a tiny child faced with a stranger, the problem is usually solved by hiding behind its mother's body and peeping out at the intruder. . . . If the mother's body is not available, then a chair or some other piece of furniture will do. (p. 133)

Of course, as we mature, subtle and often unconscious gestures begin to replace childish actions. According to Morris, we use various body-cross gestures, which range from simple arm folding to the more fleeting types of self-touching actions: one hand reaches across our torso to touch an opposing hand, arm, or shoulder. In addition to the signals noted above, many flirting behaviors include special vocal and gestural actions that invite the company of potential lovers. Examples are giggling, self-caressing, preening, and so on (Chapter 8).

In the early stages of a relationship, the extent to which we make implicit requests, show involvement, display receptivity, and flirt can help determine whether we open or close the door to future interactions. But there is yet another way we communicate positive or negative feelings toward others: the extent to which we move to the beat of their speech, a process known as *interactional synchrony*. Earlier, we introduced the concept of self-synchrony, moving to the beat of our own speech. But when seen at the interpersonal level, observers usually describe synchrony as a kind of dance that seems to be taking place between two people, with each individual moving in tandem to the beat of their own and the other's speech and, at key moments, even mirroring each other's exact movements.

As we noted earlier, William Condon was the first to study and report the existence of this phenomenon (Condon & Ogston, 1966), but Condon was not alone in seeing this kind of synchrony in everyday interactions. Another psychologist, Adam Kendon, published his first observations of similar phenomena in 1970. Unlike his predecessor, Kendon viewed the synchrony that occurs between speakers as a product of their mutual involvement in tracking and attending to the speech of the other rather than as a result of rhythmic coordination (Kendon, 1970). Both agreed, however, that the phenomenon exists.

Interactional synchrony may well be a phenomenon with profound implications for effective everyday communication, greatly affecting our capacity to bond with other individuals in all sorts of social and professional encounters (e.g., casual conversations, first dates, interviews, etc.). For this reason, we'll revisit the topic in subsequent chapters. Much of Condon's later work showing the presence of such synchrony in adult–infant interactions (Condon & Sander, 1974) raised provocative questions about its role in early childhood development and led to a sizeable body of compelling research on the matter (Bernieri & Rosenthal, 1991). Kendon (1973) was especially interested in the degree to which interactional synchrony reflects and contributes to a general state of rapport between conversants. Much of the available research suggests that it does (see Chapter 7). We should note, of course, that some researchers have been skeptical about the existence of synchrony, having failed to observe it in their own studies (McDowall, 1978). Others contend that these efforts fail only because they don't measure up, methodologically, to the original studies and because they make different assumptions about the nature of interactional synchrony (Gatewood & Rosenwein, 1981).

Have you ever been in a conversation with someone and suddenly notice that the two of you are sharing the same body posture? Perhaps you're both facing each other with arms folded across the chest. Maybe you're both leaning back in your seats with hands clasped behind the head. Psychiatrist Albert Scheflen (1964) coined the terms *postural echo* and *postural congruence* to describe what he believed was more than just a coincidence: two or more individuals sharing the same viewpoint or stance on an issue also happen to share the same body posture (*mirroring* is another term for this). According to Scheflen, their shared posture unconsciously echoes their shared point of view. As Morris (1977) explains,

> A true bond of friendship is usually only possible between people of roughly equal status. This equality is demonstrated in many indirect ways, but it is reinforced in face-to-face encounters by a matching of the postures of relaxation or alertness. In this way, the body transmits a silent message, saying: "See, I am just like you"; and this message is not only sent unconsciously but also understood in the same manner. (p. 83)

CONTROL Many of our vocal and gestural behaviors send messages that affect or merely reflect the balance of power in a relationship. Some are rather obvious and deliberate displays of dominance or submission. For instance, we might expect the bossy person in a relationship to do most of the shouting, talking, interrupting, and insulting (i.e., derogatory gestures). Other signals are less obvious and controllable yet still leave an impression: A deep-pitched voice conveys more power than a high-pitched voice, large gestures communicate more strength than small gestures, relaxed postures imply more authority than tense postures, fluent speech suggests more confidence than hesitating speech, and so on.

Like the approach–avoidance signals of gaze, touch, and personal space (see Chapter 4), we can classify vocal and gestural behaviors as territorial intrusions, threat displays, or status reminders. A territorial intrusion occurs when someone's behavior invades the private territory of another. This can happen when a person is too loud and invades the acoustic space of another (e.g., yelling, loud laughter, etc.). It can also happen when the pointing gesture of one person (remote touching) is unwelcomed by another. A threat display is a declaration of dominance in a competitive context. It says, in effect, "I can defeat you if I so choose." In an argument, for example, a speaker can mock an adversary by using sarcastic or patronizing forms of communication. Sarcastic tones (e.g., "That made a lot of sense") and gestures (e.g., a pseudo-protective "Don't hurt me" gesture) suggest that an adversary is not being taken seriously; patronizing speech (i.e., parentese or baby talk) and gestures (e.g., thumbs up, beckoning, etc.) imply that an adversary is faltering and may not be able to continue competing without some kind of help or encouragement. Modern researchers are trying to introduce gestures of appeasement to defuse confrontations due to road rage. Vocal and gestural behaviors can also become status reminders, actions that symbolize superior rank. An authoritative tone of voice, interruptions, unresponsive silence, floor-holding tactics, insulting gestures, and more are all ways of asserting dominance in this regard (see Chapter 10). In many cultures, status reminders are woven into the fabric of everyday life. Greeting rituals in which one person bows, kneels, salutes, or kisses the hand of another are good examples.

RESEARCH 6.3

FIND OUT MORE

The Gestures of Winners and Losers: Does Culture Matter?

Power and dominance can be expressed nonverbally through voice and gesture. The authors of this study focused specifically on the nonverbal cues associated with victory at the conclusion of a competitive contest; they were also interested in whether the power distance orientation of one's culture would increase the likelihood that a winner would use these nonverbal displays. The researchers studied the nonverbal expressions of winners and losers in the medal rounds of judo competitions at the 2004 and 2008 Olympics and Paralympic games. Overall, they found that the winners from high power distance countries were more likely to use nonverbal expressions of victory than were the winners from lower power distance countries.

To find out more about this study and to answer the following questions, see the full text (cited below).

1. According to the researchers, what are the nonverbal signals of victory/triumph?
2. What is the power distance orientation of a culture and why is it relevant in this study?
3. What do you believe is the most important limitation of this study?
4. What kind of research is this study? (See Appendix.)

Source: Hwang, H. C., & Matsumoto, D. (2014). Cultural differences in victory signals of triumph. *Cross-Cultural Research*, 48, 177–191.

Sometimes we alter our speech in ways that are so subtle we have no idea we're doing them. A case in point: In a conversation with his boss, Nathan's usual manner of speaking begins to change ever so slightly. He speaks just a bit louder and slower than he normally does, and he says *um* every so often, something he rarely does when talking to other individuals. This is an instance of **speech convergence**, a phenomenon that takes place when one person adopts the speaking patterns of another. Communication scholar Howard Giles began articulating the basic tenets of **speech accommodation theory** in 1973 after observing interviews in which one speaker began to pick up the accent of the other speaker (Giles, 1973). Speech accommodation theory (now expanded to a much broader theory called *communication accommodation theory*) was an attempt to explain why this and other forms of speech convergence take place. Aside from a speaker's accent, studies have shown that individuals sometimes become more alike in their speech rate (Webb, 1972), pause and utterance duration (Jaffe & Feldstein, 1970; Matarazzo, Wiens, & Saslow, 1965; Woodall & Burgoon, 1983), vocal volume (Natale, 1975), and pitch pattern (Gregory, 1990, 1994). In one interesting study, researchers found that when speaking over the phone to a person they believed was physically attractive, participants lowered the pitch of their voices, a change in tone of voice that was also rated as more pleasant and attractive by other participants in the study (Hughes, Farley, & Rhodes, 2010).

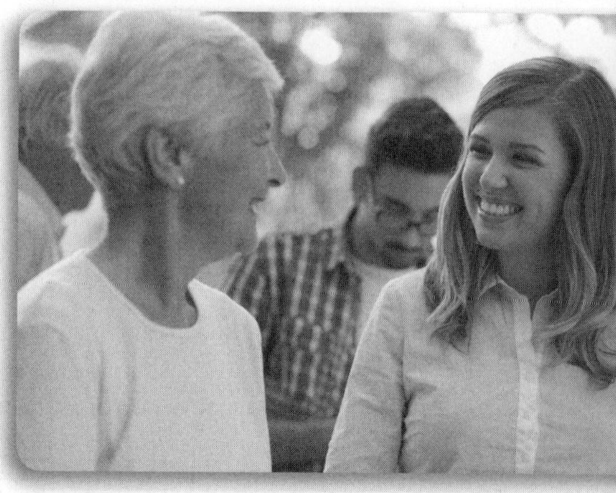

▸ Speech convergence occurs when persons deliberately or unknowingly change their usual manner of speaking to accommodate another person's manner of speaking. This may happen, for example, between persons of different generations.

istockphoto.com/simonkr

There are many reasons why a speaker converges (e.g., to gain approval, to facilitate bonding, or to try and improve communication). One explanation focuses on the relative status of the speakers, contending that the lower-status individual is more likely to converge than is the higher-status person (Giles, Mulac, Bradac, & Johnson, 1987). In the special case of speech accent accommodation, studies usually show upward convergence; that is, the low-status accented speaker is more likely to sound like the high-status accented speaker than vice versa (Giles, 1973). In the example above, Nathan altered his normal speech pattern to accommodate his boss: to gain approval from his boss, to foster identification with his boss, to enhance his own self-image, and so on. Sociologist Stanford Gregory believes that status has a lot to do with speech accommodation. In one investigation, he and colleague Stephen Webster discovered a pattern of convergence on the popular *Larry King Live* talk show. When the host, Larry King, interviewed higher-status guests (e.g., George Bush, Bill Clinton, Elizabeth Taylor, Ross Perot, etc.), he changed his voice (i.e., pitch and volume) to accommodate them more than they changed their voices to accommodate him. In contrast, when he interviewed lower-status guests (e.g., Dan Quayle, Gordon Sullivan, Robert Strauss, Arthur Ashe, etc.), they accommodated him more than he accommodated them (Gregory & Webster, 1996).

More recent research has focused on the convergence that takes place when a person's speech patterns change based on the stereotypes the person may hold about particular groups of people. Studies show a specific pattern called **over-accommodation** that occurs when someone changes his or her speech patterns more than necessary because of mistaken beliefs about a group of people. A common example is the way a young adult sometimes talks to an older adult, using speech patterns such as talking slower, using a higher-pitched delivery, talking louder, and over-pronouncing words so that the older adult will find it easier to understand what the younger adult is saying. The implication is that the older adult needs more help than a younger adult does to comprehend adult speech and must be spoken to in a more childlike fashion. But to an older adult, this pattern of speech is often seen as patronizing and insulting. Interestingly, some research shows that the more personal contact we have with unrelated older adults, the less likely we are to use most of the elements of "elderspeak" (Hehman, Corpuz, & Bugenthal, 2012).

Of course, the opposite tendency—**speech divergence**—is also possible. We can distance ourselves from others by adopting speech patterns that differ from theirs. We may slow down our speech when they speak fast, talk louder when they quiet down, emphasize our own accent when they stress their own, and so on. Whereas speech convergence may be more characteristic of a lower-status person, speech divergence may be more typical of higher-status individuals. In fact, it is also possible that speech divergence may be used in an attempt to control another, to move a person away from what may be considered undesirable behavior in a particular situation (e.g., getting someone to slow down or quiet down when you believe he or she is talking too fast or too loud).

SUMMARY

We use vocal paralanguage (the nonverbal elements of speech consisting of various voice qualities) and vocalizations, and we use an array of gestures that replace speech (emblematic and pantomimic gestures) and facilitate it (batonic, deictic, iconic, and metaphoric). Vocal and gestural communication codes can be intrinsic, iconic, or arbitrary. Intrinsic codes are the natural signaling systems we inherit at birth and include our ability to use vocal and gestural modes of communication for the delivery of spoken messages, the expression of emotion, the signaling of speaker identity, and the establishment of relationships based on intimacy and control. Iconic signals include various acts of deception and mimicry as well as the use of iconic gestures. Arbitrary codes consist of speech accents, speech-related stereotypes, speech fads (e.g., uptalk), and emblematic gestures.

Although we often regard voice and gesture as two distinct forms of nonverbal communication, it may be more appropriate to focus on how they work together as part of a speech communication system to facilitate and replace the spoken word. Most importantly, vocal and gestural behaviors assist in speech production. But we also use voice and gesture to mark speech—to emphasize, clarify, or qualify what we say and to structure the discourse into meaningful units. Voice and gesture also help us to visualize, synchronize, and replace speech.

Our voices communicate much about our identities, providing important signals and fostering all sorts of stereotypes related to individuality, age, personality, gender, race, ethnicity, culture, and social class. While not communicating our identity in the same direct way, our use of gesture varies considerably as a function of culture, gender, and personality. Our voices also express basic emotions such as anger, sadness, and joy. Some gestures, known as *adaptors*, take many forms (e.g., displacement activities) and provide information related to feelings of anxiety and inner conflict. Various vocal expressions and gestures also facilitate relationships by serving as approach–avoidance signals (e.g., involvement behaviors, interactional synchrony, postural congruence), overt expressions of dominance or submission (e.g., territorial intrustion, threat displays, status reminders), and subtle signs of status (e.g., speech convergence).

KEY TERMS

Acoustic signals 202
Adaptors 227
Articulatory signals 202
Barrier signals 241
Batonic gestures 203
Co-speech gestures 203
Deictic gestures 203
Displacement activities 240
Emblematic gestures 203
Filled pauses 210
Iconic gestures 203
Intention movements 207
Interactional synchrony 218
Metaphoric gestures 203
Multi-gesture message 231
Multi-message gesture 231
Over-accommodation 245
Parentese 205
Pantomimic gestures 203
Phonemic clauses 215
Protogestures 206
Self-synchrony 218
Speech accommodation theory 244
Speech accents 230
Speech convergence 244
Speech divergence 246
Unique gestures 231
Vocal attractiveness stereotype 226
Vocal paralanguage 202
Vocal stereotypes 225
Vocalizations 202
Voice qualities 202

PART III

APPLICATIONS

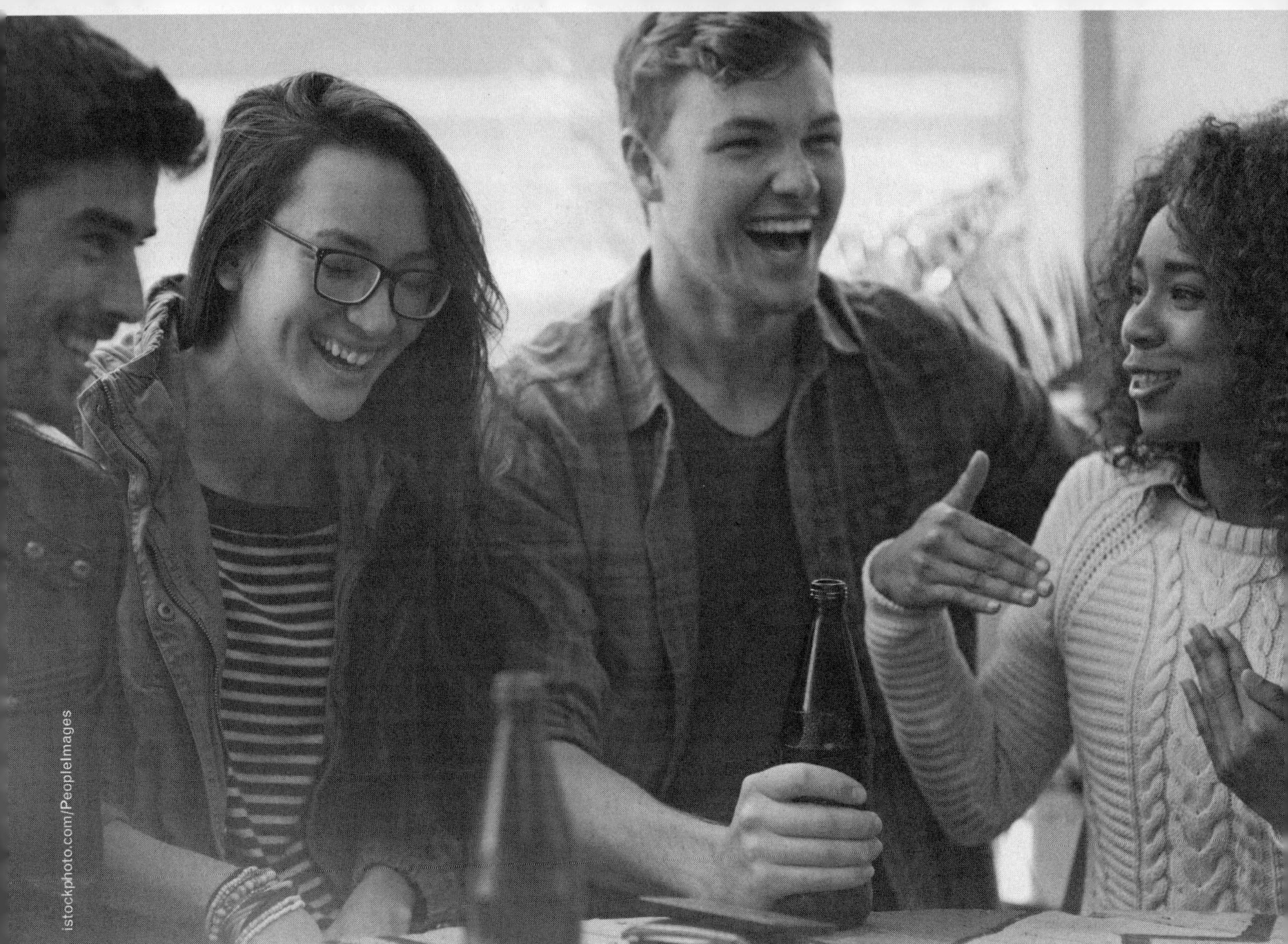

Chapter Outline

7

NONVERBAL COMMUNICATION IN NON-INTIMATE ENCOUNTERS

It is a typical day for Lucinda. On her way home from work, she stops off at the grocery store to pick up a few things for dinner. While browsing for fresh fruit in the produce section, she spots her neighbor, Susan, waiting in the checkout line. Lucinda goes over to Susan and the two strike up a lively conversation that lasts until Susan leaves.

"Excuse me! Could you do me a big favor?" Bill asks the stranger walking by. "Could you help me put a couple of boxes into the back of my truck? They're a little too heavy for me to lift by myself." The stranger, already running late for his appointment, wonders whether he should stop and help.

Learning Objectives

After reading this chapter, you will be able to do the following:

1. Understand the two basic ways that nonverbal communication affects our efforts to build rapport with others: through approach–avoidance signals and through interpersonal coordination.
2. Explain how entering and exiting a conversation and how getting involved in a conversation depend on the use of nonverbal communication.
3. Identify the two basic elements of interpersonal coordination in a conversation: turn taking and behavioral adaptation.
4. Recognize the challenges of building rapport associated with key elements of the interaction context, such as the goals of an interaction, status differences, and cultural differences.
5. Identify the various channels of nonverbal communication that influence the likelihood of compliance gaining and prosocial behavior.
6. Discuss the different explanations for why nonverbal communication influences the likelihood of compliance gaining and prosocial behavior.

CASUAL ENCOUNTERS: BUILDING CONVERSATIONAL RAPPORT

Most advice about becoming a good conversationalist stresses the importance of verbal communication—what we say rather than how we say it. Sometimes advice about what to say and what not to say can make all the difference in the world. After all, who would want to talk to us if we couldn't keep from saying things that were dull, annoying, or offensive? But the success or failure of any conversation can also hinge on the effectiveness of nonverbal communication, which includes an ability to use a wide range of approach–avoidance signals as well as an ability to coordinate our behavior with that of our conversational partner. Both abilities directly affect a conversation, providing that special blend of behaviors that leads to positive feelings of rapport (Tickle-Degnen & Rosenthal, 1990).

Approach–Avoidance Signals

Imagine this scene: You're standing in line, waiting to purchase a ticket to the concert. Suddenly, you look to your left and see someone you know, who now looks up and makes eye contact with you. She smiles, waves, and begins walking toward you. Even the most casual of conversations requires a commitment of time and energy. How much will you commit to this conversation? You don't care much for her, you're already in a conversation with someone else, and you're just about ready to purchase your ticket. In short, you don't want to encourage the conversation. Rarely, however, do we let others know how much or how little we want to converse with them—at least not in words. Can you imagine saying something like, "Sorry, but I don't want to talk to you. Goodbye"? Yet we still get the message across with a glance, a facial expression, a posture, or a vocal intonation. We exchange some of these signals to start or to forestall a conversation. We exchange others to maintain a conversation or to end it. But most of our approach–avoidance signals simply spell out some level of commitment we're willing to make to a conversation that, in turn, others may read as indicating our interest/disinterest, like/dislike, friendliness/unfriendliness, aggressiveness/timidity, and so on.

ENTERING, EXITING, AND AVOIDING A CONVERSATION For many people, getting in and out of conversations takes almost no effort at all. For others, it can be a source of real frustration. Regardless of how skillful people are, the signals they exchange during greetings and departures not only frame the conversation but also give us some insight into how committed they are to having the conversation.

▸ Greeting rituals provide an unmistakable set of cues that set the stage for conversation. These everyday greetings may contain a predictable and universal sequence of behaviors that usually involve some type of physical contact.

istockphoto.com/gremlin

Some studies suggest that **greeting rituals**, which precede most conversations, may contain a predictable and possibly universal sequence of signals. Based on their landmark investigation of American greeting behavior, psychologist Adam Kendon and family therapist Andrew Ferber claim that the customary greeting ritual contains five basic stages. The first stage, sighting and recognition, occurs when we make eye contact with another person. The second stage is distance salutation: saying hello with a wave, eyebrow flash, nod, smile, and so forth. But our intention to engage in conversation doesn't become apparent until we enter the third stage of the greeting ritual: While lowering our head and averting our gaze (to avoid staring), we approach the other person. A resumption of mutual gaze and smiling quickly follows our initial approach. In the fourth stage, close salutation, we offer an open palm and engage in some type of physical contact, such as a handshake, kiss, or hug. The fifth and final stage of the greeting sequence, backing off (e.g., taking a step back, turning to the side, etc.), orients us to the conversation and creates a certain amount of distance that varies from one relationship to another (Kendon & Ferber, 1973).

EXERCISE 7.1

TRY THIS

Observing the Greeting Ritual

OBJECTIVES: To see how people use nonverbal signals when greeting others and to test the idea that their behavior conforms to a predictable sequence of stages

INSTRUCTIONS: Visit a convenient place for watching people say hello or goodbye, such as an airport or train station, or stage a greeting encounter in which you call out to someone you've met before (bring along a friend who can observe what happens during the encounter). Record observations of three such encounters and be prepared to answer the following discussion questions.

Discussion Questions:

1. Does each encounter follow the five stages described in this chapter?
2. What specific nonverbal behaviors were involved during each stage?
3. What were some of the differences among the three encounters? Why do you think these differences occurred?

Greeting rituals provide an unmistakable set of cues that set the stage for conversation. On the other hand, when the greeting ritual doesn't move past the distance salutation stage (i.e., there is no approach), we know that a conversation is not likely. But sometimes we find ourselves in social situations that do not allow for greeting rituals, such as striking up a conversation with someone standing next to us. In these contexts, specific nonverbal signals let us know whether or not a person will be receptive to a conversation. Picking up on these signals can help us decide whether or not we want to pursue a conversation with that person. For example, at any distance and no matter where we happen to be, a simple eyebrow flash, head nod, or smile can invite conversation (Eibl-Eibesfeldt, 1975; Scheflen, 1972). But what nonverbal signals communicate the opposite message?

Sociologist Erving Goffman (1963) wrote extensively about everyday situations where people interact without having a conversation, such as standing in line at a grocery store or sitting in a waiting room. He called these situations **unfocused interactions**. In other words, people share a common presence while not exchanging any words. Goffman further described what he called the norm of **civil inattention**, a gaze pattern we follow when we don't plan to converse with someone we encounter. It consists of a brief gaze at the person, which signals interest, followed immediately by gaze aversion, a withdrawal of interest. In fact, violating the norm of civil inattention with unbroken or recurrent gaze may signal a desire to start a conversation. One researcher who videotaped men and women in a waiting room found that individuals who made eye contact and then looked away (i.e., civil inattention) were more likely to initiate a continuous conversation if mutual gaze followed their initial gaze aversion than if no mutual gaze occurred (Carey, 1978). Anthropologist David Givens (1978b) also observed the incidental encounters we have with others that do not result in conversations. His observations of people at a public market, a bar, and a university campus revealed that in more than 90% of all cases, people used a combination of signals to express their desire to avoid a conversation: gaze aversion; self-touches; constricted postures; arm crossing; and an array of facial expressions (i.e., facial adaptors) such as lip compressions (pressing lips tightly together and rolling inward), lip bites, tongue shows (slight protrusion of tongue), and tongue presses against the inside of the cheek.

▸ Wearing headphones lets others know that you do not want to be disturbed and is one way of avoiding unwanted conversation. Can you think of other "do not disturb" signals?

istockphoto.com/visionchina

We experience brief instances of civil inattention every day as we approach and walk past people we don't know, either by not looking at the other person or looking and then looking away. But to appear friendly or polite, we may smile or nod while making eye contact with the other person. How do strangers react to these nonverbal cues? And are the norms of civil inattention bound by culture? Many factors can determine how a stranger responds to a polite smile. For instance, one recent study found that we are more likely to return a stranger's smile on sunny days than we are on cloudy days (Gueguen, 2013). Cultural norms also vary. Miles Patterson and his colleagues discovered that, although Americans generally reciprocate glances and smiles, Japanese pedestrians do not. In one study, nearly half of the American pedestrians who received a glance and a smile from a trained

EXERCISE 7.2

TRY THIS

First Encounters

OBJECTIVE: To observe how individuals use nonverbal signals to encourage or discourage continued interaction with someone they don't know

INSTRUCTIONS: With a friend who agrees to observe, visit a place where close contact with others is common (e.g., standing in line, standing in an elevator, etc.). While your friend observes, try to initiate a casual conversation with a stranger. Instruct your friend/observer to note the stranger's nonverbal signals during the initiation phase of the attempted conversation. Be prepared to answer the following discussion questions.

Discussion Questions:

1. What kinds of facial expressions were observed? Did you see any of the expressions that David Givens saw in his research? Was there an eyebrow flash, head nod, smile, or frown at the start of the encounter?
2. Did the stranger avoid or make eye contact during any particular part of the encounter?
3. What bodily reactions were observed? For example, did the stranger shift positions, touch his or her face or body, or cross his or her arms?

RESEARCH 7.1

FIND OUT MORE

What Is the Cost of Civil Inattention?

How do you feel when someone walks toward you, glances in your direction, and looks at you as though you're not there, as though you're invisible? Would it make any difference if that person acknowledged your presence by making eye contact, nodding, or smiling? The researchers in this field study discovered that it does make a difference. Apparently, we feel less socially disconnected with other people when passersby at least make eye contact with us than when they look through us as though they were looking through air.

To find out more about this study and to answer the following questions, see the full text (cited below).

1. Who were the participants in this study and how did the researchers obtain their consent?
2. How did the researchers test their hypothesis with their participants (eye contact, smiles)?
3. What were the limitations of this study?
4. Does this study have any practical implications?

Source: Wesselmann, E. D., Cardoso, F. D., Slater, S., & Williams, K. D. (2012). To be looked at as though air: Civil attention matters. *Psychological Science*, 23, 166–168.

confederate responded in kind, while no more than 5% of the Japanese confederates did so (Patterson et al., 2007). These results seem to substantiate the existence of different cultural norms. As the researchers point out, the Japanese are not only less expressive in general compared to Americans but are also more sensitive to in-group and out-group distinctions. That is, while Americans may try to behave in a friendly manner to everyone in these circumstances, the Japanese may act less friendly toward strangers (out-group members) than toward people with whom they share some type of relationship (in-group members).

RESEARCH 7.2

FIND OUT MORE

Approaching Strangers: Where Would You Sit?

Using naturalistic, laboratory, and survey methods, the researchers confirmed that when given a choice, we would rather sit next to someone who is physically similar to us than someone who is physically dissimilar to us, even on seemingly trivial physical characteristics such as someone's hair length or whether someone is wearing glasses or not. Apparently, as the researchers conclude, "birds of a feather sit together."

To find out more about this study and to answer the following question, see the full text (cited below).

1. How did the researchers design their first study and what were their two hypotheses?
2. How did the researchers second study differ from their first study?
3. What conclusion did the researchers reach about why people tend to sit next to people who are physically similar?
4. What do you think were the main limitations of this research?

Source: Mackinnon, S., Jordan, C., & Wilson, A. (2011). Birds of a feather sit together: Physical similarity predicts seating choice. *Personality and Social Psychology Bulletin, 37*, 879–892.

Understanding the nonverbal script that accompanies greeting rituals can help us initiate conversations competently. The same can also be said about the farewell or leave-taking ritual. Whether it's a botched greeting or an abrupt departure, we may be seen as inept, rude, or worse when our hellos and goodbyes deviate markedly from the norm. Communication researcher Mark Knapp and his colleagues (1973) were interested in finding out how we ease our way out of a conversation with a partner who refuses to leave. Their findings show how we rely on nonverbal signals to set the stage for our departure—signals that communicate both inaccessibility (i.e., we are no longer available) and supportiveness (i.e., we enjoyed the conversation, we may want to see you again). The most frequent signals—those that occurred 45 seconds prior to departure—were breaking eye contact, pointing the legs and feet toward the exit, leaning forward, head nodding, smiling, and sweeping hand gestures. As most of us probably know from firsthand experience, subtle signals don't always work (i.e., our conversational partner may continue talking). In fact, one author on the subject goes so far as to recommend special techniques for leaving such situations as gracefully as possible (Martinet, 1992).

PERSONAL EXPERIENCE 7.1

CAN YOU RELATE TO THIS?

Exiting a Conversation Is Not Always Easy

The other day, I was stopped by one of my teachers on my way out of class. I talked to her for a few minutes and then I realized I had to leave soon or I would be late for my next class. I didn't want to be rude and say I had to leave and interrupt her because she kept talking and talking. So, I started to use nonverbal signals to try and communicate to her that I had to get going. I started by breaking eye contact with her for longer periods of time, positioning my body towards an exit, and looking out in the hall and at the clock. My teacher must have really wanted someone to talk to because she didn't really catch my drift. Finally, I had to end up increasing the distance between us and interrupted her by saying, "I'm sorry, but I'm going to be really late for my next class."

Lindsay

GETTING INVOLVED IN A CONVERSATION Once we start a conversation with someone, our commitment to that conversation is easy to see; it shows up in various **nonverbal involvement behaviors**—actions indicating our interest in the conversation and our excitement about participating in it. Based on several reviews of the research, Table 7.1 identifies the nonverbal signals of conversational involvement (Cappella, 1985; Coker & Burgoon, 1987; Edinger & Patterson, 1983). Immediacy indicates feelings of closeness, warmth, and accessibility and includes eye contact, close proximity, touch, direct body orientation, and smiling gestures. Expressiveness includes facial, vocal, and bodily displays of felt emotions. Composure implies the absence of discomfort (e.g., nervous mannerisms) and includes various signs of relaxation. Engagement indicates how involved we are in the verbal encoding or decoding process (e.g., speech rate and volume, floor holding, gestures, listener responses, etc.). Taken together, these signals offer a reasonably clear picture of one's overall commitment to a particular conversation.

Table 7.1 Nonverbal Indicators of Conversational Involvement		
Behavior	**High Involvement**	**Low Involvement**
Immediacy	Eye contact	Gaze avoidance
	Direct body and facial orientation	Indirect body and facial orientation
	Leaning toward	Leaning away
	Close distances	Far distances
	Open body positions	Closed body positions
	Touch	Absence of touch
Expressiveness	Facial expressiveness	Neutral facial expression
	Vocal expressiveness	Monotone voice
	Relaxed laughter	Absence of laughter
Composure	Absence of nervous mannerisms	Nervous mannerisms
	Vocal relaxation	Vocal tension
	Postural relaxation	Postural tension
Engagement	Floor holding	Avoidance of floor holding
	Positive reinforcers (head nods, smiling)	Absence of positive reinforcers
	High vocal energy	Low vocal energy
	Fluent speech	Hesitating speech
	Co-speech gestures	Absence of co-speech gestures

Nonverbal signs of conversational involvement may also communicate some degree of liking and disliking toward another person. People sometimes express (encode) a positive attitude through these behaviors and people sometimes infer (decode) a positive attitude when observing these behaviors in others. In one experimental study, researchers instructed three-person groups to engage in brief problem-solving discussions. Two of the persons in each group discussed the problems while the third person observed the interaction. At a designated point in each discussion, one of the participants (a confederate) had to act as though he or she "really liked" or "really disliked" the other person. As expected, the confederates encoded these messages with increases (liking) or decreases (disliking) in smiling, gazing, proximity, forward leaning, nodding, body orientation, and vocal pitch variation. In addition, observers and participants received the intended message, accurately decoding nonverbal cues of liking and disliking (Ray & Floyd, 2006).

PERSONAL EXPERIENCE 7.2

CAN YOU RELATE TO THIS?

A Lack of Nonverbal Involvement Shows Disinterest

This summer, my friend and I decided to drive to the beach. Before we left, my father wanted to give us some last-minute instructions to ensure that we would not get lost. While he was explaining the directions, which I already knew, I started making sandwiches for the ride. He stops talking and starts staring at me. He said, "Will you please listen to me so that you do not get lost?" I said, "I am listening, I'm just not looking at you." He says, "Exactly, you're not really paying attention." In his mind, he thought that because I was not making eye contact that I wasn't listening. In reality, I heard what he said, but he felt as though I was not giving him my undivided attention and, therefore, not listening.

Jilanna

It is difficult to overstate the importance of nonverbal involvement behavior. Indeed, most discussions of effective communication extol the virtues of making your conversational partner feel important, which you do by paying attention and showing interest. But this advice usually carries the caveat that more isn't necessarily better. The best examples of this are the use of eye contact, personal space, and touch, where too much can be intrusive and counterproductive (i.e., rude). And as we've seen in previous chapters, there are notable differences among people's expectations and likely reactions based on their cultural background, gender, and personality.

Interpersonal Coordination

Building conversational rapport takes a lot more than the optimal use of approach–avoidance signals by any one person. In a two-person interaction, we shouldn't expect to feel comfortable with the other person without also responding to his or her signals, whether that means giving up the floor, moving to a different beat, shifting postures, backing off, or speaking up. The key ingredient is some kind of interpersonal sensitivity by one or both participants. The result is a well-coordinated conversation that feels good to the two parties involved. This kind of **interpersonal coordination** can exist on two different levels: the first is how well we take turns speaking and listening, the second is how well we adapt our behavior to that of another person (Burgoon, Buller, & Woodall, 1996).

TURN TAKING Have you ever conversed with another person who wouldn't stop talking? If so, you may have wondered, at the time, whether that person was clueless, obnoxious, or just playing by a different set of rules. Whatever the reason for such behavior, these lopsided conversations usually remind us that turn taking is a fundamental part of the give-and-take we expect from others in most of our everyday interactions. Because we rarely verbalize our intentions to speak or listen, learning to navigate conversational currents can become a real challenge. The signals we use to regulate the flow of interactive speech consist largely of vocal and gestural actions. Much of what we know about these signals comes from the work of social scientist Starkey Duncan (1972, 1974; Duncan & Fiske, 1977). His meticulous accounts of what speakers and listeners do to keep from "bumping into each other" (i.e., talking at the same time) paved the way for those interested in exploring this subtle, taken-for-granted form of communication.

When we are speaking and we want to continue speaking, we use signals that communicate this intention to listeners, thus preventing unwanted interruptions. These **turn-maintaining signals** include numerous vocal and gestural acts: raising the volume of our voice, uttering *ums* and *ahs*, continuing to gesture, gazing away from the listener, and so on. On the other hand, if we don't want to continue speaking, we can relinquish the speaking turn by dropping the volume and pitch of our voice, slowing the tempo of our speech, pausing for an extended period, not gesturing, making eye contact with a listener, or raising our eyebrows. These are **turn-yielding signals**. Some research shows that it's much easier for individuals to switch turns when speakers use many of these signals than when they don't (Duncan, 1972).

As listeners, we also use turn-taking signals. To express a desire to speak, we employ various **turn-requesting signals**. These include an open mouth, audible inhalations, a raised index finger or hand, forward body lean, eye contact, quickened or exaggerated head nods, and simultaneous speech (i.e., listener speech that overlaps with the speaker's). But we may prefer not to take the floor—even when a speaker is inviting us to do so (i.e., turn-yielding signals). **Turn-denying signals** communicate this intention to a speaker in two different ways. One, passive listening, simultaneously sends a double message: (1) the primary message that you don't want to speak and (2) the implied, secondary message that you may not want the speaker to continue speaking either. Silence, gaze avoidance (e.g., looking at something in the surrounding environment), gaze aversion (deliberately looking away when the speaker makes eye contact as part of a turn yielding message), and indirect body orientation epitomize passive listening. Another way to deny a turn is known as active listening. Active listeners use **back-channel signals**, various vocal and gestural cues that encourage a speaker to keep speaking. Vocalizations such as *uh huh*, *mm hmm*, and *yeah* in face-to-face interactions usually combine with intermittent head nods and responsive facial gestures to keep someone talking. Table 7.2 summarizes the turn-taking signals found in most everyday conversations (Burgoon et al., 1996; Knapp & Hall, 2002).

PERSONAL EXPERIENCE 7.3

CAN YOU RELATE TO THIS?

Active Listening Requires the Use of Back Channels

I used to play in a band with a bunch of older guys, and I soon became friends with the lead singer's son. He went to school in Boston, so we spent a lot of time on the phone. Unfortunately, I soon grew to greatly dislike talking to him. When I would be speaking, he would remain completely silent; he never used "back-channel signals"—vocalizations like *uh huh*, *hm hm*, and *yeah* that listeners use to let the speaker know they're still awake! I always felt like he was completely disinterested in what I was saying. My conversations with him made me realize just how important those little vocalizations are.

Laura

Like all social activities requiring interpersonal coordination, conversational turn taking depends on how well we are attuned to others and can respond on cue. When the turn taking process breaks down, interruptions, simultaneous utterances (overlaps), and overlong silences predominate and the conversation becomes awkward and strained. In contrast, smooth listener–speaker exchanges make us feel as though we're connecting with another person. Some researchers estimate that half of all exchanges are smooth (Kendon, 1967), typically involving **switch pauses**—the time it takes to switch speaking turns—that are less than a quarter of a second in duration (Argyle, 1988). Apparently, when it's our turn to speak, there's no time to waste!

The idea that conversation is a turn taking activity generally keeps us from speaking when someone else is speaking. Our sense of fair play, apart from our interest in

Table 7.2 Turn-Taking Signals		
Intention	Audible Signals	Visual Signals
Turn maintaining	Increased volume	Continued gesticulation
	Filled pauses	Gazing away from listener
	Decreased unfilled pauses	"Stop" gestures
	Audible inhalation	Touching listener
Turn yielding	Decreased volume	Cessation of co-speech gestures
	Slowed tempo	Gazing at listener
	Dropped pitch (declaratives)	Eyebrow raising
	Raised pitch (interrogatives)	
	Extended unfilled pause	
Turn requesting	Audible inhalation	Raised index finger
	Simultaneous speech	Forward lean
		Gazing at speaker
		Quickened head nods
Turn denying	Silence	Gaze aversion
	Vocal back channels	Relaxed posture
		Head nods and shakes
		Smiles

hearing what others have to say, demands that we grant others an equal opportunity to speak their minds. Of course, this doesn't always happen. When people speak at the same time, it doesn't necessarily mean that anyone is trying to dominate the conversation, even if it appears that way to others. Overlapping speech can occur for several reasons (e.g., to show one is listening) and can reflect personalities (e.g., outgoing) and backgrounds (e.g., interrupting is expected in some cultures) that have little to do with one's desire to control the conversation. In fact, some scholars on the subject even recommend reserving the term *interruption* only for those instances in which a speaker is trying to monopolize the conversation (Tannen, 1994). So what are the consequences of speaking during someone else's turn? It seems to depend on the underling purpose of the interruption. Researchers in one recent study compared the effects of four different types of interruptions: interruptions that change the subject, interruptions that don't change the subject, interruptions that disagree with what the speaker is saying, and interruptions that support what the speaker is saying. The researchers found that when it comes to the social consequences of interrupting a speaker, all interruptions are not the same. Speakers disapproved most of interruptions that changed the subject, followed by interruptions that didn't change the subject. But speakers actually *approved* of interruptions that challenged or supported what they were saying, perhaps viewing such interruptions as a sign of involvement and engagement in the interaction (Gnisci, Sergi, DeLuca, & Errico, 2012).

EXERCISE 7.3

TRY THIS

Following the Three-Second Rule

OBJECTIVES: To experience the role of silence between speaking turns in a conversation and to minimize the likelihood of interrupting a speaker

INSTRUCTIONS: During your next conversation with someone, wait a full three seconds before taking your turn to speak. Be prepared to answer the following

Discussion Questions:

1. Was it difficult for you to wait the three seconds? If so, why?
2. How did this affect your conversation? For instance, did you lose opportunities to speak? Did it interfere with the flow of the conversation? Was it very distracting? Were there fewer interruptions?
3. Did the other person figure out what you were doing? How did the other person react?

Research on how people use nonverbal signals while taking turns in a conversation has begun to focus on turn taking as a collaborative activity. This shifts the focus away from what each individual chooses to do during his or her turn to how these choices are often the product of mutual cooperation between speaker and listener. It also encourages us to look more closely at how speakers and listeners use each other's verbal and nonverbal cues to move the conversation forward. For instance, communication researcher Janet Beavin Bavelas and her colleagues discovered what they call a ***gaze window***, a moment of mutual gaze between a speaker and a listener that the speaker initiates to encourage listener reactions (i.e., back channels) and immediately terminates after receiving a reaction. These brief reactions allow the speaker to obtain listener feedback that enhances the quality of the speaker's narrative (Bavelas, Coates, & Johnson, 2002). To illustrate: Heather is telling a story to her friend, Steve. At a certain point, she makes eye contact with Steve (opening the gaze window); he takes her gaze as a signal for him to respond in some way, which he does with a facial expression of astonishment. Heather then reacts to Steve's look of astonishment by breaking eye contact (closing the gaze window) and continuing to tell her story. But now she tells her story in a way that is more animated than it would have been in the absence of Steve's reaction. These listener reactions can also have a marked impact on the "script" a speaker ends up using. In their research on how people explain their failures (verbal accounting), for example, communication researchers Valerie Manusov and April Trees (2002) found that speakers who received negative facial expressions of confusion or disagreement from listeners tended to interpret those expressions as calls for them to offer more than just a concession (an acknowledgment that the failure occurred but not offering an excuse). Speakers who received negative facial expressions from listeners were more likely to engage in *facework*, trying to promote a positive image of themselves, than were speakers who did not receive negative facial expressions.

When participating in conversations with others, we should be mindful of the fact that conversational styles differ. For example, observations of turn taking behavior often show that men, compared to women, take more turns, hold turns longer, interrupt more frequently, and use fewer back channels (Anderson & Leaper, 1998; Bonvillain, 1993; Hall, 1984; Hannah & Murachver, 1999). One common explanation for these gender differences is that we may expect more supportive communication from women than we expect from men. A related explanation claims that men's turn taking behavior is a status reminder, a way of asserting their presumed dominance over women. Men's use of interruptions provides some support for the dominance explanation. One team of researchers examined the results of 43 published studies comparing adult women's and men's interruptions during conversations. They found that while men interrupt women more than women interrupt men, the magnitude of the difference depends on how you define the term *interruption* (Anderson & Leaper, 1998). When an interruption includes any instances of overlapping talk, there is little difference between men and women. However, when limited to instances of intrusive interruptions (i.e., attempts to take another's speaking turn), men were much more likely to interrupt than women were. Whatever the explanation, our sense of fairness should dictate that we afford everyone an equal opportunity to participate in the conversation.

There are also cultural differences in the use of back channels and interruptions (overlapping speech). For instance, some scholars claim that Japanese listeners use more back channels compared to American and British listeners (Argyle, 1988; Hall, 1959). In fact, a case study examining back channels in conversations in English between Japanese and British participants found that the Japanese used slightly more, but the British had more variety in the types of back channels they used (Cutrone, 2005). Another study showed that Germans use back channels less often and also use fewer overlapping (interrupting) back channels than Americans do (Heinz, 2003). In a study of telephone conversations between friends, family members, and strangers speaking Arabic, German, English, Japanese, Spanish, and Mandarin, one team of researchers found no differences in the use of vocal back channels, but there were differences in the number of interruptions, defined merely as instances of overlapping speech. During ten minutes of conversation, the most overlaps occurred between Japanese speakers. The Japanese averaged about 63 interruptions while the average number of interruptions for all other groups ranged between 38 and 43. However, since it isn't clear whether these interruptions indicated attempts to control the conversation or indicated only high levels of conversational involvement, we don't know the reasons for such high rates of overlapping speech between Japanese speakers (Yuan, Lieberman, & Cieri, 2007).

Some research suggests the possibility of a racial difference in conversational gaze patterns: In dyadic interactions, a white listener may look at a speaker more than a black listener will; but a black speaker may look at a listener more than a white speaker will (LaFrance & Mayo, 1976). If these claims are correct, we ought to be cautious before judging others as too aggressive or too inattentive simply because we believe they look at us too much or not nearly enough.

ADAPTATION During a conversation, we often adjust our behavior in response to the behavior of the person we're with. As we've seen in previous chapters, we may be entirely unaware of how we change from one moment to the next: leaning forward to reciprocate another's shift in body orientation (Chapter 4), mimicking another's sad facial expression (Chapter 5), synchronizing our movements to the slower beat of another's speech, mirroring another's relaxed posture, or accommodating another's louder tone of voice (Chapter 6). The common denominator is that in all these particular adaptations, our behavior becomes more similar to that of the other person.

There is considerable evidence that many of these behavioral adaptations occur automatically and outside our conscious awareness, a phenomenon called the **chameleon effect** (Bargh, Chen, & Burrows, 1996). According to this theory, the mere perception of another person's postures, gestures, expressions, and mannerisms is sometimes sufficient to produce the same behaviors in the perceiver. This perception-behavior link creates a sort of "monkey see, monkey do" stimulus-response pattern

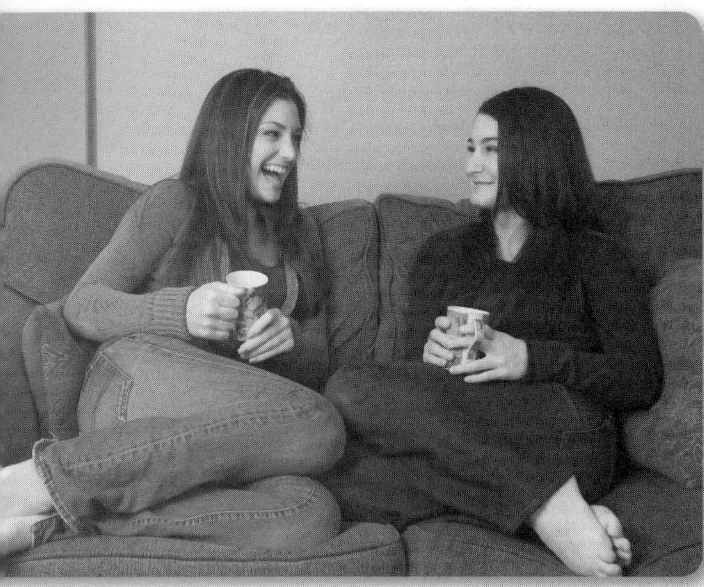

▸ During a conversation, we often adjust our behavior unknowingly in response to the behavior of the person we're with. Studies show that one type of adaptation, *posture sharing* or *mirroring*, occurs when persons are either building or trying to build conversational rapport.

istockphoto.com/leezsnow

that reflects and influences our interactions with others. For example, researchers in one experiment found that participants taking turns describing a series of pictures were much more likely to rub their face or shake their foot unknowingly when they interacted with a person who deliberately did those things than when they interacted with a person who did not (Chartrand & Bargh, 1999).

How does the chameleon effect relate to conversational rapport? As Chartrand and Lakin (2013) point out in their recent review of the research on this topic, "[M]any of the factors that increase behavioral mimicry are related in some way to affiliation and rapport" (p. 293). One of the building blocks of rapport is the feeling that you have something in common with another person—a perception of similarity; and there is evidence that mimicry is more likely to occur when someone is similar, or believes he or she is similar, to another person. For example, Gueguen and Martin (2009) found that mimicry of another person was more likely to occur when participants in their experiments (college students) were told that the person they were going to observe in a video recording shared the same first name or the same subject of study as they did. Mimicry is also more likely to occur when we have some reason to like someone than when we do not (Stel et al., 2010). So these studies suggest that mimicry may be a sign of perceived similarity and it may indicate the potential for liking between individuals. But how do these factors translate into signs of rapport?

The earliest research on posture sharing (i.e., mirroring) provided an optimistic picture of a clear and straightforward answer to the question raised above by showing that posture sharing is an indicator of rapport (Charney, 1966; LaFrance, 1979; LaFrance & Broadbent, 1976). But several follow-up studies failed to replicate these early findings, showing instead that couples who shared similar postures were actually less talkative and more likely to report feeling anxious or self-conscious during their interactions than were couples who didn't share similar postures (Bernieri, 1988; LaFrance & Ickes, 1981). Why the discrepancy? One possibility is that there were differences in how well the individuals knew each other. In the first series of studies, the participants were involved in ongoing relationships with each other, but in the follow-up studies, participants were little more than casual acquaintances. So one conclusion is that while posture sharing may reflect rapport in the later stages of a relationship (e.g., friends, coworkers, etc.), it may reflect only an attempt to build rapport—where little exists—in the early stages (Bernieri & Rosenthal, 1991; Chartrand & Lakin, 2013). In fact, studies show that the chameleon effect occurs when people are merely *trying* to build rapport with others and that various forms of mimicry reveal an unconscious effort to build positive relations with another person (Tickle-Degnen, 2006). Still, as much as mimicry may occur between strangers trying to build rapport, it is much more prevalent and a more reliable sign of rapport between friends than between strangers (Chartrand & Lakin, 2013).

Some studies also suggest that under certain circumstances, deliberately mimicking or matching another person's behavior can build rapport. One early experiment revealed that when an individual copied the postures and gestures of others, he received more positive evaluations from them than he did from persons whose postures and gestures he did not copy (Dabbs, 1969). In another experiment, researchers asked pairs of participants to take turns describing a series of photographs. In each dyad, one of the participants was a confederate instructed by the researchers to mimic the postures, movements, and mannerisms of randomly selected participants. The mimicked participants liked their partner more and also reported having smoother interactions than did the non-mimicked participants (Chartrand & Bargh, 1999). In another, more recent experiment, participants who were instructed to mimic the behavior of their interaction partner reported feeling closer to their interaction partner and experienced a generally smoother interaction compared to participants who were not told to mimic their partner (Stel et al., 2010). Recent research also shows that deliberate mimicry of another person's nonverbal behavior can trigger in that person a desire to seek affiliation, which contributes to greater rapport (Leander, Chartrand, & Wood, 2011). So there is some evidence that mimicry can lead to conversational rapport.

But even though the results of these experiments confirm the positive impact of mimicry and matching, the interaction contexts in these studies lack many of the elements found in ordinary everyday conversations, such as unclear goals and unstructured exchanges. Thus, questions remain about whether we can build rapport by simply copying someone's posture, accent, mannerisms, facial expressions, rate of speech, and so on. More likely, these patterns may reflect rapport or efforts to build rapport but do not necessarily produce it—an interpretation consistent with the fact that we usually aren't aware of our nonverbal cues in these instances. In addition, trying to mimic someone's behavior can backfire if your behavior appears phony rather than genuine, if the other person discovers what you're trying to do, or if you become self-conscious or distracted while trying to carry out the performance.

EXERCISE 7.4

TRY THIS

Sharing Postures

OBJECTIVE: To evaluate the apparent pros and cons of postural congruence

INSTRUCTIONS: The next time you have a conversation with a friend (don't try this with someone you don't know very well), try mimicking his or her postures at several points during the conversation. Hold those postures for as long as your friend does. Try not to be obvious about what you are doing—be as subtle and inconspicuous as you can. Be prepared to answer the following questions.

Discussion Questions:

1. Were you able to accomplish postural congruence? Did you encounter any difficulties trying to do it?
2. Did your friend figure out what you were doing?
3. Do you believe that posture sharing had any impact on the conversation? Explain.

We don't know how much we can build rapport in a typical conversation by strategically adapting our nonverbal behavior to that of another person. Nonetheless, it is easy to appreciate the many pitfalls that come from mismatched, incompatible conversational styles; and more than a few studies confirm the positive effects—including the favorable judgments of those who observe the conversation—of adaptations that result in reciprocity, mimicry, matching, mirroring, and speech convergence (Cappella, 1985). But like other forms of positive nonverbal communication, more is not necessarily better. In fact, research shows that a moderate degree of mimicry tends to produce more rapport between people than does a small or a large degree of mimicry (Tickle-Degnen, 2006). What this seems to imply is that while a lack of mimicry is a sign that two people in a conversation are not connecting very well, too much mimicry may mean they are trying too hard (i.e., being overly polite or accommodating).

The Interaction Context

Building conversational rapport with a stranger is no doubt more challenging for some individuals than for others and in some situations compared to others. In this concluding section, we focus on how the nonverbal encoding and decoding of conversational rapport depends on the goals we wish to achieve in a particular context. As new studies continue to shed light on how judgments of rapport depend on nonverbal cues, we are also learning that the perceptions of conversational participants often differ from those of outside observers and, ultimately, that the interpersonal context of a conversation makes a difference.

Some interaction contexts place greater demands on our nonverbal communication than other contexts do. For instance, contexts where the participants are either bored and unfocused, or anxious and overly focused, make it difficult for them to build rapport and tougher for observers to recognize it. In contrast, interaction contexts with reasonably clear goals and in which participants are focused, relaxed, and engaged make it easier for them to build rapport and easier for observers to notice high or low levels of rapport (Tickle-Degnen, 2006). In one important study, psychologist Frank Bernieri and his colleagues examined the impact of nonverbal behavior in two different dyadic contexts: one competitive (taking opposite sides on a controversial topic) and the other cooperative (planning a vacation). Their analysis of 50-second videotaped clips from each of 50 opposite-sex interactions revealed some key differences not only between the competitive and cooperative contexts but also between the judgments of participants and those of observers (Bernieri, Gillis, Davis, & Grahe, 1996). A look at Table 7.3, which summarizes their findings, shows that the competitive interactions yielded a much wider range of nonverbal indicators than did the cooperative interactions. These results suggest that it may be less demanding nonverbally to build rapport in simple cooperative tasks than in

Table 7.3 Nonverbal Predictors of Conversational Rapport

Competitive Context	Cooperative Context	
Participants	Back channels	Proximity
	Eye contact	*Interaction synchrony*
	Forward lean	
	Gestures (females only)	
	Fewer posture shifts	
	Proximity	
	Interaction synchrony	
Observers	Back channels	*Expressiveness*
	Expressiveness	Gestures (females)
	Proximity	
	Smiling	

Note: Most significant predictors are italicized.

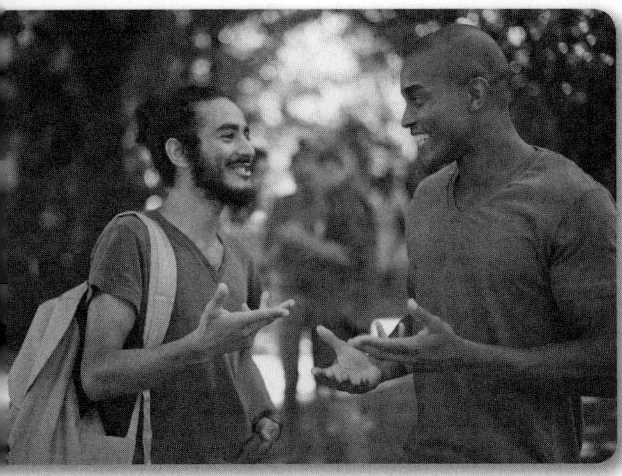

▸ It may be especially challenging to build rapport when we are interacting with someone of unequal status or with someone whose cultural background is different than our own.

istockphoto.com/PeopleImages

more complex and demanding tasks. In addition, the results show that observers' judgments of rapport, which differed from those of participants, relied heavily on how expressive (i.e., animated, emotional) the speakers were, despite the fact that expressiveness was unrelated to how much rapport the participants actually felt, particularly in the competitive context, where observer judgments were less accurate. According to the researchers, this judgment bias in favor of expressiveness leads to a halo effect that benefits expressive individuals in much the same way that it benefits good-looking people: We tend to evaluate expressive persons more positively (e.g., well liked, friendly, charismatic, etc.) than we evaluate less expressive persons.

It may be especially challenging to build rapport when we are interacting with someone of unequal status or with someone whose cultural background is much different than our own. In the case of status differences, as we will see in Chapter 10, higher-status persons generally behave toward lower-status persons in a more distant, less involved, less pleasant, and less responsive manner than lower-status persons behave toward higher-status persons—an asymmetrical or mismatched nonverbal communication pattern that interferes with the attainment of rapport. In the case of cultural differences, our lack of familiarity with the conversational norms and customs of another culture can produce tentative, awkward, and inappropriate behavior that makes rapport difficult to achieve.

Research on interracial interactions in particular also shows that feelings of prejudice, anticipating prejudice, and even making an effort to avoid the appearance of prejudice create conditions that make it difficult to build rapport. In their extensive review of this research, John Dovidio and his colleagues note that while explicit forms of bias (racist beliefs) show up in what a person says, subtler and implicit forms of bias (hidden feelings) show up in our nonverbal cues. They offer a clear and concise picture of the obstacles faced by many black and white individuals in these sometimes-uncomfortable situations:

> With respect to race relations, in particular, our analysis has revealed, Whites' self-consciousness in interracial interactions may lead them to focus primarily on the controllable aspects of their behavior, such as the verbal content of their speech, but to

> increase the signs of discomfort and other negative states they exhibit nonverbally. Because they interpret their behavior based on the behaviors they can monitor most easily, Whites tend to overestimate how favorably they are appearing. In contrast, Blacks, because of their self-consciousness, may be particularly vigilant to cues of Whites' bias in these interactions. As a result, they may rely on nonverbal behavior primarily, largely discounting the verbal content, in forming impressions of Whites and the interaction. Given their vigilance to cues of bias, Blacks are likely to attribute their White partner's negative nonverbal behavior to racial bias. (Dovidio, Hebl, Richeson, & Shelton, 2006, p. 495)

To illustrate, let's consider a hypothetical case: Michael, who is black, is meeting with Jim, who is white, to discuss a class assignment. Michael wonders if Jim is prejudiced and Jim worries about appearing prejudiced. When they get together, Michael will be attuned to subtle signs of prejudice in Jim's behavior, and Jim will be careful not to say anything that Michael could take the wrong way. Jim's self-consciousness and control over what he says will make his nonverbal behavior seem less friendly: he'll make less eye contact with Michael, fidget more, exhibit more masking/polite smiles, touch his face more, and so forth. But because Jim is more aware of what he's saying than how he's saying it, he'll think he's making a good impression. Michael, however, may be paying as much if not more attention to Jim's nonverbal cues and will therefore get a different impression. Research confirms this conversational dynamic in mixed-race encounters and also shows that in these interactions both blacks and whites are more likely to attribute nonverbal signs of anxiety from the other person as proof of unfriendliness than they would in interactions with someone of the same race (Dovidio et al., 2006). Moreover, there is some proof that blacks are more attuned to these subtle messages. In one experiment, researchers found that black observers, viewing a 20-second silent video clip of an interracial conversation, were better able than white observers to accurately estimate the implicit bias of the white participants in the videotaped interactions (Richeson & Shelton, 2005).

In sum, the nonverbal cues of conversational partners are especially important in communicating rapport. Still, we may question how important these signals are compared to what people say (verbal content). Research suggests that nonverbal communication is probably more important. In one study, Grahe and Bernieri (1999) prepared brief video clips of mixed-sex pairs of students working on a cooperative task (planning a vacation). The researchers wanted to find out how accurately the judges could assess the rapport present in each interaction (i.e., how the judge's ratings compared to the students' own ratings). Some of the judges read a transcript of the students' interactions (verbal only); some saw the video (visual only); some listened (audio only); some watched the video and read the transcript (verbal and visual); and some watched and listened (visual, verbal, and audio). The results of this experiment confirmed the overwhelming importance of nonverbal communication, particularly as it is conveyed through the visual channel. In fact, judges who only saw the video (visual only) were more accurate in assessing rapport than were any of the other judges—including those who received the full videorecorded presentation (visual, verbal, and audio). The pairs of students who reported the highest levels of rapport were those who exhibited the most expressive, synchronous, and proximate behaviors—behaviors fully accessible to judges with access to the visual channel.

INFLUENTIAL ENCOUNTERS: GETTING HELP

When was the last time that you asked someone for help? Consider the following scenario: You go to a shopping mall to purchase some clothes. After making your purchase, you head toward the exit. An individual approaches you and asks you to sign a petition in support of a local initiative about which you know little. Will your response depend on what this person looks like or on how she or he behaves while making the request? In short, does nonverbal communication in such an encounter make a difference? In the sections that follow, we'll examine the research on **compliance gaining** (when we ask a person for help), but we'll also address relevant studies on a closely related subject—**prosocial behavior** (helping someone without being asked to help).

Nonverbal Communication Makes a Difference

For more than three decades, researchers have been conducting compliance-gaining experiments to determine whether or not our appearance or our demeanor alters the likelihood that others will say yes when we ask for assistance. In nearly all these experiments, researchers place one or more individuals (confederates) into an ordinary situation in which they must ask strangers (subjects) for help. Varying their nonverbal presentation according to the researcher's specifications (the confederates might be instructed to touch some subjects but not others or to establish eye contact with some subjects but not others, and so forth), the confederates approach randomly selected subjects and ask each for some type of assistance (e.g., to give money, participate in a survey, mail a postcard, donate money, sign a petition, etc.). With the exception of the nonverbal presentation that they deliberately vary, the confederates try to keep their actions constant from one encounter to another. Recording how many subjects comply with the request, researchers compare rates of compliance for each type of nonverbal presentation (e.g., touching the subject compared to not touching the subject).

Some of these experiments focus on the appearance of the confederate, while others concentrate on the confederate's nonverbal behavior.

After completing a statistical analysis of 49 such experiments (nearly 10,000 subjects) published in scientific journals between 1971 and 1992, communication researcher Chris Segrin (1993) concluded that nonverbal communication does indeed make a difference. Notable exceptions notwithstanding, the overall finding from his analysis is that compliance with a request is more likely when the person making the request wears formal or high-status attire or uses immediacy behaviors such as eye contact, close proximity, or touch. More recent research shows that mimicking another person's behavior may also lead to greater compliance and prosocial behavior. In the sections below, we'll take a closer look at some of the experiments that have been done on compliance gaining and prosocial behavior and point out important exceptions (i.e., when nonverbal communication doesn't seem to make a difference).

ATTRACTIVENESS It might not surprise us to learn that attractive people have an edge when it comes to getting what they want. In one typical experiment, researchers placed a dime in a conspicuous place in a phone booth. As subjects (random phone callers) left the phone booth, presumably with the dime in their possession, a female confederate approached, saying, "Excuse me, I think I might have left a dime in this booth. Did you find it?" Half the time, the confederate, who was attractive, dressed to look as homely as possible. When she looked her best, 87% of the subjects complied, but when she dressed poorly, her success rate dropped to 64% (Sroufe, Chaikin, Cook, & Freeman, 1977). Many other experiments have yielded similar results (Wilson, 1978). For instance, psychologist Shelly Chaiken (1979) arranged for her students to approach other students on campus and to ask them to fill out a questionnaire and sign a petition requiring the university to stop serving meat at breakfast and lunch at all dining commons. Overall, attractive students were more successful at getting signatures than were the less-attractive students. The most striking difference occurred when males approached females: The attractive men were successful 53% of the time; the less attractive men were successful only 38% of the time.

The advantage of good looks even extends to situations in which people engage in prosocial behavior—they choose to help without being asked. In one experiment, researchers discovered that motorists were more likely to assist a woman stranded on the highway with a flat tire if she was attractive than if she wasn't (Athanasiou & Greene, 1973). In another experiment, researchers found that good looks can encourage good deeds—even when there's no one around to witness the deed. The researchers placed a completed graduate school application clipped to a stamped envelope inside a telephone booth at the Detroit airport. An attached note read, "Dear

Dad, Have a nice trip. Please remember to mail this application before you leave Detroit on your flight to New York." It was signed either "Love, Linda" or "Love, Bob." Half the time, a photograph attached to the application pictured an attractive man or woman; half the time, it pictured an unattractive man or woman. More people helped out by dropping the application into a mailbox when the attached photograph showed an attractive person than when it showed an unattractive person.

Of course, there might be an exception. Maybe looks wouldn't make any difference in an emergency situation. After all, when someone needs help badly and there's no time to play favorites, wouldn't the good Samaritan in each of us win the day? Not necessarily, according to the results of one experiment: A woman (confederate) wearing a blood-soaked bandage around one arm approached strangers, asking for their help. She told them she was just bitten by a rat while conducting an experiment and needed money for a tetanus shot. In some cases—the less severe version—there was no blood or bandage. The woman was either attractive or unattractive. Her ability to obtain help depended on both attractiveness and severity. When things looked bad (i.e., blood-soaked bandage), the attractive woman got more help; when things didn't look so bad (i.e., no blood or bandage), attractiveness didn't make any difference (West & Brown, 1975). The more we need help, the more it may help to look good.

CLOTHING The way we dress can also make a difference. Many of the experiments that have been done on clothing focus on the impact of wearing a uniform; most others consider the impact of wearing high-status as opposed to low-status or unconventional attire. In his analysis of 19 such experiments, Segrin (1993) concluded that (1) uniforms gain compliance and (2) most of the time, high-status dress is more likely to gain compliance than is low-status dress.

In the early 1970s, psychologist Leonard Bickman conducted several studies on clothing and compliance. In one of his experiments, male confederates who were dressed in a sport coat and tie, a milk company uniform, or what looked like a security guard's uniform approached individuals on a Brooklyn street and asked them to pick up some litter, give some change to a man who needed it for an expired parking meter, or (for those waiting at a bus stop) move to a different location (Bickman, 1974). Regardless of which request was made, people were more willing to comply when the request came from a man in a guard's uniform (36%) than when it came from a man in the coat and tie (20%) or in a milk company uniform (14%). Another study questioned whether people would be as deferential to a woman in uniform as they apparently are to a man (Bushman, 1988). A female confederate dressed in a dark blue uniform; a business suit; or a stained T-shirt, pants, and tennis shoes approached randomly selected pedestrians at a St. Louis shopping center. Pointing at her accomplice, she said: "This fellow is overparked at the meter and doesn't have any change. Give him a nickel." More people complied when the woman was wearing the uniform (72%) than when she was wearing either the business suit (48%) or the T-shirt (52%).

▸ Studies confirm that wearing an authoritative uniform is one of the factors that increase the likelihood of compliance and prosocial behavior.

istockphoto.com/galatapartners

An authoritative-looking uniform makes a difference. Can the same be said about dressing up? Studies comparing high-status clothing to low-status clothing, as we noted, show an overall effect favoring the former over the latter; but the findings are inconsistent enough to raise questions. For example, in the Bushman (1988) study, wearing a business suit was no better than wearing a dirty T-shirt. In another study, male and female confederates, well dressed or sloppily dressed, entered checkout lines of a department store intending to purchase a pack of batteries. Pretending to be short 37 cents, they each asked a customer standing in line behind them (subjects) for the needed amount of money. Well-dressed confederates got no more help than did the sloppily dressed confederates (Long, Mueller, Wyers, Khong, & Jones, 1996). How can we explain these results?

Psychologist Chris Kleinke (1977) offers a theory. He believes that being well dressed is an advantage only when there may be some reason to question the legitimacy of a request, when motivation is an issue. In such cases, well-dressed individuals can benefit from appearing more credible than their poorly dressed counterparts. This theory has some merit. For instance, in one of Bickman's (1971) experiments, well-dressed confederates at airport and train terminals had more success getting people to return money left in a telephone booth (77% compliance) than did poorly dressed confederates (38% compliance). Perhaps the subjects in this experiment had more reason to question the motives, and therefore the credibility, of poorly dressed individuals than those of well-dressed individuals.

Clothing not only makes a difference when asking for help. Research shows that it encourages prosocial behavior in the most ordinary everyday situations, such as crossing the street. In one study of 18,000 attempts to cross the street at legally designated crossing points, more cars stopped for well-dressed pedestrians than for poorly dressed pedestrians (North & Sheridan, 2004).

EXERCISE 7.5

TRY THIS

Dress for Success

OBJECTIVE: To find out if the help you receive depends on the way you're dressed

INSTRUCTIONS: With a friend/observer, visit a nearby shopping mall on two separate occasions. On one, wear sloppy, unattractive clothes; on the other, dress up. Pick out two comparable sets of stores to enter—one set of stores when poorly dressed, the other set of stores when dressed up. For example, on one occasion, visit one jewelry store, one clothing store, and one shoe store. On the other occasion, do the same. In each store, stand in a conspicuous place and wait until someone comes to help you. Keep track of how long it takes to receive service. Ask your friend/observer to note the salesperson's behavior (e.g., smiling, proximity, etc.). Be prepared to answer the following discussion questions.

Discussion Questions:

1. Was there any noticeable difference in the way you were treated based on your appearance?
2. What are the strengths and weaknesses of doing this kind of experiment?

IMMEDIACY BEHAVIOR For reasons we'll discuss shortly, we may be more successful getting help from others if we reach out to them than if we don't. As we learned in Chapter 4, our use of gaze, personal space, and touch makes it possible to reach people in the most rudimentary way we can and take the first step to build a relationship with them. Segrin's (1993) analysis of the research on these immediacy behaviors confirms the contribution they make. Even the simplest of human connections—a split second of eye contact, a single touch, or a close approach—can bring the help we want.

Eye contact almost always helps. In one experiment, researchers trained two young adults (a male and female confederate) to approach 100 individuals walking in a popular spot on the streets of a medium-sized city in France. While asking individuals to participate in a marketing survey, the confederates either maintained a steady gaze with the individual or used an evasive glance, first looking at the individual and then averting their gaze when the individual looked at them. With a steady gaze, the confederates succeeded in getting 66% of the individuals whom they approached to participate in the survey; with an evasive glance they were successful with only 34% (Gueguen & Jacob, 2002a). Segrin's (1993) analysis of 12 experiments shows that compliance was more likely in each one when eye contact accompanied a clear and legitimate request than when it didn't. But note the exceptions to the general rule: It doesn't help when a request is unclear or when it is illegitimate. Some studies show, in fact, that eye contact actually deters people from helping when they question the legitimacy of the request (Kleinke, 1980) or when they don't know exactly what they are being asked to do (Ellsworth & Langer, 1976). Psychologist Phoebe Ellsworth and her associates have demonstrated in a series of experiments that eye contact alone is sufficient to stimulate in others either approach behavior or avoidance behavior. In a study conducted at a shopping mall, subjects were most likely to help a female confederate who made eye contact with them—but only if they knew what she wanted. Her companion (another confederate) approached each subject and explained that her friend needed help finding a lost contact lens. When the subjects didn't know exactly what the problem was (they were just asked to help), those who received eye contact from the confederate-in-need, who was on the ground several feet away, were the least likely to help her (Ellsworth & Langer, 1976). As this study shows, the effect of eye contact depends on the situation: We avoid people who look at us when we aren't sure what they want; we approach people who look at us when we know what they want and we believe we can help.

How close we get to others and whether or not we touch them can also make a difference. Segrin's (1993) review of the research showed a slight advantage for being relatively near someone (1 to 2 feet) rather than far away (3 to 5 feet) when making a request. This was the case in five of the eight studies reviewed. However, this same research qualifies the relationship between distance and compliance. In some studies, being close produced more compliance only in high-need situations, while in low-need situations, it actually paid to be farther away. Although we don't like having a stranger invade our personal space, we may feel it's more understandable and justified in high-need situations.

The research on touch generally shows positive effects. In 11 of the 13 studies Segrin reviewed, lightly touching people on the forearm or shoulder increased their compliance with requests to sign a petition, return money, score questionnaires, volunteer time for charity, participate in a market survey, and the like. Some field studies confirm the impact of touch. In one, confederates asked passersby if they would look after a large and excited dog for ten minutes, a request more demanding than those made in most previous studies. When touched, 55% agreed; when not touched, compliance dropped to 35% (Gueguen & Fischer-Lokou, 2002). In another study, researchers found a post-compliance effect: After complying with a request to participate in a survey, respondents who were touched on the arm worked harder completing the questionnaire than did those who were not touched (Nannberg & Hansen, 1994). Psychologist Nicolas Gueguen recently discovered that touch can lead

RESEARCH 7.3

FIND OUT MORE

Do Waitresses Get Bigger Tips If They Touch Their Customers?

In one of the earliest field studies on the practical effects of touch, the researchers selected a restaurant environment as an appropriate place for their study. Specifically, they were interested in finding out whether customer reactions and tipping behavior were affected in some observable and measurable way by the brief touch of a waitress. So the researchers instructed the waitresses to briefly touch a customer on the hand or shoulder when returning the customer's change after receiving payment for the check. Although touching on the hand or shoulder made no difference, customers who were touched left a bigger tip than did the customers who were not touched.

To find out more about this study and to answer the following questions, see the full text (cited below).

1. Why did the researchers think that touch would make a difference? Did they refer to any prior theory or research to explain or justify their predictions?
2. What kind of study is this? (See Appendix.)
3. Did the effect of touch differ for men compared to women customers?
4. What were the strengths and limitations of this study?

Source: Crusco, A., & Wetzel, C. G. (1984). The Midas touch: The effects of interpersonal touch on restaurant tipping. *Personality and Social Psychology Bulletin, 10*, 512–517.

to compliance in a courtship context. One experiment found that a male confederate approaching women in a French nightclub had more success when asking women to slow dance with him when he touched the women on the arm while asking them to dance than when he didn't touch them while asking them. And a second experiment found that a male confederate approaching women on the street and asking them for their phone numbers obtained more phone numbers when he touched the women on the arm than when he didn't (Gueguen, 2007).

But touch doesn't always help. In one study, for instance, touching people at an airport while asking them to mail a postcard produced no more compliance than did not touching them at all (Remland & Jones, 1994). In another study, a female confederate asked individual shoppers ahead of her in the checkout lines of a discount store if she could move ahead of them. Her verbal justification varied from a low justification ("Excuse me. Do you mind if I get ahead of you in line?") to a high justification ("Excuse me. I just volunteered to drive my neighbor to the hospital for a lab appointment. Do you mind if I get ahead of you in line?"). Whereas the confederate's justification made a difference to the shoppers, her use of touch did not (Bohm & Hendricks, 1997). Sometimes compliance depends on the gender of the person making the request, as it did in a study where male bus drivers were only more likely to go along with a person's request to ride the bus for less than the full payment if the person was a woman who used a slight touch while making the request (Gueguen & Fischer-Lokou, 2003). Identifying homophobia as the most likely cause, a series of experiments actually found that men touched by a man were *less* likely to comply with a request than if they were not touched by the man (Dolinski, 2010). Perhaps in certain environments, with certain kinds of requests and with certain individuals, touch may not matter and may even be counterproductive. Future research may help determine the conditions under which touch is most likely to facilitate compliance and prosocial behavior.

MIMICRY In our earlier discussion of conversational rapport, we concluded that mimicry often has positive social effects. Do these effects include compliance with a request for help and prosocial behavior? Although more research needs to be done, a few studies suggest that it might. In one experiment, for instance, participants whose body orientation and arm movements were mimicked by another person were more likely to comply with a request to read and offer feedback on a written essay than were participants who were not mimicked. Specifically, 77% of the participants offered to help in the mimicry condition, while only 47% offered to help in the non-mimicry condition (Gueguen, Martin, & Meineri, 2011). Other studies show that mimicked persons are more likely to donate money to charitable causes, help a stranded person, and volunteer to fill out a tedious survey questionnaire (Ashton-James, van Baaren, Chartrand, Decety, & Karremans, 2007; Fischer-Lokou, Martin, & Guegen, 2011; Stel, van Baaren, & Vonk, 2008).

Research also shows that mimicking another person's body posture and position can produce prosocial helping behavior. For instance, researchers in the Netherlands conducted a series of experiments in which a female confederate either mimicked or did not mimic the body lean, arm position, and leg position of seated participants while the participants described their opinions of different advertisements for what they believed was a marketing study (van Baaren, Holland, Kawakami, & van Knippenberg, 2004). The results of the first experiment showed that mimicked participants were more likely to help the confederate by picking up pens that she dropped on the floor (100%) than were the participants who were not mimicked (33%). What's more, the researchers found in a second and third study that the prosocial behavior of mimicked persons went beyond helping only the person who did the mimicking. In the second study, mimicked participants were more likely to pick up pens dropped by someone who was not involved in the mimicking part of the experiment (84%) than were the non-mimicked participants (48%). And in the third study, mimicked participants were more likely to donate money to charity (76%) than were the non-mimicked participants (43%). Although we need more research before claiming that mimicry increases the likelihood of gaining compliance, these findings certainly suggest that it may have such an effect.

Why Nonverbal Communication Makes a Difference

As the above research shows, getting people to help us may depend as much, if not more, on our nonverbal communication as it does on the words we use (Segrin, 1993). Overall, it pays to look good, wear an authoritative uniform, dress up, make eye contact, get close, and use a light touch to the forearm or shoulder. Perhaps with additional research, we may be able to add other nonverbal cues—facial expressions, speech accents, vocal qualities, postures and so forth—that could also make a difference. It may surprise us to learn that seemingly trivial actions can play so prominent a role in our everyday interactions. At this point, we'll stop to consider four different reasons why nonverbal communication can determine whether or not someone comes to our aid: attraction, authority, affiliation, and arousal.

ATTRACTION Why do good looks make a difference? In their book, *Mirror, Mirror: The Importance of Looks in Everyday Life*, psychologists Elaine Hatfield and Susan Sprecher (1986) offer a straightforward explanation: We like good-looking people, we're attracted to them, and we tend to give them the benefit of the doubt (remember the halo effect from Chapter 3). As a result, they are more likely to be the beneficiary of our good intentions than are the less attractive people who seek our assistance. Even in the case of the various immediacy behaviors that produce compliance, the attraction explanation makes sense. We often interpret eye contact, close distances, and touch as indicators of liking. And research in social psychology has shown convincingly that we tend to like people who we believe like us, a simple fact of life sometimes known as the reciprocity-of-liking rule (Berscheid & Walster, 1978).

One final point is worth noting: Evidence is beginning to surface, as we noted much earlier in this chapter, that we have a bias in favor of expressive behavior (Bernieri et al., 1996). Although eye contact, proximity, and touch alone rarely convey particular emotions, they are part of the affective domain and express the attitudes and feelings we have toward others. Thus, we are likely to judge persons who use these behaviors as more expressive than persons who refrain from using such behaviors.

AUTHORITY In his now-famous experiments on obedience to authority, psychologist Stanley Milgram (1974) demonstrated dramatically how a surprising number of unsuspecting individuals (subjects) would administer to others (confederates) what they thought were painful electric shocks (in reality, none of the confederates were shocked) simply because an authority figure told them to do so (subjects were told, "The experiment must continue"). As a salient symbol of authority, a uniform can produce the same sort of knee-jerk reaction that will make us do what we are told. Less directly, high-status clothing, as well as the use of eye contact, personal space, and touch, can all serve as status reminders (see Chapter 4), cues we often associate with legitimate authority.

AFFILIATION Rooted in the concept of identification, so fundamental to the process of persuasion, this explanation says that we may be more likely to aid someone who is one of us than someone who is different from us. In fact, the results of some studies on high-status dress favor this explanation over the rival theory based on the authority of one's clothing. Communication researcher Wayne Hensley (1981) found, for instance, that well-dressed female confederates at an airport terminal were able to obtain more money to make a telephone call (they approached subjects and asked each for money) than were their poorly dressed counterparts; but at a train station in a lower-class neighborhood, they received less money. In another experiment, a team of researchers found that men were more successful in gaining compliance when they wore a necktie—but not among the working-class individuals whom they approached (Green & Giles, 1973). In these studies, at least, the message is clear: Similarity outweighs status. On a much deeper level, immediacy and mimicking behaviors can also promote affiliation. Even if just for a fleeting moment, eye contact, proximity, touch, and mimicry establish a human bond with another person and foster the recognition that a fellow human needs our help.

AROUSAL Anyone who has ever rushed to the aid of a crying infant can fully appreciate one way that arousal leads to compliance: negative reinforcement, taking action to remove an aversive stimulus (e.g., crying). This demand theory of compliance (Ellsworth & Langer, 1976) can explain why someone might go along with a request from a pushy stranger who gets too close, stares, or touches. In such cases, the best way to end the discomfort may be to comply with the request.

A second explanation, arousal-labeling theory, suggests that we may label the arousal produced by immediacy behaviors positively or negatively (Patterson, 1976). If we like being touched, for example, we might comply with the toucher's request. On the other hand, if we dislike being touched, we would not comply to avoid rewarding the toucher. Despite the intuitive appeal of this theory, its validity remains a matter of speculation. Most of the studies do not assess the attitudes or feelings of subjects, which would be necessary to test the theory.

Finally, the most elaborate arousal-based perspective, with implications for compliance gaining, is expectancy violations theory. According to this theory, we may become aroused when someone's behavior, such as standing close to us, violates our expectations. The arousal focuses our attention on the individual who violated our expectations. If this individual is highly rewarding to us (e.g., liked, respected, attractive, etc.), then the violation increases the probability that we'll comply with the request. For instance, we might be more likely to comply with the request of an attractive (high-reward) person who invades our space than with an unattractive (low-reward) person who does the same. Like the other arousal explanations, however, this promising theory has not yet been fully tested in the compliance-gaining context (Segrin, 1993).

SUMMARY

Nonverbal communication plays a major role in our everyday interpersonal encounters with anyone, anywhere, and at any time. Building conversational rapport with others involves an ability to use approach–avoidance signals as well as an ability to coordinate our behavior with that of another. We use various approach–avoidance signals to enter and exit conversations (e.g., greeting rituals), and we use a wide array of nonverbal involvement behaviors to express some degree of commitment to a conversation. Interpersonal coordination, which is vital to building rapport, includes the many signals we use to negotiate the turn taking that occurs in conversations. It also involves some degree of adaptation, an ability to adjust our behavior in response to the behavior of another (e.g., mimicking, synchronizing, mirroring, etc.).

Numerous studies have discovered a connection between certain nonverbal signals and the likelihood of obtaining compliance from a stranger. In particular, attractiveness, clothing, and immediacy behaviors generally make a difference when requesting aid from strangers. There are many possible explanations for the nonverbal communication compliance-gaining effect. The most common include increased attraction, perceptions of authority, feelings of affiliation, and physiological arousal.

KEY TERMS

Back-channel signals 261
Chameleon effect 265
Civil inattention 254
Compliance gaining 272
Gaze window 263
Greeting rituals 252
Interpersonal coordination 260
Nonverbal involvement behaviors 257
Prosocial behavior 272
Switch pauses 261
Turn-denying signals 260
Turn-maintaining signals 260
Turn-requesting signals 260
Turn-yielding signals 260
Unfocused interactions 254

istockphoto.com/AMR Image

Chapter Outine

8

NONVERBAL COMMUNICATION IN INTIMATE ENCOUNTERS

Sometimes in our relationships with others, we experience turning points—moments when something happens that dramatically alters the course of the relationship. A student in one of my classes, Matt, described such a moment that he had with his best friend at the time:

> As time went on, we hung out together more and more. But I began to like her in a way that was much more than friendship. The problem was I didn't know how to approach her about this because I didn't want to risk losing her friendship in the process. I decided that I would become more "flirty" with her when we went out. I would try to get closer to her than I normally did. You could say I was going to enter her personal space and see how she reacted, before I decided to tell her how I felt. So that night, we went for a walk after going to a movie, and I tried to stay very close to her, I held eye contact more often and much longer, and I guess you could say more intensely. I tried to do everything I could to get a feel for how she felt. As the night progressed, I noticed that she was responding the same way and wasn't opposed to the "nonverbal cues" that I was presenting. Later that night, I asked her to be my girlfriend and she said

Learning Objectives

After reading this chapter, you will be able to do the following:

1. Explain how cognitive valence theory highlights the dynamic relationship between nonverbal communication and relational intimacy.
2. Understand how intimacy affects the nonverbal communication that occurs in a relationship.
3. Recognize how nonverbal communication in successful relationships differs from nonverbal communication in less successful relationships.
4. Identify the identity signals and courtship signals that attract a potential mate and influence the development of romantic relationships.
5. Discuss the various nonverbal behaviors that affect the occurrence, escalation, and management of interpersonal conflicts in close relationships.
6. Explain how a person's attachment style influences the person's ability to provide and receive emotional support.
7. Identify the various nonverbal messages that can provide emotional support to others' communication.

> yes. She went on to tell me that she knew I was going to bring it up because of the "hints" I was giving her all night, by the way I was acting and not by what I was saying.

Matt's experience should remind us of how much we all rely on approach–avoidance signals such as eye contact, personal space, and touch to communicate our desire or lack of desire for intimacy. Rarely, do we put these intentions into words. Being able to send, receive, and respond to nonverbal signals can have a tremendous impact on our intimate relationships with other individuals.

This chapter explores the role of nonverbal communication in our most intimate encounters, those we usually reserve for family members, close friends, and romantic partners. We begin with an overview of some key concepts and principles regarding the importance of nonverbal signals in close relationships. Then we'll focus on the three types of encounters we all experience with the special people in our lives: romantic encounters, confrontational encounters, and comforting encounters.

RELATIONAL INTIMACY AND NONVERBAL COMMUNICATION

Most of us know that we don't communicate the same way with a close friend or with a sibling as we do with a new acquaintance. With a close friend, for example, we may be more open, discuss more topics, dress more casually, and act more spontaneously. In fact, we may not be completely aware of how our style of communication changes from an interaction with one person to an interaction with another. Yet the way we communicate reflects the kind of relationship we have with someone. In this section, we'll examine our nonverbal communication in intimate or close relationships, those with individuals whom we like, trust, and know well. First, we'll consider the dynamics of regulating intimate nonverbal communication. Then we'll highlight the nature of nonverbal communication in intimate or close relationships. Finally, we'll examine the role of nonverbal communication in determining the success of our close relationships.

The Dynamics of Intimacy Regulation

Jason and Melissa have been dating close to three years. They met over the summer while working the day shift at a nearby restaurant. Jason remembers their first date and how he had to muster the courage to ask Melissa out to a movie. Melissa always liked Jason's sense of humor, and they hit it off from the start. Most of their friends can't believe they haven't married. "They do practically every thing together," people who know them say. Inseparable couples, like Jason and Melissa, love being around each other. They not only enjoy each other's company, they are also free to be themselves, always feeling accepted and comfortable. This kind of closeness takes time to develop; it rarely happens overnight, even under the best of circumstances. As Jason and Melissa became closer, their communication gradually changed, reflecting the increased intimacy of their relationship.

Intimate nonverbal communication consists of behaviors that promote closeness and mutual affection in our relationships with others. These behaviors can take a relationship with someone to the next level or indicate that the relationship is moving in that direction. At a minimum, intimate nonverbal communication includes the various behaviors related to conversational rapport—signs of nonverbal involvement, smooth turn taking, and patterns of mutual adaptation—which serve as a stepping stone toward building a more intimate relationship.

Increased intimacy in a relationship doesn't take place in a vacuum. Several factors combine in an instant to determine whether or not a couple takes the next step on the path toward greater intimacy. One account of how this happens is known as **cognitive valence theory**. Proposed by communication scholar Peter Andersen (1989), it sheds light on why we welcome some attempts at intimacy and reject others. The theory predicts what will happen when one person in a relationship tries to become more intimate with the other. Beginning with a focus on nonverbal immediacy behaviors (e.g., gaze, proximity, body orientation, touch, and smiling), the theory predicts that an increase in immediacy by Person A will produce a positive response from Person B only under certain conditions: (a) Person B perceives Person A's increased immediacy; (b) Person A's behavior causes Person B to become moderately aroused, which activates Person B's **cognitive schemata** (i.e., stored knowledge determining whether or not Person B will be receptive to Person A's increased intimacy); and (c) Person B's cognitive schemata is completely positive—any negative valence will produce a negative reaction.

Like other similar theories (see Chapter 4), cognitive valence theory concentrates on the pivotal exchanges of intimacy—sometimes what become the turning points in our relationships—that occur in all sorts of everyday encounters. Three years ago, when Jason and Melissa went out on their first date, they experienced a few awkward but fateful moments. While Jason was anxious to take the relationship to the next level, Melissa was less sure and wanted to proceed more slowly. Sitting next to Melissa in his car right after the movie, Jason put his hand on her leg and slowly leaned over to kiss her, but she turned away. Later that evening, however, Melissa's unexpected goodnight kiss completely eradicated his worst fears. Jason's unmistakable increase in immediacy produced moderate arousal in Melissa (activating her cognitive schemata). Her feeling that it was too early in the relationship for sex (i.e., negatively valenced relational schemata) effectively countered her strong positive feelings for Jason, leading to compensatory behavior on her part (turning away). But later in the evening, things took a positive turn because of Melissa's belief that a goodnight kiss, but not sex, is a perfectly acceptable way to show your affection on a first date (positively valenced relational schemata).

According to the theory, many other factors could have caused Melissa to respond to Jason's advances similarly: becoming afraid (high arousal), being from a country that discourages physical contact before marriage (cultural appropriateness), having a shy personality (personal predisposition), disliking Jason (interpersonal reward), being in the wrong place at the wrong time (situational appropriateness), or having a headache (psychological or physical state). Although several key elements of the theory have not been fully tested (e.g., the hypothesized association between negative outcomes and any single negatively valenced schemata), cognitive valence theory gives us a comprehensive and intuitively sensible picture of what happens when even the most ordinary of our interactions take a turn toward greater intimacy.

Nonverbal Communication in Close Relationships

Nonverbal communication in intimate relationships includes normative behaviors and patterns of interaction that differentiate very close relationships (e.g., a ten-year marriage) from all other relationships, including those in the early stages of intimacy (e.g., a two-month courtship). In addition, it includes the nonverbal cues we expect to exchange in intimate contexts such as a romantic dinner, a family fight, or a painful self-disclosure.

Social psychologists Irwin Altman and Dalmas Taylor (1973) developed an elaborate theory to explain what happens to interpersonal relationships as the partners become more and more intimate. One element of that theory, which we focus on here, identifies eight changes in communication that take place as a relationship deepens. As Table 8.1 shows, each dimension captures a particular quality of communication that we should expect from intimates.

To illustrate some of these qualities, what might we expect from Jason and Melissa? The closeness that comes from three years of being together can show up in any number of ways: When Jason gets upset, Melissa knows immediately because of the way he sighs, stretches his neck, and touches his forehead (efficiency); when they go out together and get into one of their good conversations—the kind that can go on for hours—they go back and forth in the blink of an eye, echoing each other's postures and movements (synchrony); Melissa says that Jason has a habit of belching out loud when he wants to bug her, something he would never do in public (openness); occasionally, when Jason does something to annoy her (such as belching), Melissa screams angrily at him (spontaneity) to stop acting like a jerk. Sometimes when they're out with friends, she teases him in a good-natured way about him being a slob (evaluation).

Table 8.1 Nonverbal Communication in Intimate Relationships

Communication		
Dimensions	**Essential features**	**Examples**
RICHNESS	Exposure to a wide variety of messages, greater breadth of communication	More facial expressions (e.g., blends), subtler vocal cues, more self-presentations (e.g., wardrobe changes)
EFFICIENCY	Accuracy and speed of signals, fewer misunderstandings	Decoding symptoms of emotion (e.g., anxiety, depression, contempt, etc.) that might be missed or misunderstood by others
UNIQUENESS	Less stylized or conventional forms of communication, idiosyncratic signals	Unique emblematic messages for expressing affection, being secretive, etc.
SUBSTITUTABILITY	Different ways of expressing the same message, interchangeable signals, flexibility in signaling system	Ability to signal a feeling, such as romantic interest, with a gesture, facial expression, glance, vocalization, etc.
SYNCHRONY	Smooth exchange of messages, turn taking, interpersonal coordination, and sensitivity	Interactional synchrony, mirroring, signals, speech convergence
OPENNESS	Accessibility of self to other, witnessing private behavior	Immediacy behaviors such as gaze, proximity, and touch; less restricted display of adaptors
SPONTANEITY	Less cautious and hesitant behavior; honest, uninhibited communication	Natural facial and vocal expressions of all emotions, fewer display rule pressures to control expressions, more relaxed behavior
EVALUATION	Judgmental messages, critical feedback, controlling messages indicating a desire to change the other	Disapproving as well as approving facial and vocal expressions (e.g., showing disgust or anger, yelling, hugging, praising, etc.)

The notion that we communicate much differently with intimates than we do with nonintimates is easy to accept; most of us experience these differences every day. Because many of the differences stand out, when we witness two people interacting, we can make fairly accurate guesses about the intimacy of their relationship. In one study, for example, communication researchers Sally Planalp and Anne Benson

PERSONAL EXPERIENCE 8.1

CAN YOU RELATE TO THIS?

Unique Signaling is a Sign of Intimacy

My best friend and I have known each other for eight years. Over this time, we have developed many nonverbal signals that we both use and interpret with ease. For instance, if one of us raises our eyebrows and then looks to one side, it means that there is a person of interest in that direction. If we move our eyebrows up and down quickly before looking in a direction, it means there is a good-looking guy over there. We have many other signals for things like feeling confused, angry, anxious, or thinking that something is weird. We also have signals for things such as "We need to talk," "I have to go to the bathroom," and "I want to be alone with this guy." We've developed these signals over the course of our friendship.

Kiely

EXERCISE 8.1

TRY THIS

Nonverbal Signs of Closeness

OBJECTIVE: To identify how your nonverbal communication in a close relationship differs from your nonverbal communication in other relationships

INSTRUCTIONS: Based on one of your close relationships (e.g., a sibling, parent, close friend, etc.), try to describe an example that illustrates four of the basic dimensions of intimate nonverbal communication listed in Table 8.1.

Relationship with ___________________________

Example 1. Dimension: Description:

Example 2. Dimension: Description:

Example 3. Dimension: Description:

Example 4. Dimension: Description:

(1992) asked listeners to decide whether two-minute audiotaped excerpts from each of 36 conversations were between friends or acquaintances. The listeners had little difficulty and decided correctly 80% of the time. When asked what they based their decisions on, they had a wide range of explanations, many of which corroborated the basic dimensions of intimate communication listed in Table 8.1. Compared to acquaintances, listeners believed that friends laughed more, showed more involvement in the conversation, were more relaxed, were more spontaneous and less hesitant, had smoother conversations, paused less often, distributed floor time more equally, conversed at a faster pace, expressed more negative evaluations, used more sarcasm and **teasing**, and interrupted more often.

When researchers compare the nonverbal communication of close friends with that of strangers, they usually find differences. For example, one study demonstrated that an individual is more facially expressive in the presence of a close friend than in the presence of a stranger (Wagner & Smith, 1991). Researchers also find differences between the nonverbal cues of married couples and those of less intimate couples. One study found that married couples were more likely than dating couples to reciprocate their partner's use of touch (Guerrero & Andersen, 1994). Communication researcher Laura Guerrero (1997) compared the nonverbal involvement behaviors of friendly couples with the behaviors of romantic couples while the couples discussed impersonal and personal topics. Based on videotaped observations of six-minute interactions, she found that the romantic couples displayed more immediacy behavior—gaze, touch, and proximity—than the friendly couples did. But she also found that the romantic couples' interactions were not as smooth, raising the possibility that silences, pauses, and the like meant that the romantic partners were being more thoughtful with each other and less concerned with managing the interaction (i.e., letting their guard down). In another study comparing differences in touching (i.e., tie signs) between opposite-sex friends and dating partners, researchers found that the latter used more waist and shoulder embraces and body supports than did the former (Afifi & Johnson, 1999). Another more recent study found that listeners could tell from vocal cues alone whether a telephone caller was talking to a friend or a romantic partner after listening to a brief 20-second audio segment of the telephone caller's part of the conversation. In the same study, the researchers also found more vocal convergence between romantic partners than between friends. Romantic partners were more likely to alter the pitch of their voices to accommodate the vocal pitch of their partner. Women speakers were more likely to lower the pitch of their voices while male speakers were more likely to raise the pitch of their voices (Farley, Hughes, & LaFayette, 2013).

Research confirms that individuals in close relationships are generally more attuned to one another's emotions, though there may be some exceptions (Noller, 2006). For instance, one study compared the ability of close friends, less close friends, and strangers to accurately recognize facial expressions of emotion. The participants viewed videotapes, with the sound turned off, of individuals talking about an emotional experience when they either felt very happy, very sad, or very angry. In half of these

RESEARCH 8.1

FIND OUT MORE

Does Intimacy Improve the Ability to Read Facial Expressions?

While most of us might think we can read the facial expressions of close friends or romantic partners better than strangers can, there is little hard data to back up the claim. In fact, most studies show that strangers can recognize expressions of emotion on our close friends' and romantic partners' faces about as well as we can. Of course, prototypical (high intensity) expressions of anger, sadness, fear, and so forth are not too difficult for most people to see. But the researchers in this study speculated that subdued (moderately low intensity) expressions of emotion might be more difficult for strangers to see than for close friends or romantic partners. So the researchers designed a study to test the idea that the decoding/recognition advantage in close relationships depends on the intensity level of the facial expression.

To find out more about this study and to answer the following questions, see the full text (cited below).

1. What did the researchers discover in their study?
2. How did the researchers create different intensity levels for the facial expressions they used in this study?
3. What kind of study is this? (See Appendix.)
4. What were the main strengths and limitations of this study?

Source: Zhang, F., & Parmley, M. (2011). What your best friend sees that I don't see: Comparing female close friends and casual acquaintances on the perception of emotional facial expressions of varying intensities. *Personality and Social Psychology Bulletin, 37*, 28–39.

videos, the individuals expressed the emotion clearly and in the other half, they tried to conceal their emotion. Overall, the friends did a better job compared to the strangers at correctly identifying these emotions. But closeness doesn't always improve accuracy. Less close friends were more accurate than were the close friends at recognizing concealed sadness and anger. According to the researchers, this supports the idea that often, people in close relationships deliberately avoid receiving unintended messages from each other that are emotionally unpleasant or threatening in some way—a tendency known as **motivated inaccuracy** (Sternglanz & DePaulo, 2004). Thus, we may miss the disappointment, resentment, or frustration exhibited by a close friend, sibling, or spouse in order to avoid the emotional burdens that frequently come with such messages.

Although increased intimacy often yields communication that is rich, efficient, unique, open, spontaneous, and so on, there comes a point in every relationship when these qualities peak and then stabilize at some lower optimal level. In other words, the communication of a couple happily married for ten years is not necessarily more spontaneous, more efficient, more evaluative, and so forth than is the communication of a couple happily married for only five years. Not only does this imply that some qualities do not continue to intensify (e.g., how spontaneous can you get?) but also that more isn't necessarily better. For example, too much efficiency in signaling would remove some of the mystery and guesswork that keeps relationships interesting, too much evaluation from a partner would turn every little action into a performance, too much uniqueness would create a burdensome communication code that would insulate the couple from the outside world, too much openness would rob them of their opposing need for privacy, and so on.

Studies of immediacy behaviors show convincingly how outward signs of mutual attraction often peak and then decline as couples become increasingly intimate. Systematic observations of interpersonal touch provide the clearest and strongest evidence of this curvilinear relationship between public displays of affection and relational intimacy. Communication researchers Laura Guerrero and Peter Andersen (1991) recorded the number of times opposite-sex partners standing in line at a public zoo and at movie theaters touched each other. They found that couples that were seriously dating or marriage-bound touched the most—much more than either married couples or couples who were casually dating. In another field study of touching in public, McDaniel and Andersen (1998) found additional support for a curvilinear relationship between physical displays of affection and relational intimacy. They observed opposite-sex couples from Asian, European, and Latin American countries as well as the United States at the international terminal of a major U.S. West Coast airport. The least amount of touching occurred among strangers and acquaintances, as expected, but there were no more touches among spouses and family members. The most touching took place among close friends and lovers. Self-report studies reveal a similar pattern between immediacy behaviors and intimacy. In a cross-sectional survey of married couples, Hinkle (1999) found that couples married a year or less and couples married more than 24 years reported the greatest amounts of immediacy behavior (and liking for each other) in their marriages. One explanation for this finding is that married couples may turn their attention away from each other and to their children during the middle years of marriage but pay more attention to each other when the children are out on their own.

Another team of communication researchers documented a curvilinear relationship between the expression of negative emotions and the intimacy of a relationship, suggesting that individuals in newly formed relationships follow stereotypical display rules that discourage the expression of negative feelings, feelings that peak in moderately developed relationships and probably decline soon after. In this study, observations of couples engaged in brief problem-solving discussions revealed that the greatest suppression of negative feelings occurred in the discussions of the least and the most intimate couples: those who had been together less than five months and those who had been together more than two years (Aune, Buller, & Aune, 1996).

Nonverbal Communication and Relationship Success

One of the most important features of any successful relationship is the quality of its nonverbal communication. Researchers have been documenting a link between nonverbal communication and various indicators of marital success for quite some time. In her book, *Nonverbal Communication and Marital Interaction*, Patricia Noller (1984) reported the results of numerous studies confirming the impact of nonverbal signals on measures of marital adjustment. Most studies investigating the relationship between marital success and communication have concentrated on the impact of "positive" and "negative" communication behaviors, most often collecting data by observing couples' interactions rather than by administering questionnaires. In their review of this research, Kelly, Fincham, and Beach (2003) confirm that negative communication behavior predicts long-term declines in marital satisfaction. Research also shows that the use of positive communication behaviors while trying to solve problems and while discussing personal issues improves the quality of a couple's relationship (Julien, Chartrand, Simard, Bouthillier, & Begin, 2003). In general, negative communication behaviors weaken, while positive communication behaviors strengthen a relationship. In fact, studies confirm that emotional exchanges between spouses in a single brief interaction can predict with high degrees of accuracy whether the couple's marriage will survive (Gottman & Levenson, 1999; Waldinger, Hauser, Schulz, Allen, & Crowell, 2004). But what are some of these positive and negative forms of nonverbal communication?

Numerous studies confirm that skills in expressing, interpreting, and managing displays of emotion contribute to successful relationships (Guerrero & Floyd, 2006). The nonverbal communication of happy couples tends to be filled with more smiles and laughter than that of less happy couples (Kelly et al., 2003). Research also shows that satisfied couples use nonverbal cues more effectively when trying to influence each other, for instance, by playfully teasing one another in ways that soften the otherwise hurtful impact of personal criticism (Keltner, Young, Heerey, Monarch, & Oemig, 1998). Satisfied partners also experience less difficulty expressing their emotions nonverbally and reading the emotional cues of their partner (Cordova, Gee, & Warren, 2005; Yelsma & Marrow, 2003). Researchers in one study, for example, found that the ability of husbands to recognize and respond to their wives' depressed moods is predictive of marital success (Koerner & Fitzpatrick, 2002). As we noted earlier, however, there are times in close relationships when individuals gain more by being inaccurate; that is, by noticing positive, "relationship enhancing" messages but failing to notice negative, "relationship endangering" messages (Noller, 2006). One study of dating couples found that their relationship satisfaction increased the likelihood of noticing positive behaviors, particularly for the men in these relationships (Manusov, Floyd, & Kerssen-Griep, 1997).

Research shows that unhappy couples tend to display more antagonistic nonverbal behaviors (Noller, 2006). In one study, for example, low-adjustment couples tended to look at each other more when speaking than when listening and looked more when delivering hurtful messages than when delivering uplifting ones—a pattern that did not occur in high-adjustment couples. These findings suggest that gaze behavior in low-adjustment couples may be more indicative of competition and control than of concern and connection (Noller, 1980). Other studies as well show that nonverbal cues of avoidance (e.g., turning away) and hostility (e.g., angry voice) have a negative impact on marital satisfaction (Feeney, Noller, Sheehan, & Peterson, 1999; Newton & Burgoon, 1990). Research also confirms that negative nonverbal behavior is a good predictor of future distress. In one longitudinal study, researchers discovered that partners who went on to have unhappy relationships averaged close to two times more negative nonverbal behaviors (e.g., yelling, unpleasant facial expressions, etc.) than did partners who went on to have happy relationships (Notarius, Benson, Sloane, & Vanzetti, 1989). Studies also find that spouses in poor marriages tend to perceive their partner's actions in more negative ways than do spouses in healthier marriages. In his early research on marital communication, Gottman (1979) found that distressed spouses were more likely to infer negative feelings from messages with neutral affective intent (e.g., seeing anger in an expressionless face), whereas happy spouses tended to infer positive affective intent.

▸ Researchers have discovered that in close relationships, touch leads to long-lasting feelings of well-being and greater intimacy in the relationship.

istockphoto.com/GlobalStock

Over time, the buildup of positive and negative behaviors can determine whether a relationship succeeds or fails. Some relationship scholars use a bank account metaphor, likening the buildup of positive behaviors to deposits in a "relationship account" and the buildup of negative behaviors to withdrawals from the account. To keep their relationship in a healthy (i.e., balanced) state, partners need to make more or bigger deposits than withdrawals. For instance, based on his studies, marital expert John Gottman (1994) recommends what he calls the **magic ratio** of 5 to 1; that is, five positive behaviors for every negative behavior. In other words, over time, as long as there is five times as much positive interaction between spouses as there is negative, a marriage is likely to survive. As Gottman explains,

RESEARCH 8.2

FIND OUT MORE

How Does Interpersonal Touch Contribute to Relationship Success?

The various health benefits of interpersonal touch are well known (e.g., reduced stress, lower blood pressure, improved immune system). But does touch between individuals in close relationships improve the success of their relationship and, if it does, how does it contribute? In this study, the researchers recruited 102 romantic couples that had been dating for at least three months and asked the couples to make entries in an e-diary four times a day for one typical week. The researchers found strong support for the claim that interpersonal touch is associated with positive feelings of closeness and intimacy in the relationship. Moreover, partners who reported touching more frequently experienced higher levels of well-being six months later.

To find out more about this study and to answer the following questions, see the full text (cited below).

1. What kind of study is this? (See Appendix.)
2. Where was this study done and how did they recruit the couples that participated?
3. What are the practical implications of this study?
4. What are the strengths and limitations of this study?

Source: Debrot, A., Shoebi, D., Perrez, M., & Horn, A. B. (2013). Touch as an interpersonal emotion regulation process in couples' daily lives: The mediating role of psychological intimacy. *Personality and Social Psychology Bulletin, 39*, 1373–1385.

> As part of our research, we carefully charted the amount of time couples spent fighting versus interacting positively—touching, smiling, paying compliments, laughing, etc. Across the board, we found there was a very specific ratio that exists between the amount of positivity and negativity in a stable marriage, whether it is marked by validation, volatility, or conflict avoidance. . . . That magic ratio is 5 to 1. In other words, as long as there is five times as much positive feeling and interaction between husband and wife as there is negative, we found the marriage was likely to be stable. (p. 57)

NONVERBAL COMMUNICATION IN INTIMATE ENCOUNTERS

Thus far, we have seen how nonverbal communication changes in relationships that grow increasingly intimate. We've also considered the important role of nonverbal communication in determining the success of a relationship. Now, we begin our focus on the value of nonverbal communication in certain kinds of intimate encounters: those that attract a romantic partner, those that manage relational conflict, and those that provide emotional support.

Romantic Encounters: Attracting a Potential Partner

In their book, *Love and Sex: Cross Cultural Perspectives*, psychologist Elaine Hatfield and historian Richard Rapson (1996) remind us that throughout much of history and in many parts of the world, arranged marriages—parents deciding who their children marry—were the rule rather than the exception. In fact, only in this century have we witnessed major upheavals in the practice, leading to the now-widespread acceptance of unions based on mutual love and attraction. Even in countries with a rich tradition of arranged marriages (for example, India and China), large percentages of young people believe they should have complete freedom in choosing a mate (Sprecher & Chandak, 1992; Xu & Whyte, 1990).

With the freedom to select a romantic partner comes the added responsibility of selecting a compatible one. Few decisions are more important. Not surprisingly, the selection process whereby we attract the interest of potential mates and communicate our intentions involves an elaborate signaling system shaped by the pressures of both nature and culture. In this section, we'll examine the two kinds of signals we use in the pursuit of love: identity signals and courtship signals.

IDENTITY SIGNALS Nonverbal signals often determine whether or not we will be romantically interested in someone. A person's gender, sexual orientation, age, attractiveness, social class, ethnicity, physical fitness, dress, and so on combine to create a first impression that will make that person appealing or unappealing to others. For quite some time, social scientists have been studying the role of physical appearance—the primary source of identity signals—in determining whom we choose as a romantic partner. Based on a rather sizable body of research, two key principles have emerged: (1) Attractive people have an advantage in dating and mating and (2) we expect people to be properly matched according to their physical appearance.

Our attitude toward potential partners reflects a **beauty bias**; that is, we generally prefer attractive over less attractive individuals. We find others attractive because we see physical attributes in their faces and bodies that are signs of youthfulness, fitness, and sexual maturity—desirable qualities in a mate (see Chapter 3). This is not to imply that other factors, such as one's cultural preferences, are not just as important. Moreover, our judgments can change after one or more interactions. Communication researchers Kelly Albada, Mark Knapp, and Katheryn Theune (2002) suggested that

▸ Although many factors become important in finding a romantic partner, studies show that both men and women prefer the best-looking person available.

Allstar Picture Library / Alamy

perceptions of attractiveness in developing romantic relationships change as a direct result of positive (pleasant) or negative (unpleasant) interactions. In three studies using surveys and diaries, the researchers found support for this idea. In the diary study, for instance, dating couples over a three-week period tended to rate their partners as more physically attractive after pleasant interactions and less attractive after unpleasant interactions. Perceptions of attractiveness are even influenced by factors such as one's blood alcohol level, confirming a "beer goggles" effect in places where people socialize, flirt, and drink (Lyvers, Cholakians, Puorro, & Sundram, 2011).

Of course, the relative weight we attach to the looks of a potential mate often depends on whether we are a male or a female. This is not surprising. Throughout history, it has been more adaptive for women to seek men with resources and honorable intentions than it has been for them to seek men with good looks. On the other hand, men benefit from the pursuit of an attractive partner (Buss, 1989). This explains why, in one survey of men and women from 37 different countries, male respondents rated attractiveness in a potential mate as a more important factor than did females (Buss, 1990). In addition, physical attractiveness seems to have more staying power for men than it does for women (i.e., after marriage). For example, one longitudinal study of marital satisfaction over a four-year period showed that in the long run, having an attractive partner was more predictive of marital satisfaction for men than it was for women (Meltzer, McNulty, Jackson, & Karney, 2013).

But there is evidence that for women, as well as men, good looks matter in the short term, when sex rather than commitment and the attainment of social and economic resources are the primary goals of the relationship (Norman & Kendrick, 2006). Furthermore, research shows that women prefer more masculine features in men as they become more interested in short-term encounters. In one study, female undergraduates rated the attractiveness of pictures of male faces and physiques varying in masculinity. The women who were more receptive to short-term sexual encounters were more attracted to men with masculine physiques. The researchers replicated these results in a speed dating study where women could choose between a highly masculine male and a less masculine male (confederates). Women more open to short-term encounters were more likely to pick the more masculine man (Provost, Kormos, Kosakoski, & Quinsey, 2006). These findings seem to show that when sex matters the most, looks are important for women as well as for men.

Despite men's somewhat greater interest in the appearance of a partner, looking good still confers an advantage on those of us—male or female—looking for a date. In one classic study, psychologist Elaine Hatfield and her colleagues were interested in knowing which factors—attractiveness, personality, intelligence, or social skills—would be the best predictor of interpersonal attraction. They organized a dance for freshmen at the University of Minnesota to find out whether the students were attracted to their blind dates—they were matched randomly by the researchers—and which of the above factors accounted for that attraction. When each student purchased a ticket to the dance, he or she was unknowingly rated on attractiveness by four research assistants who were positioned nearby. These attractiveness ratings alone determined whether or not the students wanted to see their blind date again (Walster, Aronson, Abrahams, & Rottmann, 1966).

Studies in which individuals chose dating partners from photographs, after brief interactions, or following blind dates also show that attractive people—particularly women—receive more offers than do less attractive people (Brislin & Lewis, 1966; Curran & Lippold, 1975; Tesser & Brodie, 1971). In one study, researchers compared the most frequently chosen members of a videodating service with the least chosen members. The only difference between them was their physical attractiveness (Riggio & Woll, 1984). The findings of these studies corroborate survey data showing that attractive men and attractive women tend to have more dates and more sexual experiences than do less attractive persons (Hatfield & Sprecher, 1986, pp. 186–187).

There are many reasons why we desire good looks in a romantic partner—we may have an inborn preference for attractive faces, we believe attractive people possess other positive qualities (see Chapter 3), and we think that others will give us credit for being with a good-looking partner (e.g., trophy wives). As numerous studies demonstrate, however, we usually don't get what we want. The main reason, it seems, is fear of rejection. When there is little or no risk of being rejected (as was the case in the studies reported above), we tend to prefer the best-looking person available. But throw in the more realistic prospect of being turned down, and our preferences suddenly change. For instance, in one experiment, men could choose a date from among photographs of six women differing in physical attractiveness. Some men were told that all the women had already agreed to go out with them; others were told nothing about whether the women had consented. As expected, the men were more likely to choose the most attractive woman, but only if they knew she had already given her consent (Huston, 1973). In a similar experiment, researchers found that women will pick the best-looking man they can if there is little or no chance of being rejected (Shanteau & Nagy, 1979).

Of course, we shouldn't assume that everyone has the same level of interest in attractiveness. Some people (for example, individuals with traditional values about male–female relationships) are more interested than others are in finding a

RESEARCH 8.3

FIND OUT MORE

First Impressions of a Potential Partner: What Counts the Most?

In this speed-dating study, opposite sex strangers had 10-minute interactions with a possible date in mind. The data obtained from post-interaction questionnaires revealed three main findings:

1. Judgments of attractiveness/vitality were the most accurate (compared with observer ratings) and were the most significant predictors of dating interest (compared with judgments of warmth/trustworthiness and status/resources) for both men and women.
2. Women were more cautious and choosy than men were; that is, they were more likely to underestimate the interest of the men while men were more likely to overestimate the interest of the women; women were also less likely than the men to want further contact.
3. Women were less likely than men to want further contact because they perceived their interaction partner as not meeting their minimum standards of attractiveness/vitality.

To find out more about this study and to answer the following questions, see the full text (cited below).

1. How did this speed-dating study compare and contrast with prior speed-dating studies?
2. Who were the participants in the study and how did the researchers get them to participate?
3. What explanation do the researchers offer for the different perceptions of men and women?
4. What are the strengths and limitations of this study?
5. What kind of study is this? (See Appendix.)

Source: Fletcher, G. J. O., Kerr, P. S. G., Norman, P. L., & Valentine, K. A. (2014). Predicting romantic interest and decisions in the very early stages of mate selection: Standards, accuracy, and sex differences. *Personality and Social Psychology Bulletin, 40*, 540–550.

good-looking partner (Hatfield & Sprecher, 1986, pp. 124–125). Still, it seems that the fear of rejection may be the greatest equalizer, leading to a more realistic strategy of mate selection than that of going after the most attractive people. One team of researchers, in fact, found evidence that men are more likely to use a realistic rather than an idealistic strategy: Unattached good-looking women in singles bars were not approached by men any more than were the less attractive women (Glenwick, Jason, & Elman, 1978).

When our self-esteem gets a boost, however, we may become more idealistic. Psychologists Sara Kiesler and Roberta Baral (1970) recruited college men to participate in what they thought was a study on intelligence testing. After the men completed the first part of the IQ test, the researchers tried to alter the men's self-esteem: Some men were told they had done very well (raised self-esteem group); others were told they had done poorly (lowered self-esteem group). Kiesler and Baral found that during a subsequent coffee break, men in the raised self-esteem group were friendlier with an attractive woman than they were with an unattractive woman. In contrast, men in the lowered self-esteem group were friendlier with the unattractive woman.

We may like the idea of having an attractive partner, but in reality, we generally adhere to certain **matching norms**, which not only suggest how attractive our partner ought to be but prescribe for us many other physical attributes of our partner as well. Most matching norms reflect the prevailing belief that similarity breeds contentment, that couples may be better off if partners are similar rather than dissimilar in looks (Hatfield & Sprecher, 1986). In terms of attractiveness ratings, a 10 should go with another 10, a 6 should pair off with a 6, and so on, which is what happens more often than not, according to the available research (Feingold, 1988). While we may desire an attractive partner early in the dating process, we ultimately choose a partner based on matching norms (Taylor, Fiore, Mendelsohn, & Cheshire, 2011). For example, one team of researchers confirmed the matching hypothesis for couples at movie theaters, singles bars, and other social events: Most partners were remarkably similar to each other in attractiveness. The more similar they were, the more likely they were to exchange intimate touches (Silverman, 1971). Other researchers compared the photographs of intimate couples with those of randomly paired couples and found that the former are much more alike in attractiveness, and even facial features, than are the latter (Hinsz, 1989; Murstein, 1972). Studies in the United States, Canada, and Japan show that matched couples are more likely to get married and stay married than are mismatched couples (Cavior & Boblett, 1972; White, 1980).

▸ With few exceptions, for heterosexual romantic couples, the male-taller norm says that the man should be taller or at least as tall as the woman. Violations of this norm usually attract our attention.

istockphoto.com/Peeter Viisimaa

Of course, attractiveness is not the only way in which couples are physically similar. Everyday observations bear out the fact that noticeable

> differences in age, skin color, facial features, stature, and even dress are the exceptions rather than the rule. Couples mismatched in any of these ways may experience greater hardships than matched couples. In one survey of 215 newlyweds in the San Francisco area, researchers found that couples who broke up 7 to 8 years later were more likely to be mismatched on height and weight measures than were those couples who were still together. (study reported in Hatfield & Sprecher, 1986, p. 150)

Perhaps the most enduring of all heterosexual matching norms is the one pertaining to height, the male-taller norm, which practically dictates that the man be taller or at least as tall as the woman (Martel & Biller, 1987). Predicting a reversal of the norm in approximately 2% of cases, researchers in one study of married couples were surprised to find only a single instance out of 720 in which the wife was taller than the husband (Gillis & Avis, 1980). Studies show consistently that women prefer taller rather than shorter men, but there is a ceiling effect for a man's height—a point of diminishing returns for men over 6 feet 2 inches. These same studies also show that men generally want to be taller than their female partners (Graziano, Brothen, & Berscheid, 1978; Hensley, 1994; Pierce, 1996; Shepperd & Strathman, 1989).

EXERCISE 8.2

TRY THIS

Opposites Don't Attract

OBJECTIVE: Studies show that, when shown photographs of individuals, most of us accurately match them up with their intimate partners (Terry & Macklin, 1977). The purpose of this exercise is to see for yourself whether the various matching norms (similar looks, clothes, height, weight, etc.) make it easy for us to identify intimate couples.

INSTRUCTIONS: Find the engagement announcements in a local newspaper. If the section includes photographs of some couples, cut them out and then separate the two individuals. Show them to others to see how well they can correctly match the couples.

An alternative is to get your high school yearbook and identify the pictures of five males and five females who you know were dating or going together. See if others can figure out who dated whom.

Identity signals that have not received much attention from researchers, until recently, are those related to sexual orientation. Now, some social scientists are investigating how members of the gay and lesbian community are able to identify potential partners without asking potential partners about their sexual orientation. Studies indicate that accurate identifications can come from cues related to physical appearance as well as demeanor. In one study, a team of researchers found that homosexual participants were much more able than heterosexual participants to recognize other homosexuals on the basis of photographs, 10-second silent videotaped clips, and 10-second figural outline displays. An interesting gender difference that emerged in the study was that physical appearance cues such as hairstyle, jewelry, and clothing were most informative for the lesbian participants, whereas dynamic cues from nonverbal behavior were most informative for the gay men who participated in the study (Ambady, Hallahan, & Conner, 1999). This gender difference between physical appearance and behavioral cues also showed up in a recent study of sexual orientation, body shape, and walking styles. Using motion sensors that only revealed the body shape and walking style of their volunteers, the researchers created videos of 16 individuals, half of whom were gay men and lesbians and half of whom were heterosexual men and women, each walking on a treadmill. Would observers (undergraduate students) be able to guess which walkers were straight and which were gay or lesbian? The results confirmed the prevalence of stereotypical thinking about gait and sexual orientation. Observers equated shoulder movement (swaggering) with masculinity and hip movement (hip sway) with femininity. Observers also equated body shape (i.e., waist-to-hip ratio) with sexual orientation, but more so for the female walkers than for the male walkers. When it came to guessing the women walkers' sexual orientation, observers were correct much less than half the time. But for the men walkers, observers guessed correctly more than half the time (Johnson, Gill, Reichman, & Tassinary, 2007).

Eye contact and gazing patterns are probably more revealing. In a survey of gay men and lesbians, researchers found that both groups tended to rely most heavily on eye contact for identifying other gay men and lesbians, although the respondents reported that they also noticed signs of sexual orientation in clothing style and fit, jewelry, facial expressions, posture, body type, walk or gait, and types of gestures (Carroll & Gilroy, 2002). In her ethnographic study of the eye-gaze patterns used by members of gay and lesbian communities in Oklahoma City and Chicago, Nicholas (2004) identified two specific "gaydar" devices people used to exchange information about sexual orientation as well as personal interest. The first type, a *direct stare*, was prolonged eye contact, "maintained for a period of time that is considered longer than what would be customary in a social context" (p. 74). Many of the informants in the study reported that the signal was unmistakable and that holding the gaze could indicate mutual interest. The second type, a *broken stare*, consisted of a stare/look away/stare again action. "This behavior occurs when one or both of the interactants 'break' the gaze due to either trying to be polite, paying attention to someone else, or being embarrassed due to the possibility of behaving inappropriately" (p. 75). Other nonverbal cues, such as eyebrow raises, smiles, and gestures communicate levels of recognition and interest that go beyond identity recognition.

EXERCISE 8.3

TRY THIS

The Dating Game: Are Looks Most Important?

OBJECTIVE: To exchange your thoughts, feelings, and experiences about the role of appearance in romantic relationships

INSTRUCTIONS: Discuss the following questions:

1. Is appearance the most important factor in deciding to go out on a date with someone?
2. Are men more interested in the appearance of their dates than women are? If so, why?
3. Do attractive people have better social lives than less attractive people? If so, why?
4. Is it best for people to date only those who are similar to themselves in attractiveness?
5. Do attractive people have different personalities than less attractive people?
6. Is it riskier to fall for an attractive person than for an average-looking person because the attractive person—being more in demand—will have more opportunities to be with others?

COURTSHIP SIGNALS Whereas identity signals can get us interested in a potential mate, courtship signals keep us interested. When they are uncompromised by conflicting cues, these flirtatious behaviors usually communicate some romantic aspiration. Psychiatrist Albert Scheflen (1965) was the first to observe and describe systematically many of these subtle sexual behaviors. According to Scheflen, courtship consists of three basic elements. The first is **courtship readiness**, an exhilarated state of high muscle tone in which sagging disappears, bagginess around the eyes decreases, the torso becomes more erect, the belly is tightened, the eyes seem to be brighter, and so on. All sorts of preening behavior usually accompany these physical changes: Women stroke their hair, glance at their makeup in a mirror, and rearrange their clothing; men fix their hair, pull up their socks, readjust their coats, and so forth. The second element, **positioning for courtship**, occurs when individuals begin turning their bodies and heads to face each other directly. Accompanying these moves are the many arm and leg positions that frame the interaction while excluding outsiders. This element of courtship typically includes intimate topics of conversation as well. Scheflen referred to the third element of courtship as **actions of appeal or invitation**. Performed more by women than by men, these actions include coy and flirtatious glances, gaze holding, soft speech, head tilting, smiling, demure gestures, leg crossing (slightly exposing thigh), placing a hand on the hip, exhibiting the wrist or palm, body caresses (e.g., stroking arm, etc.), object caresses (e.g., stroking a glass), giggling, overloud laughter, and so on.

Scheflen's most important contribution was distinguishing between courtship behavior, which expresses a romantic attraction and an interest in some form of sexual intimacy, and what he called **quasi-courtship behavior**—flirtatious behavior that is not meant to be taken seriously. Like all forms of kidding behavior (e.g., mock fighting, teasing, put-ons, etc.), which we often do just for the fun of it, the efficacy of quasi-courtship depends on a receiver's ability to read between the lines and thus not take the behavior literally. Scheflen identified various signals that, if read properly, will keep us from thinking that others are trying to flirt with us when they probably aren't: looking around at others in the area, not blocking others out with framing leg or arm positions, using indirect body orientations (e.g., head faces you but torso doesn't), speaking in an overloud voice, discussing impersonal topics, using exaggerated or comical flirting behaviors, and so on.

According to Scheflen, quasi-courtship behavior serves a highly useful purpose, despite the possibility of misinterpretation. In the extreme, quasi-courtship may be a way of breathing some life into a dull interaction; but more often, it merely catches or keeps the attention of someone who seems to be losing interest. Without being consciously aware of it, we've probably all experienced situations in which quasi-courtship behavior changed the mood of an entire group:

> Sometimes quasi-courting and decourting seem to work together as a kind of thermostatic device to maintain group morale. Almost everyone has seen a dull party or a dull business meeting come alive with the arrival of just one vividly attractive person. Others in the room immediately become more animated and themselves more attractive. In a situation like this, a body motion analysis would reveal that the new arrival triggered whole sequences of quasi-courtship. On the other hand, if one member of the group quasi-courts too enthusiastically, raising the general level of

intimacy and excitement above what is mutually acceptable, others in the group will decourt, apparently trying to defuse the situation. (Davis, 1973, p. 18)

Other researchers, such as anthropologist David Givens (1978c, 1983) and psychologist Timothy Perper (1985), have studied human courtship from a somewhat different perspective, focusing on what they believe are the universal stages of courtship, from the first encounter to the sexual encounter. Based on countless observations of humans and animals, both researchers agree on a five-stage sequence that shows how we negotiate progress toward sexual intimacy. In courtship settings, such as singles bars and parties, much of the signaling from both men and women takes place well before the first encounter with a potential partner, during an attention-getting period. Table 8.2 provides a summary of the nonverbal signaling that would most likely promote intimacy (i.e., escalation) from one courtship stage to the next (Givens, 1978b).

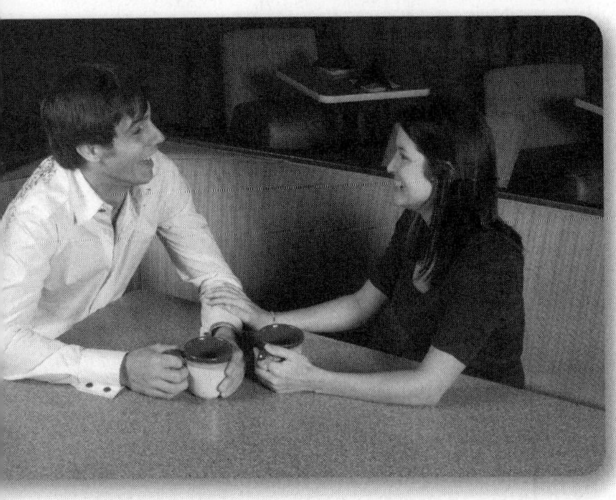

▸ Romantic intentions are rarely expressed in words.

istockphoto.com/princessdlaf

According to Givens, much of the courtship behavior, particularly during the early stages, conveys messages of ambivalence, affiliation, and submissiveness; that is, if there is some degree of mutual attraction between them, flirting partners will communicate mixed feelings (i.e., approach and avoidance tendencies), a willingness to interact, and a desire to be nonthreatening. As Table 8.2 shows, messages of ambivalence, which include all sorts of anxious and tentative behaviors, generally occur during the attention stage. Obviously, courtship requires displays of interest. But these affiliation signals, which include immediacy behaviors such as smiles, eye contact, forward leaning, and direct body orientation, remain rather ambiguous (reflecting mixed feelings) until the interaction stage, at which time they become somewhat exaggerated (reflecting self-presentation goals). Of particular interest is the observation that submissiveness is a major part of courtship for both males and females during most of the courtship stages. Shoulder shrugs, head tilts, coy smiles, downward glances, eyebrow raises, giggling, and the like make partners feel safe and secure during the early stages and invite attention and affection during the later stages. Finally, once an intimate sexual relationship forms, the need for courtship signaling diminishes. As a result, we see a dramatic decline in the flirting behavior that characterized so much of the courtship ritual.

Table 8.2 Givens' Five Stages of Nonverbal Courtship

Stage	Definition	Nonverbal Signaling
ATTENTION	Interest in a potential partner, communicating a readiness to interact	Self-conscious and conflicted body movements (preening, adaptors, displacement activities), incomplete displays of interest (e.g., direct body orientation with gaze aversion), ambivalent smiles, intermittent and sidelong glances
RECOGNITION	Responding to the expressed interest of potential partner	Availability signals that express a receptive attitude, including body orientation, eye contact, smiling, and eyebrow flashes Feminine displays include head tossing, coy smiles, eyelash batting, etc. Anxiety signals include self-touches and freezing Submissive signals include shoulder shrugs, head tilts, pouting, downward gaze, constricted postures, hand clasping, pigeon toeing
INTERACTION	Approaching a potential partner and engaging in conversation	Heightened anxiety brought about by close proximity would lead to increased displacement activities, especially near the start of speaking turns and during initial approach Preening, head tossing, stretching, yawning, throat clearing, etc. Performance anxiety would produce exaggerated displays of interest: overloud laughter, vigorous gestures, overly emphatic head nods, etc. Appearance of some interactional synchrony (if the couple is hitting it off) Continuation of submissive behaviors, especially the use of high-pitched, softer voices (parentese)
SEXUAL AROUSAL	Becoming compatible Exchanging intimacies and physical forms of affection	Intimate touching (e.g., kissing) and other forms of immediacy (e.g., prolonged gaze, close distances, direct orientation, etc.) Appearance of behaviors reminiscent of caregiver–child interactions (e.g., parentese, tickling, teasing, grooming, cuddling, clinging) Prolonged gaze Conversational behavior relaxes (e.g., decrease in displacement activity, etc.)
RESOLUTION	Sexual relationship between partners is consummated	Following sexual activity and bonding, nonverbal signaling associated with early stages of courtship ritual, flirting, begin to disappear

Anthropologist Helen Fisher (1992) endorses a similar view of nonverbal courtship behavior. Like Givens and Perper, she focuses on the stages of nonverbal courtship that are most common across species. In addition to the preliminary signaling that occurs during the early stages of courtship (such as attention getting, recognition, and some type of interaction), Fisher highlights the important roles of mutual touching and body synchrony (i.e., mimicry, mirroring, matching, reciprocity) as pivotal signs of romantic interest that take place during the latter part of the courtship ritual but prior to the stages of sexual arousal and resolution (see Table 8.2).

We exchange many of these nonverbal signals without conscious awareness. Still, they are powerful signals of romantic interest as well as disinterest. In a recent study, psychologist Sally Farley (2014) recruited heterosexual male undergraduates and asked them to participate in a structured interview. The interviewer—the same highly attractive female research assistant interviewed all of the participants—asked a series of questions that ranged from superficial ("What is your major?") to more personal ("What is your happiest childhood memory?"). The interviewer was instructed to maintain a relatively flirtatious set of behaviors (e.g., eye contact, smiling, directly facing the participant) with each participant and was automatically and unobtrusively cued to touch her face every 15 seconds. She was also instructed to touch her hair at the beginning of each question. Prior to the interviews, the men were asked questions about their relationship status and were classified as either non-exclusive daters (involved in a romantic relationship for less than three months) or exclusive daters (involved in a romantic relationship for longer than three months). The results of the experiment revealed that non-exclusive daters (especially those reporting romantic interest in the interviewer) mimicked the interviewer's head touching more than the exclusive daters did (particularly exclusive daters reporting greater love for their partners), suggesting that not only does mimicry function as a flirtatious signal but that the absence of mimicry can indicate the lack of romantic interest.

Gender also influences the nonverbal signaling that occurs during these flirtatious encounters. According to evolutionary theorists, the gender that invests the most in reproduction (usually the female) is the one who must be the most selective in choosing a mate (Trivers, 1972). In humans, the demands of pregnancy and most of the demands of child rearing fall on the female. When it comes to mate selection, she has more to lose if she gets stuck with someone who doesn't contribute to the relationship than the man does. As a result, women need to be choosier than men. An indirect signaling system, one that relies on subtle nonverbal cues, gives females more of an opportunity to assess potential mates than would a more direct approach—they can see how determined and worthwhile the man is while they remain uncommitted. Thus, contrary to what most men believe, women usually get things started and do most of the signaling (Cary, 1976; de Weerth & Kalma, 1995; Grammer & Juette, 2000; Grammer,

Kruck, & Magnusson, 1998; Moore, 1985). According to this view, the man's nonverbal behavior serves an important self-presentation function that attracts the attention of women and communicates the man's fitness and social status. In one study, researchers observed the nonverbal behavior of men in a bar before the men made successful contact with women. The nonverbal behaviors of the successful men during this precontact period differed from the behaviors of the unsuccessful men. Specifically, the successful men glanced around more, used up more space, engaged in more same-sex touching, and exhibited more open body postures—signals of dominance, social power, and interpersonal competence (Renninger, Wade, & Grammer, 2004).

Based on her extensive observations in singles bars and other social settings, anthropologist Monica Moore (1985) developed a comprehensive catalog of the nonverbal signals women regularly use to express their interest in finding and selecting a romantic partner. Among the nonverbal signals she recorded were room-encompassing glances, prolonged eye contact, head tilts, head tosses, hair flips, smiles, animated gestures, preening, various body and object caresses, body leans, provocative walks, solitary dancing, suggestive touches, and more—52 different behaviors in all. In support of these initial findings, subsequent research has shown that women use these signals more often in courtship contexts (singles bars) than they do in other social settings and that women who use many of these signals are much more likely to receive the attention of men (e.g., being asked to dance) than are women who use fewer (Canary & Cody, 1994, pp. 91–93; Moore, 1985; Moore & Butler, 1989).

If women send the signals that encourage men to approach—the "green lights" men encounter on the path to courtship—then what are the "red" or "yellow" lights that stop or slow down the approach of men? Returning to singles bars where she conducted much of her early research, Moore's (1998) trained observers recorded female behaviors that appeared to result in male disinterest: leaving, leaning or turning away, ceasing to talk, or looking away. Women's rejection behaviors included facial and head actions such as yawns, frowns, sneers, gaze avoidance, stares, and head shakes; gestures such as putting hands in pockets, crossing arms, cleaning nails, or picking teeth; and postures such as pulling away, avoiding body contact, closing legs tightly together, and tightening up the torso. In some cases, these rejection behaviors occurred along with signals of interest, combining to slow the pace of courtship (i.e., yellow lights). In other cases, rejection signals stood alone, leaving little doubt about the woman's desire to discourage the man (i.e., red lights). Others studies show that the mere absence of encouraging nonverbal cues from women, such as eye contact, is enough to keep men away (Grammer & Juette, 2000).

Despite the prevalence of nonverbal signals in courtship, men and women frequently miss or misread the signals. Moreover, men and women often see the same signals

▸ Nonverbal signaling predominates in the flirting that occurs during the early stages of courtship. All too often, men and women do not interpret these signals in the same way.

istockphoto.com/Susan Chiang

differently. Perhaps the most common difference is the greater tendency for men to infer that a woman is sexually interested in a man. In one study, men and women viewed a videotaped interaction between two actors, a man and a woman. The researchers prepared three different versions of the interaction so that the nonverbal cues varied in their suggestiveness. In one version, there was no eye contact and no touch; the actors sat far apart; and the female actor wore denim jeans, a black turtleneck sweater, and a long red jacket. In the second version, there was occasional eye contact and occasional mutual touching of legs or hands; the actors sat moderately close; and the female actor wore denim jeans and a tight T-shirt. In the third version, there was continuous mutual eye contact and hand holding; the actors sat close together; and the female actor wore a short black skirt and a black T-shirt that revealed some cleavage. Compared to the female viewers, male viewers rated the woman in all three versions as more flirtatious, seductive, promiscuous, and sexually attracted to the man (Koukounas & Letch, 2001). In another study, men and women viewed videotaped clips of a young dating couple interacting with each other. The men rated the woman's flirtatious behaviors (e.g., laughing, touching, gazing, primping, hair flipping, etc.) more positively than the women did. In addition, the men rated the woman's rejection behaviors (e.g., looking

PERSONAL EXPERIENCE 8.2

CAN YOU RELATE TO THIS?

Staring (a Threat Display) Is Not Flirting

My friend Phil likes to "make eyes" with women at bars. I understand that in this [flirting] game, you make eye contact and then look away. Phil doesn't understand this concept. He makes eye contact and the girl will look away but Phil will continue to fix his eyes on the target in almost a stalker-like manner. Plainly, he just stares at them. One time, this beautiful girl stared back at him and then disappeared. Phil thought she was coming over to talk to him, but instead, her very large guy friend came over and said, "Sara doesn't appreciate you staring at her."

David

at ceiling, frowning, head shaking, etc.) less negatively than the women (Moore, 2002). Apparently, while men may see women's "green lights" as a bit brighter than women do, men also may see the "red" and "yellow" lights as a bit duller. The results of these studies reinforce the idea that men are more likely than women to interpret a wide range of female behaviors in ways that facilitate the courtship process.

Confrontational Encounters: Managing Relational Conflict

Consider the case of Linda and Anthony: Like most couples who have been together for a long time, they quarrel about all sorts of things. Sometimes their disagreements are relatively minor—bickering about where to go for dinner or whether to wallpaper the den, for example. Other times, they get into fights that can go on for hours, leaving them both emotionally drained and simmering with resentment. The pattern for these prolonged fights is usually the same: Linda becomes angry and then criticizes Anthony for not doing some household chore, such as unloading the dishes from the dishwasher or taking out the trash. Anthony doesn't want to be bothered—he doesn't believe household chores are all that important. Linda's nagging (as he describes it) makes him upset and defensive. Feeling attacked, Anthony responds by criticizing Linda for "constantly bugging him about nothing." In the worst fights, Anthony refuses to talk and walks away.

For more than two decades, psychologist John Gottman has been studying the way couples like Linda and Anthony try to settle their differences. As one of the few social scientists who have paid close attention to the role of nonverbal communication in the conflicts of intimate couples, his work is singularly important. In this section, we'll highlight some of what he and other researchers have discovered.

NONVERBAL HOSTILITY AND CONFLICT In relationships that don't survive, couples rely on what Gottman calls *hostile styles of conflict*—they become overwhelmed by the negative emotions associated with four destructive kinds of behavior. Emphasizing the impending doom these actions bring, he refers to them as the "four horsemen of the apocalypse": criticism, contempt, defensiveness, and stonewalling (see Table 8.3).

According to Gottman, when we *complain*, we express dissatisfaction without assigning blame to our partner. *Criticism*, on the other hand, points an accusing finger and is often accompanied by nonverbal expressions of hostility, such as head shaking, a raised voice, and an angry facial expression. One curious exception is the use of teasing, an indirect form of criticism that is part play and part aggression. A playfully delivered tease employs various nonverbal cues, such as smiles, winks, laughter, odd facial expressions, exaggerated vocal intonations, and playful touches, to take the edge off the criticism. But sometimes even a playfully delivered tease, so commonplace and often

Table 8.3 Gottman's Four Horseman of the Apocalypse

Behavior	Definition	Typical Comments	Nonverbal Signals
CRITICISM	Accusing the partner of wrongdoing, blaming	"Why are you always late?" "You didn't clean the kitchen again."	Angry facial expressions, raising voice, finger pointing, head shaking, arms akimbo, staring, arm thrusting
CONTEMPT	Insulting the partner, showing disrespect	"You're such a moron." "Why are you always so irresponsible?"	Facial expression of contempt, eye rolling, smirking, laughing at other, parentese, mimicking, mocking, sarcasm, interrupting
DEFENSIVENESS	Feeling attacked by the partner, regarding self as an innocent victim	"Here we go again." "It's not my fault." "I couldn't help it."	Pouting facial expressions, masking smiles, false smiles, whining, arm folding, postural shifts, adaptors, displacement activity, gaze aversion, shoulder shrugs
STONEWALLING	Withdrawing from the conflict	No response or changing the topic "I don't have to take this." "See you later."	Blank facial expression, silence, gaze avoidance, indirect body orientation, pausing, turning away

beneficial in close relationships, carries a hostile message and may be more hurtful than amusing to the object of the tease. In fact, research shows that no matter how innocently we tease someone, the effect is usually more hurtful than the teaser thinks it is. In a series of studies, researchers asked participants to recall instances of either teasing or being teased by a roommate, partner, friend, or family member. The findings revealed that teasers tend to be egocentric in their thinking, generally regarding their teases as enjoyable whereas targets hold a much more negative view. These results were further confirmed in a subsequent experiment in which observers, targets, and teasers judged the impact of a teasing interaction. Regardless of the teasers' delivery or intentions, observers and targets had much more negative judgments of the teasing, seeing it as considerably more malicious than the teasers did. Of particular interest was the finding that having good intentions mattered far less to the targets (and observers) than it did to the teasers. As the researchers put it, teasers should be mindful that when it comes to teasing, "'just kidding' just isn't good enough" (Kruger, Kuban, & Gordan, 2006, p. 424). Interestingly, this communication gap between teasers and targets may depend on culture. In four studies, researchers confirmed that Asian Americans, representing a collectivistic orientation, attribute more positive intent to teasers, regard teasing as more beneficial, and see teasing as more pleasurable to targets than do European Americans (Campos, Keltner, Beck, Gonzaga, & John, 2007).

Although criticism in itself may be the least harmful of the four destructive behaviors, it is usually responsible for setting into motion the vicious cycles of negativity that follow. More destructive than criticism are the feelings and expressions of contempt that insult, ridicule, and belittle the person to whom they are directed. Not surprisingly, someone on the receiving end of criticism or contempt becomes defensive, feeling and acting like an innocent victim. But defensiveness can quickly turn to hostility, creating an escalating pattern of negativity in which each partner—feeling attacked—reciprocates the other's displays of criticism and contempt. At some point, when one partner has had enough (usually the man), *stonewalling* occurs: He or she simply shuts down and withdraws from the conflict. Gottman considers stonewalling the most destructive of the four horsemen because it all but eliminates any possibility of repairing the damage that has been done.

PERSONAL EXPERIENCE 8.3

CAN YOU RELATE TO THIS?

Expressions of Contempt Have Harmful Consequences

I was arguing with my girlfriend the other day and sometimes she makes these faces that totally set me off, even if what we're arguing about isn't that big a deal. She has certain faces that I take as disrespectful and that just inflame the argument. We could be arguing over which television show is better and as soon as she makes that face almost to say, "Yeah, OK, like you know what you're talking about?" I get so ticked off because I don't argue about something unless I do know what I'm talking about.

Shaun

During a conflict, what goes on inside a person is at least as important as what we can see and hear. For example, suppose Linda gets angry at Anthony and yells at him for not buying eggs at the grocery store: "What's wrong with you?" she shouts. "How can you be so forgetful? I told you a dozen times that I needed eggs." In this instance, Anthony's reaction to Linda's criticism (laced with contempt) will depend greatly on his private thoughts about Linda. According to Gottman, self-soothing thoughts ("Linda doesn't get angry very often; she must be under a lot of stress.") minimize the problem, whereas distress-maintaining thoughts, which often include beliefs about being an innocent victim ("I can't believe she's being such a jerk about this. So I forgot; big deal.") exacerbate the problem. Distressing thoughts can lead to what Gottman calls **flooding**, the point at which you just can't take it anymore:

> When people start to be flooded, they feel unfairly attacked, misunderstood, wronged, or righteously indignant. If you are being flooded, you may feel that things have gotten too emotional, that you just want things to stop, you need to calm down, or you want to run away. Or you may want to strike back and get even. . . . Under duress, we tend to release excess amounts of stress hormones such as adrenaline that lead the heart to beat faster, the sweat glands to work overtime, and respiration to speed up. These physical symptoms of stress create a feedback loop with the anxiety-provoking thoughts and emotions we are experiencing. . . . This is exactly what seems to happen when you become flooded during a marital conflict. In a sense, your negative inner thoughts and your aroused nervous system goad each other on, making it all the more difficult to break out of the cycle of negativity. (Gottman, 1994, p. 116)

Gottman discovered that men become flooded sooner than women do—when their heart rate goes up to about 80 beats per minute. On average, women don't begin to feel the same way until their heart rate reaches about 90 beats per minute. According to Gottman, this finding may explain why men are much more likely than women to withdraw from a highly emotional conflict (he estimates that 85% of stonewallers are men) and why so many male–female conflicts follow a familiar and well-documented **demand–withdraw pattern**: The woman pursues and the man withdraws; the man's withdrawal goads the woman into pursuing more, which leads to greater withdrawal by the man; and so forth—a predictable pattern that threatens the stability of the relationship (Christensen, 1988; Christensen & Heavey, 1990; Notarius & Markman, 1993). The fact that men become flooded before women do may be a contributing factor, but recent studies of this "wife-demand–husband-withdraw" pattern point to other factors as well. For instance, one study of marital conflict found that the pattern was more likely on issues of most concern to the wives than to the husbands. That is, when the conflict revolved around a course of action strongly favored by the wife, the husband was more likely to withdraw in response to the wife's demands than when the conflict revolved around an issue of great concern to the husband (Feeney et al., 1999). Thus, the occurrence of the demand–withdraw pattern may depend on whose issue instigates the conflict. The pattern may also be a negative by-product of how the husband and wife relate to each other on an emotional level. Research shows that the pattern is less likely to occur among couples who exhibit positive emotions during mundane conversations, such as in response to the question, "How was your day?" Interestingly, the same research shows that the pattern is less likely when the husband avoids communicating in an angry and whiny manner during their everyday interactions (Gottman & Levenson, 2000). In distressed marriages, research indicates that the man's withdrawal may more likely cause than result from the woman's demands (Noller, Feeney, Roberts, & Christensen, 2005) Some research also shows that in marriages marked by violence, a reverse in the pattern—the husband demands and the wife withdraws—is more likely than it is in nonviolent marriages (Noller at al., 2005).

PERSONAL EXPERIENCE 8.4

CAN YOU RELATE TO THIS?

The Demand–Withdraw Pattern Occurs among Roommates

I live with six girls, and there is drama and there are fights between us every once in a while. My one roommate has a very unique way of fighting. If something gets her upset or she is annoyed about something, she'll act like everything is fine, but she'll just sit there, emotionless. If we try to talk to her, she'll answer in a one-word, monotone voice. Her face will be just blank and empty of any type of emotion. We'll keep asking her what's wrong, but she'll just respond, "Nothing. I'm fine," while staring straight ahead.

Andrea

NONVERBAL CONFLICT MANAGEMENT How do we escape these destructive behaviors? Gottman offers numerous remedies, some to increase the positive side of a couple's "magic ratio," some to repair the damage inflicted by destructive behaviors as they arise in the midst of a conflict, and some to head off the four horsemen well before they can rear their ugly heads. According to Gottman, engaging in various positive interactions allows a couple, over the long run, to endure the effects of negative behavior—the good simply outweighs the bad. This involves showing interest and concern; being affectionate, appreciative, and empathic; joking around; and sharing joyful moments. Of course, all these actions involve various nonverbal signals but primarily immediacy behaviors such as eye contact, direct body orientation, close distances, and touch, along with laughter and smiles expressing genuine positive emotions (e.g., amusement, contentment, joy, etc.).

In addition to these positive interactions, Gottman advocates the use of what he calls **repair mechanisms**, the phrases and actions that prevent negative feelings and behaviors from spiraling out of control. While observing the conflicts of successful couples, he noticed how they were able to say or do little things that seemed to keep them out of harm's way: encouraging the partner to talk (e.g., silence; head nods and other back channels; comments such as, "Tell me more," "Go on," etc.), urging the partner to stick with the subject (e.g., "Don't bring that up now"), or asking the partner not to interrupt. Although these actions and phrases weren't always delivered congenially, they still kept the conflict from taking a turn for the worse.

Gottman offers this practical advice for heading off each of the four horsemen:

- Try complaining instead of criticizing. Don't point an accusing finger at your partner. Avoid the needless displays of anger that often accompany criticism.
- Replace contemptuous actions (verbal and nonverbal insults) with validating actions (reflecting feelings, active listening).
- Combat defensiveness and flooding by calming down—many relaxation techniques work—and by rewriting negative inner thoughts, taking responsibility, and apologizing.

Instead of withdrawing from your partner, use active listening skills to engage him or her in constructive dialogue.

Finally, Gottman stresses the need to raise issues in a way that is nonthreatening to the other person. He calls this a "soft start-up" to the conflict and argues that it can make the difference between a conflict that remains healthy and constructive as opposed to one that, because of a "harsh start-up," becomes unhealthy and destructive. "In fact," as he points out,

> studies of married couples show that 96 percent of the time, you can predict the outcome of a 15-minute conversation based on what happens in the first three minutes of that interaction. And if the first three minutes include a lot of negativity, blame, and criticism, the outcome is not going to be very good. (Gottman & DeClaire, 2001, p. 70)

Although Gottman's recommendations for soft start-ups concentrate on the importance of verbal messages (e.g., begin with something positive, express appreciation, start with "I" instead of "You"), he does not overlook the impact of an angry tone of voice or facial expression. Nonverbal cues can certainly soften the impact of criticism. In one study, for example, researchers found that participants rated a harsh criticism as more polite when it was accompanied by a pleasant facial expression, direct body orientation, a soft voice, raised eyebrows, and other warm nonverbal behaviors (Trees & Manusov, 1998).

Another highly useful approach to nonverbal conflict management focuses on the unique role and impact of **appeasement** behavior (Keltner, Young, & Buswell, 1997). Psychologists Dacher Keltner, Randall Young, and Brenda Buswell define *appeasement* as "the process by which individuals placate or pacify others in situations of potential or actual conflict" (p. 360). This process, common among primates as well as humans, unfolds when one individual (1) anticipates aggression from others and (2) displays apologetic, submissive, and affiliative behavior, which (3) prevents or reduces others' aggression, increases social approach, and reestablishes the individual's relation to others. According to this view, appeasement displays lead to reconciliation. One form, reactive appeasement, serves to reduce conflict that is already taking place and includes nonverbal signs of embarrassment and shame, such as downward head movements, gaze aversion, coy smiles, and face touches. A second form, anticipatory appeasement, prevents conflict from occurring and includes nonverbal signals of polite modesty and shyness, such as inhibited movement, gaze aversion, postural constriction, speech hesitations, head bowing, vocal back channels, head nods, and eyebrow raises. Interestingly, many of these nonverbal cues correspond to those used by romantic partners in the contexts of flirting and courtship and serve a similar bonding function in the conflicts of dating and married couples. Keltner and his colleagues found support for their theory in several studies on teasing. In one study, for example, romantic partners teased each other by making up nicknames and stories to illustrate an odd habit or a character flaw in their partner. The researchers found that partners who delivered their teases and responded to being teased with various appeasement behaviors (including flirtatious and submissive behaviors) elicited more positive emotions in their partners and were more satisfied in their relationships six months later than were the less appeasing couples (Keltner et al., 1998).

NONVERBAL CONFLICT BEHAVIOR AND MARITAL STABILITY In recent years, Gottman and his colleagues have been testing the idea that emotional communication during conflicts (and non-conflict interactions) can accurately predict divorce. The results of these studies have been quite remarkable. In one study, Carrere and Gottman (1999) coded the emotional content of a 15-minute conflict interaction using the Specific Affect Coding System, which measures the occurrence of negative emotions (e.g., anger, contempt/disgust, sadness, fear, and whining) and positive emotions (e.g., affection/caring, humor, interest/curiosity, and joy/enthusiasm). They found that it was possible to predict marital outcome over a six-year period for 124 newlywed couples, using data from just the first three minutes

▸ How a couple deals with nonverbal displays of hostility during a fight is more relevant to the success of their relationship than how often they fight or what they fight about.

istockphoto.com/laflor

of the couples' interactions. Similarly, Gottman and Levenson (1999) found that the emotional content of a couple's conflict conversation could predict, with 82.6% accuracy, the likelihood of divorce over a four-year period.

In a longitudinal study of 79 young married couples that began in 1983, Gottman and Levenson (2000) also found that the emotional content of a couple's interaction predicted whether they would divorce. But using the same data, they were also able to predict whether a couple was more likely to divorce early (about seven years after marriage) or later (about 14 years after marriage). Hostile expressions during a couple's conflict, including criticism, defensiveness, contempt, and stonewalling, predicted early divorce. In contrast, the lack of positive expressions during a conflict and during an "events-of-the-day" conversation predicted later divorce (but not early divorce). Why the difference? According to the researchers, the presence of intense negativity in a marriage makes it difficult for a couple to stay together for long. But the absence of positive expressions, on the other hand, may take its toll only after a very long time (e.g., when the children are older, when the couple drifts apart, etc.). Another finding of interest was that the wife-demand–husband-withdraw pattern predicted both early and later divorce. In a subsequent study, Gottman, Levenson, and Woodin (2001) restricted their analysis to the facial expressions of husbands and wives during conflict. They found that the wives' facial expression of disgust as well as both the husbands' and wives' facial expressions of unfelt happiness (i.e., false smiles) predicted months of separation over a four-year period.

Other researchers have also corroborated the powerful impact of emotional expressions on the quality and stability of a marriage. In one longitudinal study of 37 married and 10 cohabitating couples, researchers analyzed the nonverbal expressions of each couple as the couple interacted with one another for 10 minutes about the most important and troubling disagreements they have in their relationship. Each couple participated in two videotaped interactions—one on a disagreement of most concern to the man and another on a disagreement of most concern to the woman. Among the most common topics were disagreements over their communication, finances, and household chores. Based on observations of several 30-second video clips of each interaction, the researchers found that a couple's nonverbal expressions affected their relationship satisfaction, marital adjustment, and marital stability. For example, in more satisfied and well-adjusted relationships, men expressed less hostility and greater empathy, while women expressed more affection, less distress, and greater empathy. The single most important determinant of the couples' dissatisfaction ratings was the men's hostile expressions. Five years after these laboratory sessions, eight of the 47 couples were no longer together. The emotional expressions of the women in these sessions could predict with 83% accuracy which of the couples would stay together and which would separate. The men's expressions were slightly less accurate at 81%. The strongest predictors of separation were the women's expressions of affection and the men's expressions of empathy (Waldinger et al., 2004).

Comforting Encounters: Providing Emotional Support

Almost instinctively, we seem to know how to comfort people in need. Indeed, the experience of giving and receiving emotional support goes back to the earliest of our infant–parent interactions, setting the stage for what we crave in the years to come. Comforting encounters begin in infancy with parental communication that involves nonverbal warmth and affection (the use of immediacy behaviors such as touch, gaze, smiles, closeness, and soothing vocal tones) and patterns of mutual influence in which infant and parent engage in synchronized movement, mirroring, reciprocity, and the like.

Of course, everyone doesn't share the same childhood experiences. In one study, anthropologist David Givens (1978a) found dramatic differences in the nonverbal communication of abusive mothers compared to that of nonabusive mothers. He observed seven videotapes of abusive mothers and seven of nonabusive mothers. In each, the mother interacted with her 24- to 30-month-old child as the child tried to complete two tasks, one age-appropriate, the other advanced and more difficult. The tasks included activities such as stacking or sorting blocks, folding paper, stringing beads, drawing lines on paper, and so on. As Givens concluded,

> The abusive mothers observed in the study presented themselves much more negatively to their children than the control [nonabusive] mothers. They used significantly more dominant and aversive nonverbal signs to convey unambiguous poses of overbearance, non-concern, and emotional coldness. Over a period of years, these presentations must have devastating effects on the youngsters. (p. 42)

Specifically, abusive mothers were more likely to use a threatening voice (loud and low-pitched), harsher touches, and negative facial gestures (e.g., lip retractions). They were less likely to use a soft, high-pitched voice (i.e., baby talk); gentle touches; smiles; head tilts; and mutual eye contact. The nonabusive mother–child interactions were more coordinated and synchronized than were the abusive mother–child interactions (e.g., more reciprocated smiles, similar pacing, etc.). According to Givens, the negative cues of abusive mothers create a self-fulfilling prophecy: The mother unconsciously behaves in a way that invites the bad behavior from her child that she expects to get, justifying the abuse she then administers.

PERSONAL EXPERIENCE 8.5

CAN YOU RELATE TO THIS?

The Capacity to Comfort Others Develops Early in Life

I have always had a very strong family base and my parents have always been very loving. My family is also very affectionate. Whenever I was sad as a kid, I can remember my mother holding me and making a very comforting sound to help me stop crying. Today, I am very good at helping to comfort those who are feeling hurt. People actually tell me I am one of the first people they want to call when they are sad. My girlfriend, on the other hand, has a great family. But . . . I never to this day have seen any of them touch one another or hug at all. She is not the best at comforting me when I have a problem. In fact, most of the time, she takes my cry for attention as a personal attack.

Corey

ATTACHMENT AND NONVERBAL COMMUNICATION One of the consequences of these early experiences is the insecurity a child develops over the prospect of forming close relationships. Extending the basic principles of attachment theory (Bowlby, 1973, 1980), which regards attachment to others as a human need activated during moments of distress, researchers have been studying differences in **attachment styles**. These styles are relatively stable interpersonal orientations, developed in childhood, that reflect beliefs we have about whether we are worthy of receiving care and affection from others and whether others can be counted on to provide it (Bartholomew, 1990). A negative view of others results in avoidant attachment styles: Not wanting closeness because one is overly self-reliant (low anxiety and high avoidance) creates a dismissive style; whereas not wanting closeness because of apprehension (high anxiety and high avoidance) creates a fearful style. A positive view of self and others results in a secure attachment style. Secure persons (low anxiety and low avoidance) are comfortable with intimacy and confident and optimistic about close relationships but self-sufficient to the point of not being overly dependent on others. In contrast, a preoccupied style, which includes a negative view of self and a positive view of others (high anxiety and low avoidance), results in a lack of self-confidence combined with a desire for intimacy. Preoccupied persons may be clingy in their close relationships with others (Bartholomew & Horowitz, 1991). Table 8.4 displays the four attachment styles based on high and low levels of anxiety and avoidance.

Table 8.4 Attachment Styles Based on Anxiety and Avoidance

	Low Anxiety	High Anxiety
Low Avoidance	Secure Attachment	Preoccupied Attachment
High Avoidance	Dismissive Attachment	Fearful Attachment

Studies show that attachment security or insecurity is like a filter in the communication process that blocks a person's sensitivity to certain nonverbal messages and discourages the expression of certain messages as well (Noller, 2006). For example, people who have a secure attachment style are the most likely to seek comfort from others when they need it (Ognibene & Collins, 1998) and the best equipped to comfort others, offering more reassurance and physical comfort and showing increased gaze, more facial and vocal expressiveness, less tension, and more enjoyment than persons with other attachment styles (Becker-Stoll, Delius, & Scheitenberger, 2001; Feeney & Collins, 2001; Guerrero, 1996; Tucker & Anders, 1998). For instance, research shows that anxious and avoidant individuals are less tolerant of close interpersonal distances, a behavioral tendency that would make it difficult for them to offer contact comfort and emotional support to others (Kaitz, Bar-Haim, Lehrer, & Grossman, 2004; Yukawa, Tokuda, & Sato, 2007).

People with nonsecure attachment styles are less accurate in their assessment of emotional cues, though the precise nature of this difficulty is still being investigated. One hypothesis supported in a recent study is that persons with low avoidance styles (secure and preoccupied) have a positive view of others, which improves their judgment, while high-avoidance people (dismissive and fearful) have a negative view of others, which impedes their judgment (Cooley, 2005). A different hypothesis suggests that persons with an anxious attachment style (preoccupied and fearful) tend to focus on their own needs and vulnerabilities and are hypersensitive to cues of rejection. As a result, they are less sensitive to others' nonverbal signals of distress (Mikulincer & Shaver, 2003). There is some evidence that this hypersensitivity causes anxious individuals to be less accurate overall in recognizing facial expressions of emotion because they make hair-trigger assessments of other people's feelings. Several studies confirm that when anxious persons watch faces morph from neutral to an emotional expression or from an emotional expression to neutral and researchers ask them to indicate when they first see the emotional expression appear or disappear on the face, these anxious persons see changes in both the onset and offset of an emotion sooner than less anxious persons do, but they are also less accurate in recognizing the emotions. In other words, as the researchers point out, persons with anxious attachment styles mistakenly jump to emotional conclusions about the feelings of other people (Fraley, Niedenthal, Marks, Brumbaugh, & Vicary, 2006).

COMFORTING MESSAGES In general, we seem to be more mindful of some comforting behaviors than we are of others, agreeing on many of the obvious (i.e., stereotypical) nonverbal signals we can use to provide reassurance. Beyond that, gender may play a key role in determining how we respond to a person in need of comfort. For example, when asked to describe how they would react nonverbally to a situation in which a close same-sex friend tells them that he or she just ended a romantic relationship, college students in two separate surveys largely agreed on what they would do. Overall, hugging emerged as the number-one response, but the men in both surveys were much less likely than the women to say they would hug their troubled friend. Other high-ranking responses included being attentive, proxemics (i.e., getting close), concerned facial expressions, increased touch, and eye contact. Some responses depended mainly on the respondent's gender: Men were more likely to pat their friend on the arm or shoulder and to suggest going out and doing something (to take their mind off the problem); women were more likely to cry with their friend and to use a wider variety of comforting touches (Bullis & Horn, 1995; Dolin & Booth-Butterfield, 1993). Another study found that embraces are seen as more expected for women than for men (Floyd, 1999).

Gender differences notwithstanding, comforting others involves a lot more than giving someone a big hug. Drawing on his own studies and those of many others from various disciplines, communication researcher Brant Burleson, with his colleague Daena Goldsmith, developed a theory of **comforting messages** that focuses on how our involvement in a conversation with another person can help alleviate that person's emotional distress (Burleson & Goldsmith, 1998). Beginning with the premise that our emotional reactions to a particular situation stem from the way we interpret and evaluate its relevance and importance to us (a premise derived from appraisal theories of emotion), Burleson and Goldsmith view comforting messages as those that facilitate reappraisals; that is, they encourage us to see situations differently.

Consistent with Burleson and Goldsmith's views on comforting messages, this section introduces six nonverbal communication skills that can help us become a valuable source of emotional support for the people we care about, which we do by helping them see situations in a better light (i.e., facilitating reappraisals). Imagine the following scenario: A close friend of yours, Jeremy, just found out that he did not make the shortlist of applicants for a job he wanted and one for which he thought he was extremely qualified. Aside from some bitterness about not being a finalist, he is now starting to seriously question his own competence and career goals. His confidence is badly shaken. Jeremy is about to tell you his bad news.

RECOGNIZING DISTRESS Before we can help someone, we need to know if they need or want our help. This decoding skill is important because many people who need or want help don't come out and ask for it—at least, not in words. Decoding skills are also important because a person may be too upset and not emotionally ready to reappraise the situation. Finally, we need decoding skills to decide what someone is feeling. The same event—in Jeremy's case, not getting a job—can produce more than a single negative emotion: sadness, anger, fear, embarrassment, and so on. Since the topics we should pursue with a distressed individual depend on what he or she is feeling, it behooves us to know what those feelings are. As we noted earlier in the chapter, studies show that happy and well-adjusted couples also happen to be more accurate decoders of each other's nonverbal messages than are less happy and not as well-adjusted couples (Noller, 1992).

Whether Jeremy calls on the phone or comes to see you, he shouldn't have to say "I'm very upset" in order for you to recognize his SOS signals. If he is depressed, for instance, nonverbal symptoms of distress may include slow, hesitating speech; a low-pitched, soft, and monotone voice; sad facial expressions; gaze avoidance; indirect body orientations; constricted, slumped postures; displacement activity (fidgeting); and self-touching. The fact that Jeremy is a close friend and not merely an acquaintance should make it easier for you to notice the signs that something is wrong, that he is not acting the way he normally does.

REFLECTING FEELINGS Communication that provides emotional support begins with expressions of empathy, messages that show we understand, accept, and appreciate what another person is experiencing. Of the many benefits such messages provide, perhaps the most important is that they let a distressed person know that it's okay here and now to express negative feelings. Given the many pressures on us (i.e., display rules) to suppress negative emotions in most social situations, we aren't likely to vent these feelings without some reassurance that we have nothing to lose if we do.

Although we can empathize with someone verbally with utterances that show we understand what someone is feeling (e.g., "I can see that this is making you angry"), facial and vocal expressions, gestures, postures, and more combine to create a much more powerful empathic message. Research on emotional contagion, facial feedback, and self-perception theories demonstrate that we may begin to feel the way we act, thus putting us a step closer to feeling another person's distress (see Chapter 5).

PERSONAL EXPERIENCE 8.6

CAN YOU RELATE TO THIS?

Expressing Unfelt Emotions Can Be Comforting

When I broke up with my ex-boyfriend, he was pretty upset about it. I wasn't really that upset because I had been contemplating doing it for a while, and I just didn't feel the same way about him anymore. But when I saw how upset he got when I told him, it made me feel bad that I wasn't feeling the same way or showing the same emotions in return. I wanted him to think that I was also upset so I tried to show sadness and cry. I pretended to be upset by burying my face in my hands and shaking my head. I tried to make my facial expression mimic the look of sadness but it was not genuine. I think it made him feel better that he wasn't the only one crying. Today, we are still friends.

Leighann

When you encounter Jeremy, it may be obvious from his facial expressions, tone of voice, and posture what he is feeling. You can reflect his feelings by mirroring some of these nonverbal expressions. Mirroring not only shows Jeremy what he is feeling, but it lets him know in an instant that it's okay to feel that way. Mirroring also shows him that you can relate to those feelings, that you understand what his emotions are. And it enables you to sharpen your focus on what needs to be the primary topic of conversation: Jeremy's emotional reactions to the loss of a possible job.

REACHING OUT Sometimes offering to help is enough. As Burleson and Goldsmith (1998) point out,

> The recognition by distressed others that such an environment is present—that trustworthy, caring others are available, that the expression and exploration of feelings is possible and legitimate—may itself be curative. Indeed, research has found that the perception of support availability, especially in stressful contexts, has facilitative effects on coping, health, and psychological well-being. (p. 265)

Of course, reaching out is more than just offering to help. It's an expression of caring and concern, demonstrated most often through some form of physical affection, from a gentle pat on the shoulder to a loving embrace. Does reaching out, touching, and getting close to someone make a difference? The available evidence indicates that it does.

There is a great deal of research that most forms of touch, particularly those that occur in the context of helping someone, convey and elicit strong positive emotions (Jones, 1994; Montagu, 1986). Such touches in close relationships can stimulate the release of chemicals in the brain, such as oxytocin, that reduce stress and promote comfort and intimacy (Goleman, 2006). Aside from touch, studies show that other nonverbal immediacy and involvement behaviors express caring and concern. In one study, undergraduate students and their mothers discussed problems of concern to the students. After each interaction, the students rated their mother's supportiveness during the interaction. Overall, mothers who exhibited more vocal warmth, attentiveness, and movement synchrony with their children received higher ratings from their children (Trees, 2000). In another study, individuals discussed an emotionally distressing event with a confederate who was instructed by the researcher to use nonverbal involvement behaviors at high, moderate, or low levels. In the high-involvement condition, for instance, the confederate leaned forward, moved closer, maintained eye contact and a direct body orientation, spoke in a warm manner, nodded often, and showed emotion when appropriate. As expected, participants rated high-involvement behaviors more positively than moderate- or low-involvement behaviors (Jones & Guerrero, 2001). In a similar experiment, Jones and Wirtz (2006) found that participants discussing an upsetting event with a stranger (confederate) felt better after the interaction if they interacted with a stranger who exhibited high rather than moderate or low levels of nonverbal involvement (close proximity, forward lean, direct body orientation, and expressiveness).

PERSONAL EXPERIENCE 8.7

CAN YOU RELATE TO THIS?

Touch Provides Comfort and Builds Intimacy

My girlfriend and my mother were friendly, but never really seemed to hit it off for quite some time. After several months into the relationship, they were sitting together talking and the topic of divorce came up. My mother began discussing her separation from my father nearly 12 years before. The situation became somewhat emotional, and my girlfriend recognized my mother's distress. My girlfriend was very comforting and leaned in to hug my mother just as the first tear rolled down her face. A new bond was formed between the two as soon as she reached out. My girlfriend used to be a little scared of my mother, but ever since they shared that intimate encounter, she is at ease in her presence.

Matt

The impact of these nonverbal involvement behaviors extends even further, changing the nonverbal behaviors of the person receiving the comfort. In one study, researchers found that distressed persons interacting either with a helper (confederate) who displayed high levels, moderate levels, or low levels of nonverbal involvement liked the helper displaying high levels of involvement the most but tended to match the involvement behaviors of their helper regardless of the involvement level. In other words, participants paired with a helper who exhibited high levels of involvement, such as smiling, moving closer, facing the person, head nodding, and so forth, tended to respond in a similar manner; likewise, participants paired with a helper who exhibited low levels of involvement (e.g., not smiling or nodding) responded by exhibiting low levels of involvement themselves. This effect was most pronounced when women interacted with other women. As the researchers noted, this tendency to match a helper's nonverbal involvement would be quite beneficial in cases where helpers exhibit high levels of involvement, but severely counterproductive in situations where a helper may be verbally concerned but nonverbally uninvolved and distant, causing the distressed person's nonverbal behavior to become more uninvolved and distant as well (Jones & Wirtz, 2007). In cases where neither person is aware of these nonverbal cues and their unintended consequences, the emotional damage could be especially difficult to prevent or repair

In our hypothetical case, Jeremy feels depressed about missing what he thought was a golden job opportunity. After boasting about his credentials, he's a little embarrassed about being rejected. Now he faces, with some fear and trepidation, the prospect of not getting the kind of job he wanted. In his present condition, he would most likely welcome the concern and warmth of a close friend.

RELINQUISHING CONTROL We often use communication to get others to do what we want them to do: We argue, cajole, intimidate, demand, beg, threaten, and so on. But even with the best of intentions, these actions may do more to serve our own self-interests than those of the people we're trying to help. In contrast, comforting messages encourage the distressed person to come up with his or her own reappraisals. According to Burleson and Goldsmith (1998), this requires the helper to resist the impulse to do most of the talking and the temptation to offer most of the solutions:

> Participants in comforting conversations must work to overcome two natural inclinations that may inhibit the process of reappraisal. Helpers may experience pressure to fix the other's distress by telling her or him what to think, do, or feel. At the same time, distressed others may experience pressure to keep their conversational turns brief rather than extended. Each of these

> natural inclinations is at odds with what we suspect are the optimal conversational features for facilitating reappraisals: the elicitation by helpers and the performance by distressed others of extended talk about feelings and coping options. (p. 270)

In this sense, relinquishing control means exercising restraint and empowering the person we're trying to help. It means, for the most part, giving up the speaking floor, suppressing the urge to evaluate what we hear, and, most important, being relatively deferential rather than controlling. With Jeremy, this means that you would (1) allow him to do most of the talking; (2) avoid rendering judgments with facial or vocal expressions; (3) give him your undivided attention with behaviors such as eye contact, direct body orientation, and forward lean; and (4) avoid dominant behaviors such as staring, interrupting, talking loudly, turning away, taking up space, and so on.

REINFORCING SPEECH As we noted earlier, a vital part of the comforting process is getting someone who may be reluctant to talk to do so. We can do this verbally with the use of open-ended and probing questions, which give the distressed individual an opportunity to elaborate on his or her condition. Nonverbally, we can encourage someone to speak by being attentive and patient and by using back-channel signals—vocalizations (such as *uh huh* or *hm hm*), head nods, smiles, and other responsive facial gestures. Your conversation with Jeremy should include an array of questions and nonverbal signals that will get him talking and keep him talking about what happened, why, how he feels about it, and what he plans to do. As Burleson and Goldsmith (1998) emphasize,

> If distress is to be alleviated, a change in appraisal must take place, and this is more likely to occur if the other articulates and elaborates a new way of viewing things or new ways of coping for herself or himself. (p. 271)

REWARDING OPTIMISM Of course, in reappraising the situation, some things that a distressed person says will be more helpful than others. Insights that lead to optimistic rather than pessimistic reappraisals—one indicator of what some call *emotional intelligence*—are those most likely to alleviate distress. As psychologist Daniel Goleman (1994) points out:

> People who are optimistic see a failure as due to something that can be changed so that they can succeed next time around, while pessimists take the blame for failure, ascribing it to some lasting characteristic they are helpless to change. These differing explanations have profound implications for how people respond

> to life. For example, in reaction to disappointment such as being turned down for a job, optimists tend to respond actively and hopefully, by formulating a plan of action, say, or seeking out help and advice; they see the setback as something that can be remedied. Pessimists, by contrast, react to such setbacks by assuming there is nothing they can do to make things go better the next time, and so do nothing about the problem; they see the setback as due to some personal deficit that will always plague them. (p. 88)

We can reward a distressed person nonverbally each time he or she thinks of an optimistic reappraisal, one that alleviates or softens the impact of negative emotions such as grief, anger, fear, guilt, or embarrassment. With smiles, congratulatory and approving gestures, vocal enthusiasm, head nods, forward leans, and the like, we can encourage Jeremy to stay focused on those things that will allow him to be optimistic about his future.

SUMMARY

Nonverbal communication often reflects the intimacy of a relationship. Intimate couples are more likely than non-intimate couples to use nonverbal signals in ways that demonstrate the presence of certain distinct qualities: richness, efficiency, uniqueness, substitutability, pacing/synchrony, openness, spontaneity, and evaluation. But the link between intimacy and these various qualities of intimate nonverbal communication is not linear—increased intimacy does not continue to produce increased openness, spontaneity, efficiency, and so forth. At some point in the development of a relationship, these qualities tend to peak and then stabilize at some lower level. Couples experience changes in the intimacy of their relationships during interactions (turning points) in which one partner responds to the nonverbal immediacy behaviors of the other. Attempts to explain the dynamics of intimacy regulation, such as cognitive valence theory, include a host of factors—culture, personality, interpersonal reward, and so forth—that may predict the outcome of these interactions.

Nonverbal communication has a powerful and cumulative impact on the success of a close relationship, where expressions of hostility reduce and expressions of affection enhance the satisfaction and stability of a relationship. Accurately reading nonverbal messages and avoiding overly negative inferences also have a positive impact. Nonverbal signals play an important role in romantic encounters and help us attract a potential partner. Identity signals related to physical appearance often set the stage for the courtship sequence that follows. While we may be attracted to good-looking people—a beauty bias—we generally follow matching norms that recommend a partner who is similar to us in physical appearance. Nonverbal courtship signals communicate a readiness to interact with another person and facilitate a couple's progression through key stages in the courtship ritual. Whether we engage in conflicts with others or try to comfort them, our nonverbal communication makes a difference. In conflicts, the destructive effects of nonverbal behaviors accompanying criticism, contempt, defensiveness, and stonewalling can be minimized by avoiding such behaviors as much as possible and by using other, more positive behaviors, such as the use of appeasement displays that promote reconciliation and bonding. Attachment security influences our ability to offer and receive emotional support. During attempts to comfort distressed individuals, we can help most by recognizing the distress, reflecting feelings, reaching out, relinquishing control, reinforcing speech, and rewarding optimism.

KEY TERMS

Actions of appeal or invitation 305
Appeasement 317
Attachment styles 320
Beauty bias 297
Cognitive schemata 287
Cognitive valence theory 287
Comforting messages 322
Courtship readiness 304
Demand–withdraw pattern 314
Flooding 314
Magic ratio 295
Matching norms 301
Motivated inaccuracy 292
Positioning for courtship 305
Quasi-courtship behavior 305
Repair mechanisms 316
Teasing 291

Chapter Outline

9

NONVERBAL COMMUNICATION IN DECEPTIVE ENCOUNTERS

Ben is talking to Julia as they leave class. He's trying to find out why she didn't call or text him the night before as she said she would. The truth is that she didn't call him because she was partying with some of her friends and just didn't get around to it; but she doesn't want to tell him the truth because she knows it would make him upset. So she lies and tells him she was very tired last night and went to bed early. But there's something about the *way* she tells him (not *what* she tells him) that makes him question her truthfulness.

Should Ben trust his instincts? What is it about Julia's demeanor that might betray the lie she is telling? These are difficult questions to answer. Nevertheless, as we will see in this chapter, researchers have been trying to answer questions like these for a long time. We begin this chapter by discussing the everyday occurrence of **lying** as well as the differences between lying and the more general category of **deception**. Then we consider some theoretical approaches to the thesis that nonverbal communication often betrays the liar by exposing the liar's intent to deceive or by revealing what the liar is trying to hide. Following this discussion of theory, we take a look at what the research tells us about the nonverbal signs of lying; and in the concluding sections, we consider some of the factors that influence our ability to catch a liar and whether training or the use of modern technology makes it more difficult for liars to succeed in their deception.

Learning Objectives

After reading this chapter, you will be able to do the following:

1. Discuss the prevalence and nature of lying and deception in everyday life.
2. Identify and differentiate the four major theories scholars rely on to explain the nonverbal signs of lying and deception.
3. Highlight what researchers have discovered about the nonverbal cues associated with lying and deception and identify the limitations of this research.
4. Address the main factors that limit the success of lie catching.
5. Review the research on the effectiveness of training programs designed to enhance the ability of lie catchers.

LYING AND DECEPTION IN EVERYDAY LIFE

Unlike our efforts to build rapport with others or to seek help from strangers (Chapter 8), we rarely interact with people for the sole purpose of catching them in the act of lying. On the contrary, most of us give people the benefit of the doubt, trusting that what they tell us is true. This presumption of innocence, or **truth bias**, as some call it (McCornack & Parks, 1986), is one of the reasons why liars can dupe us more than we might like. Another reason, among those that we will address later in this chapter, is that many people are quite adept at lying, making it nearly impossible for even the best lie catcher to detect the lie. In fact, most studies show that we are not very good at catching liars, performing at a level slightly better than the toss of a coin (around 54%). For the most part then, the odds of catching a liar are not much better than the odds of getting away with a lie. In this chapter, we will focus on the lies that are not so immune to scrutiny (i.e., detectable lies), where we are most likely—with the right knowledge, training, and practice—to increase the odds in favor of the lie catcher over the liar (Frank & Svetieva, 2013).

Lying is, in fact, a part of everyday life. But how often do people lie? Surveys say that the average person admits to lying about once or twice a day. But some of this research also says that the average number of lies may be misleading because a small percentage of people (prolific liars) report doing most of the lying (Serota, Levine, & Boster, 2010). On the other hand, one study suggests that people can't resist telling a few lies, even in a very short conversation, let alone an entire day (Feldman, Forrest, & Happ, 2002). Researchers asked participants (undergraduate students) to take part in a 10-minute interaction for the purpose of getting to know someone they have never met before. One group was asked to include things they liked about themselves, another group was asked to stress their own competence, and the final group received no specific instructions on how to present themselves. As each of the participants viewed their own videotape—the participants were not aware they were being videotaped—they were asked to indicate when they said something that was not true. The researchers found that 60% of the participants confessed to lying at least once—on average, two to three times during their interaction. So it would appear that people most likely *underestimate* the frequency of their own lies—particularly polite lies and little white lies, which tend to go unnoticed or may not even be seen as lies.

People probably lie to or deceive others more than they care to admit, but is there a difference between lying and deception? One answer is that, while lying is an act of deception, deceiving a person is not the same as lying to that person. In other words, a person can be deceptive without telling a lie. Think of a basketball or football player, for example, who tricks an opponent with a fake to the right and a move to the left.

Or think about the professional magician using deception in a performance to fool an audience. Are any of these persons lying? While *deception* usually refers to any act that misleads someone, *lying* is not only a deliberate attempt to mislead someone but also an attempt to do so *without prior notification*. In other words, lying comes without any advance notice (Frank & Svetieva, 2013). In sports competitions, the players realize in advance that deception is part of the game. In a magician's act, the audience knows in advance that deception is part of the performance. In addition, the idea that a liar doesn't want to be caught, that lying is a *deliberate* act of deception, means that being sarcastic or facetious (i.e., saying one thing but meaning another) and not telling the truth without realizing it (i.e., believing false information) are not lies even though both instances are deceptive acts.

THEORIES OF NONVERBAL COMMUNICATION AND DECEPTION

Over the years, there have been several attempts to offer theories that explain the connection between lying, deception, and nonverbal communication. This section introduces four of the most prominent theories.

Nonverbal Leakage and Clues to Deception

Psychologists Paul Ekman and Wallace Friesen (1969a, 1974) developed the earliest account of how lying can influence nonverbal behavior. According to their theory, we may be able to catch a liar because (1) the truth will come out, despite the liar's best efforts, or (2) something in the liar's performance is insincere and provides us with clues that deception is occurring. To illustrate, Alex is angry that someone just insulted him, but he smiles to cover up his true feelings. Still, we see the hint of a frown flash across his face. This is an example of what Ekman and Friesen call **leakage**, one or more signals that convey the truth behind the lie. In this case, Alex's frown leaked his true feelings. More often than not, however, we may suspect that someone is lying, but that is all (i.e., there is no leakage). For example, Yolanda concocts a bogus excuse for not attending her friend Tara's party. A few minutes later, while answering Tara's queries, Yolanda stumbles over her own words. In this instance, Yolanda's halting speech is a deception clue, a signal that she might have been lying.

A liar must be careful to avoid saying the wrong things. In addition, a liar's demeanor (i.e., nonverbal behavior) must not arouse any suspicion. While liars may be able to choose their words carefully and avoid any hint of deception, the same is not true of their nonverbal communication, which represents a mode of expression much more difficult to control. When someone tells a lie, the control of a communication channel—the ability to control words, face, voice, or body—determines whether that channel will help the liar deliver a convincing performance or help the lie catcher discover the truth. According to this theory, the verbal channel is the most easily controlled. Among the various nonverbal channels, the face is the most controllable and, therefore, the least likely to betray a lie (although there are many exceptions that we'll discuss later).

In their classic study of deception, Ekman and Friesen (1974) obtained some support for this theory. In the first part of the study, student nurses viewed a film of the ocean and a film of gruesome surgical procedures. They were videotaped at the same time describing to an interviewer how each film made them feel. But they followed the researchers' instructions and described feeling good regardless of which film they were watching, thus lying about the unpleasant film and telling the truth about the other. To add a measure of realism to the study, raise the stakes, and motivate the nurses to lie, the researchers explained that they were testing the nurses' ability to conceal their true feelings, something nurses must occasionally do with their patients. The nurses were also told that their scores on the test would be made available to members of the nursing school faculty. In the second part of the study, observers watched the videotapes and judged the truthfulness of the nurses. But the researchers restricted the communication channels available to the observers: Some saw only the nurses' faces, some saw only their bodies, some heard the voices but not the words, and some heard the words. The ability of observers to catch the lies depended on which channel they received. Those who saw just the nurses' faces or who only heard the words—the most controllable channels—were least able to catch the lies. The most accurate judges were those who saw only the body. More recent studies also show that we are misled more

RESEARCH 9.1

FIND OUT MORE

Does a Poker Player Need More Than a Good Poker Face?

Most of us are probably familiar with the importance of a good "poker face" when trying to conceal our true emotions. Nowhere is this skill expected to be practiced more than in the card game of poker, where players don't want other players to know when they have a winning hand or when they have a losing hand of cards. So any skilled poker player must be able to control their facial expressions of emotion. But do other channels of nonverbal communication betray the quality of the player's hand? In this study, researchers were interested in discovering if there are other such "tells" in the game of poker. In three studies, researchers studied professional poker players at the

World Series of Poker Championship and found that the players' arm motions when placing a bet and pushing their chips on the table predicted the quality of their hand.

To find out more about this study and to answer the following questions, see the full text (cited below).

1. The researchers used videorecordings of the poker players. What versions of these recordings did they show to the three groups of judges?
2. The researchers did three studies of the poker players. How did these studies differ and why were they done (i.e., why wasn't one study enough)?
3. How do the results of this study relate to Ekman's theory of leakage and clues to deception?
4. What were the strengths and limitations of this research?

Source: Slepian, M. L., Young, S. G., Rutchick, A. M., & Ambady, N. (2013). Quality of professional players' poker hands is perceived accurately from arm motions. *Psychological Science, 24*, 2335–2338.

RESEARCH 9.1

by a liar's face than we are by a liar's voice or body (DePaulo, Stone, & Lassiter, 1985). Even when observers were presented with facial signs of anxiety in one study, they were still fooled by a smile (Harrigan & Taing, 1997).

The Four-Factor Theory of Deception

The notion that difficult-to-control actions are more honest than easy-to-control actions makes sense. But what do these uncontrollable signals actually tell us? Do they tell us that someone is lying? The answer is no. There are no unambiguous signals of deception—only signals of some underlying internal process associated with deceptive behavior. Psychologists Miron Zuckerman, Bella DePaulo, and Robert Rosenthal (1981) proposed a **four-factor theory** that lying can produce various signs of attempted control, physiological arousal, displays of emotion, and cognitive processing. These signs may communicate deception—that someone is lying or only appears to be lying.

ATTEMPTED CONTROL A liar's attempts to look and sound truthful can in themselves be clues to deception. The controlled behavior may look or sound unnatural (e.g., an awkward gesture, a poorly timed facial expression, a flat tone of voice, etc.) or it may contradict some other behavior that is more difficult to control, producing an inconsistent overall performance (e.g., a smiling face contradicted by nervous gestures). The importance of controlling one's presentation also suggests that leakage and **deception clues** will depend on the characteristics of the liar and of the situation. For instance, some individuals are highly motivated or possess certain personality traits or skills and may be better at getting away with a lie than

▸ Lie detection is based on the idea that when the stakes are high, a liar will be unable to suppress many of the signals associated with deception. Physiological signs of arousal, such as the ones recorded on a polygraph test, are among the signals that can betray a lie.

Photofest

others are. In addition, a planned lie—where the liar has time to prepare and rehearse—is often tougher to catch than is an unplanned lie (Littlepage & Pineault, 1982).

PHYSIOLOGICAL AROUSAL For most individuals, telling a lie is a stressful event. The use of polygraph testing is based on the idea that various measures of physiological arousal—blood pressure, respiration, and skin resistance—will pick up the amount of stress someone is experiencing. Of course, if a liar is not stressed while telling a lie, no measure of physiological arousal will be effective. Human lie detectors can choose to operate on the same basic principle, trying to pick up visible or audible signs of arousal that may be linked to deception. These signals include pupil dilation, eye blinking, vocal pitch, and speech hesitations.

DISPLAYS OF EMOTION When a person lies about how he or she feels, leakage and deception clues can show up in countless ways (Ekman & Friesen, 1975). While trying to conceal an emotion, difficult-to-control facial muscles may leak one's true feelings. Some examples include the following: a micro-expression flashes across a person's face in a fraction of a second, revealing suppressed rage; an expression of glee begins to appear on someone's face but is quickly squelched; a partial expression of fear shows around a person's eyes, betraying an otherwise confident demeanor; a quick shoulder shrug accompanies a strongly stated opinion. In all of these cases, an attempt to hide an emotion fails. When trying to fabricate an emotion one doesn't feel, the liar's face or voice might not portray the emotion genuinely. A false smile—pretending to be happy or amused—is the best example. As we learned in Chapter 5, a false smile doesn't activate the muscles around the eyes. It also tends to produce an asymmetrical expression (right and left sides differ). In addition, the timing of the expression is unnatural. As Ekman (1986) points out,

> The offset time of the false smile may appear inappropriate. The smile may drop off the face too abruptly, or there may be a stepped offset, in which the smile decreases, and then is held, before either disappearing or going through another stepped decrease as it leaves the face. (p. 158)

Thus, a lie may consist of a concealed emotion or a fabricated one. But another way a lie can cause an emotional reaction is when the liar has feelings about the very act of lying: fear of being caught, guilt about not telling the truth, glee about getting away with a lie (Ekman, 1986). Any of these emotions can produce nonverbal clues to deception. Aside from the physiological symptoms of arousal brought on by emotions, signs of fear and guilt can include an increase in the use of adaptors (i.e., self-touching often signals negative emotions), avoidance behaviors (e.g., gaze avoidance, distance, indirect body orientation, shorter speaking turns, etc.), and masking smiles (i.e., to conceal feelings of fear and guilt). Signs of glee—produced by an emotional condition known *as duping delight*—might leak out in fairly obvious ways (e.g., a squelched facial expression) or not-so-obvious ways (e.g., increased involvement behavior).

Liars and the situations they face are not all the same. Table 9.1 presents Ekman's (1986) summary of the many factors that will cause a liar to feel apprehension (i.e., fear), guilt, or delight. These factors underscore the importance of diagnosing the situation. A guilty liar is not necessarily a fearful or apprehensive liar. The signs of duping delight do not resemble the signs of apprehension. Most important, the more a liar experiences these emotions, the less likely it is that he or she will escape detection.

Table 9.1 Some Factors Increasing the Emotional Reactions of a Liar

Detection Apprehension (Fear)	Deception Guilt	Duping Delight
The target has a reputation for being tough to fool.	The target is unwilling.	The target poses a challenge, having a reputation for being difficult to fool.
The target starts out being suspicious.	The deceit is totally selfish.	The lie is a challenge because of either what must be concealed or the nature of what must be fabricated.
The liar has had little practice and no record of success.	The deceit is unauthorized.	Others are watching or know about the lie and appreciate the liar's skillful performance.
The liar is especially vulnerable to the fear of being caught.	The liar and target share social values.	
The stakes are high.	The liar is personally acquainted with the target.	
The target does not benefit from the lie.	The target cannot be faulted as mean or gullible.	

RESEARCH 9.2

FIND OUT MORE

Does a Liar's Face Give the Liar Away?

We learned in Chapter 5 that micro-expressions of emotion occur in a fraction of a second and can reveal our true feelings. We also learned that people follow display rules when they want to cover up how they really feel with a blank face (neutralizing) or with a phony face (masking one emotion with a different emotion). In this study, the researchers wanted to find out more about the prevalence and timing of micro-expressions as well as the ability of people to neutralize and mask facial expressions of emotion. Although observers were not very good at detecting emotional deception (just slightly above-chance levels), there was clear evidence of emotional deception, supporting the idea that emotional deception, particularly neutralizing, is difficult for untrained observers to catch.

The researchers also found emotional leakage in all of the dishonest participants, but with facial expressions that did not occur quickly enough to be classified as micro-expressions.

To find out more about this study and to answer the follow questions, see the full text (cited below).

1. Who were the participants in this study and how did the researchers get them to mask and neutralize facial expressions of emotion?
2. How did the findings about masking an emotion differ from the findings about neutralizing?
3. What kind of study is this? (See Appendix.)
4. How often did micro-expressions occur?
5. In your opinion, what is the most important weakness in the methods used in this study?

Source: Porter S., & ten Brinke, L. (2008). Reading between the lies: Identifying concealed and falsified emotions in universal facial expressions. *Psychological Science*, 19, 508–514.

COGNITIVE PROCESSING Telling a lie, particularly an elaborate one, presents the liar with a cognitive task that is usually more demanding than is telling the truth, a mental challenge for the liar referred to as **cognitive load.** This is certainly the case for spontaneous lies, when the liar isn't prepared and must think fast. But any lie that involves a good deal of fabrication (e.g., making up an elaborate story) requires more cognitive effort than does telling truth. As a result, nonverbal signs of thinking (eye movements, pupil dilation, response latencies, and speech hesitations) can be reliable clues to deception.

The four-factor theory provides a useful account of how unscripted **high-stakes deception** (i.e., when a liar has a lot to lose if caught) can produce an array of nonverbal signals. Of course, a major limitation of the theory is that it cannot distinguish between the nonverbal behavior of a liar and the nonverbal behavior of a truth teller when circumstances put either no pressure or a great deal of pressure on both liars and truth tellers to look and sound truthful.

PERSONAL EXPERIENCE 9.1

CAN YOU RELATE TO THIS?

Signs of Thinking May Be Clues to Deception

In our class exercise, my partner and I participated in an interview during which I asked her questions and she responded truthfully or lied, according to instruction. I found it rather easy to tell when she was lying because when she gave a false answer she would look away and think for a moment or two before responding. This told me that she must be fabricating the answer, otherwise the answer would have come more easily to her.

Kirsten

Self-Presentation Theory

Taking a somewhat different approach, DePaulo and her colleagues acknowledge that most of the lies we tell—the "little white lies," for instance—do not quicken our pulse, arouse feelings of guilt or fear, force us to think too much, or make us work too hard on our presentation. Under these circumstances, nonverbal behaviors will usually not betray the liar. Still, as they claim, people generally tell lies in less convincing and more deliberate ways than they tell the truth. As a result, according to their **self-presentation perspective**, the nonverbal communication of liars will tend to be less forthcoming (e.g., not speaking as much), less compelling (e.g., less nonverbal involvement, less fluent speech, more discrepancies), less positive (e.g., fewer enjoyment smiles), and more tense (e.g., vocal stress, fidgeting) than will the nonverbal communication of truth tellers (DePaulo et al., 2003). This perspective also predicts a **motivation impairment effect**: The more a liar wants to succeed, the more a liar will fail. High levels of motivation create feelings of anxiety and carefully monitored verbal presentations but also create overlooked or overmanaged nonverbal presentations—all of which increase the chance of detection.

Interpersonal Deception Theory

One limitation of both the four-factor theory and the self-presentation perspective is that they focus on deception as a noninteractive phenomenon. That is, they don't

▸ Being deceptive by tricking someone is not the same thing as telling a lie.

istockphoto.com/Thomas_EyeDesign

address deception as an interpersonal exchange between a sender and a receiver, both of whom respond to the demands of the situation. Instead, they focus on a person's deception as more of a monologue than as a dialogue. Communication researchers David Buller and Judee Burgoon proposed **interpersonal deception theory** as an alternative way of conceptualizing and studying the communication of liars and truth tellers (Buller & Burgoon, 1994, 1996). Their theory emphasizes (a) the skills, goals, expectations, and relational history that interactants bring with them to a deceptive encounter; (b) the different types of deception that may occur; (c) the pattern of give and take between a deceiver (sender) and a target (receiver) that characterizes the encounter; and (d) the range of behaviors that differentiate liars from truth tellers. The hallmark of their approach lies in the reminder that the communication of deception is inherently complex and will vary considerably from one context to another. Interpersonal deception theory, like the self-presentation perspective, emphasizes the strategic behavior of deceivers—how they manage their information, behavior, and image so as to appear truthful (e.g., not saying too much, suppressing nervous movements, maintaining eye contact, etc.). The theory also considers the nonstrategic behavior of deceivers, the inadvertent behaviors usually labeled as *leakage* (e.g., a micro-expression) or *deception clues* (e.g., averting gaze, eye blinking, speech hesitations, etc.). But, unlike the four-factor theory, Buller and Burgoon's theory views nonstrategic behavior as less telling in most situations than strategic behavior and shifts in behavior as potentially more useful in detecting deception than the mere presence or absence of particular behaviors.

In the next section, we'll present the results of literally hundreds of scientific studies on nonverbal communication and deception. Before doing so, however, a few words of caution: First, we should bear in mind that these findings, at best, give us some idea of how the average liar, usually in laboratory conditions, differs most often from the average truth teller. This overlooks the fact that no two individuals will lie in the same way. It also obscures the many situational influences on deception (e.g., the stakes involved, the type of lie, the speaking environment, etc.) that will make one case different from the next. Second, for the most part, the studies do not duplicate the emotional conditions—feelings of both fear and guilt—that we associate with high-stakes deception. Third, few of the early studies took into account how difficult-to-see facial reactions (e.g., micro-expressions, partial expressions) can often reveal deception, particularly when a liar is concealing or falsifying an emotion. But as long as we are cautious about how we apply these findings to our everyday encounters, there is value in the ability to identify the nonverbal cues most often associated with lying. As researchers continue to include the individual and situational factors that are most likely to make a difference, we may soon reach a point when our judgments about individual cases of deception are more informed than they are today.

STUDIES COMPARING LIARS AND TRUTH TELLERS

Trying to compare the nonverbal communication of liars and truth tellers is no simple task. For scientific, practical, and ethical reasons, researchers generally make these controlled comparisons in the laboratory rather than in real-life situations. Regardless of the procedures that researchers use—how they get participants to lie, for instance—these studies involve comparing the nonverbal behaviors of the same persons' or of different persons' truthful and deceptive presentations (Miller & Stiff, 1993). Several extensive reviews of this research have been available for many years, while more recent reviews continue to illuminate (and complicate) this growing body of research (DePaulo et al., 1985; DePaulo et al., 2003; Sporer & Schwandt, 2007; Vrij, 2000; Vrij, Granhag, & Porter, 2010b; Zuckerman & Driver, 1985; Zuckerman et al., 1981).

The results of these in-depth analyses confirm the difficulties of trying to offer simplistic claims about nonverbal signals of deception. For instance, the earliest reviews of the research showed that liars blink more, have more dilated pupils, use more adaptors (self-touching), speak in a higher-pitched voice, give shorter responses, speak less fluently, and make more speech errors (e.g., verbal slips, repetitions, and grammatical errors). But more subsequent reviews dispute some of these findings, most notably rejecting the claim that adaptors increase while lying, but also qualifying or dismissing claims about increased blinking and less fluent speech. In one of the most extensive reviews to date, DePaulo and her colleagues (2003) found no overall evidence of increased blinking, speech pauses, or increased use of adaptors. But there was evidence that liars look and sound more detached, tense, and uncertain; deliver inconsistent messages; use less talking time; have more dilated pupils; exhibit fewer genuine smiles; gesture less; press their lips more; raise their chin more; and speak in a higher-pitched and more repetitive manner. They also concluded that these and other nonverbal signs of deception become more noticeable when liars are highly motivated to get away with their lie than when they are not.

In another review of the research, Sporer and Schwandt (2007) analyzed more than fifty studies but limited their review to assessments of the most common visual cues: blinking; eye contact; gaze aversion; head, hand, leg, and foot movements; nodding;

smiling; adaptors; gestures; and postural shifts. They found that liars nodded less and moved their legs, feet, and hands less than truth tellers did and that liars smiled more, but only when they were highly motivated to get away with the lie.

Recent studies on eye contact further illustrate the difficulties of offering simple generalizations about nonverbal signs of lying. For example, a study comparing children and adults found that gaze aversion when lying was more common among younger children (seven- and nine-year-olds) than it was among older children and adults (McCarthy & Lee, 2009). Other studies suggest that liars in high-stakes situations use *more* deliberate eye contact than truth tellers (Frank & Svetieva, 2013; Mann et al., 2012).

Although the results of these studies are not entirely consistent, one conclusion we can draw from them is that highly motivated liars in high-stakes situations will *usually* provide more nonverbal cues of deception than will liars who have little to gain from their deception or nothing to lose if their deception fails. Of course, motivation doesn't always hurt a liar's performance (Stromwall, Hartwig, Granhag, 2006) and may even help in some cases (Burgoon & Floyd, 2000). The effect of motivation probably depends in part on the type of reward and punishment at stake. In fact, a limitation of previous studies is their failure to fully replicate the emotional consequences of high-stakes deception (fear and guilt). Researchers usually increase their participants' motivation to lie by offering money, issuing threats, or describing the deception as a test of an important skill. But studies show that these motivations have different effects. For instance, liars perform less convincingly when they lie to protect themselves than when they lie to get money (DePaulo et al., 2003). The effect of motivation on a liar may also be no different than the effect of motivation on a truth teller in certain situations. In one study where researchers found no differences in the nonverbal behavior of liars and truth tellers, the participants had to convince professional interrogators over an extended period of time that they were telling the truth about their lack of involvement in a mock crime. While the liars reported being more nervous than the truth tellers, both groups of participants seemed highly motivated, saying that they tried to avoid the stereotypical behaviors of a liar (e.g., fidgeting, gaze aversion) and suppress movements that could be revealing (Stromwall et al., 2006). Importantly, this same strategy of controlling and inhibiting nonverbal cues produced stark contrasts between liars and truth tellers in arguably the most comprehensive study of high-stakes deception to date (Mann, Vrij, & Bull, 2002). Based on their analysis of videotaped police interviews of individuals suspected of serious crimes, such as murder, rape, and arson, the researchers found that the suspects appeared more controlled and deliberate rather than nervous while lying than while telling the truth. When lying, they exhibited more vocal pauses, fewer eye blinks, and fewer hand and arm movements.

CATCHING LIARS

Social scientists have been testing our ability to detect lies for decades. The results of these laboratory studies show that the odds of catching a lie are only a little better than those of winning a coin toss (Kraut, 1980; Vrij, 2000). In the next section, we consider some of the factors that influence our ability to catch a liar.

RESEARCH 9.3

FIND OUT MORE

Lie Detection: Are We Thinking Too Much?

The authors of this study begin with the premise that lie catchers are not very good at catching liars. They claim that our unconscious mind may in fact be better at catching lies than our conscious mind because lie catching is a natural ability that developed in all of us over the course of evolution and that conscious deliberation does little more than interfere with this natural ability. In two experiments, the authors found evidence that indirect, less conscious measures of lie detection were more accurate then were direct, conscious measures, such as asking judges if they thought a person was lying or telling the truth.

To find out more about this study and to answer the following questions, see the full text (cited below).

1. What evidence do the researchers offer to support their claim that unconscious lie detection is superior to conscious lie detection?
2. What were on the videos shown to the participants in these experiments?
3. How did the researchers measure unconscious lie detection in their two experiments?
4. Do the researchers identify and discuss any weaknesses in their studies? What are they?

Source: ten Brinke, L., Stimson, D., & Carney D. R. (2014). Some evidence for unconscious lie detection. *Psychological Science, 25,* 1098–1105.

Factors Influencing the Success of Lie Catching

Even under the best of circumstances, lie catching may still be more of an art than a science. That is, it may take the kind of ability that some people have and others do not—a knack that eludes any kind of precise measurement and testing. But to be at all successful in the practice of lie catching, there are certain bottom-line conditions that must be met by the lie catcher. Frank and Svetieva (2013) offer four such conditions:

1. The person being judged must display behavior relevant to lying. In other words, *the stakes must be high enough to produce emotional clues relevant to deception.*
2. *The behaviors must be accessible to the judge.* For example, is the lie catcher close enough to detect micro-expressions of emotion or other subtle behaviors?
3. *The judge must detect these behaviors.* When we are a participant in an interaction (rather than an observer, for instance), we often miss telling behaviors because we aren't looking in the right place at the right time or because we may not want to be seen as impolite (e.g., staring).
4. *The judge must correctly interpret the behavior.* What does the behavior in this context mean? Could it be a sign of anything other than lying? Many people telling the truth can look like they are lying, either because they are afraid of not being believed or because they tend to behave in a way that is consistent with the stereotype of a liar (e.g., avoiding eye contact, nervous mannerisms, etc.).

The absence of these conditions means that all bets are off when it comes to the success of lie catching. But there are other factors as well— some that affect the performance of the liar and some that affect the ability of the lie catcher—that can change the odds of catching a liar in favor of the liar or the lie catcher.

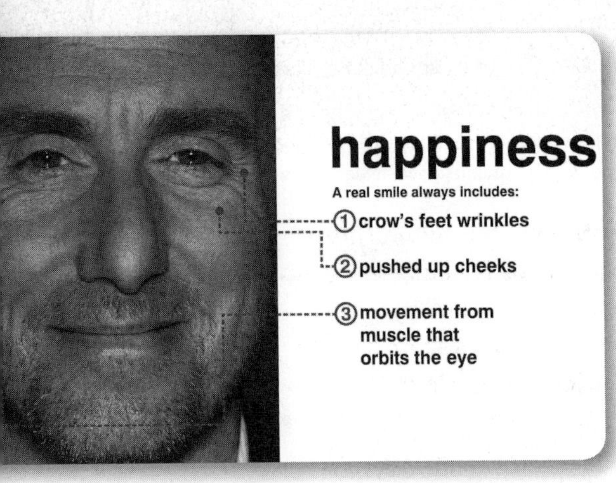

▸ Paying attention to someone's face for signs of lying can be helpful. Suppressed or falsified expressions of emotion may provide clues to deception.

Photofest

COMMUNICATION SKILLS: GOOD LIARS AND BAD LIARS The fact that nonverbal signs of deception vary from one situation to the next challenges even the very best of human lie detectors. Research also shows that the traits and abilities of a liar make a difference. Some individuals are better liars than others simply because they are able to act naturally in a sincere and believable manner more than others can, avoiding behaviors associated with the stereotype of a liar. This ability capitalizes on what researchers refer to as a **demeanor bias** that favors some people and penalizes others in lie detection situations (Levine et al., 2011; Vrij et al., 2010a). To some degree, this demeanor bias is related to personality differences. Introverts, for example, are more likely than extroverts to fit the stereotype of a liar because introverts tend to exhibit more signs of nervousness and speak with less fluency. They also tend to move more when they lie, which is one of the more common behavioral patterns associated with stereotype of deception (Vrij, 2000). Acting ability has an effect as well. The more one can act, the less likely one is to show stereotypical deceptive behaviors, such as gaze aversion and nervousness (Vrij et al., 2010a). Similarly, when socially skilled individuals deceive, they tend to engage in strategic behaviors that defy the stereotype of a liar (e.g., fewer hesitations and signs of nervousness), whereas unskilled individuals are less able to do so (Burgoon & Buller, 1995). Good liars feel less emotion in a high-stakes situation, think better on their feet, have a better memory, take more time to rehearse and prepare a strategy, and have more experience getting away with their lies compared to poor liars (Vrij et al., 2010a).

PERSONAL EXPERIENCE 9.2

CAN YOU RELATE TO THIS?

Anxious Truth Tellers May Appear to Be Deceptive

I am terrible liar and sometimes I think that others feel that I am lying even when I'm telling the truth. This past weekend, I was at a bar with some friends. The next day, I went over to my girlfriend's house and she asked if my friends and I had met any girls. I told her no, but I felt like I had to elaborate so that she would believe me, even though I was telling the truth. I started to break eye contact and hesitate primarily because I was thinking of what to say. I felt tense and anxious for fear that she would not believe me. She didn't, and we got into a big argument.

Bryan

WHAT ARE THE STAKES? WHAT IS THE RISK? THE CONTEXT IN WHICH LYING OCCURS As noted above, it is very difficult to detect any signs of deception except in high-stakes situations. But most lies are just not very stressful to the liars (including those told by research participants in laboratory studies). When asked about the kinds of lies they tell, respondents in one survey reported that their lies were generally not serious, involved little effort and planning, didn't make them worry about being caught, and resulted in little regret. Most said they would tell the lies again if given a second chance (DePaulo, Kashy, Kirkeodol, Wyer, & Epstein, 1996). Under such circumstances, there is no reason to expect the telltale signs of fear, guilt, physiological arousal, inhibition, or heavy thinking that we need in order to catch a liar (Frank & Svetieva, 2013). In addition, liars are more likely to provide nonverbal clues to deception in situations that increase the risk of detection. In fact, research shows that the risk of detection may cause the liar to behave in a manner that is similar to high-stakes situations where the liar has a lot to lose if caught. One study compared the nonverbal behavior of liars and truth tellers in three different contexts designed to increase the risk of detection (Zhang, Frumkin, Stedmon, & Lawson, 2013):

1. Lying in front of peers in a semipublic space (a classroom)
2. Lying during interaction with another person in a private space (a laboratory)
3. Lying and reconnaissance while passing through a security control point in a public space (the corridor of a building)

Similar to high-stakes contexts, liars were more likely, as the risk of detection became greater, to restrict their hand movements in a manner that indicated heightened tension, attempted control, and greater cognitive load.

BELIEFS, PERCEPTIONS, AND BEHAVIOR OF THE LIE CATCHER Another reason why people are poor lie detectors is the prevalence of false beliefs about the behavior of liars. Countless studies confirm the existence of a deeply ingrained stereotype of a liar's nonverbal cues, which includes looking away, stuttering and stammering, shifting positions, self-touching, nervous movements, and more (Global Deception Research Team, 2006). Unfortunately for lie detectors, while some of these beliefs correspond to what liars actually do, most do not. Very few lie detectors pay attention to the more revealing signs of deception, such as inhibited movement, micro-expressions of emotion, discrepant verbal and nonverbal messages, and vocal cues (Vrij, 2000). False beliefs about nonverbal signs of lying extend to the workplace, where a recent study found that most employees held incorrect beliefs (Hart, Fillmore, & Griffin, 2010). Another study found that police interrogators overestimated their lie-detection skills and were misled by incorrect beliefs about the nonverbal signs of lying (Elaad, 2009).

People can also be poor lie detectors because of the existence of a truth bias that prompts them to believe what they are told and thus to overlook signs of deception. In fact, when researchers look closely at the results of deception detection studies, they find clear evidence of this truth bias. When they separate the task of detecting a truth from that of detecting a lie, the tendency for people to lean toward the truth inflates the overall accuracy rates for truth detection. For instance, Vrij (2000) found a truth detection rate of 67% and a lie detection rate of only 44%.

On the other hand, not believing a liar can lead the lie catcher to behave in a way that signals suspicion. Some research indicates that liars who believe the receiver is suspicious are more likely to move less, take longer to speak, speak for shorter periods of time,

RESEARCH 9.4

FIND OUT MORE

Will Reducing Cross-Cultural Bias Help Us Catch a Lie?

Borrowing from previous theory, the researchers in this study argue that when someone's behavior in a given situation violates our expectations (e.g., less smiling than we expect), we may become suspicious of that person and wonder why he or she is behaving in this way (especially if no reason for the behavior is offered). If we are asked to judge the truthfulness of this person, we are less likely to believe a person acting in an unexpected manner than a person acting in an expected manner.

The researchers tested the notion that cultural bias can determine whether a behavior is expected or unexpected and can therefore influence our judgments of a person's truthfulness.

For example, we are more likely to mistrust a person who uses less eye contact, smiles more, and moves his or her arms and hands more if these behaviors are inconsistent with the norms of our culture than if they are consistent with the norms of our culture. The results of the study not only supported this hypothesis but also supported the idea that we can reduce the cultural bias that causes people to mistrust someone who behaves in an unexpected manner if people are given specific information about the behavioral norms of other cultural groups.

To find out more about this study and to answer the following questions, see the full text (cited below).

1. How did the researchers prepare the video clips shown to the participants in the study?
2. What was the culture of the participants who viewed the video clips?
3. Why did the researchers select the nonverbal behaviors that they did?
4. Why did the researchers randomly assign participants to three different conditions?

Source: Castillo, P. A., & Mallard, D. (2012). Preventing cross-cultural bias in deception judgments: The role of expectancies about nonverbal behavior. *Journal of Cross-Cultural Psychology*, 43, 967–978.

and express less positive affect (e.g., less laughing and more head shaking) than liars who do not feel they are under such scrutiny (Buller, Strzyzewski, & Hunsaker, 1991). So a receiver's suspicion may itself prompt a liar to behave, at least initially, in a more guarded or detached manner. In contrast, when a receiver's nonverbal feedback becomes favorable, liars are likely to gain confidence and reciprocate with positive nonverbal behaviors, such as those associated with increased involvement and immediacy (Buller et al., 1991; Burgoon, Buller, White, Afifi, & Buslig, 1999; White & Burgoon, 2001).

Whether a lie catcher is too trusting or suspicious of a liar can also depend on the mood of the lie catcher at a given moment. One study found that being in a good mood decreased whereas being in a bad mood increased the skepticism of the lie catcher (Forgas & East, 2008).

PERSONAL EXPERIENCE 9.3

CAN YOU RELATE TO THIS?

Suspicion Can Make an Innocent Person Act Like a Guilty Person

I'm one of those people who have a difficult time with anxiety under scrutiny, no matter how truthful I'm being. If I think that someone doesn't believe me, I'll immediately begin to feel guilty and send out the stereotypical nonverbal "liar" signals. One day, someone threw a cup of coffee into the trashcan in the kitchen I share with my six roommates. It ended up spilling out and leaking all over the inside of the can. My roommates know I love coffee and drink it every day, but that day, I had been running around and hadn't gotten a chance to get any. But when they started questioning me, I started smiling nervously and kept looking away and fidgeting, so they were convinced I was guilty.

Andrea

EXPERIENCE AND EXPERTISE OF THE LIE CATCHER Does experience in the practice of lie detection make a difference? Surprisingly, the answer to this question is less straightforward than you might think. It appears that so-called professional lie detectors, such as police officers, detectives, military intelligence instructors, and customs inspectors, do not perform the task of lie detection any better than college students do (Burgoon, Buller, Ebesu, & Rockwell, 1994; DePaulo & Pfeifer, 1986; Ekman & O'Sullivan, 1991b; Garrido, Masip, Herrero, Tabernero, & Vega, 1998; Vrij & Graham, 1997; Vrij & Mann, 1999, 2001). While there is no difference in overall accuracy rates, studies show that when we separate the task of truth detection from that of lie detection, professionals are more accurate in detecting lies (55%) than nonprofessionals (44%) but less accurate (55%) than nonprofessionals (67%) in detecting the truth. The reason for this is that professionals are less biased in favor of seeing someone as truthful (Vrij, 2006). Researchers have also discovered that when compared to their nonprofessional counterparts, police officers tend to report feeling more confident about their ability to catch a liar (DePaulo & Pfeifer, 1986; Garrido et al., 1998). But some professionals may have more reason to feel confident than others do. In one study, secret service agents outperformed all other groups, with more than half of the agents achieving an accuracy rate of at least 70% (Ekman & O'Sullivan, 1991a). The researchers attributed the success of the agents to the fact that they noticed micro-expressions of emotion, treated each case as unique, and did not rely on stereotypical behaviors. Moreover, in a study of police officers that viewed videotapes of a murder suspect being interrogated in a foreign language, researchers found that the most accurate lie detectors were the officers who did not rely on stereotypical behaviors such as fidgeting and looking away (Vrij & Mann, 2001). In another study involving the detection of high-stakes lies, researchers found a positive correlation between the ability to detect a lie and the ability to identify micro-expressions of emotion (Frank & Ekman, 1997). In addition, research shows that professionals detect lies more accurately in actual cases of high-stakes deception than they do in laboratory studies. In one such study, police officers achieved an average accuracy rate of 66% for catching the lies of criminal suspects and 63% for recognizing the truth (Mann, Vrij, & Bull, 2004).

Does familiarity with the liar make a difference? Familiarity with a person's behavior should make a difference, since it provides a lie detector with a baseline of truthful behavior against which to judge instances of behavior that may be deceptive. Research reported by Andersen (1999) indicates that this is in fact the case. Familiarity improves lie detection. For instance, in one study, researchers found that exposing lie detectors to an individual's truthful behavior resulted in greater accuracy—a 72% rate for those exposed to the truthful behavior compared to a 56% rate for those who were not exposed (Feeley, deTurck, & Young, 1995). Because familiarity with a liar makes the task of lie detection easier, it is tempting to conclude that catching a friend or lover in a lie must be less challenging than catching a stranger is. Yet, according to studies comparing detection rates for these groups of deceivers, there is virtually no support for such a claim (Anderson, Ansfield, & DePaulo, 1999; Millar & Millar, 1995; Vrij, 2000). Why is this so? One explanation is our eagerness to believe and trust people with whom we have close relationships—a strong truth bias against seeing the lies of friends and lovers (Burgoon et al., 1994; Levine, McCornack, & Parks, 1999; McCornack & Parks, 1986). Other explanations include overconfidence in thinking that we know someone well enough to catch them and the offsetting advantage of being familiar with the lie detector (i.e., knowing what the other person thinks is honest or dishonest behavior and then behaving accordingly).

In general, then, most people are not very good at catching liars. Still, some people are better than others, and it seems they have mastered techniques that work more often than not. In addition, some situations create circumstances that favor the lie catcher over the liar.

Does participation instead of observation make a difference? Will you be in a better position to catch a liar if you interact with that person—asking questions, giving feedback, expressing opinions—than if you just observe their presentation? The answer to this question is no. Studies indicate that passive observers are at least as accurate and often more accurate in their judgments than participants are. In one study, interviewers were correct in their judgments only 29% of the time, whereas passive observers were correct 49% of the time (Buller et al., 1991). In another study, observers were also more accurate judges (50% score) than interviewers (43% score) (Feeley & deTurck, 1997). It may seem odd that being able to ask questions doesn't benefit the lie detector. Perhaps it depends on the type of lie being told and how good the questions are. But there are reasons why passive observation may be more effective, as Vrij (2000) points out in his review of these studies. First, passive observers can focus more on the task of lie detection than interviewers can; they are less distracted by other concerns such as phrasing questions and making a good impression. Second, researchers have found that passive observers are less susceptible to the effects of a truth bias than interviewers are. Third, passive observers have much greater access to nonverbal cues than interviewers have (i.e., they can look more closely and longer without being rude). One team of researchers claims that participation benefits the liar more than the lie catcher because it gives the liar an opportunity over time to improve his or her performance, thereby making a better impression (Burgoon, Buller, & Floyd, 2001).

The practice of lie detection involves two possible errors in judgment: (1) believing the lie and (2) not believing the truth (Ekman, 1986). In the first case, we may be victimized by an accomplished liar and by our own gullibility (recall the truth bias) or by an inability to spot the telltale signs of deception. In the second case, we may be unduly swayed by the false stereotypes we hold about lying (e.g., lack of eye contact). Or, just as likely, we may render a verdict based on the idea that a particular cue or set of cues cannot indicate anything other than deception. Of course, when we encounter people for the first time, we cannot rule out the possibility that what may seem like a clue to deception is just a feature of their normal speaking style. If you meet someone who blinks a lot, for example, would you immediately suspect that person of lying? But even when we know someone well, mistakes are still possible. Consider the following scenario: Jeff suspects his wife Vicky of having an affair with one of her coworkers. When he questions her about why she was late for dinner the night before, her fearful eyes, nervous mannerisms, and hesitating speech convince him that she's hiding the truth. But what else might explain Vicky's behavior? In this particular case, she might be an anxious truth teller, someone afraid of not being believed. Recall that many nonverbal clues to deception are only indicators of fear and anxiety.

Training People to Catch Liars

Studies show that very few people can tell with a high degree of accuracy (correct more than 70% of the time) whether someone is lying or not. But over the years, after testing more than 12,000 people, psychologists Maureen O'Sullivan and Paul Ekman discovered a small number of individuals, 29 people to be exact, who have an uncanny ability to do better than that, with accuracy rates above 80%. These lie detection "wizards" as O'Sullivan and Ekman called them, are all in the 40–60 age range, come from a variety of occupations, are highly motivated and emotionally intelligent, and, surprisingly, tend to have introverted personalities. Their unique talent for catching liars includes a knack for picking up nonverbal cues that most people miss. Here is a brief summary of what they do and don't do (Ekman & O'Sullivan, 1991b; Ekman, O'Sullivan, & Frank, 1999):

- They do not look for the nonverbal cues associated with the stereotype of a liar, such as lack of eye contact, fidgeting, or self-touches.
- They do not exhibit a truth bias in their judgments; their accuracy rates for detecting the truth are similar to their accuracy rates for detecting lies.
- They notice fleeting facial expressions (micro-expressions) and other cues that don't go along with what a person is saying.
- They pick up idiosyncratic mannerisms that seem out of place.
- They do not make judgments based on any simple list of nonverbal cues.
- They observe authentic but subtle nonverbal signs of sincerity, such as speech-gesture synchrony, that others might ignore.
- They notice the quality rather than the quantity of nonverbal behaviors, such as whether a person's eye contact or movements seem genuine or deliberate.

While it is highly doubtful that any training program can produce wizard-like abilities to catch liars, is there evidence that training improves one's ability to catch a liar? The results of studies on training are decidedly mixed and do not offer much encouragement that people can readily improve their lie detection abilities without considerable effort on their part and improvements in the training they receive (Knapp, 2008). Still, the most promising approach seems to be one that trains people to recognize the emotional leakage (i.e., micro-expressions) that may occur in high-stakes situations and trains people to use interview techniques that force the respondent to fear detection, talk a lot, and think hard before answering questions.

First, there is growing evidence that trained observers are better able to detect micro-expressions of emotion than are untrained observers. Studies of participants with wide-ranging backgrounds and across a number of demographic categories (e.g., age, gender, occupation, etc.) that receive such training improve their detection abilities after the training program (Hurley, 2012; Hurley, Anker, Frank, Matsumoto, & Hwang, 2014). There is also evidence that persons who receive micro-expression training are better able to detect micro-expressions than persons who do not receive any training (Matsumoto & Hwang, 2011).

Most scholars and practitioners also recommend an interviewing approach, such as the use of open-ended questions, that encourages a liar to speak so there is enough time to spot signs of deception (Frank & Svetieva, 2013). Another approach is to make the interview more difficult for the liar (i.e., increasing cognitive load) than it would be for a truth teller (Vrij, Granhag, Mann, & Leal, 2011). This approach involves interview techniques such as asking the person to tell the facts of his or her story in reverse order, asking unanticipated questions that the person probably didn't prepare for, taking on the role of a devil's advocate and asking the person to express an opinion that counters their own expressed opinion, and so forth.

Deception is part of everyday life. People lie for all sorts of reasons, and they learn to lie at a young age. While not all high-stakes lies are malicious or self-serving, many are. Despite the perils of trying to catch a liar, the value of critical listening demands that we at least consider the possibility that someone is not telling us the whole truth. Armed with the knowledge that nonverbal communication is usually more honest than words, we may find ourselves better equipped to make informed judgments about the truthfulness of what we hear.

SUMMARY

Many of our everyday encounters involve some degree of deception. Despite its prevalence, a presumption of innocence or *truth bias* hinders our efforts to detect deception when it does occur. The most widely cited theory of nonverbal communication and deception—the leakage theory—attempts to identify the nonverbal cues most likely to betray a lie. An elaboration on the theory identifies four factors that determine a liar's ability to deceive: attempted control, degree of physiological arousal, displays of emotion, and the need for cognitive processing. Studies comparing liars and truth tellers have found some relatively consistent differences between the two that may indicate the incidence of deception, but the findings also obscure the many factors that make each situation an exceptional and potentially difficult case. Many factors influence the success of lie catching, including the skills of the liar; the context in which lying occurs; and the beliefs, perceptions, knowledge and expertise of the lie catcher. However, there is evidence that training programs in the detection of micro-expressions as well as interviewing techniques can improve our ability, under the right circumstance, to catch someone telling a lie.

KEY TERMS

Cognitive load 338
Deception 338
Deception clues 335
Demeanor bias 344
Four-factor theory 335
High-stakes deception 338
Interpersonal deception theory 340
Leakage 333
Lying 331
Motivation impairment effect 339
Self-presentation perspective 339
Truth bias 332

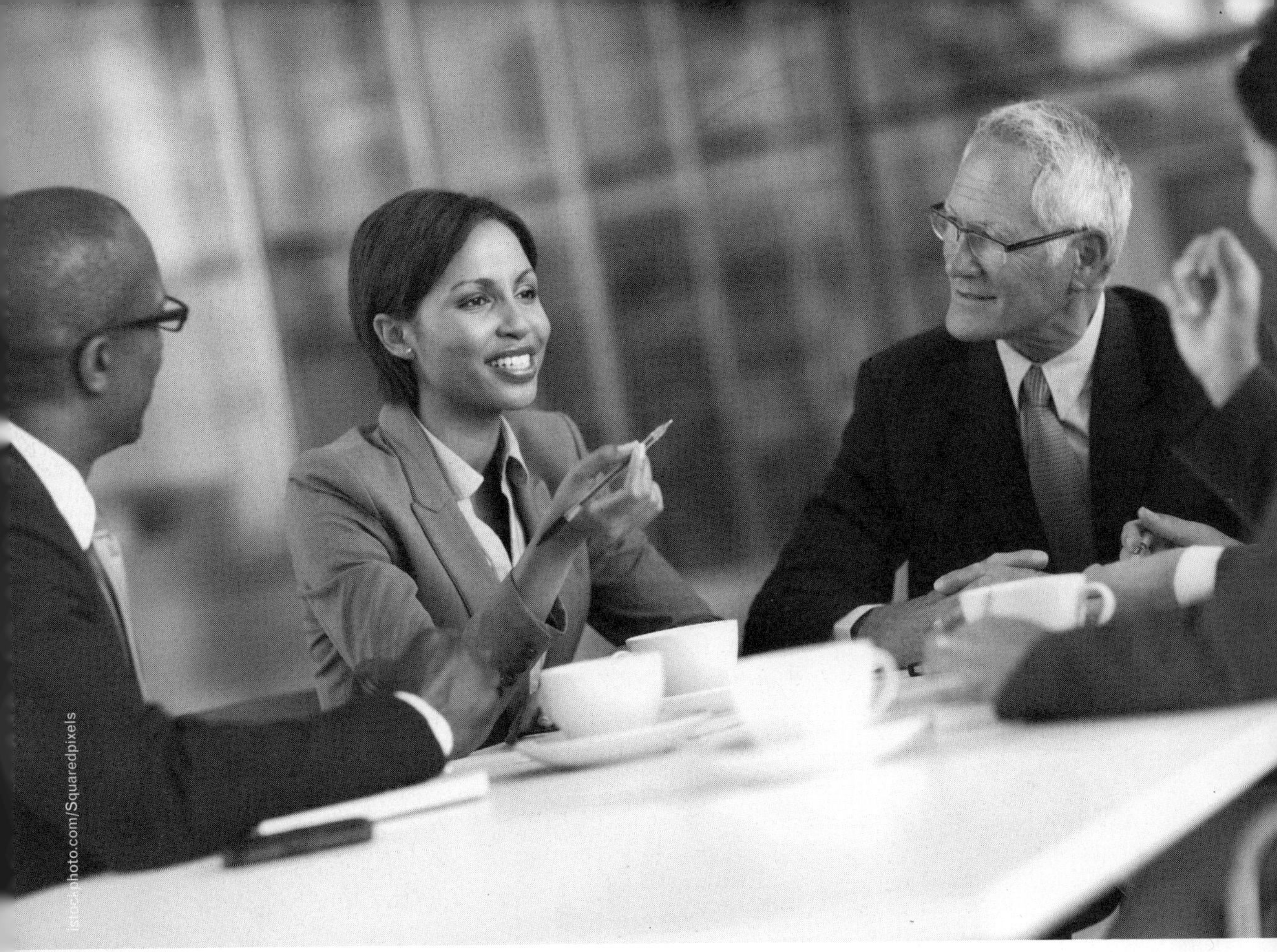

Chapter Outline

10

NONVERBAL COMMUNICATION IN WORKPLACE ENCOUNTERS

In the Dilbert cartoon on the facing page, Scott Adams keenly portrays what for many individuals in the workplace is an all-too-familiar sight: bosses who don't treat their employees with respect. Sometimes this lack of respect shows up in ways that are neither subtle nor inconsequential (e.g., verbal abuse). But even when the put-downs are barely noticed, the communication of contempt in the workplace can have an insidious effect, creating an atmosphere that jeopardizes the goals of any organization. In this chapter, we'll examine the many different ways that nonverbal communication, mainly in the form of **status reminders**, can contribute to such an atmosphere. Then we'll concentrate on how nonverbal communication can make or break the many task-oriented encounters we have with others in the workplace (e.g., interviews and presentations).

Learning Objectives

After reading this chapter, you will be able to do the following:

1. Identify the many different ways that the members of an organization can nonverbally signal their rank and status (i.e., status reminders).
2. Explain how the misuse of nonverbal status reminders can lead to problems related to dysfunctional leadership, sexual harassment, cross-cultural misunderstanding, and workplace discrimination.
3. Explain how nonverbal communication in an organization can create self-fulfilling prophecies that interfere with an individual's job performance.
4. Understand the role of emotional exchanges in the workplace and how emotional contagion, emotional labor, and emotion recognition skills can have a positive or negative impact on the attainment of an organization's goals.
5. Indicate how nonverbal communication improves the performance of individuals in customer service transactions, professional interviews, and oral presentations.

SUPERIOR–SUBORDINATE ENCOUNTERS: COMMUNICATING STATUS

As you already know from previous chapters, one of the primary functions of nonverbal communication is facilitating relationships. With nonverbal signals, we can encourage or discourage intimacy. We can also address fundamental issues of power and control, making it clear to everyone concerned who the take-charge person is or is going to be. Even in the workplace, where the pecking order is firmly entrenched and the chain of command is a matter of public record, nonverbal

Universal Uclick

communication announces and reinforces the status hierarchy. Sometimes, whether deliberate or not, these status reminders also contribute to serious organizational problems: dysfunctional leadership, sexual harassment, workplace discrimination, and cross-cultural misunderstandings.

Status Reminders: The Nonverbal Dimension

When you see two or more individuals engaged in conversation and one of them is the boss, you can probably guess which one it is. When viewed from a rules-of-conduct perspective, much of the behavior we witness in an organization results from our willingness to abide by various sets of rules, some more explicit (i.e., formally acknowledged) than others (Shimanoff, 1980). In any organization, our actions become both predictable and understandable when they are guided by the rules of organizational life. Many of these contextual rules define the way an individual is obliged to behave in the presence of others and the way others are expected to respond.

EXERCISE 10.1

TRY THIS

Status Reminders at Work

OBJECTIVE: To identify nonverbal status reminders

INSTRUCTIONS: Visit a convenient location where you can inconspicuously observe interactions between superiors and subordinates. (You might be able to do this by observing interactions between professors and students.) Observe a single interaction for about five minutes. Of the twelve basic status reminders discussed in this chapter, how many of them can you spot in this interaction?

Even the most trivial action in a face-to-face encounter can say something about the balance of power in that relationship. This is readily apparent in the military, where an enlisted person or junior officer will salute an officer of higher rank out of deference to his or her rank; in a corporate office, where an executive vice president freely interrupts the plant manager to tell her a joke; or in a university library, where the college dean approaches a faculty member and pats him on the back. In each case, an image of one's self in relation to another is symbolized by certain nonverbal behaviors, behaviors that communicate the relative status of the respective individuals in the organization's hierarchy.

▸ Nonverbal status reminders reinforce the pecking order that characterizes organizational life and include those aspects of physical appearance and demeanor that clarify superior–subordinate relations between individuals in different contexts. What status reminders do you see in the picture shown here?

istockphoto.com/steex

According to sociologist Erving Goffman (1967), when the rules of a group lead individuals to act similarly toward each other, the relationships that form are symmetrical. In contrast, **asymmetrical relationships** are those in which group members act differently toward one another. In most formal organizations, persons of unequal status due to their relative positions in the chain of command develop asymmetrical relationships. Below, we summarize research findings on the many nonverbal signals (i.e., status reminders) that call attention to the asymmetrical nature of superior–subordinate relationships. We reported the results of some of these studies in each of the chapters in Part II of this text. Several excellent reviews of this research can also be found elsewhere (Andersen, 1999, Chapter 12; Andersen & Bowman, 1990; Burgoon, Buller, & Woodall, 1996, pp. 305–320; Edinger & Patterson, 1983; Henley, 1977, 2001; Remland, 1981, 1984). Based on this body of research, we present 12 status reminders that all of us have witnessed in our everyday lives.

DRESSING UP AND DRESSING DOWN One way of communicating status is through dress. Military personnel and police officers wear uniforms that make status identifications easy. More typically, higher-status persons in an organization wear more expensive clothes and accessories than do their lower-status counterparts. In fact, it is possible in many instances to spot the higher-ranking individual in an interaction between two people by noticing the quality of the suits, coats, shoes, or jewelry each is wearing.

Dressing up isn't the only way to communicate status. In some cases, grooming can be an indicator of status as well: clean, manicured fingernails; polished shoes; styled hair; whitened teeth; and so on imply that an individual has both the time and the money for attention to detail. Paradoxically, low-status appearances can also signal high status.

When the wearing of inappropriate, unfashionable, or even dirty clothes flies in the face of convention, it implies that the wearer is somehow above the concerns of others (i.e., the boss doesn't have to follow the company dress code).

SIZE MATTERS Height conveys status. Studies show, for example, that we are more likely to ascribe higher status to a tall man than we are to a shorter man (Wilson, 1968). The way a person positions his or her body in relation to others can also result in a height advantage, such as when one person stands over another. Some formal settings are designed to bestow a height advantage on higher-status persons. The elevated bench of a judge in a courtroom places her above everyone else, the raised platform of a teacher in a lecture hall places him above the students, and so on. In the absence of any real height advantage, one person may still try to gain the advantage over another by symbolically looking down at that person with a disdainful gaze (e.g., head tilted back, eyes downward).

PERSONAL EXPERIENCE 10.1

CAN YOU RELATE TO THIS?

Height Can Communicate Status

I worked at a store where the store manager was literally the smallest person in the store. He was 5 feet 2 inches tall. However, the assistant manager was 6 feet tall. One day, a customer asked me if she could speak to the manager. I told her what aisle he was in and she then left to find him. A few seconds later she came back and said he was not there. I went down the same aisle and low and behold there he was. She probably didn't think he was the store manager because he didn't have the stature of a manager, being so short. She said to me in a surprised tone, "Oh, so he's the manager."

Camise

In addition to height, higher-status persons tend to use more space than persons of lower status. Often, what they own is larger and thus occupies more space. Large homes, cars, boats, and so forth symbolize status. When interacting with subordinates face to face, superiors generally take more liberties with the space around them than their subordinates do; they are more mobile and might walk around while their subordinates stay in the same place. Even their gestures tend to be more expansive than those of their subordinates. As we noted in previous chapters (see Chapter 3 and 4), body enlargement (i.e., puffing up) is one of the most common displays of dominance throughout the animal kingdom. In fact, a number of studies confirm that among humans, expansive postures express power and the emotion of pride, leading to judgments of high status, dominance, and expertise, whereas constrictive postures express powerlessness and the emotion of shame, leading to judgments of low status, submissiveness, and lack of expertise (Carney, Cuddy, & Yapp, 2010; Martens & Tracy, 2012; Shariff, Tracy, & Markusoff, 2012).

"DO NOT DISTURB" SIGNS The territory of higher-status individuals is generally much less accessible than is the territory of lower-status personnel. We grant superiors more privacy than we do their subordinates. Organizational environments tend to be structured in ways that insulate the highest-status people against unwanted intrusions (e.g., remote locations, gatekeepers, etc.). In universities, like most organizations, the inaccessibility of an individual is directly related to his or her place in the pecking order: The president is harder to reach than the vice president, the vice president is harder to reach than the dean, the dean is harder to reach than the department chairperson, and so on. To underscore these status differences, even restrooms are more or less accessible to others based on one's position in the organization: Top executives often have restrooms in their own offices, managers have shared but private restrooms, and workers usually share a common public restroom.

UP CLOSE AND PERSONAL While high-status individuals may enjoy the luxury that comes from the services of gatekeepers and the privacy of remote locations, low-status individuals in an organization are rarely so privileged. Such persons tend to be at the mercy of nearly any intrusion that comes down from above. In many instances, they occupy a cubicle, a space-saving substitute for a private office that affords them very little if any real protection against the distractions swirling around them. In face-to-face encounters with the boss, they may find themselves on the receiving end of close approaches, uninvited touches, prolonged gazes, or intrusive commands—none of which they would think of initiating with the boss. As author Michael Korda (1975) aptly observes in his book, *Power!*, some people become embroiled in the various power games that define territoriality:

> Many powerful people, particularly the aggressive ones, prefer to go to other people's offices, since they are then invading the other person's turf. Thus a man who wants to establish his precedence over another may go into the other person's office, sit down, and put his feet on the desk, thus infringing on the intimate territory of his inferior. These small signs of conquest are numerous and include using objects as ashtrays when that's obviously not what they were intended for, giving orders to someone else's

▸ In most organizations, high-status persons get more privacy than lower-status persons.

istockphoto.com/ntmw

> secretary, spilling coffee, and even lying down on someone else's carpet to do back exercises when the other person is seated at his or her desk. The important thing in such games is to simultaneously establish territorial rights and appear more casual than your opponent, giving the impression that you believe his office belongs to you by making yourself at home there. Generally speaking, people playing the power game on subordinates will call them into their own power spot to give orders, and go into their subordinates' offices to issue warnings, threats, and denunciations. (p. 164)

It doesn't take much to demonstrate the basic connection that exists between movement toward a person and the power one has over that person. In one recent series of experiments, for example, researchers found that even moving toward rather than moving away from an object increased one's sense of power and status (Smith, McCulloch, & Shouwstra, 2013).

THE CENTER OF ATTENTION Group leaders usually sit at the head of a table, so designated to symbolize the leader's authority over those assembled. But in a practical sense, sitting at the head of a table gives a group leader the best opportunity to command the attention of group members than sitting elsewhere; the head of a table puts the leader in a position to see and be seen by others. In fact, research confirms that one measure of a person's relative status is the amount of attention the person receives from group members while speaking compared to the amount of attention the person gives while listening, referred to as the **visual dominance ratio** of a group member (Koch, Bahne, Kruse, & Zimmermann, 2010).

For similar reasons, high-status individuals may also gravitate toward the center of a room, where they are in the best position to command the attention of others. At an office party, this display of status might not happen right away. Based on his observations of such gatherings, Korda (1975) described what he often saw as two distinct phases: (1) On arrival, the most powerful persons will tend to occupy separate corners of the room, each one attracting a small circle of supporters; (2) after some time, these high-status persons will abandon their corner positions, move slowly toward neutral territory, and form a circle near the center of the room with other high-status persons. As Korda says, "Their first act is to display themselves and seek confirmation of power from the rank and file. Once this has been accomplished, they move naturally toward one another and close ranks, the powerful separating themselves instinctively from the non-powerful" (p. 96).

THE COLD SHOULDER Politeness norms usually compel us to give a speaker our undivided attention. As is the case with many other actions indicative of high status, however, not paying attention stems from one's ability to disregard the rules.

Picture this scene: Ben, a 20-year employee of a large manufacturing plant, is talking to his supervisor, Tino, about some problems he has been having with one of his coworkers. While Ben is talking, Tino is looking over his mail. Occasionally, he glances over at one of his other workers as though he is amused by what she is doing. He looks at his watch a few times. When he hears a phone ringing, he walks off in the direction of his office without excusing himself. Giving someone the cold shoulder, what Tino does to Ben, is a prerogative of higher-status individuals who don't have to worry about the consequences of being impolite.

THE SILENT TREATMENT Choosing not to speak can be a status signal in certain situations. In other situations, silence conveys lower status, such as when waiting for one's turn to speak or choosing not to interrupt. According to communication researchers Judee Burgoon, David Buller, and W. Gill Woodall (1996),

> Silence shows respect for authority. Protocol dictates that subordinates must wait for superiors to break the silence first, and their refusal to do so can be a very potent reminder of the status difference. The ultimate form of silence—failing to acknowledge another's presence with a greeting—is a powerful symbolic message of status inequality, even if unintentional. A person who receives no greeting from a preoccupied equal or superior can easily stew for a week about the perceived snub. (pp. 316–317)

KICKING BACK For obvious reasons, talking to a higher-status person will make us more tense and anxious than will talking to a peer or a lower-status person. Generally, higher status is associated with an easygoing demeanor. When watching two individuals—one higher in status than the other—conversing with each other, we would probably have little difficulty correctly identifying the higher-status person if we based our decision solely on which of the two individuals seemed to be the most relaxed. In his early and well-known experiments, psychologist Albert Mehrabian (1972) found that the postures and movements of superiors generally differed from those of subordinates: Superiors were more likely to lean back in their chairs, to use open arm positions, to stretch out, and to place their arms and legs in relaxed, asymmetrical positions. To Mehrabian, these signs of relaxation suggest a fearlessness that is normally reserved for individuals in positions of power.

THE VOICE OF AUTHORITY Throughout the animal kingdom, the sound of status is loud and low-pitched (indicating large size). Not surprisingly, we associate power and dominance with the same vocal signals. We seem to understand instinctively that we will be much less threatening to children if we alter our voice by speaking in a soft, high-pitched tone (i.e., parentese or baby talk). Research indicates that in addition to vocal pitch and volume, higher-status speech is moderately fast, articulate, expressive, and relatively accent free.

BELATED APPEARANCES It's okay to be late if you're the boss, but don't try being late for an appointment with one of your superiors. This is one of the many double standards that pervades the workplace and reminds us of who's in charge. As communication researcher Peter Andersen (1999) concludes,

> Like money and property, the rich, the powerful, and the dominant control time. By contrast, the lives of the less privileged are filled with waiting—in crowded health care clinics and in long lines for unemployment checks, welfare, food stamps, and temporary employment. Waiting time decreases as status increases. (p. 321)

Julius Fast, author of the book, *Body Language in the Workplace* (1991), sees a connection between how long someone makes us wait and what that person thinks of us. In the United States, according to Fast,

> a wait of about five minutes to see someone on business when you have an appointment is considered normal. If someone keeps a client waiting beyond ten minutes, the subtext is clear—"[M]y time is valuable." Fifteen minutes, and the subtext is "I am more important than you." Twenty minutes and the subtext becomes "I am contemptuous of you." (p. 140)

Of course, such observations are difficult to substantiate (there are many other reasons why someone may be 15 minutes late for a meeting), but they nonetheless show how time communicates. At the very least, someone who makes us wait longer than we expected owes us a sincere apology.

MONOPOLIZING A CONVERSATION No doubt, all of us have had the experience of being in a conversation in which we never had the chance to talk. Of course, not everyone who monopolizes a conversation is higher in status than their listeners—many of them just love to talk. But talking can become self-indulgent, a privilege that comes with one's rank in an organization. Holding the floor is such a strong indicator of status, in fact, that we can correctly identify the leader of a group or the higher-ranking person in an organization based entirely on which person does most of the talking. Interrupting a speaker often occurs as an attempt to monopolize a conversation, as a turn taking behavior (i.e., taking the floor from another person) can serve as a status reminder in any conversation (Farley, 2008; Farley, Ashcraft, Stasson, & Nussbaum, 2010).

AN EMOTIONAL ROLLER COASTER While display rules constrain the emotional expressions of most people in various social situations, these rules, like many others, can be cast aside when interacting with lower-status individuals because display rule violations in the company of lower-status individuals generally won't produce the same kind of condemnation that they will in the company of one's peers or that they most certainly will in the company of one's superiors. Thus, higher status allows one to show how he or she really feels: to yell, frown, stare angrily, smirk, not join in the laughter, yawn, and so on. By not following the display rules that conceal all sorts of negative emotions and put phony smiles on our faces, high-status individuals are free to show us how they really feel whenever they feel like it. They may end up being much more expressive than their lower-status counterparts, pushing the latter onto what could be an emotional roller coaster.

RESEARCH 10.1

FIND OUT MORE

How Do Workers Respond to Angry Bosses? It Depends

The researchers in this study distributed questionnaires to 100 supervisors and 243 subordinates from 40 companies in Taiwan. The companies included a range of industries: banking, retail, high tech, manufacturing, service, transportation, and more. They found that expressing negative emotions sometimes helped supervisors, and sometimes it hurt. For instance, expressing negative emotions improved the performance of subordinates if the subordinates were highly conscientious and agreeable. The researchers also discovered, among other findings, that expressing negative emotions lowered the performance of subordinates when the subordinates held a low-power orientation and viewed their supervisor as relatively powerless.

To find out more about this study and to answer the following questions, see the full text (cited below).

1. According to the authors, why is it important to study the negative expressions of leaders?
2. How did the researchers recruit and gain the cooperation of their participants?
3. Did the researchers find what they expected to find? What explanations were given for their results?
4. What are the practical implications of this study?
5. What kind of study is this? (See Appendix.)

Source: Chin, N., & Ho, T. (2014). Understanding when leader negative emotional expression enhances follower performance: The moderating role of follower personality traits and perceived leader power. *Human Relations, 67*, 1051–1072.

Nonverbal Displays of Status: Mishaps and Misunderstandings

Status reminders serve a useful function: They clarify the roles and relationships in an organization while simultaneously reducing much of our behavior to actions that are simply appropriate or inappropriate. If we know the standard script (i.e., proper etiquette) for such interactions, it can make our lives a bit easier and keep us out of trouble. But there is another side: Unlike verbal reminders of who the boss is, the inherent ambiguity of nonverbal reminders can create all sorts of mishaps and misunderstandings that imperil an organization. In this section, we focus on four such perils: dysfunctional leadership, sexual harassment, workplace discrimination, and cross-cultural misunderstandings.

DYSFUNCTIONAL LEADERSHIP In a well-known essay, management scholar Robert Tannenbaum (1961) defined leadership as "interpersonal influence, exercised in situations and directed through the communication process, toward the attainment of a specific goal or goals" (p. 24). To anyone who has ever been in a leadership position, this definition probably sounds accurate. A leader must influence his or her followers, communicate effectively, and accomplish certain goals. No two situations are exactly alike. In this section, we'll examine how a leader's nonverbal communication can diminish his or her influence over subordinates in certain situations and thus interfere with the attainment of organizational goals. The problem comes in two forms: The first arises when a leader ignores the danger of mismatched behavior and the second arises when a leader succumbs to **sex-role stereotyping**.

Often, only a fine line separates a status reminder from an act of contempt. The ambiguity of many nonverbal signals raises the stakes for leaders who happen to have a dominant communication style. If a leader's inattentiveness, fits of anger, spatial intrusions, booming voice, floor hogging, and so on demeans his or her subordinates, the leader may lose a great deal of influence over them. Collectively, these actions greatly influence our perceptions of a leader—in particular, his or her consideration of others. For example, one study found a strong positive correlation between how much subordinates liked their supervisor and the extent to which they believed their supervisor used nonverbal involvement behaviors (Hinkle, 2001). A leader's use of dominant behaviors, on the other hand, leads to negative evaluations. Participants in one study viewed videotapes of a supervisor giving instructions to a subordinate. Asked to imagine they were the subordinate in the interaction, the participants responded to one version of either a male or female supervisor delivering a neutral or dominant message in a neutral or dominant delivery. The supervisor's neutral message was, "Please check these figures and submit any changes when you are done." The dominant message was, "You have to improve your work or there is not going to be a place for you in this organization." The neutral delivery included moderate eye contact and a relaxed facial expression and tone of voice while the dominant delivery consisted of glaring with a loud, angry tone of voice and an angry facial expression. Participants rated the supervisor as much less competent and likeable when the supervisor's delivery was dominant. More importantly, the negative impact of the supervisor's delivery was greater than that of the supervisor's verbal message (Driskell & Salas, 2005).

PERSONAL EXPERIENCE 10.2

CAN YOU RELATE TO THIS?

Nonverbal Displays of Status Can Foster Resentment

The first semester I attended the university full time (as a continuing education/nontraditional student) was a bit unnerving for me. I was attending classes with freshmen, mostly traditional students, and taking 100-level courses. I encountered an instructor in one department who seemed to thrive on letting his young students know who was in charge. The first day of class, he went over his rules, one of which was a zero-tolerance policy for lateness. He sat in front of the class with his feet propped up on the desk and arms clasped behind his head. He spoke in a very loud authoritative voice and made very little eye contact with us. I only made it two weeks and felt that his "power trip" was much more than I could tolerate. In that two weeks, he did not arrive on time for class even once!

Susan

Of course, these findings are not surprising because, as we have seen in previous chapters, nonverbal behaviors carry powerful messages about our attitudes toward others. In the workplace, subordinates are likely to form impressions based on their observations of leaders in a variety of interpersonal encounters. But some of these judgments may depend less on the leader's behavior than they do on how the leader's behavior compares with that of his or her subordinates' (i.e., degree of asymmetry). This is what I discovered in a laboratory experiment on first impressions and nonverbal displays of status (Remland, 1984). I produced four videotapes of the same two male actors playing a scene in which a superior reprimands his subordinate. Although the script was the same in each role-play, the actors changed their nonverbal presentations so that each actor had a high-status and a low-status performance. In the high-status performance, the actors used a relaxed posture, an indirect body orientation, a loud voice, inattentive behavior, and an act of spatial invasion. In the low-status performance, each actor used a tense posture, direct body orientation, soft and hesitating speech, and attentive gaze. Four versions of the superior–subordinate scenario resulted from these performances: (1) high-status superior with high-status subordinate, (2) low-status superior with low-status subordinate, (3) high-status superior with low-status subordinate, and (4) low-status superior with high-status subordinate. Judges rated the superior on how considerate he was toward his subordinate and how well he solved the particular problem. As it turned out, what mattered most was the asymmetry in the actors' performances—how mismatched their behavior was. When their performances were symmetrical (i.e., both high status or both low status), it made no difference to the judges whether the superior used high-status displays or low-status displays. But when their performances were asymmetrical, judges rated the superior's high-status displays as much less considerate than his low-status displays. Apparently, it's not what the boss does but what the boss does in relation to what his or her subordinates do.

Large asymmetries in superior–subordinate interactions—where there is a big difference between the way the superior acts and the way the subordinate acts—may be less desirable than more symmetrical or matched behavior. As we have seen in previous chapters, matching, reciprocity, synchrony, and mimicry often reflect or lead to positive feelings and rapport. If an employee feels uncomfortable interacting with the boss because of these mismatches in their behavior, that employee may choose to avoid the boss as much as possible. This could foster an organizational climate in which management inadvertently discourages the open and free-flowing exchange of ideas that is so necessary for organizational success (Remland, 1988). On the other hand, if the boss abandons the use of status reminders in a well-intentioned effort to empower his or her subordinates or gain their affection, the boss may find that the subordinates rarely do what they're told (i.e., they see the boss as more of a friend and coworker than as an authority figure). Thus, the double bind of status reminders, from the leader's perspective, is that conveying too much status may make the leader abusive in some situations while not conveying enough status may compromise the leader's legitimate authority in other situations. The best remedy, of course, is for the leader to become aware of his or her nonverbal signals and to use them judiciously, using more status reminders when the situation calls for it (as in cases of insubordination) and using fewer in other situations (such as when one is interacting with a timid or insecure employee).

Reflecting an awareness of the need to be polite or supportive—which varies according to factors such as culture, gender, and context—it seems unlikely that most leaders in American organizations would avoid the use of some low-status behaviors. Even the most casual observations of bosses interacting with their employees probably confirm this. In one study, researchers found that higher-status persons spoke more, used more hand gestures, and leaned forward less than lower-status persons did. But the higher-status persons also nodded more frequently (Hall & Friedman, 1999).

PERSONAL EXPERIENCE 10.3

CAN YOU RELATE TO THIS?

Low-Status Nonverbal Signals Can Weaken a Leader

I used to work at this plant where the supervisor didn't get any respect from most of the workers. He never acted like he was in charge and so he didn't command much respect. We just never took him very seriously even though he was our boss. He seemed to be unsure of himself half the time when he talked to us. He hesitated, looked intimidated, and seemed sort of nervous, like he was afraid we wouldn't like him or agree with him. Needless to say, he didn't last very long at the job.

Tim

Unlike the first set of behaviors, all of which signal higher status, head nodding (which implies attentiveness, agreement, or the desire for approval), tends to signal lower status. One especially interesting finding in the study was that the greater the disparity was between the high-status person and the low-status person, the less the high-status person spoke. As the researchers point out, "This seemingly paradoxical pattern is understandable if the [high-status] person is motivated to downplay his or her own status in the service of comfortable social interaction by (as one example) encouraging the partner to speak more" (p. 1088). Still, subordinates, through their own behavior, may encourage status differences. One study found that persons in low-status positions often choose low-status behaviors (which may be more comfortable for them), when they interact with higher-status persons, particularly in task-oriented contexts (Tiedens & Fragale, 2003). In the case of male–female interactions, this tendency to complement dominant behavior with submissive behavior can in itself create difficulties, which we discuss later in the next section on sexual harassment (see Research 10.2 for more on this).

Using nonverbal behavior to reinforce status differences also varies according to one's culture. Hofstede (1983) argues that cultures classified as high in **power distance** tend to embrace authoritarian values and encourage actions that perpetuate status distinctions. For example, researchers in one study asked Japanese and American respondents to imagine various interactions between high-status and lower-status individuals. Though there was considerable agreement on the specific behaviors differentiating high- from low-status persons, the magnitude of the differences varied, with Japanese (a more hierarchical, collectivistic people) reporting greater differences than did Americans (a more egalitarian, individualistic society) (Kowner & Wiseman, 2003). Thus, what seems excessive in one culture may seem quite ordinary in another.

There is another obstacle that leaders must face, the one that comes from sex-role stereotyping. A great deal of scientific research supports the idea that the nonverbal communication of women differs from that of men. We have already reviewed many of these studies in Part II, studies showing differences in physical appearance, approach–avoidance signals, facial expressions, voice, and gesture. Table 10.1 summarizes these differences. In addition, several in-depth reviews of this research are readily available (Andersen, 1999, Chapter 5; Burgoon et al., 1996, pp. 232–239; Hall, 1984, 1985).

Table 10.1 Gender Differences in Nonverbal Communication

Signals	Males	Females
Physical appearance		
	Taller	Shorter
	More muscular	Less muscular
	Wider shoulders	Narrower shoulders
	More body hair	Less body hair
	Stronger jaw and chin	Weaker jaw and chin
	Thicker neck	Thinner neck
	Thicker eyebrows	Thinner eyebrows
Approach–avoidance		
	More control touching	Less control touching
	More staring	Less staring
	Closer approaches	More distant approaches
	Discourages closeness	Invites closeness
	Less attentive gazing	More attentive gazing
Facial expression		
	Less expressive	More expressive
	Less smiling	More smiling
	More displays of anger	Fewer displays of anger
	Less crying	More crying
	Fewer displays of fear, shame, and embarrassment	More displays of fear, shame, and embarrassment
	Less responsive	More responsive
	Less head tilting	More head tilting

Signals	Males	Females
Voice and gesture		
	More interrupting	Less interrupting
	More floor holding	Less floor holding
	Louder voice	Softer voice
	Lower-pitched voice	Higher-pitched voice
	Less rising intonations	More rising intonations
	Infrequent giggling	More frequent giggling
	Fewer back channels (head nods, *uh huhs*)	More back channels (head nods, *uh huhs*)
	More expansive gestures	Less expansive gestures
	More use of insulting gestures	Less use of insulting gestures
	More relaxed postures	Less relaxed postures

Although researchers continue to test the validity of these gender differences (some depend on the situation; others are no longer as pronounced or as widespread as they once were), the overall picture still remains the same. Even a cursory examination of Table 10.1 reveals a stunning parallel between these findings and those reviewed earlier on status reminders. Nonverbal communication between men and women continues to remind us of the traditional sex-role expectations that place men in charge of women: Men act as leaders, women act as subordinates. Yet researchers also find that many of these differences disappear when women assume leadership positions. The influence of status and power on nonverbal communication may be greater than that of gender (Johnson, 1994). In addition, studies show that women's nonverbal behaviors become more powerful than men's when men and women work together on tasks seen as traditionally feminine (Dovidio, Brown, Heltman, Ellyson, & Keating, 1988). But women often find themselves penalized no matter what they do. As communication and gender researcher Deborah Tannen (1994) writes,

> [W]omen in positions of authority face a special challenge. Our expectations for how a person in authority should behave are at odds with our expectations for how a woman should behave. If a woman talks in ways expected of women, she is more likely to be liked than respected. If she talks in ways expected of men, she

> is more likely to be respected than liked. It is particularly ironic that the risk of losing likability is greater for women in authority, since evidence indicates that so many women care so much about whether or not they are liked. (p. 202)

In the long run, some degree of **behavioral flexibility** (doing what the situation demands) may be the best course of action for both men and women. Most organizational communication experts, in fact, usually recommend a situational approach in which the communication techniques depend on the goals we wish to achieve. The skills needed to interview a job applicant effectively differ from those needed to deliver a forceful presentation, the skills needed to counsel a troubled employee differ from those needed to reprimand a difficult one, those needed to run a meeting differ from those needed to motivate a work group, and so on. In short, submissive signals sometimes work best, dominant signals work best at other times, and a combination of submissive and dominant signals work best at still other times.

Overall, it makes sense to focus on the task at hand and achieve a competent communication style for that task instead of focusing on the use of high- or low-status behaviors. In one study, researchers compared the effectiveness of a task style (i.e., competent) of nonverbal communication with that of a dominant style, submissive style, and social style (i.e., friendly and competent) (Carli, LaFleur, & Loeber, 1995). They prepared four sets of four videotapes: a set for each of two male speakers and a set for each of two female speakers. On each tape, the speaker used one of the four styles to deliver the same persuasive message to a seated listener (who was only partially visible so the person's gender could not be identified). Each speaker altered his or her nonverbal style as follows:

1. *Task style*—used a rapid rate of speech; spoke in a firm tone of voice with moderate voice volume; had few hesitations; used an upright posture, calm hand gestures, and a moderately high amount of eye contact
2. *Social style*—spoke in a moderately loud tone of voice, used a relaxed posture with the body leaning toward the other person, had a friendly facial expression, and used a moderately high amount of eye contact
3. *Dominant style*—spoke in a loud and angry tone of voice, pointed intrusively at the other person, maintained almost constant eye contact, and had a stern facial expression
4. *Submissive style*—spoke in a soft and pleading voice with many hesitations and stumbles, had a slumped posture, made nervous hand gestures, and averted his or her gaze from the other person

As expected, the judges who watched the tapes were persuaded most by male and female speakers when those speakers used the task and social styles. Contrary to what we might expect, female speakers were not penalized any more than were male speakers for using a dominant (i.e., masculine) style—male and female speakers using this style were equally ineffective. However, female speakers who used a task style were less effective with male judges than were male speakers who used the same task style. Again, with male judges, when female speakers injected some warmth and friendliness into their presentations (a social style), they were more persuasive than when they used the cooler task style; this wasn't true for the male speakers. The male judges also rated female speakers using the task style as less likable and more threatening than the male speakers who used the same style. Although the results of this study show that women succeed using a task-oriented style rather than one that highlights feminine (submissive) or masculine (dominant) traits, it still reveals the presence of a double standard. For the same performance, women apparently get less credit from men than do their male counterparts.

Other studies also show support for the presence of a double standard. For instance, observations of group members' nonverbal reactions to male and female leaders suggest unequal treatment of a leader's performance based solely on gender. In one laboratory experiment, researchers observed that in small group discussions, the same behavior of the group leader (male or female confederates) elicited more negative facial expressions from group members when the leader was a woman rather than a man, even though group members rated male and female leaders as equally competent (Butler & Geis, 1990). A more recent study replicated these results in a laboratory setting as well as in organizational field settings where female team leaders generally received more negative facial expressions from group members but not more negative ratings of competence (Koch, 2005).

SEXUAL HARASSMENT Sexual harassment occurs in the workplace for several reasons. Some of these reasons, particularly those that involve the deliberate abuse of power, are obvious (e.g., offers to exchange job opportunities for sexual favors). But it is equally obvious that many cases of sexual harassment occur because one person misreads the nonverbal cues of another. These are the cases we focus on here.

An unwelcome sexual advance can occur when the perpetrator mistakes quasi-courtship behavior, which is little more than innocent flirting, for actual courtship behavior (see Chapter 8). Since many of the signals are the same—prolonged eye contact, smiling, touch, body orientation, and so forth—it may not be easy for everyone to spot the telltale signs that these courtship signals are not supposed to be taken seriously (e.g., signs of incomplete involvement, references to the context, etc.). Compounding the problem is the long history of male–female relationships

▸ Many cases of sexual harassment occur because one person misses or misreads the nonverbal signals of another person. How can you tell that the woman shown here is uncomfortable with the nonverbal communication of her coworker?

istockphoto.com/Alina Solovyova-Vincent

in the workplace, which still encourages individuals to view a superior, subordinate, or coworker as a potential mate. But the landscape in which men and women now work is no longer the same.

Explanations of sexual harassment usually refer to the actions of both the perpetrator and the victim: inappropriate sexual behavior by the perpetrator and some form of resistance or at least disapproval by the victim. Studies show that judgments of whether an individual is guilty of sexual harassment depend on the actions of both parties. The more inappropriate a behavior is and the more unwelcome the behavior seems to be, the more likely we are to define it as an instance of sexual harassment. But studies also show that men and women frequently don't see eye to eye about what actions constitute sexual harassment. In general, men are less likely than women are to see the same scenario as a case of sexual harassment, particularly when there is some degree of ambiguity in the actions of either party (Jones & Remland, 1998). For example, a recent experiment demonstrates how a smile in response to sexually provocative questions can lead to misunderstandings and inappropriate sexual conduct (Woodzicka & LaFrance, 2005). Based on the idea that women use social smiles for a variety of reasons, the researchers discovered that female job applicants were more likely to use *masking smiles* (concealing negative feelings) in response to questions such as "Do you have a boyfriend?" than in response to questions such as, "Do you have a best friend?" These non-enjoyment smiles led to perceptions of the interviewer as sexist and sexually harassing. But men were less able to read these uncomfortable smiles correctly than women were, and men who scored higher on an instrument that measures likelihood to sexually harass were the most likely to interpret the smiles as flirtatious!

The danger of being misunderstood is especially serious in asymmetrical relationships, where a status reminder can quickly take on sexual overtones. A superior's use of immediacy behaviors—touching, looking, and getting close, for example—has long been the prerogative of higher-status individuals. But since these actions are subject to all sorts of interpretations (e.g., friendliness, intimidation, sexual interest), there is always the chance of misreading the signals. In addition, a subordinate's use of submissive or low-status behaviors, such as smiling, head nodding, silence, eye contact, direct body orientation, and the like, can make it equally difficult to tell whether the subordinate is welcoming the superior's advances (if that's what they are) or is simply acting as a subordinate. The ambiguity of nonverbal signals also makes it possible for offending harassers to deny the charges against them. Yet, holding people who engage in harassment accountable means letting them know as unequivocally as possible, in words and actions, that their behavior is unacceptable. Anything less is unlikely to deter the harassment. The risks of sexual harassment to the organization and the individuals involved make restraint a prudent policy. We must think about the consequences before we say or do something that may be offensive.

As noted above, the inherent ambiguity of nonverbal signals in the context of superior–subordinate interactions may lead to cases of sexual harassment. But nonverbal behavior may also reveal whether someone is prone to engage in sexual harassment. Studies on the attitudes, beliefs, and perceptions of persons likely to sexually harass show that such persons tend to describe themselves in ways that emphasize social and sexual dominance (Pryor, 1987). And some studies indicate that nonverbal behavior (i.e., displays of status) is part of the behavioral profile. In one study, participants viewed silent clips of videotaped interviews of men being interviewed by an attractive female subordinate (who could not be seen by the viewers). While only observing the men's nonverbal behavior, the participants were able to predict which men scored high on a test that measured likelihood to sexually harass and which men scored low (Driskell, Kelly, & Henderson, 1998). In a follow-up study, male undergraduate participants, classified as high or low on likelihood to sexually harass (based on their test scores), were interviewed individually by a female confederate posing as a high school senior (Murphy, Driscoll, & Kelly, 1999). To put the men in a more powerful position relative to the interviewer, the researchers told them that they would be evaluating the performance of the female interviewer following the interview. Men classified as more likely to sexually harass expressed greater dominance through their nonverbal behavior (e.g., less time in the interview, less forward leaning, more indirect body orientation, and more direct eye contact) compared to those less likely to sexually harass. Underscoring the idea that sexual harassment is more about power and control than it is about sexual attraction, the researchers found no differences between the two groups in any nonverbal signals of sexual interest (e.g., smiles, sexual glances). In more recent studies, researchers have discovered that a male supervisor's dominant nonverbal behavior not only leads to perceptions of the behavior as more sexual and more likely to be harassing than other forms of nonverbal behavior (e.g., flirtatious behavior) but that such behavior actually hinders the task performance of female subordinates (Kelly, Murphy, Craig, & Driscoll, 2005).

RESEARCH 10.2

FIND OUT MORE

How Do Women Respond to the Dominant Nonverbal Cues of Men?

The researchers in these experiments raised the question of how women respond to the nonverbal behavior of men, particularly when the man occupies a more powerful position than the woman in an organizational environment. They found support for their hypothesis that a woman's nonverbal behavior would tend to *complement* rather than *reciprocate* (match) that of the man's. That is, when the man's nonverbal cues were dominant (using expansive postures as opposed to constricted postures), the woman's nonverbal cues were more submissive (using constricted postures rather than expansive) than they were when the man's nonverbal cues were not dominant. This was especially the case when the man was instructed to smile—even when he used a sexist remark. As the researchers concluded, "[I]t seems that overt sexism can promote behavior in a way that actually promotes women's submissiveness or lack of resistance when the bitter pill of sexism is given the sugar coating of a smile" (p. 1492).

To find out more about this study and to answer the following questions, see the full text (cited below):

1. Who were the participants in these experiments? What did the researchers ask them to do?
2. What is gender salience and how did the researchers include this in their experiments? Why did they include it in their experiments?
3. How did the researchers measure the women's nonverbal behavior?
4. What are the main limitations of this research?

Source: de Lemus, S., Spears, R., & Moya, M. (2012). The power of a smile to move you: Complementary submissiveness in women's posture as a function of gender salience and facial expression. *Personality and Social Psychology Bulletin, 38*, 1480–1494.

WORKPLACE DISCRIMINATION Jim wasn't promoted because he doesn't speak up as much as Shelly does. Frank was well qualified for the job, but he didn't get it because he's only 5 feet 3 inches tall. Barbara didn't get a prestigious work assignment because of her wardrobe. Mario's accent kept him off an important committee. Sandy wasn't hired because the other applicant was more attractive. In each case, no one—including the victim—was aware of any discrimination. How can this happen? It usually happens not because of any overt discrimination but because of our automatic tendency to think less of someone whose looks or actions are indicative of lower status rather than of higher status. For example, an employer ordinarily wouldn't consciously reject a job applicant because he has a high-pitched voice or a foreign accent. Yet these cues may still influence the employer's perception of the applicant (e.g., "I think she's pretty unreliable,"

"He doesn't seem very intelligent," etc.). Numerous scientific studies demonstrate that we form all sorts of negative impressions of individuals simply because those individuals in some way communicate a low-status identity. For instance, one study of regional accents found clear evidence of workplace discrimination. The study involved 56 potential employers listening to 10 males reading the same 45-second passage. Readers with southern accents (Georgia and Louisiana) and a New Jersey accent received the most negative ratings from the employers. In particular, listeners evaluated the southern accents as friendly but less educated, cultured, and energetic (Brinson, 2000). (We reviewed many of these studies in Part II of the text.)

Research shows that **powerless stereotypes**—being seen as weak, ineffectual, incompetent, nonauthoritative, and so on—afflict people who share certain physical features considered to be low-status, such as being unattractive, obese, short (men), dark skinned, poorly dressed, baby faced, and physically handicapped. Research also suggests the presence of a demeanor bias (supporting the same kind of powerless stereotyping) against low-status behaviors: not speaking up; speaking in a high-pitched voice, nasal tones, and with certain accents; having a slouched posture; giggling; looking down; not gesturing; being interrupted; smiling nervously; wearing certain attire; and so on. These unflattering appraisals can undermine a person's opportunities to succeed in the workplace. In one set of experiments, for example, researchers found that both male and female job applicants with feminine-sounding voices were judged as less competent for a job than were male and female applicants with more masculine-sounding voices (Ko et al., 2009). One's choice of attire can also trigger negative stereotypes and biases that lead to discrimination. In one study, researchers found that female job applicants dressed in Muslim attire (i.e., black robe, black shoes, and black hijab) received more negative evaluations and less time in the job interview that the same female job applicants dressed in nonreligious attire (i.e., black shoes, black pants, and black shirt) (King & Ahmad, 2010).

This kind of discrimination generally goes unnoticed or, as is often the case when judging one's behavior rather than one's physical appearance, is accepted as part of the evaluation process. Of course, bona fide job qualifications that require an employee to be good looking, to wear certain clothes, to speak up, and so forth are neither rare nor unreasonable. In the case of a speaker's accent, for instance, an employer might claim that the accent jeopardizes the speaker's ability to do the job. On the other hand, such claims can also be used to perpetuate an unwarranted policy of discrimination.

Lawsuits alleging "accent discrimination" have accused employers of denying jobs to individuals with foreign accents; the employers claim that the accent would interfere with effective job performance. Similarly, there have been some efforts to keep teachers with accents from being assigned to teach in the early grades on the grounds that

RESEARCH 10.3

FIND OUT MORE

When Is It Bad to Be Beautiful?

As the research reported in this book illustrates, the well-known halo effect for attractiveness, sometimes referred to as the "what is beautiful is good" hypothesis, usually extends to most situations, including those in organizational contexts. But are there any exceptions? In this series of studies (evaluating job applicants, evaluating applicants for admission to a university), the researchers found support for the idea that people may feel threatened by attractive members of the same sex more than attractive members of the opposite sex and that this would lead to differences in the evaluations of attractive and less attractive persons. They also found that persons with high self-esteem were less likely to downgrade attractive same-sex applicants.

To find out more about this study and to answer the following questions, see the full text (cited below):

1. Who were the participants in these studies? Do you think a different sample would produce different results?
2. What did the researchers do in these studies to obtain evaluations of applicants? How realistic were the studies?
3. Is there anything other than self-esteem that you think might have a similar effect on the results?
4. How do the results of these studies compare with any work-related experiences you've had?

Source: Agthie, M., Sporrle, M., & Maner, J. (2011). Does being attractive always help? Positive and negative effects of attractiveness on social decision making. *Personality and Social Psychology Bulletin, 37*, 1042–1054.

their accents would interfere with teaching the English language. Attorneys and civil rights activists are concerned that this is ethnic discrimination in disguise, pointing to instances where the foreign-born applicant was denied a job in spite of speaking accurate and perfectly intelligible English (Knapp & Hall, 2002, p. 412).

Women, in particular, often find themselves in a precarious position. Since many feminine behaviors turn out to be low-status behaviors in the workplace, women are prime targets of discriminatory practices that can keep them from climbing the corporate ladder.

CROSS-CULTURAL MISUNDERSTANDINGS In Brazil, as author and business consultant Roger Axtell (1998) observes,

> Most touching, as well as sustained eye contact (a sign of courtesy), occurs between peers. A younger person would not touch an older

PERSONAL EXPERIENCE 10.4

CAN YOU RELATE TO THIS?

Giggling Can Send a "Powerless" Message

About two months ago, I was going on an internship interview for FOX news. On the way to the interview, I asked my mom for any advice because she is the executive director of her company and oversees all of the hiring. The only advice she gave me was, "Don't giggle." She elaborated by saying that girls who giggle aren't taken seriously and even appear to be stupid. I had never really thought about my nervous behavior before this, but during the interview, I consciously did not giggle. The interview went well and I got the internship, even though I ended up turning it down for another one!

Denise

> person informally, and strangers do not touch. Similarly, there is little eye contact between people of different ages or status. Usually the younger or less powerful person looks down and away. Many Americans mistakenly interpret this indirect eye contact as evasiveness or deceit. (p. 211)

As we have seen in earlier chapters, the meanings we attach to many nonverbal signals, particularly emblematic gestures, vary dramatically from culture to culture. In addition, the learned scripts that account for much of our communication behavior vary according to the traditional beliefs and values of a cultural group (e.g., individualistic versus collectivistic cultures). In this section, we'll examine how cultural differences in the communication of status can lead to all sorts of mishaps and misunderstandings.

People in all societies must occasionally interact with others whose social standing differs from their own. To avoid blunders that might give offense and to act properly, they must learn the rules that govern such interactions (i.e., etiquette). According to psychologists Marianne LaFrance and Clara Mayo (1978),

> Some cultures have very few status distinctions; in many so-called primitive societies, only the tribal chief is set apart from all the other members. Most complex societies have many status distinctions based on wealth, power, age, sex, family, occupation, and other reasons. Some cultures have evolved very elaborate nonverbal rules for monitoring and regulating status. (p. 178)

But even among industrialized societies, the weight attached to status distinctions varies considerably. The term *power distance* refers to a culture's preoccupation with the maintenance of status differences between groups of people and with how important or unimportant those differences are (Hofstede, 1980). Countries classified as high in power distance embrace authoritarian values and encourage actions that perpetuate status distinctions. The top ten countries on this list are the Philippines, Mexico, Venezuela, India, Yugoslavia, Singapore, Brazil, France, Hong Kong, and Colombia (most African and Arab cultures are also included in this category). In contrast, low power distance countries embrace egalitarian values and place much less emphasis on the expression of status. The top ten low power distance countries are Austria, Israel, Denmark, New Zealand, Ireland, Sweden, Norway, Finland, Switzerland, and Great Britain. Although not near the top of the list, the United States, Canada, and Australia are also considered low power distance cultures.

The power distance orientation of a culture exerts a strong influence over its members' nonverbal communication. Elevated to a fine art, the whole business of communicating status is much more serious and complex in high power distance cultures, where even the simplest of transactions may be orchestrated carefully to signal differences in status (e.g., proper attire, greeting rituals, demeanor, etc.) and where any failure to follow the rules can have undesirable consequences. Certainly, as we noted earlier, Americans have their share of status reminders. But Americans visiting a high power distance culture might be inclined to view the expression of status in that culture as excessive and even unpleasant (e.g., "abusive" bosses, "groveling" employees). Yet how would visitors to the United States react to the way our superiors and subordinates interact? A visitor from Thailand (higher power distance), for example, would probably think that we are too permissive while a visitor from Finland (lower power distance) would probably think that we are too strict.

Another cultural difference with implications for communicating status involves the use of time. Struck by the significant differences he observed in the way people in various cultures scheduled their everyday activities, anthropologist Edward Hall (1983) concluded that some cultures have a preference for doing many things at once (polychronic or P-time cultures), whereas other cultures prefer doing one thing at a time (monochronic or M-time cultures). Hall elaborates on how this fundamental difference can produce a message of status where clearly none is intended.

TASK-ORIENTED ENCOUNTERS: GETTING THE JOB DONE

Thus far, we have addressed the importance of nonverbal communication in expressing and perpetuating status differences in the workplace. We've also considered how the communication of status can jeopardize the goals of an organization, leading to problems of dysfunctional leadership, sexual harassment, workplace discrimination, and cross-cultural misunderstanding. In this section, we focus on how nonverbal communication can help or hinder our performance in various task-oriented encounters, highlighting the ones for which we need preparation to be successful: interviews and presentations.

RESEARCH 10.4

FIND OUT MORE

Dress for Success: How Much Self-Sacrifice Is Required?

The authors of this study interviewed men and women, aged 26–45, about how they cope with the demands of the workplace that keep them from wearing clothes and accessories that express their personal affiliation with the punk subculture. The authors found that the interviewees adopted a number of different coping strategies. For example, one strategy was maintaining two closets: one for work, the other for outside of work. Another strategy was deciding to either blend in or to stand out. Tattoo coverage was a common theme among many interviewees. One interviewee, Bill, a sales representative, remarked, "[T]he main thing is just covering up the tattoos. That's about it. I mean, I have one on the back of my neck that people still see. People see them. So it's not a big deal, but . . . you get some older clients that you don't want to freak out" (p. 293).

To find out more about this study and to answer the following questions, see the full text (cited below).

1. What is the punk subculture and how does it influence one's appearances?
2. What do the authors mean by *appearance labor?*
3. How did the authors find persons to interview for this study?
4. What were the main methods of accommodation used by the interviewees?
5. What kind of study is this? (See Appendix.)

Source: Sklar, M., & DeLong, M. (2012). Punk dress in the workplace: Aesthetic expression and accommodation. *Clothing and Textiles Research Journal, 30,* 285–299.

Of course, no matter how much we prepare, the subtleties of nonverbal communication can sabotage even our best-laid plans. In the sections that follow, we'll first consider the role of self-fulfilling prophecies, then the impact of emotional exchanges, and finally, we'll focus on successful nonverbal communication in various workplace interactions.

Self-Fulfilling Prophecies: Expectancy Effects in the Workplace

In the 1960s, psychologist Robert Rosenthal (1966) showed how a researcher's nonverbal cues could unwittingly prod human subjects into behaving the way the researcher hoped they would rather than the way they might in the absence of the researcher's influence, a finding that demonstrated how the nonverbal signals of a researcher can damage the validity of a scientific experiment. Turning his attention to the classroom, Rosenthal discovered that a teacher's nonverbal cues could produce a similar kind of self-fulfilling prophecy. When a teacher believes that a student is bright (whether or not the student really is), the teacher will expect great things from that student. In many subtle ways, the teacher will unknowingly telegraph these expectations to that student. Emboldened by these positive messages from the teacher, the student rises to the teacher's expectations (Rosenthal & Jacobsen, 1968).

When they are made aware of this phenomenon, teachers try their best to monitor the messages they send to their students, trying to signal the same high expectations to everyone, including low-achieving students. But researchers continue to uncover these **expectancy effects** in the classroom. Unbeknownst to them and contrary to what they report when asked, teachers' feelings still leak out to their students—positive feelings toward the good students, which encourage them to excel, and negative feelings toward the poor students, which invite them to fail (Babad, 1992). Interestingly, research shows that young students, but not adults, have so much implicit knowledge of and are so attuned to teachers' differential treatment of students in the classroom that they can make accurate guesses from a 10-second video clip of a teacher's nonverbal communication in a single lecture as to whether that teacher is likely to show favoritism to some students or not (Babad, 2005a).

Researchers have found sufficient evidence of expectancy effects in other workplace environments as well. Research suggests that in the courtroom context, jurors are highly attuned to a judge's negative nonverbal cues (Burnett & Badzinski, 2005). These signals can influence the outcome of a trial. In fact, judges often get the verdicts they expect after signaling their expectations to members of the jury (Blanck & Rosenthal, 1992). The same process influences the outcome of job interviews. One study found that an interviewer could inadvertently elicit from a job applicant the undesirable behavior he expected to see (Word, Zanna, & Cooper, 1974). These self-fulfilling prophecies can easily interfere with the effectiveness of most formal workplace encounters. Information-gathering interviews (e.g., job interviews, survey interviews, etc.) become tainted when an interviewer gets hoped-for rather than truthful answers to questions. Business meetings become dysfunctional when attendees say what they think the boss wants to hear instead of what they honestly believe (this phenomenon is called *groupthink*). Oral presentations deteriorate when speakers, fearing audience disapproval and signaling that fear to the audience, begin to get the negative feedback they expected in the first place.

Certainly, part of our preparation for interviews and presentations should include some assessment of how our performance might suffer from expectancy effects. Becoming aware of how we unintentionally signal our expectations—through facial expressions, head nods, eye contact, body movement, and so on—is the first step toward correcting the problem. Trying to suppress and counteract these signals, the second step, requires that we also make some effort to monitor our behavior during the performance.

Emotional Exchanges in the Workplace

As in all of our everyday face-to-face interactions, we send and receive emotional messages in the workplace, expressing how we feel and picking up the feelings of others. The study of these exchanges in the workplace is beginning to show that sharing emotions, following display rules, and being attuned to the emotions of others are basic components of one's emotional intelligence and play an important role in determining the effectiveness of our workplace interactions (Côté & Hideg, 2011).

EMOTIONAL CONTAGION *Emotional contagion* refers to a phenomenon in which emotions spread from person to person (see Chapter 5). The implications of emotional contagion for organizations have not escaped the attention of scholars and practitioners, who consider it a ubiquitous process that leaders should harness for the good of the organization (Goleman, Boyatzis, & McKee, 2002). In one study, researchers observed 70 work teams across diverse industries and found that members who sat in meetings together ended up sharing moods in a relatively short period of time (Bartel & Saavedra, 2000). Some evidence supports the claim that the more cohesive a work group is, the more contagious the emotional displays will be (Goleman et al., 2002). Further, leaders are most likely to control the contagion that takes place because group members generally see the leader's emotional reaction as the most appropriate response and, therefore, members tend to model their own reactions on the leader's, particularly in emotionally ambiguous situations. In other words, if the boss is laughing, maybe it's okay for us to laugh, too. Just such a scenario occurs in the popular Jim Carrey movie, *Liar, Liar*, in which Carrey plays Fletcher Reede, an attorney and habitual liar who falls prey to his son's wish that he must tell the truth for 24 hours. In one hilarious scene, Reede walks in on a meeting that his boss, the head of the firm, is having with members of the firm. When asked what he thinks about the boss, Reede reveals everything he despises about his boss while everyone listens in stunned disbelief. All eyes then turn to the boss, awaiting his reaction. When the boss begins laughing hysterically, everyone instantly joins in. As this scene illustrates, the leader may be the one who activates the emotional contagion process. Of course, a leader's ability to spread emotions probably depends on his or her capacity to convey those emotions. That is, a leader with a highly expressive face, voice, and body is more likely to activate the process than is a leader who doesn't show much emotion.

Emotional contagion may occur wherever individuals work together in face-to-face groups or meet directly with the public. But does it affect task performance? Some research suggests that the spread of positive emotions can boost the performance of work groups (Barsade, 2002), predict job satisfaction among employees (Fisher, 2000), increase cooperation and minimize conflict (Barsade, 2002), improve sales performance, and increase customer satisfaction (Homburg & Stock, 2004; Verbeke, 1997). Researchers have also discovered, however, that the spread of negative emotions is a contributing factor to stress and burnout among physicians (Bakker, Schaufeli, Sixma, & Bosveld, 2001), nurses (Omdahl & O'Donnel, 1999), teachers (Bakker & Schaufeli, 2000), and sales personnel (Verbeke, 1997). Thus, studies show that emotional contagion in the workplace may have positive and negative effects on employee performance, health, and well-being.

EMOTIONAL LABOR The contagion process described above depends to a large degree on the genuine (i.e., spontaneous) expression of emotions. But the workplace also demands that individuals engage in various kinds of emotional deception, pretending to be cheerful when they are really annoyed or frustrated, for instance. Expressing an unfelt emotion, exaggerating a felt emotion, and suppressing a felt emotion are acts of **emotional labor** in the workplace, which the sociologist Arlie Hochschild (1983) defined as "the management of feeling to create a publicly observable facial and bodily display [that] is sold for a wage [and] therefore has exchange value" (p. 7). The management of emotions, according to Hochschild, requires a worker to engage in either surface acting or deep acting. *Surface acting* only requires the actor to display an emotion with no attendant feelings. On the other hand, *deep acting* requires the actor to elicit the corresponding emotion in some way, as a method actor might do to prepare for an emotionally charged scene. Curiously, the short-term effort involved in deep acting may surpass that needed for surface acting, as it requires more long-term effort and takes a heavier toll (Grandey, 2003; Totterdell & Holman, 2003).

In her early research, Hochschild (1983) estimated that "roughly one-third of American workers have jobs that subject them to substantial demands for emotional labor" (p. 11). Mann (1999) surveyed twelve UK companies and found moderate levels of emotional labor in almost two-thirds of the communications reported by respondents and high levels in about one-third of the reported communications. More than half of the participants reported that they laughed or frowned not because they wanted to but because they were expected to. Sixty percent of the reported communications involved suppressing an emotion, mostly anger. In addition, those higher up in the organization reported less emotional labor than did those lower in the chain of command, supporting Van Maanen and Kunda's (1989) astute observation that "only the dominant and the dormant have relative freedom from emotional constraints in organizational life" (p. 55). Other surveys show that American employers and employees tend to agree that emotional labor is a job requirement, though more involved and satisfied employees share this perception to a greater degree than do less involved and satisfied employees (Diefendorff, Richard, & Croyle, 2006).

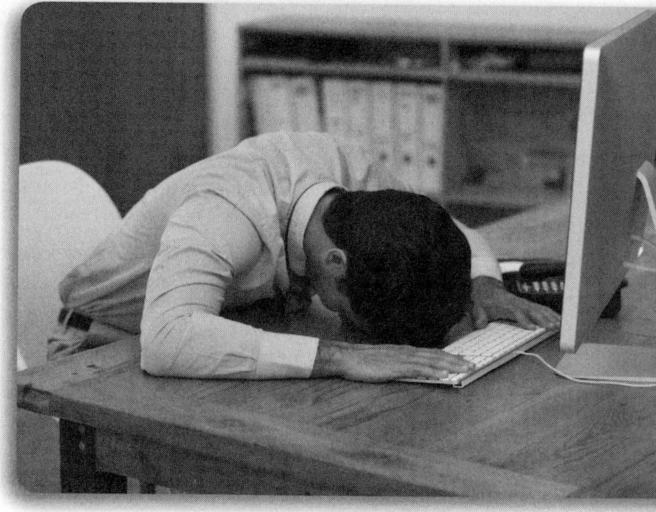

▸ Jobs that require workers to display emotions they do not feel or inhibit emotions they do can lead to emotional exhaustion and job burnout.

istockphoto.com/PeopleImages

Studies of flight attendants, nurses, cashiers, and others show that emotional labor consists of four basic elements: (1) the frequency, duration, and intensity of emotional displays; (2) the variety of emotions displayed; (3) attentiveness to display rules; and (4) the discrepancy between the felt and the displayed emotion, referred to as **emotional dissonance** (Mann, 1999; Morris & Feldman, 1996). Subsequent surveys have identified emotional dissonance as a strong predictor of job dissatisfaction, emotional exhaustion, depersonalization, and other factors contributing to job burnout (Diefendorff & Richard, 2003; Lee & Ashforth, 1996; Pugliesi, 1999). There is also evidence that emotional dissonance, particularly the suppression of negative emotions, can produce health consequences related to prolonged stress. But the research also points to factors that lessen the impact of these negative consequences, such as job autonomy, social support, and cultural climate (Grandey, Fisk, & Steiner, 2005; Morris & Feldman, 1996; Wharton, 1996).

Despite the sometimes-damaging effects of emotional labor, research identifies benefits that arise under certain conditions. For example, the use of deep acting and the regular display of positive emotions can result in lessened dissonance, improved performance, and increased satisfaction (Diefendorff & Richard, 2003; Grandey, 2003; Totterdell & Holman, 2003). Other researchers contend that any requirement to display positive emotions leads ultimately to improved performance (e.g., increased sales) and a heightened sense of accomplishment (Rafaeli & Sutton, 1987). In a qualitative study of sales workers, for example, Abiala (1999) found that emotional labor was most likely to produce positive effects when interacting with customers was a small part of the workers' day, there were few rules to follow, the intent to sell was not concealed, and the workers were hired for their training and experience rather than for their looks or demeanor. Regardless of the circumstances, however, managing emotions is an essential and often inescapable part of one's job in an organization. So it may not be surprising to find that it is also one of the strongest predictors of job performance and organizational commitment (Kluemper, DeGroot, & Choi, 2013).

EMOTION RECOGNITION Whereas the research on emotional contagion and emotional labor generally focuses on the expression and management of emotion, other studies have examined the recognition of emotion. The ability to recognize emotions in others is a mainstay in the research on interpersonal sensitivity, which is necessary for leadership success, personnel functions of hiring and performance appraisal, the development and functioning of work teams, and successful customer service (Goleman et al., 2002; Riggio, 2001). In one review of the research on emotion recognition ability, researchers found a consistently positive correlation between job performance and the emotion recognition accuracy (Elfenbein, Beaupré, Lévesque, & Hess, 2007). For instance, one study found that the ability to recognize posed facial expressions of emotion predicted the outcome of a negotiation exercise. Participants with greater ability performed better than participants with less ability to recognize expressions of emotion (Elfenbein et al., 2007).

But some studies have also raised questions about the benefits of emotion recognition in all situations, finding support for the counter-intuitive claim that "people reading" has a downside. Using the Diagnostic Analysis of Nonverbal Accuracy (DANVA), one study found that the ability to read negative emotions conveyed through the voice rather than the face damaged workplace evaluations received from peers and supervisors (Elfenbein & Ambady, 2002). Similarly, another study found a negative correlation between the ability to read body cues and ratings of rapport from an interaction partner but a positive correlation between the ability to read facial cues and these same ratings of rapport (Puccinelli & Tickle-Degnen, 2004). Apparently, as the researchers claim, the ability to pick up emotions from less controllable nonverbal communication channels (such as the voice and the body), which the researchers refer to as *emotional eavesdropping*, may burden individuals with difficult or unpleasant information that was not meant to be shared. Certainly, more studies of this kind will continue to clarify the costs as well as the benefits of reading emotions in the workplace.

Successful Nonverbal Communication in Task-Oriented Encounters

The effectiveness of our nonverbal communication in most formal workplace encounters depends on the particular goals we want to achieve. Much of what we have already addressed in earlier chapters applies here as well. Skills in building conversational rapport, gaining compliance, detecting deception, providing emotional support, and managing interpersonal conflict are all highly useful in various workplace encounters, from sales interviews to counseling sessions. In the remainder of this chapter, we survey the research on how nonverbal communication contributes directly to the immediate success or failure of these encounters, whether we are communicating to an audience of one or to an audience of one hundred. Does nonverbal communication affect the outcome of these encounters? In recent years, mounting evidence shows that it does.

CUSTOMER SERVICE TRANSACTIONS Even in workplace encounters that involve little or no preparation and where the participants have had no prior contact with each other, nonverbal communication can make a difference. As we saw in Chapter 7, our physical appearance and even our use of a single immediacy behavior such as touch, eye contact, or close proximity can help us gain the compliance of a complete stranger. A similar effect sometimes occurs on the job during customer service transactions. In one well-known study, for instance, researchers discovered that people, especially women, who were touched on the hand by a librarian while she returned their library card had a more positive attitude toward the librarian and the library in general than did those who were not touched (Fisher, Rytting, & Heslin, 1976). The use of touch also had a positive effect in another widely cited study. Waitresses received bigger tips from diners they touched on the hand than from those they didn't touch (Crusco & Wetzel, 1984). Researchers in another study found that patrons in public taverns who were touched on the shoulder by their server ordered more drinks than did patrons who were not touched (Kaufman & Mahoney, 1999). In retail sales interactions, touch also has a positive impact; but as one recent study shows, the impact may depend as much on the customer as it does on the use of touch alone. Researchers compared the impact of a salesperson's brief touch on the shoulder of customers in a high-contact culture (France) and a low-contact culture (Germany). Customers trusted the salesperson more, rated the product more favorably, and were more likely to purchase the product when the salesperson touched them—but only in low-contact cultures or only when the customer had a greater need for touch (Orth, Chameeva, & Brand, 2013). So

▸ Research shows that in customer service transactions, customers who receive smiles from service employees are likely to reciprocate these smiles and report more satisfaction with the service they receive compared to customers who do not receive smiles.

istockphoto.com/piksel

it appears that the benefits of touch may be lost in places where the use of touch is relatively common (high-contact cultures) or with customers that have little need or desire for touch.

Customer service professionals may benefit from other immediacy behaviors as well, such as getting close and making eye contact. For example, in one study, waiters and waitresses in family-style restaurants in a small Midwestern town and in a large urban area received bigger tips when they squatted and made eye contact with diners than when they stood and made eye contact (Davis, Schrader, Richardson, Kring, & Kieffer, 1998). As another researcher concluded from interviews with numerous waitresses, good service is synonymous with friendly, deferential, and even flirtatious behaviors (Hall, 1993).

Customer service employees are probably inundated with advice about being friendly and courteous. In fact, observations of customer service encounters confirm that smiling has beneficial effects, sometimes due to the process of emotional contagion. Customers who receive smiles from service employees are likely to mimic or reciprocate these smiles and report more satisfaction with the service they receive compared to customers who do not receive smiles (Pugh, 2006; Tan, Foo, & Kwek, 2004). Moreover, the strength and authenticity of the employee's smile makes a difference, with more genuine and fuller smiles producing more beneficial effects (Barger & Grandey, 2006; Hennig-Thurau, Groth, Paul, & Gremier, 2006). While few can deny the importance of friendly service, employees who follow emotional display rules have to continually monitor their own nonverbal behavior and work to keep difficult-to-control signals (e.g., a smirk, an angry tone, etc.) from betraying their true feelings.

PERSONAL EXPERIENCE 10.5

CAN YOU RELATE TO THIS?

Gender Discrimination Occurs in Customer Service

When I used to waitress and serve a male/female couple, I often went out of my way to treat the man nicer because he usually was the one paying and I wanted a bigger tip. I would smile at the male customers, compliment them, and sometimes touch then on the shoulder. Because men responded more generously with their money than women did, I made sure I worked the men real good to make more money. I wasn't mean to the women; I just didn't treat them the same.

Julia

But even when they try, customer service employees don't treat everyone in the same friendly manner. For example, some research documents a gender bias that favors male customers. A researcher found in one study that although female salesclerks gave friendlier service (more greetings, smiles, and eye contact) than their male counterparts did, male customers received friendlier service than did female customers (Rafaeli, 1988). In another study, researchers discovered that when a man and a woman approached a salesclerk at the same time, the clerk served the man first 61% of the time and the woman first 32% of the time (in the remaining cases, either no one was served or the clerk inquired who was first). While dressing up improved the male customer's chances of being served first, it did not do the same for the female customer (Stead & Zinkhan, 1986). But not all studies show a customer service bias favoring male customers. The occurrence of gender discrimination may in fact depend on other factors. For example, based on more than 300 observations of customer service encounters in various businesses and retail stores, researchers in one study found that employees were least likely to exhibit friendly behavior (e.g., smiling, eye contact, thanking, etc.) toward customers who were male, white, young, or casually dressed (Martin & Adams, 1999). Another study showed that black vendors were friendlier (e.g., smiles, pleasant tone of voice, speaking, touch) to black customers than they were to white customers (Amsbary & Powell, 2007).

PROFESSIONAL INTERVIEWS Most of the face-to-face interactions that occur in the workplace are dyadic encounters, one person communicating to another. These interactions include formal interviews between employers and job applicants, doctors and patients, researchers and respondents, attorneys and clients, and so on. Although we need much more research to understand fully the role of nonverbal communication in each of these encounters, the research that has been done gives us some idea of what helps and what doesn't.

Studies show that nonverbal communication affects the outcomes of all sorts of interviews. In many types of interviews, nonverbal signs of involvement (see Table 7.1) produce positive results. Most information-gathering interviews, for example, depend on the interviewer's ability to gain the cooperation of an individual and encourage him or her to talk freely. Research indicates that touching and making eye contact with a person increases the likelihood that the person will comply with a request to participate in a survey (Hornik & Ellis, 1988). Research also shows that even apprehensive respondents will talk much more and will like their interviewer more when the interviewer uses high levels of nonverbal involvement (direct body orientation, forward lean, head nods, back channels, and gazing while listening) as opposed to much lower levels (Remland & Jones, 1989).

RESEARCH 10.5

FIND OUT MORE

How Important Is Nonverbal Communication in the Sales Interview?

According to the authors of this study, nonverbal communication is at least as important for a successful sales interview as the verbal content of the interview. With regards to the sales interview context in particular, prior research confirms five distinct phases: approach (e.g., greeting, building rapport), needs identification (i.e., active listening), presentation (i.e., making the pitch), overcoming objections, and closing the sale. Using the National Collegiate Sales Contest scoring instrument (which includes an evaluation of each of the five phases), undergraduate business and marketing majors participated in role-plays of sales interviews. Subsequent evaluations indicated that the students needed a balance of effective verbal and nonverbal communication order to maximize their persuasiveness, especially during the approach and needs identification phases of the sales interviews.

To find out more about this study and to answer the following questions, see the full text (cited below).

1. How were the students motivated to participate in the sales interviews?
2. How realistic do you think the sales interviews and the evaluation of the sales interviews were?
3. Why didn't nonverbal communication improve the performance of sales interviewers during the overcoming objections phase of the interviews?
4. Specifically, what are the nonverbal behaviors that sales interviewers should use during the first two phases of the sales interview?
5. What kind of research is this? (See Appendix.)

Source: Taute, H. A., Heiser, R. S., & McArther, D. N. (2011). The effect of nonverbal signals on student role-play evaluations. *Journal of Marketing Education, 33*, 28–40.

PERSONAL EXPERIENCE 10.6

CAN YOU RELATE TO THIS?

Nonverbal Communication Gains Survey Compliance

I hate when those people with clipboards come up to you at the mall with those questionnaires. But one day while walking through the mall, this little old lady was doing the survey. I felt bad for her so I decided to do it. During the interview, she was so friendly—smiling, touching me on the arm, and making eye contact—that I really loosened up and dropped my previous thoughts about loathing mall interviews.

Jilanna

Research also confirms the positive effects of nonverbal involvement behaviors in counseling sessions (Barak, Patkin, & Dell, 1982; Fretz, Corn, Tuemmler, & Bellet, 1979; Tepper & Haase, 1978). One study found that clients rated counselors as having greater expertise when the counselors used high levels of involvement (such as forward lean, eye contact, and hand gestures) directed toward the client than when they used fewer of these behaviors, an effect that outweighed the impact of conspicuously displayed diplomas (Siegel & Sell, 1978). In another early study, counselors were judged as more trustworthy, attractive, and expert when they used responsive nonverbal behaviors, which included head nodding, vocal variety, facial expressiveness, eye contact, and gestures, than when they used less responsive nonverbal behaviors (Claiborn, 1974). Other studies show that congruent postures (i.e., matching) as well as a counselor's forward lean are indicative of greater rapport between counselor and client (Charney, 1966; Sandhu & Reeves, 1993; Sharpley & Sagris, 1995; Stafford, 2001; Trout & Rosenfeld, 1980).

In medical consultations, research confirms that a physician's nonverbal communication has important consequences for patient satisfaction and clinical outcomes (Roter, Frankel, Hall, & Sluyter, 2006). In one study, investigators found that physicians who were better able to express their emotions tended to have more satisfied patients (DiMatteo, Hays, & Prince, 1986). For example, when a physician or nurse conveys emotion (i.e., concern, warmth, enthusiasm) through their tone of voice, patients tend to adhere more to their treatment and to be more satisfied with the treatment they receive (Haskard, Williams, DiMatteo, Heritage, & Rosenthal, 2008).

Many more studies show a link between a physician's use of nonverbal involvement behaviors and patient satisfaction (Conlee, Olvera, & Vagim, 1993; Hall, Roter, & Katz, 1988; Harrigan, Oxman, & Rosenthal, 1985; Harrigan & Rosenthal, 1983; Larsen & Smith, 1981; Richmond, Smith, Heisel, & McCroskey, 2001; Schorr, 2000; Street & Buller, 1988). For instance, one study examined the nonverbal behavior of physicians in three different 15-minute standardized patient interviews, each requiring a different set of communication skills (e.g., gathering information, counseling). The researchers found that in all three interviews, the physician's tone of voice, smiles, open postures, body lean, eye contact, head nods, and facial expressivity had a much greater influence on patient satisfaction than did the actual quality of the interview content, as evaluated by other physicians (Griffith, Wilson, Langer, & Haist, 2003). A similar study in Japan corroborates these findings. In standardized patient interviews, medical students received more favorable evaluations from patients, regardless of the medical faculty's ratings of interview content, when they used higher levels of nonverbal involvement behaviors (nodding, direct body orientation, eye contact) and when they adapted their speech rate and volume to match that of their patient (Ishikawa et al., 2006)

Of course, more positive nonverbal behavior is not always better and can backfire when doctors use excessive amounts of touch, too much eye contact, or positive vocal tones that downplay the seriousness of the visit (Hall, Roter, & Rand, 1981; Harrigan et al., 1985; Larsen & Smith, 1981). Cultural and gender differences in the use and interpretation of nonverbal cues also matter. As we have seen in previous chapters, some cultures are more comfortable with nonverbal displays of closeness and affection than other cultures are. In addition, the same behaviors do not always carry the same meanings, which can cause misunderstanding in doctor–patient interactions. For example, one study discovered that Canadian and Chinese physicians' and patients' use of back-channel responses while listening to one another (head nods, vocalizations) improved their recall of information in intracultural interactions but hindered communication, leading to less recall of information, in intercultural interactions. While a Chinese listener may have nodded to say "I am paying attention," a Canadian speaker may have interpreted the head nod as "I understand what you are saying." This kind of misleading feedback could make it more difficult to exchange information in an accurate manner (Li, 2006). Gender also makes a difference. Research also shows, for instance, that female physicians are more likely than their male counterparts to use and consequently to benefit from the use of nonverbal immediacy behaviors: They obtain more medical information from their patients and receive higher evaluations from persons who observe them interacting with patients (Hall, Irish, Roter, & Ehrlich, 1994; Koss & Rosenthal, 1997).

When doctors don't use a variety of nonverbal involvement behaviors, they run the risk of communicating a lack of interest in their patients. One specific way that physicians communicate a lack of interest is by not actively encouraging, and sometimes even not allowing their patients to speak. One observational study of 60 routine primary care office visits found a disturbing tendency for physicians to interrupt their patients. On average, patients spoke uninterrupted for 12 seconds after the resident physician entered the room. One fourth of the time, physicians interrupted patients before they finished speaking. The average visit lasted 11 minutes with the patient speaking for about four minutes. During this time, physicians interrupted patients an average of two times. Interestingly, the researchers observed gender differences in how physicians treated patients. Female physicians interrupted patients less often than did their male counterparts, and females patients were interrupted more often than were the male patients. Not surprisingly, the more patients were interrupted, the less they liked their visits (Rhoades, McFarland, Finch, & Johnson, 2001). Obviously, not interrupting is one way to get patients to speak. Another way is through active listening (i.e., the use of back channels). Researchers in another study found that a physician's use of reinforcing facial expressions and head nods increased patients' self-disclosures during their interactions (Duggan & Parrott, 2000).

Patients recognize the importance of a doctor's communication style. In one survey, 85% of the respondents said that what they looked for in a physician was whether the doctor communicated well and demonstrated a caring attitude. The doctor's experience and credentials were not nearly as important (Makoul & Schofield, 1999). According to some studies, differences in the nonverbal (and verbal) communication styles of physicians are important enough to explain why some doctors get sued and others don't. Researchers in one study examined the differences between frequently sued obstetricians and those who had no claims against them. The patients of frequently sued doctors said they felt rushed, ignored, or ill-informed during visits. One of their biggest complaints was that the doctor did a poor job of listening to them (Hickson, Clayton, & Entman, 1994). Participants in another study viewed a videotape of a physician treating a patient. In one version the doctor used positive communication behaviors, which included eye contact, a friendly tone of voice, appropriate touch, smiles, responsive facial expressions, and a relatively long period of contact time. In the other version, the doctor refrained from using positive communication behaviors and did not spend much time with the patient. Participants were more likely to judge the doctor in the second version as less professional, caring, friendly, trustworthy, and competent. Perhaps most importantly, they saw that doctor as more to blame, more negligent, and more liable for possible mistreatment of the patient (Lester, 1993).

Social scientists have also investigated nonverbal communication in the employment interview. These studies, along with countless insights from personnel professionals, employment interviewers, communication consultants, management specialists, and others, give us a fairly accurate and comprehensive view of how nonverbal communication affects the performances of both the interviewer and the interviewee (Arvey & Campion, 1982; DeGroot & Motowidlo, 1999; DePaulo, 1992; Fleischmann, 1991; Forsythe, 1990; Forsythe, Drake, & Cox, 1985; Gifford, Ng, & Wilkinson, 1985; Hickson & Stacks, 1993, pp. 246–252; Imada & Hakel, 1977; Leathers, 1997, Chapter 14; McGovern & Tinsley, 1978; Riggio & Throckmorton, 1988; Tessler & Sushelsky, 1978; Young & Beier, 1977).

Interviewers are quite susceptible to the nonverbal messages they receive from job applicants. Like the rest of us, highly trained interviewers have all sorts of biases and preconceptions about what a person's appearance and behavior reveals about that person. As we have seen throughout this text, we form instantaneous impressions of people—favorable and unfavorable—based on their facial features, body shape, height, clothing, tone of voice, gaze behavior, use of space, facial expressions, and so on. Usually knowing little about the applicant except what's on the résumé, employment interviewers often have little choice but to follow their gut reactions. Evidence that most interviewers make up their minds after only the first few minutes of an interview seems to confirm this (Hickson & Stacks, 1993, Chapter 12). The apparent similarities that exist among large numbers of qualified applicants results in a **negativity bias**, a tendency for the interviewer to attach more significance to what he or she dislikes about the applicant than to what he or she likes. Thus, salient and undesirable features of the applicant's performance, such as a sloppy appearance, poor manners, halting speech, nervousness, or tardiness, can undermine the applicant's chance of success. Moreover, the nonverbal cues of the interviewer—signaling a positive or negative attitude—can greatly influence the performance of the applicant, weakening it when the signals are negative and improving it when the signals are positive (see *expectancy effects*).

In a relatively short time, the applicant tries to create a favorable image in the mind of the interviewer. To be successful, an applicant's communication should project the image of someone who is motivated, enthusiastic, composed, responsive, and assertive. Table 10.2 summarizes the nonverbal signals most likely to help the job applicant communicate such an image.

The image a job applicant conveys through vocal and physical cues has a significant impact on the judgments of interviewers. In fact, some research suggests that the effect of the applicant's nonverbal communication is greater than that of the applicant's verbal abilities (Goldberg & Cohen, 2004). Research also raises the possibility that an applicant's nonverbal communication may predict performance on the job. Using videotaped interviews with managers in utility companies, researchers found that a composite of vocal cues (pitch, pitch variability, speech rate, pauses, and variations in volume) correlated with supervisory ratings of job performance. Similarly, the researchers found a positive correlation between the same vocal cues and job performance ratings for a sample of videotaped interviews with managers in a news-publishing company. In this latter sample, the researchers also found a positive correlation between visual cues (physical attractiveness, smiling, gaze, hand movements, and body orientation) and job performance ratings (DeGroot & Motowidlo, 1999).

Building rapport—an important goal of most researchers, counselors, physicians, employment interviewers, and others—may require a friendly and nonthreatening demeanor that is not entirely compatible with the goals of all professional interviewers in all interview contexts. Although most sales professionals strive to establish positive relations with their clients, for example, the circumstances of a particular situation may call for an interviewer to use a hard-sell rather than a soft-sell approach, intimidating a client with a loud voice, steady gaze, disapproving face, and more. In fact, one contingency theory of the sales interview recommends the use of a hard-sell approach for certain clients (e.g., less knowledgeable and educated) and when the likelihood of making a sale is either very good or very bad (Poppleton, 1981).

Similarly, in police interrogations (or in many attorney–client interviews), the goal of an interviewer may be at odds with the use of a friendly and nonthreatening style. When trying to assess the honesty of a criminal suspect who is highly motivated to lie, an interviewer may be more likely to elicit truthful statements or to pick up

Table 10.2 Successful Nonverbal Communication in the Employment Interview

Image	Nonverbal Signals
MOTIVATED	Wearing proper business attire
	Knowledge of proper etiquette (handshake, punctuality)
	Fluent speech, floor holding (i.e., preparation)
ENTHUSIASTIC	Animated gestures
	Pleasant facial expressions
	Expressive voice
	Moderately fast speaking rate
	Moderately close distances
COMPOSED	Avoiding closed postures
	Avoiding self-touch
	Avoiding nervous mannerisms (displacement activity)
	Avoiding negative facial expressions (anger, disgust, contempt, fear, shame, boredom, etc.)
	Avoiding tense, rigid postures
	Avoiding interruptions (i.e., showing patience)
RESPONSIVE	Short but thoughtful response latencies
	Back channels (e.g., head nods, saying *uh huh*)
	Responsive facial gestures (e.g., smiles, eyebrow raises, etc.)
	Attentive eye contact and body orientation
	Some mirroring
	Adapting to nonverbal feedback
ASSERTIVE	Masculine attire
	Strong, confident voice
	Direct eye contact, avoiding downward gaze
	Firm handshake
	Erect posture
	Strong, full gestures

nonverbal clues to deception (i.e., signs of guilt and anxiety) by making the suspect uncomfortable rather than comfortable. Indeed, the stress-inducing techniques of police interrogators—the use of silence, staring, shouting, close proximity, and so on—may sometimes facilitate lie detection. In his work with police interrogators, communication researcher Dale Leathers (1997) found that they often rely heavily on nonverbal signs of stress such as gaze avoidance, perspiration, fidgeting, unusual breathing patterns, abnormal swallowing, and the like. On the other hand, studies also show that many of these professional lie detectors may be overconfident in assessing their own ability to detect deception, performing no better than the rest of us when they are put to the test (Feeley & Young, 1998).

Police interviewers are also vulnerable to **deception stereotypes**: actions believed to be (though usually not) associated with lying, such as avoiding eye contact, and fidgeting. In one series of studies with considerable implications for cross-cultural police–citizen interactions everywhere, researchers in the Netherlands discovered evidence of racial discrimination in police–citizen interviews: a tendency for police interrogators to judge black citizens' nonverbal communication, which typically includes more speech hesitations, smiling, and gesturing, as more deceptive than that of white citizens (Vrij & Winkel, 1991, 1992, 1994). Adding further support to this finding, recent study of 120 videotaped noncriminal police interactions with law-abiding citizens showed that black and Hispanic citizens in these encounters exhibited more "suspicious" nonverbal cues, such as gaze aversion, speech hesitations, smiles, and hand gestures, than did the white citizens (Johnson, 2006).

ORAL PRESENTATIONS Many people in the workplace must sometimes give oral presentations. The delivery of those presentations—the speaker's nonverbal communication—can determine whether or not the audience pays attention to or cares about the speaker's message. What constitutes an effective delivery?

There is no shortage of advice in the popular and academic literature about delivering an effective speech. Typical recommendations include making eye contact with individual audience members; using smooth, forceful gestures; not standing too far from the audience; using pauses for emphasis; adjusting vocal volume; enunciating; expressing emotions through the face and voice; dressing to gain respect; speaking fluently; and so on. While most of these recommendations seem to reflect a consensus among experts and probably resonate with beginning and experienced public speakers alike, many have never been tested adequately in scientific studies, leaving unanswered questions about the relative impact of nonverbal signals on various indexes of speaking effectiveness—comprehension, attraction, credibility, attitude change, and the like.

Research recommends the use of nonverbal involvement behaviors. In one study, for example, communication researchers Judee Burgoon, Thomas Birk, and Michael Pfau (1990) studied the nonverbal communication of undergraduate students who were assigned to give in-class persuasive speeches. They found that the student speakers most likely to be evaluated by audience members as credible and persuasive were the ones who exhibited nonverbal immediacy and expressiveness: facial expressiveness, facial pleasantness, pitch variety, eye contact, vocal fluency, body lean, and body relaxation. Other studies indicate that speakers are also likely to be persuasive if they speak moderately fast and loud and move toward their audience. While these findings seem to imply that a single style of public speaking is most successful, other research suggests that a dynamic style of speaking (e.g., rapid, loud, high-pitched speech) is especially effective for well-liked and highly respected speakers, whereas a more conversational style (e.g., slower, softer, calmer, lower-pitched speech) may be best for everyone else (Burgoon et al., 1996).

Some studies highlight the impact of a speaker's delivery in workplace settings. One study of a salesperson's nonverbal communication in an industrial sales call found that professional buyers rated the salesperson as more believable when he used a steady gaze and more interesting and persuasive when he avoided speech hesitations in his presentation (Leigh & Summers, 2002). Another study found that the speech delivery of a bogus CEO was more effective with eye contact, fluency, smiles, and dynamic gestures and that the speaker's delivery was a more important predictor of his performance than either his vision for the company or the success of the company (Awamleh & Gardner, 1999). Other studies also show that the delivery of a leader is more predictive of a leader's charisma than is the "visionary content" of a leader's message (Holladay & Coombs, 1993, 1994).

The most ambitious and groundbreaking program of research to date has been exploring the use of "social sensing" technology developed at MIT's digital media laboratory (including mobile sensors called *sociometers*) to capture, measure, and analyze the effects of nonverbal communication—tone of voice, rate of speech, body posture, gestures, proximity, and more—in a variety of naturally occurring face-to-face interactions, including brief oral presentations. Led by management scholar and computer scientist Alex Pentland, researchers have been able to quantify the impact of speech delivery with greater precision than ever before. In one study, for example, Pentland and his colleagues arranged a contest for students in MIT's Executive MBA program to determine who would do the best job of pitching a complex business plan to a group of their peers and charged them with the task of deciding which of the plans to submit for consideration to a panel of venture finance experts (Pentland, 2008). As a requirement for participation in the contest, each student had to wear one of the MIT lab-developed mobile sensors while delivering his or her presentation (these badge-like devices were attached to their clothing). The results of the study confirmed the powerful impact of a speaker's delivery. As Pentland concludes,

> The executives thought they were evaluating the plans based on rational measures, such as: How original is this idea? How does it fit the current market? How well developed is this plan? While listening to the pitches, though, another part of their brain was registering other crucial information such as: How much does this person believe in this idea? How confident are they when speaking? How determined are they to make this work? And the second set of information—information that the business executives didn't even know they were assessing—is what influenced their choice of business plans to the greatest degree. (p. 71)

Few people in the workplace give more oral presentations than teachers do. If there is a link between successful speaking and nonverbal communication, the classroom could be an ideal place to find out. Numerous studies show that teachers who use an array of involvement behaviors in their classroom presentations—making a lot of eye contact, getting close to students, using touch, exhibiting open body positions, showing emotion through facial and vocal expressions, gesturing, smiling, and so on—tend to receive higher student evaluations (i.e., the students like the course more) and tend to have students who believe they learn more. A teacher's nonverbal communication during an oral presentation has such a powerful effect on student attitudes that observers can make accurate predictions of a college instructor's end-of-term student evaluations after exposure to just a few seconds of the instructor's content-free nonverbal behavior during a single lecture (Babad, Avni-Babad, & Rosenthal, 2004). Despite these effects, there is little evidence that a teacher's nonverbal communication directly affects students' learning of course content (Witt, Wheeless, & Allen, 2004). For instance, one controlled experiment compared the impact of a fluent and a non-fluent style of delivering the same lecture. One group of students was randomly assigned to the fluent lecture, where the instructor stood upright in front of a desk, gestured, maintained direct eye contact, and spoke in a fluent manner without the use of notes; another group of students was randomly assigned to the non-fluent lecture, where the instructor hunched over a podium behind the desk, read from notes, intermittently looked at her notes and her audience, read haltingly and flipped through her notes several times. Although the students assigned to the fluent lecture gave the instructor higher evaluations and felt they learned more than the students assigned to the non-fluent lecture, there were no differences in what the students actually learned (Carpenter, Wilford, Kornell, & Mullaney, 2013).

SUMMARY

In everyday workplace encounters, nonverbal communication announces and reinforces the differences in status that exist between members of an organization. These status reminders, common in most asymmetrical relationships, come in many different forms: dressing up or dressing down, size, "do not disturb" signs, getting close (invading another's personal space), holding the center of attention, the cold shoulder, the silent treatment, kicking back, the voice of authority, tardiness, monopolizing a conversation, and an emotional roller coaster. Although the use of these signals is inevitable and necessary, their misuse can lead to serious problems. Dysfunctional leadership can result when a leader ignores the danger of mismatched behavior or when a leader succumbs to sex-role stereotyping. Sexual harassment can occur when one person misreads the nonverbal signals of another. Workplace discrimination can occur when employers favor high-status nonverbal signals over lower-status signals. Cross-cultural misunderstandings can occur when persons from different cultures overlook each other's interpretations of status signals.

The success of many task-oriented encounters often depends on the use of nonverbal communication. Becoming aware of nonverbal expectancy effects—the nonverbal cues that create counterproductive, self-fulfilling prophecies—requires an individual to monitor the subtle signals that can reveal his or her expectations. Emotional exchanges also have important consequences in the workplace. These exchanges include the process of contagion, emotional labor, and emotion recognition. In addition, the use of nonverbal involvement behaviors—smiling, leaning forward, eye contact, touch, facial and vocal expressiveness, speech fluency, and so forth—can contribute in varying degrees to the success of customer service transactions, professional interviews, and oral presentations.

KEY TERMS

Asymmetrical relationships 357
Behavioral flexibility 370
Deception stereotypes 394
Emotional dissonance 383
Emotional labor 382
Expectancy effects 380
Negativity bias 391
Power distance 367
Powerless stereotypes 375
Sex-role stereotyping 364
Status reminders 355
Visual dominance ratio 360

Getty

Chapter Outline

11

NONVERBAL COMMUNICATION IN MEDIATED ENCOUNTERS

It was a remarkable achievement. Responding to allegations that he was improperly using a secret campaign fund, Republican vice-presidential candidate Richard Nixon went before the American people in 1952. What followed was an unprecedented speech in which Nixon, taking the offensive and denying the charges against him, confessed only to accepting a single personal gift—a cocker spaniel named Checkers. Making little use of his handwritten notes, his gaze focused almost continuously on the camera, Nixon won the hearts of the American people. While fewer than half of the electorate could name the Republican candidate for vice president before the speech, Nixon was a household name after it (Bochin, 1990).

This chapter focuses on the importance of nonverbal communication in mediated encounters, those we have each time we turn on a television, answer a phone, or go online. In the sections that follow, we'll examine three basic kinds of media encounters: those that keep us connected to the outside world, those that seek to influence us, and those that assimilate us into the popular culture.

INFORMATIVE ENCOUNTERS: STAYING CONNECTED

To some extent, all of us rely on mediated communication to maintain the ties we have with the outside world: keeping up with the news of the day, sharing information with family and friends, doing business, getting an education, building

Learning Objectives

After reading this chapter, you will be able to do the following:

1. Describe the role of nonverbal communication in media coverage of the news.
2. Compare and contrast the differences between face-to-face and online forms of communication in the context of everyday interactions.
3. Discuss how the relative absence of nonverbal cues affects new media efforts to build and manage social relationships.
4. Analyze how reduced social presence affects the success of distance education programs.
5. Review and explain the impact of physical appearance and nonverbal behavior on the persuasiveness of political speakers and the success of commercial advertisers.
6. Discuss how media images of physical appearance and nonverbal behavior become part of the popular culture.

relationships, and so on. Whether it's through a television program, magazine, Internet site, or text messaging account, mediated communication is part of our everyday lives. While clearly no substitute for the immediacy of being there, modern technology lets us stay connected in ways that improve the overall quality of our lives. Of course, some media bring us closer to the real thing than others do. A news story presented on television gives us a richer and more immediate sense of the story than does a printed version reported in the newspaper. Text messaging doesn't give us the vocal or visual cues we need to appreciate fully the presence of another person, but the availability of vocal cues in a phone conversation represents a decided edge over an e-mail message. We begin this section by examining the importance of nonverbal communication in television news. Then we turn our attention to interactive uses of media.

Media Coverage of the News

Of the media sources available to us, television gives us the most graphic account of the day's news. Aside from witnessing an event firsthand, watching a live telecast is the next best thing. In addition, unlike print news, television news includes the nonverbal communication—the physical appearance, facial expressions, vocal cues, gestures, and so forth—of the people featured in a news story as well as those who report it. The presence of these nonverbal cues, as we'll see shortly, also brings a special set of challenges for those who produce the news and for those who deliver it.

NONVERBAL COMMUNICATION OF THE NEWS As we've seen in previous chapters, one way we communicate nonverbally is through physical appearance, which signals multiple identities (e.g., gender, age, ethnicity, etc.). Despite a steady increase in the hiring of women and minorities for various positions in the industry, the face of television news anchors at the highest levels generally remains stereotypically male, white, and middle aged. In addition, an implicit if not outright acceptance of the belief that what is beautiful is good seemingly forbids the hiring of unattractive persons—particularly so for women—for highly visible anchor positions (see section below on media bias). The demand for attractiveness also requires anchors to have an attractive on-air voice, one that conforms to contemporary standards (e.g., low pitched, fluent, accent free).

Television journalists also communicate nonverbally with approach–avoidance signals and with facial and vocal expressions of emotion. In the case of newscasters sitting behind a desk, the need for ratings conflicts with the need for clear and impartial reporting to produce a highly restricted and somewhat paradoxical set of cues: approachability and detachment. Moderately close proximity, nearly continuous eye contact (levels that would be uncomfortable in a face-to-face encounter), carefully placed smiles (i.e., after an amusing story), and relaxed vocal tones enhance the apparent warmth and accessibility of news anchors while at the same time, restricted movement, minimal vocal intonation, and a neutral facial expression add to the clarity and objectivity of the presentation. The format of most local news programs also allows for lighthearted banter—laughter, smiles, sarcasm, an occasional touch, and so on—between anchors as a way of moving from one segment to the next (e.g., sports to weather). On rare occasions, such as when reporting tragic and horrific events, nonverbal displays of emotion belie the detached reserve of most television anchors. Yet even these moments reflect the routine demands of objective journalism. A study of television reporting during the first 24 hours following the 9/11 attacks found a "crisis management" style of emotional communication that unfolded in three distinct stages. Examining facial and bodily signs of emotion, researchers determined that nonverbal leakage varied across these stages, with the least emotion shown during the first stage of reporting, when describing events and staying on task is paramount, and the third stage of reporting, when journalists regain their composure and professional demeanor. Reporters were most expressive during the second stage, when making sense of the event for the public is most likely to evoke strong emotional reactions (Coleman & Wu, 2006).

▸ Television talk show host Chris Matthews interviews Barack Obama during the 2008 presidential campaign. The nonverbal communication of today's television interviewers ranges from polite and deferential to impolite and confrontational. Studies suggest that nonverbal cues may reveal an interviewer's bias in ways that escape the interviewer's awareness.

AP Images

Of course, the script-like nature of most broadcast news presentations doesn't apply to the many television interviewers who analyze the news. On talk shows, for instance, where there is little need to follow the emotional display rules that are supposed to preserve the integrity of straight news and where advocacy journalism often blurs the line between news and entertainment, we regularly see a wide range of nonverbal behaviors, from the active listening of style of CNN's former host Larry King (e.g., eye contact, close proximity, forward lean, smiles, laughter, soft vocal tones, friendly touches) to the more antagonistic questioning of MSNBC's Chris Matthews (e.g., few back channels, interruptions, frowns, harsh vocal tones, etc.) and the sarcastic, joking style of John Stewart, Bill Mahr, and others (smirking, eye rolling, jeering, etc.). Although some critics have accused former television hosts such as Larry King of doing more casual conversing than professional interviewing, media critic Howard Kurtz (1997) acknowledges the pros and cons of such a style:

> The benefits of a softer talk show are obvious. If guests don't have to stay in a defensive crouch, sparring with the host and fending off hostile queries, they can reveal more of themselves as real

> people. The downside is that they don't have to entertain tough questions—indeed, any uncomfortable question—that might make the program more than a publicity tool for whatever policy or product they are pushing at the moment. (p. 77)

If the "Larry King style" typifies a talk show in which an interviewer uses nonverbal cues to build a friendly relationship with a guest, The FOX News Channel's Bill O'Reilly and Shawn Hannity represent an opposing view, a television talk show in which interviewers set aside the usual display rules that urge them to be as polite and respectful as possible.

NONVERBAL COMMUNICATION IN THE NEWS Media coverage of the news sometimes includes headlines in which nonverbal communication plays a prominent role. After the jury acquittal of a white police office in the 2014 Ferguson, Missouri shooting of an unarmed black man, protestors across the country frequently were seen using a *hands up, don't shoot* gesture to represent what the protestors saw as another instance of police brutality against young black men. In one highly publicized case, for example, members of the St. Louis Rams football team came on to the playing field of a game using this protest gesture.

In political reporting, the media spin on these stories not only shapes our understanding of the nonverbal messages involved in a particular event but can also shape the course of future events. This talk or discourse about nonverbal communication, what some scholars call *meta-discourse*, offers a glimpse into how the media interpret nonverbal forms of expression and how these interpretations enter the public consciousness (Manusov & Jaworski, 2006). The fate of many politicians rests on how the media portray them to the public, and a politician's demeanor and looks sometimes count as much—if not more—in the minds of news reporters and analysts than a politician's words. The now historic "Dean Scream" is a case in point. While delivering a speech intended to rally a crowd of supporters following a disappointing result in the Iowa Caucus during the 2004 Presidential campaign, Democratic frontrunner Howard Dean shouted enthusiastically into his microphone over the loud cheering audience. Because his microphone filtered out the sound of the audience, leaving only the sound of his "scream" for television audiences to hear, his shrill display of emotion created a brief dramatic (and ridiculed) moment that television stations, in their lust for attention, broadcast over and over again, effectively ending any chance of success for the Dean campaign. In his book on the role of emotion in politics, Drew Westen (2007) offers this assessment of the media's coverage:

> Dean's famous "scream" was not the scream of an unbalanced, raving lunatic, as it was portrayed on television. It was a failed attempt to use a style of political rhetoric (the old-fashioned,

> pre-microphone style of yelling into a megaphone) with which he wasn't comfortable, to fire up his base on an evening that was a tremendous disappointment to both him and those who participated in his meteoric rise. The interpretation spun by the media was deeply unfair. (p. 298)

Likewise, during the 2008 Presidential debates, the Republican nominee, Senator John McCain rarely made eye contact with his Democratic rival, Senator Barack Obama. Many in the media were quick to call our attention to McCain's gaze avoidance, which they interpreted as an unmistakable sign of condescension (McKenzie, 2008). Before the debates, there were other examples of media headlines regarding the nonverbal behavior of the candidates. For example, the media paid a lot of attention to a "teary eyed" Hillary Clinton at a campaign stop in New Hampshire answering an audience member's question about how Clinton remained so "upbeat and wonderful." Most media accounts either framed the event as an instance of a woman showing genuine emotion, or, more cynically, as an instance of a politician manipulating her audience for political gain (Manusov & Harvey, 2011).

This type of discourse about nonverbal communication also appears in print accounts of the news. Like television broadcasts, these accounts can shape our understanding of important political events as well as the motivations of those ultimately responsible for the accounts. Communication researchers Valerie Manusov and her colleagues examined the media's coverage of the historic 1993 handshake between the Israeli Prime Minister Yitzhak Rabin and the Palestinian leader Yasser Arafat on the White House lawn in Washington. The occasion for the handshake was the signing of a Declaration of Principles for peace between Arabs and Israelis. Press coverage of the event offered commentary on the meanings of the handshake, the first-ever between the two men, as well as the meanings of other nonverbal cues surrounding the event. This commentary framed the event through representations and transformative meanings. Representations focused on how the handshake and other nonverbal cues symbolized something embedded in the event or context that is greater and more abstract than what those same behaviors would otherwise represent. These representations, depending on the source of the account, included messages of peace/hope/optimism, violence, betrayal, anguish, authority/legitimacy, agreement/promise, and dislike. Transformative meanings offered visions of what the future could bring, such as gaining legitimacy, increasing status, working as a cure, and taking a step backward (Manusov & Bixler, 2003; Manusov & Milstein, 2005).

In another discourse analysis study, researchers examined British press accounts of President Clinton's videotaped testimony to the grand jury in the Monica Lewinsky affair (Jaworski & Galasinski, 2002). The study examined newspaper descriptions and interpretations of Clinton's nonverbal behavior in the video and the extent to which a newspaper presented images with accompanying text to support their claims about Clinton's appearance during the testimony. The researchers found that newspapers focused more on constructing a version of Clinton's facial expressions, eye contact, tone of voice, gestures, and so forth that advanced the newspaper's own political agenda, sometimes favorable to Clinton and sometimes critical of Clinton, than on providing the most objective and accurate account of Clinton's behavior. As expected, some of the tabloids contained the most sensational depictions of Clinton's behavior.

NONVERBAL COMMUNICATION OF MEDIA BIAS The results of some studies raise questions about a newscaster's ability to inhibit facial signs of bias (eyebrow movements, smiles, and other idiosyncratic displays) while reporting the news (Friedman, DiMatteo, & Mertz, 1980; Mullen et al., 1986; Remmers, 1980; Tankard et al., 1977). In one study, for example, researchers found that some network newscasters (David Brinkley, Walter Cronkite, and Harry Reasoner) exhibited more positive facial expressions during their coverage of the 1976 presidential campaign while referring to Jimmy Carter than while referring to Gerald Ford (Friedman et al., 1980). In a similar investigation, another team of researchers confirmed the presence of a facial bias, this time during network coverage of the 1984 presidential campaign: ABC anchor Peter Jennings, but not NBC's Tom Brokaw or CBS's Dan Rathers, displayed more positive expressions while referring to Ronald Reagan than he did while referring to Walter Mondale. The researchers also found a connection between viewers' choice of candidates and their choice of network news programs: A greater percentage of ABC viewers voted for Reagan than did NBC or CBS viewers (Mullen et al., 1986). Although these results are intriguing, we still don't know how much bias of this kind actually exists and what impact, if any, it has on the attitudes and actions of viewers.

Nonverbal signs of preference go beyond the facial bias of news anchors. In the most extensive study of television news interviewers' nonverbal behavior to date, communication researcher Elisha Babad (1999) looked at the performance of seven Israeli television interviewers. Groups of American students, none of whom understood the language of the interviews (all in Hebrew), evaluated the behavior of each interviewer without seeing the interviewee. The interviewees represented one or the other of the two major political parties in Israel. Babad found significant differences in how each interviewer acted toward different interviewees (e.g., friendly, respectful, warm, agrees with, etc.). In particular, the ratings of two high-profile interviews of the candidates for prime minister, Shimon Peres and Benjamin Netanyahu, during the 1996 election campaign, showed that the same prominent interviewer treated one of the candidates much better than the other. As Babad concludes,

> [M]y interpretation is that [the interviewer's] differential conduct was preferential and predisposed, that his own personal liking and political preference shaped his nonverbal behavior, and that he intended to influence viewers to favor [one candidate] and to demean [the other candidate]. (p. 346)

An analysis of the interviewers' nonverbal behavior revealed that each interviewer had a unique style for expressing positive and negative attitudes. But in general, they tended to signal their preferences with smiles, a relaxed face, head nods, forward lean, rhythmical hand gestures, blinking, head thrusts, sarcasm, and attempts to control the interviewee. Interestingly, more dominant and aggressive interviewers showed more preferential behavior, perhaps suggesting that these interviewers felt more justified in going after disliked interviewees.

In another study, Babad (2005b) found that the nonverbal bias of an interviewer could shape viewers' perceptions of the interviewee. In this experiment, non-Hebrew-speaking British and American students viewed one of two versions of an edited videotaped interview spoken in Hebrew, one with the interviewer using friendly nonverbal behaviors or another with the same interviewer using unfriendly nonverbal behaviors. Both versions of the video contained the same video clips of the interviewee, described as a politician, as though he was responding directly to the interviewer presented in the video. Viewers rated the politician as more genuine, convincing, optimistic, cheerful, more likely to win election, and even as more handsome, when they saw him with the friendly interviewer than with the unfriendly interviewer. While an in-depth analysis of similar experiments in seven other countries confirms the impact of this nonverbal interviewer bias, studies document various ways of minimizing and even counteracting its effects (Babad & Peer, 2010). For instance, an audience is less likely to be influenced by interviewer bias if they are instructed to ignore the interviewer, if the interviewee adopts a more relaxed demeanor in response to the interviewer, and if the audience regards the interviewee as "one of us" (in-group member) rather than "one of them" (out-group member).

Another nonverbal indicator of media bias is the physical appearance of newscasters. In the past, for example, when women and minorities simply weren't hired, the exclusive presence of white male journalists constituted an unequivocal sign of sexist and racist policies. Although few women and minorities occupy the most prestigious positions, their on-air presence cannot be overlooked. Nearly two decades ago, one study reported that 11 of the 13 stations among the nation's 25 largest markets employed at least one black in a coanchor role (Entman, 1990). As communications researcher Robert Entman argues, the presence of black news anchors, which signals an end to what he calls "old-fashioned racism" (i.e., the belief that blacks are inferior), belies the prevalence of "modern racism," a media bias favoring stories that are likely to fuel negative attitudes toward blacks (e.g., black crime, self-serving black politics). Some studies also confirm the existence of a local news bias that favors negative stories of young blacks over positive stories (Woodruff, 1998).

As we've seen in previous chapters, a beauty bias favors attractive people in all walks of life. In the workplace specifically, attractive individuals are more likely than less attractive individuals to be hired for all sorts of jobs (Hatfield & Sprecher, 1986, pp. 55–67). The need for audience approval makes it unlikely that television news anchors will ever escape this beauty bias. Consider the landmark case of Christine Craft. Nine months after being hired in 1981 as a news anchor for KMBC-TV in Kansas City, Missouri, 37-year-old Christine Craft was demoted from anchor to reporter because, as she put it, she was "too old, too unattractive, and not deferential enough to men." Craft filed a $1.2 million lawsuit against the station for alleged sex discrimination and was awarded $500,000 in 1983, but she lost it on appeal three years later. (During the same week, the California state senate unanimously adopted a resolution honoring her in connection with the state's observance of Women's History Week!) The case sparked a great deal of controversy at the time over the treatment of women in broadcasting.

Interactive Uses of Media

Whether it's a cell phone call, a text message, an e-mail, or an Internet site, every day we rely on mediated forms of communication to exchange information with others. The various uses of social media platforms continue to grow. The most recent Pew Research survey of adults (18 years of age or older) reported the following trends (Duggan, 2015):

- 85% of adults are Internet users and 67% are smartphone users.
- 31% of online adults use Pinterest, with women users far exceeding men users by a wide margin of 44% to 16%.
- 28% of online adults use Instagram, a number that has doubled since the Pew Research Center first started tracking social media platform adoption in 2012. Women users outnumber men users 31% to 24%.
- Facebook remains the most popular social media site; 72% of online adults are Facebook users, amounting to 62% of all American adults. But there has not been a significant change in the overall share of users since 2012. Those on Facebook remain highly engaged, with 70% saying they log on daily, including 43% who log on several times a day.

- 25% of online adults use LinkedIn, up from 20% in 2012.
- 20% of online adults use Twitter; a 4% increase from the 16% who did so in 2012. Twitter is more popular among adults under age 50 (30%) than among those over age 50 (11%).

The relationship between nonverbal communication and our use of media is obvious—some types of media provide access to more nonverbal cues than other types do. Face-to-face communication provides the greatest access, followed by video, audio, and text-only communication modalities. In a well-known and widely cited series of experiments, psychologist Albert Mehrabian compared the relative weight we attach to facial, vocal, and verbal channels of communication when judging a speaker's feelings; that is, whether the speaker likes or dislikes something. The results from these studies showed a heavy reliance on nonverbal over verbal messages: The speaker's facial expression accounted for 55% of the meaning attributed to the spoken message, the speaker's voice accounted for 38%, and the speaker's words accounted for the remaining 7% (Mehrabian & Ferris, 1967; Mehrabian & Weiner, 1967). Although these studies may exaggerate somewhat the relative impact of nonverbal cues (other studies suggest that nonverbal signals account for about 65% rather than 93% of the message), one overall conclusion still remains: When we need to exchange messages that convey our feelings, some communication channels are clearly more revealing than others (Burgoon, Buller, & Woodall, 1996; Hegstrom, 1979; Philpott, 1983).

COMPARING COMMUNICATION MEDIA One way of comparing communication media is in terms of **social presence**, our awareness of another person during an interaction. As an attribute, it refers to a medium's capacity to approximate the conditions of face-to-face communication (Short, Williams, & Christie, 1976). Differences in social presence can sometimes lead to differences in communication outcomes. Early research comparing interactions with relatively few nonverbal cues (e.g., not being able to see the other person) with face-to-face interactions discovered some key differences. For example, one study found that removing visual cues from an interaction generally made it more task-oriented, more impersonal, and less spontaneous than when visual cues were available (Argyle, 1988, p. 119). To some degree, research corroborates these findings when comparing computer-mediated with face-to-face communication (Hiltz, Johnson, & Turoff, 1986; Rice & Love, 1987). What makes the difference?

▸ Recent surveys confirm that most adults are now using smartphones to share information with others.

istockphoto.com/Petar Chernaev

Freed from distracting social cues, participants in voice-only or text-only interactions may find it easier to concentrate on the task at hand, which may partly explain why researchers in one early study found that negotiation sessions were more efficient—the person with the stronger case usually prevailed—when the participants worked in a low social presence environment (no visual cues) than in a face-to-face encounter (Morley & Stephenson, 1969). The near absence of nonverbal cues in most mediated forms of communication can make it difficult to form impressions of others, contributing to judgments that such interactions are relatively cold and impersonal. Yet research shows that we form many of the same kinds of impressions using online communication that we do in face-to-face conversations—it just takes longer and involves different sets of cues (Walther, 1993, 2006). Communication researcher Joe Walther and his colleagues have demonstrated how individuals adapt to the situation by using the communication resources available to achieve their interaction goals. For instance, one study compared computer-mediated communication (CMC) and face-to-face "get-acquainted" meetings and found that CMC users asked more personal questions and disclosed more information about themselves during their meetings than did the people in face-to-face meetings (Tidwell & Walther, 2002). Another study showed that when

RESEARCH 11.1

FIND OUT MORE

Online Pauses and Silences: Do They Leave a Bad Impression?

One exception to the lack of nonverbal cues in e-mail communications is the use and interpretation of time. For instance, not responding to an e-mail—or not responding to an e-mail in a timely fashion—can create a bad impression in the mind of the person who sent the e-mail. In this study, the researchers hypothesized that waiting 12 days to respond or not responding even after a month, compared to a more expected single-day response, would leave a much worse impression of a job applicant. They found, however, that it didn't matter much if the person who sent the e-mail had an unfavorable impression of the job applicant in the first place.

To find out more about this study and to answer the following questions, see the full text (cited below).

1. What is EVT and how was it used in this study?
2. Who were the participants in this study and what did they do?
3. What were the main limitations of this study?
4. What kind of study is this? (See Appendix.)

Source: Kalman, Y. M., & Rafaeli, S. (2011). Online pauses and silence: Chronemic expectancy violations in written computer-mediated communication. *Communication Research*, 38, 54–69.

prompted to convey greater liking toward a conversational partner, computer chat users were just as able to get the message across to their partner as were participants in face-to-face conversations. In contrast to the CMC users, participants in the face-to-face conversations got their message across not by *what* they said but by *how* they said it (Walther & Bunz, 2005).

One theory seems to be that text-based media users, at first, form impressions that lack the scope of those they form in face-to-face and telephone interactions, but the impressions are more intense (Lea & Spears, 1992, 1995; Spears & Lea, 1994; Walther, 1996, 1997). That is, given the lack of nonverbal cues, CMC users don't have the social information to make *as many* judgments about the person with whom they are interacting as do individuals who participate in face-to-face or phone conversations. Additionally, this lack of social information prompts CMC users to rely more heavily on simple and exaggerated stereotypes. This is, in fact, what researchers discovered in one study comparing the first impressions of interaction partners who used CMC to work on a cooperative task with those who used face-to-face interaction (Hancock & Dunham, 2001).

PERSONAL EXPERIENCE 11.1

CAN YOU RELATE TO THIS?

Sometimes We Need Face-to-Face Communication

I recently got together with a group of guys and girls I knew from high school that I didn't get along with. First we were friends, then we were enemies. My girlfriend, who used to be friends with them, too, was the first person I called after I saw them. I began telling her what each person said, along with their gestures and expressions. We always ask each other for these clues. It was so hard to describe them to her that I had to drive over to her house and start the story from the beginning. It was so much more effective being face-to-face than trying to tell the story over the phone. The visual cues helped my girlfriend get the full effect.

Connie

Other studies also show that CMC can produce more simplistic first impressions. In one interesting series of experiments, researchers found that the same verbal responses to interviewers' questions led to more biased first impressions and racial stereotyping if the interviewers received the answers to their questions in the form of an e-mail than if they received the answers over the telephone. In the first experiment, the researchers gave some of these interviewers (college undergraduate participants) the impression that the person they were about to interview is intelligent, while they gave other interviewers the opposite impression, that the person is unintelligent. These bogus expectancies left more of a lasting impression on the interviewers in the e-mail condition, where they had less social information to use, than in the telephone condition, where they could use vocal cues to alter their preconceived notions. A second experiment provided further support for the idea that we are more vulnerable to simplistic first impressions when the media we use deprives us of nonverbal social cues. The researchers gave the interviewers bogus photographs leading them to believe that the interviewee was either an Asian American woman or a black woman. Racial stereotyping was more pronounced over e-mail than over the telephone. That is, using e-mail, interviewers were more likely to describe the same woman as shy and timid (a racial stereotype) if they thought she was Asian American than if they thought she was black (Epley & Kruger, 2005).

Over time, new media users find ways to compensate for the lack of nonverbal cues, adapting to the resources available. One way, the use of **emoticons**, lets users express emotions by constructing facial expressions from various combinations of keyboard characters, such as :-) for smiling and :-(for frowning. One study found that including emoticons in an e-mail had limited effects. Smiley faces made no difference in readers' interpretations of positive or negative verbal statements about a college course. A winking emoticon ;) did manage to turn a positive message into a sarcastic one. Overall, the researchers found a negativity bias that led readers to interpret any e-mail message about the college course in a negative way if it contained either a frowning emoticon or a negative statement about the course (Walther & D'Addario, 2001). But a similar study, with Dutch secondary school students as participants, found that emoticons added intensity to a positively worded message (making it seem more positive) or a negatively worded message (making it seem more negative). In addition, a contradictory emoticon (i.e., a smiley face along with a negatively worded message; a frowning face with a positive message) succeeded in adding an element of sarcasm to the interpretation of the message (Derks, Bos, & Grumbkow, 2008).

Without the benefit of facial expressions, tone of voice, or emoticons, how well do we exchange sarcastic text-only messages? Apparently, we aren't as good as we think we are. One team of researchers conducted a series of experiments to test their hunch that e-mail users, well aware of the difficulties they face, are consistently overconfident in their ability to get their messages across (Kruger, Epley, Parker, & Ng, 2005). In one experiment, pairs of participants (undergraduates) selected a list of statements, half serious and half sarcastic, about a variety of topics. Their task was to communicate the intended meaning of each statement to their partner by using either e-mail or speech. As expected, participants using speech were far more successful (73%) than were those using e-mail (56%). But, while the speakers were realistic in their expectations (78% predicted success), the e-mail users were not (78% also predicted success). In another experiment, the researchers found that e-mail users were also more overconfident in their ability to express anger and sadness than were participants who had access to either speech-only or face-to-face channels of communication. Why the overconfidence? It appears that egocentrism is to blame. Thinking about how a statement sounds to us, we assume it will sound that way to others, even if there's nothing for them to hear. When e-mail users in another experiment had to first say their statement out loud and in a way that was opposite of how it was intended (saying a sarcastic statement in a serious one and a serious statement in a sarcastic tone), they were no longer overconfident.

▸ Are emojis an adequate substitute for the emotional cues we exchange in face-to-face interactions?

istockphoto.com/yuoak

So emoticons may enhance or contradict the verbal content of a message, but they may also reveal the cultural affiliation of the user. In a recent study of twitter messages, researchers found an interesting cultural difference in the construction of emoticons. Persons from collectivist cultures, particularly the East Asian countries of Japan, Korea, China, and Thailand, tend to use vertical emoticons that emphasize the eye region of the face for expressing an emotion such as ^_ ^ whereas persons from individualistic cultures tend to use horizontal emoticons that emphasize changes in the mouth region of the face, such as :) (Park, Baek, & Cha, 2014).

Other methods of conveying emotion with standard keyboard characters include embedded texts that bracket an expression (e.g., <smile>, <frown>) and explicit statements such as, "I'm kidding!" (Jacobson, 1996). There are many ways of using textual cues to replace nonverbal cues, such as the use of exclamation points to add emphasis or express excitement, a repeated vowel to inject a sarcastic tone, or capital letters to intensify an emotion.

In recent years, keyboards on computers, smartphones, and tablets have made it easy for users to insert an array of colorful pictographs called **emojis** into their text-based messages. Emojis can represent human faces, animal faces, and a variety of objects for the purpose of expressing the feelings, thoughts, intentions, and moods of the user. According to one study, the most popular emojis around the world are happy faces, followed by sad faces, hearts, and hand gestures (Goldsborough, 2014). Over time, users find that emojis can serve a variety of functions. Based on interviews of individuals around the world, one team of researchers found that respondents reported using emojis to conceal or mask how they really felt about something, to let someone know they were thinking of them without having to put it in words (like a touch, smile, or glance they might use in face-to-face situations), to play or act silly with someone, and to communicate in a special way that is exclusive to a particular relationship (Kelly & Watts, 2015).

PERSONAL EXPERIENCE 11.2

CAN YOU RELATE TO THIS?

Social Media Users Find Ways to Account for Kidding and Sarcasm

When AOL came out, my family was one of the last families to get a computer and to use the Internet. Most of my friends were seasoned pros at instant messaging. When I got [an instant message], I found that I would get very confused about knowing whether someone was kidding. For example, I was typing to a friend and he said something mean. After he finished; he typed "JK!" I was confused by this and thought that he was insulting me again. I asked him what *JK* meant and he sent back a message saying it meant "Just kidding." I was relieved that he wasn't insulting me.

Rob

Naturally, new media users do not have the same access to the social cues and spontaneous emotional exchanges that accompany face-to-face and, to a lesser degree, phone conversations. This puts added pressure on users to compensate with strategies aimed at acquiring information about a person's identity, attitudes, and feelings (Ramirez, Walther, Burgoon, & Sunnafrank, 2001). It also puts pressure on message senders to think of ways that heighten the social presence of their communication. For instance, researchers in one study found that including a digital photograph along with an e-mail request to participate in a survey was sufficient to increase their compliance rate from 58% to 84% (Gueguen & Jacob, 2002b).

Developers of new technologies continue to enrich the online and mobile messaging environment with products and services that help us connect with others. **Social networking sites**, such as **Facebook**, enable users to exchange information that goes beyond the text-based messages of the past. For more than a decade, Facebook has been giving subscribers an opportunity to post photographs that can provide a visual image of how they see themselves and how they want others to see them, thereby contributing to the identification function of nonverbal communication that we explored in Chapter 3. One recent study of 1,744 Facebook users from 20 different countries found that profile photos conveyed important information about the user's identity and included photos representing the following categories: face shot, interests, special occasion, posing alone, humorous, family, playing sports, socializing, romantic, supporting a cause, and unique location. The photos also reflected the user's personality, the feedback they received from their peers, and how people reacted to the photo choices of their peers (Wu, Chang, & Yuan, 2015).

Facebook profile photos also reveal information about the cultural orientation and gender of the user. In a study comparing East Asian, collectivistic societies and the individualistic orientation of Americans, for example, researchers found that East Asians were more likely to use photographs that highlighted various contextual features (deemphasizing the face of the user) while Americans, consistent with a more self-focused perspective, were more likely to use images that highlighted their faces (Huang & Park, 2013). Gender also influences one's selection of profile photos. While men tend to select pictures that highlight their status (e.g., objects and clothing) and risk-taking experiences in outdoor settings, women are more likely to use pictures that highlight family relationships and emotional expression (Tifferet & Vilnai-Yavetz, 2014).

The growing popularity of **avatars**, graphic two-dimensional images users can move around a computer screen, demonstrates an interest in continuing to reduce the impersonal dimensions of text-based communication. One study of instant messaging comparing the effects of avatars and emoticons found that the use of facially expressive avatars increased participants' levels of involvement in but not their overall enjoyment of an interactive problem-solving task. Of particular interest was the occurrence of some facial mimicry between avatars, raising the possibility that expressive avatars may heighten levels of empathy among users. Moreover, the researchers found that participants who did engage in more of these emotional exchanges rated and described their experience as more entertaining and liked their partner more than did the other participants (Fabri, Moore, & Hobbs, 2005). Some research reveals other interesting parallels between the nonverbal behavior of avatars and that of their human counterparts. For example, in an observational study of Second Life, a virtual community, researchers found that gender differences transferred into the virtual environment. Male dyads maintained greater distances and made less eye contact than did female dyads, and decreases in interpersonal distance were compensated with gaze aversion (Yee, Bailenson, Urbanek, Chang, & Merget, 2007). Similarly, another study using avatars found that females high in social anxiety were more likely to avert the steady gaze of an approaching male avatar than were females who were

▸ Technological innovations in computer-mediated forms of communication continue to recognize the importance of social presence.

istockphoto.com/Zinkevych

lower in social anxiety (Wieser, Pauli, Grosseible, Molzow, & Mulberger, 2010). Cultural differences in approach–avoidance signals may also appear in virtual environments. Researchers in one study of dyadic avatar interactions found that Asians preferred greater distances in their avatar interactions that Europeans did, which is consistent with what one would expect in human face-to-face interactions (Hasler & Friedman, 2012). So there is evidence that interactions with avatars in a virtual environment may mirror some of the nonverbal behavior we would expect in real face-to-face interactions. But there is far less evidence that avatars are capable of creating the kind of social presence we often desire in our interactions with others. Perhaps the closest we can come to achieving a high degree of social presence with mediated forms of communication may be with face-to-face video chat applications (e.g., Skype, Facetime).

Social presence may not always be advantageous, however. The absence of visual cues in some situations, for example, may facilitate lie detection. In fact, the greater likelihood that certain kinds of lies, such as fabricating a story, produce more verbal and vocal than facial or body clues suggests that lie catchers use a telephone rather than a face-to-face conversation. Reducing social presence can also be desirable in research interviews, where even the slightest nonverbal signal from an interviewer can bias respondents' answers to questions (Persichitte et al., 1997). Moreover, certain people may benefit from a communication environment that minimizes social presence. Whereas shy and socially anxious individuals typically avoid face-to-face contact with others, one study found that shy persons were no less likely to use Internet services such as e-mail and chat rooms than persons who are not shy (Scealy, Phillips, & Stevenson, 2002). And a survey of university undergraduates found that nearly half felt less shy on the Internet than they did in face-to-face situations (Knox, Daniels, Sturdivant, & Zusman, 2001).

Another consequence of reduced social presence that has both desirable and undesirable consequences is a phenomenon known as **disinhibition**—being less concerned with self-presentation and the judgment of others and acting accordingly (Joinson, 1998). Armed with a sense of personal anonymity and shielded from the instantaneous and unpleasant emotional reactions of others (e.g., a look of hurt, embarrassment, anger, fear, shame), people often say things online they would never say in a face-to-face encounter (Donn & Sherman, 2002; Levine, 2000). On the positive side, this can produce more open and honest communication. But on the negative side, it can produce hurt feelings, resentment, and more (Turner, 1998).

Performance feedback is one example. Research shows that an evaluator is more likely to give a negative appraisal of someone's work when delivering it through e-mail than when delivering it face-to-face (Hebert & Vorauer, 2003). Despite the many advantages of using media to reduce social presence, the usual test for new media is how successfully they approximate the look and feel of face-to-face communication. The next section briefly considers some everyday applications.

APPLICATIONS OF INTERACTIVE MEDIA As we move further into the twenty-first century, technological innovations will continue to give us more opportunities to meet new people and to stay in touch with people we know. Whether for business or pleasure, these developments can produce convenient and cost-saving alternatives to face-to-face meetings. This section considers two applications of interactive media that are changing the landscape of our everyday lives: building personal relationships and pursuing an education.

Despite the opportunities afforded by social media, most studies confirm that we use mobile devices and social networking sites mainly for communication with a small handful of people: close friends, family members, and intimate partners. Also, instead of using them to start up new relationships, we tend to use them for maintaining or deepening already-existing offline relationships (Chambers, 2013). At times, mobile devices can actually lessen the chances of meeting new people. For example, one study found that using a mobile device can disrupt the simple exchange of friendly smiles that often occurs during brief moments of eye contact as pedestrians approach and pass each other (Patterson, Lammers, & Tubbs, 2014). Even the mere presence of a mobile device can impair the quality and likelihood of starting a conversation and building a relationship by interfering with the nonverbal signals we may otherwise use to establish a face-to-face connection and build conversational rapport (Pryzbylski & Weinstein, 2012).

Still, social uses of mediated interaction have changed the way we develop and maintain personal relationships. For teens, in particular, talking face-to-face has become the exception rather than the rule. According to the latest Pew Research Center survey (Lenhart, Madden, Macgill, & Smith, 2015), texting is their preferred method of communicating with close friends (49%), followed by social media (20%), and phone calls (13%). But teens are aware of the risks involved in relying on social media. The survey reports that 77% of teens agree that social media allows people to be less authentic than they would be offline. Among teens with dating experience, 76% say they have never dated or hooked up someone they first met online.

In the general population, one in ten Americans have used an online dating site or mobile dating app themselves, and many people know someone who uses online dating or who has found a spouse or long-term partner through online dating. Public attitudes toward online dating have also become much more favorable in recent years, and social networking sites are now playing a major role when it comes to navigating and documenting romantic relationships. Online dating is most common among Americans in their mid-20s through mid-40s. Compared with eight years ago, online daters in 2013 are more likely to actually go out on dates with the people they meet on these sites. Some 66% of online daters have gone on a date with someone they met through an online dating site or application, a four-fold increase since 2005 (Smith & Duggan, 2013).

In face-to-face encounters, physical appearance and courtship signals play a prominent role in the initial stages, determining who gets together. In contrast, online courtship, what some call *cyber-flirting*, is more likely to begin with an exchange of text messages or a simple exchange of digital pictures. Individuals get to know each other and then decide whether to meet face-to-face (Levine, 2000). In a recent focus group interview study of Facebook users who had experience using the site to build intimacy, researchers found that it was helpful during the early stages of a relationship when the profile photos could be used as a source of information about a person and when the online messaging could be used as a way to avoid the discomfort, embarrassment, and anxiety that often accompanies face-to-face interactions (Fox, Warber, & Makstaller, 2013).

Online courtship has its costs and benefits. On the positive side, disinhibition may lead to more revealing and rewarding self-disclosures during the initial stages of an online courtship compared to a face-to-face courtship (Merkle & Richardson, 2000; Wysocki, 1998). But disinhibition can also result in the one thing people say they fear most about Internet romance: deception (Donn & Sherman, 2002). The feeling of anonymity coupled with the desire to make a good impression can tempt individuals to lie. In one survey of undergraduates, 40% admitted that they lied—mostly about their age, weight, appearance, and marital status (Knox et al., 2001). Yet a study that compared first impressions formed online and second impressions formed offline found little evidence of deception. Results showed that people were honest with each other online and most respondents reported being as or more attracted to their online partners with additional information obtained from phone calls, photographs, and face-to-face meetings (Albright, 2002). One survey reported a gender difference in online flirting. Women were more likely than men to use emoticons and other devices to convey their feelings (Whitty, 2004).

Jealousy is a potential source of conflict in a romantic relationship, and social networking sites such as Facebook can provide a source of threatening information capable of arousing jealous feelings. Researchers have shown how Facebook photos can arouse such feelings. In one study, researchers found that wall photos sent by a romantic partner's "rival" were especially threatening when the text message contained a suggestive emoticon (e.g., a winking emoticon attached to the text message, "It was great seeing you last night") than when it didn't. Not surprisingly, jealous feelings were greater if the rival happened to be attractive (Fleuriet, Cole, & Guerrero, 2014). In another study, participants became more jealous when they saw photos of their partner touching an opposite-sex friend (Miller et al., 2014.). In both studies, however, not everyone experienced the same jealous feelings. Women tended to feel more jealous than men; and individuals with dismissive attachment styles (i.e., positive sense of self, negative sense of others) were less jealous than individuals with insecure attachment styles (e.g., fear of rejection).

RESEARCH 11.2

FIND OUT MORE

What Do Facebook Profile Pictures Say about Our Relationships?

One of the signs of an intimate relationship is the feeling that you and your partner are connected in ways that reflect a shared identity, that you see your partner as an important part of who you are. In fact, research shows that this sense of shared or overlapping identities may indicate greater satisfaction with the relationship. Would there be any evidence of this in the photographs that people selected for their Facebook profiles? In this series of studies, researchers found that individuals who are happier in their relationships were more likely to post images of themselves and their partner as their main profile photo on Facebook compared to individuals who were not as happy in their relationships

To find out more about this study and to answer the following questions, see the full text (cited below):

1. Why did the researchers decide to study Facebook profiles in particular?
2. Was one study enough? Why did they decide to do three studies? In what ways did the research methods of these three studies differ?
3. How did the researchers recruit persons to participate in these studies?
4. How was relationship satisfaction measured in these studies?
5. Is there any reason to think that future studies might not replicate the result of these studies?

Source: Saslow, L. R., Muise, A., Impett, E. A., & Dubin, A. (2012). Can you see how happy we are? Facebook images and relationship satisfaction. *Social Psychological and Personality Science*, 4, 411–418.

Distance education is another application of interactive media. With the aid of online computer technology and video-conferencing systems, modern distance education programs create a real-time, multimedia, two-way communication-learning environment.

Early studies comparing distance education courses with traditional courses did not find different outcomes in terms of student learning—at least as far as grades are concerned (Storck & Sproull, 1995; Whittington, 1987). Studies also support the claim that students learn as much in online courses as they do in traditional classrooms (Francescato et al., 2006). Research continues to raise important questions, however, about the impact of distance learning environments on various social-emotional measures of success. In one early study, researchers found that students at remote locations perceived the instructor as behaving more distantly—less eye contact, fewer gestures, and more time behind the desk—than did students in the same classroom with the instructor (Freitas, Myers, & Avtgis, 1998). Such perceptions, a likely consequence of the instructor's reduced social presence, can have a negative impact on student evaluations of the course and the instructor (Geurrero & Miller, 1998; Hackman & Walker, 1990). Other early studies also found that students were less likely to form positive relationships with peers in a mediated environment than in a face-to-face setting (Storck & Sproull, 1995).

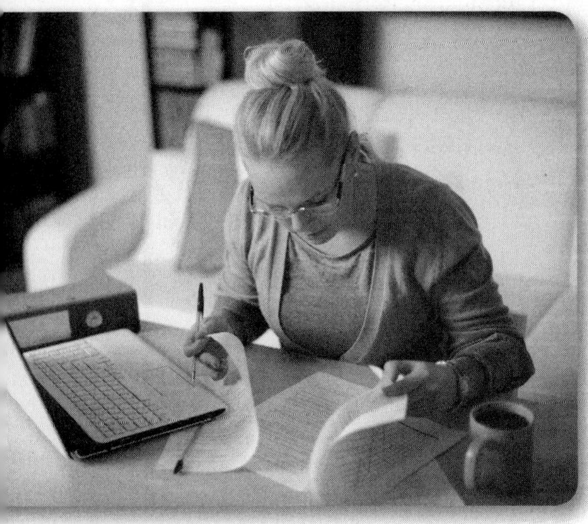

▸ Distance education is one important application of interactive media.

istockphoto.com/elenaleonova

Despite these early cautionary signs, there is no consistent evidence that the negative effects of reduced social presence are serious enough to outweigh the many tangible benefits of distance education offerings. Moreover, as new technology continues to enrich the social-emotional climate of these courses, student evaluations and other related outcomes are likely to improve. In fact, there is growing evidence that students and instructors adapt to these new learning environments, compensating in ways that produce social-emotional outcomes comparable in some ways to those of face-to-face settings. One study comparing online and face-to-face seminars taught by the same instructor over a two-month period found no differences in student perceptions of social presence and in their overall satisfaction with the course (Francescato et al., 2006). Research also suggests that student attitudes probably vary as a function of how much technology an instructor uses and how effectively an instructor uses nonverbal behaviors and other instructional resources to build rapport and intimacy with students (Schrodt & Witt, 2006).

In addition to the incorporation of synchronous forms of communication (i.e., teleconferences, video conferences), instructors can work to enhance the social presence of online learning environments with video recordings of lectures, personalized e-mail contact as early as possible, personal pictures of instructor and students, and coffee-shop exchanges that might occur outside the confines of the traditional classroom (Keengwe, Adjai-Boatng, & Diteeyont, 2013). Some researchers have also found that in collaborative virtual environments, the use of avatars to assist learning improved evaluations of the course and increased participants' involvement in their interactions and perceptions of others, although there was no direct evidence that their use increased the social presence of the learning experience (Allmendinger, 2010). Social presence is an ongoing concern, but as with other applications of interactive media, users continue to find innovative ways to compensate for the relative absence of nonverbal cues.

PERSUASIVE ENCOUNTERS: RESISTING INFLUENCE

Eight years after Richard Nixon's stunning triumph on national television (see the introduction to this chapter), he was eager once again to address the American people. But this time, television cameras recorded the birth of a new media star. It was September 26, 1960. Several points behind in the latest polls and projected as a near-certain loser in the upcoming election, Senator Kennedy had much to gain and little to lose from his decision to confront the vice president in a nationally televised debate. As history confirms, it was a good decision. Based on surveys conducted at the time, Nixon fared better among those who heard it on the radio than those who saw it on television (Bochin, 1990). Less physically attractive than his rival—a condition worsened by his pale complexion (he was recuperating from a knee infection), lack of rest, and unflattering attire—Nixon looked much worse than the tan, younger senator. No would-be persuader has disregarded the impact of television ever since. And no other single event gets more credit for changing the face of American political rhetoric and ushering in a new age of image consultants, media advisors, television ads, sound bites, and spin doctors—what many decry as an age of style over substance.

Politicians aren't the only ones on television trying to influence people. Perhaps nothing attests more to the persuasive power of television than does the amount of money advertisers spend to televise their messages. But even though the commercials might be more entertaining than some of the shows, how many turn on the television to watch an entertaining commercial? The fact that we don't choose to be influenced by much of what we see and hear makes the effect of these appeals—which rely heavily on the subtleties of nonverbal communication—all the more insidious. We begin this section with a brief review of the research on the persuasive effects of nonverbal communication and then we offer an explanation.

The Impact of Nonverbal Communication

How many people would say they decided to buy a product because of the voice-over in a television commercial or that they voted for a political candidate because of that candidate's facial expressions? Not many. Yet there is an abundance of evidence that people are influenced in ways that might surprise them. All things being equal, sometimes a single nonverbal cue can make a difference. Sometimes, in fact, the nonverbal message is the only message we receive. First, we'll consider the impact of physical appearance, and second, we'll examine the effects of nonverbal behavior.

PHYSICAL APPEARANCE How important is it to look good? Research reported in previous chapters showed that physical attractiveness has a significant impact on others, producing positive first impressions (Chapter 3), gaining the compliance of strangers (Chapter 7), attracting romantic partners (Chapter 8), and helping in the workplace (Chapter 10). It should come as no surprise, therefore, that good looks can also help a company sell a product or help a politician win an election.

In her review of the research on good looks and social influence, psychologist Shelly Chaiken (1986) cites several studies in which beauty paid off. In one study, for instance, researchers found that endorsements of a disposable razor by attractive celebrities elicited more positive attitudes and intentions to use the product than did endorsements by less attractive celebrities. In another study, student volunteers were more interested in a new

PERSONAL EXPERIENCE 11.3

CAN YOU RELATE TO THIS?

Good Looks Sell Products

When I go to the drugstore to buy a box of hair dye, I usually pick a color I like, but mostly I look at the attractive woman on the box, sometimes without even realizing that's what I'm doing. One time, my girlfriend picked out this nice hair color for me that probably would have looked pretty good. But I couldn't help noticing that I didn't like the woman on the box; I didn't think she was very attractive. I refused to buy the hair dye just because of that.

Daniela

pain reliever when the ad displayed an attractive person than when it showed an unattractive one. Men in another study were more receptive to the purchase of a brand of cologne when it was advertised by an attractive rather than by an unattractive woman. More recently, when researchers showed participants images of the same female model wearing different colored T-shirts, they found that the participants who saw the model when she had a genuine smile on her face evaluated the T-shirts more favorably than did participants who saw the model with a posed smile or with a neutral expression (Peace, Miles, & Johnston, 2006).

▸ The use of sexy and attractive models to sell products is well known and has been a part of the advertising industry for a long time. Are some consumers more likely to be influenced by these ads than other consumers?

istockphoto.com/travelif

Studies also show that politicians benefit from being attractive. In one experiment, researchers designed a mock election. They distributed campaign flyers to their subjects, each containing the picture, party affiliation, and issue positions of a candidate. They discovered that the photograph affected the candidate's perceived image, which in turn influenced the outcome of the election (Rosenberg, Bohan, McCafferty, & Harris, 1986). In fact, the impact of a candidate's looks may be too much for the public to resist. Researchers in one experiment were surprised to discover that people made stereotypical judgments about the personality of a political candidate based on that candidate's physical attractiveness, even when they were given more reliable and objective information on which to base their judgments (Budesheim & DePaola, 1994). Another study found that evaluations of a hypothetical politician's competency, trustworthiness, leadership ability, and qualifications varied along with the facial attractiveness of the politician (Surawski & Ossoff, 2006).

Another element of physical appearance related to good looks is sexiness. The use of attractive and sexy models in advertising is well known. But does sex sell? The answer seems to depend more on the gender of both the model and the targeted consumer than it does on the sexiness of the model. Even taking those factors into account, however, the effect of sexiness on attitudes does not necessarily correspond with its effect on other measures of advertising success, such as brand-name recognition and information recall. For instance, researchers in one study of magazine ads found that when an ad for a cross-training bicycle contained a sexy female model, males liked the ad and the product more than females did, but males recalled less about the claims made in the ad. Females who judged the ad had more negative attitudes toward both the ad and the product than did females who judged the same ad without a sexy female model. When the same ad had a sexy male model, male and female judges did not differ in any of their attitudes (Jones, Stanaland, & Gelb, 1998). For both men and women, sex appeal does not seem to have the completely positive effects advertisers would like. Sex appeal is also a cultural phenomenon, accepted as appropriate in some cultures more than in others. For example, one survey found that Asians regarded sex appeal in advertising as much less appropriate than did North American survey respondents (Sawang, 2010). Gender and cultural differences notwithstanding, as long as they catch the attention of consumers, the use of sexy models in advertising is not likely to diminish any time soon.

The impact of attractiveness and sex appeal may not come as much of a surprise. But we may be less aware of how we are influenced by other nonverbal signals related to physical appearance. In one study, researchers found that a woman received more pledges from her audience to contribute money for leukemia research when she wore a nurse's uniform than when she delivered the same message in a business suit. The woman's attire also affected her ability to obtain support for a local crime-stopping program. Audience members who saw her when she delivered the appeal in a sheriff's uniform pledged more support than did audience members who saw her make the same appeal in a business suit (Lawrence & Watson, 1991).

Some research suggests that the credibility of a speaker may depend on his or her facial features. Psychologists Sheila Brownlow and Leslie Zebrowitz (1990) hypothesized that a baby-faced speaker will have a more innocent-looking appearance than a speaker with mature facial features. As a result, the baby-faced speaker might be judged as having less expertise than a speaker with mature facial features, but the baby-faced features might make the speaker appear more trustworthy. Using videotaped broadcasts of weekday television commercials, Brownlow and Zebrowitz obtained independent ratings of the commercial spokespersons' facial maturity (baby face versus mature), attractiveness, age, smiling, trustworthiness, and expertise. As Table 11.1 shows, the results of their study provided clear support for their predictions: baby-faced men and women lost points on expertise but gained points on trustworthiness, and the results had nothing to do with differences in age, attractiveness, or amount of smiling. The effects of gender paralleled the effects of facial features: Men got higher ratings on expertise than women did, but they also got lower ratings on trustworthiness.

In the context of political negotiations, a recent study confirmed the impact of baby-faced features. Researchers gave Jewish-Israeli participants a news item containing a peace proposal along with a photograph identified as the Palestinian leader offering the proposal. The photograph included a digitized face that was altered to appear baby faced or mature faced by altering the size of the eyes and lips. Participants judged the peace proposal more favorably and rated the Palestinian leader as more trustworthy when he was baby faced than when he was mature faced (Maoz, 2012).

Table 11.1 Ratings of Male and Female Baby-Faced and Mature-Faced Commercial Spokespersons (on a Seven-Point Scale)

	Male Baby Face	Male Mature Face	Female Baby Face	Female Mature Face
Expertise	3.18	4.39	1.64	2.44
Trustworthiness	4.21	2.96	5.50	4.98

Research shows that split-second judgments of facial appearance carry a great deal of weight in predicting the outcome of political elections (Olivola & Todorov, 2010). For example, in one study, psychologist Alexander Todorov and his students discovered that facial appearance alone produces snap judgments of politicians' competence and trustworthiness and that these judgments can predict with much better-than-chance accuracy the outcome of an election. In one study, the researchers determined that 100 millisecond exposures to photographs of the faces of the winner and runner-up in each of the 2006 gubernatorial and Senate elections was sufficient for participants (who only saw the faces they did not recognize) to make competency judgments about the faces that, in turn, predicted the winner of the election about 70% of the time. Asking participants to take some time and make "good" judgments about which of the two persons in each photograph is the most competent decreased the accuracy of their judgments (Ballew & Todorov, 2007). In fact, these snap judgments are so consistently reliable and automatic that even young children aged five to 13 years are able to predict election outcomes based on nothing more than the facial appearance of the candidates (Antonakis & Dalgas, 2009).

Another promising line of inquiry with startling political implications focuses on the appeal of a digitally altered face that resembles our own. Just prior to the 2004 presidential election, Jeremy Bailenson and his colleagues conducted an intriguing experiment with a national sample of voting-age individuals. The participants were instructed to complete a survey of their attitudes toward President Bush and Senator Kerry while viewing side-by-side photos of the two candidates. The photos were altered so that a third of the participants viewed photos of themselves that were morphed at a 40–60 ratio into the photo of Bush, another third viewed photos of themselves morphed into the photo of Kerry, and another third, the control group, viewed the unaltered photos. The control group ended up favoring Bush by about the same margin as that of the election. But the participants morphed into the Bush photo favored Bush by five times the expected margin, while the participants morphed into the Kerry photo favored Kerry by a significant six-point spread (Bailenson & Yee, 2005). Considering the ease with which we can digitally alter an image and the potentially alarming practical consequences of such doctoring, future studies are likely to shed more light on how facial features affect our political judgments.

NONVERBAL BEHAVIOR The way a person looks can be persuasive. Research also shows that a speaker's nonverbal behavior can exert a strong influence on audience attitudes and perceptions. Reviews of the scientific literature usually conclude that several nonverbal behaviors can enhance in some way the persuasiveness of a speaker by creating an image of someone who is involved, enthusiastic, concerned, and responsive. These behaviors typically include eye contact, forceful gestures, open body positions, head nodding, close distances, touch, facial pleasantness, fluent speech, moderately loud vocal tones, moderately fast speech, and pitch variation (Burgoon et al., 1996).

EXERCISE 11.1

TRY THIS

Infomercial Persuasion

OBJECTIVE: To identify the persuasive nonverbal behaviors typically used in infomercials

INSTRUCTIONS: Watch part of a popular infomercial on television (e.g., sports equipment, diet programs, cleaning appliances, hair or skin care products, etc.). Use the checklist below to note how many of the 11 persuasive nonverbal behaviors are used by the spokesperson.

___ Close-ups	___ Head nodding	___ Moderately loud voice
___ Direct eye contact	___ Smiling	___ Pitch variety
___ Open body positions	___ Touch	___ Moderately fast speech
___ Big, forceful gestures	___ Fluent speech	

The nonverbal communication of political leaders becomes especially important during televised debates, where their every move is observed and judged by millions of voters. Even subtle signals contained in their voices may have unanticipated effects. In one study, researchers measured the vocal dominance expressed in voice samples obtained from 19 presidential debates, including the 1960 Kennedy–Nixon debate. Surprisingly, these measures were able to predict the popular vote outcome of all eight presidential elections (Gregory & Gallagher, 2002). Although we cannot calculate the persuasive impact of nonverbal cues on such a large scale, most political speakers realize the importance of conveying the best image possible. Prior to the 1976 presidential election, Jimmy Carter and Gerald Ford engaged in a series of nationally televised debates. Concerned about his image after the first debate, Carter's media advisor asked communication scholar Dale Leathers to offer some recommendations. Based on his analysis of the first debate, Leathers concluded that Carter could enhance his credibility by looking down less often before answering questions, paying more attention to Ford when Ford was speaking, shifting his gaze less often, slowing down his rate of speech, injecting more emotion into his voice, and hesitating less often (Leathers, 1997).

The 1996 presidential campaign offered a stark contrast in styles between the nonverbal communication of Bill Clinton and that of his rival Bob Dole. In his analysis of the two candidates, Leathers focuses on the nonverbal immediacy behaviors of both:

> Clinton's posture is open and relaxed. Moreover, Clinton looks like he is enjoying himself while interacting with an audience. If you had to choose a single word to characterize Clinton's nonverbal communication style, it would probably be pleasant. In contrast, Senator Dole often looks stern, serious, and unapproachable during his appearances in public. Clinton's great edge in pleasantness and likability may certainly be traced to the fact that he seems to minimize the distance between himself and those with whom he interacts, and he does so with a style that accentuates informality and close personal contact. Dole, in contrast, appears to cultivate a stiff informality that makes it difficult for people to get close to him at least in a figurative sense. (p. 241)

In his book, *The Political Brain*, Drew Westen (2007) suggests that the nonverbal demeanor of a political candidate can offer subtle cues to the candidate's character that can have an impact on voters:

> When the younger Bush's pollsters detected in early 2000 that his infamous smirk was creating "the wrong impression," they rapidly coached him on how to reflect gravitas instead of hubris. As it turns out, voters were not being "irrational" in their initial negative "take" on Bush's facial movements. They were detecting what turned out to be perhaps the central character defect that colored his presidency, a pathological certainty and smugness without regard to the facts. No one appears to have systematically coached Dukakis on the wooden use of his hands, Gore on the hinds of condescension in his demeanor, or Kerry on the emotional messages conveyed by his periodic lack of vocal intonation or facial movement. What candidates' faces, tone of voice, and gestures often reveal are aspects of their character to which voters

respond—and to which they sometimes should respond because they may provide a window into the soul of a person who can only be seen through a television glass darkly.

Sometimes the impact of nonverbal communication can be remarkably subtle. Researchers in political psychology have discovered, for example, that even a brief exposure to a political leader's facial expressions can evoke emotions in observers that lead to changes in attitudes toward that leader. In one series of experiments, they found evidence of empathy and emotional contagion (see Chapter 5). The facial muscle activity of students who were shown brief videotaped excerpts (with no sound) of then-President Ronald Reagan's and former senator Gary Hart's facial expressions mirrored each of the expressions they saw (McHugo, Lanzetta, & Bush, 1991; McHugo, Lanzetta, Sullivan, Masters, & Englis, 1985). In another experiment, researchers showed students videotaped excerpts of happy and reassuring facial expressions of all the Democratic candidates in the 1984 presidential election. The students' emotional responses to these facial expressions were more likely to produce changes in attitudes toward the candidates than were the students' party affiliation, stand on the issues, or assessment of the candidates' leadership abilities (Sullivan & Masters, 1988).

The idea that emotional contagion may be implicated in the process of political persuasion prompted one team of researchers to study what might be the "essence" of charismatic leadership (Cherulnik, Donley, Wiewel, & Miller, 2001). In their first experiment, college undergraduates role-played a candidate for president of student government at their university by giving a brief campaign speech. The researchers selected both charismatic and noncharismatic speakers (male and female) based on the speakers' nonverbal style (facial expressiveness, smiles, and eye contact). Observations of audience members' reactions to the speakers showed that when they were listening to the charismatic speakers, they smiled more often, displayed more intense smiles, looked away from the speaker less often, and spent more time looking at the speaker. In a second experiment, the researchers used videotaped excerpts from the first presidential debate between George Bush and Bill Clinton. Students watched the most and least charismatic excerpts for both Bush and Clinton. Whereas a contagion effect generally occurred for Clinton, it did not occur for Bush. Students smiled more and looked away less while watching the charismatic Clinton than while watching the noncharismatic Clinton. In contrast, a reversed pattern occurred for Bush: Students smiled and looked less during the charismatic Bush than during the noncharismatic Bush. The researchers concluded that Bush's charismatic style might not have been as genuine as that of Clinton's and was therefore less likely to produce an emotional contagion effect. One implication of this study is that coaching a speaker to act charismatic may not yield the desired effect if the speaker's nonverbal communication seems deliberate rather than spontaneous.

Even the facial expressions of a political rival can affect audience perceptions. Communication researcher John Seiter and his colleagues studied these perceptions in a series of laboratory experiments in which audience members view videotaped debates prepared by the researchers in a split-screen format so viewers can simultaneously view both debaters. In one experiment, they found that the facial expressions of a speaker's opponent during a debate affected judgments of the speaker. When the opponent displayed disagreement by rolling his eyes, shaking his head, and so forth, viewers had more positive attitudes toward the speaker, rating him higher on competence, character, composure, and sociability (Seiter, Abraham, & Nakagama, 1998). In another experiment, Seiter (2001) found that when a nonspeaking debater expressed nearly continuous disbelief by frowning, head shaking, mouthing "No" or "What?" audience members regarded him as deceptive and the speaker as truthful. However, moderate signs of disbelief lowered the truthfulness ratings for both speakers. Another study found that audience members regard even moderate expressions of disbelief as inappropriate, most likely viewing such behavior as a violation of the turn-taking rules expected in formal debates (Seiter & Weger, 2005). The mediated format of these debates heightens viewers' awareness of these nonverbal reactions. In an experiment using live rather than videotaped debates, the researchers still found some support for the idea that moderate expressions of disbelief have a negative effect. When expressing disbelief (compared to being stone-faced), viewers judged the nonspeaking debater as behaving inappropriately and as having a weaker speaking delivery. On the other hand, viewers did not judge her overall as any less competent nor did they downgrade the quality of her arguments (Seiter, Kinzer, & Weger, 2006).

Perhaps the best advice for a nonspeaking debater is to remain composed and wait until it's your turn to speak. Indeed, this is precisely the advice offered to former Vice President Al Gore after one of his presidential debates with George W. Bush. During one of the debates, Gore's occasional sighs of exasperation were easy to hear, leading reporters and others to speculate about how much this kind of "rude" behavior may have damaged his performance (Smith, 2000). Similarly, President Bush's smirks, grimaces, and contorted facial expressions during one of his presidential debates with John Kerry were so pronounced that they actually undermined his support among many undecided voters (reported in Seiter, Kinzer, & Weger, 2006).

Explaining the Impact of Nonverbal Communication

Psychologists Richard Petty and John Cacioppo (1986) believe that nonverbal signals alone can be persuasive. According to their **elaboration likelihood model**, targets of persuasion generally take one of two different routes on their way to accepting a persuasive message: the **central route** or the **peripheral route**. Listeners who are willing and able to grapple with a speaker's ideas (individuals who know a lot or care a lot about the speaker's message, for instance) tend to take the central route, which involves *message elaboration* or rational thinking about issue-relevant arguments (i.e., weighing the pros and cons of a speaker's position). In contrast, listeners who are relatively unwilling or unable to engage in message elaboration tend to take the peripheral route—they rely on various decision rules about when to accept or reject a speaker's message. These decision rules represent a default option that listeners can use when they need or desire a simple way to make up their minds; thus, not much thinking is needed.

When a listener takes the peripheral route, situational circumstances determine which of many different rules the listener will follow. Many of these rules are not relevant to nonverbal communication, such as agreeing with a speaker because most people do or because it is personally advantageous. But many nonverbal cues reinforce decision rules that recommend accepting the message of a credible speaker, a speaker you happen to like, or a speaker who appeals to your emotions. Thus, nonverbal cues that convey expertise and trustworthiness, that are personally appealing (e.g., good looks), or that arouse emotions become especially influential when listeners cannot or will not engage in issue-relevant thinking.

The value of the elaboration likelihood model is that it helps us understand why nonverbal cues may be persuasive with some listeners but not with others. The more likely a listener is to focus on the issues, the less likely it is that he or she will succumb to the influence of nonverbal cues. Research indicates that the persuasive impact of nonverbal communication decreases with listeners who (1) are involved in the topic, (2) enjoy thinking about issues, (3) hear opposing positions from different sources, (4) are able to concentrate without distractions, and (5) have prior knowledge of the topic (O'Keefe, 1990).

ENTERTAINING ENCOUNTERS: ABSORBING POPULAR CULTURE

When MTV first appeared in 1981, the marriage of music and fashion became more prominent than ever before. Consider Madonna's impact. Before 1983 (the year she became a hit on MTV), the oversized tailored shirt and tight jeans were among the most conspicuous garments of young teenagers. Madonna's videos *Borderline*, *Lucky Star*, and *Like a Virgin* introduced her first look:

> a short black dress, big cross earrings, silver and rubber bracelets, black crosses, and many silver chains worn around the neck, and a bare midriff. The short tube skirt, tank tops, cropped leggings, and fingerless gloves that Madonna wore became "required attire" among the younger teenage set. (Rubinstein, 1995, p. 214)

Buying a few new outfits is one thing, but sometimes mimicking the look of a media idol is not so benign. In the early 1990s, for example, one study estimated that 250,000 to 500,000 high school male seniors had used or were then using dangerous anabolic steroids not to enhance athletic performance but to emulate the muscularity of their media idols ("Deadly Search for Beautiful Bodies," 1993). Another example is the growing international trade in unsafe and potentially deadly skin-bleaching products that claim to turn dark-skinned individuals into more popular and successful lighter-skinned individuals, a claim boosted by media images linking status and celebrity with skin color. For example, one widely viewed television commercial seen on Indian satellite channels and on YouTube features a superstar Indian actress promoting a skin cream called Fair & Handsome. The commercial shows a glum dark-skinned Indian man who, after using the cream, becomes light skinned, confident, and attractive to women (Van Marsh, 2007).

PERSONAL EXPERIENCE 11.4

CAN YOU RELATE TO THIS?

Mimicking a Media Icon

As a high school student, I was very involved in various musical and theatrical groups at my school. We all had our favorite stars that we tried to emulate, but only a few people would go so far as to try and be just like them. I remember one girl who wanted to be just like Mariah Carey. She tried to sing like her, dress like her, and did her hair the same way. I thought that was totally pathetic, but a lot of teenagers do things like that.

Katie

In this section, we'll focus on one important way that entertaining encounters with the media become socializing encounters as well—through a process known as *modeling*. Mass media scholars Melvin DeFleur and Everette Dennis (1998) explain:

> The mass media, and especially television and movies, present many depictions of people acting out patterns of behavior in various ways. These can be ways of speaking, relating to members of the opposite sex, dressing, walking, or virtually any form of meaningful action. These depictions can serve as "models" of behavior that can be imitated, and people who see the action depicted may adopt it as part of their own behavioral repertoire. (p. 471)

The most straightforward explanation of how and why individuals adopt behaviors depicted in the media is **modeling theory**, a derivation of psychologist Albert Bandura's (1977) more general social learning theory. Modeling theory contains five basic propositions: (1) an individual encounters a media portrayal of someone (model) performing an action; (2) the individual identifies with the model; (3) at some point, the individual imitates the action of the model; (4) performing the action is rewarding to the individual (i.e., positive reinforcement); (5) having been rewarded for imitating the model, the individual is likely to perform the action again (DeFleur & Dennis, 1998).

EXERCISE 11.2

TRY THIS

Mimicking Media Icons

OBJECTIVE: To identify instances of modeling for class discussion

INSTRUCTIONS: Can you think of specific cases where the actions or look of a well-known celebrity or other media personality became part of the popular culture? Try to come up with examples for a media icon who popularized:

1. A hair style
2. An article of clothing
3. A distinct gesture
4. A speech mannerism
5. An accessory

Whether in sitcoms or dramas, talk shows or reality programs, sporting events or musical productions, television offers countless opportunities to witness performances that are relevant to our everyday lives. By giving us idealized images of how we should look and act in all sorts of situations, television invites us to join the crowd. Despite the pressures to conform, not everyone accepts the invitation. For those who do, a belief that the benefits outweigh the risks is often motivation enough. In the sections that follow, we'll examine modeling theory in action. First, we'll consider media portrayals of physical appearance, and then, we'll examine media portrayals of nonverbal interaction.

Media Portrayals of Physical Attractiveness

▸ Media icons like Lady Gaga can have a great deal of influence over large segments of the population.

istockphoto.com/EdStock

The mass media play a significant role in the modeling of attractiveness, not only by presenting various images of beauty but by creating in consumers the desire to emulate those images. According to the results of one study, which examined the contents of nearly 4,300 television commercials, approximately one out of every four television commercials we see contains some form of attractiveness-based message, selling us on the importance of good looks (Downs & Harrison, 1985). Media portrayals in film and television that repeatedly equate attractiveness with positive qualities—the protagonists are usually good looking—contribute to the halo effect we bestow on attractive people (see Chapter 3). Media representations of good looks also vary by culture. For example, a study of advertisements from fashion and beauty magazines in Singapore, Taiwan, and the U.S. found that women's faces predominated in Asian ads with their emphasis on cosmetics and facial beauty products. But women's bodies were the focus in the clothing ads that dominated U.S. magazines (Frith, Shaw, & Cheng, 2005).

Although both men and women want to be attractive, research generally confirms what most of us probably suspect: The media perpetuates the stereotype that being attractive is more important for the well-being of women than it is for men. Of course, there is a long history of such stereotyping. Television advertisements from the 1950s through the 1970s consistently used women for decorative purposes and portrayed women as more concerned than men with their personal appearance (Ferrante, Haynes, & Kingsley, 1988; Sullivan & O'Connor, 1988). Although the gap has narrowed somewhat in recent years, research also shows that network television ads and MTV commercials are more likely to present women rather than men as young and attractive and as sex objects (Lin, 1998; Signorielli, McLeod, & Healy, 1994; Sullivan & O'Connor, 1988). And it's not just true of commercials. A study of primetime comedy, drama, action-adventure, and magazine television programs arrived at the same conclusion (Davis, 1990).

What are these attractive female images that we see in the media every day? Marketing researchers Basil Englis and Michael Solomon and psychologist Richard Ashmore

(1994) reject any notion of a single image. While certain universal standards of facial beauty may exist (see Chapter 3), there is tremendous cultural diversity as well. Cultural gatekeepers (fashion editors, film directors, and so on) often have the final say about the images on magazine covers or in the movies. Based on the terms these cultural gatekeepers use to distinguish among beautiful models (incorporating both appearance and behavior), the researchers proposed a typology of female good looks:

1. The feminine/classic image typically has light hair, Nordic features, and a soft image; is not heavily accessorized; and is usually slightly older.
2. The sensual/exotic image is sexual in a classy, understated way and is ethnic looking (deviating from white European norms).
3. The cute image is youthful and shorter, wears casual attire, and looks awkward but natural.
4. The girl-next-door image is outdoorsy, casual, active, and athletic.
5. The sex kitten image wears skin-revealing attire, seems cool and detached, and strikes uncomfortable-looking poses.
6. The trendy image wears current and faddish clothes, strikes challenging poses, and is often ethnic looking.

In their study of fashion magazines and music videos, the researchers found that the media favored the classic/feminine, sensual/exotic, and trendy images over the others. They also found that the prevalence of an image varied according to type of magazine (*Cosmopolitan* favored classic/feminine, *Seventeen* favored trendy), and in the music videos, the image varied according to the type of music (classic rock favored classic/feminine, new wave favored trendy, and so forth).

While there may be some diversity in the media's portrayal of good looks, thinness is still popular when it comes to their depictions of the ideal feminine physique (White, Ginsburg, & Brown, 1999). The slightest attention to female performers in any of the media confirms the presence of this ideal—the result of a steady emphasis on being slender. As one researcher concluded over twenty years ago:

> [P]resent day women who look at the major mass media are exposed to a standard of bodily attractiveness that is slimmer than that presented for men and that is less curvaceous than that presented for women since the 1930s. This standard may not be promoted only in the media and it may not even originate in the media, but given the popularity of television, movies and

> magazines . . . the media are likely to be among the most influential promoters of such thin standards. (Silverstein, Perdue, Peterson, & Kelly, 1986, p. 531)

Children absorb media images promoting thinness at an early age. One study of popular animated cartoons showed that underweight characters were more likely than overweight characters to possess all sorts of good qualities, such as intelligence, attractiveness, emotional well-being, and good judgment (Klein & Shiffman, 2006).

Studies show that these media images leave a lasting impression. One team of researchers discovered that even 30 minutes of exposure is enough to alter a woman's image of her own body. They found that viewers felt thinner than they normally felt after watching 30 minutes of television commercials containing thin models (which is usually an overestimation of their body size). The research suggests that the desire to lose weight comes at a later stage. First, viewers identify with the thin models—even imagining that they look more like the models than they really do. But when reality sets in, they begin to experience dissatisfaction with their bodies (Myers & Biocca, 1992). Of course, these results do not take individual differences into account. Some viewers will feel more dissatisfaction than others will. Perhaps the single most important factor is the degree to which a viewer has internalized the media conception of beauty. Research shows that for males and females alike, the more a viewer embraces the media ideal, the more he or she is likely to be dissatisfied (Durkin & Paxton, 2002; Hargreaves & Tiggemann, 2002). One exception may be whether a person is taking steps to achieve the ideal, such as dieting or exercising. Then, according to some research, that person may actually feel better after seeing ideal media images (Mills, Polivy, Herman, & Tiggeman, 2002).

For those who do not reject the media ideal, an important factor is the discrepancy between one's own body and the ideal media image. For many women, thin media images activate this discrepancy and make them feel heavier than they really are (Lavine, Sweeney, & Wagner, 1999). Studies show that the greater the perceived discrepancy is, the more dissatisfaction one feels (Posovac & Posovac, 2002). Since the ideal media image for females of all ages is thin, it's not surprising that heavier girls and women feel more dissatisfaction after viewing these media images (Durkin & Paxton, 2002; Henderson-King & Henderson-King, 1997). Generally, women who are dissatisfied with their bodies have a tougher time coping with exposure to media images of thin and attractive people. One team of researchers examined women's feelings about their bodies after exposure to images of attractive professional models as well as attractive non-models. They found that, compared to satisfied women, dissatisfied women felt much worse after making these comparisons. In addition, while dissatisfied women felt worse about themselves after seeing images of professional models as well as non-models, satisfied women only felt worse after seeing images of the non-models,

▸ While there may be some diversity in the media's portrayal of physical attractiveness, being thin is still in when it comes to depictions of the ideal feminine physique. What are the consequences of these media images?

istockphoto.com/Yaromir_M

suggesting that satisfied women don't compare themselves to images of attractive women with whom they have little in common, such as professional models, whereas dissatisfied women do. The researchers also found that dissatisfied women spend more time comparing themselves to other women than satisfied women do (Trampe, Siero, & Stapel, 2007). Finally, research shows that race plays a part. One study found that black women with low levels of body-esteem reported less satisfaction with their own bodies after exposure to advertisements containing images of thin and attractive black models, but not after similar exposure to thin and attractive white models (Frisby, 2004).

The impact of these images is far reaching, extending to virtually all parts of the globe. In fact, a study of female body dissatisfaction in 26 countries across 10 world regions found that exposure to Western media, combined with body mass index (BMI), predicted body dissatisfaction among women, particularly in high socioeconomic environments. As the authors of the study warn,

> The implications of the present work are clear: Across the globe, societies now face the urgent task of promoting more realistic and healthier body weight ideals, and challenging associations between extreme thinness and femininity, success and health. Only a response at the sociopolitical and economic levels, in combination with the current focus on the individual, can be expected to result in more positive body images among women and men in different cultural spheres. (Swami et al., 2010, p. 321)

If mere exposure to these images takes its toll, we might expect that people who see more of them in their everyday lives would feel more dissatisfied with their appearance than would people who see much less. Researchers found support for this in a study of 382 students in the ninth and tenth grades. More frequent TV viewers and magazine readers expressed greater dissatisfaction with their bodies, idealized body types like those found in the popular media, and were more likely to adopt dieting and exercise programs (Hofschire & Greenberg, 2002). More dramatic support comes from a study comparing the body images of 20 sighted women, 20 women who lost their eyesight after age 15, and 20 women who had been blind since birth. The researchers found that the congenitally blind women had the most positive view of their bodies while the sighted women had the least positive view ("Out of Sight," 1999).

Gender differences in the desire to be attractive also surface at an early age. In one study of elementary school children, communication researcher Cynthia Hoffner (1996) asked the children to identify their favorite television character, to indicate how much they wanted to be like that character, and to indicate what particular traits the character had in five different areas: attractiveness, strength, humor, intelligence, and social behavior. For the boys, the best predictor of how much they identified with the character was the character's intelligence; for the girls, the best predictor was the character's attractiveness.

Media images of physical appearance create and sustain many of the stereotypes we use in our snap judgments of other people. Research shows that increased exposure to these images brings an increased reliance on stereotypical judgments (see Research 11.3). For instance, a study of 10- to 13-year-old boys and girls found that the more time they spent watching television, playing videogames, and reading magazines, the more likely they were to have negative attitudes toward obese girls and boys (Latner, Rosewall, & Simmonds, 2007).

RESEARCH 11.3

FIND OUT MORE

How Do Media Images of Racial Stereotypes Influence Public Policy?

Research has shown for a long time that media portrayals of minority groups often reinforce stereotypes about those groups. In these two experiments, the researchers were interesting in finding out whether media images of black stereotypes influence support for public assistance programs when those programs would be assisting blacks. In the first experiment, the researchers found that participants who viewed images of black looters during Hurricane Katrina (representing the "black criminal" stereotype) were less likely to feel empathy for and less likely to support assistance programs for black evacuees in need of assistance than for white evacuees in need of assistance compared to those participants who viewed images of non-looting black evacuees or those participants who saw no images of evacuees at all.

The second experiment examined the impact of the "promiscuous black female" stereotype. One group of participants listened to a rap song with many references to explicit sexual acts and degrading comments about the sexual performance of men, a second group of participants listened to a rap song with no sexual references, and a final group of participants listened to a non-rap song with no sexual references. As in the first experiment, participants primed with a black stereotype (the "promiscuous black female") showed less empathy for a black woman in need of help and were less inclined to support social programs that offered assistance than did the other two groups of participants. The same effect was not found when the woman in need of help was described as white rather than black.

(Continued)

RESEARCH 11.3

(Continued)

To find out more about this study and to answer the following questions, see the full text (cited below).

1. How was this research described as different than the research that had already been done?
2. Who were the participants in these experiments? Do you think the results might have been different with a different group of participants?
3. Why did the researchers decide to do a second experiment, following up on the first?
4. What did the researchers do in the second experiment to find out whether the music would affect empathy and help for a woman in need?
5. What were some of the limitations of these experiments?

Source: Johnson, J. D., Olivo, N., Gibson, N., Reed, W., & Ashburn-Nardo, N. (2009). Priming media stereotypes reduces support for social welfare policies: The mediating role of empathy. *Personality and Social Psychology Bulletin*, 35, 463–476.

Media Portrayals of Nonverbal Interaction

Whether in daytime soaps or primetime sitcoms, movies or magazines, media portrayals of everyday life give us an endless stream of images about how to relate to one another: parents with children, superiors with subordinates, men with women, and so on. How does a steady diet of such images affect us? According to modeling theory, we may pick up the behaviors of characters we identify with. We can only wonder how far-reaching the consequences are and how much modeling actually takes place.

Social scientists are a long way from offering any definitive answers. Many researchers are interested in learning about the implicit messages contained in media images rather than in how much we are affected by them. When focused on nonverbal interaction, these studies show how media reflect and perpetuate various stereotypes— how men interact with women, for example. Whether the portrayal appears in a feature film, an action-adventure series, a music video, or a television commercial, the male/female stereotype is relatively clear and consistent: Female characters are more likely than male characters to exhibit deferential and nurturing behavior (Wood, 1994, Chapter 9). In the extreme, these images are not inconsequential. Many of the classic films of the 1940s featuring screen idols such as Clark Gable, Errol Flynn, and John Wayne, for instance, rarely showed the male stars taking no for an answer from their leading ladies.

When the world discovered, soon after his death in 1985, that media idol Rock Hudson was gay, people were stunned that a movie star known for his portrayals of tough, masculine men could be homosexual. He didn't fit the stereotype. But even today, the media stereotype of a gay man persists. For example, a recent study of North American television shows found that male actors playing the part of a gay man tend to change the tone and pitch of their voice to fit the feminine-sounding stereotype of a gay man (Cartei & Reby, 2012).

Media depictions of women's behavior often differ from those of men. Music videos, for example, tend to portray male characters as adventuresome, domineering, and aggressive but female characters as affectionate, dependent, nurturing, and fearful (Seidman, 1992). These differences even turn up in children's television ads. One study found that girls were more likely than boys in Saturday morning commercials to engage in all sorts of shy and submissive behaviors: nervous giggling, face covering, gaze aversion, snuggling, peeking out from behind an object, showing fear, and so forth (Browne, 1998). Gender differences also appear in news photographs. One study of a major daily newspaper showed that the photos of women were more likely to picture the women as smiling and submissive than were the photos of men (Rodgers, Kenix, & Thorson, 2007).

Another media portrayal of nonverbal interaction that may lead to extensive modeling among viewers is that of expressing emotions. Some stereotypical portrayals are easy to see, such as those that encourage us to follow well-known cultural display rules: not laughing at another's misfortune, not being a sore loser, not showing fear to an adversary, being humble, exhibiting shame during a confession, and so on. These portrayals also include gender-appropriate displays, such as men showing anger or concealing their emotions, and women showing a greater range of emotions and typically showing greater vulnerability with displays of fear, sadness, shame, and the like.

According to one estimate, in a typical 30-minute television sitcom, viewers are exposed to 68 instances of emotional expressions (Houle & Feldman, 1991). What are we learning from these portrayals? In one study of the most popular prime-time family sitcoms among two- to 11-year-olds, communication researchers Audrey Weiss and Barbara Wilson (1996) discovered that episodes usually centered on incidents that evoked negative emotions such as fear, anger, or embarrassment in the main characters (often child characters). Humor often accompanied these incidents and, more often than not, other characters did not respond directly to the individuals who experienced negative emotions. As the researchers concluded,

> The prevalence of nonresponsive reactions in family sitcoms could convey either harmful or beneficial information to children. On the one hand, frequent ignoring responses may suggest to a child viewer that negative feelings are unimportant to other family members. Such disconfirmation of negative emotions among

> television families might influence expectations that children themselves develop about their own family's support and concern when they feel bad. On the other hand, young viewers may learn from family sitcoms which emotional responses are inappropriate or unacceptable. For example, if family sitcom characters ignore a child who is misbehaving or throwing a temper tantrum, young viewers may learn that such negative emotional reactions are inappropriate. (p. 22)

Research often shows that television portrayals are not very realistic. Emotional expressions in particular do not mirror the frequency, context, or range of those expressed in real life. One study found that television characters tend to show emotions much more often than people do in everyday life. They also show certain emotions (such as anger and sadness) much more often, while other emotions (such as disgust and fear) are shown much less often. Interestingly, the researchers observed that television characters tend to show their true emotions regardless of the context (Coats, Feldman, & Philippot, 1999). In other words, they rarely mask their emotions and thus do not follow the display rules most of us take for granted (e.g., don't be a sore loser; don't gloat, etc.). What impact do these portrayals have on children who watch a lot of television? In a series of follow-up studies, the researchers found that frequent viewers (as much as 40 hours a week or more) exhibited different nonverbal strengths and weaknesses compared to infrequent viewers. Frequent viewers were more expressive when genuinely experiencing emotions but less expressive when trying to pose an emotion. Frequent viewers were better able to express emotions common on television (happiness and sadness) than emotions uncommon on television (fear and disgust). Frequent viewers demonstrated greater skill at decoding others' facial expressions. Finally, frequent viewers tended to share television characters' inclination to show true emotions regardless of the context (Coats et al., 1999). As the authors conclude, "[C]hildren whose primary source of information about nonverbal behavior is learned from television do not appear to fully appreciate the complexities of emotional dissemblance" (p. 172).

In recent years, scholars have been implicating the media in the unintended transmission of intergroup bias. According to one perspective, media consumers may pick up or, to use their concept of contagion, become "infected" with the nonverbal bias exhibited by the persons they observe on mainstream television programs (Weisbuch & Pauker, 2011). Nonverbal bias includes more negative, unfriendly nonverbal cues and fewer positive, friendly nonverbal cues directed toward particular social groups. Exposure to nonverbal bias may cause individuals to adopt a bias of their own through implicit learning or some other relatively unconscious process. One study examined the presence of nonverbal bias found in television programs watched by more than 100 million weekly viewers (Weisbuch, Paulker, & Ambady, 2009). They found that black characters were more likely to be the targets of nonverbal bias from their co-characters than were white characters. Another study of 18 popular television programs found a similar bias exhibited toward overweight characters (Weisbuch & Ambady, 2009). Furthermore, correlational studies as well as controlled experiments have revealed that observers of programs exhibiting this kind of nonverbal bias are more likely to show signs of bias compared to observers who are not exposed to nonverbal bias (Weisbuch & Pauker, 2011). These studies suggest that efforts to remove explicit (i.e., verbal) signs of discrimination may not be sufficient to eradicate the continuing problems resulting from intergroup bias.

SUMMARY

Few things in life will replace the satisfaction we derive from face-to-face encounters with others, yet we find ourselves in an ever-shrinking world that relies more and more on mediated communication. Informative encounters, those that keep us connected to the outside world, include traditional uses of the media (such as getting the daily news) and modern uses that include interactive media (such as e-mail, texting, and videoconferencing). Nonverbal communication is an important part of news broadcasts, and attention to it reflects the need for viewer ratings as well as for objective reporting, a set of constraints not found on many talk shows. Nonverbal cues can reveal subtle newscaster bias or they can overshadow other forms of inadvertent discrimination. News presentations reflect a beauty bias: Reporters, especially women, are more likely to be attractive.

We use various forms of media to exchange information with others; some exhibit greater social presence—a closer approximation to face-to-face communication—than do other forms. Although social presence is not always desirable, it remains the most important criterion for judging the effectiveness of new media. People often go online or rely on mobile messaging for social reasons, which continues to change the way people go about building their relationships with others. Distance education is also becoming increasingly popular, placing demands on instructional designers to incorporate new technologies that facilitate the social presence of the learning environment.

Nonverbal communication in the media may also influence us in various ways. Studies show that attractive individuals in advertisements and in politics are more persuasive than their less attractive counterparts. Sexy models in advertising may succeed only in getting our attention. Clothing, such as wearing a uniform, can be persuasive. Baby-faced individuals may appear more trustworthy but are also seen as less competent than mature-faced individuals. Faces that resemble our own may also be influential. Certain nonverbal behaviors tend to be more persuasive than others, such as those reflecting greater immediacy and expressiveness. Research shows that a political leader's facial expressions can be persuasive, creating an emotional reaction that affects our attitude toward the leader. As an explanation of why nonverbal signals are persuasive, the elaboration likelihood model helps us understand when people are most likely to resist or succumb to the influence of these signals.

Media presentations do more than inform, persuade, and entertain—they socialize. Media consumers absorb the images of popular culture through *modeling*, a process that begins when a consumer identifies with a media portrayal, retains it, tries it out, and likes the results. Modeling theory can explain why media consumers often want to alter their looks by becoming more fashionable or thinner, for example. It can also provide some insight into the widespread acceptance of certain patterns of nonverbal interaction, such as those that are typical of male–female relationships, those that involve the expression of emotion, and those that may inadvertently transmit bias toward marginalized social groups.

KEY TERMS

Avatars 413
Central route 427
Disinhibition 414
Elaboration likelihood model 427
Emojis 411
Emoticons 410
Facebook 412
Modeling theory 430
Peripheral route 427
Social networking sites 412
Social presence 407

APPENDIX

Approaches to the Study of Nonverbal Communication

TWO COMPETING PARADIGMS

Two of my students, Karen and Larry, were both interested in studying tattoos for their class research project. Although their general topics were the same, each had an entirely different interest in the subject of tattoos: Karen wanted to find out why people get them; Larry wanted to find out how people react to them. Each was asking a different question about the same topic. In the end, this also meant that each would carry out a very different kind of investigation. Karen interviewed individuals who had tattoos. In their own words, she reported why they decided to get a tattoo and what it meant to them. She did a study that exemplifies the *humanistic* approach to communication research. Larry ended up showing people photographs of individuals who were either displaying or not displaying tattoos. He asked the people to record on a series of rating scales their first impressions of the individuals shown in the photographs. Larry did a study that represents the *scientific* approach to communication research. Similarly, there are many ways of studying nonverbal communication. In the communication discipline, we often characterize the research someone does as either scientific or humanistic in nature. Each of these approaches, or *paradigms*, embraces a different set of assumptions about the kind of research that will make the greatest contribution to the discipline.

THE SCIENTIFIC PARADIGM

At its core, this paradigm views communication as a set of behaviors that are shaped by a combination of genetic and environmental factors—a point of view known as *determinism*. The study of communication is reduced to the study of *variables*, concepts that can be measured by the researcher. The chief aim of the researcher is to discover universal laws that determine how these variables affect one another. For example, Larry's question was "How are first impressions affected by tattoos?" In this case, the concept of *first impressions* is a variable and the concept of *tattoos* is another variable.

The implicit assumption underlying the question is that our first impressions of others may not be a matter of individual choice but may in fact be determined by the appearance (i.e., tattoo) of another person. If that turns out to be the case, knowing someone's physical appearance may allow the researcher to predict (or at least explain) the first impressions of others in a particular situation. This deterministic philosophy requires the researcher to seek out cause–effect relationships and thus dictates the kinds of questions that will be investigated. Once the question is raised, the researcher must use the most appropriate methods available for answering that question. As we'll see in the next section, the experimental method of research is best suited for the discovery of cause–effect relationships. Moreover, it is the most appropriate method to use for the study of intrinsic signaling systems, since the use of these signals is not a matter of personal choice.

THE HUMANISTIC PARADIGM

Humanistic researchers view communication as a matter of free will guided by the development of rules. A belief in free will means a commitment to the idea that communication behavior is much more a product of what we choose to do in a given situation than it is the result of uncontrollable genetic and environmental pressures. Thus, researchers are interested in finding out why individuals make the choices they do and how they make sense of their own lives. Yet humanists accept the fact that individuals do not operate in a vacuum; they are members of some culture and may choose to act in ways that conform to the norms of that culture. Often, the researcher seeks to identify the implicit rules of a culture and to codify the actions performed by its members. This paradigm encourages a researcher to ask questions that are fundamentally different from those of the scientist. In stark contrast to cause–effect questions, a researcher might wonder about how individuals interpret their own actions. In the example above, Karen wants to find out the answer to the question "Why do people get tattoos?" If she accepts the principle that our actions are guided by personal choice and that individuals are unique members of some culture, it makes sense for her to do an ethnographic study (see below). Whereas the scientific paradigm is well suited for the study of intrinsic communication codes, the humanistic paradigm is a good fit for the investigation of arbitrary communication systems.

METHODS OF RESEARCH

Nonverbal communication researchers use a variety of methods. Each of the methods listed below has a distinct purpose and may be the only way for a researcher to seek an answer to a particular question. Let's examine each in turn.

The Anecdotal Method

The least rigorous of the methods, anecdotal research relies on personal observation and experience. The researcher merely collects and reports firsthand accounts of some phenomenon. For instance, if the question of interest is "Are short people discriminated against in the workplace?" then the researcher would look for incidents of such discrimination and then report the details of those incidents. Obviously, there are many serious problems with this method of investigation, not the least of which is researcher bias (i.e., the researcher might only collect incidents that confirm his or her beliefs). Moreover, the casual manner in which accounts are collected makes it virtually impossible for the researcher to form any generalizations about discrimination. And even the truthfulness of the accounts that are collected may be suspect, since the method lacks any procedures for objectively reporting the details of an account or corroborating the accuracy of any details. Often, our willingness to accept or even consider the results of such research depends on the credibility of the researcher. Still, many of the most provocative ideas about nonverbal communication originated from anecdotal evidence at a time when no other information was available. Thus, as a starting point and when the findings are examined critically, the anecdotal method can provide a rich and useful source of data.

The Ethnographic Method

Ethnographers explore the rules, routines, practices, and symbols that unify a particular culture. They accept most of the assumptions and are guided by most of the procedures associated with humanistic inquiry: They do their work in the field (they go where the action is), they immerse themselves in the actual phenomenon being investigated (naturalistic inquiry), they put a premium on studying the meanings people attach to things (interpretive research), they trust their own observations and insights (they allow for subjectivity), they develop theories during and after collecting data (inductive method), and they analyze narrative rather than statistical data (qualitative analysis). The ethnographic method, which relies on long-term observation and/or in-depth interviews, is especially well suited to exploring the subtleties and intricacies of the nonverbal communication used by members of particular cultures or institutions. David Efron's research on the gestural styles of Italian and Jewish immigrants living in New York City during World War II typifies this approach. Similarly, Erving Goffman used ethnographic methods to study the way people use nonverbal behavior to enact the roles they perform in public.

The Experimental Method

This method of research, which epitomizes the scientific method, concentrates on whether a cause–effect relationship exists between two or more variables. Experiments are designed to examine the effect of one or more independent variables on one or more dependent variables. The researcher exposes subjects (participants) to a stimulus (an independent variable) and measures quantitatively their reactions to the stimulus (dependent variable). Since these reactions might be caused by something other than the stimulus, the study is conducted in a *controlled environment*, which means that the researcher sets things up to reduce the danger that other variables may affect the dependent variable. These other variables are referred to as *confounding variables*. Most often, a technique known as *random assignment* is used to minimize the possibility that ordinary differences between the subjects who are exposed to the stimulus and those who are not are responsible for different reactions. The technique does this by creating roughly equivalent groups (the subjects in one group should be very similar to the subjects in other groups). Much of the research on nonverbal communication uses this basic method. Early studies by Michael Argyle and his colleagues on the effects of immediacy behaviors are good examples of this research methodology. To further clarify the kind of experiments researchers do, we can distinguish between two approaches: encoding experiments and decoding experiments.

Encoding experiments focus on the factors that affect the use of nonverbal signals. These factors, which may include things such as attitudes, culture, the situation, characteristics of another person, and so on, serve as independent variables in the experiment. Certain nonverbal signals, such as facial expression, gestures, eye contact, and so forth, are dependent variables. For example, the researcher might design an experiment to see if subjects use more eye contact when they interact with a higher-status person than with a lower-status person. In this example, the status of the other person is the independent variable and eye contact is the dependent variable. In contrast, decoding experiments study the effects of nonverbal signals. They seek to answer questions such as *How do we react to another's stare? What is the effect of voice quality on first impressions? How do we regard someone with body piercings? Are speakers who use gestures judged more favorably than speakers who don't use gestures?* In all decoding experiments, the independent variables are one or more nonverbal signals; the dependent variables are the reactions of the subjects who participate in the experiment.

The Discourse–Analysis Method

Some researchers believe the best way to study nonverbal communication is in context. They maintain that the true meaning of a nonverbal behavior or the actual structure of nonverbal interaction cannot be discovered by removing nonverbal signals from their natural state. To that end, the discourse–analysis method focuses on the interdependence that exists among all forms of communication in a given situation; it regards communication as an event rather than as a collection of isolated behaviors. A researcher who is interested in studying the meaning of gestures, facial expressions, or gazing patterns, for instance, would be inclined to examine these things only by studying the larger discourse (e.g., a conversation, a dispute, a group discussion, etc.) of which they are a part. William Condon and Adam Kendon's research on the synchrony of speech and body movement is a good example of this method of investigation (see Chapter 6). Another is Albert Scheflen's research on quasi-courtship behavior (see Chapter 8). In addition, Ray Birdwhistell's pioneering study of kinesics stressed the importance of the context in which nonverbal communication takes place.

The Textual-Analysis Method

Researchers can learn about communication that has already occurred by studying records of that communication. A *text* is any artifact that contains one or more instances of communication. Video recordings, transcripts, films, audio recordings, electronic images, printed documents, and so on are all examples of texts. Many researchers, both scientific and humanistic, use this method. Whereas the scientist might use a procedure known as *content analysis*, which quantifies the frequency of communicative behaviors in a text, humanists take a critical stance: They might interpret the hidden meanings embedded in the communication, they might choose to place the communication in some larger social or political context, or they might evaluate the impact of the communication. A very common method among nonverbal communication researchers is to analyze videotaped interactions, often for the purpose of quantifying the frequencies of various nonverbal signals (e.g., comparing the number of times people blink while telling a lie with the number of times they blink while telling the truth to see if blinking is an indicator of deception).

The Survey Method

Survey researchers administer standardized questionnaires to a sample of respondents who are selected from some larger population. If they use a scientific sampling procedure, which gives each person in the population an equal chance of being selected, they can generalize about the results of their survey. They can claim that what's true of the sample is probably true of the population. Using mailed questionnaires or personal interviews, nonverbal communication researchers sometimes use this method to study people's attitudes or opinions about clothing, the use of touch, the meaning of gestures, what they find attractive in others, and so forth. Researcher often use this method to do correlational research, which examines the degree to which a change in one variable is associated with a change in some other variable. For example, a researcher might administer a series of questionnaires that contain various personality assessments to respondents from different cultures, along with some questions about how emotional they are in certain situations. This would allow the researcher to see if the respondents' culture influences how emotional they say they are. But the researcher could also find out if respondents who score high on certain personality traits also score high on emotional expressiveness. Many researchers use this method. In their early research, Paul Ekman and Wallace Friesen used this method to study the universality of facial expressions by asking people from different cultures to interpret the meaning of photographed facial expressions.

REFERENCES

Abiala, K. (1999). Customer orientation and sales situations: Variations in interactive service work. *Acta Sociologica, 42*, 207–222.

Acredolo, L. P., & Goodwyn, S. W. (1996). *Baby signs: How to talk with your baby before your baby can talk*. Chicago, IL: Contemporary Books.

Addington, D. W. (1968). The relationship of selected vocal characteristics to personality perception. *Speech Monographs, 35*, 492–503.

Addison, W. E. (1989). Beardedness as a factor in perceived masculinity. *Perceptual and Motor Skills, 68*, 921–922.

Afifi, W. A., & Johnson, M. L. (1999). The use and interpretation of tie signs in a public setting: Relationship and sex differences. *Journal of Social and Personal Relationships, 16*, 9–38.

Aiello, J. R., & Aiello, T. D. (1974). The development of personal space: Proxemic behavior of children 6 through 16. *Human Ecology, 2*, 177–189.

Aiello, J. R., & Jones, S. E. (1971). Field study of the proxemic behavior of young school children in three subcultural groups. *Journal of Personality and Social Psychology, 19*, 351–356.

Akechi, H., Senju, A., Uibo, H., Kikuchi, Y., Hasegawa, T., & Hietanen, J. K. (2013). Attention to eye contact in the West and East: Autonomic responses and evaluative ratings. *PLOS One, 8*, e59312.

Albada, K. F., Knapp, M. L., & Theune, K. E. (2002). Interaction appearance theory: Changing perceptions of physical attractiveness through social interaction. *Communication Theory, 12*, 8–40.

Albright, J. M. (2002). Impression formation and attraction in computer-mediated communication. *Dissertation Abstracts International A: The Humanities and Social Sciences, 62*, 3199.

Algoe, S. B., Buswell, B. N., & DeLamater, J. D. (2000). Gender and job status as contextual cues for the interpretation of facial expression of emotion. *Sex Roles, 42*, 183–208.

Alibali, M. W., Kita, S., & Young, A. J. (2000). Gesture and the process of speech production. *Language and Cognitive Processes, 15*, 593–613.

Allmendinger, K. (2010). Social presence in synchronous virtual learning situations: The role of nonverbal signals displayed by avatars. *Educational and Psychological Review, 22*, 41–56.

Altman, I., & Taylor, D. A. (1973). *Social penetration: The development of interpersonal relationships*. New York, NY: Holt, Rinehart, & Winston.

Ambady, N., Hallahan, M., & Conner, B. (1999). Accuracy of judgments of sexual orientation from thin slices of behavior. *Journal of Personality and Social Psychology, 77*, 538–547.

Amsbary, J. H., & Powell, L. (2007). Nonverbal behavior of vendors in customer-vendor interaction. *Perceptual and Motor Skills, 104*, 366–370.

Andersen, J. F., Andersen, P. A., & Lustig, M. (1987). Opposite-sex touch avoidance: A national replication and extension. *Journal of Nonverbal Behavior, 11*, 89–109.

Andersen, P. A. (1989, May). *A cognitive valence theory of intimate communication*. Paper presented at the International Network on Personal Relationships Conference, Iowa City, IA.

Andersen, P. A. (1991). When one cannot not communicate: A challenge to Motley's traditional communication postulates. *Communication Studies, 42*, 309–325.

Andersen, P. A. (1999). *Nonverbal communication: Forms and functions*. Mountain View, CA: Mayfield.

Andersen, P. A., & Bowman, L. (1990). Positions of power: Nonverbal influence in organizational communication. In J. A. DeVito & M. L. Hecht (Eds.), *The nonverbal communication reader* (pp. 391–411). Prospect Heights, IL: Waveland.

Andersen, P. A., Guerrero, L K., Buller, D. B., & Jorgensen, P. F. (1998). An empirical comparison of three theories of nonverbal immediacy exchange. *Human Communication Research, 24*, 501–535.

Andersen, P. A., & Leibowitz, K. (1978). The development and nature of the construct touch avoidance. *Environmental Psychology and Nonverbal Behavior, 3*, 89–106.

Anderson, D. E., Ansfield, M. A., & DePaulo, B. M. (1999). Love's best habit: Deception in the context of relationships. In P. Philippot, R. S. Feldman, & E. J. Coats (Eds.), *The social context of nonverbal behavior* (pp. 372–409). Cambridge, England: Cambridge University Press.

Anderson, K. J., & Leaper, C. (1998). Meta-analysis of gender effects on conversational interruption: Who, what, when, where, and how. *Sex Roles, 39*, 225–250.

Antonakis, J., & Dalgas, O. (2009). Predicting elections: Child's play. *Science, 27*, 1183.

Arce, C. H., Murguia, E., & Frisbie, W. P. (1987). Phenotype and life chances among chicanos. *Hispanic Journal of Behavioral Sciences, 9*, 19–32.

Argyle, M. (1975). *Bodily communication*. London, England: Methuen.

Argyle, M. (1988). *Bodily communication*. Madison, CT: International Universities Press.

Argyle, M., & Dean, J. (1965). Eye contact, distance, and affiliation. *Sociometry, 28*, 289–304.

Arvey, R. D., & Campion, J. E. (1982). The employment interview: A critical summary and review of recent research. *Personnel Psychology, 35*, 281–322.

Ashton-James, C., van Baaren, R. B., Chartrand, T. L., Decety, J., & Karremans, J. (2007). Mimicry and me: The impact of mimicry on self-construal. *Social Cognition, 25*, 518–535.

Athanasiou, R., & Greene, P. (1973). Physical attractiveness and helping behavior. *Proceedings of the 81st Annual Convention of the American Psychological Association (Montreal, Canada), 8*, 289–290.

Atkinson, M. (2004). Tattooing and civilizing processes: Body modification as self-control. *Canadian Review of Sociology and Anthropology, 41*, 125–146.

Aune, K. S., Buller, D. B., & Aune, R. K. (1996). Display rule development in romantic relationships: Emotion management and perceived appropriateness of emotions across relationship stages. *Human Communication Research, 23*, 115–145.

Awamleh, R., & Gardner, W. L. (1999). Perceptions of leader charisma and effectiveness: The effects of vision content, delivery, and organizational performance. *Leadership Quarterly, 10*, 345–373.

Axtell, R. (1998). *Gestures: The do's and taboos of body language around the world*. New York, NY: Wiley.

Babad, E. (1992). Teacher expectancies and nonverbal behavior. In R. S. Feldman (Ed.), *Applications of nonverbal behavioral theories* (pp. 167–190). Hillsdale, NJ: Lawrence Erlbaum.

Babad, E. (1999). Preferential treatment in television interviewing: Evidence from nonverbal behavior. *Political Communication, 16*, 337–358.

Babad, E. (2005a). Guessing teachers' differential treatment of high- and low-achievers from thin slices of their public lecturing behavior. *Journal of Nonverbal Behavior, 29*, 125–134.

Babad, E. (2005b). The psychological price of media bias. *Journal of Experimental Psychology: Applied, 11*, 245–255.

Babad, E., & Peer, E. (2010). Media bias in interviewers' nonverbal behavior: Potential remedies, attitude similarity and meta-analysis. *Journal of Nonverbal Behavior, 34*, 57–78.

Babad, E., Avni-Babad, D., & Rosenthal, R. (2004). Prediction of students' evaluations from brief instances of professors' nonverbal behavior in defined instructional situations. *Social Psychology of Education, 7*, 3–33.

Bahrick, H. P., Bahrick, P. O., & Wittlinger, R. P. (1975). Fifty years of memory for names and faces: A cross-sectional approach. *Journal of Experimental Psychology: General, 104*, 54–75.

Bailenson, J. N., & Yee, N. (2005). Digital chameleons. *Psychological Science, 16*, 814–819.

Bakker, A. B., & Schaufeli, W. B. (2000). Burnout contagion processes among teachers. *Journal of Applied Social Psychology, 30*, 2289–2309.

Bakker, A. B., Schaufeli, W. B., Sixma, H. J., & Bosveld, W. (2001). Burnout contagion among general practitioners. *Journal of Social and Clinical Psychology, 20*, 82–98.

Ballew, C. C., & Todorov, A. (2007, November 13). Predicting political elections from rapid and unreflective face judgments. *Proceedings of the National Academy of Sciences, 104*, 17948–17953.

Bandura, A. (1977). *Social learning theory*. Englewood Cliffs, NJ: Prentice Hall.

Banse, R., & Scherer, K. R. (1996). Acoustic profiles in vocal emotion expression. *Journal of Personality and Social Psychology, 70*, 614–636.

Barak, A., Patkin, J., & Dell, D. M. (1982). Effects of certain counselor behaviors on perceived expertness and attractiveness. *Journal of Counseling Psychology, 29*, 261–267.

Barber, N. (2001). Mustache fashion co-varies with a good marriage market for women. *Journal of Nonverbal Behavior, 25*, 261–272.

Barger, P. B., & Grandey, A. A. (2006). Service with a smile and encounter satisfaction: Emotional contagion and appraisal mechanisms. *Academy of Management Journal, 48*, 1229–1238.

Bargh, J. A., Chen, M., & Burrows, L. (1996). Automaticity of social behavior: Direct effect of trait construct and stereotype priming on action. *Journal of Personality and Social Psychology, 71*, 230–244.

Barnhill, G. P., Cook, K. T., Tebbenkamp, K., & Myles, B. S. (2002). The effectiveness of social skills intervention targeting nonverbal communication for adolescents with Asperger syndrome and related pervasive developmental delays. *Focus on Autism and Other Developmental Disabilities, 17*, 112–118.

Baron, N. S. (1992). *Growing up with language: How children learn to talk*. Reading, MA: Addison-Wesley.

Baron-Cohen, S. (1995). *Mindblindness: An essay on autism and theory of mind*. Cambridge, MA: MIT Press.

Baroni, M. R., & D'Urso, V. (1984). Some experimental findings about the question of politeness and women's speech (research note). *Language in Society, 13*, 67–72.

Barrett, K. C. (1993). The development of nonverbal communication of emotion: A functionalist perspective, *Journal of Nonverbal Behavior, 17*, 145–170.

Barsade, S. G. (2002). The ripple effect: Emotional contagion and its influence on group behavior. *Administrative Science Quarterly, 47*, 644–675.

Bar-Tal, D., & Saxe, L. (1976). Perceptions of similarly and dissimilarly attractive couples and individuals. *Journal of Personality and Social Psychology, 33*, 772–781.

Bartel, C. A., & Saavedra, R. (2000). The collective construction of work group moods. *Administrative Science Quarterly, 45*, 197–242.

Bartholomew, K. (1990). Avoidance of intimacy: An attachment perspective. *Journal of Social and Personal Relationships, 7*, 147–178.

Bartholomew, K., & Horowitz, L. M. (1991). Attachment styles among young adults: A test of a four-category model. *Journal of Personality and Social Psychology, 61*, 226–244.

Basso, K. (1972). To give up on words: Silence in Western Apache culture. In P. Giglioli (Ed.), *Language in social context* (pp. 67–86). Harmondsworth, England: Penguin.

Bates, E., Thal, D., Fenson, L., Whitesell, K., & Oakes, L. (1989). Integrating language and gesture in infancy. *Developmental Psychology, 25*, 1004–1019.

Bavelas, J. B. (1994). Gestures as part of speech: Methodological implications. *Research on Language and Social Interaction, 27*, 201–221.

Bavelas, J. B., Black, A., Lemery, C. R., & Mullett, J. (1986). "I show how you feel": Motor mimicry as a communicative act. *Journal of Personality and Social Psychology, 50*, 322–329.

Bavelas, J. C., & Chovil, N. (2006). Nonverbal and verbal communication: Hand gestures and facial displays as part of language use in face-to-face dialogue. In V. Manusov & M. L. Patterson (Eds.), *The SAGE handbook of nonverbal communication* (pp. 97–115). Thousand Oaks, CA: SAGE.

Bavelas, J. C., Coates, L., & Johnson, T. (2002). Listener responses as a collaborative process: The role of gaze. *Journal of Communication, 52*, 566–580.

Beattie, G., & Coughlin, J. (1999). An experimental investigation of the role of iconic gestures in lexical access using the tip-of-the-tongue phenomenon. *British Journal of Psychology, 90*, 35–56.

Beattie, G., & Shovelton, H. (1999a). Do iconic hand gestures really contribute anything to the semantic information conveyed by speech? An experimental investigation. *Semiotica, 123*, 1–30.

Beattie, G., & Shovelton, H. (1999b). Mapping the range of information contained in the iconic hand gestures that accompany spontaneous speech. *Journal of Language and Social Psychology, 18*, 438–462.

Beaulieu, C. (2004). Intercultural study of personal space: A case study. *Journal of Applied Social Psychology, 34*, 794–805.

Beck, L., & Feldman, R. S. (1989). Enhancing children's decoding of facial expression. *Journal of Nonverbal Behavior, 13*, 269–278.

Becker-Stoll, F., Delius, A., & Scheitenberger, S. (2001). Adolescents' nonverbal emotional expressions during negotiation of a disagreement with their mothers: An attachment approach. *International Journal of Behavioral Development, 25*, 344–353.

Behling, D. U. (1988). T-shirts as communicators of attitudes. *Perceptual and Motor Skills, 66*, 846.

Behne, T., Carpenter, M., & Tomasello, M. (2005). One-year-olds comprehend the communicative intentions behind gestures in a hiding game. *Developmental Science, 8*, 492–499.

Bell, S. (1999). Tattooed: A participant observer's exploration of meaning. *Journal of American Culture, 22*, 53–58.

Benjamin, B. C. (1986). Dimensions of the older female voice. *Language and Communication, 6*, 35–45.

Berman, P. W., & Smith, V. L. (1984). Gender and situational differences in children's smiles, touch, and proxemics. *Sex Roles, 10*, 347–356.

Bernieri, F. J. (1988). Coordinated movement and rapport in teacher-student interactions. *Journal of Nonverbal Behavior, 12*, 120–138.

Bernieri, F. J., & Rosenthal, R. (1991). Interpersonal coordination: Behavior matching and interactional synchrony. In R. S. Feldman & B. Rime (Eds.), *Fundamentals of nonverbal behavior* (pp. 401–432). Cambridge, England: Cambridge University Press.

Bernieri, F. J., Gillis, J. S., Davis, J. M., & Grahe, J. E. (1996). Dyad rapport and the accuracy of its judgment across situations: A lens model analysis. *Journal of Personality and Social Psychology, 71*, 110–129.

Berry, D. S. (1990). Vocal attractiveness and vocal babyishness: Effects on stranger, self, and friend impressions. *Journal of Nonverbal Behavior, 14*, 141–153.

Berscheid, E., & Walster, E. H. (1978). *Interpersonal attraction.* Reading, MA: Addison-Wesley.

Bickman, L. (1971). The effect of social status on the honesty of others. *Journal of Social Psychology, 85*, 87–92.

Bickman, L. (1974). The social power of a uniform. *Journal of Applied Social Psychology, 4*, 47–61.

Birdwhistell, R. (1970). *Kinesics and context: Essays on body motion communication*. Philadelphia, PA: University of Pennsylvania Press.

Bjorkland, D. F. (1987). A note on neonatal imitation. *Developmental Review,* 7, 86–92.

Blair, I. V., Judd, C. M., Sadler, M. S., & Jenkins, C. (2002). The role of Afrocentric features in person perception: Judging by features and categories. *Journal of Personality and Social Psychology, 83*, 5–23.

Blanck, P. J., & Rosenthal, R. (1992). Nonverbal behavior in the courtroom. In R. S. Feldman (Ed.), *Applications of nonverbal behavioral theories* (pp. 167–190). Hillsdale, NJ: Lawrence Erlbaum.

Bloom, K., Zajac, D., & Titus, J. (1999). The influence of nasality of voice on sex-stereotyped perceptions. *Journal of Nonverbal Behavior, 23*, 271–281.

Blurton-Jones, N. G. (1967). An ethological study of some aspects of social behavior of children in nursery school. In D. Morris (Ed.), *Primate ethology* (pp. 347–368). London, England: Weidenfeld & Nicholoson.

Bochin, H. (1990). *Richard Nixon: Rhetorical strategist.* New York, NY: Greenwood Press.

Bohm, J. K., & Hendricks, B. (1997). Effects of interpersonal touch, degree of justification, and sex of participant on compliance with a request. *Journal of Social Psychology, 137*, 460–469.

Bonvillain, N. (1993). *Language, culture, and communication*. Englewood Cliffs, NJ: Prentice Hall.

Boomer, D. S. (1978). The phonemic clause: Speech unit in human communication. In A. W. Siegman & S. Feldstein (Eds.), *Nonverbal behavior and communication* (pp. 245–262). Hillsdale, NJ: Erlbaum.

Boothroyd, L., & Brewer, G. (2014). Self-reported impulsivity, rather than sociosexuality, predicts women's preferences for masculine features in male faces. *Archives of Sexual Behavior, 43*, 983–988.

Bothwell, R. K., Brigham, J. C., & Malpass, R. S. (1989). Cross-racial identification. *Personality and Social Psychology Bulletin, 15*, 19–25.

Bowen, E., & Nowicki, S. (2007). The nonverbal decoding ability of children exposed to family violence or maltreatment: Prospective evidence from a British cohort. *Journal of Nonverbal Behavior, 31*, 169–184.

Bower, B. (2000). Building blocks of talk: When babies babble, they may say a lot about speech. *Science News, 157*, 344–346.

Bower, B. (2001). Babies may thrive on wordless conversation. *Science News, 159*, 390.

Bower, B. (2002). The eyes have it: Newborns prefer faces with a direct gaze. *Science News, 162*, 4–5.

Bowlby, J. (1973). *Attachment and loss: Separation, anxiety and anger*. New York, NY: Basic Books.

Bowlby, J. (1980). *Attachment and loss: Sadness and depression*. New York, NY: Basic Books.

Boyatzis, C. J., & Satyaprasad, C. (1994). Children's facial and gestural decoding and encoding: Relations between skills and with popularity. *Journal of Nonverbal Behavior, 18*, 37–55.

Boyatzis, C. J., & Watson, M. W. (1993). Preschool children's symbolic representation of objects through gestures. *Child Development, 64*, 729–735.

Bradford, A., Ferrer, D., & Bradford, G. (1974). Evaluation reactions of college students to dialect differences in the English of Mexican-Americans. *Language and Speech, 17*, 255–270.

Breed, A. G. (1997, January 1). Girl returns sans lipstick. *Philadelphia Inquirer*.

Brennan-Parks, K., Goddard, M., Wilson, A. E., & Kinnear, L. (1991). Sex differences in smiling as measured in a picture taking task. *Sex Roles, 24*, 375–382.

Bretherton, I., Fritz, J., Zahn-Waxler, C., & Ridgeway, D. (1986). Learning to talk about emotions: A functionalist perspective. *Child Development, 57*, 529–548.

Brigham, J. C., & Malpass, R. S. (1985). The role of experience and contact in the recognition of faces of own and other-race faces. *Journal of Social Issues, 41*, 139–155.

Brinson, C. S. (2000, August 28). Ya'll don't like my accent? Song of the south isn't music to everyone's ears. *The State*.

Brislin, R. W., & Lewis, S. A. (1966). Dating and physical attractiveness: A replication. *Psychological Reports, 22*, 976.

Broadstock, M., Borland, R., & Gason, R. (1992). Effects of suntan on judgments of healthiness and attractiveness by adolescents. *Journal of Applied Social Psychology, 22*, 157–172.

Brown, B. L., & Bradshaw, J. M. (1985). Toward a social psychology of voice variations. In H. Giles & R. N. St. Clair (Eds.), *Recent advances in language communication and social psychology* (pp. 144–181). London, England: Lawrence Erlbaum.

Brown, B. L., & Lambert, W. E. (1976). A cross-cultural study of social status markers in speech. *Canadian Journal of Behavioural Science, 8*, 39–55.

Brown, W. M., Palameta, B., & Moore, C. (2003). Are there nonverbal cues to commitment? An exploratory study using the zero-acquaintance video presentation paradigm. *Evolutionary Psychology, 1*, 42–69.

Browne, B. A. (1998). Gender stereotypes in advertising on children's television in the 1990s: A cross-national analysis. *Journal of Advertising, 27*, 83–96.

Brownlow, S., & Zebrowitz, L. A. (1990). Facial appearance, gender, and credibility in television commercials. *Journal of Nonverbal Behavior, 14*, 51–60.

Buck, R. (1975). Nonverbal communication of affect in children. *Journal of Personality and Social Psychology, 31*, 644–653.

Buck, R. (1977). Nonverbal communication of affect in preschool children: Relationships with personality, and skin conductance. *Journal of Personality and Social Psychology, 35*, 225–236.

Buck, R. (1981). The evolution and development of emotion expression and communication. In S. S. Brehm, S. S. Kassin, & F. X. Gibbons (Eds.), *Developmental social psychology* (pp. 127–151). New York, NY: Oxford University Press.

Buck, R. (1984). *The communication of emotion*. New York, NY: Guilford.

Buck, R. (1991). Social factors in facial display and communication: A reply to Chovil and others. *Journal of Nonverbal Behavior, 15*, 155–161.

Buck, R., & VanLear, C. A. (2002). Verbal and nonverbal communication: Distinguishing symbolic, spontaneous, and pseudo-spontaneous nonverbal behavior. *Journal of Communication, 52*, 522–541.

Buck, R., Miller, R. E., & Caul, W. F. (1974). Sex, personality, and physiological variables in the communication of emotion via facial expression. *Journal of Personality and Social Psychology, 30*, 587–596.

Buck, R., Savin, V., Miller, R. E., & Caul, W. F. (1972). Nonverbal communication of affect in humans. *Journal of Personality and Social Psychology, 23*, 362–371.

Budesheim, T. L., & DePaola S. J. (1994). Beauty or the beast? The effects of appearance, personality, and issue information on evaluations of political candidates. *Personality and Social Psychology Bulletin, 20*, 339–348.

Buisine, S., & Martin, J. (2007). The effects of speech-gesture cooperation in animated agents' behavior in multimedia presentations. *Interacting with Computers, 19*, 484–493.

Bull, P., & Connelly, G. (1985). Body movement and emphasis in speech. *Journal of Nonverbal Behavior, 9*, 169–187.

Buller, D. B., & Burgoon, J. K. (1994). Interpersonal deception VII: Behavioral profiles of falsification, equivocation, and concealment. *Journal of Language and Social Psychology, 13*, 366–395.

Buller, D. B., & Burgoon, J. K. (1996). Interpersonal deception theory. *Communication Theory, 6*, 203–242.

Buller, D. B., Strzyzewski, K. D., & Hunsaker, F. G. (1991). Interpersonal deception II: The inferiority of conversational participants as deception detectors. *Communication Monographs, 58*, 25–40.

Bullis, C., & Horn, C. (1995). Get a little closer: Further examination of nonverbal comforting strategies. *Communication Reports, 8*, 10–17.

Burger, T. D., & Finkel, D. (2002). Relationships between body modifications and very high-risk behaviors in a college population. *College Student Journal, 36*, 203–213.

Burgess, J. W. (1983). Developmental trends in proxemic spacing behavior between surrounding companions and strangers in casual groups. *Journal of Nonverbal Behavior*, 7, 158–169.

Burgoon, J. K. (1978). A communication model of personal space violations: Explication and an initial test. *Human Communication Research, 4*, 129–142.

Burgoon, J. K. (1980). Nonverbal communication in the 1970s: An overview. In D. Nimmo (Ed.), *Communication yearbook 4* (pp. 179–197). New Brunswick, NJ: Transaction.

Burgoon, J. K. (1991). Relational message interpretations of touch, conversational distance, and posture. *Journal of Nonverbal Behavior, 15*, 233–259.

Burgoon, J. K., & Buller, D. B. (1995). Interpersonal deception IX: Effects of social skill and nonverbal communication on deception success and detection accuracy. *Journal of Language and Social Psychology, 14*, 289–311.

Burgoon, J. K., & Floyd, K. (2000). Testing for the motivation impairment effect during deceptive and truthful interaction. *Western Journal of Communication, 64*, 243–267.

Burgoon, J. K., Birk, T., & Pfau, M. (1990). Nonverbal behaviors, persuasion, and credibility. *Human Communication Research, 17*, 140–169.

Burgoon, J. K., Buller, D. B., & Floyd, K. (2001). Does participation affect deception success? A test of the interactivity principle. *Human Communication Research, 27*, 503–534.

Burgoon, J. K., Buller, D. B., & Woodall, W. G. (1996). *Nonverbal communication: The unspoken dialogue*. New York, NY: McGraw-Hill.

Burgoon, J. K., Buller, D. B., Ebesu, A. S., & Rockwell, P. (1994). Interpersonal deception

V: Accuracy in deception detection. *Communication Monographs, 61*, 303–325.

Burgoon, J. K., Buller, D. B., Hale, J. L., & deTurck, M. A. (1984). Relational messages associated with nonverbal behaviors. *Human Communication Research, 10*, 351–378.

Burgoon, J. K., Buller, D. B., White, C. H., Afifi, W., & Buslig, A. L. S. (1999). The role of conversational involvement in deceptive interpersonal interactions. *Personality and Social Psychology Bulletin, 25*, 669–686.

Burgoon, J. K., Stern, L. A., & Dillman, L. (1995). *Interpersonal adaptation: Dyadic interaction patterns*. Cambridge, England: Cambridge University Press.

Burleson, B. R., & Goldsmith, D. J. (1998). How the comforting process works: Alleviating emotional distress through conversationally induced reappraisals. In P. A. Andersen & L. K. Guerrero (Eds.), *Handbook of communication and emotion* (pp. 245–280). San Diego, CA: Academic Press.

Burnett, A., & Badzinski, D. M. (2005). Judge nonverbal communication on trial: Do mock trial jurors notice? *Journal of Communication, 55*, 209–224.

Bush, L. K., Barr, C. L., McHugo, G. J., & Lanzetta, J. T. (1989). The effects of facial control and facial mimicry on subjective reactions to comedy routines. *Motivation and Emotion, 13*, 31–52.

Bushman, B. J. (1988). The effects of apparel on compliance: A field experiment with a female authority figure. *Personality and Social Psychology Bulletin, 14*, 459–467.

Buss, D. (1989). Sex differences in human mate selection: Evolutionary hypotheses tested in 37 countries. *Behavioral and Brain Sciences, 12*, 1–49.

Buss, D. (1990). International preferences in selecting mates. *Journal of Cross-Cultural Psychology, 21*, 5–47.

Butler, D., & Geis, F. L. (1990). Nonverbal affect responses to male and female leaders: Implications for leadership evaluations. *Journal of Personality and Social Psychology, 58*, 48–59.

Cahoon, D. D., & Edmonds, E. M. (1987). Estimates of opposite-sex first impressions related to females' clothing style. *Perceptual and Motor Skills, 65*, 406.

Calvo, M. G., Gutierrez-Garcia, A., Fernandez-Martin, A., & Nummenmaa, L. (2014). Recognition of facial expressions of emotion is related to their frequency in everyday life. *Journal of Nonverbal Behavior, 38*, 549–567.

Camargo, S. P. H., Rispoli, M., Ganz, J., Hong, E. R., Davis, H., & Mason, R. A. (2014). Review of the quality of behaviorally-based intervention research to improve social interaction skills of children with ASD in inclusive settings. *Journal of Autism Developmental Disorders, 44*, 2096–2116.

Cameron, H., & & Xu, X. (2011). Representational gesture, pointing gesture, and memory recall of preschool children. *Journal of Nonverbal Behavior, 35*, 155–171.

Campbell, D. A., & Urgo, J. L. (1997, February 18). After fatal beating, shock and disbelief. *Philadelphia Inquirer*, p. B1.

Campos, B., Keltner, D., Beck, J. M., Gonzaga, G. C., & John, O. P. (2007). Culture and teasing: The relational benefits of reduced desire for positive self-differentiation. *Personality and Social Psychology Bulletin, 33*, 3–16.

Camras, L. A. (1985). Socialization of affect communication. In M. Lewis & C. Saarni (Eds.), *The socialization of emotions* (pp. 141–160). New York, NY: Plenum.

Camras, L. A., Grow, J. G., & Ribordy, S. C. (1983). Recognition of emotional expression by abused children. *Journal of Clinical Child Psychology, 12*, 325–328.

Camras, L. A., Sullivan, J., & Michel, G. (1993). Do infants express discrete emotions? Adult judgments of facial, vocal, and body actions. *Journal of Nonverbal Behavior, 17*, 171–186.

Canary, D. J., & Cody, M. J. (1994). *Interpersonal communication: A goals-based approach*. New York, NY: St. Martin's.

Canli, T., Silvers, H., Gotlib, I. H., & Gabrieli, I. D. E. (2002). Amygdala response to happy faces as a function of extraversion. *Science, 296*, 2191.

Caplan, F. (1973). *The first twelve months of life*. New York, NY: Grosset & Dunlap.

Cappella, J. N. (1983). Conversational involvement: Approaching and avoiding others. In J. M. Wiemann & R. P. Harrison (Eds.), *Nonverbal interaction* (pp. 113–148). Beverly Hills, CA: SAGE.

Cappella, J. N. (1985). The management of conversations. In M. L. Knapp & G. R. Miller (Eds.), *Handbook of interpersonal communication* (pp. 393–438). Beverly Hills, CA: SAGE.

Cappella, J. N., & Greene, J. O. (1982). A discrepancy-arousal explanation of mutual influence in expressive behavior for adult-adult and infant-adult dyadic interaction. *Communication Monographs, 49*, 89–114.

Carello, C., Grosofsky, A., Shaw, R. E., Pittenger, J. B., & Mark, L. S. (1989). Attractiveness of facial profiles is a function of distance from archetype. *Ecological Psychology, 1*, 227–251.

Carey, M. S. (1978). The role of gaze in the initiation of conversation. *Social Psychology, 41*, 269–271.

Carli, L. L., LaFleur, S. J., & Loeber, C. C. (1995). Nonverbal behavior, gender, and influence. *Journal of Personality and Social Psychology, 68*, 1030–1041.

Carney, D. R., Cuddy, A. J., & Yapp, A. J. (2010). Power posing: Brief nonverbal displays affect neuroendocrine levels and risk tolerance. *Psychological Science, 10*, 1363–1368.

Carpenter, S. K., Wilford, M., Kornell, N., & Mullaney, K. M. (2013). Appearances can be deceiving: Instructor fluency increases perceptions of learning without increasing actual learning. *Psychonomic Bulletin & Review, 20*, 1350–1356.

Carrere, S., & Gottman, J. M. (1999). Predicting divorce among newlyweds from the first three minutes of a marital conflict. *Family Process, 38*, 293–301.

Carroll, J. M., & Russell, J. A. (1996). Do facial expressions signal specific emotions? Judging emotion from the face in context. *Journal of Personality and Social Psychology, 70*, 205–218.

Carroll, L., & Gilroy, P. J. (2002). Role of appearance and nonverbal behaviors in the perception of sexual orientation among lesbians and gay men. *Psychological Reports, 91*, 115–122.

Carroll, S. T., Riffenburgh, R. H., Roberts, T. A., & Myhre, E. B. (2002). Tattoos and body piercings as indicators of adolescent risk-taking behaviors. *Pediatrics, 109*, 1021–1027.

Cartei, V., & Reby, D. (2012). Acting gay: Male actors shift the frequency components of their voices toward female values when playing homosexual characters. *Journal of Nonverbal Behavior, 36*, 79–93.

Carton, J. S., & Kessler, E. A. (1999). Nonverbal decoding skills and relationship well-being in adults. *Journal of Nonverbal Behavior, 23*, 91–100.

Cary M. S. (1976). *Talk? Do you want to talk? Negotiation for the initiation of conversation between the unacquainted* (Unpublished doctoral dissertation). University of Pennsylvania, Philadelphia.

Cash, T. F. (1990). Losing hair, losing points? The effects of male pattern baldness on social impression formation. *Journal of Applied Social Psychology, 20*, 154–167.

Cash, T. F., Dawson, K., Davis, P., Bown, M., & Galumbeck, C. (1989). Effects of cosmetics use on the physical attractiveness and body image of American college women. *The Journal of Social Psychology, 129*, 349–355.

Cashdan, E. (1995). Hormones, sex, and status in women. *Hormones and Behavior, 29*, 354–366.

Cassidy, C. M. (1991). The good body: When big is better. *Medical Anthropology, 13*, 181–213.

Catford, M. (1964). Phonation types: The classification of some laryngeal components of speech production. In D. Abercrombie, D. B. Fry, P. A. D. MacCarthy, N. C. Scott, & J. L. M. Trim (Eds.), *In honour of Daniel Jones* (pp. 26–37). London, England: Longmans.

Cavior, N., & Boblett, P. J. (1972). Physical attractiveness of dating versus married couples. *Proceedings of the 80th Annual Convention of the American Psychological Association, 7*, 175–176.

Chaiken, S. (1979). Communicator physical attractiveness and persuasion. *Journal of Personality and Social Psychology, 37*, 1387–1397.

Chaiken, S. (1986). Physical appearance and social influence. In C. P. Herman, M. P. Zanna, & E. T. Higgins (Eds.), *Physical appearance, stigma, and social behavior: The Ontario symposium*

(Vol. 17, pp. 143–177). New York, NY: Academic Press.

Chambers, D. (2013). *Social media and personal relationships*. New York, NY: Palgrave Macmillan.

Chandler, J., & Schwarz, N. (2009). How extending your middle finger affects your perception of others: Learned movements influence concept accessibility. *Journal of Experimental Social Psychology, 45*, 123–128.

Chapell, M. S., & Beltran, W. (1999). Men and women holding hands II: Whose hand is uppermost? *Perceptual and Motor Skills, 89*, 537–549.

Chaplin, W. F., Phillips, J. B., Brown, J. D., Clanton, N. R., & Stein, J. L. (2000). Handshaking, gender, personality, and first impressions. *Journal of Personality and Social Psychology, 19*, 110–117.

Charney, E. J. (1966). Psychosomatic manifestations of rapport in psychotherapy. *Psychosomatic Medicine, 28*, 305–315.

Chartrand, T. L., & Bargh, J. A. (1999). The chameleon effect: The perception-behavior link and social interaction. *Journal of Personality and Social Psychology, 76*, 893–910.

Chartrand, T. L., & Lakin, J. L. (2013). The antecedents and consequences of behavioral mimicry. *Annual Review of Psychology, 64*, 285–308.

Chawla, P., & Krauss, R. M. (1994). Gesture and speech in spontaneous and rehearsed narratives. *Journal of Experimental Social Psychology, 30*, 580–601.

Chen, N. Y., & Shaffer, D. R. (1997). On physical attractiveness stereotyping in Taiwan: A revised sociocultural perspective. *Journal of Social Psychology, 137*, 117–124.

Cherulnik, P. D., Donley, K. A., Wiewel, T. S. R., & Miller, S. R. (2001). Charisma is contagious: The effect of leaders' charisma on observers' affect. *Journal of Applied Social Psychology, 31*, 2149–2159.

Chevrie-Muller, C., Perbos, J., & Guilet, C. (1983). Automated analysis of the electroglottographic signal: Application to the study of phonation in the elderly. *Aging Communication Bulletin Audiophonology, 16*, 121–144.

Chovil, N. (1989). *Communicative functions of facial displays in conversations* (Unpublished dissertation). University of Victoria, Victoria, British Colombia.

Chovil, N. (1991). Social determinants of facial displays. *Journal of Nonverbal Behavior, 15*, 141–154.

Christenfeld, N. (1996). Effects of a metronome on the filled pauses of fluent speakers. *Journal of Speech and Hearing Research, 39*, 1232–1238.

Christenfeld, N., & Creager, B. (1996). Anxiety, alcohol, aphasia, and ums. *Journal of Personality and Social Psychology, 70*, 451–460.

Christensen, A. (1988). Dysfunctional interaction patterns in couples. In P. Noller & M. A. Fitzpatrick (Eds.), *Perspectives on marital interaction* (pp. 31–52). Philadelphia, PA: Multilingual Matters.

Christensen, A., & Heavey, C. L. (1990). Gender, power and marital conflict. *Journal of Personality and Social Psychology, 59*, 73–85.

Church, R. B., Garber, P., & Rogalski, K. (2007). The role of gesture in memory and social communication. *Gesture, 7*, 137–158.

Claiborn, C. D. (1974). Counselor verbal intervention, nonverbal behavior, and social power. *Journal of Counseling Psychology, 26*, 378–383.

Clay, Z., Pople, S., Hood, B., & Kita, S. (2014). Young children make their gestural communication systems more language-like. *Psychological Science, 25*, 1518–1525.

Clayson, D. E., & Maughan, M. R. C. (1986). Redheads and blondes: Stereotypic images. *Psychological Reports, 59*, 811–816.

Coats, E. J., & Feldman, R. S. (1996). Gender differences in nonverbal correlates of social status. *Personality and Social Psychology Bulletin, 22*, 1014–1022.

Coats, E. J., Feldman, R. S., & Philippot, P. (1999). The influence of television on children's nonverbal behavior. In P. Philippot, R. S. Feldman, & E. J. Coats (Eds.), *The social context of nonverbal behavior* (pp. 156–181). Cambridge, England: Cambridge University Press.

Cogan, J. C., Bhalla, S. K., Sefa-Dedeh, A., & Rothblum, E. D. (1996). A comparison study of United States and African students on perceptions of obesity and thinness. *Journal of Cross-Cultural Psychology, 27*, 98–113.

Cohen, A. A. (1977). The communicative functions of hand gestures. *Journal of Communication, 27*, 54–63.

Coker, D. A., & Burgoon, J. K. (1987). The nature of conversational involvement and nonverbal encoding patterns. *Human Communication Research, 13*, 463–494.

Coleman, B. (1994, July 13). Obese teen girls, short boys earn less as adults, study says. *Philadelphia Inquirer.*

Coleman, R., & Wu, H. D. (2006). More than words alone: Incorporating broadcasters' nonverbal communication into the stages of crisis coverage theory—evidence from September 11th. *Journal of Broadcasting and Electronic Media, 50*, 1–17.

Condon, W. S., & Ogston, W. D. (1966). Sound film analysis of normal and pathological behavior patterns. *Journal of Nervous and Mental Disease, 143*, 338–347.

Condon, W. S., & Sander, L. W. (1974). Synchrony demonstrated between movements of the neonate and adult speech. *Child Development, 45*, 456–462.

Conlee, C. J., Olvera, J., & Vagim, N. M. (1993). The relationship among physician nonverbal immediacy and measures of patient satisfaction with physician care. *Communication Reports, 6*, 25–33.

Cook, S. W., & Goldin-Meadow, S. (2006). The role of gesture in learning: Do children use their hands to change their minds? *Journal of Cognition and Development, 7*, 211–232.

Cooley, E. L. (2005). Attachment style and decoding of nonverbal cues. *North American Journal of Psychology, 7*, 25–33.

Corballis, M. (2001, February 6). Do animals have language? *Lingua Franca*, 1–5.

Cordova, J. V., Gee, C. B., & Warren, L. Z. (2005). Emotional skillfulness in marriage: Intimacy as a mediator of the relationship between emotional skillfulness and marital satisfaction. *Journal of Social and Clinical Psychology, 24*(2), 218–235.

Costa, M. (2010). Interpersonal distances in group walking. *Journal of Nonverbal Behavior, 34*, 15–26.

Costanzo, M. (1992). Training students to decode verbal and nonverbal cues: Effects on confidence and performance. *Journal of Educational Psychology, 84*, 308–313.

Costanzo, M., & Archer, D. (1989). Interpreting the expressive behavior of others: The Interpersonal Perception Task (IPT). *Journal of Nonverbal Behavior, 13*, 225–245.

Côté, S., & Hideg, I. (2011). The ability to influence others via emotion displays: A new dimension of emotional intelligence. *Organizational Psychology Review, 1*, 53–71.

Cramer, P., & Steinwert, T. (1998). Thin is good, fat is bad: How early does it begin? *Journal of Applied Developmental Psychology, 19*, 429–451.

Crane, E. A., & Gross, M. M. (2013). Effort-shape characteristics of emotion-related body movement. *Journal of Nonverbal Behavior, 37*, 91–108.

Croft, J. B., Strogatz, D. S., James, S. A., & Keenan, N. L. (1992). Socioeconomic and behavioral correlates of body mass index in black adults: The Pitt County study. *American Journal of Public Health, 82*, 821–826.

Cronkhite, G. (1986). On the focus, scope, and coherence of the study of human symbolic activity. *Quarterly Journal of Speech, 72*, 231–246.

Crusco, A. H., & Wetzel, C. G. (1984). The Midas touch: The effects of interpersonal touch on restaurant tipping. *Personality and Social Psychology Bulletin, 10*, 512–517.

Cunningham, M. R., Roberts, A. R., Barbee, A. P., Druen, P. B., & Wu, C. H. (1995). Their ideas of beauty are, on the whole, the same as ours: Consistency and variability in the cross-cultural perception of female physical attractiveness. *Journal of Personality and Social Psychology, 68*, 261–279.

Curran, J. P., & Lippold, S. (1975). The effects of physical attractiveness and attitude similarity on attraction in dating dyads. *Journal of Personality, 43*, 528–539.

Cutica, I., & Bucciarelli, M. (2011). "The more you gesture, the less I gesture": Co-speech gestures as a measure of mental model quality. *Journal of Nonverbal Behavior, 35*, 173–187.

Cutler, W. B., & Genovese, E. (2002). Pheromones, sexual attractiveness and quality of life in menopausal women. *Climacteric: The Journal of the International Menopause Society, 5*, 112–121.

Cutrone, P. (2005). The backchannel norms of native English speakers: A target for Japanese L2 English learners. *Language Studies Working Papers, 2*, 28–37.

D'Entremont, B., & Muir, D. (1999). Infant responses to adult happy and sad vocal and facial expressions during face-to-face interactions. *Infant Behavior and Development, 22*, 527–539.

Dabbs, J. M. (1997). Testosterone, smiling, and facial appearance. *Journal of Nonverbal Behavior, 21*, 45–55.

Dabbs, J. M., Hargrove, M. F., & Heusel, C. (1996). Testosterone differences among college fraternities: Well behaved vs. rambunctious. *Personality and Individual Differences, 20*, 157–161.

Dabbs, J. M., Jr. (1969). Similarity of gestures and interpersonal influence. *Proceedings of the 77th annual convention of the American Psychological Association, 4*, 337–338.

Darden, C. (1996). *In contempt*. New York, NY: HarperCollins.

Darwin, C. (1872). *Expression of the emotions in man and animals*. London, England: Albemarle.

Davis, D. M. (1990). Portrayals of women in primetime network television: Some demographic characteristics. *Sex Roles, 23*, 325–332.

Davis, F. (1973). *Inside intuition: What we know about nonverbal communication*. New York, NY: McGraw Hill.

Davis, S. F., Schrader, B., Richardson, T. R., Kring, J. P., & Kieffer, J. C. (1998). Restaurant servers influence tipping behavior. *Psychological Reports, 83*, 223–226.

Davis, T. L. (1996). Gender differences in masking negative emotions: Ability or motivation? *Developmental Psychology, 31*, 660–667.

de Gelder, B. (2006, March). Towards the neurobiology of emotional body language. *Nature Reviews Neuroscience*, 7, 242–249.

de Meijer, M. D. (1989). The contribution of general features of body movement to the attribution of emotions. *Journal of Nonverbal Behavior, 13*, 247–267.

De Sonneville, L. M., Verschoor, C., Nijokiktjien, C., Ophet Veld, V., Toorenaar, N., & Vranken, M. (2002). Facial identity and facial emotions: Speed, accuracy and processing strategies in children and adults. *Journal of Clinical Experimental Neuropsychology, 2*, 200–213.

de Waal, F. B. M. (2001, January 19). Pointing primates: Sharing knowledge . . . without language. *Chronicle of Higher Education, 47*, B7–B9.

de Weerth, C., & Kalma, A. (1995). Gender differences in awareness of courtship initiation tactics. *Sex Roles, 32*, 717–734.

de Wied, M., van Boxtel, A., Zaalberg, R., Goudena, P. P., & Matthys, W. (2006). Facial EMG responses to dynamic emotional facial expressions in boys with disruption behavior disorders. *Journal of Psychiatric Research, 40*, 112–121.

Deadly search for beautiful bodies. (1993). *USA Today Magazine, 121*, 14–15.

DeBruine, L. M., Jones, B. C., Crawford, J. R., Welling, L. M., & Little, A.C. (2010). The health of a nation predicts their mate preferences: Cross-cultural variation in women's preferences for masculinized male faces. *Proceeding of the Royal Society B: Biological Sciences, 277*, 2405–2410.

Deck, L. (1968). Buying brains by the inch. *Journal of College and University Personnel Association, 29*, 33–37.

DeFleur, M. L., & Dennis, E. E. (1998). *Understanding mass communication*. Boston, MA: Houghton Mifflin.

DeGroot, T., & Motowidlo, S. J. (1999). Why visual and vocal interview cues can affect interviewers' judgments and predict job performance. *Journal of Applied Psychology, 84*, 986–993.

Del Giudice, M., & Colle, L. (2007). Differences between children and adults in the recognition of enjoyment smiles. *Developmental Psychology, 43*, 796–803.

Demopoulos, C., Hopkins, J., & Davis, A. (2013). A comparison of social cognitive profiles of children with autism spectrum disorders and attention deficit/hyperactivity disorder: A matter of quantitative but not qualitative difference? *Journal of Autism and Developmental Disorders, 43*, 1157–1170.

DePaulo, B. M., & Jordan, A. (1982). Age changes in deceiving and detecting deceit. In R. Feldman (Ed.), *Development of nonverbal behavior in children* (pp. 151–180). New York, NY: Springer-Verlag.

DePaulo, B. M., & Pfeifer, R. L. (1986). On-the-job experience and skill at detecting deception. *Journal of Applied Social Psychology, 16*, 249–267.

DePaulo, B. M., Kashy, D. A., Kirkeodol, S. E., Wyer, M. M., & Epstein, J. A. (1996). Lying in everyday life. *Journal of Personality and Social Psychology, 70*, 979–995.

DePaulo, B. M., Lindsay, J. L., Malone, B. E., Muhlenbruck, L., Charlton, K., & Cooper, H. (2003). Cues to deception. *Psychological Bulletin, 129*, 74–118.

DePaulo, B. M., Rosenthal, R., Green, C. R., & Rosenkrantz, J. (1982). Diagnosing deceptive and mixed messages from verbal and nonverbal cues. *Journal of Experimental Social Psychology, 18*, 433–446.

DePaulo, B. M., Stone, J. I., & Lassiter, G. D. (1985). Deceiving and detecting deceit. In B. R. Schlenker (Ed.), *The self and social life* (pp. 323–370). New York, NY: McGraw-Hill.

DePaulo, P. J. (1992). Applications of nonverbal behavior research in marketing and management. In R. S. Feldman (Ed.), *Applications of nonverbal behavioral theories* (pp. 63–87). Hillsdale, NJ: Lawrence Erlbaum.

Derks, D., Bos, A. E. R., & Grumbkow, J. (2008). Emoticons and online message interpretation. *Social Science Computer Review, 76*, 379–388.

Derlega, V. J., Lewis, R. J., Harrison, S., Winstead, B. A., & Costanzo, R. (1989). Gender differences in the initiation and attribution of tactile intimacy. *Journal of Nonverbal Behavior, 13*, 83–96.

Derntl, B., Habel, U., Robinson, S., Windischberger, C., Krispin-Exner, I., Gur, R. C., & Moser, E. (2012). Culture but not gender modulates amygdala activation during explicit emotion recognition. *BMC Neuroscience, 13*, 54.

Desantis, M., & Sierra, N. (2000). Women smiled more often and openly than men when photographed for a pleasant, public occasion in 20th century United States Society. *Psychology: A Journal of Human Behavior, 37*, 21–28.

deTurck, M. A., & Miller, G. R. (1990). Training observers to detect deception: Effects of self-monitoring and rehearsal. *Human Communication Research, 16*, 603–620.

Deutsch, F. M., LeBaron, D., & Fryer, M. M. (1987). What is in a smile? *Psychology of Women Quarterly, 11*, 341–352.

Devereux, P. G., & Ginsberg, G. P. (2001). Sociality effects on the production of laughter. *Journal of General Psychology, 128*, 227–240.

DiBiase, R., & Gunnoe, J. (2004). Gender and culture differences in touching behavior. *The Journal of Social Psychology, 144*, 49–62.

Didillon, H., Bounsana, D., & Vandewiele, M. (1988). The maquillage practice in Brazzaville. *Psychological Reports, 62*, 307–316.

Diefendorff, J. M., & Richard, E. M. (2003). Antecedents and consequences of emotional display rule perceptions. *Journal of Applied Psychology, 88*, 284–294.

Diefendorff, J. M., Richard, E. M., & Croyle, H. H. (2006). Are emotional display rules formal job requirements? Examination of employee and supervisor perceptions. *Journal of Occupational and Organizational Psychology, 79*, 273–298.

DiMatteo, M. R., Hays, R. D., & Prince, L. M. (1986). Relationship of physicians' nonverbal communication skill to patient satisfaction, appointment noncompliance, and physician workload. *Health Psychology, 5*, 581–594.

Dimberg, U. (1982). Facial reactions to facial expressions. *Psychophysiology, 19*, 643–647.

Dimberg, U., & Ohman, A. (1996). Behold the wrath: Psychophysiological responses to facial stimuli. *Motivation and Emotion, 20*, 149–182.

Dimitrovsky, L. (1964). The ability to identify the emotional meaning of vocal expressions at successive age levels. In J. R. Davitz (Ed.), *The communication of emotional meaning* (pp. 69–86). New York, NY: McGraw-Hill.

Dindia, K., Fitzpatrick, M. A., & Attridge, M. (1989, November). *Gaze and mutual gaze: A social relations analysis*. Paper presented at the annual convention of the Speech Communication Association, San Francisco, California.

Dittman, A. T. (1972). Developmental factors in conversational behavior. *Journal of Communication, 22*, 404–423.

Dittman, A. T., & Llewellyn, L. G. (1967). The phonemic clause as a unit of speech decoding. *Journal of Personality and Social Psychology, 6*, 341–349.

Doherty, R. W. (1997). The emotional contagion scale: A measure of individual differences. *Journal of Nonverbal Behavior, 21*, 131–154.

Doherty, R. W., Orimoto, L., Singelis, T. M., Hatfield, E., & Hebb, J. (1995). Emotional contagion: Gender and occupational differences. *Psychology of Women Quarterly, 19*, 355–371.

Dolgin, K. G., & Azmita, M. (1985). The development of the ability to interpret emotional signals—what is and is not known. In G. Zivin (Ed.), *The development of expressive behavior* (pp. 319–346). Orlando, FL: Academic Press.

Dolgin, K. M., & Sabini, J. (1982). Experimental manipulation of a human nonverbal display: The tongue show affects an observer's willingness to interact. *Animal Behaviour, 30*, 935–936.

Dolin, D. J., & Booth-Butterfield, M. (1993). Reach out and touch someone: Analysis of nonverbal comforting responses. *Communication Quarterly, 41*, 383–393.

Dolinski, D. (2010). Touch, compliance, and homophobia. *Journal of Nonverbal Behavior, 34*, 179–192.

Dongieux, J., & Sassouni, V. (1980). The contribution of mandibular positioned variation to facial esthetics. *Facial Esthetics, 50*, 334–339.

Donn, J. E., & Sherman, R. C. (2002). Attitudes and practices regarding the formation of romantic relationships on the internet. *Cyberpsychology and Behavior, 5*, 107–123.

Doody, J. P., & Bull, P. (2011). Asperger's syndrome and the decoding of boredom. *Journal of Nonverbal Behavior, 35*, 87–100.

Douglis, C. (1987). The beat goes on. *Psychology Today, 21*, 37–42.

Dovidio, J. F., Brown, C. E., Heltman, K., Ellyson, S. L., & Keating, C. F. (1988). Power displays between women and men in discussions of gender-linked tasks: A multichannel study. *Journal of Personality and Social Psychology, 55*, 580–587.

Dovidio, J. F., Hebl, M., Richeson, J. A., & Shelton, N. (2006). Nonverbal communication, race, and intergroup interaction. In V. Manusov & M. L. Patterson (Eds.), *The SAGE handbook of nonverbal communication* (pp. 481–500). Thousand Oaks, CA: SAGE.

Downs, A. C., & Harrison, S. K. (1985). Embarrassing age spots or just plain ugly? Physical attractiveness stereotyping as an instrument of sexism on American television commercials. *Sex Roles, 13*, 9–19.

Drews, D. R., Allison, C. K., & Probst, J. R. (2000). Behavioral and self-concept differences in tattooed and nontattooed college students. *Psychological Reports, 86*, 475–481.

Driskell, D. M., & Salas, E. (2005). The effect of content and demeanor on reactions to dominance behavior. *Group Dynamics: Theory, Research, and Practice, 9*, 3–14.

Driskell, D. M., Kelly, J. R., & Henderson, W. M. (1998). Can perceivers identify likelihood to sexually harass? *Sex Roles, 38*, 557–588.

Drummond, P. D., & Bailey, T. (2013). Eye contact evokes blushing independent of negative affect. *Journal of Nonverbal Behavior, 37*, 207–216.

Ducci, L., Arcuri, L., Georgis, T., & Sineshaw, T. (1982). Emotion recognition in Ethiopia: The effect of familiarity with Western culture on accuracy of recognition. *Journal of Cross-Cultural Psychology, 13*, 340–351.

Duggan, A. P., & Parrott, R. L. (2000). Research note: Physicians' nonverbal rapport building and patients' talk about the subject component of illness. *Human Communication Research, 27*, 299–311.

Duggan, M. (2015, August). Mobile messaging and social media. *Pew Research Center*. Retrieved February 9, 2016, from http://www.pewinternet.org/2015/08/19/mobile-messaging-and-social-media-2015/

Duke, M. P., Nowicki, S., & Martin, E. A. (1996). *Teaching your child the language of social success*. Atlanta, GA: Peachtree.

Duncan, S. D., Jr. (1972). Some signals and rules for taking speaking turns in conversations. *Journal of Personality and Social Psychology, 23*, 283–292.

Duncan, S. D., Jr. (1974). On the structure of speaker-auditor interaction during speaking turns. *Language in Society, 2*, 161–180.

Duncan, S. D., Jr., & Fiske, D. W. (1977). *Face-to-face interaction: Research, methods, and theory*. Hillsdale, NJ: Erlbaum.

Durkin, S. J., & Paxton, S. J. (2002). Predictors of vulnerability to reduced body image satisfaction and psychological well-being in response to exposure to idealized female media images in adolescent girls. *Journal of Psychosomatic Research, 53*, 995–1005.

Eakins, B. W., & Eakins, R. G. (1978). *Sex differences in human communication*. Boston, MA: Houghton Mifflin.

Edinger, J. A., & Patterson, M. L. (1983). Nonverbal involvement and social control. *Psychological Bulletin, 93*, 30–56.

Edwards, K. (1987). Effects of sex and glasses on attitudes toward intelligence. *Psychological Reports, 60*, 590.

Efron, D. (1941). *Gesture and environment*. New York, NY: Kings Crown Press.

Eibl-Eibesfeldt, I. (1972). Similarities and differences between cultures in expressive movements. In R. Hinde (Ed.), *Non-verbal communication* (pp. 297–314). Cambridge, England: Cambridge University Press.

Eibl-Eibesfeldt, I. (1973). The expressive behavior of the deaf-and-blind born. In M. von Cranach & I. Vine (Eds.), *Social communication and movement*. New York, NY: Academic Press.

Eibl-Eibesfeldt, I. (1975). *Ethology: The biology of behavior* (2nd ed.). New York, NY: Holt, Rinehart and Winston.

Einav, S., & Hood, B. N. (2006). Children's use of the temporal dimension of gaze for inferring preference. *Developmental Psychology, 42*, 142–152.

Ekman, P. (1972). Universals and cultural differences in facial expressions of emotion. In J. Cole (Ed.), *Nebraska symposium on motivation* (pp. 207–283). Lincoln: University of Nebraska Press.

Ekman, P. (1973). Cross-cultural studies of facial expression. In P. Ekman (Ed.), *Darwin and facial expression: A century of research in review* (pp. 169–222). New York, NY: Academic Press.

Ekman, P. (1976). Movements with precise meanings. *Journal of Communication, 26*, 14–26.

Ekman, P. (1979). About brows: Emotional and conversational signals. In M. von Cranach, K. Foppa, W. Lepenies, & D. Ploog (Eds.), *Human ethology* (pp. 169–248). Cambridge, England: Cambridge University Press.

Ekman, P. (1982). *Emotion in the human face*. Cambridge, England: Cambridge University Press.

Ekman, P. (1986). *Telling lies*. New York, NY: Berkeley Books.

Ekman, P. (1992). Facial expression of emotion: New findings, new questions. *Psychological Science, 3*, 34–38.

Ekman, P. (1994). All emotions are basic. In P. Ekman & R. J. Davidson (Eds.), *The nature of emotion: Fundamental questions* (pp. 15–19). New York, NY: Oxford University Press.

Ekman, P., & Friesen, W. V. (1969a). Nonverbal leakage and clues to deception. *Psychiatry, 32*, 88–106.

Ekman, P., & Friesen, W. V. (1969b). The repertoire of nonverbal behavior: Categories, origins, usage, and coding. *Semiotica, 1*, 49–98.

Ekman, P., & Friesen, W. V. (1971). Constants across cultures in the face and emotion. *Journal of Personality and Social Psychology, 17*, 124–129.

Ekman, P., & Friesen, W. V. (1974). Nonverbal behavior and psychopathology. In R. J. Friedman & H. M. Katz (Eds.), *The psychology of depression: Contemporary theory and research*. New York, NY: Wiley.

Ekman, P., & Friesen, W. V. (1975). *Unmasking the face: A guide to recognizing emotions from facial clues*. Englewood Cliffs, NJ: Prentice Hall.

Ekman, P., & Friesen, W. V. (1976). Measuring facial movement. *Environmental Psychology and Nonverbal Behavior, 1*, 56–75.

Ekman, P., & Friesen, W. V. (1978). *Investigator's guide to the facial action coding system, part*

II. Palo Alto, CA: Consulting Psychologists Press.

Ekman, P., & Friesen, W. V. (1986). A new pan-cultural facial expression of emotion. *Motivation and Emotion, 10*, 159–168.

Ekman, P., & Heider, K. (1988). The universality of a contempt expression: A replication. *Motivation and Emotion, 12*, 303–308.

Ekman, P., & Keltner, D. (1997). Universal facial expressions of emotion: An old -controversy and new findings. In U. Segerstrale & P. Molnar (Eds.), *Nonverbal communication: Where nature meets culture* (pp. 27–46). Mahwah, NJ: Lawrence Erlbaum.

Ekman, P., & O'Sullivan, M. (1991a). Facial expression: Methods, means, and moues. In R. S. Feldman & B. Rime (Eds.), *Fundamentals of nonverbal behavior* (pp. 163–199). Cambridge, England: Cambridge University Press.

Ekman P., & O'Sullivan, M. (1991b). Who can catch a liar? *American Psychologist, 46*, 913–920.

Ekman, P., Friesen, W. V., & Ancoli, S. (1980). Facial signs of emotional experience. *Journal of Personality and Social Psychology, 39*, 1125–1134.

Ekman, P., Friesen, W. V., & Ellsworth, P. C. (1972). *Emotion in the human face*. New York, NY: Pergamon.

Ekman, P., Friesen, W. V., O'Sullivan, M., Chan, A., Diacoyanni-Tarlatzis, I., Heider, K., Krause, R., . . . & Tzauaras, A. (1987). Universals and cultural differences in the judgments of facial expressions of emotion. *Journal of Personality and Social Psychology, 53*, 712–717.

Ekman, P., Levenson, R. W., & Friesen, W. V. (1983). Autonomic nervous system activity distinguishes between emotions. *Science, 221*, 1208–1210.

Ekman, P., O'Sullivan, M., & Frank, M. (1999). A few can catch a liar. *Psychological Science, 10*, 263–266.

Ekman, P., Sorenson, R. E., & Friesen, W. V. (1969). Pan-cultural elements in facial displays of emotions. *Science, 164*, 86–88.

Elaad, E. (2009). Lie detection bias among male police interrogators, prisoners, and laypersons. *Psychological Reports, 105*, 1047–1056.

Elfenbein, H. A. (2006). Learning in emotion judgments: Training and the cross-cultural understanding of facial expressions. *Journal of Nonverbal Behavior, 30*, 21–36.

Elfenbein, H. A. (2013). Nonverbal dialects and accents in facial expressions of emotion. *Emotion Review, 13*, 90–96.

Elfenbein, H. A., & Ambady, N. (2002). On the universality and cultural specificity of emotion recognition: A meta-analysis. *Psychological Bulletin, 128*, 203–235.

Elfenbein, H. A., & Ambady, N. (2002). Predicting workplace outcomes from the ability to eavesdrop on feelings. *Journal of Applied Psychology, 87*, 963–971.

Elfenbein, H. A., & Eisenkraft, N. (2010). The relationship between displaying and perceiving nonverbal cues of affect: A meta-analysis to solve an old mystery. *Journal of Personality and Social Psychology, 98*, 301–318.

Elfenbein, H. A., Beaupré, M., Lévesque, M., & Hess, U. (2007). Toward a dialect theory: Cultural differences in the expression and recognition of posed facial expressions. *Emotion, 7*, 131–146.

Ellsworth, P. C., & Langer, E. J. (1976). Staring and approach: An interpretation of the stare as a nonspecific activator. *Journal of Personality and Social Psychology, 33*, 117–122.

Ellsworth, P. C., Carlsmith, J. M., & Henson, A. (1972). The stare as a stimulus to flight in human subjects: A series of field experiments. *Journal of Personality and Social Psychology, 21*, 302–311.

Englis, B. G., Solomon, M. R., & Ashmore, R. D. (1994). Beauty before the eyes of the beholders: The cultural encoding of beauty types in magazine advertising and music television. *Journal of Advertising, 23*, 49–64.

Entman, R. M. (1990). Modern racism and the image of blacks in local television news. *Critical Studies in Mass Communication, 7*, 332–345.

Epley, N., & Kruger, J. (2005). When what you type isn't what they read: The perseverance of stereotypes and expectancies over e-mail. *Journal of Experimental Social Psychology, 41*, 414–422.

Eskritt, M., & Lee, K. (2003). Do actions speak louder than words? Preschool children's use of the verbal-nonverbal consistency principle during inconsistent communications. *Journal of Nonverbal Behavior, 27*, 25–41.

Etcoff, N. (1999). *Survival of the prettiest*. New York, NY: Doubleday

Ewing, E. (1975). *Women in uniform through the centuries*. Totowa, NJ: Rowman & Littlefield.

Exline, R. V. (1963). Explorations in the process of person perception: Visual interaction in relation to competition, sex, and need for affiliation. *Journal of Personality, 31*, 1–20.

Fabri, M., Moore, D., & Hobbs, D. (2005, September). Empathy and enjoyment in instant messaging. In L. McKinnon, O. Bertelsen, & N. Bryan-Kinns (Eds.), *Proceedings of the 19th British HCI Group Annual Conference*, Edinburgh, England.

Farley, S. D. (2008). Attaining status at the expense of likeability: Pilfering power through conversational interruption. *Journal of Nonverbal Behavior, 32*, 241–260.

Farley, S. D. (2014). Nonverbal reactions to an attractive stranger: The role of mimicry in communicating preferred social distance. *Journal of Nonverbal Behavior, 38*, 195–208.

Farley, S. D., Ashcraft, A. M., Stasson, M. F., & Nussbaum, R. L. (2010). Nonverbal reactions to conversational interruption: A test of complementarity theory and the gender/status parallel. *Journal of Nonverbal Behavior, 34*, 193–206.

Farley, S. D., Hughes, S. M., & LaFayette, J. N. (2013). People will know we are in love: Evidence of differences between vocal samples directed toward lovers and friends. *Journal of Nonverbal Behavior, 37*, 123–138.

Fast, J. (1991). *Body language in the workplace*. New York, NY: Penguin.

Feeley, T. H., & deTurck, M. A. (1997). *Perceptions of communication as seen by the actor and as seen by the observer: The case of lie detection*. Paper presented at the International Communication Association Annual Conference, Montreal, Canada.

Feeley, T. H., & Young, M. J. (1998). Humans as lie detectors: Some more second thoughts. *Communication Quarterly, 46*, 109–126.

Feeley, T. H., deTurck, M. A., & Young, M. J. (1995). Baseline familiarity in lie detection. *Communication Research Reports, 12*, 160–169.

Feeney, B. C., & Collins, N. L. (2001). Predictors of caregiving in adult intimate relationships: An attachment theoretical perspective. *Journal of Personality and Social Psychology, 80*, 972–994.

Feeney, J. A., Noller, P., Sheehan, G., & Peterson, C. (1999). Conflict issues and conflict strategies as contexts for nonverbal behavior in close relationships. In P. Philippot, R. S. Feldman, & E. J. Coats (Eds.), *The social context of nonverbal behavior* (pp. 348–371). Cambridge, England: Cambridge University Press.

Fein, G. G. (1975). Children's sensitivity to social contexts at 18 months of age. *Development Psychology, 11*, 853–854.

Feingold, A. (1988). Matching for attractiveness in romantic partners and same-sex friends: A meta-analysis and theoretical critique. *Psychological Bulletin, 104*, 226–235.

Feldman, R. S., & White, J. B. (1980). Detecting deception in children. *Journal of Communication, 30*, 121–139.

Feldman, R. S., Devin-Sheehan, L., & Allen, V. N. (1978). Nonverbal cues as indicators of verbal dissembling. *American Educational Research Journal, 15*, 217–231.

Feldman, R. S., Forrest, J. A., & Happ, B. R. (2002). Self-presentation and verbal deception: Do self-presenters lie more? *Basic and Applied Social Psychology, 24*, 163–170.

Feldman, R. S., Jenkins, L., & Popola, O. (1979). Detection of deception in adults and children via facial expressions. *Child Development, 50*, 350–355.

Feldman, R. S., Tomasian, J. C., & Coats, E. J. (1999). Nonverbal deception abilities and adolescents' social competence: Adolescents with higher social skills are better liars. *Journal of Nonverbal Behavior, 23*, 237–249.

Fernandez-Dols, J. (2013). Emotion and expression: Naturalistic studies. *Emotion Review, 13*, 24–29.

Fernandez-Dols, J., & Ruiz-Belda, M. (1995). Are smiles a sign of happiness? Gold medal winners at the Olympic games. *Journal of Personality and Social Psychology, 69*, 1113–1119.

Fernandez-Dols, J., Sanchez, F., Carrera, P., & Ruiz-Belda,

M. (1997). Are spontaneous expressions and emotions linked? An experimental test of coherence. *Journal of Nonverbal Behavior, 21*, 163–177.

Ferrante, C. L., Haynes, A. M., & Kingsley, S. M. (1988). Image of women in television advertising. *Journal of Broadcasting and Electronic Media, 32*, 231–237.

Fiedler, K., & Walka, I. (1993). Training lie detectors to use nonverbal cues instead of global heuristics. *Human Communication Research, 20*, 199–223.

Field, T. (1982). Individual differences in the expressivity of neonates and young children. In R. S. Feldman (Ed.), *Development of nonverbal behavior in children* (pp. 279–298). New York, NY: Springer-Verlag.

Field, T. (1999). American adolescents touch each other less and are more aggressive toward their peers as compared with French adolescents. *Adolescence, 34*, 753–758.

Field, T., Woodson, R., Greenberg, R., & Cohen, D. (1982). Discrimination and imitation of facial expressions by neonates. *Science, 218*, 179–181.

Fink, B., & Penton-Voak, I. (2002). Evolutionary psychology of facial attractiveness. *Current Directions in Psychological Science, 11*, 154–158.

Fink, G., Neave, N., Manning, J., & Grammer, K. (2006). Facial symmetry and judgments of attractiveness, health and personality. *Personality and Individual Differences, 41*, 491–499.

Fischer-Lokou, J., Martin, A., & Guegen, N. (2011). Mimicry and propagation of prosocial behavior in a natural setting. *Psychological Reports, 108*, 599–605.

Fisher, C. D. (2000). Mood and emotions while working: Missing pieces of job satisfaction? *Journal of Organizational Behavior*, 21, 185–202.

Fisher, H. (1992). *Anatomy of love*. New York, NY: Fawcett-Columbine.

Fisher, J. D., Rytting, M., & Heslin, R. (1976). Hands touching hands: Affective and evaluative effects of an interpersonal touch. *Sociometry, 39*, 416–421.

Fisher, M., & Voracek, M. (2006). The shape of beauty: Determinants of female physical attractiveness. *Journal of Cosmetic Dermatology, 5*, 190–194.

Fishman, P. (1983). Interaction: The work women do. In B. Thorne, N. Henley, & C. Kramarae (Eds.), *Language, gender and society* (pp. 89–101). Rowley, MA.: Newbury House.

Fleischmann, S. T. (1991). The messages of body language in job interviews. *Employment Relations Today, Summer*, 161–166.

Fleuriet, C., Cole, M., & Guerrero, L. (2014). Exploring Facebook: Attachment style and nonverbal message characteristics as predictors of anticipated emotional reactions to Facebook postings. *Journal of Nonverbal Behavior, 38*, 429–450.

Floyd, K. (1999). All touches are not created equal: Effects of form and duration on observers' interpretations of an embrace. *Journal of Nonverbal Behavior, 23*, 283–299.

Floyd, K. (2000). Affectionate same-sex touch: The influence of homophobia on observers' perceptions. *Journal of Social Psychology, 140*, 774–788.

Fogel, A., Nelson-Goens, G., & Hsu, H-C. (2000). Do different infant smiles reflect different positive emotions? *Social Development, 9*, 497–520.

Forbes, G. B. (2001). College students with tattoos and piercings: Motives, family experiences, personality factors, and perception by others. *Psychological Reports, 89*, 774–786.

Ford, W. S., & Wolvin, A. D. (1993). The differential impact of a basic communication course on perceived communication competencies in class, work, and social contexts. *Communication Education, 42*, 215–222.

Forden, C. (1981). The influence of sex-role expectations on the perception of touch. *Sex Roles*, 7, 889–894.

Forgas, J. P., & East, R. (2008). How real is that smile? Mood effect on accepting or rejecting the veracity of emotional facial expressions. *Journal of Nonverbal Behavior, 32*, 157–170.

Forston, R. F., & Larson, C. U. (1968). The dynamics of space: An experimental study in proxemic behavior among Latin Americans and North Americans. *Journal of Communication, 18*, 109–116.

Forsythe, S. M. (1990). Effect of applicant's clothing on

interviewer's decision to hire. *Journal of Applied Social Psychology, 20*, 1579–1595.

Forsythe, S. M., Drake, M. F., & Cox, C. E. (1985). Influence of applicant's dress on interviewer's selection decisions. *Journal of Applied Psychology, 70*, 374–378.

Fortenberry, J. H., Maclean, J., Morris, P., & O'Connell, M. (1978). Mode of dress as a perceptual cue to deference. *Journal of Social Psychology, 104*, 139–140.

Fox, J., Warber, K. M., & Makstaller, D. C. (2013). The role of Facebook in romantic relationship development: An exploration of Knapp's relational stage model. *Personal Relationships, 30*, 771–794.

Fraley, R. C., Niedenthal, P. M., Marks, M., Brumbaugh, C., & Vicary, A. (2006). Adult attachment and the perception of emotional expressions: Probing the hyperactivating strategies underlying anxious attachment. *Journal of Personality, 74*, 1163–1190.

Francescato, D., Porcelli, R., Mebane, M., Cuddetta, M., Klobas, J., & Renzi, P. (2006). Evaluation of the efficacy of collaborative learning in face-to-face and computer-supported university contexts. *Computers in Human Behavior, 22*, 163–176.

Frank, M. G., & Ekman, P. (1993). Not all smiles are created equal: The differences between enjoyment and nonenjoyment smiles. *International Journal of Humor Research, 6*, 9–26.

Frank, M. G., & Ekman, P. (1997). The ability to detect deceit generalizes across different types of high-stakes lies. *Journal of Personality and Social Psychology, 72*, 1429–1439.

Frank, M. G., & Stennett, J. (2001). The forced-choice paradigm and the perception of facial expressions of emotion. *Journal of Personality and Social Psychology, 80*, 75–85.

Frank, M. G., & Svetieva, E. (2013). Deception. In D. Matsumoto, M. G. Frank, & H. Hwang (Eds.), *Nonverbal communication: Science and applications* (pp. 121–144). Thousand Oaks, CA: SAGE.

Frederick, C. M., & Bradley, K. A. (2000). A different kind of normal? Psychological and motivational characteristics of young adult tattooers and body piercers. *North American Journal of Psychology, 2*, 380–383.

Freedman, D. G. (1969). The survival value of the beard. *Psychology Today, 3*, 36–39.

Freedman, N. (1972). The analysis of movement behavior during the clinical interview. In A. Siegman & B. Pope. (Eds.), *Studies in dyadic communication* (153–175). New York, NY: Pergamon.

Freedman, N., & Hoffman, S. P. (1967). Kinetic behavior in altered clinical states: Approach to objective analysis of motor behavior during clinical interviews. *Perceptual and Motor Skills, 24*, 527–539.

Freeman, J. B., Johnson, K. L., Ambady, N., & Rule, N. O. (2010). Sexual orientation perception involves gendered facial cues. *Personality and Social Psychology Bulletin, 36*, 1318–1331.

Freitas, F. A., Myers, S. A., & Avtgis, T. A. (1998). Student perceptions of instructor immediacy in conventional and distributed learning classrooms. *Communication Education, 47*, 366–372.

Fretz, B. R., Corn, R., Tuemmler, J. M., & Bellet, W. (1979). Counselor nonverbal behaviors and client evaluations. *Journal of Counseling Psychology, 26*, 304–311.

Frick-Horbury, D., & Guttentag, R. (1998). The effects of restricting hand gesture production on lexical retrieval and free recall. *American Journal of Psychology, 111*, 43–62.

Fridlund, A. J. (1994). *Human facial expression: An evolutionary view*. San Diego, CA: Academic Press.

Fridlund, A. J. (1997). The new ethology of human facial expressions. In J. A. Russell & J. M. Femandez-Dols (Eds.), *The psychology of facial expression* (pp. 103–129). London, England: Cambridge University Press.

Friedman, H. S. (1979). The concept of skill in nonverbal communication: Implications for understanding social interaction. In R. Rosenthal (Ed.), *Skill in nonverbal communication: Individual differences* (pp. 68–103). Cambridge, MA: Oelgeschlager, Gunn & Hain.

Friedman, H. S., DiMatteo, M. R., & Mertz, T. J. (1980). Nonverbal communication on television news: The facial expressions of broadcasters during coverage of a presidential election campaign. *Personality and Social Psychology Bulletin, 6,* 427–435.

Friedman, H. S., Nelson, B. C., & Harris, M. J. (1984). *The training of personal charisma* (Unpublished manuscript). University of California, Riverside.

Friedman, H. S., Prince, L. M., Riggio, R. E., & DiMatteo, M. R. (1980). Understanding and assessing nonverbal expressiveness: The Affective Communication Test. *Journal of Personality and Social Psychology, 39,* 333–351.

Friedman, H. S., Riggio, R. E., & Casella, D. F. (1988). Nonverbal skill, personal charisma, and initial attraction. *Personality and Social Psychology Bulletin, 14,* 203–211.

Friedman, M., Brown, A. E., & Rosenman, R. H. (1969). Voice analysis test for detection of behavior pattern. *Journal of the American Medical Association, 208,* 828–836.

Frisby, C. M. (2004). Does race matter? Effects of idealized images on African American women's perceptions of body esteem. *Journal of Black Studies, 34,* 323–347.

Frith, K., Shaw, P., & Cheng, H. (2005). The construction of beauty: A cross-cultural analysis of women's magazine advertising. *Journal of Communication, 55,* 56–70.

Fromme, D. K., Jaynes, W. E., Taylor, D. K., Hanold, E. G., Daniell, J., Rountree, R., & Fromme, M. L. (1989). Nonverbal behaviors and attitudes toward touch. *Journal of Nonverbal Behavior, 13,* 3–14.

Fry, A. M., & Willis, F. N. (1971). Invasion of personal space as a function of the age of the invader. *Psychological Record, 21,* 385–389.

Fujita, B. N., Harper, N., & Wiens, A. N. (1980). Encoding-decoding of nonverbal emotional messages: Sex differences in spontaneous and enacted expressions. *Journal of Nonverbal Behavior, 4,* 131–145.

Furnham, A., & Baguma, P. (2002). A cross-cultural study on the role of weight and waist-to-hip ratio on female attractiveness. *Personality and Individual Differences, 32,* 729–745.

Galati, D., Scherer, K. R., & Ricci-Bitti, P. E. (1997). Voluntary facial expression of emotion: Comparing congenitally blind with normally sighted encoders. *Journal of Personality and Social Psychology, 73,* 1363–1379.

Gallagher, D., & Shuntich, R. J. (1981). Encoding and decoding of nonverbal behavior through facial expressions. *Journal of Research in Personality, 15,* 241–252.

Garner, D. M., Garfinkel, P. E., Schwartz, D., & Thompson, M. (1980). Cultural expectations of thinness in women. *Psychological Reports, 47,* 483–491.

Garner, G., Mogg, K., & Bradley, B. (2006). Orienting and maintenance of gaze to facial expressions in social anxiety. *Journal of Abnormal Psychology, 115,* 760–770.

Garrido, E., Masip, J., Herrero, C., Tabernero, C., & Vega, M. T. (1998). *Policemen's ability to discern truth from deception of testimony.* Paper presented at the 7th European Conference on Psychology and Law, Stockholm, Sweden.

Gatewood, J. B., & Rosenwein, R. (1981). Interactional synchrony: Genuine or spurious? A critique of recent research. *Journal of Nonverbal Behavior, 6,* 12–29.

Gerwing, J., & Bavelas, J. (2004). Linguistic influences on gesture's form. *Gesture, 4,* 157–195.

Gibbins, K. (1969). Communication aspects of women's clothes and their relation to fashionability. *British Journal of Social and Clinical Psychology, 8,* 301–312.

Gifford, R., Ng, F. N., & Wilkinson, M. (1985). Nonverbal cues in the employment interview: Links between applicant qualities and interviewer judgments. *Journal of Applied Psychology, 4,* 729–736.

Giles, H. (1973). Accent mobility: A model and some data. *Anthropological Linguistics, 15,* 87–105.

Giles, H., Mulac, A., Bradac, J. J., & Johnson, P. (1987). Speech accommodation theory: The next decade and beyond. In M. McLaughlin (Ed.), *Communication yearbook 10* (pp. 13–48). Newbury Park, CA: SAGE.

Gillis, J. S., & Avis, W. E. (1980). The male-taller norm in mate selection. *Personality and Social Psychology Bulletin, 6,* 396–401.

Givens, D. (1978a). Contrasting nonverbal styles in mother-child interaction: Examples from a study of child abuse. *Semiotica, 24*, 33–47.

Givens, D. (1978b). Greeting a stranger: Some commonly used nonverbal signals of aversiveness. *Semiotica, 24*, 351–367.

Givens, D. (1978c). The nonverbal basis of attraction: Flirtation, courtship, and seduction. *Psychiatry, 41*, 246–259.

Givens, D. (1983). *Love signals: How to attract a mate*. New York, NY: Crown.

Glenwick, D. S., Jason, L. A., & Elman, D. (1978). Physical attractiveness and social contact in the singles bar. *Journal of Social Psychology, 105*, 311–312.

Global Deception Research Team. (2006). A world of lies. *Journal of Cross-Cultural Psychology, 27*, 60–74.

Gnepp, J., & Hess, D. (1986). Children's understanding of verbal and facial display rules. *Developmental Psychology, 22*, 103–108.

Gnisci, A., Sergi, I., DeLuca, E., & Errico, V. (2012). Does frequency of interruptions amplify the effects of various types of interruptions? Experimental evidence. *Journal of Nonverbal Behavior, 36*, 39–57.

Godoy, R., Reyes-Garcia, V., Huanca, T., Tanner, S., Leonard, W. M., McDade, T., & Valdez, V. (2005). Do smiles have a face value? Panel evidence from Amazonian Indians. *Journal of Economic Psychology, 26*, 469–490.

Goffman, E. (1963). *Behavior in public places*. New York, NY: The Free Press.

Goffman, E. (1967). *Interaction ritual*. Garden City, NY: Anchor Press.

Goffman, E. (1971). *Relations in public: Microstudies of the public order*. New York, NY: Basic Books.

Goldberg, C., & Cohen, D. J. (2004). Walking the walk and talking the talk: Gender differences in the impact of interviewing skills on applicant assessments. *Group and Organization Management, 29*, 369–384.

Goldin-Meadow, S. (2003). *Hearing gesture: How our hands help us think*. Cambridge, MA: Belknap Press of Harvard University Press.

Goldman-Eisler, F. (1968). *Psycholinguistics: Experiments in spontaneous speech*. New York, NY: Academic.

Goldsborough, M. (2014). Putting your emotions on screen. *Teacher Librarian, 43*, 64.

Goleman, D. (1994). *Emotional intelligence*. New York, NY: Bantam.

Goleman, D. (2006). *Social intelligence: The new science of human relationships*. New York, NY: Bantam Books.

Goleman, D., Boyatzis, R., & McKee, A. (2002). *Primal leadership*. Boston, MA: Harvard Business School Press.

Gooden, B. R., Smith, M. U., Tattersall, S. J., & Stockler, N. S. W. (2001). Hospitalized patients' views on doctors and white coats. *Medical Journal of Australia, 175*, 219–222.

Goodwyn, S. W., Acredolo, L. P., & Brown, C. A. (2000). Impact of symbolic gesturing on early language development. *Journal of Nonverbal Behavior, 24*, 81–103.

Gosselin, P., Kirouac, G., & Dore, F. Y. (1995). Components and recognition of facial expression in the communication of emotion by actors. *Journal of Personality and Social Psychology, 68*, 1–14.

Gottman, J. (1979). *Marital interactions: Experimental investigations*. New York, NY: Academic Press.

Gottman, J. (1994). *Why marriages succeed and fail*. New York, NY: Simon & Schuster.

Gottman, J. M., & DeClaire, J. (2001). *The relationship cure*. New York, NY: Crown.

Gottman, J. M., & Levenson, R. W. (1999). Rebound from marital conflict and divorce prediction. *Family Process, 38*, 287–292.

Gottman, J. M., & Levenson, R. W. (2000). The timing of divorce: Predicting when a couple win divorce over a 14-year period. *Journal of Marriage and the Family, 62*, 737–745.

Gottman, J. M., Levenson, R. W., & Woodin, E. (2001). Facial expressions during marital conflict. *The Journal of Family Communication, 1*, 37–57.

Grace, M., Kivlighan, D. M., & Kunce, J. (1995). The effect of nonverbal skills training on counselor trainee nonverbal sensitivity and responsiveness and on session impact and working alliance ratings. *Journal of Counseling and Development, 73*, 547–552.

Grady, K. E., Miransky, L. J., & Mulvey, M. A. (1976, August). *A nonverbal measure of dominance*. Paper presented at the meeting of the American Psychological Association, Washington, DC.

Graham, J. A., & Argyle, M. (1975). A cross-cultural study of the communication of extra-verbal meaning by gestures. *International Journal of Psychology, 10*, 56–67.

Graham, J. A., & Heywood, S. (1975). The effects of elimination of hand gestures and of verbal codability on speech performance. *European Journal of Social Psychology, 5*, 189–195.

Graham, J. A., & Jouhar, A. J. (1981). The effects of cosmetics on person perception. *International Journal of Cosmetic Science, 3*, 199–210.

Grahe, J. E., & Bernieri, F. J. (1999). The importance of nonverbal cues in judging rapport. *Journal of Nonverbal Behavior, 23*, 253–269.

Grammer, K., & Juette, A. (2000). Non-verbal behavior as courtship signals: The role of control and choice in selecting partners. *Evolution and Human Behavior, 21*, 371–390.

Grammer, K., & Thornhill, R. (1994). Human (homo sapiens) facial attractiveness and sexual selection: The role of symmetry and averageness. *Journal of Comparative Psychology, 108*, 233–242.

Grammer, K., Fink, B., Moller, A. P., & Manning, J. T. (2005). Physical attractiveness and health: Comment on Weeden and Sabini. *Psychological Bulletin, 131*, 658–661.

Grammer, K., Kruck, K. B., & Magnusson, M. S. (1998). The courtship dance: Patterns of nonverbal synchronization in opposite-sex encounters. *Journal of Nonverbal Behavior, 22*, 3–29.

Grandey, A. A. (2003). When "the show must go on": Surface acting and deep acting as determinants of emotional exhaustion and peer-rated service delivery. *Academy of Management Journal, 46*, 86–96.

Grandey, A. A., Fisk, G. M., & Steiner, D. D. (2005). Must "service with a smile" be stressful? The moderating role of personal control for American and French employees. *Journal of Applied Psychology, 90*, 893–904.

Graziano, W., Brothen, T., & Berscheid, E. (1978). Height and attraction: Do men and women see eye-to-eye? *Journal of Personality, 46*, 128–145.

Green, W. P., & Giles, H. (1973). Reactions to a stranger as a function of dress style: The tie. *Perceptual and Motor Skills, 37*, 676.

Greene, J. O., & Ravizza, S. M. (1995). Complexity effects on temporal characteristics of speech. *Human Communication Research, 21*, 390–421.

Gregory, S. W. (1990). Analysis of fundamental frequency reveals covariation in interview partners' speech. *Journal of Nonverbal Behavior, 14*, 237–251.

Gregory, S. W. (1994). Sounds of power and deference: Acoustic analysis of macro social constraints on micro interaction. *Sociological Perspectives, 37*, 497–526.

Gregory, S. W., & Gallagher, T. J. (2002). Spectral analysis of candidates' nonverbal vocal communication: Predicting U.S. presidential election outcomes. *Social Psychology Quarterly, 65*, 298–308.

Gregory, S. W., & Webster, S. (1996). A nonverbal signal in voices of interview partners effectively predicts communication accommodation and social status perceptions. *Journal of Personality and Social Psychology, 70*, 1231–1240.

Griffin, A. M., & Langlois, J. H. (2006). Stereotype directionality and attractiveness stereotyping: Is beauty good or is ugly bad? *Social Cognition, 24*, 187–206.

Griffith, C. H., Wilson, J. F., Langer, S., & Haist, S. A. (2003). House staff nonverbal communication skills and standardized patient satisfaction. *Journal of General Internal Medicine, 18*, 170–174.

Gross, A. L., & Ballif, B. (1991). Children's understanding of emotion from facial expression and situations: A review. *Developmental Review, 11*, 368–398.

Guaitella, I., Santi, S., Lagrue, B., & Cave, C. (2009). Are eyebrow movements linked to voice variations and turn-taking in dialogue? An experimental investigation. *Language and Speech, 52*, 207–222.

Gueguen, N. (2007). Courtship compliance: The effect of touch on women's behavior. *Social Influence, 2*, 81–97.

Gueguen, N. (2010). Smile and gender in student's yearbook:

A cultural replication. *Research Journal of International Studies, 14*, 4–7.

Gueguen, N. (2013). Weather and smiling contagion: A quasi-experiment with the smiling sunshine. *Journal of Nonverbal Behavior, 37*, 51–55.

Gueguen, N., & Fischer-Lokou, J. (2002). An evaluation of touch on a large request: A field setting. *Psychological Reports, 90*, 267–269.

Gueguen, N., & Fischer-Lokou, J. (2003). Another evaluation of touch and helping behavior. *Psychological Reports, 92*, 62–64.

Gueguen, N., & Jacob, C. (2002a). Direct look versus evasive glance and compliance with a request. *Journal of Social Psychology, 142*, 393–396.

Gueguen, N., & Jacob, C. (2002b). Social presence reinforcement and computer-mediated communication: The effect of the solicitor's photography on compliance to a survey request made by e-mail. *Cyberpsychology and Behavior, 5*, 139–142.

Gueguen, N., & Martin, A. (2009). Incidental similarity facilitated behavioral mimicry. *Social Psychology, 40*, 88–92.

Gueguen, N., Martin, A., & Meineri, S. (2011). Mimicry and helping behavior: An evaluation of mimicry on explicit helping request. *Journal of Social Psychology, 151*, 1–4.

Guerrero, L. K. (1996). Attachment-style differences in intimacy and involvement: A test of the four-category model. *Communication Monographs, 63*, 269–292.

Guerrero, L. K. (1997). Nonverbal involvement across interactions with same-sex friends, opposite-sex friends and romantic partners. *Journal of Social and Personal Relationships, 14*, 31–58.

Guerrero, L. K., & Andersen, P. A. (1991). The waxing and waning of relational intimacy: Touch as a function of relational stage, gender, and touch avoidance. *Journal of Social and Personal Relationships, 8*, 147–165.

Guerrero, L. K., & Andersen, P. A. (1994). Patterns of matching and initiation: Touch behavior and touch avoidance across romantic relationship stages. *Journal of Nonverbal Behavior, 18*, 137–153.

Guerrero, L. K., & Floyd, K. (2006). *Nonverbal communication in close relationships*. Mahwah, NJ: Lawrence Erlbaum.

Guerrero, L. K., & Miller, T. A. (1998). Associations between nonverbal behaviors and initial impressions of instructor competence and course content in videotaped distance education courses. *Communication Education, 47*, 30–42.

Gunnery, S. D., Hall, J., & Ruben, M. A. (2013). The deliberate Duchenne smile: Individual differences in expressive control. *Journal of Nonverbal Behavior, 37*, 29–41.

Guthrie, R. D. (1976). *Body hot spots*. New York, NY: Pocket Books.

Hackman, M. Z., & Walker, K. M. (1990). Instructional communication in the televised classroom: The effects of system design and teacher immediacy on student learning and satisfaction. *Communication Education, 39*, 196–206.

Hai, D. M., Khairullah, Z. Y., & Coulmas, N. (1982). Sex and the single armrest: Use of personal space during air travel. *Psychological Reports, 51*, 743–749.

Haidt, J., & Keltner, D. (1999). Culture and facial expression: Open-ended methods find more expressions and a gradient of recognition. *Cognition and Emotion, 13*, 225–266.

Halberstadt, A. G. (1991). Toward an ecology of expressiveness: Family socialization in particular and a model in general. In R. S. Feldman & B. Rime (Eds.), *Fundamentals of nonverbal behavior* (pp. 106–162). New York, NY: Cambridge University Press.

Halberstadt, A. G., Dennis, P. A., & Hess, U. (2011). The influence of family expressiveness, individuals' own emotionality, and self-expressiveness on perceptions of others' facial expressions. *Journal of Nonverbal Behavior, 35*, 35–50.

Halberstadt, A. G., Grotjohn, D. K., Johnson, C. A., Furth, M. A., & Greig, M. M. (1992). Children's abilities and strategies in managing the facial display of affect. *Journal of Nonverbal Behavior, 16*, 215–230.

Halberstadt, A. G., Hayes, C. W., & Pike, K. M. (1988). Gender and gender role differences in smiling and communication consistency. *Sex Roles, 19*, 589–604.

Hall, C. W. (2006). Self-reported aggression and the perception of anger in facial expression photos. *The Journal of Psychology, 140*, 255–267.

Hall, E. J. (1993). Smiling, deferring, and flirting: Doing gender by giving "good service." *Work and Occupations, 20*, 452–471.

Hall, E. T. (1959). *The silent language*. Garden City, NY: Anchor/Doubleday.

Hall, E. T. (1966). *The hidden dimension*. Garden City, NY: Anchor/Doubleday.

Hall, E. T. (1983). *The dance of life: The other dimension of time*. New York, NY: Anchor.

Hall, E. T., & Whyte, W. F. (1966). Intercultural communication: A guide to men of action. In A. G. Smith (Ed.), *Communication and culture* (pp. 567–575). New York, NY: Holt, Rinehart & Winston.

Hall, J. A. (1984). *Nonverbal sex differences: Communication accuracy and expressive style*. Baltimore, MD: Johns Hopkins University Press.

Hall, J. A. (1985). Male and female nonverbal behavior. In A. W. Siegman & S. Feldstein (Eds.), *Multichannel integrations of nonverbal behavior* (pp. 195–225). Hillsdale, NJ: Lawrence Erlbaum.

Hall, J. A. (1996). Touch, status, and gender at professional meetings. *Journal of Nonverbal Behavior, 20*, 23–44.

Hall, J. A., & Friedman, G. (1999). Status, gender, and nonverbal behavior: A study of structured interactions between employers of a company. *Personality and Social Psychology Bulletin, 25*, 1082–1091.

Hall, J. A., & Veccia, E. M. (1990). More "touching" observations: New insights on men, women, and interpersonal touch. *Journal of Personality and Social Psychology, 59*, 1155–1162.

Hall, J. A., Horgan, T. G., & Carter, J. D. (2002). Assigned and felt status in relation to observer-coded and participant-reported smiling. *Journal of Nonverbal Behavior, 26*, 63–81.

Hall, J. A., Irish, J. T., Roter, D. L., & Ehrlich, C. M. (1994). Gender in medical encounters: An analysis of physician and patient communication in a primary care setting. *Health Psychology, 13*, 384–392.

Hall, J. A., LeBeau, L. S., Reinoso, J. G., & Thayer, F. (2001). Status, gender, and nonverbal behavior in candid and posed photographs: A study of conversations between university employees. *Sex Roles, 44*, 677–692.

Hall, J. A., Roter, D. L., & Katz, N. R. (1988). Meta-analysis of correlates of provider behavior in medical encounters. *Medical Care, 26*, 657–675.

Hall, J. A., Roter, D. L., & Rand, C. S. (1981). Communication of affect between patient and physician. *Journal of Health and Social Behavior, 22*, 18–30.

Halliday, T. (1983). Information and communication. In T. Halliday & P. Slater (Eds.), *Animal Behavior* (pp. 43–81). New York, NY: W. H. Freeman.

Hamid, P. (1972). Some effects of dress cues on observational accuracy: A perceptual estimate and impression formation. *Journal of Social Psychology, 86*, 279–289.

Hancock, J. T., & Dunham, P. J. (2001). Impression formation in computer-mediated communication revisited: An analysis of the breadth and intensity of impressions. *Communication Research, 28*, 325–347.

Hannah, A., & Murachver, T. (1999). Gender and conversational style as predictors of conversational behavior. *Journal of Language and Social Psychology, 18*, 153–174.

Hargreaves, D., & Tiggemann, M. (2002). The effect of television commercials on mood and body dissatisfaction: The role of appearance-schema activation. *Journal of Social and Clinical Psychology, 21*, 287–308.

Harker, L., & Keltner, D. (2001). Expressions of positive emotion in women's college yearbook pictures and their relationship to personality and life outcomes across adulthood. *Journal of Personality and Social Psychology, 80*, 112–124.

Harper, R. G., Wiens, A. N., Fujita, B. N., & Kallgren, C. (1981). Affective-behavioral correlates of the test of emotional styles. *Journal of Nonverbal Behavior, 5*, 264–267.

Harrigan, I. (1984). The effects of task order on children's identification of facial expressions. *Motivation and Emotion, 8*, 157–169.

Harrigan, J. A., & Rosenthal, R. (1983). Physicians' head and body positions as determinants of perceived rapport. *Journal of Applied Social Psychology, 13*, 496–509.

Harrigan, J. A., & Taing, K. T. (1997). Fooled by a smile: Detecting anxiety in others. *Journal of Nonverbal Behavior, 21*, 203–221.

Harrigan, J. A., Oxman, T. E., & Rosenthal, R. (1985). Rapport expressed through nonverbal behavior. *Journal of Nonverbal Behavior, 9*, 95–110.

Hart, C. L., Fillmore, D., & Griffin, J. (2010). Deceptive communication in the workplace: An examination of beliefs about verbal and paraverbal cues. *Individual Differences Research, 8*, 176–183.

Haskard, K. B., Williams, S. L., DiMatteo, M., Heritage, J., & Rosenthal, R. (2008). The provider's voice: Patient satisfaction and the content-filtered speech of nurses and physicians in primary medical care. *Journal of Nonverbal Behavior, 32*, 1–20.

Hasler, B. S., & Friedman, D. A. (2012). Sociocultural conventions in avatar-mediated nonverbal communication: A cross-cultural analysis of virtual proxemics. *Journal of Intercultural Communication Research, 41*, 238–259.

Hassin, R. R., Aviezer, H., & Benin, S. (2013). Inherently ambiguous: Facial expressions of emotion in context. *Emotion Review, 5*, 60–65.

Hatfield, E., & Rapson, R. (1996). *Love and sex: Cross-cultural perspectives*. Boston, MA: Allyn & Bacon.

Hatfield, E., & Sprecher, S. (1986). *Mirror, mirror: The importance of looks in everyday life*. Albany, NY: SUNY Press.

Hatfield, E., Cacioppo, J. T., & Rapson, R. (1994). *Emotional contagion*. Cambridge, England: Cambridge University Press.

Haviland, J. M., & Lelwica, M. (1987). The individual affect responses to three emotion expressions. *Developmental Psychology, 23*, 97–104.

Hawkes, D., Senn, C., & Thorn, C. (2004). Factors that influence attitudes toward women with tattoos. *Sex Roles, 50*, 593–604.

Hayduk, L. A. (1983). Personal space: Where we stand now. *Psychological Bulletin, 94*, 293–335.

Hebert, B. G., & Vorauer, J. D. (2003). Seeing through the screen: Is evaluative feedback communicated more effectively in face-to-face or computer-mediated exchanges? *Computers in Human Behavior, 19*, 25–38.

Hegstrom, T. J. (1979). Message impact: What percentage is nonverbal? *Western Journal of Speech Communication, 43*, 134–142.

Hehman, J. A., Corpuz, R., & Bugenthal, D. (2012). Patronizing speech to older adults. *Journal of Nonverbal Behavior, 36*, 249–261.

Heinz, B. (2003). Backchannel responses as strategic responses in bilingual speakers' conversations. *Journal of Pragmatics, 35*, 1113–1142.

Henderson-King, E., & Henderson-King, D. (1997). Media effects on women's body esteem: Social and individual difference factors. *Journal of Applied Social Psychology, 27*, 167–173.

Henley, N. M. (1973). Status and sex: Some touching observations. *Bulletin of the Psychonomic Society, 2*, 91–93.

Henley, N. M. (1977). *Body politics: Power, sex, and nonverbal communication*. Englewood Cliffs, NJ: Prentice Hall.

Henley, N. M. (1995). Body politics revisited: What do we know today? In P. J. Kalbfleisch & M. J. Cody (Eds.), *Gender, power, and communication in human relationships* (pp. 27–62). Hillsdale, NJ: Lawrence Erlbaum.

Henley, N. M. (2001). Body politics. In A. Branaman (Ed.), *Self and society: Blackwell readers in sociology* (pp. 288–297). Maiden, MA: Blackwell Publishers

Hennig-Thurau, T., Groth, M., Paul, M., & Gremier, D. D. (2006). Are all smiles created equal? How emotional contagion and emotional labor affect service relationships. *Journal of Marketing, 70*, 58–73.

Hensley, W. E. (1981). The effects of attire, location, and sex on aiding behavior: A similarity explanation. *Journal of Nonverbal Behavior, 6*, 3–11.

Hensley, W. E. (1994). Height as a basis for interpersonal attraction. *Adolescence, 29*, 469–474.

Henss, R. (1991). Perceiving age and attractiveness in facial photographs. *Journal of Applied Social Psychology, 21*, 933–946.

Herba, C. M., Landau, S., Russell, T., Ecker, C., & Phillips,

M. L. (2006). The development of emotion processing in children: Effects of age, emotion, and intensity. *Journal of Child Psychology and Psychiatry, 47*, 1098–1106.

Hermans, E. J., Putman, P., & van Honk, J. (2006). Testosterone administration reduces empathetic behavior: A facial mimicry study. *Psychoneuroendocrinology, 31*, 859–866.

Hertenstein, M., Keltner, D., App, B., Bulleit, B., & Jaskolka, A. (2006). Touch communicates distinct emotions. *Emotion, 6*, 528–533.

Heslin, R. (1974). *Steps toward a taxonomy of touching*. Paper presented at the annual convention of the Midwestern Psychological Association, Chicago, IL.

Heslin, R., & Alper, T. (1983). Touch: A bonding gesture. In J. M. Weimann & R. P. Harrison (Eds.), *Nonverbal interaction* (pp. 47–75). Beverly Hills, CA: SAGE.

Heslin, R., Nguyen, T. D., & Nguyen, M. L. (1983). Meaning of touch: The case of touch from a stranger or same-sex person. *Journal of Nonverbal Behavior, 7*, 147–157.

Hess, E. (1975). *The tell-tale eye*. New York, NY: Van Nostrand Reinhold Co.

Hess, U. (2001). Facial mimicry and emotional contagion to dynamic emotional facial expressions and their influence on decoding accuracy. *International Journal of Psychophysiology, 40*, 129–141.

Hess, U., Banse, R., & Kappas, A. (1995). The intensity of facial expressions is determined by underlying affective state and social situation. *Journal of Personality and Social Psychology, 69*, 280–288.

Hess, U., Blairy, S., & Kleck, R. E. (1997). The intensity of emotional facial expressions and decoding accuracy. *Journal of Nonverbal Behavior, 21*, 241–257.

Hickson, G., Clayton, E., & Entman, S. (1994). Obstetricians' prior malpractice experience and patients' satisfaction with care. *Journal of the American Medical Association, 272*, 1583–1587.

Hickson, M. L., & Stacks, D. W. (1993). *Nonverbal communication: Studies and applications*. Dubuque, IA: Brown and Benchmark.

Hiltz, S. R., Johnson, K., & Turoff, M. (1986). Experiments in group decision making: Communication process and outcome in face-to-face versus computerized conferences. *Human Communication Research, 13*, 225–252.

Hinkle, L. L. (1999). Nonverbal immediacy communication behaviors and liking in marital relationships. *Communication Research Reports, 16*, 81–90.

Hinkle, L. L. (2001). Perceptions of supervisor nonverbal immediacy, vocalics, and subordinate liking. *Communication Research Reports, 18*, 128–136.

Hinsz, V. B. (1989). Facial resemblance in engaged and married couples. *Journal of Social and Personal Relationships, 6*, 223–229.

Hinsz, V. B., & Tomhave, J. A. (1991). Smile and (half) the world smiles with you, frown and you frown alone. *Personality and Social Psychology Bulletin, 17*, 586–592.

Hochschild, A. (1983). *The managed heart: Commercialization of human feeling*. Berkeley: University of California Press.

Hodgins, H. S., & Belch, C. (2000). Interparental violence and nonverbal abilities. *Journal of Nonverbal Behavior, 24*, 3–24.

Hodgins, H. S., & Zuckerman, M. (1990). The effect of nonverbal sensitivity on social interaction. *Journal of Nonverbal Behavior, 14*, 155–170.

Hoffner, C. (1996). Children's wishful identification and parasocial interaction with favorite television characters. *Journal of Broadcasting and Electronic Media, 40*, 389–402.

Hoffner, C., & Badzinski, D. (1989). Children's integration of facial and situational cues to emotion. *Child Development, 60*, 411–422.

Hofschire, L. J., & Greenberg, B. S. (2002). Media's impact on adolescents' body dissatisfaction. In J. D. Brown & J. R. Steele (Eds.), *Sexual teens, sexual media: Investigating media's influence on adolescent sexuality* (pp. 125–149). Hillsdale, NJ: Lawrence Erlbaum.

Hofstede, G. (1980). *Culture's consequences*. Beverly Hills, CA: SAGE.

Hofstede, G. (1983). Dimensions of national cultures in fifty countries and three regions. In J. Deregowski, S. Dziurawiec, & R. Annis (Eds.), *Explorations in cross-cultural psychology*. Lisse, The Netherlands: Swets & Zeitlinger.

Holladay, S. J., & Coombs, W. T. (1993). Communicating visions: An exploration of the role of delivery in the creation of leader charisma. *Management Communication Quarterly, 6*, 405–427.

Holladay, S. J., & Coombs, W. T. (1994). Speaking of visions and visions being spoken: An exploration of the effects of content and delivery on perceptions of leader charisma. *Management Communication Quarterly, 8*, 165–189.

Holland, R. W., Roeder, U., van Baaren, R., Brandt, A., & Hannover, B. (2004). Don't stand so close to me: The effects of self-construal on interpersonal closeness. *Psychological Science, 15*, 237–241.

Holler, J., & Stevens, R. (2007). The effect of common ground on how speakers use gestures and speech to represent size information. *Journal of Language and Social Psychology, 26*, 4–27.

Hollien, H. (1987). "Old voices": What do we really know about them? *Journal of Voice, 1*, 2–17.

Hollien, H., & Tolhurst, G. (1978). The aging voice. In V. Lawrence & B. Weinberg (Eds.), *Transactions of the 7th Symposium on the care of the professional voice* (pp. 67–73). New York, NY: Voice Foundation.

Homburg, D., & Stock, R. M. (2004). The link between salespeople's job satisfaction and customer satisfaction in a business-to-business context: A dyadic analysis. *Journal of the Academy of Marketing Science, 32*, 144–159.

Horgan, T. G., & Smith, J. L. (2006). Interpersonal reasons for interpersonal perceptions: Gender-incongruent purpose goals and nonverbal judgment accuracy. *Journal of Nonverbal Behavior, 30*, 127–140.

Horn, M. J. (1975). *The second skin: An interdisciplinary study of clothing*. Boston, MA: Houghton Mifflin.

Hornik, J., & Ellis, S. (1988). Strategies to secure compliance for a mall intercept interview. *Public Opinion Quarterly, 52*, 539–551.

Hortacsu, N., & Ekinci, B. (1992). Children's reliance on situational and vocal expression of emotions: Consistent and conflicting cues. *Journal of Nonverbal Behavior, 16*, 231–247.

Houle, R., & Feldman, R. S. (1991). Emotional displays in children's television programming. *Journal of Nonverbal Behavior, 15*, 261–271.

Huang, C., & Park, D. (2013). Cultural influences on Facebook photographs. *International Journal of Psychology, 48*, 334–343.

Hughes, S. N., Farley, S. D., & Rhodes, B. C. (2010). Vocal and physiological changes in response to the physical attractiveness of conversational partners. *Journal of Nonverbal Behavior, 34*, 155–167.

Huguet, P., Croizet, J, & Richetin, J. (2004). Is "what has been cared for" necessarily good? Further evidence for the negative impact of cosmetics use on impression formation. *Journal of Applied Social Psychology, 34*, 1752–1771.

Hummert, M. L., Mazloff, D., & Henry, C. (1999). Vocal characteristics of older adults and stereotyping. *Journal of Nonverbal Behavior, 23*, 111–132.

Hunter, M., & Ahlers, M. (2014, August, 27). Leg room fight diverts flight. *CNN.*

Hurley, C. M. (2012). Do you see what I see? Learning to detect micro expressions of emotion. *Motivation and Emotion, 36*, 371–381.

Hurley, C. M., Anker, A. E., Frank, M. G., Matusmoto, D., & Hwang, H. C. (2014). Background factors predicting accuracy and improvement in micro expression recognition. *Motivation and Emotion, 38*, 700–714.

Huston, T. L. (1973). Ambiguity of acceptance, social desirability and dating choice. *Journal of Experimental Social Psychology, 9*, 32–42.

Hutt, C., & Vaizey, M. J. (1967). Differential effects of group density on social behavior. *Nature, 209*, 1371–1372.

Hwang, H., & Matsumoto, D. (2014). Cultural differences in victory signals of triumph. *Cross Cultural Research, 48*, 177–191.

Ickes, W. (1984). Compositions in black and white: Determinants of interaction in interracial dyads. *Journal of Personality and Social Psychology, 47*, 330–341.

Imada, A. S., & Hakel, M. D. (1977). Influence of nonverbal communication and rater proximity on impressions and decisions in simulated employment interviews. *Journal of Applied Psychology, 62*, 295–300.

Isaacowitz, D. M, & Stanley, J. T. (2011). Bringing an ecological perspective to the study of aging and recognition of emotional facial expressions: Past, current and future methods. *Journal of Nonverbal Behavior*, *35*, 261–278.

Ishii, S., & Bruneau, T. (1988). Silence and silences in cross-cultural perspective: Japan and the United States. In L. Samovar & R. Porter (Eds.), *Intercultural communication* (pp. 310–315). Belmont, CA: Wadsworth.

Ishikawa, H., Hashimoto, H., Kinoshita, M., Fujimori, S., Shimizu, T., & Yano, E. (2006). Evaluating medical students' non-verbal communication during the objective structured clinical examination. *Medical Education*, *40*, 1180–1187.

Iverson, J. N., & Goldin-Meadow, S. (2001). The resilience of gesture in talk: Gesture in blind speakers and listeners. *Developmental Science*, *4*, 416–422.

Izard, C. E. (1971). *The face of emotion*. New York, NY: Appleton-Century-Crofts.

Izard, C. E. (1977). *Human emotions*. New York, NY: Plenum.

Izard, C. E. (1978). Emotions as motivations: An evolutionary developmental perspective. In R. A. Dienstbier (Ed.), *Nebraska symposium on motivation* (Vol. 25, pp. 163–200). Lincoln: University of Nebraska Press.

Jacobs, D. R., & Schucker, B. (1981). Type A behavior pattern, speech, and coronary heart disease. In J. K Darby (Ed.), *Speech evaluation in medicine*. New York, NY: Grune & Stratton.

Jacobs, N., & Garnham, A. (2007). The role of conversational hand gestures in a narrative task. *Journal of Memory and Language*, *56*, 291–303.

Jacobson, D. (1996). Contexts and cues in cyberspace: The pragmatics of naming in text-based virtual realities. *Journal of Anthropological Research*, *52*, 461–479.

Jaffe, J., & Feldstein, S. (1970). *Rhythms of dialogue*. New York, NY: Academic Press.

Jakobs, E., Fischer, A. G., & Manstead, A. S. R. (1997). Emotional experience as a function of social context: The role of the other. *Journal of Nonverbal Behavior*, *21*, 103–130.

Jakobs, E., Manstead, A. S. R., & Fischer, A. H. (2001). Social context effects on facial activity in a negative emotional setting. *Emotion*, *1*, 51–69.

James, W. (1890). *The principles of psychology*. New York, NY: Holt.

Jaworski, A., & Galasinski (2002). The verbal construction of non-verbal behaviour: British press reports of President Clinton's grand jury testimony video. *Discourse & Society*, *13*, 629–649.

Johnson, C. (1994). Gender, legitimate authority, and leader-subordinate conversations. *American Sociological Review*, *59*, 122–135.

Johnson, H. G., Ekman, P., & Friesen, W. V. (1975). Communicative body movements: American emblems. *Semiotica*, *15*, 335–353.

Johnson, K. L., Gill, S., Reichman, V., & Tassinary, L. G. (2007). Swagger, sway, and sexuality: Judging sexual orientation from body motion and morphology. *Journal of Personality and Social Psychology*, *93*, 321–334.

Johnson, R. R. (2006). Confounding influences on police detection of suspiciousness. *Journal of Criminal Justice*, *34*, 435–442.

Johnston, L., Miles, L., & Macrae, C. N. (2010). Why are you smiling at me? Social functions of enjoyment and non-enjoyment smiles. *British Journal of Social Psychology*, *49*, 107–127.

Johnston, V. S., & Franklin, M. (1993). Is beauty in the eye of the beholder? *Ethology and Sociobiology*, *14*, 183–199.

Joinson, A. N. (1998). Causes and implications of disinhibited behavior on the Internet. In J. Gackenbach (Ed.), *Psychology and the Internet: Intrapersonal, interpersonal, and transpersonal implications* (pp. 43–60). San Diego, CA: Academic Press.

Jones, B. C., DeBruine, L. M., Little, A. C., Conway, C. A., & Feinberg, D. R. (2006). Integrating gaze direction and expression in preferences for attractive faces. *Psychological Science*, *17*, 588–591.

Jones, B. C., Little, A. C., Penton-Voak, I. S., Tiddeman, B. P., Burt, D. M., & Perrett, D. I. (2001). Facial symmetry and judgements of apparent health: Support for a "good genes" explanation of the attractiveness-symmetry relationship. *Evolution and Human Behavior*, *22*, 417–429.

Jones, M. Y., Stanaland, A. J. S., & Gelb, B. D. (1998). Beefcake and cheesecake: Insights for advertisers. *Journal of Advertising, 27*, 33–51.

Jones, N., Kearins, J., & Watson, J. (1987). The human tongue show and observers' willingness to interact: Replication and extensions. *Perceptual and Motor Skills, 60*, 759–764.

Jones, S. E. (1971). A comparative proxemics analysis of dyadic interaction in selected subcultures of New York City. *Journal of Social Psychology, 84*, 35–44.

Jones, S. E. (1994). *The right touch: Understanding and using the language of physical contact.* Cresskill, NJ: Hampton Press.

Jones, S. E., & Aiello, J. R. (1973). Proxemic behavior of black and white first-, third-, and fifth-grade children. *Journal of Personality and Social Psychology, 25*, 21–27.

Jones, S. E., & Yarbrough, A. E. (1985). A naturalistic study of the meanings of touch. *Communication Monographs, 52*, 19–56.

Jones, S. M., & Guerrero, L. K. (2001). The effects of nonverbal immediacy and verbal person centeredness in the emotional support process. *Human Communication Research, 27*, 567–596.

Jones, S. M., & Wirtz, J. G. (2006). How does the comforting process work? An empirical test of an appraisal-based model. *Human Communication Research, 32*, 217–243.

Jones, S. M., & Wirtz, J. G. (2007). "Sad monkey see, monkey do": Nonverbal matching in emotional support networks. *Communication Studies, 58*, 71–86.

Jones, T. S., & Remland, M. S. (1998). An ounce of prevention: Suggestions for training to prevent sexual harassment. In C. D. Brown, C. Snedeker, & B. Sykes (Eds.), *Conflict and diversity* (pp. 251–266). Cresskill, NJ: Hampton Press.

Joorman, J., & Gotlib, I. H. (2006). Is this happiness I see? Biases in the identification of emotional facial expressions in depression and social phobia. *Journal of Abnormal Psychology, 115*, 705–714.

Josephs, I. E. (1994). Display rule behavior and understanding in preschool children. *Journal of Nonverbal Behavior, 18*(4), 301–326.

Jourard, S. M. (1966). An exploratory study of body accessibility. *British Journal of Social and Clinical Psychology, 5*, 221–231.

Julien, D., Chartrand, E., Simard, M., Bouthillier, D., & Begin, J. (2003). Conflict, social support, and relationship quality: An observational study of heterosexual, gay male, and lesbian couples' communication. *Journal of Family Psychology, 17*(3), 419–428.

Kafestios, K., & Hess, U. (2013). Effects of activated and dispositional self-construal on emotion decoding. *Journal of Nonverbal Behavior, 37*, 191–205.

Kaitz, M., Bar-Haim, Y., Lehrer, M., & Grossman, E. (2004). Adult attachment style and interpersonal distance. *Attachment and Human Development, 6*, 285–303.

Kalick, S. M. (1988). Physical attractiveness as a status cue. *Journal of Experimental Social Psychology, 24*, 469–489.

Kalick, S. M., Zebrowitz, L. A., Langlois, J. H., & Johnson, R. M. (1997). Does human facial attractiveness honestly advertise health? Longitudinal data on an evolutionary question. *Psychological Science, 9*, 8–13.

Kampe, K. K. W., Frith, C. D., Dolan, R. J., & Firth, U. (2001). Reward value of attractiveness and gaze. *Nature, 413*, 589.

Kappas, A., Hess, U., & Scherer, K. R. (1991). Voice and emotion. In B. Rime & R. S. Feldman (Eds.), *Fundamentals of nonverbal behavior* (pp. 208–238). Cambridge, England: Cambridge University Press.

Kaufman, D., & Mahoney, J. M. (1999). The effect of waitresses' touch on alcohol consumption in dyads. *Journal of Social Psychology, 139*, 261–267.

Kawamura, S., & Kageyama, K. (2006). Smiling faces rated more feminine than serious faces in Japan. *Perceptual and Motor Skills, 103*, 210–214.

Keating, C. F., & Doyle, J. (2002). The faces of desirable mates and dates contain mixed social status cues. *Journal of Experimental Social Psychology, 38*, 414–424.

Keating, C. F., & Heltman, K. R. (1994). Dominance and deception in children and adults: Are leaders the best misleaders? *Personality and Social Psychology Bulletin, 20*, 312–321.

Keating, C. F., & Keating, E. G. (1980). Distances between pairs of acquaintances and strangers on public benches in Nairobi, Kenya. *The Journal of Social Psychology, 110*, 285–286.

Keengwe, J., Adjai-Boatng, E., & Diteeyont, W. (2013). Facilitating active social presence and meaningful interactions in online learning. *Education and Information Technology, 18*, 597–607.

Keith, V. M., & Herring, C. (1991). Skin tone and stratification in the black community. *American Journal of Sociology, 97*, 760–778.

Kelly, A. B., Fincham, F. D., & Beach, S. R. H. (2003). Communication skills in couples: A review and discussion of emerging perspectives. In J. O. Greene & B. R. Burleson (Eds.), *Handbook of communication and social interaction skills* (pp. 723–751).

Kelly, J. R., Murphy, J. D., Craig, T. Y., & Driscoll, M. (2005). The effect of nonverbal behaviors associated with sexual harassment proclivity on women's performance. *Sex Roles, 53*, 689–701.

Kelly, R., & Watts, L. (2015). Characterizing the inventive appropriation of emotion as relationally meaningful in mediated close personal relationships. *Proceedings of CSCS, Companion*, 191–194.

Keltner, D. (1995). Signs of appeasement: Evidence for the distinct displays of embarrassment, amusement, and shame. *Journal of Personality and Social Psychology, 68*, 441–454.

Keltner, D., Young, R. C., & Buswell, B. N. (1997). Appeasement in human emotion, social practice, and personality. *Aggressive Behavior, 23*, 359–374.

Keltner, D., Young, R. C., Heerey, E. A., Monarch, N. D., & Oemig, C. (1998). Teasing in hierarchical and intimate relations. *Journal of Personality and Social Psychology, 75*, 1231–1247.

Kendon, A. (1967). Some functions of gaze-direction in social interaction. *Acta Psychologica, 26*, 22–63.

Kendon, A. (1970). Movement coordination in social interaction: Some examples described. *Acta Psychologica, 32*, 1–25.

Kendon, A. (1973). The role of visible behavior in the organization of social interaction. In M. von Cranach & I. Vine (Eds.), *Social communication and movement* (pp. 29–74). New York, NY: Academic Press.

Kendon, A. (1981). A geography of gesture. *Semiotica, 37*, 129–163.

Kendon, A., & Ferber, A. (1973). A description of some human greetings. In P. Michael & J. Crook (Eds.), *Comparative ecology and behaviour of primates* (pp. 591–668). London, England: Academic Press.

Kenny, C., & Fletcher, D. (1973). Effects of beardedness on person perception. *Perceptual and Motor Skills, 37*, 413–414.

Kiesler, C. A., & Baral, R. L. (1970). The search for a romantic partner: The effects of self-esteem and physical attractiveness on romantic behavior. In K. G. Gerger & D. Marlow (Eds.), *Personality and social behavior* (pp. 155–165). Reading, MA: Addison-Wesley.

Kilbride, J. E., & Yarczower, M. (1983). Ethnic bias in the recognition of facial expressions. *Journal of Nonverbal Behavior, 8*, 27–41.

King, E. B., & Ahmad, A. S. (2010). An experimental field study of interpersonal discrimination toward Muslim job applicants. *Personnel Psychology, 63*, 881–906.

King, K. A., & Vidourek, R. A. (2013). Getting inked: Tattoo and risky behavioral involvement among university students. *The Social Science Journal, 50*, 540–546.

King, M. G. (1966). Interpersonal relations in preschool children and average approach distance. *Journal of Genetic Psychology, 109*, 109–116.

Kirouac, G., & Dore, F. Y. (1985). Accuracy of the judgment of facial expression of emotions as a function of sex and level of education. *Journal of Nonverbal Behavior, 9*, 3–7.

Kirsh, S. J., Mounts, J. R., & Olczak, P. V. (2006). Violent media consumption and the recognition of dynamic facial expressions. *Journal of Interpersonal Violence, 21*, 571–584.

Kleck, R., & Nuessle, W. (1968). Congruence between the indicative and communicative functions of eye contact in interpersonal relations. *British Journal of Social and Clinical Psychology, 7*, 241–246.

Klein, H., & Shiffman, K. S. (2006). Messages about physical attractiveness in animated cartoons. *Body Image, 3*, 353–363.

Kleinke, C. L. (1977). Compliance to requests made by gazing and touching experimenters in field settings. *Journal of Experimental Social Psychology, 13*, 218–223.

Kleinke, C. L. (1980). Interaction between gaze and legitimacy of request on compliance in a field setting. *Journal of Nonverbal Behavior, 5*, 3–12.

Kleinke, C. L. (1986). Gaze and eye contact: A research review. *Psychological Bulletin, 100*, 78–100.

Kleinke, C. L., Lenga, M. R., & Beach, T. A. (1974). *Effects of talking rate on first impressions: Do sex and attractiveness make a difference?* Paper presented at the meeting of the Western Psychological Association, San Francisco, California.

Klineberg, O. (1940). Emotional expression in Chinese literature. *Journal of Abnormal and Social Psychology, 33*, 517–520.

Kluemper, D. H., DeGroot, T., & Choi, S. (2013). Emotion management ability: Predicting task performance, citizenship, and deviance. *Journal of Management, 39*, 878–905.

Knapp, M. L. (1983). Dyadic relationship development. In J. M. Weimann & R. P. Harrison (Eds.), *Nonverbal interaction* (pp. 179–207). Beverly Hills, CA: SAGE.

Knapp, M. L. (2008). *Lying and deception in human interaction.* Boston, MA: Pearson.

Knapp, M. L., & Hall, J. A. (2002). *Nonverbal communication in human interaction*. Stamford, CT: Thomson Learning, Inc.

Knapp, M. L., Hart, R. P., Friederich, G. W., & Schulman, G. M. (1973). The rhetoric of goodbye: Verbal and nonverbal correlates of human leave-taking. *Speech Monographs, 40*, 182–198.

Knox, D., Daniels, V., Sturdivant, L., & Zusman, M. E. (2001). College student use of the Internet for mate selection. *College Student Journal, 35*, 158–160.

Knutson, B. (1996). Facial expressions of emotion influence interpersonal trait inferences. *Journal of Nonverbal Behavior, 20*, 165–182.

Ko, S. J., Judd, C. M., & Blair, I. V. (2006). What the voice reveals: Within- and between-category stereotyping on the basis of voice. *Personality and Social Psychology Bulletin, 32*, 806–819.

Ko, S. J., Judd, C. M., & Stapel, D. A. (2009). Stereotyping based on voice in the presence of individuating information: Vocal femininity affects perceived competence but not warmth. *Personality and Social Psychology Bulletin, 40*, 132–135.

Koch, J. R., Roberts, A. E., Armstrong, M. L., & Owen, D. C. (2009). Body art, deviance, and American college students. *The Social Science Journal, 47*, 151–161.

Koch, S. C. (2005). Evaluative affect display toward male and female leaders of task-oriented groups. *Small Group Research, 36*, 678–703.

Koch, S. C., Bahne, C. G., Kruse, L., & Zimmermann, F. (2010). Visual dominance and visual egalitarianism: Individual and group-level influences of sex and status in group interactions. *Journal of Nonverbal Behavior, 34*, 137–153.

Koerner, A. F., & Fitzpatrick, M. (2002). Nonverbal communication and marital adjustment and satisfaction: The role of decoding relationship relevant and relationship irrelevant affect. *Communication Monographs, 69*, 31–51.

Korda, M. (1975). *Power! How to get it, how to use it*. New York, NY: Ballantine.

Kornreich, C., Blairy, S., Philippot, P., Hess, U., Noel, X., Streel, E., LeBon, O., . . . & Verbanck, P. (2001). Deficits in recognition of emotional facial expressions are still present in alcoholics after mid- to long-term abstinence. *Journal of Studies on Alcohol, 62*, 533–542.

Koss, T., & Rosenthal, R. (1997). Interactional synchrony, positivity and patient satisfaction in the physician-patient relationship. *Medical Care, 35*, 1158–1163.

Koukounas, E., & Letch, N. (2001). Psychological correlates of perceptual of sexual intent in women. *Journal of Social Psychology, 141*, 443–456.

Kowner, R., & Wiseman, R. (2003). Culture and status-related behavior: Japanese and American perceptions of interaction in asymmetric dyads. *Cross-Cultural Research, 37*, 178–210.

Krauss, R., Morrel-Samuels, P., & Colasante, C. (1991). Do conversational hand gestures communicate? *Journal of Personality and Social Psychology, 61*, 743–754.

Kraut, R. E. (1980). Humans as lie detectors: Some second thoughts. *Journal of Communication, 30*, 209–216.

Kraut, R. E., & Johnson, R. E. (1979). Social and emotional messages of smiling: An ethological approach. *Journal of Personality and Social Psychology, 42*, 853–863.

Kruger, J., Epley, N., Parker, J., & Ng, Z. (2005). Egocentrism over e-mail: Can we communicate as well as we think we can? *Journal of Personality and Social Psychology, 89*, 925–936.

Kruger, J., Kuban, J., & Gordan, C. L. (2006). Intentions in teasing: When "just kidding" just isn't good enough. *Journal of Personality and Social Psychology, 90*, 412–425.

Krumhuber, E., & Manstead, A. S. R. (2009). Are you joking? The moderating role of smiles in the perception of verbal statements. *Cognition and Emotion, 23*, 1504–1515.

Krumhuber, E., Likowski, K., & Weyers, P. (2014). Facial mimicry of spontaneous and deliberate Duchenne and non-Duchenne smiles. *Journal of Nonverbal Behavior, 38*, 1–11.

Krumhuber, E., Manstead, A., & Kappas, A. (2007). Temporal aspects of facial displays in person and expression perception. *Journal of Nonverbal Behavior, 31*, 39–56.

Krys, K., Hansen, K., Xing, C., Szarota, P., & Yang, M. (2014). Do only fools smile at strangers? Cultural differences in social perception of intelligence of smiling individuals. *Journal of Cross-Cultural Psychology, 45*, 314–321.

Kumin, L., & Lazar, M. (1974). Gestural communication in preschool children. *Perceptual and Motor Skills, 38*, 708–710.

Kurtz, H. (1997). *Hot air: All talk all the time*. New York, NY: Basic Books.

Kutscher, M. L. (2002). *Autistic spectrum disorders: Sorting it out.* Retrieved January 30, 2016, from http://www.pediatricneurology.com/autism.htm

LaBarre, W. (1947). The cultural basis of emotions and gestures. *Journal of Personality, 16*, 49–68.

Labov, W. (1966). *The social stratification of English in New York City*. Washington, D C: Center for Applied Linguistics.

Labov, W. (1972). *Sociolinguistic patterns*. Philadelphia: University of Pennsylvania Press.

LaFrance, M. (1979). Nonverbal synchrony and rapport: Analysis by the cross-lag panel technique. *Social Psychology Quarterly, 42*, 66–70.

LaFrance, M., & Broadbent, M. (1976). Group rapport: Posture sharing as a nonverbal indicator. *Group and Organization Studies, 1*, 328–333.

LaFrance, M., & Hecht, M. A. (1999). Option or obligation to smile: The effects of power and gender on facial expression. In P. Philippot, R. S. Feldman, & E. J. Coats (Eds.), *The social context of nonverbal behavior* (pp. 45–70). Cambridge, England: Cambridge University Press.

LaFrance, M., & Ickes, W. (1981). Postural mirroring and interactional involvement: Sex and sex-typing effects. *Journal of Nonverbal Behavior, 5*, 139–154.

LaFrance, M., & Mayo, C. (1976). Racial differences in gaze behavior during conversations: Two systematic observational studies. *Journal of Personality and Social Psychology, 33*, 547–552.

LaFrance, M., & Mayo, C. (1978). *Moving bodies: Nonverbal communication in social relationships*. Belmont, CA: Wadsworth.

LaFrance, M., & Mayo, C. (1979). A review of nonverbal behaviors of women and men. *Western Journal of Speech Communication, 43*, 96–107.

Lander, K., & Metcalfe, S. (2007). The influence of positive and negative facial expressions on face familiarity. *Memory, 15*, 63–69.

Langlois, J. H., & Roggman, L. A. (1990). Attractive faces are only average. *Psychological Science, 1*, 115–121.

Langlois, J. H., Ritter, J. M., Roggman, L. A., & Vaughn, L. S. (1991). Facial diversity and infant preferences for attractive faces. *Developmental Psychology, 27*, 79–84.

Lanzetta, J. T., Cartwright-Smith, J., & Kleck, R. E. (1976). Effects of nonverbal dissimulation on emotional experience and autonomic arousal. *Journal of Personality and Social Psychology, 33*, 354–370.

Lapidus, L., Bengtsson, C., Haellstroem, T., & Bjoerntorp, P. (1989). Obesity, adipose tissue distribution and health in women: Results from a population study in Gothenburg, Sweden. *Appetite, 13*, 25–35.

LaPoint, V., Holloman, L. O., & Alleyne, S. I. (1992). The role of dress codes and uniforms in urban schools. *NASSP Bulletin, 76*, 20–26.

Larrance, D. T., & Zuckerman, M. (1981). Facial attractiveness and vocal likeability as determinants of nonverbal sending skills. *Journal of Personality, 49*, 346–362.

Larsen, K. M., & Smith, C. K. (1981). Assessment of nonverbal communication in the patient-physician interview. *The Journal of Family Practice, 12*, 481–488.

Larsen, R. J., & Shackelford, T. K. (1996). Gaze avoidance: Personality and social judgments of people who avoid direct face-to-face contact. *Personality and Individual Differences, 21*, 907–917.

Lasky, R. E., Klein, R. E., & Martinez, S. (1974). Age and sex discriminations in five- and six-month-old infants. *Journal of Psychology, 88*, 317–324.

Lass, N. J., Hughes, K. R., Bowyer, M. D., Waters, L. T., & Broune, V. T. (1976). Speaker sex identification from voiced, whispered, and filtered isolated vowels. *Journal of the Acoustical Society of America, 59*, 675–678.

Lass, N. J., Tecca, J., Mancuso, R., & Black, W. (1979). The effect of phonetic complexity on speaker race and sex identification. *Journal of Phonetics*, 7, 105–118.

Lass, N. J., Trapp, D. S., Baldwin, M. K., Scherbick, K. A., & Wright, D. L. (1982). Effect of vocal disguise on judgments of speakers' sex and race. *Perceptual and Motor Skills, 54*, 1235–1240.

Latner, J. D., Rosewall, J. K., & Simmonds, M. B. (2007). Childhood obesity stigma: Association with television, videogame, and magazine exposure. *Body Image, 4*, 147–155.

Lau, S. (1982). The effect of smiling on person perception. *Journal of Social Psychology, 117*, 63–67.

Laukka, P., Juslin, P. N., & Breslin, R. (2005). A dimensional approach to vocal expression of emotion. *Cognition and Emotion, 19*, 633–653.

Laukka, P., Linnman, C., Ahs, F., Pissiota, A., Frans, O., Faria, V., Michelgard, A., . . . & Furmark, T. (2008). In a nervous voice: Acoustic analysis and perception of anxiety in social phobics' speech. *Journal of Nonverbal Behavior, 32*, 195–214.

Laver, J. (1945). *Taste and fashion*. London, England: George G. Harrap & Co.

Laver, J. (1969). *Modesty in dress: An inquiry into the fundamentals of fashion*. Boston: Houghton Mifflin.

Lavine, H., Sweeney, D., & Wagner, S. H. (1999). Depicting women as sex objects in television advertising: Effects on body dissatisfaction. *Personality and Social Psychology Bulletin, 25*, 1049–1058.

Lavrakas, P. J. (1975). Female preferences of male physiques. *Journal of Research in Personality, 9*, 324–334.

Lawrence, S. G., & Watson, M. (1991). Getting others to help: The effectiveness of professional uniforms in charitable fund raising. *Journal of Applied Communication Research, 19*, 170–185.

Lea, M., & Spears, R. (1992). Paralanguage and social perception in computer-mediated communication. *Journal of Organizational Computing, 2*, 321–342.

Lea, M., & Spears, R. (1995). Love at first byte? Building personal relationships over computer networks. In J. T. Wood & S. Duck (Eds.), *Understudied relationships: Off the beaten track* (pp. 197–133). Thousand Oaks, CA: SAGE.

Leach, P. (1995). *Your baby and child: From birth to age five*. New York, NY: Alfred A. Knopf.

Leander, N. P., Chartrand, T. L., & Wood, W. (2011). Mind your mannerisms; Behavioral mimicry elicits stereotype conformity. *Journal of Experimental Social Psychology, 47*, 195–201.

Leathers, D. (1997). *Successful nonverbal communication: Principles and applications*. Boston, MA: Allyn and Bacon.

Lee, R. T., & Ashforth, B. E. (1996). A meta-analytic examination of three dimensions of job burnout. *Journal of Applied Psychology, 81*, 123–133.

Leeb, R. T., & Rejskind, F. G. (2004). Here's looking at you, kid: A longitudinal study of perceived gender differences in mutual gaze behavior in young infants. *Sex Roles, 50*, 1–14.

Lefkowitz, M., Blake, R., & Mouton, J. (1955). Status factors in pedestrian violation of traffic signals. *Journal of Abnormal and Social Psychology, 51*, 704–706.

Leigh, T. W., & Summers, J. O. (2002). An initial evaluation of industrial buyers' impressions of salespersons' nonverbal cues. *Journal of Personal Selling and Sales Management, 22*, 41–53.

Lenhart, A., Madden, M., Macgill, A. R., & Smith, A. (2007, December 19). Teens and social media. *PEW Internet & American life project*. Retrieved February 9, 2016, from http://www.pewinternet.org/2007/12/19/teens-and-social-media/

Lerner, R. M., & Korn, S. J. (1972). The development of body build stereotypes in males. *Child Development, 43*, 908–920.

Lester, G. (1993). Listening and talking to patients: A remedy for malpractice suits? *Western Journal of Medicine, 158*(3), 268–272.

Levine, D. (2000). Virtual attraction: What rocks your boat. *Cyberpsychology and Behavior, 3*, 565–573.

Levine, T. R., McCornack, S. A., & Parks, H. S. (1999). Accuracy in detecting truths and lies: Documenting the "veracity effect." *Communication Monographs, 66*, 125–144.

Levine, T. R., Serota, K. B., Shulman, H., Clare, D. D., Park, H., Shaw, A. S., Shim, J. C., & Lee, J. (2011). Sender demeanor: Individual differences in sender believability have a powerful impact on deception detection judgments. *Human Communication Research, 37*, 377–403.

Li, H. Z. (2006). Backchannel responses as misleading feedback in intercultural discourse. *Journal of Intercultural Communication Research, 35*, 99–116.

Lieberman, D. A., Rigio, T. G., & Campain, R. F. (1988). Age-related differences in nonverbal decoding ability. *Communication Quarterly, 36*, 290–297.

Lieberman, M. D., & Rosenthal, R. (2001). Why introverts can't always tell who likes them: Multitasking and nonverbal decoding. *Journal of Personality and Social Psychology, 80*, 294–310.

Lieberman, P. (1967). *Intonation, perception, and language*. Cambridge, MA: MIT Press.

Lightfoot, C., & Bullock, M. (1990). Interpreting contradictory communications: Age and context effects. *Developmental Psychology, 26*, 830–836.

Likowski, K. U., Weyers, P., Seibt, P., Stohr, C., Pauli, P., & Muhlberger, A. (2011). Sad and lonely? Sad mood suppresses facial mimicry. *Journal of Nonverbal Behavior*, 35, 101–117.

Lin, C. A. (1998). Uses of sex appeals in primetime television commercials. *Sex Roles, 38*, 461–475.

Lishner, D. A., Cooter, A. B., & Zald, D. H. (2008). Rapid emotional contagion and expressive congruence under strong test conditions. *Journal of Nonverbal Behavior, 32*, 225–239.

Liska, J. (1993). Bee dances, bird songs, monkey calls, and cetacean sonar: Is speech unique? *Western Journal of Communication, 57*, 1–26.

Liszkowski, U., Carpenter, M., & Tomasello, M. (2007). Pointing out new news, old news, and absent referents at 12 months of age. *Developmental Science, 10*, 1–7.

Littlepage, G. E., & Pineault, M. A. (1982). *Detection of deception of planned and spontaneous communications* (Unpublished paper). Department of Psychology, Middle Tennessee State University, Murfreesboro, Tennessee.

Lomax, C. M. (1994, April). *Proxemics in public: Space violations as a function of dyad composition*. Paper presented at the annual Meeting of the Southeastern Psychological Association, New Orleans, Louisiana.

Lomranz, J., Shapira, A., Choresh, N., & Gilat, Y. (1975). Children's personal space as a function of age and sex. *Developmental Psychology, 11*, 541–545.

Long, D. A., Mueller, J. C., Wyers, R., Khong, V., & Jones, B. (1996). Effects of gender and dress on helping behavior. *Psychological Reports, 78*, 987–994.

Lorenz, K. (1950). Part and parcel in animal and human societies. *Studium Generale, 3*(9). Berlin, Germany: Springer Verlag.

Lucker, G. W., & Graber, L. W. (1980). Physiognomic features and facial appearance judgments in children. *Journal of Psychology, 104*, 261–268.

Lyon, D. (2008). *Father knows best*. Guilford, CT: The Lyons Press.

Lyons, M., Lynch, A., Brewer, G., & Bruno, D. (2014). Detection of sexual orientation ("gaydar") by homosexual and heterosexual women. *Archives of Sexual Behavior, 43*, 345–352.

Lyvers, M., Cholakians, E., Puorro, M., & Sundram, S. (2011). Beer goggles: Blood alcohol concentration in relation to attractiveness ratings for unfamiliar opposite sex faces in naturalistic settings. *The Journal of Social Psychology, 151*, 105–112.

Macrae, C. N., Hood, B. M., Milne, A. B., Rowe, A. C., & Mason, M. F. (2002). Are you looking at me? Eye gaze and person perception. *Psychological Science, 13*, 460–464.

Maestripier, D., Schino, G., Aureli, F., & Troisi, A. (1992). A modest proposal: displacement activities as an indicator of emotions in primates. *Animal Behavior, 44*, 967–979.

Major, B., & Heslin, R. (1982). Perceptions of cross-sex and same-sex nonreciprocal touch: It is better to give than to receive. *Journal of Nonverbal Behavior, 6*, 148–162.

Makoul, G., & Schofield, T. (1999). Communication teaching and assessment in medical education: An international consensus statement. *Patient Education and Counseling, 37*, 191–195.

Malatestra, C. Z. (1985). Developmental course of emotion expression in the human infant. In G. Zivin (Ed.), *The development of expressive behavior*. Orlando, FL: Academic Press.

Maner, J. K., Delton, A., Kenrick, D., Becker, D., Robertson, T., Hofer, B., Neuberg, S., & Butner, J. (2005). Functional projection: How fundamental social motives can bias interpersonal perception. *Journal of Personality and Social Psychology, 88*, 63–78.

Mann, S. (1999). Emotion at work: To what extent are we expressing, suppressing, or faking it? *European Journal of Work and Organizational Psychology, 8*, 347–369.

Mann, S., Vrij, A., & Bull, R. (2002). Suspects, lies, and videotape: An analysis of authentic high-stakes liars. *Law and Human Behavior, 26*, 365–376

Mann, S., Vrij, A., & Bull, R. (2004). Detecting true lies: Police officers' ability to detect deceit. *Journal of Applied Psychology, 89*, 137–149.

Mann, S., Vrij, A., Leal, S., Granhag, P., Warmelink, L., & Forrester, D. (2012). Windows to the soul? Deliberate eye contact as a cue to deceit. *Journal of Nonverbal Behavior, 36*, 205–214.

Manusov, V., & Bixler, N. R. (2003, November). *The polysemous nature of nonverbal behavior: Variety in media framing of the Rabin–Arafat handshake*. Paper presented to the National Communication Association, Miami, Florida.

Manusov, V., & Harvey, J. (2011). Bumps and tears on the road to the Presidency: Media framing of key nonverbal events in the 2008 Presidential election. *Western Journal of Communication, 75*, 282–303.

Manusov, V., & Jaworski, A. (2006). Casting nonverbal behavior in the media. In V. Manusov & M. L. Patterson (Eds.), *The SAGE handbook of nonverbal communication* (pp. 237–255). Thousand Oaks, CA: SAGE

Manusov, V., & Milstein, T. (2005). Interpreting nonverbal behavior: Representation and transformation frames in Israeli and Palestinian coverage of the 1993 Rabin–Arafat handshake. *Western Journal of Communication, 69*, 183–201.

Manusov, V., & Patterson, M. L. (Eds.). (2006). *The SAGE handbook of nonverbal communication*. Thousand Oaks, CA: SAGE.

Manusov, V., & Trees, A. (2002). "Are you kidding me?": The role of nonverbal cues in the verbal accounting process. *Journal of Communication, 52*, 640–656.

Manusov, V., Floyd, K., & Kerssen-Griep, J. (1997). Yours, mine, and ours: Mutual attributions for nonverbal behaviors in couples' interactions. *Communication Research, 24*, 234–260.

Maoz, I. (2012). The face of the enemy: The effects of press-reported visual information regarding the facial features of opponent politicians on support for peace. *Political Communication, 29*, 243–256.

Maringer, M., Krumhuber, E. G., Fischer, A. H., & Niedenthl, P. M. (2011). Beyond smile dynamics: Mimicry and beliefs in judgments of smiles. *Emotion, 11*, 181–187.

Markham, R., & Wang, L. (1996). Recognition of emotion by Chinese and Australian children. *Journal of Cross-Cultural Psychology, 27*, 616–643.

Marlowe, F., Apicella, C., & Reed, D. (2005). Men's preferences for women's profile waist-to-hip ratio in two societies. *Evolution and Human Behavior, 26*, 458–468.

Marsh, A. A., Ambady, N., & Kozak, M. N. (2007). Accurate identification of fear facial expressions predicts prosocial behavior. *Emotion, 7*, 239–251.

Marsh, A. A.., Ambady, N., & Kleck, R. E. (2005). The effects of fear and anger facial expressions on approach- and avoidance-related behaviors. *Emotion, 5*, 119–124.

Martel, L. F., & Biller, H. B. (1987). Stature and stigma. Lexington, MA: Lexington Books.

Martens, J. P., & & Tracy, J. L. (2012). The emotional origins of a social learning bias: Does the pride expression cue copying? *Social Psychology and Personality Science, 4*, 492–499.

Martin, A. (1997). On teenagers and tattoos. *Journal of the American Academy of Child and Adolescent Psychiatry, 36*, 860–861.

Martin, C. L., & Adams, S. (1999). Behavioral biases in the service encounter: Empowerment by default? *Marketing Intelligence and Planning, 17*, 192–201.

Martinet, J. (1992). *The art of mingling*. New York, NY: St. Martin's.

Mason, M. F., Tatkow, E. P., & Macrae, C. N. (2005). The look of love: Gaze shifts and person perception. *Psychological Science, 16*, 236–239.

Masson, J. M., & McCarthy, S. (1995). *When elephants weep: The emotional lives of animals*. New York, NY: Delacourt.

Mast, S. M. (2002). Dominance as expressed and inferred through speaking time: A meta-analysis. *Human Communication Research, 28*, 420–450.

Masuda, T., Ellsworth, P. C., Mesquita, B., Leu, J., Tanida, S., & Veerdonk, E. (2008). Placing the face in context: Cultural differences in the perception of facial emotion: *Journal of Personality and Social Psychology, 94*, 365–381.

Matarazzo, J. D., Wiens, A. N., & Saslow, G. (1965). Studies in interview speech behavior. In L. Krasner & L. P. Ullmann (Eds.), *Research in behavior modification: New developments and implications* (pp. 179–210). New York, NY: Holt, Rinehart & Winston.

Matsumoto, D. (1989). Cultural influences on the perception of emotion. *Journal of Cross-Cultural Psychology, 20*, 92–105.

Matsumoto, D. (1990). Cultural similarities and differences in display rules. *Motivation and Emotion, 14*, 195–214.

Matsumoto, D. (1991). Cultural influences on facial expressions of emotion. *Southern Communication Journal, 56*, 128–137.

Matsumoto, D. (1992). More evidence for the universality of a contempt expression. *Motivation and Emotion, 16*, 363–368.

Matsumoto, D. (2005). Scalar ratings of contempt expressions. *Journal of Nonverbal Behavior, 29*, 91–105.

Matsumoto, D., & Ekman, P. (1989). American–Japanese cultural differences in intensity ratings of facial expressions of emotion. *Motivation and Emotion, 13*, 143–157.

Matsumoto, D., & Hwang, H. (2011). Evidence for training the ability to read microexpressions of emotion. *Motivation and Emotion, 35*, 181–191.

Matsumoto, D., & Hwang, H. (2012). Cultural similarities and differences in emblematic gestures. *Journal of Nonverbal Behavior, 37*, 1–27.

Matsumoto, D., & Hwang, H. (2014). Judgments of subtle facial expressions of emotion. *Emotion, 14*, 349–357.

Matsumoto, D., & Kishimoto, H. (1983). Developmental characteristics in judgments of emotion from nonverbal vocal cues. *International Journal of Intercultural Relations, 7*, 415–424.

Matsumoto, D., & Willingham, B. (2006). The thrill of victory and the agony of defeat: Spontaneous expressions of medal winners of the 2004 Athens Olympic games. *Journal of Personality and Social Psychology, 91*, 568–581.

Matsumoto, D., Kasri, F., & Kooken, K. (1999). American–Japanese cultural differences in judgments of expression intensity and subjective experience. *Cognition and Emotion, 13*, 201–218.

Matsumoto, D., Olide, A., & Willingham, B. (2009). Is there an in-group advantage in recognizing spontaneously expressed emotions? *Journal of Nonverbal Behavior, 33*, 181–191.

Matsumoto, D., Yoo, S., Hirayama, S., & Petrova, G. (2005). Development and validation of a measure of display rule knowledge. *Emotion, 5*, 23–40.

Mazur, A. (1977). Interpersonal spacing on public benches in contact vs. noncontact cultures. *The Journal of Social Psychology, 101*, 53–58.

McAleer, P., Todorov, A., & Belin, P. (2014). You had me at hello: Personality impressions from brief novel voices. *PLOS One, 9*, e90779.

McCallmont, L. (2014). Lawmakers make "hands up" gesture on House floor. *Politico*. Retrieved January 17, 2016, from http://www.politico.com/story/2014/12/lawmakers-ferguson-hands-up-113254

McCarthy, A., & Lee, K. (2009). Children's knowledge of deceptive gaze cues and its relation to their actual lying behavior. *Journal of Experimental Child Psychology, 103*, 117–134.

McCarthy, A., Lee, K., Itakura, S., & Muir, D. (2006). Cultural display rules drive eye gaze during thinking. *Journal of Cross-Cultural Psychology, 37*, 717–722.

McClure, E. B. (2000). A meta-analytic review of sex differences in facial expression processing and their development in infants, children, and adolescents. *Psychological Bulletin, 126*, 424–453.

McClure, E. B., & Nowicki, S. (2001). Associations between social anxiety and nonverbal processing skill in preadolescent boys and girls. *Journal of Nonverbal Behavior, 25*, 3–19.

McConnell-Ginet, S. (1983). Intonation in a man's world. In B. Thorne, N. Henley, & C. Kramarae (Eds.), *Language, gender and society* (pp. 69–88). Rowley, MA: Newbury House.

McCornack, S. A., & Parks, M. R. (1986). Deception detection and relationship development: The other side of trust. In M. McLaughlin (Ed.), *Communication yearbook 9* (pp. 377–389). Beverly Hills, CA: SAGE.

McCoy, N. L., & Pitino, L. (2002). Pheromonal influences on sociosexual behavior in young women. *Physiology and Behavior, 75*, 367–375.

McDaniel, E., & Andersen, P. A. (1998). International patterns of interpersonal tactile communication: A field study. *Journal of Nonverbal Behavior, 22*, 59–75.

McDowall, J. J. (1978). Interactional synchrony: A reappraisal. *Journal of Personality and Social Psychology, 36*, 963–975.

McGovern, T. V., & Tinsley, H. E. A. (1978). Interviewer evaluations of interviewee nonverbal behavior. *Journal of Vocational Behavior, 13*, 163–171.

McGrew, P. L., & McGrew, W. C. (1975). Interpersonal spacing behavior in preschool children during group formation. *Man-Environment Systems, 5*, 43–48.

McHugo, G. J., & Smith, C. A. (1996). The power of faces: A review of John T. Lanzetta's research on facial expression and emotion. *Motivation and Emotion, 20*, 85–120.

McHugo, G. J., Lanzetta, J. T., & Bush, L. (1991). The effect of attitudes on emotional reactions to political leader's expressive displays. *Journal of Nonverbal Behavior, 15*, 19–41.

McHugo, G. J., Lanzetta, J. T., Sullivan, D. G., Masters, R. D., & Englis, B. G. (1985). Emotional reactions to political leader's expressive displays. *Journal of Personality and Social Psychology, 49*, 1513–1529.

McIntosh, D. N. (1996). Facial feedback hypotheses: Evidence, implications, and directions. *Motivation and Emotion, 20*, 121–147.

McIntosh, D. N., Reichmann-Decker, A., Winkielman, P., & Wilbarger, J. L. (2006). When the social mirror breaks: Deficits in automatic, but not voluntary, mimicry of emotional facial expressions in autism. *Developmental Science, 9*, 295–302.

McKenzie, B. A. (2008, October 20). McCain's lack of eye contact condescending. *HuffPost Politics*. Retrieved February 9, 2016, from http://www.huffingtonpost.com/brett-ashley-mckenzie/mccains-lack-of-eye-conta_b_129826.html

McNeil, D. (1995). *Hand and mind: What gestures reveal about thought*. Chicago, IL: University of Chicago Press.

Meeren, H. K., van Heijnsbergen, C. C., & Gelder, B. D. (2005). Rapid perceptual integration of facial expression and emotional body language. *Proceedings of the National Academy of Sciences of the United States of America, 102*, 16518–16523.

Mehrabian, A. (1968). Inference of attitude from the posture, orientation, and distance of a communicator. *Journal of Consulting and Clinical Psychology, 32*, 296–308.

Mehrabian, A. (1969). Significance of posture and position in the communication of attitude and status relationships. *Psychological Bulletin, 71*, 359–372.

Mehrabian, A. (1972). *Nonverbal communication*. Chicago, IL: Aldine-Atherton.

Mehrabian, A., & Ferris, S. R. (1967). Inference of attitudes from nonverbal communication in two channels. *Journal of Consulting Psychology, 31*, 248–252.

Mehrabian, A., & Friar, J. T. (1969). Encoding of attitude by a seated communicator via posture and position cues. *Journal of Consulting and Clinical Psychology, 33*, 330–336.

Mehrabian, A., & Wiener, M. (1967). Decoding of inconsistent communications. *Journal of Personality and Social Psychology, 6*, 108–114.

Melfsen, S., & Florin, I. (2002). Do socially anxious children show deficits in classifying facial expressions of emotions? *Journal of Nonverbal Behavior, 26*, 109–126.

Meltzer, A. L., McNulty, J. K., Jackson, G. L., & Karney, B. R. (2013). Sex differences in the implications of partner physical attractiveness for the trajectory of marital satisfaction. *Journal of Personality and Social Psychology, 106*(3), 418–428.

Meltzoff, A. N., & Moore, M. K. (1977). Imitation of facial and manual gestures by human neonates. *Developmental Psychology, 198*, 75–78.

Men Acting Badly. (1997, November 27). *Philadelphia Inquirer*, p. C3.

Merkle, E. R., & Richardson, R. A. (2000). Digital dating and virtual relating: Conceptualizing computer mediated romantic relationships. *Family Relations, 49*, 187–192.

Mesko, N., & Bereczkei, T. (2004). Hairstyle as an adaptive means of displaying phenotypic quality. *Human Nature, 15*, 251–270.

Messinger, D. S., Fogel, A., & Dickson, K. L. (2001). All smiles are positive, but some smiles are more positive than others. *Developmental Psychology, 37*, 642–653.

Michael, G., & Willis, F. N., Jr. (1969). The development of gestures in three subcultural groups. *Journal of Social Psychology, 79*, 35–41.

Michelman, S. O., & Erekosima, T. V. (1992). Kalabari dress in Nigeria: Visual analysis and gender implications. In R. Barnes & J. B. Eicher (Eds.), *Dress and gender* (pp. 164–182). Providence, RI: Berg.

Mikulincer, M., & Shaver, P. R. (2003). The attachment behavioral system in adulthood: Activation, psychodynamics, and interpersonal processes. In M. P. Zanna (Ed.), *Advances in experimental social psychology* (Vol. 35, pp. 53–152). New York, NY: Academic Press.

Milgram, S. (1974). *Obedience to authority*. New York, NY: Harper & Row.

Milius, S. (1999). When lizards do push-ups. *Science News, 155*(9), 142–145.

Millar, M. G., & Millar, K. (1995). Detection of deception in familiar and unfamiliar persons: The effects of information restriction. *Journal of Nonverbal Behavior, 19*, 69–84.

Miller, A. G., Ashton, W. A., McHoskey, J. W., & Gimbel, J. (1990). What price attractiveness? Stereotype and risk factors in suntanning behavior. *Journal of Applied Social Psychology, 20*, 1272–1300.

Miller, G. R., & Stiff, J. B. (1993). *Deceptive communication*. Newbury Park, CA: SAGE.

Miller, H. C., Chabriac, A., & Molet, M. (2013). The impact of facial emotional expression and sex on interpersonal distancing as evaluated in a computerized stop-distance task. *Canadian Journal of Experimental Psychology, 67*, 188–194.

Miller, M. J., Denes, A., Diaz, B., & Buck, R. (2014). Attachment style predicts jealous reactions to viewing touch between *Journal of Nonverbal Behavior, 38*, 451–476.

Mills, J. (1984). Self-posed behaviors of females and males in photographs. *Sex Roles, 10*, 633–637.

Mills, J. S., Polivy, J., Herman, C. P., & Tiggeman, M. (2002). Effects of exposure to thin media images: Evidence of self-enhancement among restrained eaters. *Personality and Social Psychology Bulletin, 28*, 1687–1699.

Misailidi, P. (2006). Young children's display rule knowledge: Understanding the distinction between apparent and real emotions and the motives underlying the use of display rules. *Social Behavior and Personality, 34*, 1285–1296.

Molinsky, A. L., Krabbenhoft, M. A., Ambady, N., & Choi, Y. S. (2005). Cracking the nonverbal code: Intercultural competence and gesture recognition across cultures. *Journal of Cross-Cultural Psychology, 36*, 380–395.

Montagne, B., Schutters, S., Westenberg, H. G. M., van Honk, J., Kessels, R. P. C., & de Haan, E. H. (2006). Reduced sensitivity in the recognition of anger and disgust in social anxiety disorder. *Cognitive Neuropsychiatry, 11*, 401–414.

Montagu, A. (1986). *Touching: The human significance of the skin* (2nd ed.). New York, NY: Harper & Row.

Montague, D. P. F., & Walker-Andrews, A. S. (2001). Peekaboo: A new look at infants' perception of emotion expressions. *Developmental Psychology, 37*, 836–838.

Montepare, J. M. (1995). The impact of variations in height on young children's impressions of men and women. *Journal of Nonverbal Behavior, 19*, 31–47.

Montepare, J. M., & Zebrowitz-McArthur, L. (1987). Perceptions of adults and children with childlike voices in two cultures. *Journal of Experimental Social Psychology, 23*, 331–349.

Montepare, J. M., Goldstein, S. B., & Clausen, A. (1987). The identification of emotion from gait information. *Journal of Nonverbal Behavior, 11*, 33–42.

Montepare, J., & Koff, E. (1999). The use of body movement and gestures as cues to emotions in younger and older adults. *Journal of Nonverbal Behavior, 23*, 133–152.

Moody, E. J., McIntosh, D. N., Mann, L. J., & Weisser, K. R. (2007). More than mere mimicry? The influence of emotion on rapid facial reactions to faces. *Emotion, 7*, 447–457.

Moore, M. M. (1985). Nonverbal courtship patterns in women. Context and consequences. *Ethology and Sociobiology, 6*, 237–247.

Moore, M. M. (1998). Nonverbal courtship patterns in women: Rejection signaling—an empirical investigation. *Semiotica, 13*, 201–214.

Moore, M. M. (2002). Courtship communication and perception. *Perceptual and Motor Skills, 94*, 97–105.

Moore, M. M., & Butler, D. L. (1989). Predictive aspects of nonverbal courtship behavior in women. *Semiotica, 3*, 205–215.

Morency, L., & Krauss, R. M. (1982). Children's nonverbal encoding and decoding of affect. In R. S. Feldman (Ed.), *Development of nonverbal behavior in children* (pp. 181–199). New York, NY: Springer-Verlag.

Morin, R. (2002, April 28). Do babes make the bucks? *The Washington Post*, p. BO5.

Morley, I. E., & Stephenson, G. M. (1969). Interpersonal and interparty exchange: A laboratory simulation of an industrial negotiation at the plant level. *British Journal of Psychology, 60*, 543–545.

Morrel-Samuels, P., & Krauss, R. (1992). Word familiarity predicts temporal asynchrony of hand gestures. *Journal of Experimental Psychology, 18*, 615–622.

Morris, D. (1967). *The naked ape*. London, England: Cape.

Morris, D. (1977). *Manwatching: A field guide to human behavior*. New York, NY: Harry N. Abrahms.

Morris, D. (1994). *Bodytalk: The meaning of human gestures*. New York, NY: Crown.

Morris, J. A., & Feldman, D. C. (1996). The dimensions, antecedents, and consequences of emotional labor. *Academy of Management Review, 21*, 986–1010.

Morsella, E., & Kraus, R. M. (2004). The role of gestures in spatial working memory and speech. *American Journal of Psychology, 117*, 411–424.

Motley, M. T. (1990). On whether one can(not) communicate: An examination via traditional communication postulates. *Western Journal of Speech Communication, 54*, 1–20.

Motley, M. T. (1993). Facial affect and verbal context in conversation: Facial expression as interjection. *Human Communication Research, 20*, 3–40.

Motley, M. T., & Camden, C. T. (1988). Facial expression of emotion: A comparison of posed expressions versus spontaneous expressions in an interpersonal communication setting. *Western Journal of Speech Communication, 52*, 1–22.

Mueller, E., & Rich, A. (1976). Clustering and socially directed behavior in a playgroup of one-year-olds. *Journal of Child Psychology and Psychiatry, 17*, 315–322.

Muhammad, L. (2001, June 5). More men opt for plastic surgery. *Cincinnati Enquirer*.

Mulac, A., Studley, L. B., Weimann, J. M., & Bradac, J. J. (1987). Male/female gaze in same-sex and mixed-sex dyads: Gender-linked differences in mutual influence. *Human Communication Research, 13*, 323–343.

Mullen, D. M., Futrell, D., Stairs, D., Tice, D., Baumeister, R., Dawson, K., Riordan, C. A., . . . & Rosenfeld, P. (1986). Newscasters' facial expressions and voting behavior of viewers: Can a smile elect a president? *Journal of Personality and Social Psychology, 51*, 291–295.

Munhall, K. G., Jones, J. A., Callan, D. E., Kuratate, T., & Vatikiotis-Bateson, E. (2004). Visual prosody and speech intelligibility: Head movement improves auditory speech perception. *Psychological Science, 15*, 133–137.

Murphy, J. D., Driscoll, D. M., & Kelly, J. R. (1999). Differences in the nonverbal behavior of men who vary in the likelihood to sexually harass. *Journal of Social Behavior and Personality, 14*, 113–128.

Murstein, B. I. (1972). Physical attractiveness and marital choice. *Journal of Personality and Social Psychology, 22*, 8–12.

Muscarella, F., & Cunningham, M. R. (1996). The evolutionary significance and social perception of male pattern baldness and facial hair. *Ethology and Sociobiology, 17*, 99–117.

Myers, P. N., Jr., & Biocca, F. A. (1992). The elastic body image: The effect of television advertising and programming on body image distortions in young women. *Journal of Communication, 42*, 108–133.

Mysak, E. D. (1959). Pitch and duration characteristics of older males. *Journal of Speech and Hearing Research, 2*, 46–54.

Nannberg, J. C., & Hansen, C. H. (1994). Post compliance touch: An incentive for task performance. *Journal of Social Psychology, 134*, 301–307.

Nash, J. M. (2007, January 19). The gift of mimicry. *Time.com*

Nash, R., Feldman, G., Hussey, T., Leveque, J., & Pineau, P. (2006). Cosmetics: They influence more than Caucasian female facial attractiveness. *Journal of Applied Social Psychology, 36*, 493–504.

Natale, M. (1975). Convergence of mean vocal intensity in dyadic communication as a function of social desirability. *Journal of Personality and Social Psychology, 32*, 790–804.

Navy Issues Warning on the Dangers of Hugging. (2002, May 25). *The Dominion* (Wellington), p. 6.

Nelson, N., & Russell, J. A. (2013). Universality revisited. *Emotion Review, 13*, 8–15.

Newton, D. A., & Burgoon, J. K. (1990). Nonverbal conflict behaviors: Functions, strategies, and tactics. In D. D. Cahn (Ed.), *Intimates in conflict: A communication perspective* (pp. 77–104). Hillsdale, NJ: Lawrence Erlbaum.

Ng, W., & Lindsay, R. C. L. (1994). Cross-race facial recognition. *Journal of Cross-Cultural Psychology, 25*, 217–232.

Nguyen, M. L., Heslin, R., & Nguyen, T. (1975). The meaning of touch: Sex differences. *Journal of Communication, 25*, 92–103.

Nicholas, C. I. (2004). Gaydar: Eye-gaze as identity recognition among gay men and lesbians. *Sexuality & Culture, 8*, 60–86.

Nixon, Y., & Bull, P. (2005). The effects of cultural awareness on nonverbal perceptual accuracy: British and Japanese training programmes. *Journal of Intercultural Communication, 9*, 63–80.

No Hugging or Kissing—They're Counsellors. (2002, May 16). *The Straits Times* (Singapore), p. 15.

Noesjirwan, J. (1978). A laboratory study of proxemic patterns of Indonesians and Australians. *British Journal of Social and Clinical Psychology, 17*, 333–334.

Noller, P. (1980). Gaze in married couples. *Journal of Nonverbal Behavior, 5*, 115–129.

Noller, P. (1981). Gender and marital adjustment level differences in decoding messages from spouses and strangers. *Journal of Personality and Social Psychology, 41*, 272–278.

Noller, P. (1984). *Nonverbal communication and marital interaction*. Oxford, England: Pergamon Press.

Noller, P. (1992). Nonverbal communication in marriage. In R. S. Feldman (Ed.), *Applications of nonverbal behavioral theories and research* (pp. 31–59). Hillside, NJ: Lawrence Erlbaum.

Noller, P. (2006). Nonverbal communication in close relationships. In V. Manusov & M. L. Patterson (Eds.), *The*

SAGE handbook of nonverbal communication (pp. 403–420). Thousand Oaks, CA: SAGE.

Noller, P., Feeney, J. A., Roberts, N., & Christensen, A. (2005). Withdrawal in couple interactions: Exploring the causes and consequences. In R. E. Riggio & R. S. Feldman (Eds.), *Applications of nonverbal communication* (pp. 199–218). Mahwah, NJ: Lawrence Erlbaum.

Norman, P. L., & Kendrick, D. T. (2006). Sex similarities and differences in preferences for short-term mates: What, whether and why. *Journal of Personality and Social Psychology, 90*, 468–489.

North, A. C., & Sheridan, L. (2004). The effect of pedestrian clothing in 18,000 road-crossing episodes. *Journal of Applied Social Psychology, 34*, 1878–1882.

Notarius, C., & Markman, H. (1993). *We can work it out*. New York, NY: Berkley.

Notarius, C., Benson, P. R., Sloane, D., & Vanzetti, N. A. (1989). Exploring the interface between perception and behavior: An analysis of marital interaction in distressed and non-distressed couples. *Behavioral Assessment, 11*, 39–64.

Nowicki, S., & Duke, M. (2002). *Will I ever fit in? The breakthrough program for conquering adult dyssemia*. New York, NY: The Free Press.

Nowicki, S., & Duke, M. P. (1992a). *Helping the child who doesn't fit in*. Atlanta, GA: Peachtree Press.

Nowicki, S., & Duke, M. P. (1992b). The association of children's nonverbal decoding abilities with their popularity, locus of control, an academic achievement. *Journal of Genetic Psychology, 153*, 385–394.

Nowicki, S., & Duke, M. P. (1994). Individual differences in the nonverbal communication of affect: The diagnostic analysis of nonverbal accuracy scale. *Journal of Nonverbal Behavior, 18*, 9–35.

Nowicki, S., Glanville, D., & Demertzis, A. (1998). A test of the ability to recognize emotion in the facial expressions of African American adults. *Journal of Black Psychology, 24*, 335–350.

Nowoseleski, K., Sipinski, A., Kuczerawy, I., Kozlowska, D., & Skrzpulec, V. (2012). Tattoos, piercings, and sexual behavior among young adults. *Journal of Sexual Medicine, 9*, 2307–2314.

Nurmsoo, E., Einav, F., & Hood, B. M. (2012). Best friends: Children use gaze to identify friendships in others. *Developmental Science, 15*, 417–425.

O'Keefe, D. J. (1990). *Persuasion: Theory and research*. Newbury Park, CA: SAGE.

Ognibene, T. C., & Collins, N. L. (1998). Adult attachment styles, perceived social support, and coping strategies. *Journal of Social and Personal Relationships, 15*, 323–345.

Olivola, C. Y., & Todorov, A. (2010). Elected in 100 milliseconds: Appearance-based trait inferences and voting. *Journal of Nonverbal Behavior, 34*, 83–110.

Olson, I. R., & Marshuetz, C. (2005). Facial attractiveness is appraised at a glance. *Emotion, 5*, 498–502.

Omdahl, B. L., & O'Donnel, C. (1999). Emotional contagion, empathic concern, and communicative responsiveness as variables affecting nurses' stress and occupational commitment. *Journal of Advanced Nursing, 29*, 1351–1360.

Orth, U. R., Chameeva, T., & Brand, K. (2013). Trust during retail encounters: A touchy proposition. *Journal of Retailing, 89*, 301–314.

Oster, H., & Ekman, P. (1978). Facial behavior in child development. In W. A. Collins (Ed.), *Minnesota symposia on child psychology* (pp. 231–276). Hillsdale, NJ: Erlbaum.

Oster, H., Hegley, D., & Nagel, L. (1992). Adult judgments and fine-grained analysis of infant facial expressions. *Developmental Psychology, 28*, 1115–1131.

Otta, E., Abrosio, F. F. E., & Hoshino, R. L (1996). Reading a smiling face: Messages conveyed by various forms of smiling. *Perceptual and Motor Skills, 82*, 1111–1121.

Out of sight. (1999, April). *Allure*, 79.

Palanica, A., & Itier, R. J. (2012). Attention capture by direct gaze is robust to context and task demands. *Journal of Nonverbal Behavior, 36*, 123–134.

Pancer, S. M., & Meindl, J. R. (1978). Length of hair and beardedness as determinants of personality impressions. *Perceptual and Motor Skills, 46*, 1328–1330.

Park, J., Baek, Y. M., & Cha, M. (2014). Cross-cultural comparison of nonverbal cues in emoticons on Twitter: Evidence from big data analysis. *Journal of Communication, 64*, 333–354.

Parkinson, B. (2005). Do facial movements express emotions or communicate motives? *Personality and Social Psychology Review, 9*, 278–311.

Parkinson, B. (2013). Contextualizing facial activity. *Emotion Review, 5*, 97–103.

Parzuchowski, M., & Wojciski, B. (2014). Hand over heart primes moral judgments and behavior. *Journal of Nonverbal Behavior, 38*, 145–165.

Patterson, M. L. (1976). An arousal model of interpersonal intimacy. *Psychological Review, 83*, 235–245.

Patterson, M. L. (1977). Interpersonal distance, affect, and equilibrium theory. *Journal of Social Psychology, 101*, 205–214.

Patterson, M. L. (1983). *Nonverbal behavior: A functional perspective*. New York, NY: Springer-Verlag.

Patterson, M. L. (1995). A parallel process model of nonverbal communication. *Journal of Nonverbal Behavior, 19*, 3–29.

Patterson, M. L., Iizuka, Y., Tubbs, M. E., Ansel, J., Tsutsumi, M., & Anson, J. (2007). Passing encounters east and west: Comparing Japanese and American pedestrian interactions. *Journal of Nonverbal Behavior, 31*, 155–166.

Patterson, M. L., Lammers, V. M., & Tubbs, M. E. (2014). Busy signal: Effects of mobile device usage on pedestrian encounters. *Journal of Nonverbal Behavior, 38*, 313–324.

Patterson, M. L., Mullens, S., & Romano, J. (1971). Compensatory reactions to spatial intrusions. *Sociometry, 34*, 114–121.

Paunonen, S. (2006). You are honest, therefore I like you and find you attractive. *Journal of Research in Personality, 40*, 237–249.

Peace, V., Miles, L., & Johnston, L. (2006). It doesn't matter what you wear: The impact of posed and genuine expressions of happiness on product evaluation. *Social Cognition, 24*, 137–168.

Peck, H., & Peck, S. (1970). A concept of facial esthetics. *Angle Orthodontics, 40*, 289.

Pedersen, E. L., Markee, N. L., & Salusso, C. J. (1994). Gender differences in characteristics reported to be important features of physical attractiveness. *Perceptual and Motor Skills, 79*, 1539–1544.

Pelc, K., Kornreich, C., Foisy, M., & Dan, B. (2006). *Pediatric Neurology, 35*, 93–97.

Pell, M., Monetta, L., Paulman, S., & Kotz, S. A. (2009). Recognizing emotions in a foreign language. *Journal of Nonverbal Behavior, 33*, 107–120.

Pentland, A. (2008). *Honest signals: How they shape our world*, Cambridge, MA: MIT Press.

Perper, T. (1985). *Sex signals: The biology of love*. Philadelphia, PA: ISI Press.

Persichitte, K. A. (1997, February 14–18). *Conducting research on the Internet: Strategies for electronic interviewing*. Proceedings of selected research and development presentations at the 1997 National Convention of the Association for Educational Communications and Technology, Albuquerque, New Mexico.

Peterson, K., & Curran, J. P. (1976). Trait attribution as a function of hair length and correlates of subjects' preferences for hair style. *Journal of Psychology, 93*, 331–339.

Peterson, R. (2005). An examination of the relative effectiveness of training in nonverbal communication: Personal selling implications. *Journal of Marketing Education, 27*, 143–150.

Pettenati, P., Sekene, K., Congestri, E., & Volterra, E. (2012). A comparative study on representational gestures in Italian and Japanese children. *Journal of Nonverbal Behavior, 36*, 149–164.

Petty, R. E., & Cacioppo, J. T. (1986). *Communication and persuasion: Central and peripheral routes to attitude change*. New York, NY: Springer-Verlag.

Philippot, P., & Feldman, R. S. (1990). Age and social competence in preschoolers' decoding of facial expressions. *British Journal of Social Psychology, 29*, 43–54.

Philippot, P., Komreich, C., Blairy, S., Baert, I., Den, D. A., Le Bon, O., Streel, O., . . . & Verbanck, P. (1999). Alcoholics' deficits in the decoding of emotional facial expression. *Alcoholism, Clinical and Experimental Research, 23*, 1031–1038.

Phillips, R. D., Wagner, S. H., Fells, C. A., & Lynch, M. (1990). Do infants recognize emotions in facial expressions? Categorical and metaphorical evidence. *Infant Behavior and Development, 13*, 71–84.

Philpott, J. S. (1983). *The relative contribution to meaning of verbal and nonverbal channels of communication* (Unpublished master's thesis). University of Nebraska, Lincoln, Nebraska.

Picariello, M. L., Greenberg, D. N., & Pillemer, D. B. (1990). *Child Development, 61*, 1453–1460.

Pickett, C. L., Gardner, W. L., & Knowles, M. (2004). Getting a cue: The need to belong and enhanced sensitivity to social cues. *Personality and Social Psychology Bulletin, 30*, 1095–1107.

Pierce, C. A. (1996). Body height and romantic attraction: A meta-analytic test of the male-taller norm. *Social Behavior and Personality, 24*, 143–149.

Pine, K. J., Gurney, D. J., & Fletcher, B. (2010). The semantic specificity hypothesis: When gestures do not depend upon the presence of a listener. *Journal of Nonverbal Behavior, 34*, 169–178.

Pittam, J. (1994). *Voice in social interaction: An interdisciplinary approach*. Thousand Oaks, CA: SAGE.

Pittam, J., & Scherer, K. R. (1993). Vocal expression and communication of emotion. In M. Lewis & J. Haviland (Eds.), *The handbook of emotion* (pp. 185–197). New York, NY: Guilford.

Planalp, S., & Benson, A. (1992). Friends' and acquaintances' conversations I: Perceived differences. *Journal of Social and Personal Relationships, 9*, 483–506.

Plant, E. A., Hyde, J. S., Keltner, D., & Devine, P. G. (2000). The gender stereotyping of emotion. *Psychology of Women Quarterly, 24*(1), 81–92.

Plant, E. A., Kling, K. C., & Smith, G. L. (2004). The influence of gender and social role on the interpretation of facial expressions. *Sex Roles, 51*, 187–196.

Plutchik, R. (1980). *Emotion: A psychoevolutionary synthesis*. New York, NY: Harper & Row.

Polit, D., & LaFrance, M. (1977). Sex differences in reaction to spatial invasion. *Journal of Social Psychology, 102*, 59–60.

Poppleton, S. E. (1981). The social skills of selling. In M. Argyle (Ed.), *Social skills and work* (pp. 59–83). London, England: Methuen.

Posovac, S. S., & Posovac, H. D. (2002). Predictors of women's concern with body weight: The role of perceived self-media ideal discrepancies and self-esteem. *Eating Disorders, 10*, 153–160.

Post, B., & Hetherington, E. M. (1974). Sex differences in the use of proximity and eye contact in judgments of affiliation in preschool children. *Developmental Psychology, 10*, 881–889.

Preuschoft, S., & van Hooff, J. A. R. A. M. (1997). The social function of "smile" and "laughter": Variations across primate species and societies. In U. Segerstrale & P. Molnar (Eds.), *Nonverbal communication: Where nature meets culture* (pp. 171–189). Mahwah, NJ: Lawrence Erlbaum

Prkachin, K. M., & Silverman, B. E. (2002). Hostility and facial expression in young men and women: Is social regulation more important than negative affect? *Health Psychology, 21*, 33–139.

Profyt, L., & Whissell, C. (1991). Children's understanding of facial expression of emotion: I. Voluntary creation of emotion faces. *Perceptual and Motor Skills, 73*, 199–202.

Provost, M. P., Kormos, C., Kosakoski, G., & Quinsey, V. L. (2006). Sociosexuality in women and preference for facial masculinization and somatotype in men. *Archives of Sexual Behavior, 35*, 305–312,

Pryor, J. B. (1987). Sexual harassment proclivities in men. *Sex Roles, 17*, 269–290.

Pryzbylski, A. K., & Weinstein, N. (2012). Can you connect with me now? How the presence of mobile computer technology influences the face-to-face conversation quality. *Journal of Personal and Social Relationships, 30*, 337–246.

Puccinelli, N. M., & Tickle-Degnen, L. (2004). Knowing too much about others: Moderators of the relationship between eavesdropping and rapport in social interaction. *Journal of Nonverbal Behavior, 28*, 223–243.

Pugh, S. D. (2006). Service with a smile: Emotional contagion in the service encounter. *Academy of Management Journal, 44*, 1018–1027.

Pugliesi, K. (1999). The consequences of emotional labor: Effects on work stress, job satisfaction, and well-being. *Motivation and Emotion, 23*, 125–154.

Quadflieg, S., Vermeulen, N., & Rossion, B. (2013). Differential reliance on the Duchenne marker during smile evaluations and person judgments. *Journal of Nonverbal Behavior, 37*, 69–77.

Quinn, R. P. (1978). *Physical deviance and occupational mistreatment: The short, the fat, and the ugly*. Master's thesis. Ann Arbor: University of Michigan Survey Research Center.

Rafaeli, A. (1988). *When clerks meet customers: A test of variables related to emotional expression on the job*. A revision of a paper presented at the Annual Convention of the American Psychological Association, New York, NY.

Rafaeli, A., & Sutton, R.I. (1987). Expression of emotion as part of the work role. *Academy of Management Review, 12*, 23–37.

Ramirez, A., Walther, J. B., Burgoon, J. K., & Sunnafrank, M. (2001). Information-seeking strategies, uncertainty, and computer-mediated communication: Toward a conceptual model. *Human Communication Research, 28*, 213–228.

Rauscher, F. B., Krauss, R. M., & Chen, Y. (1996). Gesture, speech, and lexical access: The role of lexical movements in speech production. *Psychology Science*, 7, 226–231.

Ray, G. B., & Floyd, K. (2006). Nonverbal expressions of liking and disliking in initial interaction: Encoding and decoding perspectives. *Southern Communication Journal, 71*, 45–65.

Reeve, J. (1993). The face of interest. *Motivation and Emotion, 17*, 353–375.

Regan, P. C., Jerry, D., Marysia, N., & Johnson, D. (1999). Public displays of affection among Asian and Latino heterosexual couples. *Psychological Reports, 84*, 1201–1202.

Reis, H. T., Wilson, I. M., Monestere, C., Bernstein, S., Clark, K., Seidl, E., Franco, M., . . . & Radoane, K. (1990). What is smiling is beautiful and good. *European Journal of Social Psychology, 20*, 259–267.

Reisenzein, R., Bordgen, S., Holtbernd, T., & Matz, D. (2006). Evidence for strong dissociation between emotion and facial displays: The case of surprise. *Journal of Personality and Social Psychology, 91*, 295–315.

Reisenzein, R., Studtmann, M., & Horstmann, G. (2013). Coherence between emotion and facial expression: Evidence from laboratory experiments. *Emotion Review, 5*, 16–23.

Relethford, J. H., Stern, M. P., Gaskill, S. P., & Hazuda, H. P. (1983). Social class, admixture, and skin color variation in Mexican-American and Anglo-Americans living in San Antonio, Texas. *American Journal of Physical Anthropology, 61*, 97–102.

Remland, M. S. (1981). Developing leadership skills in nonverbal communication: A situational perspective. *Journal of Business Communication, 18*, 17–29.

Remland, M. S. (1984). Leadership impressions and nonverbal communication in a superior–subordinate interaction. *Communication Quarterly, 32*, 41–48.

Remland, M. S. (1988). Adaptive leadership and nonverbal displays of status in small groups. In R. S. Cathcart & L. A. Samovar (Eds.), *Small group communication* (pp. 515–531). Dubuque, IA: W. C. Brown.

Remland, M. S., & Jones, T. S. (1989). The effect of nonverbal involvement and communication apprehension on state anxiety, interpersonal attraction, and speech duration. *Communication Quarterly, 37*, 170–183.

Remland, M. S., & Jones, T. S. (1994). The influence of vocal intensity and touch on compliance gaining. *Journal of Social Psychology, 134*, 89–97.

Remland, M. S., Jones, T. S., & Brinkman, H. (1991). Proxemic and haptic behavior in three European countries. *Journal of Nonverbal Behavior, 15*, 215–232.

Remland, M. S., Jones, T. S., & Brinkman, H. (1995). Interpersonal distance, body orientation, and touch: Effects of culture, gender, and age. *Journal of Social Psychology, 135*, 281–298.

Remland, M. S., Jones, T. S., & Brinkman, H. (1999). *Use of touch as a function of culture* (Unpublished manuscript). West Chester University, West Chester, Pennsylvania.

Remmers, F. L. (1980, November). *A kinesic analysis of perceived bias in television anchormen: Two case studies*. Paper presented at the annual meeting of the Speech Communication Association Convention, New York, NY.

Renninger, L. A., Wade, J. T., & Grammer, K. (2004). Getting that female glance: Patterns and consequences of male nonverbal behavior in courtship contexts. *Evolution and Human Behavior, 25*, 416–431.

Rhoades, D. R., McFarland, K. F., Finch, W. H., & Johnson, A. O. (2001). Speaking and interruptions during primary care office visits. *Family Medicine*, 7, 528–532.

Rhodes, G. (2006). The evolutionary psychology of facial beauty. *Annual Review of Psychology*, 57, 199–226.

Rhodes, G., Proffitt, F., Grady, J. M., & Sumich, A. (1998). Facial symmetry and the perception of beauty. *Psychonomic Bulletin, 5*, 659–669.

Rhodes, G., Zebrowitz, L. A., Clark, A., Kalick, S. M., Hightower, A., & McKay, R. (2001). Do facial averageness and symmetry signal health? *Evolution and Human Behavior, 22*, 31–46.

Rice, R. E., & Love, G. (1987). Electronic emotion: Socioemotional content in a computer-mediated network. *Communication Research, 14*, 85–108.

Richeson, J. A., & Shelton, N. N. (2005). Thin slices of racial bias. *Journal of Nonverbal Behavior, 25*, 75–86.

Richmond, V. P., Smith, R. S., Heisel, A. D., & McCroskey, J. C. (2001). Nonverbal immediacy in the physician/patient relationship. *Communication Research Reports, 18*, 211–216.

Riggio, R. E. (1987). *The charisma quotient*. New York, NY: Dodd, Mead.

Riggio, R. E. (1992). Social interaction skills and nonverbal behavior. In R. S. Feldman (Ed.), *Applications of nonverbal behavioral theories and research* (pp. 3–30). Hillsdale, NJ: Lawrence Erlbaum.

Riggio, R. E. (2001). Interpersonal sensitivity and organizational psychology: Theoretical and methodological applications. In J. A. Hall & F. J. Bernieri (Eds.), *Interpersonal sensitivity: Theory and measurement* (pp. 305–318). Mahwah, NJ: Lawrence Erlbaum Associates.

Riggio, R. E., & Friedman, H. S. (1982). The interrelationships of self-monitoring factors, personality traits, and nonverbal social skills. *Journal of Nonverbal Behavior*, 7, 33–45.

Riggio, R. E., & Throckmorton, B. (1988). The relative effects of verbal and nonverbal behavior, appearance, and social skills on evaluations made in hiring interviews. *Journal of Applied Social Psychology, 18*, 331–348.

Riggio, R. E., & Woll, S. B. (1984). The role of nonverbal cues and physical attractiveness in the selection of dating partners. *Journal of Social and Personal Relationships, 1*, 347–357.

Rime, B., & Schiaratura, L. (1991). Gesture and speech. In R. S. Feldman & B. Rime (Eds.), *Fundamentals of nonverbal behavior* (pp. 239–281). Cambridge, England: Cambridge University Press.

Rime, B., Schiaratura, L., Hupet, M., & Ghysselinckx, A. (1984). Effects of relative immobilization on the speaker's nonverbal behavior and on the dialogue imagery level. *Motivation and Emotion, 8*, 311–325.

Robbins, O., Devoe, S., & Weiner, M. (1978). Social patterns of turn taking: Nonverbal regulators. *Journal of Communication, 28*, 38–46.

Roberti, J. W., Storch, E. A., & Bravata, E. (2004). Sensation-seeking, exposure to psychosocial stressors, and body modification in a college population. *Personality and Individual Differences, 37*, 1167–1177.

Roberts, M. (1966). *The pronunciation of vowels in Negro speech* (Unpublished doctoral dissertation). Ohio State University, Columbus, Ohio.

Roberts, M. (1987). No language but a cry. *Psychology Today, 21*, 57–58.

Rodgers, S., Kenix, L. J., & Thorson, E. (2007). Stereotypical portrayals of emotionality in news photos. *Mass Communication and Society, 10*, 119–138.

Roese, N. J., Olson, J. M., Borenstein, M. N., Martin, A., & Shores, A. L. (1992). Same-sex touching behavior: The moderating role of homophobic attitudes. *Journal of Nonverbal Behavior, 16*, 249–260.

Rogers, L. J., & Kaplan, G. (2000). *Songs, roars, and rituals: Communication in birds, mammals, and other animals*. Cambridge, MA: Harvard University Press.

Rosenberg, E. L., & Ekman, P. (1995). Conceptual and methodological issues in the judgment of facial expressions of emotion. *Motivation and Emotion, 19*, 111–138.

Rosenberg, S. W., Bohan, L., McCafferty, P., & Harris, K. (1986). The image and the voter: The effect of candidate presentation on voter preference. *American Journal of Political Science, 30*, 108–127.

Rosenfeld, L. B., & Plax, T. G. (1977). Clothing as communication. *Journal of Communication, 27*, 24–31.

Rosenthal, R. (1966). *Experimenter effects in behavioral research*. New York, NY: Appleton-Century-Crofts.

Rosenthal, R., & DePaulo, B. M. (1979). Sex differences in accommodation in nonverbal communication. In R. Rosenthal (Ed.), *Skill in nonverbal communication: Individual differences* (pp. 68–103). Cambridge, MA: Oelgeschlager, Gunn & Hain.

Rosenthal, R., & Jacobson, L. (1968). *Pygmalion in the classroom*. New York, NY: Holt, Rinehart, & Winston.

Rosenthal, R., Hall, J. A., DiMatteo, M. R., Rogers, P. L., & Archer, D. (1979). *Sensitivity to nonverbal communication: The PONS test*. Baltimore, MD: Johns Hopkins University Press.

Roter, D. L., Frankel, R. M., Hall, J. A., & Sluyter, D. (2006). The expression of emotion through nonverbal behavior in medical visits: Mechanism and outcomes. *Journal of General Internal Medicine, 21*, S28–S34.

Rothbart, M., Ziaie, H., & O'Boyle, C. (1992). Self-regulation and emotion in infancy. In N. Eisenberg & R. Fabes (Eds.), *Emotion and its regulation in early development. New directions for child development, no. 55* (pp. 7–23), San Francisco, CA: Jossey Bass.

Rotter, N. G., & Rotter, G. S. (1988). Sex differences in the encoding and decoding of negative facial expressions. *Journal of Nonverbal Behavior, 12*, 139–148.

Ruback, R. B., & Juieng, D. (1997). Territorial defense in parking lots: Retaliation against waiting drivers. *Journal of Applied Social Psychology, 27*, 821–834.

Rubin, R. B. (1985). Validity of the Communication Competency Assessment instrument. *Communication Monographs, 52*, 173–185.

Rubin, R. B., Rubin, A. M., & Jordan, F. F. (1997). Effects of instruction on communication apprehension and communication competence. *Communication Education, 46*, 104–114.

Rubin, R. B., Welch, S. A., & Buerkel, R. (1995). Performance-based assessment of high school speech instruction. *Communication Education, 44*, 30–39.

Rubinstein, R. P. (1995). *Dress codes: Meanings and messages in American culture*. Boulder, CO: Westview Press.

Ruch, W., & Deckers, L. (1993). Do extraverts like to laugh? An analysis of the Situational Humor Response Questionnaire (SHRQ). *European Journal of Personality, 7*, 211–220.

Ruffman, T. (2011). Ecological validity and age-related change in emotion recognition. *Journal of Nonverbal Behavior, 35*, 297–304.

Ruggieri, V., Celli, C., & Crescenzi, A. (1982). Self-contact and gesturing in different stimulus conditions. *Perceptual and Motor Skills, 54*, 1002–1010.

Rule, N. O., & Ambady, N. (2008). Brief exposures: Male sexual orientation is accurately perceived at 50 ms. *Journal of Experimental Social Psychology, 44*, 1100–1105.

Rusciewicz, H. L., Shaiman, S., Iverson, J. M., & Szuminski, N. (2013). Effects of prosody and position on the timing of deictic gestures. *Journal of Speech, Language, and Hearing Research, 56*, 458–470.

Russell, J. A. (1980). A circumplex model of affect. *Journal of Personality and Social Psychology, 39*, 1161–1178.

Russell, J. A. (1983). Pancultural aspects of the human conceptual organization of emotions. *Journal of Personality and Social Psychology, 45*, 1281–1288.

Russell, J. A. (1994). Is there universal recognition of emotion from facial expression? *Psychological Bulletin, 115*, 102–141.

Russell, J. A., & Bullock, M. (1986). Fuzzy concepts and the perception of emotion in facial expressions. *Social Cognition, 4*, 309–341.

Russell, J. A., Suzuki, N., & Ishida, N. (1993). Canadian, Greek, and Japanese freely produced emotion labels for facial expressions. *Motivation and Emotion, 17*, 337–351.

Russo, N. F. (1967). Connotation of seating arrangement. *Cornell Journal of Social Relations, 2*, 37–44.

Ryan, E. B. (1979). Why do low-prestige language varieties exist? In H. Giles & R. N. St. Clair (Eds.), *Language and social psychology* (pp. 15–157). Oxford, England: Basil Blackwell.

Ryan, M., Murphy, J., & Ruffman, T. (2010). Aging and the perception of emotion: Processing vocal expressions alone and with faces. *Experimental Aging Research, 36*, 1–22.

Saarni, C. (1979). Children's understanding of display rules for expressive behavior. *Developmental Psychology, 15*, 424–429.

Saarni C. (1984). An observational study of children's attempts to monitor their expressive behavior. *Child Development, 55*, 1504–1513.

Sabatelli, R. M., & Rubin, M. (1986). Nonverbal expressiveness and physical attractiveness as mediators of interpersonal perceptions. *Journal of Nonverbal Behavior, 10*, 120–133.

Sagi, A., & Hoffman, M. L. (1976). Empathic distress in the newborn. *Developmental Psychology, 12*, 175–176.

Sandhu, D. S., & Reeves, T. G. (1993). Cross-cultural counseling and neurolinguistics mirroring with Native American adolescents. *Journal of Multicultural Counseling and Development, 21*, 106–118.

Sasson, N. J., Pinkham, A. E., Hughett, P., Gur, R. E., & Gur, R. C. (2010). Controlling for response biases clarifies age and sex differences in facial affect recognition. *Journal of Nonverbal Behavior, 34*, 207–221.

Sauter, D. A. (2013). The role of motivation and cultural dialects in the in-group advantage for emotional vocalizations. *Frontiers in Psychology, 4*, 1–9.

Sauter, D. A., & Scott, S. K. (2007). More than one kind of happiness: Can we recognize vocal expressions of different positive states? *Motivation and Emotion, 31*, 192–199.

Sawang, S. (2010). Sex appeal in advertising: What consumers think. *Journal of Promotion Management, 16*, 167–187.

Sawyer, A., Williamson, P., & Young, R. L. (2012). Can gaze avoidance explain why individuals can't recognize emotions from facial expressions? *Journal of Autism and Developmental Disorders, 42*, 606–618.

Sawyer, A., Williamson, P., & Young, R. L. (2014). Metacognitive processes in emotion recognition: Are they different in adults with Asperger's disorder? *Journal of Autism and Developmental Disorders, 44*, 1373–1382.

Scaife, M., & Bruner, J. S. (1975). The capacity for joint visual attention in the infant. *Nature, 253*, 265–266.

Scealy, M., Phillips, J. G., & Stevenson, R. (2002). Shyness and anxiety as predictors of patterns of Internet usage. *Cyberpsychology and Behavior, 5*, 507–515.

Schachter, S., Christenfeld, N., Ravina, B., & Bilous, F. (1991). Speech dysfluency and the structure of knowledge. *Journal of Personality and Social Psychology, 60*, 362–367.

Scheflen, A. (1964). The significance of posture in communication systems. *Psychiatry, 27*, 316–331.

Scheflen, A. (1965). Quasi-courtship behavior in psychotherapy. *Psychiatry, 28*, 245–257.

Scheflen, A. (1972). *Body language and the social order*. Englewood Cliffs, NJ: Prentice Hall.

Scheflen, A. (1973). *Communicational structure: An analysis of a psychotherapy transaction*. Bloomington: Indiana University Press.

Scherer, K. R. (1978). Personality inference from voice quality: The loud voice of extroversion. *European Journal of Social Psychology, 8*, 467–487.

Scherer, K. R. (1986). Vocal affect expression: A review and a model for future research. *Psychological Bulletin, 99*, 143–165.

Scherer, K. R. (1989). Vocal correlates of emotion. In A. Manstead & H. Wagner (Eds.), *Handbook of psychophysiology: Emotion and social behavior* (pp. 165–197). London, England: Wiley.

Schmidt, K., Ambadar, Z., Cohn, J., & Reed, L. (2006).

Movement differences between deliberate and spontaneous facial expressions: Zygomatic major action in smiling. *Journal of Nonverbal Behavior, 30*, 37–52.

Schorr, A. J. (2000). Just what the doctor ordered: The effects of nonverbal immediately on the satisfaction of obstetric midwifery. *Dissertation Abstracts International Section B: The Science and Engineering, 61*, 1700.

Schrodt, P., & Witt, P. (2006). Students' attributions of instructor credibility as a function of students' expectations of instructional technology use and nonverbal immediacy. *Communication Education, 55*, 1–20.

Segrin, C. (1993). The effects of nonverbal behavior on outcomes of compliance gaining attempts. *Communication Studies, 44*, 169–187.

Seibold, D. R., Kudsi, S., & Rude, M. (1993). Does communication training make a difference? Evidence for the effectiveness of a presentational skills program. *Journal of Applied Communication Research, 21*, 111–131.

Seidman, S. A. (1992). An investigation of sex-role stereotyping in music videos. *Journal of Broadcasting and Electronic Media, 36*, 209–216.

Seiter, J. S. (2001). Silent derogation and perceptions of deceptiveness: Does communicating nonverbal disbelief during an opponent's speech affect perceptions of debaters' veracity? *Communication Research Reports, 18*, 334–344.

Seiter, J. S., & Weger, H. (2005). Audience perceptions of candidates' appropriateness as a function of nonverbal behaviors displayed during televised political debates. *The Journal of Social Psychology, 145*, 225–235.

Seiter, J. S., Abraham, J. A., & Nakagama, B. T. (1998). Split screen versus single screen formats in televised debates: Does access to an opponent's nonverbal behaviors affect viewers' perceptions of a speaker's credibility? *Perceptual and Motor Skills, 86*, 491–497.

Seiter, J. S., Kinzer, H. J., & Weger, H. (2006). Background behavior in live debates: The effect of the implicit ad hominem fallacy. *Communication Reports, 19*, 57–69.

Sell, A., Bryant, G. A., Cosmides, L., Tooby, J., Snycert, D., von Rueden, C., Krauss, A., & Gurven, M. (2010). Adaptations in humans for assessing physical strength from the voice. *Proceedings of Biological Sciences, 277*, 3509–3518.

Selye, H. (1956). *The stress of life*. New York, NY: McGraw-Hill.

Serota, K. B., Levine, T. R., & Boster, F. (2010). The prevalence of lying in America: Three studies in self-reported lying. *Human Communication Research, 36*, 2–25.

Shackelford, T. K., & Larsen, R. J. (1997). Facial asymmetry as an indicator of psychological, emotional, and physiological distress. *Journal of Personality and Social Psychology*, 72, 456–466.

Shaffer, D. R., & Sadowski, C. (1975). This table is the mine: Respect for marked barroom tables as a function of gender of spatial marker and desirability of locale. *Sociometry, 38*, 408–419.

Shaffer, D. R., Crepaz, N., & Sun, C. (2000). Physical attractiveness stereotyping in cross-cultural perspective: Similarities and differences between Americans and Taiwanese. *Journal of Cross-Cultural Psychology, 31*, 557–582.

Shanteau, J., & Nagy, G. F. (1979). Probability of acceptance in dating choice. *Journal of Personality and Social Psychology, 37*, 522–533.

Shapiro, P. N., & Penrod, S. (1986). Meta-analysis of facial identification studies. *Psychological Bulletin, 100*, 139–156.

Shariff, A., Tracy, J. L., & Markusoff, J. L. (2012). (Implicitly) judging a book by its cover: The power of pride and shame expressions in shaping judgments of social status. *Personality and Social Psychology Bulletin, 38*, 1178–1192.

Sharpley, C. F., & Sagris, A. (1995). When does counselor forward lean influence client-perceived rapport? *British Journal of Guidance and Counseling, 23*, 387–394.

Sheldon, W. H. (1940). *The varieties of human physique*. New York, NY: Harper & Row.

Sheldon, W. H., Dupertuis, C. V., & McDermott, E. (1954). *Atlas of men: A guide for somatotyping the adult male of all ages*. New York, NY: Harper & Row.

Shepperd, J. A., & Strathman, A. J. (1989). Attractiveness and height: The role of stature in dating preference, frequency of dating, and perceptions of attractiveness. *Personality and Social Psychology Bulletin, 15*, 617–627.

Shimanoff, S. (1980). *Communication rules: Theory and research*. Beverly Hills, CA: SAGE.

Shipp, T., & Hollien, H. (1969). Perception of the aging male voice. *Journal of Speech and Hearing Research, 12*, 704–710.

Short, J., Williams, E., & Christie, B. (1976). *The social psychology of telecommunications*. New York, NY: Wiley.

Shuter, R. (1976). Proxemics and tactility in Latin America. *Journal of Communication*, 26, 46–52.

Shuter, R. (1977). A field study of nonverbal communication in Germany, Italy, and the United States. *Communication Monographs, 44*, 298–305.

Siegel, J. C., & Sell, J. M. (1978). Effects of objective evidence of expertness and nonverbal behavior on client perceived expertness. *Journal of Counseling Psychology, 25*, 188–192.

Siegman, A. W. (1987). The telltale voice: Nonverbal messages of verbal communication. In A. W. Siegman & S. Feldstein (Eds.), *Nonverbal behavior and communication* (2nd ed.; pp. 351–434). Hillsdale, NJ: Lawrence Erlbaum.

Siegman, A. W., & Pope, B. (1965). Effects of question specificity and anxiety producing messages on verbal fluency in the initial interview. *Journal of Personality and Social Psychology, 4*, 188–192.

Signorielli, N., McLeod, D., & Healy, E. (1994). Gender stereotypes in MTV commercials: The beat goes on. *Journal of Broadcasting and Electronic Media, 38*, 91–101.

Silveira, J. (1972). Thoughts on the politics of touch. *Women's Press, 1*, 13.

Silverman, A. F., Pressman, H. E., & Bartell, H. W. (1973). Self-esteem and tactile communication. *Journal of Humanistic Psychology, 13*, 73–77.

Silverman, I. (1971). Physical attractiveness. *Sexual Behavior, September*, 22–25.

Silverstein, B., Perdue, L., Peterson, B., & Kelly, E. (1986). The role of the mass media in promoting a thin standard of bodily attractiveness for women. *Sex Roles, 14*, 519–532.

Silvia, P. J., Allan, W. D., Beauchamp, D. L., Maschauer, E. L., & Workman, J. O. (2006). Biased recognition of happy facial expressions in social anxiety. *Journal of Social and Clinical Psychology, 25*, 585–602.

Singh, D. (1993). Adaptive significance of female physical attractiveness: Role of waist-to-hip ratio. *Journal of Personality and Social Psychology, 65*, 293–307.

Slane, S., & Leak, G. (1978). Effects of self-perceived nonverbal immediacy behaviors on interpersonal attraction. *Journal of Psychology, 98*, 241–248.

Smith, A., & Duggan, M. (2013, October 21). Online dating and relationships. *Pew Research Center*. Retrieved February 9, 2016, from http://www.pewinternet.org/2013/10/21/online-dating-relationships/

Smith, L. (2000, October 15). A sigh isn't just a sigh, but indicates a range of emotions. *Milwaukee Journal Sentinel*, 02L.

Smith, P. K., McCulloch, K. C., & Shouwstra, A. (2013). Moving closer to reach the top: Approach behavior increases one's sense of power. *Social Cognition, 31*, 519–529.

Smith, W. J., Chase, J., & Leiblich, A. N. (1974). Tongue showing: A facial display of humans and other primate species. *Semiotica, 11*, 201–246.

Snyder, M. (1974). The self-monitoring of expressive behavior. *Journal of Personality and Social Psychology, 30*, 526–537.

Sobal, J., & Stunkard, A. J. (1989). Socioeconomic status and obesity: A review of the literature. *Psychological Bulletin, 105*, 260–275.

Soppe, H. J. (1988). Age differences in the decoding of affect authenticity and intensity. *Journal of Nonverbal Behavior, 12*, 107–119.

Sorce, J., Emde, R., & Klinnert, M. (1981, April). *Maternal emotional signaling: Its effect on the visual cliff behavior on one-year-olds*. Paper presented at the meeting of the Society for Research in Child Development, Boston, Massachusetts.

Spears, R., & Lea, M. (1994). Panacea or panopticon? The hidden power in computer-mediated communication. *Communication Research, 21*, 427–459.

Spence, S. H. (1987). The relationship between social-cognitive skills and peer sociometric status. *British Journal of Developmental Psychology, 5*, 347–356.

Spicer, C. H. (1981). *The comment-provoking potential of T-shirts: A nonverbal dimension of communication apprehension*. Paper presented at the annual meeting of the Western Communication Association, San Jose, California.

Spitz, R., & Wolf, K. (1946). The smiling response: A contribution to the ontogenesis of social relations. *Genetic Psychology Monographs, 34*, 57–125.

Sporer, S. L., & Schwandt, B. (2007). Moderators of nonverbal indicators of deception: A meta-analytic synthesis. *Psychology, Public Policy, and Law, 13*, 1–34.

Sprecher, S., & Chandak, R. (1992). Attitudes about arranged marriages and dating among men and women from India. *Free Inquiry in Creative Sociology, 20*, 1–11.

Sroufe, R., Chaikin, A., Cook, R., & Freeman, V. (1977). The effects of physical attractiveness on honesty: A socially desirable response. *Personality and Social Psychology Bulletin, 3*, 59–62.

Stafford, J. E. (2001). Standard posture, postura1 mirroring and client-perceived rapport. *Counselling Psychology Quarterly, 14*, 267–280.

Stark, R. E., Bernstein, L. E., & Demorest, M. E. (1993). Vocal communication in the first 18 months of life. *Journal of Speech and Hearing Research, 36*, 548–558.

Stead, B. A., & Zinkhan, G. M. (1986). Service priority in department stores: The effects of customer gender and dress. *Sex Roles, 15*, 601–611.

Stel, M., van Baaren, R. V., & Vonk, R. (2008). Effects of mimicking: Acting prosocially by being emotionally moved. *European Journal of Social Psychology, 38*, 965–976.

Stel, M., van Baaren, R. V., Blaskovich, J., van Dijk, E., McCall, C., Pollmann, M. M. H., van Leeuwen, M. L., . . . & Vonk, R. (2010). Effects of a priori liking on the elicitation of mimicry. *Experimental Psychology, 57*, 412–418.

Stephan, W. G., Stephan, C. W., & DeVargas, M. C. (1996). Emotional expression in Costa Rica and the United States. *Journal of Cross-Cultural Psychology, 27*, 147–160.

Stern, C., West, T. V., Jost, J. T., & Rule, N. O. (2013). The politics of gaydar: Ideological differences in the use of gendered cues in categorizing sexual orientation. *Journal of Personality and Social Psychology, 104*, 520–541.

Sternglanz, R. W., & DePaulo, B. M. (2004). Reading nonverbal clues to emotions: The advantages and liabilities of relationship closeness. *Journal of Nonverbal Behavior, 28*, 245–266.

Stevanoni, E., & Salmon, K. (2005). Giving a memory a hand: Instructing children to gesture enhances their event recall. *Journal of Nonverbal Behavior, 29*, 217–233.

Stevens, D., Charman, T., & Blair, R. J. R. (2001). Recognition of emotions in facial expressions and vocal tones in children with psychopathic tendencies. *Journal of Genetic Psychology, 162*, 201–211.

Stewart, M. A., Ryan, E. B., & Giles, H. (1985). Accent and social class effects on status and solidarity evaluations. *Personality and Social Psychology Bulletin, 11*, 98–105.

Stier, D. S., & Hall, J. A. (1984). Gender differences in touch: An empirical and theoretical review. *Journal of Personality and Social Psychology, 47*, 440–459.

Stifter, C., & Fox, N. (1986). Preschool children's ability to identify and label emotions. *Journal of Nonverbal Behavior, 10*, 255–266.

Stirling, L. J., Eley, T. C., & Clark, D. M. (2006). Preliminary evidence for an association between social anxiety symptoms and avoidance of negative faces in school-age children. *Journal of Clinical Child and Adolescent Psychology, 35*, 431–439.

Storck, J., & Sproull, L. (1995). Through a glass darkly: What do people learn in videoconferences? *Human Communication Research, 22*, 197–219.

Storrs, D., & Kleinke, C. L. (1990). Evaluation of high and equal status male and female touchers. *Journal of Nonverbal Behavior, 14*, 87–96.

Strack, R., Martin, L. L., & Stepper, S. (1988). Inhibiting and facilitating conditions of facial expressions: A non-obtrusive test of the facial feedback hypothesis. *Journal of Personality and Social Psychology, 54*, 768–777.

Street, R. L., & Buller, D. B. (1988). Patients' characteristics affecting physician–patient nonverbal communication. *Human Communication Research, 15*, 60–90.

Striano, T., Kopp, F., Grossman, T., & Reid, V. M. (2006). Eye contact influences neural processing of emotional expressions in 4-month-old infants. *Social Cognitive and Affective Neuroscience, 1*, 87–94.

Stromwall, L. A., Hartwig, M., Granhag, P. A. (2006). To act truthfully: Nonverbal behaviour and strategies during a police interrogation. *Psychology, Crime, and Law, 12*, 207–219.

Sullivan, D. G., & Masters, R. D. (1988). "Happy warriors": Leaders' facial displays, viewers' emotions, and political support. *American Journal of Political Science, 32*, 345–368.

Sullivan, G. L., & O'Connor, P. J. (1988). Women's role portrayals in magazine advertising: 1958–1983. *Sex Roles, 18*, 181–188.

Sullivan, S., Ruffman, T., & Hutton, S. B. (2007). Age differences in emotion recognition skills and the visual scanning of emotion faces. *Journal of Gerontology Series B: Psychological Sciences and Social Sciences, 62B*, 53–60.

Summerhayes, D. L., & Suchner, R. W. (1978). Power implications of touch in male-female relationships. *Sex Roles, 4*, 103–110.

Surawski, M. K., & Ossoff, E. P. (2006). The effect of physical and vocal attractiveness on the impression formation of politicians. *Current Psychology, 25*, 15–27.

Surcinelli, P., Codispoti, M., Montebarocci, O., Rossi, N., & Baldaro, B. (2006). Facial emotion recognition in trait anxiety. *Journal of Anxiety Disorders, 20*, 110–117.

Suris, J., Jeannin, A., Chossis, I., & Michaud, P. (2007). Piercing among adolescents: Body art as risk marker: A population-based survey. *The Journal of Family Practice, 56*, 126–130.

Sussman, N. M., & Rosenfeld, H. M. (1982). Influence of culture, language, and sex on conversational distance. *Journal of Personality and Social Psychology, 42*, 66–74.

Swami, V. (2012a). Personality differences between tattooed and non-tattooed individuals. *Psychological Reports, 111*, 97–106.

Swami, V. (2012b). Written on the body: Individual differences between British adults who do and do not obtain a first tattoo. *Scandinavian Journal of Psychology, 53*, 407–412.

Swami, V., Caprario, C., Tovee, M., & Furnham, A. (2006). Female physical attractiveness in Britain and Japan: A cross-cultural study. *European Journal of Personality, 20*, 69–81.

Swami, V., Frederick, D. A., Aaivic, T., Alcalay, L., Allik, J., Anderson, D., . . . & Becirevic, I. (2010). The attractive female body weight and female body dissatisfaction in 26 countries across 12 world regions. Results of the international body project I. *Personality and Social Psychology Bulletin, 36*, 309–325.

Swami, V., Smith, J., Tsiokris, A., Georgiades, C., Sangareau, Y., Tovee, M., & Furnham, A. (2007). Male physical attractiveness in Britain and Greece: A cross-cultural study. *Journal of Social Psychology, 147*, 15–26.

Swenson, J., & Casmir, F. L. (1998). The impact of culture-sameness, gender, foreign travel, and academic background on the ability to interpret facial expressions of emotion in others. *Communication Quarterly, 46*, 214–230.

Szarota, P. (2010). The mystery of the European smile: A comparison based on individual photographs provided by Internet users. *Journal of Nonverbal Behavior, 34*, 249–256.

Talwar, V., & Lee, K. (2002). Emergence of white-lie telling in children between 3 and 7 years of age. *Merrill-Palmer Quarterly, 48*, 160–181.

Tamura, R., & Kameda, T. (2006). Are facial expressions contagious in the Japanese? *Japanese Journal of Psychology, 77*, 377–382.

Tan, H. H., Foo, M. D., & Kwek, M. H. (2004). The effects of customer personality traits on the display of positive emotions. *Academy of Management Journal, 487*, 287–296.

Tankard, J. W., Jr., McClenegahan, J. S., Ganju, V., Lee, E. B., Olkes, C., & DuBose, D. (1977). Nonverbal cues and television news. *Journal of Communication, 27*, 106–111.

Tannen, D. (1990). *You just don't understand: Women and men in conversation*. New York, NY: Ballantine.

Tannen, D. (1994). *Talking from 9 to 5*. New York, NY: Avon.

Tannenbaum, R. (1961). *Leadership and organization*. New York, NY: McGraw-Hill.

Taylor, L. S., Fiore, A. T., Mendelsohn, G. A., & Cheshire, C. (2011). "Out of my league": A real-world test of the matching hypothesis. *Personality and Social Psychology Bulletin*, 7, 942–954.

Tepper, D. T., Jr., & Haase, R. F. (1978). Verbal and nonverbal communication of facilitative conditions. *Journal of Counseling Psychology, 25*, 35–44.

Terburg, D., Aarts, H., & van Honk, J. (2012). Memory and attention for social threat: Anxious hypercoding-avoidance and submissive gaze avoidance. *Emotion, 12*, 666–672.

Terry, R. L., & Krantz, J. H. (1993). Dimensions of trait attributions associated with eyeglasses, men's facial hair, and women's hair length. *Journal of Applied Social Psychology, 23*, 1757–1769.

Terry, R. L., & Krofer, D. L. (1976). Effects of eye correctives on ratings of attractiveness. *Perceptual and Motor Skills, 42*, 562.

Terry, R. L., & Macklin, E. (1977). Accuracy of identifying married couples on the basis of similarity of attractiveness. *Journal of Psychology, 97*, 15–20.

Tesser, A., & Brodie, M. (1971). A note on the evaluation of a computer date. *Psychonomic Science, 23*, 300.

Tessler, R., & Sushelsky, L. (1978). Effects of eye contact and social status on the perception of a job applicant in an employment interview situation. *Journal of Vocational Behavior, 13*, 338–347.

Thakerar, J. N., & Giles, H. (1981). They are—so they spoke: Noncontent speech stereotypes. *Language and Communication, 1*, 255–261.

Than, K. (2007, April). Apes point to origins of human language. *LiveScience, MSNBC.com.*

Thompson, L. A., Aidinehad, M. R., & Ponte, J. (2001). Aging and the effects of facial and prosodic cues on emotional intensity ratings and memory reconstructions. *Journal of Nonverbal Behavior, 25*, 101–125.

Thunberg, M., & Dimberg, U. (2000). Gender differences in facial reactions to fear-relevant stimuli. *Journal of Nonverbal Behavior, 24*, 44–51.

Tickle-Degnen, L. (2006). Nonverbal behavior and its functions in the ecosystem of rapport. In V. Manusov & M. L. Patterson (Eds.), *The SAGE handbook of nonverbal communication* (pp. 381–400). Thousand Oaks, CA: SAGE.

Tickle-Degnen, L., & Rosenthal, R. (1990). The nature of rapport and its nonverbal correlates. *Psychological Inquiry, 1*, 285–293.

Tidwell, L. C., & Walther, J. B. (2002). Computer-mediated communication effects on disclosure, impressions, and interpersonal evaluations: Getting to know one another a bit at a time. *Human Communication Research, 28*, 317–348.

Tiedens, L. Z., & Fragale, A. R. (2003). Power moves: Complementarity in dominant and submissive nonverbal behavior. *Journal of Personality and Social Psychology, 84*, 558–568.

Tifferet, S., & Vilnai-Yavetz, I. (2014). Gender differences in Facebook presentation: An international randomized study. *Computers in Human Behavior, 38*, 388–399.

Tiggemann, M., & Golder, F. (2006). Tattooing: An expression of uniqueness in the appearance domain. *Body Image, 3*, 309–315.

Tinbergen, N. (1952). Derived activities; their causation, biological significance, origin, and emancipation during evolution. *Quarterly Review of Biology, 27*, 1–32.

Tomasello, M., & Camaioni, L. (1997). A comparison of the gestural communication of apes and human infants. *Human Development, 40*, 7–24.

Tompkins, S. S. (1962). *Affect, imagery, consciousness* (Vols. 1 and 2). New York, NY: Springer.

Totterdell, P., & Holman, D. (2003). Emotion regulation in customer service roles: Testing a model of emotional labor. *Journal of Occupational Health Psychology, 8*, 55–73.

Trager, G. L. (1958). Paralanguage: A first approximation. *Studies in Linguistics, 13*, 1–12.

Trampe, D., Siero, F. W., & Stapel, D. A. (2007). On models and vases: Body dissatisfaction and proneness to social comparison effects. *Journal of Personality and Social Psychology, 92*, 106–118.

Trees, A. R. (2000). Nonverbal communication and the support process: Interactional sensitivity in interactions between mothers and young adults. *Communication Monographs, 67*, 239–261.

Trees, A. R., & Manusov, V. (1998). Managing face concerns in criticism: Integrating nonverbal behaviors as a dimension of politeness in female friendship dyads. *Human Communication Research, 24*, 564–582.

Trevarthen, C. (1977). Descriptive analysis of infant communicative behavior. In H. R. Schaffer (Ed.), *Studies in mother-infant interaction* (pp. 227–270). London, England: Academic Press.

Trivers, R. L. (1972). Parental investment and sexual selection. In B. Campbell (Ed.), *Sexual selection and the descent of man 1871–1971* (pp. 136–179). New York, NY: Aldine de Gruyter.

Tronick, E. Z., Als, H., & Brazelton, T. B. (1980). Monadic phases: A structural descriptive analysis of infant-mother face-to-face interaction. *Merrill Palmer Quarterly, 26*, 3–24.

Trotter, R. J. (1987). The play's the thing. *Psychology Today, 21*, 27–34.

Trout, D. L., & Rosenfeld, H. M. (1980). The effects of postural lean and body congruence on the judgment of psychotherapeutic rapport. *Journal of Nonverbal Behavior, 4*, 176–190.

Trudgill, P. (1974). *The social differentiation of English in Norwich*. New York, NY: Cambridge University Press.

Trujillo, L. T., Jankowitsch, J. M., & Langlois, J. H. (2014). Beauty is in the ease of the beholding: A neurophysiological test of the averageness theory of facial attractiveness. *Cognitive, Affective, and Behavioral Neuroscience, 14*, 1061–1075

Tucker, J. S., & Anders, S. L. (1998). Adult attachment style and nonverbal closeness in dating couples. *Journal of Nonverbal Behavior, 22*, 89–107.

Tucker, J. S., & Riggio, R. E. (1988). The role of social skills in encoding posed and spontaneous facial expressions. *Journal of Nonverbal Behavior, 12*, 87–97.

Turner, J. (1998, October 29). Internet's illusion of intimacy leaves a lot of red faces. *Christian Science Monitor, 90*, B4.

Tusing, K. J., & Dillard, J. P. (2000). The sounds of dominance: Vocal precursors of perceived dominance during interpersonal influence. *Human Communication Research, 26*, 148–171.

Undersheriff Fired for Hugging. (1999, December 18). *Rocky Mountain News*, 7A.

Unzner, L., & Schneider, K. (1990). Facial reactions in preschoolers: A descriptive study. *Journal of Nonverbal Behavior, 14*, 19–33.

Uzzell, D., & Horne, N. (2006). The influence of biological sex, sexuality, and gender role on interpersonal distance. *British Journal of Social Psychology, 45*, 579–597.

Van Baaren, R. B., Holland, R. W., Kawakami, K., & van Knippenberg, A. (2004). Mimicry and prosocial behavior. *Psychological Science, 15*, 71–74.

van Dijk, E. T., Torta, E., & Cuijpers, R. H. (2013). Effects of eye contact and iconic gestures on message retention in human-robot interaction. *International Journal of Social Robotics, 5*(4), 491–501.

van Hooff, J. A. R. A. M. (1972). A comparative approach to the phylogeny of laughter and smile. In R. A. Hinde (Ed.), *Nonverbal communication* (pp. 209–241). Cambridge, England: Cambridge University Press.

Van Lacker, D. (1981). Speech behavior as a communication process. In J. K. Darby (Ed.), *Speech evaluation in psychiatry* (pp. 5–38). New York, NY: Grune & Stratton.

Van Lancker, D. (1987). Old familiar voices. *Psychology Today, 21*, 12–13.

Van Maanen, J., & Kunda, G. (1989). Real feelings: Emotional expression and organizational culture. In L. L. Cummings & B. M. Staw (Eds.), *Research in organizational behavior* (Vol. 11, pp. 43–103). Greenwich, CT: JAJ Press.

Van Marsh, A. (2007). UK's skin bleaching trade exposed. *CNN.com*. Retrieved November 26, 2007, from http://www.cnn.com/2007/HEALTH/11/26vanmarsh.skinbleaching/index.html

Verbeke, W. (1997). Individual differences in emotional contagion of salespersons: Its effect on performance and burnout. *Psychology and Marketing, 14*, 617–637.

Vrij, A. (2000). *Detecting lies and deceit: The psychology of lying and implications for professional practice*. Chichester, England: John Wiley and Sons.

Vrij, A. (2006). Nonverbal communication and deception. In V. Manusov & M. L. Patterson (Eds.), *The SAGE handbook of nonverbal communication* (pp. 341–359). Thousand Oaks, CA: SAGE.

Vrij, A., & Graham, S. (1997). Individual differences between liars and the ability to detect lies. *Expert Evidence: The International Digest of Human Behaviour Science and Law, 5*, 144–148.

Vrij, A., & Mann, S. (1999). *Who killed my relative? Police officers' ability to detect real-life high-stakes lies* (Unpublished manuscript). Psychology Department, University of Portsmouth, Portsmouth, UK.

Vrij, A., & Mann, S. (2001). Telling and detecting lies in a high-stakes situation: The case of a convicted murderer. *Applied Cognitive Psychology, 15*, 187–203.

Vrij, A., & Winkel, F. W. (1991). Cultural patterns in Dutch and Surinam nonverbal behavior: An analysis of simulated police/citizen encounters. *Journal of Nonverbal Behavior, 15*, 169–184.

Vrij, A., & Winkel, F. W. (1992). Cross-cultural police-citizen interactions: The influence of race, beliefs, and nonverbal communication on impression formation. *Journal of Applied Social Psychology, 22*, 1546–1559.

Vrij, A., & Winkel, F. W. (1994). Perceptual distortions in cross-cultural interrogations: The impact of skin color, accent, speech style, and spoken fluency on impression formation. *Journal of Cross-Cultural Psychology, 25*, 284–295.

Vrij, A., Granhag, P., & Mann, S. (2010a). Good liars. *The Journal of Psychiatry and Law, 38*, 77–98.

Vrij, A., Granhag, P., & Porter, S. (2010b). Pitfalls and opportunities in nonverbal and verbal lie detection. *Psychological Science in the Public Interest, 11*, 89–121.

Vrij, A., Granhag, P., Mann, A., & Leal, A. (2011). Outsmarting the liars: Toward a cognitive lie detection approach. *Current Directions in Psychological Science, 20*, 28–32.

Wagner, H. L. (1990). The spontaneous facial expression of differential positive and negative emotions. *Motivation and Emotion, 14*, 27–43.

Wagner, H. L. (2000). The accessibility of the term "contempt" and the meaning of the unilateral lip curl. *Cognition and Emotion, 14*, 689–710.

Wagner, H. L., & Smith, J. (1991). Facial expression in the presence of friends and strangers. *Journal of Nonverbal Behavior, 15*, 201–214.

Wagner, H. L., Buck, R., & Winterbotham, M. (1993). Communication of specific emotions: Gender differences in sending accuracy and communication measures. *Journal of Nonverbal Behavior, 17*, 29–53.

Waldinger, R. J., Hauser, S. T., Schulz, M. S., Allen, J. P., & Crowell, J. A. (2004). Reading others' emotions: The role of intuitive judgments in predicting marital satisfaction, quality, and stability. *Journal of Family Psychology, 18*, 58–71.

Walker, M. B., & Trimboli, C. (1983). The expressive function of the eye flash. *Journal of Nonverbal Behavior, 8*, 3–13.

Walster, E., Aronson, V., Abrahams, D., & Rottmann, L. (1966). Importance of physical attractiveness in dating behavior. *Journal of Personality and Social Psychology, 4*, 508–516.

Walther, J. B. (1993). Impression development in computer-mediated interaction. *Western Journal of Communication, 57*, 381–398.

Walther, J. B. (1996). Computer-mediated communication: Impersonal, interpersonal, and hyperpersonal interaction. *Communication Research, 23*, 3–43.

Walther, J. B. (1997). Group and interpersonal effects in international computer-mediated collaboration. *Human Communication Research, 23*, 342–369.

Walther, J. B. (2006). Nonverbal dynamics in computer-mediated communication or :(and the net :('s with you, :) and you :) alone. In V. Manusov & M. L. Patterson (Eds.), *The SAGE handbook of nonverbal communication* (pp. 461–480). Thousand Oaks, CA: SAGE.

Walther, J. B., & Bunz, U. (2005). The rules of virtual groups: Trust, liking, and performance in computer-mediated communication. *Journal of Communication, 55*, 828–846.

Walther, J. B., & D'Addario, K. P. (2001). The impacts

of emoticons on message interpretation in computer-mediated communication. *Social Science Computer Review, 19*, 321–345.

Walton, J. H., & Orlikoff, R. F. (1994). Speaker race identification from acoustic cues in the vocal signal. *Journal of Speech and Hearing Research, 37*, 738–745.

Wang, H., Hahn, A. C., Fisher, C. I., DeBruine, L. M., & Jones, B. C. (2014). Women's hormone levels moderate the motivational salience of facial attractiveness and sexual dimorphism. *Psychoneuroendocrinology*, 50, 246–251.

Watson, J. B. (1928). *Psychological care of infant and child*. New York, NY: Norton.

Watson, O. M. (1970). *Proxemic behavior: A cross cultural study*. The Hague, the Netherlands: Mouton.

Watson, O. M., & Graves, T. D. (1966). Quantitative research in proxemic behavior. *American Anthropologist, 68*, 971–985.

Weathers, M. D., Frank, E. M., & Spell, L. A. (2002). Differences in the communication of affect: Members of the same race versus members of a different race. *Journal of Black Psychology, 28*, 66–77.

Webb, J. T. (1972). Interview synchrony: An investigation of two speech rate measures. In A. W. Siegman & B. Pope (Eds.), *Studies in dyadic communication* (pp. 115–133). New York, NY: Pergamon.

Weeden, J., & Sabini, J. (2005). Physical attractiveness and health in Western societies: A review. *Psychological Bulletin, 131*, 635–653.

Weiner, M., Devoe, S., Rubinow, S., & Geller, J. (1972). Nonverbal behavior and nonverbal communication. *Psychological Review, 79*, 185–214.

Weisbuch, M., & Ambady, N. (2009). Unspoken cultural influence: Exposure to and influence of nonverbal bias. *Journal of Personality and Social Psychology, 96*, 1104–1119.

Weisbuch, M., & Pauker, K. (2011). The nonverbal transmission of intergroup bias: A model of bias contagion with implications for social policy. *Social Issues and Policy Review, 5*, 257–291.

Weisbuch, M., Paulker, K., & Ambady, N. (2009). The subtle transmission of race bias via televised nonverbal behavior. *Science, 326*, 1711–1714.

Weisbuch, M., Slepian, M. L., Clarke, A., Ambady, N., & Veenstra-VanderWeele, J. (2010). Behavioral stability across time and situations: Nonverbal versus verbal consistency. *Journal of Nonverbal Behavior, 34*, 43–56.

Weiss, A. J., & Wilson, B. J. (1996). Emotional portrayals in family television series that are popular among children. *Journal of Broadcasting and Electronic Media, 40*, 1–29.

Wellens, A. R., & Goldberg, M. L. (1978). The effects of interpersonal distance and orientation upon the perception of social relationships. *Journal of Psychology, 99*, 39–47.

Wells, W., & Siegel, B. (1961). Stereotyped somatypes. *Psychological Reports, 8*, 77–78.

Wesp, R., Hesse, J., Keutmann, D., & Wheaton, K. (2001). Gestures maintain spatial imagery. *American Journal of Psychology, 114*, 591–600.

West, S. G., & Brown, T. J. (1975). Physical attractiveness, the severity of the emergency and helping: A field experiment and interpersonal simulation. *Journal of Experimental Social Psychology, 11*, 531–538.

Westen, D. (2007). *The political brain*. New York, NY: Public Affairs.

Whale Chat. (1999, June). *Discover, 20*, 30–31.

Wharton, A. S. (1996). Service with a smile: Understanding the consequences of emotional labor. In C. L. McDonald & C. Sirianni (Eds.), *Working in the service society* (pp. 91–112). Philadelphia, PA: Temple University Press.

Whately, M. A. (2005). The effect of participant sex, victim dress, and traditional attitudes on causal judgments for marital rape victims. *Journal of Family Violence, 20*, 191–200.

White, C. H., & Burgoon, J. K. (2001). Adaptation and communicative design: Patterns of interaction in truthful and deceptive conversations. *Human Communication Research, 27*, 9–37.

White, G. L. (1980). Physical attractiveness and courtship progress. *Journal of Personality and Social Psychology, 39*, 660–668.

White, S. E., Ginsburg, S. L., & Brown, N. J. (1999). Diversity of body types in network television programming: A content analysis. *Communication Research Reports, 16*, 386–392.

Whittington, N. (1987). Is instructional television educationally effective? A research review. *The American Journal of Distance Education, 1*, 47–57.

Whitty, M. (2004). Cyber-flirting: An examination of men's and women's flirting behaviour both offline and on the Internet. *Behaviour Change, 21*, 115–126.

Wieser, M. J., Pauli, P., Grosseible, M., Molzow, I., & Mulberger, A. (2010). Virtual social interactions in social anxiety—the impact of sex, gaze, and interpersonal distance. *Cyberpsychology, Behavior, and Social Networking, 13*, 547–554.

Wild, B., Erb, M., & Bartels, M. (2001). Are emotions contagious? Evoked emotions while viewing emotionally expressive faces: Quality, quantity, time course and gender differences. *Psychiatry Research, 102*, 109–124.

Wiley, R. H. (1983). The evolution of communication: Information and manipulation. In T. R. Halliday & P. J. B. Slater (Eds.), *Animal behavior* (pp. 156–189). New York, NY: W. H. Freeman.

Wilkowski, B. M., & Meier, B. P. (2010). Bring it on: Angry facial expressions potentiate approach-motivated motor behavior. *Journal of Personality and Social Psychology, 98*, 201–210.

Willis, F. N., & Briggs, L. E. (1992). Relationship and touch in public settings. *Journal of Nonverbal Behavior, 16*, 55–62.

Willis, F. N., & Dodds, R. A. (1998). Age, relationship, and touch initiation. *Journal of Social Psychology, 138*, 115–123.

Willis, F. N., & Rawdon, V. A. (1994). Gender and national differences in attitudes toward same-gender touch. *Perceptual and Motor Skills, 78*, 1027–1034.

Willis, F. N., & Reeves, D. L. (1976). Touch interactions in junior high students in relation to sex and race. *Developmental Psychology, 12*, 91–92.

Wilson, D. W. (1978). Helping behavior and physical attractiveness. *Journal of Social Psychology, 104*, 313–314.

Wilson, P. R. (1968). Perceptual distortion of height as a function of ascribed academic status. *Journal of Social Psychology, 10*, 97–102.

Witt, P., Wheeless, L. R., & Allen, M. (2004). A meta-analytic review of the relationship between teacher immediacy and student learning. *Communication Monographs, 71*, 184–207.

Wogalter, M. S., & Hosie, J. A. (1991). Effects of cranial and facial hair on perceptions of age and person. *Journal of Social Psychology, 131*, 589–591.

Wohlrab, S., Stahl, J., Rammsayer, T., & Kappeler, P. M. (2007). Differences in personality characteristics between body-modified and non-modified individuals: Associations with individual personality traits and their possible evolutionary implications. *European Journal of Personality, 21*, 931–951.

Wolfe, M., & Laufer, R. (1974). The concept of privacy in childhood and adolescence. In S. T. Margulis (Ed.), *Privacy* (pp. 29–54). Stony Brook, NY: Environmental Design Research Association.

Wolff, C. (1945). *A psychology of gesture*. London, England: Methuen.

Wolff, P. H. (1963). Observations on the early development of smiling. In B. M. Foss (Ed.), *Determinants of infant behavior* (Vol. I). London, England: Metheun.

Wolff, P. H. (1969). The natural history of crying and other vocalizations in early infancy. In B. M. Foss (Ed.), *Determinants of infant behavior* (Vol. IV). London, England: Metheun.

Wood, J. T. (1994). *Gendered lives: Communication, gender, and culture*. Belmont, CA: Wadsworth.

Woodall, W. G., & Burgoon, J. K. (1983). Talking fast and changing attitudes: A critique and clarification. *Journal of Nonverbal Behavior, 8*, 126–142.

Woodruff, K. (1998). Youth and race on local TV news. *Nieman Reports, 52*, 43.

Woodzicka, J. A., & LaFrance, M. (2005). Working on a smile: Responding to sexual provocation in the workplace. In R. E. Riggio & R. S. Feldman (Eds.), *Applications of nonverbal communication* (pp. 141–160). Mahwah, NJ: Lawrence Erlbaum.

Word, C. O., Zanna, M. P., & Cooper, J. (1974). The nonverbal mediation of self-fulfilling prophecies in interracial interaction. *Journal of*

Experimental Social Psychology, 10, 109–120.

Workman, J. E., & Johnson, K. P. (1991). The role of cosmetics in impression formation. *Clothing and Textile Research Journal, 10,* 63–67.

Wu, Y. J., Chang, W., & Yuan, C. (2015). Do Facebook profile pictures reflect users' personality. *Computers in Human Behavior, 51,* 880–889.

Wysocki, D. K. (1998). Let your fingers do the talking: Sex on an adult chat line. *Sexualities, 1,* 425–452.

Xu, X., & Whyte, M. K. (1990). Love matches and arranged marriages: A Chinese replication. *Journal of Marriage and the Family, 52,* 709–722.

Yee, N., Bailenson, J. N., Urbanek, M., Chang, F., & Merget, D. (2007). The unbearable likeness of being digital: The perseverance of nonverbal social norms in online virtual environments. *CyberPsychology and Behavior, 10,* 115–121.

Yelsma, P., & Marrow, S. (2003). An examination of couples' difficulties with emotional expressiveness and their marital satisfaction. *Journal of Family Communication, 3*(1), 41–62.

Young, A. E., & Guile, M. N. (1987). Departure latency to invasion of personal space: Effects of status and sex. *Perceptual and Motor Skills, 64,* 700–702.

Young, D. M., & Beier, E. G. (1977). The role of applicant nonverbal communication in the employment interview. *Journal of Employment Counseling, 14,* 154–165.

Yuan, J., Lieberman, M., & Cieri, C. (2007, August). *Towards an integrated understanding of speech overlaps in conversation.* Retrieved April 16, 2008, from http://icphs2007.de/conference/Papers

Yukawa, S., Tokuda, H., & Sato, J. (2007). Attachment style, self-concealment, and interpersonal distance among Japanese undergraduates. *Perceptual and Motor Skills, 104,* 1255–1261.

Zaidel, D., & Deblieck, C. (2007). Attractiveness of natural faces compared to computer constructed perfectly symmetrical faces. *International Journal of Neuroscience, 117,* 423–431.

Zajonc, R. B., Murphy, S. T., & Inglehart, M. (1989). Feeling and facial experience: Implications of the vascular theory of emotions. *Psychological Review, 96,* 395–416.

Zakahi, W. R., & Gross, B. (1995). Loneliness and interpersonal decoding skills. *Communication Quarterly, 43,* 75–85.

Zebrowitz, L. A. (1997). *Reading faces: Window to the soul?* Boulder, CO: Westview.

Zebrowitz, L. A., & Rhodes, G. (2004). Sensitivity to "bad genes" and the anomalous face overgeneralization effect: Cue validity, cue utilization, and accuracy in judging intelligence and health. *Journal of Nonverbal Behavior, 28,* 167–185.

Zebrowitz, L. A., Andreoletti, C., Collins, M. A., Lee, S. Y., & Blumenthal, J. (1998). Bright, bad, baby-faced boys: Appearance stereotypes do not always yield self-fulfilling prophecy effects. *Journal of Personality and Social Psychology, 75,* 1300–1320.

Zebrowitz, L. A., Collins, M. A., & Dutta, R. (1998). The relationship between appearance and personality across the life span. *Personality and Social Psychology Bulletin, 24,* 736–749.

Zebrowitz, L. A., Kikuchi, M., & Fellous, J. (2010). Facial resemblance to emotions: Group differences, impression effects, and race stereotypes. *Journal of Personality and Social Psychology, 89,* 175–189

Zhang, K., Frumkin, L., Stedmon, A., & Lawson, G. (2013). Deception in context: Coding nonverbal cues, situational variables and risk of detection. *Journal of Police and Criminal Psychology, 28,* 150–161.

Zimmerman, A. (1998, June, 25). A mother and child reunion. *Dallas Observer.* Retrieved January 24, 2016, from http://www.dallasobserver.com/news/a-mother-and-child-reunion-6401785

Zuckerman, M., & Driver, R. E. (1985). Telling lies: Verbal and nonverbal correlates of deception. In A. W. Siegman & S. Feldstein (Eds.), *Nonverbal communication: An integrated perspective* (pp. 129–147). Hillsdale, NJ: Lawrence Erlbaum.

Zuckerman, M., & Driver, R. E. (1989). What sounds beautiful is good: The vocal attractiveness stereotype. *Journal of Nonverbal Behavior, 13,* 67–82.

Zuckerman, M., & Miyake, K. (1993). The attractive voice: What makes it so? *Journal of Nonverbal Behavior, 17*, 119–135.

Zuckerman, M., & Przewuzman, S. (1979). Decoding and encoding facial expressions in preschool-age children. *Environmental Psychology and Nonverbal Behavior, 3*, 147–163.

Zuckerman, M., & Sinicropi, V. (2011). When physical and vocal attractiveness differ: Effects on favorability of interpersonal impressions. *Journal of Nonverbal Behavior, 35*, 75–86.

Zuckerman, M., DePaulo, B. M., & Rosenthal, R. (1981). Verbal and nonverbal communication of deception. In L. Berkowitz (Ed.), *Advances in experimental social psychology* (Vol. 14, pp. 1–59). New York, NY: Academic Press.

Zuckerman, M., Hall, J. A., DeFrank, R. S., & Rosenthal, R. (1976). Encoding and decoding of spontaneous and posed facial expressions. *Journal of Personality and Social Psychology, 34*, 966–977.

Zuckerman, M., Hodgins, H., & Miyake, K. (1990). The vocal attractiveness stereotype: Replication and elaboration. *Journal of Nonverbal Behavior, 14*, 97–112.

Zuckerman, M., Larrance, D. T., Hall, J. A., DeFrank, R. S., & Rosenthal, R. (1979). Posed and spontaneous communication of emotion via facial and vocal cues. *Journal of Personality, 47*, 712–733.

INDEX